River Through Time

Time

THE COURSE OF WESTERN CIVILIZATION

River Through Time

THE COURSE OF WESTERN CIVILIZATION

C. WARREN HOLLISTER
UNIVERSITY OF CALIFORNIA, SANTA BARBARA

JOHN F. H. NEW
UNIVERSITY OF WATERLOO

JAMES D. HARDY, JR.
LOUISIANA STATE UNIVERSITY, BATON ROUGE

ROGER L. WILLIAMS
UNIVERSITY OF WYOMING

JOHN WILEY & SONS, INC., NEW YORK • LONDON • SYDNEY • TORONTO

Library of Congress Cataloging in Publication Data:

Main entry under title:

River through time.

    Includes bibliographical references.
    1. Civilization—History. I. Hollister, Charles
Warren.
CB69.R58   910′.03   74-14972
ISBN 0-471-40695-3 (pbk.)

Printed in the United States of America

10 9 8 7 6 5 4 3 2 1

Preface

In this short history of Western Civilization our goal has been to strike a proper balance between factual narrative and interpretation, to maintain the highest possible level of accuracy, to present sound, current, sometimes original interpretations, and to write clearly and, if possible, vividly. Above all, we have sought brevity, in the belief that the beginning college student needs a genial and agile guide through Western Civilization rather than an encyclopedic, overillustrated catalogue of details. With the conviction that the great text-book in Western Civilization is yet to be written, we have written a succinct one that will leave adequate time for the student to pursue extensive collateral reading. Bibliographies are provided at the end of the book's various sections.

We have exchanged many ideas with one another, and with the general editor, and some of these ideas flow through the entire book. In general, the sections on ancient and medieval history are the work of C. Warren Hollister, the chapters on the Renaissance and Reformation are by John F. H. New, those on the seventeenth and eighteenth centuries are by James Hardy, and the concluding portions—since 1815—are by Roger Williams.

C. WARREN HOLLISTER
JOHN F. H. NEW
JAMES D. HARDY, JR.
ROGER L. WILLIAMS

Contents

PROLOGUE: THE LEGACY OF THE
ANCIENT NEAR EAST 1

PART 1   THE LEGACY OF GREECE 11

1   The Rise and Decline of Classical Greece 13
2   The Thought and Culture of Classical
    Greece 31
3   The Hellenistic Age 44

PART 2   THE LEGACY OF ROME 53

4   The Rise of Rome: Kingdom, Republic,
    Empire 55
5   Rome and Jerusalem 75
6   The Waning of the Western Empire 90

PART 3   THE EARLY MIDDLE AGES: THE
GENESIS OF WESTERN CIVILIZATION 99

7   Byzantium, Islam, and Western
    Christendom 101
8   Carolingian Europe and the New
    Invasions 113
9   Europe Survives the Siege 121

PART 4   THE HIGH MIDDLE AGES:
THE FIRST FLOWERING OF EUROPEAN
CULTURE 131

10   Economic Revolution and New
     Frontiers 133
11   The Politics of High-Medieval
     Europe 142
12   New Dimensions in Medieval
     Christianity 152
13   Thought, Letters, and the Arts 161

PART 5   LATE-MEDIEVAL AND RENAISSANCE
EUROPE: THE ORDEAL OF TRANSITION 177

14   Church and State in the Fourteenth and
     Fifteenth Centuries 179
15   Economic and Cultural Change 193
16   The Culture of the Renaissance 199

PART 6   THE AGE OF THE
REFORMATION 217

17   The Transformation of Europe 219
18   The Protestant Reformation 226
19   The Catholic Reformation and the
     Counterreformation 243

PART 7 EUROPE IN CRISIS: FROM REFORMATION TO ENLIGHTENMENT 255

20 State Churches and Religious Wars: 1560–1648 257

21 Europe Overseas: The Growth of Empire 270

22 Hard Times: The Great Depression— 1590–1660 285

23 The World Reconsidered: The Development of Modern Science 297

PART 8 ENLIGHTENMENT, REVOLUTION, INDUSTRIALIZATION 313

24 State Building and State-Craft: 1648–1789 315

25 Diplomacy and Warfare: 1648–1789 330

26 The Age of Enlightenment 343

27 The Eighteenth Century: The Crisis of the Old Order 353

28 Industrialization 371

29 Europe in Revolution: 1789–1814 385

PART 9 THE NINETEENTH CENTURY: 1814-1914 407

30 The Vienna Settlement and the Metternich Era: 1815–1848 409

31 The Replacement of the Vienna Settlement: 1848–1871 420

32 The Road to Total War: 1871–1914 432

33 The Gathering Centraization of Power 443

34 The Two Cultures of the Nineteenth Century 454

PART 10 THE TWENTIETH CENTURY 477

35 World War I and its Aftermath 479

36 The Uneasy Peace 495

37 The Great Dictatorship and the Crisis of the 1930s 505

38 World War II 520

39 From Hot to Cold War and Beyond 531

40 The Cultures of the Twentieth Century 550

Index 561

River Through Time

Time

THE COURSE OF WESTERN CIVILIZATION

Prologue: The Legacy of the Ancient Near East

There are those who believe that history is obsolete. The present is said to be so radically different from the past that we have nothing to learn from former generations or previous ages. This view, which finds its most ardent supporters among those most ignorant of the past, cuts us off from the flow of history and prevents our seeing human society in its proper perspective: as a river through time.

The ideas, experiments, blunders, and labors of many generations underlie the modern technological marvels that have revolutionized our standard of living and our means of polluting and killing. Our political and economic institutions—parliamentary, capitalist, communist, socialist, fascist—are products of long historical processes. The same is true of our ways of thinking about religion, social justice, urban planning, and astrophysics, our achievements in medicine with their by-product of overpopulation, and our sense of what is moral and what is obscene. These are not matters unique to us but are, rather, aspects of our own moment in the evolution of an age-old civilization. Only the most indifferent can fail to wonder about the roots of the culture that surrounds us, shapes our assumptions, defines our options, and governs the very categories in which we judge and perceive. For once we grasp that we are products of a transitory moment in the flow of human culture, we can raise our vision from the features of the passing shoreline to the whole course of the river. We can begin to see past the blinders of our own generation, class, and nation, and to view our lives—and the lives of our contemporaries—in historical dimension. Stretching our minds and imaginations across an immense panorama of diverse, interconnected human experiences, we deepen our understanding of our own society, and of ourselves.

The Formation of Ancient Near-Eastern Civilization

The Western cultural tradition reaches back some 1200 years into the European past. It rose from the debris of a still older civilization — the Greco-Roman — from which is derived much of its political, artistic and philosophical orientation. Western Civilization drew also from the Judeo-Christian tradition of the Ancient Near East which was inspired in turn by the more ancient religious thought of Mesopotamia, Egypt and the lands between. Greco-Roman civilization was itself a child of former cultures: Minoan, Etruscan, and, behind them, Egyptian and Mesopotamian. This connected sequence of civilizations extends, like an immense chain, backward some six thousand years to Mesopotamia's emergence from the Stone Age, and forward into an unknown future.

What do we mean by civilization? Various simple definitions have been suggested at one time or another, but none is entirely satisfactory. Civilization is usually associated with the town or city (the Latin *civitas*), yet the people of ancient Egypt were more or less evenly spread through the Nile valley. The population of the valley was dense, but there were few cities. Do we associate civilization with writing? This art was unknown among some of the ancient civilizations of the Americas.

Civilization can only be regarded as a configuration of several elements, all of which are products of a fairly high degree of social organization. It is best understood not in the abstract but in the concrete, as a convenient label for a whole series of related developments such as

were occurring in the Nile and Tigris-Euphrates valleys between about 4000 and 3000 B.C. As the fourth millennium opened, the Near East was a mosaic of Neolithic farming communities,* nomadic herdsmen, and peoples whose livelihood still depended on hunting and fishing. By 3000 B.C. in Mesopotamia the village was giving way to the city-state, a political unit that was far larger and more complex than the Neolithic community. This momentous process was accompanied by a remarkable series of fundamental discoveries and inventions: writing; mathematics; the widespread use of copper and, shortly afterward, bronze; monumental architecture; a calendar; large-scale irrigation systems; and administrative bureaucracies. Collectively, these developments mark the transformation from primitive society to civilization.

These same processes were occurring in the Nile basin. Although the city was far less prominent in Egypt than in Mesopotamia, the Egyptians were centuries ahead of the Mesopotamians in achieving political unity. By 3000 B.C. the entire Nile valley had been organized into a single state. The fourth millennium, which witnessed the birth of civilization in Mesopotamia and Egypt, was in some respects the most fundamentally creative era in human history.

The early civilizations of Egypt and Mesopotamia evolved the basic social structures that came to characterize all subsequent civilizations up to the industrial revolution of the late eighteenth century. They were built on a broad human base of agricultural slaves (or serfs), living more or less at the subsistence level, whose economic productivity made possible the emergence of a small commercial and manufacturing class—usually of low social status—and of a tiny elite group of landed nobles and priests. At the top of the social pyramid was a prince—a king, pharaoh or emperor, usually absolute in

* The Neolithic Age, or "New Stone Age," was itself the product of a revolutionary change in the Near East, thousands of years earlier, from the traditional hunting economy to a new agrarian and pastoral economy.

his political power and claiming kinship or association with the gods. It has become commonplace in recent times to condemn these civilizations as "exploitative," "repressive," and "superstitious." And in an evident sense, they were. Yet this was the pattern that all large-scale ancient civilizations followed, in the East and in the West, in the New World as well as in the Old. To condemn them all is a childish indulgence that blocks any serious effort at deeper understanding. Civilizations have doubtless imposed a tragic burden on humanity. Freud argued that they are the sources of some of our basic neuroses. But they also became avenues of creative human expression to a degree unknown before. And they provided the large-scale political and economic organizations whereby food production could be significantly increased and, with it, the security of human lives. If the preindustrial civilizations were a kind of bondage, the profound insecurity of the previous hunting, gathering, and primitive pastoral and agrarian societies amounted to a bondage far greater—a bondage to the whims of wilderness nature. For it is only from the perspective of a secure, developed civilization that the wilderness can be viewed with romance and nostalgia. Only an advanced industrial society is inclined to produce national parks. To precivilized peoples—lacking camp stoves, forest rangers, grocery stores, and comfortable homes to return to after vacation —the wilderness would have been a world of desperate insecurity and dark terror.

It was industrialization that made possible our present-day dream of economic abundance, justly shared by all. Preindustrial peoples, lacking the necessary productivity, would have found a welfare state like modern Sweden beyond conceiving. The universality of vast social and economic cleavages in ancient civilizations, suggests that a slave society was the only available means of escape from the shared starvation of primitive culture. If there were other options, they were never taken—not, at least, until the High and Late Middle Ages, when slavery and, afterwards serfdom gradually disappeared from large portions of Western Europe. And deep social inequalities contined long thereafter. Indeed, they persist today, even in the most advanced and affluent societies of our world—and with far less excuse.

The pattern of agrarian slavery-serfdom and privileged elites moulded the social orders of Egypt's and Mesopotamia's successor civilizations, down to the Greek, Roman, Islamic, Byzantine, and medieval European. Each had its own characteristic variations, but these were variations on a single theme: a wealthy minority and an impoverished, economically productive, politically voiceless majority. Understanding this reality, we will perhaps have the wisdom not to single out and castigate the ancient Athenians for having slaves, or the medieval nobility for living off the toil of peasants. The system was thousands of years old, deeply ingrained, and omnipresent. It is perhaps the ancient Near East's most fundamental legacy to Greece, Rome, and the civilization of Western Europe.

But there are other legacies as well, far too numerous to discuss. There was the invention of writing, the subsequent development of methods of working iron, the study of the stars by Babylonian astrologers, discoveries in practical chemistry by Egyptians as they mummified their pharaohs, advances in engineering, dike building, temple construction, road building, and administrative organization. The ancient Persians developed a remarkably efficient postal system. The ancient Canaanites invented the alphabet, reducing the hundreds of syllabic signs of earlier scripts to 29 symbols representing the consonants, and thus opened the way to a vast expansion of literacy.

Religion

Beyond all these contributions, the ancient Near East shaped the religious concepts of Western Europe, Byzantium, and Islam. And whatever one's personal attitude toward religion might be, no sensitive student would ignore religion's tremendous role in human history. The civilizations of Egypt and Mesopotamia, no less than the primitive societies that preceded them, were god-ridden. Early peoples tended to regard all inanimate objects as personalities with wills of their own. Mountains, trees, rivers, even sticks and stones, were alive. The more spectacular aspects of nature—the wind, the sky, the sun, the earth—were commonly regarded as gods. Thus, whereas modern peoples regard the world around them as inanimate—as an "it"—primitive and early civilized peoples thought of it as animate —as a "thou." To them, human beings were linked to nature in an "I-Thou" relationship.

The various ancient civilizations, each in its distinctive way, gave expression to these attitudes and, in a few instances, went beyond them. The Mesopotamians, awed and terrorized by nature—and by the incessant threat of barbarian invasion —viewed themselves as playthings of the gods—as tragic figures subject to the whims of nature. "Mere man—," the Mesopotamians observed, "his days are numbered. Whatever he may do, he is but wind." The Egyptians on the other hand, protected by the deserts that surrounded their Nile valley, regarded the gods more optimistically, believing that nature had blessed them and would continue to do so. Much later on, the Persians made a sharp break with the Near Eastern religious tradition, replacing it with a doctrine known as Zoroastrianism. The Persian Zoroastrians viewed the world as an arena of combat between a god of goodness, light and spirit and a god of evil and darkness who created the physical universe. The great Zoroastrian goal was to liberate the soul from the physical body and thus escape from the realm of evil and matter into the world of spirit. This Zoroastrian dualism between good and evil exerted a powerful influence on various important religions of the Greco-Roman world—including Christianity. But far greater was the influence of the Israelites, whose contribution to religious thought is altogether unique in the history of the ancient world.

The Israelites

No other ancient Near Eastern people are as familiar to us as the Israelites. Their Bible has been studied by scholars and men of faith throughout the centuries of Western civilization. It is the fountainhead of Judaism, Islam, and Christianity, and a crucial element in the heritage of modern man. As a historical source it enables us to endow the dry bones of ancient Israel with flesh and life. But it also raises serious problems of historical criticism. The Biblical critics of the nineteenth century rejected the traditional belief in divine inspiration and subjected the Bible to painstaking scrutiny of the sort that historians normally apply to their documents. These critics doubted the historical existence of Abraham, Jacob—even Moses —and concluded that the Bible was not especially good history. More recently, however, certain Biblical episodes that were previously rejected as mere myth have been corroborated by new archaeological discoveries and by comparisons with non-Biblical sources. Scholars are now inclined to regard the Bible as a relatively reliable body of ancient historical documents.

According to the Bible, the history of the Jews begins when the patriarch Abraham entered into an agreement or *Covenant* with a specific deity, "the God of Abraham." Abraham promised not to recognize or worship any other god, and, in return, he and his family were taken under the special protection of the God of Abraham. The Covenant was renewed by all succeeding generations of Abraham's clan, and became a basic ingredient of Jewish religious thought. It seems unlikely that Abraham viewed his God as the only god. Had he been asked, he would probably have conceded the existence of other deities, yet from the *practical* standpoint even Abraham was a monotheist. The existence of other gods was irrelevant to him, for it was his God alone that Abraham honored.

Under Jacob, Abraham's grandson, the clan is said to have been driven by famine from Palestine to Egypt. This migration, sometime around 1600 B.C., was probably not limited to Jacob and his immediate family, but included kindred folk who would be known henceforth as Hebrews. The Hebrews seem to have prospered in Egypt for a time, but around 1570 the Egyptians enslaved all foreigners, forcing them to labor for the state. During this prolonged period of bondage, the Covenant of Abraham was extended to include more and more of the Hebrews.

At length, perhaps sometime in the fourteenth century B.C., a Hebrew, trained in the Egyptian bureaucracy and bearing the Egyptian name of Moses, led a band of his own and other enslaved peoples to freedom. For a long generation they wandered in the wilderness of the Sinai Desert. Under Moses' superb leadership they were forged into a unified people and the personal Covenant was transformed into a Covenant between God and the whole Hebrew nation. The God of Abraham was given the name "Yahweh" (traditionally translated as Jehovah). It is to this Sinai period that the Bible ascribes the divine dictation of the Ten Commandments.

Moses had promised to lead his people to the "promised land" of Palestine or Canaan, but when the Hebrews emerged at last from the wilderness, Moses was dead, and a new generation had arisen. Under the leadership of Joshua, the Hebrews entered the land of the Canaanites, perhaps around the beginning of the thirteenth century, and won a series of important victories. The best known of Joshua's battles was fought at the ancient city of Jericho whose walls, we are told, came tumbling down. But the struggle with the Canaanites did not end with these initial battles. It continued with many ups and downs for another two centuries during which the Hebrews were deeply influenced by Canaanite civilization. They adopted a Canaanite dialect and used the Canaanite alphabet. Some even began to worship Canaanite gods, much to the chagrin of the orthodox. During these centuries the Hebrews were loosely organized into tribes under local military leaders known inappropriately as "judges." The epoch of the judges gave way at length to a unified monarchy which was made necessary by the increasing military pressure of an aggresive tribe of invaders: the Philistines.

The United Israelite Kingdom and Its Aftermath

In 1020, the priest Samuel anointed Saul, Israel's first king. Saul waged war against the Philistines with some success but was far outshone by his able successor, David (1005 to 965), who is said to have demonstrated his prowess even as a child by slaying the great Philistine, Goliath, with a slingshot. Under David and his son Solomon (965-925), Israel reached its political zenith. Their kingdom dominated the area of modern Syria and Israel and extended inland toward the Euphrates River. This was the golden age that etched itself on Israel's imagination for all time to come—the age that for endless generations the Jews never despaired of recovering.

It was David's great hope to build a permanent, central temple for Yahweh in

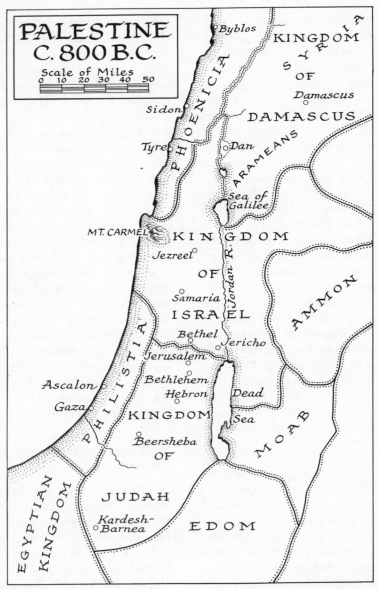

Jerusalem, a city that he had recently conquered, and under Solomon the temple was completed. Jerusalem itself became the cosmopolitan capital of a wealthy empire. Solomon surrounded himself with all the trappings of Near Eastern monarchy from bureaucrats to concubines. But Solomon's subjects were obliged to pay for all this imperial glory with heavy taxes and forced labor, and many of them concluded that the price was too high. Upon Solomon's death (925 B.C.) Israelite particularism reasserted itself, and the kingdom split into two halves: a large state to the north known thenceforth as Israel, and a much smaller but more coherent state to the south, centering on Jerusalem, that was called Judah.

This political schism brought an early end to Hebrew imperialism. Around 900 B.C., the Near East entered a new age of great empires. The first of these, the Assyrian Empire, exerted increasing military pressure against both Israel and

Judah. Israel fell to the Assyrians in 722, and her people were scattered across the Near East where they faded into the local populations and vanished from history. Judah survived the Assyrian attacks only to fall to Assyria's imperial successor, the Babylonian Empire, in 586. Judah's political and intellectual leaders were banished to Babylon where they and their children endured that tragic epoch in Biblical history, the Babylonian Captivity (586-539 B.C.). The bitterness of exile is captured in the opening lines of the 137th Psalm:

By the rivers of Babylon,
There we sat down, yea, we wept,
When we remembered Zion.

The Prophets

The devastating experience of divided kingdom and Babylonian Captivity evoked a profound religious response. The moral initiative now passed from kings and priests to inspired individuals known as prophets whose boldly original spiritual insights—arising out of an age of agony and despair—deepened and ennobled the Hebrew religion immeasurably. To the prophets, law and ritual were insufficient without sincerity of purpose and righteousness of life. The prophet Micah expressed this insight with striking brevity:

It has been shown to you, O man, what is good
and what the Lord requires of you:
Only to do justice
and live loyally
and walk humbly with your God [6:8].

The teachings of the prophets were based on two fundamental concepts: (1) the covenant between God and his Hebrew people, and (2) the consequent obligation of Israelites to treat one another justly. Their vision of justice and righteousness was not applied to mankind at large but only to the Israelite community; yet even with that important qualification it was a profound affirmation of human dignity. The prophetic teachings became a fundamental component of Hebrew thought. More than that, they underlie the tradition of social justice that has developed in Western Civilization. The prophets' insistence that all Israelites were equal in the sight of God would ultimately be expanded into the doctrine of universal human equality.

In the hands of the prophets, the concept of Yahweh was universalized. They explained the collapse of Solomon's empire and the Assyrian and Babylonian conquests by asserting that Yahweh had used the Hebrews' enemies to punish his chosen people for their transgressions and to prepare them for a triumphant future. But if this was so, then Yahweh's power was evidently not limited to the Hebrews, but embraced all peoples. Wheras Yahweh had formerly been the only God that *mattered*, he was now proclaimed as the only God that *existed*. The prophet Amos quotes the Lord as saying,

Did I not bring up Israel
from the land of Egypt
and the Philistines from Caphtor
and the Syrians from Kir? [9:7].

Yahweh was the Lord of nations, yet the Hebrews remained His chosen people. History itself could be understood only in terms of Israel's encounter with God. The Hebrews were unique among the peoples of the Ancient Near East in their sensitivity toward history, for to them, God's relations with man occurred in a historical dimension, and history itself was directed by God toward certain predetermined goals. Thus, it was Yahweh, not the Babylonians, who sent the Hebrews into exile, and in the fullness of time, so the prophets said, Yahweh would build their kingdom anew. A divinely appointed leader of the house of David—a Messiah—would one day be sent to consummate the divine plan by reestablishing the political glory of Israel. This assurance sustained the Hebrew exiles in Babylon, and they preserved their integrity and their faith against the lures of a powerful alien culture. A few succumbed to the temptations of Babylon, but the majority held fast in the conviction that history was on their side.

Later Jewish History

In 539 B.C. the Babylonian Empire gave way to the Persian Empire, and the Hebrews were permitted to return to their homeland and rebuild the temple of Jerusalem. They could now practice their faith without interference, but they remained under Persian political control. Two centuries thereafter Persian rule gave way to Greek rule, and in time the Greeks were replaced by the Romans. During these postexilic centuries, the Hebrew sacred writings were collected, sifted, and expanded, and the Old Testament acquired its final form. As always, the Israelites were torn between the desire to preserve the purity of their heritage and the impulse to accommodate themselves to outside cultural influences. From time to time they rebelled against their political masters but never with lasting success. Their final rebellion, in A.D. 70, prompted the Romans to destroy their temple and scatter them throughout the Empire. There followed an exile far more prolonged than their earlier ones in Egypt and Babylonia, lasting until the present century. But the Jews had demonstrated long before that they could survive as a people and a faith without political unity.

The impact of the ancient Hebrews on future civilizations has been immense. The Old Testament, a tremendous literary monument in itself, has been of incalculable importance in the development of European culture. The Hebrews' sense of history—as a dynamic, purposive, morally-significant process of human-divine interaction—went far beyond the histor-

ical concepts of other Near Eastern peoples and became a fundamental element in the historical vision of Western Civilization. But at the core of everything is their ethical monotheism—their vision of a single God of incredible power who is also a God of righteousness and mercy. The Hebrew confronted his universe in a new way. The world was no longer pregnant with spirits; nature was no longer a "Thou," but rather the handiwork of a far greater "Thou." The myriad spooks and demons of tree, rock, and mountain dissolved before the unutterable holiness of the God of Israel.

CHRONOLOGY OF THE ANCIENT HEBREWS

All dates except the last are B.C.

?1600–1350:	Migration to Egypt and bondage there
?1350–1310	Moses and the Sinai
?1300–1020	Era of the Judges
1020–925:	United Kingdom of Israel
925–722:	Political split: Israel and Judah
722:	Israel falls to the Assyrians
586–539	Judah falls: Babylonian captivity
539:	Establishment of Persian Empire; Babylonian captives return to Palestine
330:	Greek domination replaces Persian
c.189:	Roman domination replaces Greek
A.D. 70	Last Hebrew rebellion; Romans destroy Temple of Jerusalem and scatter the Jews throughout the Empire

SUGGESTED READINGS

The asterisk indicates a paperback edition.

Chester G. Starr, *Early Man: Prehistory and the Civilizations of the Ancient Near East* (*New York: Oxford Press, 1973).

V. Gordon Childe, *What Happened in History* (*Baltimore, Md.: Penguin, 1964).

Stuart Piggott, ed., *The Dawn of Civilization* (New York: McGraw-Hill, 1961).

Sabatino Moscati, *The Face of the Ancient Orient* (*New York: Doubleday, 1962).

John A. Wilson, *The Culture of Egypt* (*Chicago: University of Chicago Press, 1959).

Robert C. Zaehner, *The Dawn and Twilight of Zoroastrianism* (New York: Putnam, 1961).

H. M. Orlinsky, *Ancient Israel* (*Ithaca, N. Y.: Cornell Press, 1954).

T. J. Meek, *Hebrew Origins* (*New York: Harper, 1960).

Part 1 The Legacy of Greece

1
The Rise and Decline of Classical Greece

The World of the Ancient Aegean

One of the supreme Greek epic poems, Homer's *Odyssey*, tells of the perils and adventures of the ancient Greek chieftain Odysseus as he returned home by sea from the fall of Troy. As a tale of a hero's conquest of the terrors of the ocean, the *Odyssey* symbolizes a central quality of the Greek experience. For the Greeks were, above all, a seafaring people. Sailing out from their barren, mountainous homeland, they planted colonies far and wide and eventually came to dominate the commerce of the eastern Mediterranean. In the end they, like their mythical hero Odysseus, conquered the sea and gained fame and sorrow in the process.

The two great Homeric epics, the *Odyssey* and the *Iliad*, originated in the eighth century B.C. Both epics tell of the conclusion and aftermath of a half-legendary, long-ago war between the Greeks and the Trojans—a struggle that ended with the Greek conquest of Troy. The *Iliad* and the *Odyssey* mark the dawn of written Greek literature, and yet hark back to a civilization far older than that of classical Greece. Archaeologists have found independent evidence of such a civilization—or, more properly, two closely related cultures. The earlier of the two, centering on the large Aegean island of Crete, is known as the Minoan (after Minos, a legendary king of Crete). The other, related culture flourished on the nearby Greek mainland and is called Mycenaean (after an ancient fortress town in southern Greece). The memory of the Minoan-Mycenaean era lingered on in later Greek literature like a half-remembered dream.

Archaeologists have concluded that Minoan civilization arose on the island of Crete in the third millennium B.C. The Minoans derived their technological and artistic skills from the still earlier civilizations of Mesopotamia, Egypt, and Asia Minor but developed them in novel and vitally creative directions. Excavations on Crete have unearthed ruins of great, rambling

Bull-leaping; fresco from Palace at Cnossus.   (Alison Frantz/Art Reference Bureau)

palaces, their walls decorated with vivacious paintings, their rooms containing exquisite statuettes and delicate polychromatic pottery fashioned with consummate skill and taste. Minoan art is light and flowing: plants, animals, marine life, youths playing games—all are portrayed with stylistic flair and stunning naturalism. Like the later Greeks, the Minoans were a commercial, seafaring people. The absence of fortifications in the Cretan ruins suggests that the island was politically unified under the Minoan "sea kings" of Greek legend, and that its navy was regarded as an adequate defense. Its agriculture was devoted chiefly to the production of grain, wine, and olive oil—the so-called "Mediterranean triad"—which were also to be the major agricultural commodities of classical Greece.

The Mycenean Greeks

The Minoans of Crete were not a Greek-speaking people at all. Not until someone after about 2000 B.C. did the first Greeks begin settling the peninsula that would

later bear their name. Bringing little or no civilization with them, they gradually passed under the influence of Minoan culture, though retaining their political independence. After about 1580 B.C. great fortress cities began to arise in the district of southwestern Greece known as the Peloponnesus—cities such as Mycenae, Tiryns, and Pylos. With time, the political power of these cities spread, until at length all the princes of southern Greece may have come to recognize the supremacy of the warrior-kings of Mycenae.

These early Greeks were divided into tribes that were themselves subdivided into clans. Each clan consisted of a number of related families that had their own distinctive religious cult and held their lands and wealth in common. The Mycenaean Greeks learned much from the Minoans. Their culture differed from that of Crete chiefly in its emphasis on weapons and fortifications. They adapted the Minoan script to their own, very different language. Their art, architecture and customs were all strongly influenced by the Minoans, and Greek women began adopting Minoan dress, hairdos, and cosmetics. (The painted face is traditionally a mark of primitivism in men; of sophistication in women.)

Before long Mycenaean sailors were challenging the Cretan supremacy in the Aegean Sea. During the 1400s Minoan civilization was devastated by invasions that left the Cretan towns, villas and palaces in ruins. The great palaces were never rebuilt on their former scale, and the Minoan state seems to have disintegrated. The Mycenaean Greeks fell heir to the Minoan mastery of the Aegean.

Between about 1400 and 1200 the Greeks grew rich on their commerce and flourished exceedingly. It is at the end of this period, perhaps around 1200, that King Agamemnon of Mycenae led the Greeks against Troy. But even at the time of the Trojan War the political stability of Mycenaean Greece was being disturbed by the initial attacks and migrations of the Dorian Greeks and other tribes that were largely untouched by the civilizing effects of Minoan-Mycenaean culture. About 1120 B.C. the Dorian invasion of the Peloponnesus began in earnest. The writing inscribed on tablets found in Mycenaean cities of this era discloses frantic but vain preparations for defense. One after another, the cities of Greece were sacked and burned, and the civilization that had begun in Crete and later spread to the mainland came to an end at last.

The Greek Dark Age (c. 1120–800 B.C.)

Between Mycenaean and classical Greece lies a gap of several centuries known as the "dark age" of Hellenic history.* The Greeks lapsed into illiteracy, and when they began to write once again it was not in the old Minoan syllabary but in an alphabet derived from that of the Canaanites. The Mycenaean Greeks were violently displaced by the invasions. Most of the Peloponnesus became Dorian, and in time

* Hellenic means Greek; Hellas means Greece.

the leadership of that area, once exercised by Mycenae, passed to the new Dorian city of Sparta. Athens, as yet an unimportant town, held out against the invaders and became a haven for refugees. A group of mainland Greeks known as Ionians fled across the Aegean and settled along the western coast of Anatolia (Asia Minor) and on the islands offshore. Thenceforth, that region was known as Ionia and became an integral part of Greek civilization (see the map on p. 28). Throughout most of dark-age Greece, political conditions were chaotic, and sovereignty descended to the level of the village and the clan.

Homer

With the appearance of the Homeric epics in eighth-century Ionia the darkness began to lift. Both the *Iliad* and the *Odyssey* are the products of a long oral tradition carried on by the minstrels of Mycenaean and post-Mycenaean times who recited their songs of heroic deeds at the banquets of the nobility. Whether the epics in their final form were the work of one man or several is in dispute. Someone has suggested facetiously that the epics should not be associated with Homer at all but with an entirely different person of the same name.

Both epics are filled with vivid accounts of battle and adventure, but at heart both are concerned with ultimate problems of human life. The *Iliad* depicts the tragic consequences of the quarrel between two sensitive and passionate Greek leaders, Agamemnon and Achilles, toward the end of the Trojan War:

Divine Muse, sing of the ruinous wrath of Achilles, Peleus' son, which brought ten thousand sorrows to the Greeks, sent the souls of many brave heroes down to the world of the dead, and left their bodies to be eaten by dogs and birds: and the will of Zeus was fulfilled. Begin where they first quarrelled, Agamemnon the King of Men, and great Achilles.†

Despite Homer's allusion to the will of Zeus, his characters are by no means puppets of the gods, even though divine intervention occurs repeatedly in his narrative. Rather they are intensely—sometimes violently—human, and they are doomed to suffer the consequences of their own deeds. In this respect, as in many others, Homer foreshadows the great Greek tragic dramatists of the fifth century.

Achilles' dazzling career no less than that of the seagoing Odysseus, prefigures the career of Greece itself. The gods were said to have offered Achilles the alternatives of a long but mediocre life or glory and an early death. His choice symbolizes the tragic, meteoric course of Hellenic history.

Homer was the first European poet known to us and he has never been surpassed. The *Iliad* and the *Odyssey* were the Old and New Testament of ancient Greece, studied by every Greek schoolboy and cherished by Greek writers and artists as an inexhaustible source of inspiration. The epics were typically Greek in their rigorous and economical organization around a single great theme, their lucidity, their moments of tenderness that never slip into sentimentality—in short, their brilliantly successful synthesis of intellectualism and humanity.

The Homeric Gods

The gods of Mt. Olympus, who play such a significant role in the Homeric poems, had a great variety of individual backgrounds. Poseidon, the sea god, was Minoan; Zeus, the hurler of thunderbolts and ruler of Olympus, was a Dorian god; Aphrodite, the goddess of love, was an astral deity from Babylonia; Apollo was from Asia Minor; and a number of other gods were local deities long before they

† Translated by H. D. F. Kitto in *The Greeks* (rev. ed., Penguin, 1957), p. 45.

entered the divine assemblage of Olympus. By Homer's time these diverse gods had been arranged into a coherent hierarchy of related deities common to all Greeks. The Olympic gods were anthropomorphic; that is, they were human in form and personality, capable of rage, lust, jealousy, and all the other traits of the warrior-hero. But they also possessed immortality and various other superhuman attributes. The universality of the Olympic cult served as an important unifying force that compensated in part for the localism that always characterized Greek politics. Yet each clan and each district also honored its own special gods, many of whom, like Athena the patron goddess of Athens, were represented in the Olympic pantheon. The worship of these local gods was associated with feelings of family devotion or regional and civic pride. The gods were concerned chiefly with the well-being of social groups rather than the prosperity or salvation of the individual, and their worship was therefore almost indistinguishable from patriotism.

Among the lower classes ancient fertility deities remained immensely popular. Demeter, the goddess of grain, and Dionysus, the god of wine, were almost ignored in the Homeric epics but seem to have been far more important to the Greek peasantry than were the proud, aristocratic deities of Olympus. Eleusis, a small town near Athens, became the chief religious center for the worship of Demeter, and the rites celebrated there, the Eleusinian Mysteries, dramatized the ancient myth of death and resurrection. The worship of Dionysus was characterized by wild orgies during which female worshipers would dance and scream through the night. (In time these rites became more sedate and respectable.) Both Demeter and Dionysus offered their follower the hope of personal salvation and immortality that was lacking in Olympic religion. At the bottom of the social order animism persisted in all its bewildering and exotic forms: the world of the Greek peasant, like that of his Near-Eastern contemporaries, was literally crawling with gods.

The Polis

By Homer's time, Greek culture was developing throughout the area surrounding the Aegean Sea—in Ionia along the coast of Anatolia, on the Aegean islands, in Athens and its surrounding district of Attica, in the Peloponnesus, and in other regions of mainland Greece. (See the map on p. 28). The roughness of the Ionian Coast, the obvious insularity of the islands, and the mountains and inlets that divided Greece itself into a number of semi-isloated districts discouraged the development of a unified pan-Hellenic state, but the existence of the myriad city-states of classical Greece cannot be explained entirely by the environment. There are numerous examples of small independent states separated by no geographical barriers whatever—of several autonomous districts, for example, on a single island. Perhaps the Greeks lived in city-states simply as a matter of choice. Whatever the reason, classical Greek culture without the independent city-state is inconceivable.

We have used the term "city-state" to describe what the Greeks knew as the "polis." Actually, "polis" is untranslatable, and "city-state" fails to convey its full meaning. In classical times the word was packed with emotional and intellectual content. Each polis had its own distinctive customs and its own gods and was an object of intense religious-patriotic devotion. More than a mere region, it was a community of citizens—the inhabitants of both town and surrounding district who enjoyed political rights and played a role in government. Words such as "political," "politics," and "polity" come from the Greek "polis"; to the Greeks, politics without the polis would be impossible. Aristotle is often quoted as saying that man is a political animal; what he really said was

that man was a creature who belonged in a polis. In a vast empire like that of Persia, so the Greeks believed, slaves could live—barbarians could live—but not free and civilized men. The polis was the Greeks' answer to the perennial conflict between man and the state, and perhaps no other human institution has succeeded in reconciling these two concepts so satisfactorily. The Greek expressed his intense individualism *through* the polis, not in spite of it. The polis was sufficiently small that its members could behave as individuals rather than mass men. The chief political virtue was participation, not obedience. Accordingly, the polis became the vessel of Greek creativity and the matrix of the Greek spirit. A unified pan-Hellenic state might perhaps have eliminated the inter-city warfare that was endemic in classical Greece. It might have brought peace, stability, and power, but at the sacrifice of the very institution that made classical Greece what it was.

Still, the system of independent warring "city-states" was a remarkably inefficient basis for Greek political organization. The Greeks were able to evolve and flourish only because they developed in a political vacuum. The Minoans were only a memory, and Macedonian and Roman imperialism lay in the future. During the formative period of the polis system in the ninth, eighth, and seventh centuries the Assyrians were concerned primarily with maintaining their land empire, and the seafaring Phoenicians* were not a dangerous military power. The chief threat to the Greek of the dark age was the violence of his own people. As a matter of security the inhabitants of a small district would often erect a citadel on some central hill which they called an acropolis (high town). The acropolis was the natural assembly

---

* Settled on a narrow coastal strip along the eastern Mediterranean, the Phoenicians were a commercial people descended from the ancient Canaanites. It was they who introduced the Canaanite aphabet to dark-age Greece.

place of the district in time of war and its chief religious center. As local commerce developed, an agora or marketplace usually arose at the foot of the acropolis, and many of the farmers whose fields were nearby built houses around the market, for reasons of sociability and defense.

The Social Orders

At about the time that the polis was emerging, descendants of the original tribal elders were evolving into a hereditary aristocracy. An occasional polis might be ruled by a king (*basileus*) but, generally speaking, monarchy died out with Mycenae or was reduced to a ceremonial office. By about 700 B.C., or shortly thereafter, virtually every Greek king had been overthrown or shorn of all but his religious functions, leaving the aristocracy in full control. The aristocrats had meanwhile appropriated to themselves the lion's share of the lands that the clan members had formerly held in common. Slowly the polis was replacing the clan as the object of primary allegiance and the focus of political activity, but the aristocracy rode out the waves of change, growing in wealth and power.

Below the aristocracy was a class of small farmers who had managed to acquire fragments of the old clan common lands or who had developed new farms on virgin soil. These Greek farmers had no genuine voice in political affairs, and their economic situation was always hazardous. The Greek soil is the most barren in Europe, and while the large-scale cultivation of vine and olive usually brought a profit to the aristocrat, the small farmer tended to sink gradually into debt. His deplorable condition was portrayed vividly by the eighth-century poet Hesiod, a peasant himself, who wrote in a powerful, down-to-earth style. In his *Works and Days* Hesiod describes a world that had declined from a primitive golden age to the present "age of iron," characterized by a corrupt nobility and a downtrodden peasantry. For the common farmer, life was "bad in winter, cruel in summer—never good." Yet Hesiod insists that righteousness will triumph in the end. In the meantime the peasant must work all the harder: "In the sweat of your face shall you eat bread." Out of an age in which the peasant's lot seemed hopeless indeed, Hesiod proclaimed his faith in the ultimate victory of social justice and the dignity of toil.

Colonization (750–550 B.C.)

Even as Hesiod was writing his *Works and Days*, a movement was beginning that would bring a degree of relief to the small farmer and the still lower classes of the landless and dispossessed. By 750 B.C. the Greeks had once again taken to the sea—as pirates in search of booty or as merchants in search of copper and iron (rare in Greece) and the profits of trade. In this adventurous age a single crew of Greek seamen might raid and plunder one port and sell the loot as peaceful merchants in the next. During the course of their voyaging they found many fertile districts ripe for colonization, and during the two centuries between about 750 and 550 B.C. a vast movement of colonial expansion occurred that was to transform not only Greece itself but the whole Mediterranean world. Most of the more important Greek city-states sent bands of colonists across the seas to found new communities on distant shores, and in time some of these colonies sent out colonists of their own to establish still more settlements. The typical colonial polis, although bound to its mother city by ties of kinship, sentiment, and commerce and a common patriotic cult, was politically independent. We cannot speak of colonial empires in this period; even the word "colony" is a little misleading.

The motives behind the colonial movement are to be found in the economic and social troubles afflicting the Greek homeland. Colonization meant new opportunities for the landless freeman and the struggling peasant. It provided the aristocracy with a useful safety valve against the revolutionary pressures of rising population and accumulating discontent. And there were always a few disaffected aristocrats to lead the enterprise. In the rigorous environment of the pioneer colony hard work was much more likely to bring its reward than in the Greece of Hesiod. Here were all the opportunities for rapid social and economic advancement commonly associated with a frontier society.

Accordingly, in the course of two centuries or so the Greek polis spread from the Aegean region far and wide along the coasts of the Mediterranean and the Black Sea. The great Ionian polis of Miletus alone founded some 80 colonies. So many Greek settlements were established in southern Italy and Sicily that the whole area became known as *Magna Graecia*— Great Greece. The small colonial polis of Byzantium, dominating the trade route between the Black Sea and the Mediterranean, became, a millennium later, the capital of the East Roman Empire (under the name of Constantinople) and remained throughout the Middle Ages one of the greatest cities in the world. The Greek colony of Neopolis (New Polis) in southern Italy became the modern Napoli or Naples; Nikaia on the Riviera became the modern Nice; Massilia became Marseilles; Syracuse in Sicily remains to this day one of the island's chief cities. Through the city-states of *Magna Graecia* Greek culture and the Greek alphabet were transmitted to the Romans, but this was merely one important episode in a process that saw the diffusion of Greek civilization all along the shores of Southern Europe, North Africa, and Western Asia.

The colonial experience was profoundly significant in the evolution of the Greek way of life. The flourishing commerce that developed between the far-flung Hellenic settlements brought renewed prosperity to Greece itself. The homeland became an important source of wine, olive oil, and manufactured goods for the colonies. The needs of the new settlements stimulated the growth of industrial and commercial classes: smiths and potters, stevedores and sailors, transformed many Greek city-states from quiet agrarian communities into bustling mercantile centers. A new elite of merchants and manufacturers began to rival the old landed aristocrats in wealth and to challenge their traditional monopoly of political power. During the seventh and sixth centuries many of these wealthy upstarts forced their way into the councils of government alongside the old noble families.

The Tyrants

The century from about 650 to 550 was an age of fundamental economic and political change: the introduction of coinage from Lydia (in Asia Minor) was a boon to the mercantile elite, but tended to sharpen and amplify differences in wealth. It was in this age that the Ionian poet Pythermus wrote the golden line that alone of all his works has survived: "There's nothing else that matters—only money." The ever-increasing abundance of metal brought the heavy armor necessary in the warfare of the day within the financial reach of the middle class, and the mounted aristocratic army of earlier times began to give way in the early seventh century to a citizens' army of well-drilled, mailed infantrymen called hoplites. It was not long before the classes who fought for the polis began to demand a voice in its affairs.

At length the colonial movement began to wane. The best colonial sites were gradually preempted, and the rise of new powers like Carthage in the west and Lydia and Persia in the east prevented further expansion. As the safety valve slowly closed, the old pressures of economic and social discontent asserted themselves with renewed fury. One after another the city-states of

Greece and Ionia were torn by bloody civil strife as the middle and lower classes rose against the wealthy and privileged. In many instances these conflicts resulted in the overthrow of aristocratic control by "tyrants" who, like many of their modern counterparts, claimed to govern in the interests of the common people.

To the Greeks a tyrant was not necessarily an evil man but simply a ruler who rose to power without hereditary or legal claim. Typically, the tyrants did not smash the machinery of government but merely controlled it. They were new men, attuned to the currents of their age, who used the new coined money to hire armies of mercenaries and manipulated social discontent to their own advantage. Since they owed their power to the masses they sought to retain their support by canceling or scaling down debts, sponsoring impressive public works projects, redistributing the lands of aristocrats, and reforming taxation. But in most Greek communities tyranny did not last long. Some tyrants were overthrown by the older privileged classes; others, by the middle and lower classes who, as they became increasingly self-confident, sought to assume direct control of political affairs. By the opening of the fifth century the Greek political structure displayed every imaginable configuration of upper, lower, and middle class rule.

Sparta

Sparta and Athens, the two dominant city-states of fifth century Greece, stood at opposite ends of the Greek political spectrum. Neither played an important role in the colonization movement, for both adopted the alternative course of territorial expansion in their own districts. But while Athens evolved through the traditional stages of monarchy, aristocracy, tyranny, and democracy, Sparta acquired a peculiar mixed political system that discouraged commerce, cultural inventiveness and the amenities of life for the sake of iron discipline and military efficiency.

During the eighth and seventh centuries Sparta underwent the same political and social processes as other Greek states and played a vigorous role in the development of Greek culture. Yet from the beginning the Spartan spirit was singularly sober and masculine, and military concerns were always central to Spartan life. The stern severity of its art and its Dorian architecture contrasted sharply with the charming elegance of Ionia and the cultural dynamism of Attica. Politically, Sparta had always been conservative. When the aristocracy rose to power, the monarchy was not abolished but merely weakened. With the rise of the commoners certain democratic features were incorporated into the Spartan constitution yet the monarchy and aristocracy endured. Sparta could adapt cautiously to new conditions but found it terribly difficult to abandon anything from its past.

Toward the end of the eighth century, when other Greek states were beginning to relieve their social unrest and land hunger by colonization, Sparta conquered the fertile neighboring district of Messenia, appropriating large portions of the conquered land for its own citizens and reducing many Messenians to slavery. These unfortunate people, described by a Spartan poet as "asses worn by loads intolerable," were Greeks themselves and were too proud to accept their enslavement with resignation. In the late seventh century the Spartans crushed a Messenian revolt only after a desperate struggle. It became clear that the Messenians could be held down only by strong military force and constant watchfulness. It was at this point that Sparta transformed herself into a garrison state whose citizens became a standing army. Culture declined to the level of the barracks; the good life became the life of basic training.

Sparta became a tense, humorless society dedicated to the perpetuation, by force, of the status quo. Fear of Messenian rebellion grew into a collective paranoia as some 8000 Spartan citizens assumed the task of keeping 200,000 restless slaves in a state of permanent repression. Between the citizens and the slaves was a group of freemen without political rights who engaged in commercial activities (forbidden to the citizens themselves). The state slaves themselves—the helots—included not only Messenians but other Greek families as well, some of whom had been enslaved during the original Dorian conquests. The Spartan state divided its lands into numerous lots, one for each citizen, and the helots who worked these lots relieved the citizens of all economic responsibility, freeing them for a life of military training and service to the state.

The Constitution of "Lycurgus"

The writers of antiquity ascribed the Spartan constitution to a legendary lawgiver named Lycurgus, and despite its evolutionary elements the constitution operated with such rigorous logical consistency as to suggest the hand of a single author. Sparta had two kings whose powers had been greatly reduced by the sixth century. One or the other of them served as supreme commander on every military campaign, but at home their authority was overshadowed by that of three other bodies: (1) an aristocratic council of elders, (2) an executive board of five *ephors* elected from the whole citizenry, and (3) an assembly that included every Spartan citizen over thirty. Thus, if one counts only her handful of citizens, Sparta was a democracy, although a limited one. The assembly had the function of approving or disapproving all important questions of state, but it did so by acclamation rather than ballot, and its members were not permitted to debate the issues. Accordingly, this democratic assembly was by no means an arena of rough and tumble political conflict. It was characterized rather by the same dreary conformity that overhung all Spartan life.

The lives of Sparta's citizens were tended and guided by the state from cradle to grave, always for the purpose of producing strong, courageous, highly disciplined soldiers. The introduction of styles, luxuries, and ideas from without was rigorously controlled. At a time when coinage was stimulating economic life elsewhere Sparta used simple iron bars as her medium of exchange. Spartan citizens seldom left their homeland except on campaigns, and outsiders were discouraged from visiting Sparta. Spartan infants were abandoned to die of exposure if they were puny or malformed. At the age of seven the Spartan boy was turned over to the state and spent his next thirteen years in a program of education in military skills, physical training, the endurance of hardships, and unquestioning devotion to the polis. The typical product of this system was patriotic, strong, and courageous, but incurious. At twenty he entered the citizen army and lived his next ten years in a barracks. He might marry, but he could visit his wife only if he was sufficiently resourceful to elude the barracks guards (this seems to have been regarded as a test of skill). At thirty he became a full-fledged citizen. He could now live at home, but he ate his meals at a public mess to which he was obliged to contribute the products of his assigned fields. The fare at these public messes was Spartan in the extreme. One visitor, after eating a typical meal, remarked, "Now I understand why the Spartans do not fear death."

The Spartan citizen had almost no individual existence; his life was dedicated to the state. If the helot's life was hard, so was the citizen's. Life in Sparta would seem to be a violent negation of Greek individualism, yet many Greeks were unashamed admirers of the Spartan regime. To them,

Sparta represented the ultimate in self-denial and commitment to a logical idea. The Greeks admired the ordered life, and nowhere was life more ordered than in Sparta. To the Greek, there was a crucial difference between the helot and the Spartan citizen: the helot endured hardships because he had to; the citizen, because he *chose* to. And the Spartans always remembered that the object of their heroic efforts was the maintenance of the status quo—not aggressive imperialism. They were the best warriors in Greece, yet they employed their military advantage with restraint. To the accusation of artistic sterility a Spartan might reply that his state was artistic in the most basic sense of the word—that Sparta, with all its institutions directed uncompromisingly toward a single ideal, was itself a work of art.

Athens

Athens dates from the Mycenaean Age, but not until much later did it become prominent in Greek politics and culture. By about 700 B.C. the earlier monarchy had been deprived of political power by the aristocracy, and the entire district of Attica had been united into a single state whose political and commercial center was Athens itself. But the free inhabitants of Attica became Athenian citizens, not Athenian slaves, and the district was held together by bonds of mutual allegiance rather than military might. To be an Attican was to be an Athenian.

The unification of Attica meant that the polis of Athens comprised a singularly extensive area, and consequently the Athenians suffered less severely from land hunger than many of their neighbors. Athens therefore sent out no colonists, yet as a town only four miles from the coast it was influenced by the revival of Greek commerce. Very slowly, new mercantile classes were developing. Athenian political institutions were gradually modified, first to extend political power to the lesser landed gentry, next to include the merchants and manufacturers, and finally to accommodate the increasing demands of the common citizens.

Solon and Pisistratus

In the 590s a wise and moderate aristocratic poet-statesman named Solon was given extraordinary powers to reform the laws of Athens. His reforms left the preponderance of political power in the hands of the wealthy but nevertheless moved significantly in the direction of democracy. Solon's laws abolished enslavement for default of debts and freed all debtors who had previously been enslaved. More important, the lowest classes of free Athenians were now admitted into the popular assembly (whose powers were yet distinctly limited), and a system of popular courts was established whose judges were chosen by lot from among the entire citizenry without regard to wealth. For the Athenian, selection by lot was simply a means of putting the choice into the hands of the gods. Its consequence was to raise to important offices men who were their own masters and owed nothing to wealthy and influential political backers. Of course the system also produced a predictable quota of asses and nincompoops, but recent history attests that the elective principle is by no means immune to that fault. On the whole, selection by lot worked well in Athens and gradually became a characteristic feature of Athenian democracy.

Solon's laws were seen by many among the privileged classes as dangerously radical, but the lower classes demanded still more reforms. The consequence of this continued popular unrest was the rise of tyranny in Athens. Between 561 and 527 a colorful tyrant named Pisistratus dominated the Athenian government. Twice he was expelled by angry aristocrats; twice he returned with the support of the commoners. At length he achieved the elusive goal of all despots: he died in power and in bed. Pisistratus was the best of all possible tyrants: he sponsored a magnificent building program, patronized the arts, revolutionized agriculture by confiscating vast estates of recalcitrant noblemen and redistributing them among the small farmers, and established Athenian commercial outposts in the Dardanelles, thereby taking the first crucial steps along the road to empire. He gave Athens peace, prosperity, and a degree of social and economic harmony that it had long needed.

The Constitution of Cleisthenes

Pisistratus' two sons and successors proved incompetent and oppressive. One was assassinated; the other was driven from power by exiled nobles who returned with Spartan military support. But many of the aristocrats had grown wise in exile and were willing to accept popular rule. Under the leadership of a statesmanlike aristocrat named Cleisthenes a new and thoroughly democratic constitution was established in the closing decade of the sixth century which became the political basis of Athens' most glorious age. Cleisthenes administered the final blow to the aristocratic leaders of the old tribes and clans. Until the time of his reforms loyalty to clan and tribe had remained strong. Now, Cleisthenes abolished these ancient groups, replacing them with ten new "tribes" whose membership was no longer based on kinship. Each of the ten tribes was made up of numerous small territorial districts scattered throughout Attica. Consequently, members of every class—commercial, industrial, rural, and aristocratic—were about evenly divided among the ten tribes.

Cleisthenes may also have been responsible for introducing the principle of ostracism, which provided a further safeguard against the evils of violent factionalism. In any case, its first recorded use was in 488.

Each year thereafter the Athenians decided by vote whether or not they would ostracize one of their number. If they decided affirmatively, then any citizen might propose the name of a person whom he considered a threat to the well-being of the polis. Whichever candidate received the most votes in the Assembly was banished from Athens for ten years. He kept his citizenship and his property but was no longer in a position to interfere with the operation of the polis.

All matters of public policy were decided by the Assembly whose membership included all Athenian citizens from landless laborers to great aristocrats. Citizenship was given to every Athenian freeman of eighteen years or over, and in the mid-fifth century the total citizenry has been estimated at about 50,000 men. There were also, exclusive of women and children, about 25,000 resident aliens called "metics" who were free but without political rights, and perhaps some 55,000 adult male slaves. When we speak of Athenian democracy we must always remember that a considerable group of Athens' inhabitants were enslaved and had no voice in politics whatever, while another large group, including every nonenslaved Attican woman, was "free" but without the rights and status of a citizen. The philosopher Aristotle was expressing a deep Hellenic (and Near Eastern) bias when he "proved" the natural inferiority of women and slaves. Nevertheless, citizenship was far less exclusive in Athens than in Sparta, and with respect to the citizenry itself Athens was more thoroughly democratic than any modern state. The citizens did not elect the legislators; they *were* the legislators.

For the transaction of day-to-day business, Cleisthenes provided a smaller body —a Council of Five Hundred—for which every Athenian citizen over thirty was eligible. The Council was made up of 50 men from each tribe chosen annually by lot from a list of tribal nominees. Each of these

50-man tribal groups served for one-tenth of the year. Their order of rotation was determined by a crude machine that archaeologists have recently discovered. It worked much like our modern bubble gum machines: a stone for each of the ten tribes was put in the machine, and each month one stone was released, thus preventing any tribe except the last from knowing in advance when its term would begin.

Random selection pervaded the Athenian constitution. Every day a different chairman for the 50-man panel was chosen by lot. Most of the various magistrates and civil servants also came to be selected by lot for limited terms and were strictly responsible to the Council of Five Hundred and the Assembly. This was a citizens' government in every sense of the word—a government of amateurs rather than professional bureaucrats.

But neither Council nor Assembly could provide the long-range personal leadership essential to the well-being of the state. The Assembly was too unwieldy, the Council too circumscribed by rotation and lot. Consequently, the chief executive power in Athens came to be exercised by a group of ten generals (strategoi), one from each tribe, who were elected annually by the Assembly and were eligible for indefinite reelection. Even the most zealous democrat could scarcely wish to see his generals chosen by lot or rotated every year. These were offices for which special talent was essential, and the Athenians wisely tended to choose as their strategoi men from the aristocracy who had behind them a long tradition of military and political experience. The greatest Athenian strategos of the fifth century, Pericles, was precisely such a man, and his extended tenure in office illustrates the remarkable equilibrium achieved in the golden age between aristocratic leadership and popular sovereignty. Even Pericles was subject to the Assembly on which he depended for support and reelection. He could exercise his authority only by persuasion or political manipulation—never by force.

Sixth-Century Ionia and the Expansion of Persia

During the sixth century, while Solon, Pisistratus, and Cleisthenes were transforming Athens into a prosperous democracy, the cultural center of the Hellenic world was Ionia. Here on the shores of Anatolia the Greeks came into direct contact with the ancient Near East. The results of this contact were fruitful indeed, for the Ionian Greeks adapted Near Eastern art, architecture, literature, and learning to their own different outlook, creating a brilliant, elegant culture, far more gracious and luxurious than any that existed in Greece itself. It was in this setting that Greek philosophy, science, and lyric poetry were born. Ionian polises underwent much the same political and economic developments as those of Greece, and by the sixth century the lower classes were attempting to overthrow the control of the aristocrats. In Miletus the aristocrats and commoners went to the extreme of burning one another alive.

These internal social struggles were affected drastically by the intervention of outside powers. During the 560s and 550s the coastal cities of Ionia fell one by one under the control of the Lydians, and when Lydia was conquered by the Persian Empire in 546 they passed under Persian control. In 499 there occurred a general Ionian rebellion against Persian rule during which the Athenians were persuaded to send 20 ships to aid their desperate kinsmen. But the Athenian aid proved insufficient and by 494 the Persians had crushed the insurrection, punctuating their victory by sacking Miletus. Ionia's gamble for independence had failed and, even more important, Darius the Great, king of Persia, was now bent on revenge against Athens. The Persian Wars, the Greek historian Herodotus observes, were precipitated by the sending of 20 ships.

The Persian Wars   (490–479 B.C.)

In 490 Darius led an army across the Aegean to teach the Greeks a lesson in respect. As was so often the case, the Greeks, even in the face of this calamity, found it impossible to unite. The Spartans held aloof in the Peloponnesus, claiming that they could not send their army until the moon's phase was auspicious, and other states preferred to await further developments. Consequently Athens was obliged to face the Persians almost alone. At Marathon in Attica the two armies met, and the Athenian hoplites, fighting shoulder to shoulder for the preservation of their homes and their polis, won a brilliant victory that not only postponed the Persian threat but also stirred up in Athens a powerful sense of pride and self-confidence. The sovereign of the world's greatest empire had been defeated by a small army of free Athenian citizens. For such men as these, so it seemed, nothing was impossible.

The buoyant optimism that filled Athens in the wake of Marathon was tempered by the sobering thought that the Persians were likely to return in far greater numbers. Darius the Great spent his last years planning a devastating attack against Greece, but when the new invasion came in 480 it was led by Darius' successor, Xerxes. A Persian army of about 180,000 fighting men, stupendous by the standards of the age, moved by land around the northern Aegean shore accompanied by a powerful armada. Xerxes had paved his way into Greece by alliances with a number of opportunistic Greek cities such as Argos and Thebes. In the meantime Athens had been preparing for the onslaught under the enterprising leadership of Themistocles, a statesman of great strategic imagination, who saw clearly that Athens' one hope was

to build a strong fleet and seize control of the Aegean from the Persian Empire. By the time Xerxes led his forces into Greece, Themistocles' fleet was ready.

Sparta had by now awakened to the danger of a Persian conquest and was equally alarmed at the possibility of Athens winning additional prestige from another miraculous, single-handed victory. As Xerxes moved southward through northern Greece a small army of Spartans and other Greeks placed itself across the Persian path at Thermopylae, a narrow pass between sea and mountains through which Xerxes' host had to move before breaking into the south. When the two armies met, the Persians found that their immense numerical superiority was of little use on so restricted a battlefield and that man for man they were no match for the Greeks. But at length a Greek turncoat led a contingent of the Persian army along a poorly defended path through the mountains to the rear of the Greek position. Now completely surrounded, the Greeks continued to fight and died to the last man in defense of the field. Although the battle of Thermopylae was a defeat for the Spartans, it was also a symbol of their dedication. The inscription that was later placed over their graves is a model of Spartan brevity and understatement:

Tell them the news in Sparta, passer by,
That here, obedient to their words, we lie.

Much delayed, Xerxes' army now moved against Athens. The Athenians, at Themistocles' bidding, evacuated Attica and took refuge elsewhere, some in the Peloponnesus, others on the island of Salamis just off the Attican coast. The refugees on the island had to look on helplessly as the Persians plundered Athens and burned the temples on the Acropolis. But Themistocles' strategy was vindicated when the Greek and Persian fleets fought a decisive naval engagement in the Bay of Salamis. The bay provided insufficient room for the huge Persian armada to maneuver, and the lighter, faster Greek fleet, with the new Athenian navy as its core, won an overwhelming victory. Persia's navy was decimated before the eyes of Xerxes, who witnessed the disaster from a rocky headland. Commanding his army to withdraw to northern Greece for the winter, Xerxes himself departed for Asia, never to return.

In the following spring (479) the Persian army was routed at Plataea on the northern frontier of Attica by a Pan-Hellenic army under Spartan command, and the Greeks won a final victory over the tattered remnants of the Persian army and fleet at Cape Mycale in Ionia. Now, one after another, the Ionian cities were able to break loose from Persian control. Hellas had preserved its independence and was free to work out its own destiny. As an ironic postscript to the momentous struggle, Themistocles, the key figure in Athens' triumph at Salamis, fell from power shortly thereafter, was exiled, and ended his days in the service of the king of Persia.

The Athenian Empire

To some historians the moment of truth for classical Greece was not Marathon, Salamis, or Plataea but rather the brief period immediately afterward when the possibility of establishing the Spartan-led Pan-Hellenic League on a permanent basis was allowed to slip by. Yet as more recent history attests, it is far easier to unite against a common foe than to hold together a wartime confederation in the absence of military necessity. Common fear is a stronger cement than common hope, and the creation of a Pan-Hellenic state from the Greek alliance of 480 to 479 was of the same order of difficulty as the creation of a viable world state from the United Nations of World War II. Considering the intense involvement of the typical Greek in his polis, it seems doubtful that Greek federalism was ever a genuine option.

Nevertheless, the Greek world in 479 could not be certain that the Persian invasions were truly over. Sparta, always fearful of a helot revolt at home, withdrew from the league to concentrate on its own affairs, and Sparta's Peloponnesian confederates withdrew also. Athens, however, was unwilling to lower its guard. A large fleet had to be kept in readiness, and such a fleet could not be maintained by Athens alone. Consequently a new alliance was formed under Athenian leadership which included most of the maritime cities on the coasts and islands of the Aegean from Attica to Ionia. The alliance was known as the Delian League because its headquarters and treasury were on the island of Delos, an ancient Ionian religious center. Athens and a few other cities contributed ships to the Delian fleet; the remaining members contributed money. All were entitled to a voice in the affairs of the Delian League, but Athens, with its superior wealth and power, gradually assumed a dominant position.

Slowly the Delian League evolved into an Athenian Empire. In 454 the league treasury was transferred from Delos to Athens, where its funds were diverted to the welfare and adornment of Athens itself. The Athenians justified this extraordinary policy of financial juggling by the argument that their fleet remained always vigilant and ready to protect league members from Persian aggression. But their explanation was received unsympathetically in some quarters. An Ionian visiting Athens might well admire the magnificent new temples being erected on the Acropolis. But his admiration would be chilled by the reflection that his own polis was contributing financially toward their construction. Certain members decided to withdraw from the league only to find that Athens regarded secession as illegal and was ready to enforce the continued membership of disillusioned cities by military action. With the development of this policy in the 460s the transformation from Delian League to Athenian Empire was complete.

The half century (480 to 431) between

Salamis and the beginning of the show-down with Sparta was the Athenain Golden Age. The empire rose and flourished, bringing Athens unimagined wealth, not merely from imperial assessments but also from the splendid commercial opportunities offered by Athenian domination of the Aegean. Athens was now the commercial capital of the Mediterranean world and the great power in Greece. Sparta and her Peloponnesian allies held aloof, yet Athenian statesmen such as Pericles hoped that one day they, too, would be brought by force under Athens' sway.

The Golden Age

The economic and imperialistic foundations of Athens' Golden Age are interesting to us chiefly as a backdrop for the momentous cultural explosion that has echoed through the centuries of Mediterranean and European civilizations. Through a rare and elusive conjunction of circumstances a group of some 50,000 politically conscious Athenian citizens created in the decades after Salamis a unique, many-sided culture of superb taste and unsurpassed excellence. The culture of the Golden Age was anticipated in the sixth and even earlier centuries, and the period of creativity continued, especially in the intellectual sphere, into the fourth. But the zenith of Greek culture was reached in imperial Athens during the administration of Pericles in the middle decades of the fifth century. We will examine this achievement more closely later. For now, suffice it to say that fifth century Athens showed what the human spirit at its best is capable of attaining.

The Athenian achievement is so glittering that one is in danger of viewing the Golden Age as a utopia. In reality the architecture and sculpture of the Acropolis, the tragic dramas, the probing philosophical speculation, were produced against a background of large-scale slavery, petty politics, commercial greed, and growing imperial arrogance. Pericles, who remained in pow-

er almost continuously from shortly after 460 to his death in 429, provided much-needed direction to democratic Athens, but he maintained the support of the commercial classes by advocating an ever-expanding empire. His policy of extending Athenian imperialism to dominate the entire Greek world aroused the fear and hostility of Sparta and its Peloponnesian League. Corinth, the second greatest city in the league and Athens' chief commercial rival, was especially apprehensive of Pericles' imperialism. In 431 these accumulating tensions resulted in a war between the Peloponnesian League and the Athenian Empire—a protracted, agonizing struggle that ultimately destroyed the Athenian Empire and shook the Greek political structure to its foundations. The fifth century saw the polis system at its best and at its worst: on the one hand, the culture of Periclean Athens; on the other, the Peloponnesian War.

The Peloponnesian War

The war ran from 431 to 404. Athens dreamed of bringing all Hellas under its sway, and Sparta and its allies were determined to end the threat of Athenian imperialism. Athens was coming to be regarded as a tyrant among the states of its own empire, but so long as Athenian ships patrolled the Aegean, rebellion was minimized. Ironically, the mother of democracies was driven to ever more despotic expedients to hold its empire together.

In 430 and 429 Athens, crowded with refugees, was struck by a plague that carried off perhaps a quarter of its population, including Pericles himself. The loss of this far-sighted statesman, combined with the terrible shock of the plague, led to a rapid deterioration in the quality of Athenian government. Leadership passed into the hands of extremists, and the democracy acquired many of the worst characteristics of mob rule. A general who, through no fault of his own, failed to win some battle

Pericles the Athenian statesman.   (Trustees of the British Museum)

island of Melos, an innocent neutral in the struggle, all its men were slaughtered and its women and children sold as slaves.

Pericles had observed on the eve of the war that he was more afraid of Athens' mistakes than of Sparta's designs. His fear was well founded, for as the war progressed along its dreary course Athenian strategy became increasingly reckless. The better part of the Athenian fleet was lost when two ill-planned expeditions against distant Syracuse ended in complete disaster. As Athens' grip on the Aegean loosened, its subjects cities began to rebel, and at length a Peloponnesian fleet, financed in part by Persian gold, destroyed what was left of Athens' navy. In 404 Athens surrendered—its wealth lost, its spirit broken, and its empire in ruins. Long thereafter it remained the intellectual and cultural center of the Greek world—it was even able to make something of an economic and political recovery—but its years of imperial supremacy were gone forever.

The Fourth Century

might be sent to exile. (Such was the experience of Thucydides, Athens' greatest historian.) When the Athenians captured the

The period between the end of the Peloponnesian War in 404 and the Macedonian

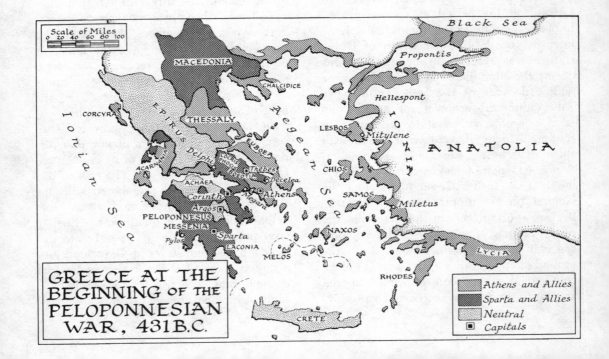

GREECE AT THE BEGINNING OF THE PELOPONNESIAN WAR, 431 B.C.

Scale of Miles
0 20 40 60 80 100

Athens and Allies
Sparta and Allies
Neutral
■ Capitals

conquest of Greece in 338 was an age of chaos and anticlimax during which the polis system was drained of its creative force by incessant intercity warfare and a disastrous decline in social responsibility. The immediate result of Athens' surrender was Spartan power over the Greek world. The victorious Spartan fleet had been built with Persian money, and Sparta paid its debt by allowing Persia to reoccupy Ionia. The Spartans were much too conservative to be successful imperialists, and although for a time they followed a policy of establishing oligarchic regimes* in the city-states of Athens' former empire—indeed, in Athens itself—they quickly proved incapable of giving coherence and direction to Hellas. In Athens and in many other states the oligarchies were soon overthrown, and Greece passed into a bewildering period of military strife and shifting centers of power. For a brief period Thebes rose to supremacy. Athens itself began to form a new Aegean league, only to be frustrated by Persian intervention. In the middle decades of the fourth century power tended to shift between Sparta, Athens, and Thebes, while the Greek colony of Syracuse dominated Sicily and southern Italy. Envoys from Persia, always well supplied with money, saw to it that no one state became too powerful. A Greece divided and decimated by incessant warfare could be no threat to the Persian Empire.

Ironically, Persia's diplomacy paved the way for an event its rulers had been determined at all costs to avoid: the unification of Greece. The debilitating intercity wars left Greece unprepared for the intervention of a new power on its northern frontier. Macedon was a backward mountain kingdom whose inhabitants, although distantly related to the Greeks, knew little of Hellenic culture. In 359 a talented opportunist named Philip became king of Macedon. He tamed and unified the wild Macedonian

tribes, secured his northern frontiers, and then began a patient and artful campaign to bring Greece under his control. Having spent three years of his boyhood as a hostage in Thebes he had acquired a full appreciation of both Greek culture and Greek political instability. He hired the philosopher Aristotle as tutor for his son Alexander, and he exploited the ever-increasing Greek distaste for war by bluffing and cajoling his way into the south. His conquests of Greek towns were accompanied by declarations of his peaceful intentions, and when at last Athens and Thebes resolved their ancient rivalry and joined forces against him it was much too late. In 338 Philip won the decisive battle and Greece lay at his feet.

Philip allowed the Greek states to run their own internal affairs but he organized them into a league whose policies he controlled. With the subordination of Greek freedom to the will of King Philip the classical age of Greek history came to an end. With the accession of Philip's illustrious son, Alexander the Great, two years later, a new age began which would see the spread of Greek culture throughout the Near East and the transformation of Greek life into something drastically different from what it had been before.

The Decline of the Polis

Classical Greece was a product of the polis, and when the polis lost its meaning classical Greece came to an end. The essence of the polis was participation in the political and cultural life of the community. The citizen was expected to take care of his private business and at the same time attend the assembly, participate in decisions of state, serve in the administration, and fight in the army or navy whenever necessary. Statesmen such as Pericles were at once administrators, orators, and generals. The polis at its best was a community of well-rounded men—men who had many interests and capabilities—in short, amateurs

---

* An *oligarchy* is a state governed by a small, privileged minority.

In the sixth and early fifth centuries, when Greek life had been comparatively simple, it was possible for one man to play many roles. But as the fifth century progressed the advantages of specialization grew. Military tactics became more complex. Administrative procedures became increasingly refined. Oratory became the subject of specialized study. As the various intellectual disciplines progressed it became more and more difficult to master them. The age of the amateur gradually gave way to the age of the professional. The polis of the fourth century was filled with professional administrators, orators, scholars, bankers, sailors, and businessmen whose demanding careers left them time for little else. Citizens were becoming absorbed in their private affairs, and political life, once the very embodiment of the Greek spirit, was losing its fascination. Citizen-soldiers gave way increasingly to mercenaries, partly because civic patriotism was running dry but also because fighting was now a full-time career. The precarious equilibrium achieved in the Golden Age between competence and versatility—between individual and community—could only be momentary, for the intense creativity of the fifth century led inevitably to the specialization of the fourth. It has been said that "Progress broke the Polis,"* yet progress was a fundamental ingredient of the way of life that the polis created.

* Kitto, *The Greeks*, p. 161.

2
The Thought and Culture of Classical Greece

The Hellenic Mind

The civilizations of the ancient Near East did significant pioneer work in mathematics, engineering, and practical science; the Hebrews developed a profound ethical system based on divine revelation; but it was the Greeks who first took the step of examining man and his universe from a rational standpoint. It was they who transcended the mythical and poetic approach to cosmology and began to look at the universe as a natural rather than a supernatural phenomenon, based on discoverable principles of cause and effect rather than on divine will. It was they who first attempted to base morality and the good life on reason rather than revelation. Accordingly, the Greeks were the first philosophers—the first logicians—the first theoretical scientists. The Babylonians had studied the stars to prophesy; the Egyptians had mastered geometry to build tombs, and chemistry to create mummies. The Greeks had much to learn from their predecessors, but they turned their knowledge and their investigation toward a new end: a rational understanding of man and the universe. Their achievement has been described as "the discovery of the mind."

This is not to say that the Greeks were irreligious. Their dramas, their civic festivals, their Olympic Games were all religious celebrations; their art and architecture were devoted largely to honoring the gods; their generals sometimes altered their strategy on the basis of some divine portent. But the Greek philosophers succeeded by-and-large in holding their gods at bay and untangling the natural from the supernatural. Like the Jews, they rejected the "I-thou" relationship of man and nature, but unlike the Jews they were not intensely involved in the worship of a single, omnipotent deity. The Greeks had no powerful official priesthood to enforce correct doctrine. To them as to other ancient peoples the cosmos was awesome, but they possessed the open-mindedness and the audacity to probe it with their intellects.

Ionia: the Lyric Poets

Open-mindedness and audacity—so alien to the despotisms of the Middle East—were nourished by the free and turbulent atmosphere of the polis. Greek rationalism was a product of Greek individualism, and among the first manifestations of this new spirit of self-awareness and irreverence for tradition was the development of lyric poetry in seventh and sixth century Ionia. Greek lyric poetry was a notable literary achievement, but its importance transcends the realm of letters. The works of lyric poets such as Archilochus in the seventh century and Sappho of Lesbos in the sixth disclose self-consciousness and intensity of experience far exceeding anything known before. At a time when Spartan mothers were sending their sons to war with the stern admonition, "Return with your shield —or on it," the Ionian Archilochus was expressing a far more individualistic viewpoint:

Some lucky Thracian has my shield,
For, being somewhat flurried,
I dropped it by a wayside bush,
As from the field I hurried;
Thank God, I made it clear away,
To blazes with the shield!
I'll get another just as good
When next I take the field.

With such lines as these Archilochus ceases to be a mere name and emerges as a vivid, engaging personality. He is history's first articulate coward.

The most intensely personal of the lyric poets was Sappho, an aristocratic lady of sixth-century Lesbos, who became the directress of a school for young girls— apparently a combination finishing school and religious guild dedicated to Aphrodite, the goddess of Love. Her passionate love lyrics to her students used to raise eyebrows and have given enduring meaning to the word "lesbian," but the people of antiquity saw Sappho as the equal of Homer. Never before had human feelings been expressed with such perception and sensitivity:

Love has unbound my limbs and set me shaking
A monster bitter-sweet and my unmaking.*

The Ionian Philosophers

The same surge of individualism that produced lyric poetry gave rise to mankind's first effort to understand rationally the physical universe. So far as we know the first philosopher and theoretical scientist in human history was the sixth-century Ionian, Thales of Miletus, who set forth the proposition that water was the primal element of the universe. This hypothesis, although crude by present standards, constitutes a significant effort to impose a principle of intellectual unity on the diversity of experience. The world was to be understood as a single physical substance. Presumably solid objects were made of compressed water and air of rarefied water. Empty space was perhaps composed of dehydrated water. Thales' hypothesis did not commend itself to his successors, but the crucial point is that Thales had successors—that other men, following his example, would continue the effort to explain the physical universe through natural rather than supernatural principles. Intellectual history had taken a bold new turn and was headed into a fruitful, uncharted land.

The Ionian philosophers after Thales continued to speculate about the primal substance of the universe. One suggested that air was the basic element, another, fire. The Ionian Anaximander set forth a primitive theory of evolution and declared that men were descended from fish. But these intellectual pioneers, their originality notwithstanding, disclose a basic weakness that characterized Greek thought throughout the classical age: an all-too-human

* Greek Literature in Translation, ed. Oates and Murphy, p. 972.

tendency to rush into sweeping generalizations on the basis of a grossly inadequate factual foundation. Beguiled by the potentialities of rational inquiry they failed to appreciate how painfully difficult it is to arrive at sound conclusions. Consequently, the hypotheses of the Ionians are of the nature of inspired guesses. Anaximander's theory of evolution, for example, was quickly forgotten because, unlike Darwin's it had no significant supporting data.

The Pythagorean School

Pythagoras (c. 582–507 B.C.) represents a different intellectual trend. A native of Ionia, he migrated to southern Italy where he founded a strange brotherhood, half scientific, half mystical. He drew heavily from the mystery cults of Dionysus and Demeter and was influenced especially by Orphism, a salvation cult that was becoming popular in the sixth century. The cult of Orpheus stressed guilt and atonement, a variety of ascetic practices, and an afterlife of suffering or bliss depending on the purity of one's soul. This and similar cults appealed to those who found inadequate solace in the heroic but worldly gods of Olympus. Following the basic structure of Orphic dogma, Pythagoras and his followers advocated the doctrine of transmigration of souls and the concept of a quasi-monastic communal life. Entangled in this was their profoundly significant notion that the basic element in nature was neither water, air, nor fire, but *number*. The Pythagoreans studied the intervals between musical tones and worked out basic laws of harmony. Having demonstrated the relationship between music and mathematics, they next applied these principles to the whole universe, asserting that the cosmos obeyed the laws of harmony and, indeed, that the planets in their courses produced musical tones that combined into a cosmic rhapsody: the music of the spheres. Implicit in this bewildering mixture of insight and fancy is the pregnant concept that

nature is best understood mathematically.

The mathematical thought of the Pythagoreans included a mystical reverence for the number ten, which they saw as magical. But despite their number mysticism, which modern science rejects, they played a crucial role in the development of mathematics and mathematical science. They produced the Pythagorean theorem and the multiplication table, and their notions contributed to the development of modern science in the sixteenth and seventeenth centuries. The Greeks were at their best in mathematics, for here they could reason deductively—from self-evident concepts—and their distaste for the slow, patient accumulation of data was no hindrance.

The Fifth Century

In the course of the fifth century a great many of the central problems that have occupied philosophers ever since were raised and explored: whether the universe is in a state of constant flux or eternally changeless; whether it is composed of one substance or many; whether or not the nature of the universe can be grasped by the reasoning mind. Democritus set forth a doctrine of materialism that anticipated several of the views of modern science. He maintained that the universe consists of countless atoms in random configurations —that it has no center and no periphery but is much the same one place as another. In short, the universe is infinite and the earth is in no way unique. Like Anaximander's theory of evolution, Democritus' atomism was essentially a philosophical assertion rather than a scientific hypothesis based on empirical evidence. And since infinity was not a concept congenial to the Greek mind, atomism long remained a minority view. But in early modern times Democritus' notion of an infinite universe contributed to the development of a new philosophical outlook and to the rise of modern astronomy.

It was in medicine and history rather

than in cosmology that the Greeks of the fifth century were able to resist the lure of the spectacular generalization and concentrate on the humble but essential task of accumulating verified facts. In the field of medicine, Hippocrates and his followers recorded case histories with scrupulous care and avoided the facile and hasty conclusion. Their painstaking clinical studies and their rejection of supernatural causation started medicine upon its modern career.

A similar reverence for the verifiable fact was demonstrated by the Greek historians of the period. History, in the modern sense, begins wtih Herodotus, a man of boundless curiosity who, in the course of his extensive travels, gathered a vast accumulation of data for his brilliant and entertaining history of the Persian Wars. Herodotus made a serious effort to separate fact from fable, but he was far surpassed in this regard by Thucydides, a disgraced Athenian general who wrote his masterly account of the Peloponnesian War with unprecedented objectivity and an acute sense of historical criticism. "Of the events of the war," writes Thucydides, " . . . I have described nothing but what I either saw myself or learned from others whom I questioned most carefully and specifically. The task was laborious, because eyewitnesses of the same events gave different accounts of them, as they remembered or were interested in the actions of one side or the other." To Thucydides, the polis was a fascinating arena where diverse political views contended, and since he was inclined to view political issues as the central problems of existence, he ascribed to the polis a dominant role in the dynamics of history.

The Sophists

In philosophy, history, and science, reason was winning its victories at the expense of the supernatural. The anthropomorphic gods of Olympus were especially suscep-

tible to rational criticism, for few people who were acquainted with Ionian philosophy or the new traditions of scientific history and medicine could seriously believe that Zeus hurled thunderbolts or that Poseidon caused earthquakes. Some philosophical spirits came to see Zeus as a transcendent god of the universe; others rejected him altogether. But if one doubts that Zeus tosses thunderbolts one is also likely to doubt that Athena protects Athens, and the rejection of Athena and other civic deities was bound to be subversive to the traditional spirit of the polis. Religious skepticism was gradually undermining civic patriotism, and as skepticism advanced, patriotism receded. Once again we are brought face to face with the dynamic and paradoxical nature of the Greek experience: the polis produced the inquiring mind, but in time the inquiring mind eroded the most fundamental traditions of the polis.

The arch skeptics of fifth-century Athens were the Sophists, a heterogeneous group of professional teachers drawn from every corner of the Greek world by the wealth of the great city. Much of our information about the Sophists comes from the writings of Plato, who disliked them heartily and portrayed them as intellectual prostitutes and tricksters. In reality most of them were dedicated to the life of reason and the sound argument. Unlike the Ionian philosophers, they were chiefly in-

A Greek classroom.   (Staatsliche Museen, Berlin)

terested in man rather than the cosmos. They investigated ethics, politics, history, and psychology and have been called the first social scientists. In applying reason to these areas and teaching their students to do the same they aroused the wrath of the conservatives and doubtless encouraged an irreverent attitude toward tradition. Of course, the Greeks were not nearly so tradition-bound as their predecessors and contemporaries, but there is a limit to the amount of skepticism and change that any soical system can absorb. Many of the Sophists taught their pupils techniques of debating and getting ahead, while questioning the traditional doctrines of religion, patriotism, and dedication to the welfare of the community. One of them is described by Plato as advocating the maxim that might makes right. In other words, the Sophists as a whole stimulated an attitude of iconoclasm, relativism, and ambitious individualism, thereby contributing to the dissolution of the polis spirit.

Socrates (469–399 B.C.)

Socrates, the "patron saint" of intellectuals, was at once a part of this movement and an opponent of it. During the troubled years of the Peloponnesian war he wandered the streets of Athens teaching his followers to test their beliefs and preconceptions with the tool of reason. "An uncriticized life," he observed, "is scarcely worth living." Like the Sophists Socrates was interested in human rather than cosmic matters, but unlike many of them he was dissatisfied merely with tearing down traditional beliefs. He cleared the ground by posing seemingly innocent questions to his listeners which invariably entangled them in a hopeless maze of contradictions. But having devastated their opinions he substituted closely-reasoned conclusions of his own on the subject of ethics and the good life. Knowledge, he taught, was synonymous with virtue, for a person who

knew the truth would act righteously. Impelled by this optimistic conviction he continued to attack cherished beliefs—to play the role of "gadfly" as he put it.

Gadflies have seldom been popular. The Athenians, put on edge by their defeat at Sparta's hands (which was hastened by the treachery of one of Socrates' pupils) could at last bear him no longer. In 399 he was brought to trial for denying the gods and corrupting youth and was condemned by a close vote. In accordance with Athenian law, he was given the opportunity to propose his own punishment. He suggested that the Athenians punish him by giving him free meals at public expense for the rest of his life. By refusing to take his trial seriously he was in effect condemning himself to death. Declining an opportunity to escape into exile, he was executed by poison and expired with the cheerful observation that at last he had the opportunity of discovering for himself the truth about the afterlife.

Plato (427–347 B.C.)

Socrates would not have made good on an American university faculty, for although he was a splendid teacher, he did not publish.* We know of his teachings largely through the works of his student Plato, one of history's towering intellects and a prolific and graceful writer. In his *Republic*, Plato outlined the perfect polis—the first utopia in literary history. Here, ironically, the philosopher rejected the democracy that he knew and described an ideal state far more Spartan than Athenian. The farmers, workers, and merchants were without political rights; a warrior class was trained with Spartan rigor to defend the state; and an intellectual elite, schooled in mathematics and philosophy, constituted a ruling class. At the top of the political pyramid was a philosopher-king, the wisest and most virtuous product of a state-training

* Jesus would not have qualified for tenure either.

program that consumed the better part of his life. Culture was not encouraged in the Republic; dangerous and novel ideas were banned, poets were banished, all music was prohibited except the martial, patriotic type.

What are we to make of a utopia that would encourage Sousa but ban Brahms—a polis that could never have produced a Plato? We must remember that democratic Athens was in decline when Plato wrote. He could not love the polis that had executed his master, nor was he blind to the selfish individualism and civic irresponsibility that characterized fourth-century Greece. Plato had the wit to recognize that through the intensity of its cultural creativity and the freedom and breadth of its intellectual curiosity the polis was burning itself out. Achilles had chosen a short but glorious life; Plato preferred long-lived mediocrity, and stability was therefore the keynote of his Republic. There would be no Sophists to erode civic virtue, no poets to exalt the individual over the community (or abandon their shields as they fled from battle). Plato's cavalier treatment of the mercantile classes represents a deliberate rejection of the lures of empire. Like a figure on a Grecian urn, his ideal polis would be frozen and rigid—and enduring.

There remains the paradox that this intellectually static commonwealth was to be ruled by philosophers. We tend to think of philosophy as a singularly disputatious subject, but Plato viewed truth as absolute and unchanging and assumed that all true philosophers would be in essential agreement—that future thinkers would simply affirm Plato's own doctrines. This assumption has proven to be resoundingly false, yet Plato's conception of reality has nevertheless exerted an enormous influence on the development of thought. His purpose was to reconcile his belief in a perfect, unchanging universe with the kaleidoscopic diversity and impermanence of the visible world. He stated that the objects that we perceive through our senses are merely pale, imperfect reflections of ideal models or archetypes that exist in a world invisible to man. For example, we observe numerous individual cats, some black, some yellow, some fat, some skinny. All are imperfect particularizations of an ideal cat existing in the Platonic heaven. Again, we find in the world of the senses many examples of duality: twins, lovers, pairs of jackasses, and so forth, but they merely exemplify more or less inadequately the idea of "two" which, in its pure state, is invisible and intangible. We cannot see "two." We can only see two *things*. But—and this is all important—we can *conceive* of "twoness" or abstract duality. Likewise, with sufficient effort, we can conceive of "catness," "dogness" and "rabbitness"—of the archetypal cat, dog or rabbit. If we could not, so Plato believes, we would have no basis for grouping individual cats into a single category. In short, the world of phenomena is not the *real* world. The phenomenal world is variegated and dynamic; the real world—the world of archetypes—is clear-cut and static. We can discover this real world through introspection, for knowledge of the archetypes is present in our minds from birth, dimly remembered from a previous existence. (Plato believed in a beforelife as well as in an afterlife.) So the philosopher studies reality not by *observing* but by *thinking*.

Plato illustrates this doctrine with a vivid metaphor. Imagine, he says, a cave whose inhabitants are chained in such a position that they can never turn toward the sunlit opening but can only see shadows projected against an interior wall. Imagine further that one of the inhabitants (the philosopher) breaks his chains, emerges from the cave, and sees the real world for the first time. He will have no wish to return to his former shadow world, but he will do so nevertheless out of a sense of obligation to enlighten the others. Similarly, the philosopher-king rules the Republic unwillingly through a sense of duty. He would prefer to contemplate reality undisturbed.

Yet he alone can rule wisely, for he alone has seen the truth.

Plato's doctrine of ideas has always been alluring to people who seek order and unity, stability and virtue, in a universe that appears fickle and chaotic. Plato declared that the greatest of the archetypes is the idea of the Good, and this notion has had great appeal to men of religious temperament ever since. His theory of knowledge, emphasizing contemplation over observation, is obviously hostile to the method of experimental science, yet his archetypal world is perfectly compatible with the world of the mathematician—the world of pure numbers. Plato drew heavily from the Pythagorean tradition—"God is a geometer," he once observed—and Platonic thought, like Pythagorean thought, has contributed profoundly to the development of mathematical science. As for philosophy, it developed for almost the next two thousand years in the shadow of two giants. One of them is Plato; the other, Aristotle, Plato's greatest pupil.

Aristotle (384–322 B.C.)

Plato founded a school in Athens called the Academy (from which arises our word, *academic*). To this school came the young Aristotle, the son of a Thracian physician in the service of the king of Macedon. Aristotle remained at the Academy for nearly two decades. Then, after serving at the Macedonian court as tutor to Alexander the Great, he returned to Athens, founded a school of his own (the Lyceum), and wrote most of his books. At length he was condemned by the Athenians for impiety, fled into exile, and died shortly thereafter in 322, one year after the death of Alexander. Thus Aristotle's life is concurrent with the final phase of Classical Greece.

Aristotle was nearly a universal scholar. He wrote definitively on a great variety of topics including biology, politics, literature, ethics, logic, physics, and metaphysics. He brought Plato's theory of ideas down to earth by asserting that the archetype exists in the particular—that one can best study the archetypal cat by observing and classifying individual cats. Thus observation of things in this world takes its place alongside contemplation as a valid avenue to knowledge. Like Hippocrates and Thucydides, but on a much broader scale, Aristotle advocated the painstaking collection and analysis of data, thereby placing himself at odds with the main body of Greek thought. Although his political studies included the designing of an ideal commonwealth, he also investigated and classified the political systems of many existing city-states and demonstrated that several different types were conducive to the good life. His splendid biological studies followed the same method of observation and classification, and he set forth the concepts of genus and species which, with modifications, are still used. His work on physics has been less durable since it was based on an erroneous concept of motion, a fundamental belief in *purpose* as the organizing factor in the material universe, and an emphasis on qualitative rather than quantitative differences (for example, that the heavenly bodies were more perfect than objects on the earth.) Mathematics had no genuine role in his system; in general, early modern science was to draw its experimental method from the Aristotelian tradition and its mathematical analysis from the Pythagorean-Platonic tradition.

Aristotle's physics and metaphysics were based on the concept of a single God who was the motive power behind the universe —the unmoved mover and the uncaused cause to which all motion and all causation must ultimately be referred. Hence, Aristotelian thought was able to serve as a philosophical framework for the later religious thought of Islam and Christianity. Aristotle's immense significance in intellectual history arises from his having done some of the best thinking up to his time in so many significant realms of thought. It was he who first set forth a systematic logic, who first (so far as we know) produced a rigorous, detailed physics, who literally founded biology. A pioneer in observational method, he has been criticized for basing conclusions on insufficient evidence. Even Aristotle was not immune to the tendency toward premature conclusions, yet he collected data as no Greek before him had done. His achievement, considered in its totality, is without parallel in the history of thought.

Plato and Aristotle represent the apex of Greek philosophy. Both were religious men —both, in fact, were monotheists at heart. But both were dedicated also to the life of reason, and, building on a rational heritage that had only begun in the sixth century, both produced philosophical systems of unprecedented sophistication and depth. Their thought climaxed and completed the intellectual revolution that brought such glory and such turmoil to Greece.

Periclean Culture and Life

History has never seen anything like the intense cultural creativity of fifth-century Athens. It has been said that the Athenians of the Golden Age were incapable of producing anything ugly or vulgar. Everything from the greatest temple to the simplest ornament was created with unerring taste and assurance. Emotions ran strong and deep, but they were controlled by a sure sense of form that never permitted ostentation yet never degenerated into formalism. The art of the period was an incarnation of the Greek maxim: "nothing in excess"—a perfect embodiment of the taut balance and controlled excitement that we call "the classical spirit."

It is not difficult to understand how Greek citizens, whose freedom far exceeded that of any previous civilized people, produced such a dynamic culture. It is less easy to explain the harmony and restraint of Greek classicism, for no people had ever before lived with such intensity and fervor.

Herodotus tells us that even the barbaric Scythians lamented the Greek impulse toward frenzy, and a speaker in Thucydides observes that the Athenians "were born into the world to take no rest themselves and to give none to others." The Greek ideal was moderation and restraint precisely because these were the qualities most needed by an immoderate and unrestrained people. A degree of cooperation and self-control was essential to the communal life of the polis, and civic devotion acted as a brake on rampant individualism. During its greatest years the polis stimulated individual creativity but directed it toward the welfare of the community. Individualism and civic responsibility achieved a momentary and precarious balance.

The achievement of this equilibrium in the fifth century was a precious but fleeting episode in the evolution of the polis from the aristocratic conservatism of the previous age to the irresponsible individualism of the fourth century and thereafter, hastened by the growth of religious doubt and the tendency toward specialization. This process is illustrated clearly in the evolution of Greek art from the delicate, static elegance of the "archaic style" through the serious, balanced classical style of the fifth century to the increasing individualism, naturalism and particularism of the late-classical fourth century. In sculpture, for example, one observes a development from aristocratic stiffness to a harmonious serenity that gradually displays signs of increasing tension and individualization. The works of the fifth-century sculptors were idealized human beings—we might almost say Platonic archetypes. The fourth-century sculptors tended to abandon the archetype for the specific and the concrete. In short, as Greek life was evolving from civic allegiance to individualism, from traditionalism to originality and self-expression, from aristocracy to democracy, there was a moment when these opposites were balanced—and the moment was frozen and immortal-ized in some of the most superb works of architecture, sculpture, and dramatic literature the world has known.

In Periclean Athens individualism was still strongly oriented toward the polis. One of the most basic differences between the daily life of the fifth-century Athenian citizen and that of the modern American is the Athenian's emphasis on public over privite affairs. The private life of even the most affluent Athenian was simple: his clothing was plain, his home was humble, his furniture was rudimentary. With the intensification of individualism in the fourth century, private homes became much more elaborate, but during the Golden Age the Athenian's private life was, by our standards, almost as Spartan as the Spartan's. The plainness of private life was counterbalanced, however, by the brilliant diversity of public life. Under Pericles, imperial Athens lavished its wealth and its genius on its own adornment. The great works of art and architecture were dedicated to the polis and its gods. Life was enriched by the pageantry of civic religious festivals, by spirited conversation in the marketplace (the agora), by exercise in elaborate civic gymnasiums complete with baths and dressing rooms, and of course by participation in political affairs. The Greeks socialized the amenities of life. The pursuit of excellence in body and mind, so typical of Greek culture, was carried on in a communal atmosphere. The good life was not the life of the individual but the life of the citizen.

Only a minority of the inhabitants of Athens were actually citizens. As we have seen, slaves, metics (resident aliens), women and children were all excluded from the privileges of citizenship. Although many metics prospered in business, many slaves were well-treated, and many women had loving husbands, only the citizens could participate fully in the life of the polis. The citizen's wife in Periclean Athens remained in the home. She had heavy domestic duties but few social responsibilities, and was legally under her husband's control. Since her education was confined to the level of "home economics," her husband was not likely to find her especially interesting. At the parties and festive gatherings of the citizens the only ladies present were foreigners, often Ionians, who were more notable for their charm and wit than for their virtue. Typical of these ladies was Pericles' mistress, Aspasia, a sophisticated, well-educated Ionian whose name, appropriately enough, means "welcome." The wives of Athens were denied the rich public life of the Golden Age, and their lot is expressed eloquently in one of the tragedies of Euripides: "For a man may go, when home life palls, to join with friends and raise his spirits in companionship. But for us poor wives it is solitary communion with the one same soul forever."

Drama

The civic culture of the Golden Age achieved its most notable triumphs in drama, architecture, and sculpture. All three illustrate the public orientation of Greek cultural life. Greek tragedy arose out of the worship of Dionysus, as the songs and dances of the worshipers gradually evolved into a formalized drama with actors and a chorus. The sixth-century Athenian tyrant Pisistratus gave vigorous support to the Dionysian drama, and by the fifth century it had become a great civic institution. Wealthy citizens were expected to finance the productions, and each year a body of civic judges would award prizes to the three best tragedies. By modern standards the performances were far from elaborate. The most important of them took place in an outdoor "Theater of Dionysus" on the southern slope of the Acropolis. The chorus sang and danced to a simple musical accompaniment and commented at intervals on the action of the drama. Behind the chorus were low, broad steps on which the actors performed. There were never more than three actors on the stage at one time, and the sets behind them were simple in the extreme. The dramas themselves were based on mythological or historical themes, often dealing with semi-legendary royal families of early Greece, but the playwrights went beyond the realm of historical narrative to probe deeply some of the fundamental problems of morality and religion. The immense popularity of these stark, profound, and uncompromising productions testifies to the remarkable cultural elevation of fifth-century Athens. The citizens who flocked to the Theater of Dionysus constituted a critical and sophisticated audience. Many had themselves participated in the numerous dramas that were constantly being performed both in the city and in the surrounding Attican countryside. It has been estimated that each year some 3000 citizens had the experience of performing in a dramatic chorus, and thousands more had been trained, as a part of the normal Athenian curriculum, in singing, dancing, declamation, and acting. The drama was a central and meaningful element in the life of the polis and serves as an added illustration of the many-sidedness of human experience in the Golden Age.

The three great tragedians of fifth-century Athens were Aeschylus, who wrote during the first half of the century; Sophocles, whose productive period covered the middle and later decades of the century; and Euripides, a younger contemporary of Sophocles. All three exemplify the seriousness, the order, the controlled tension that we identify as "classical," yet they also illustrate the changes the classical spirit was undergoing. Aeschylus, the first of the three, tended to emphasize traditional values. Deeply devoted to the polis and the Greek religious heritage, he probed with majestic dignity the fundamental relationships of man and his gods, the problem of injustice in a righteous universe, and the terrible consequences of overweening pride. Sophocles was less intellectually rigorous, less traditional than Aeschylus, but he was a supreme dramatic artist with an unerring sense of plot structure and characterization. His plays treat the most violent and agonizing emotional situations with restraint and sobriety. In Sophocles the perfect classical equilibrium is fully achieved. Never have passions been so intense yet under such masterly control. The younger dramatist Euripides displays the logic, the skepticism, and the hard-headed rationalism of the Sophists who were then the rage of Athens. One of his characters makes the audacious statement, "There are no gods in heaven; no, not one!" and Euripides, far more than his predecessors, demonstrated a deep, sympathetic understanding for the hopes and fears, the unpredictability and irrationality, the *individuality* of human nature. Aeschylus' characters were chiefly types rather than individuals; in Sophocles the individual emerges with much greater clarity; but Euripides portrays his characters with profound insight and psychological realism. With the tragedies of Euripides the new age of skepticism and acute individualism has dawned.

The depth and power of fifth-century tragedy is exemplified in Sophocles' *Antigone* which deals with the perennial problem of individual conscience and state authority. Antigone's brother has betrayed his country and has been killed. Her uncle, the king of Thebes, refuses to permit her brother's burial even though burial was regarded as mandatory in the Greek religious tradition. Torn by the conflict between the royal decree and her sense of religious obligation, Antigone defies the king, buries her brother, and is condemned to death. She addresses the king in these words:

I did not think that thy decrees were of such force as to override the unwritten and unfailing laws of heaven. For their duration is

The Parthenon, the Temple of Athena at Athens.   (Camera Press/Transworld Feature Syndicate)

not of today or yesterday, but from eternity, and no man knows when they were first put forth. And though men rage I must obey those laws. Die I must, for death must come to all. But if I am to die before my time, I'll do it gladly; for when one lives as I do, surrounded by evils, death can only be a gain. So death for me is but a trifling grief, far better than to let my mother's son lie an unburied corpse.

The lighter side of the fifth-century theater is represented by the great comic playwright Aristophanes who, taking advantage of the freedom of the Athenian theater, subjected his fellow citizens great and small to merciless ridicule as he exposed the pretension and follies of imperial Athens during the Peloponnesian War. A product of the age of Socrates and the Sophists, Aristophanes expressed his deep-rooted conservatism by lampooning them. Socrates appears in a comedy called *The Clouds* hanging from a basket suspended in the air so that he could contemplate the

heavens at closer range, while his students below studied geology, their noses in the earth and their posteriors upraised toward the sky. Aristophanes was an ardent pacifist who condemned Athenian participation in the Peloponnesian War and mocked the war leaders with a frankness that would seldom be tolerated by a modern democracy during wartime. The audacity of his criticism illustrates the degree of intellectual freedom that existed in fifth-century Athens, yet his plays betray a yearning for the dignity and traditionalism of former years and a disturbing conviction that all was not well.

Architecture and Sculpture

Every aspect of fifth-century culture displays the classical spirit of restrained excitement. We find it in Athenian drama where the most violent deeds and passions are presented in an ordered and unified framework. We find it in the history of Thucydides, who treats with penetrating and Pericles, against the opposition of a conservative minority, pursued a lavish policy of civic beautification as a part of his effort to make Athens the cultural center of Hellas. The age of Pericles was therefore a period of feverish public building. Its supreme architectural monument was the central temple on the reconstructed Acropolis—the Parthenon. This superb structure, dedicated to the patron goddess Athena, is the ultimate expression of the classical ideal. It creates its effect not from a sense of fluidity and upward-reaching as in the much later Gothic cathedral, but from an almost godlike harmony of proportions. Here indeed was "nothing in excess."

The genius of the architects was matched by that of the sculptors who decorated the temples and created the great statues that were placed inside them. The most distinguished of the fifth-century sculptors was Phidias, the master sculptor of the Parthenon, who was responsible either directly or through his helpers for its splendid reliefs. Phidias made a majestic statue of Athena in ivory and gold for the interior of the

The Charioteer of Delphi.   (Alinari/Art Reference Bureau)

The god Zeus or Poseidon.   (Marburg/Art Reference Bureau)

and dispassionate analysis the impetuous and often childish excesses of the Peloponnesian War. And we find it in the architecture and the art of fifth-century Athens: deeply moving yet perfectly balanced and controlled. When Xerxes burned the Acropolis he left the next generation of Athenians with a challenge and an opportunity: to rebuild the temples in the new, classical style—to crown the polis with structures of such majesty and perfection as the world had never seen. Athenian imperialism provided the money with which to rebuild,

Hermes with infant Dionysus; a masterpiece by Praxiteles. (Alinari/Art Reference Bureau)

Parthenon and a still larger statue of the same goddess which was placed in the open and could be seen by ships several miles at sea. The work of Phidias and his contemporaries comes at the great moment of classical balance. Their works portray man as a type, without individual problems or cares, vigorous yet serene, ideally proportioned, and often in a state of controlled tension.

The architecture and sculpture of the Parthenon and its surrounding temples exemplify perfectly the synthesis of religious feeling, patriotic dedication, artistic genius, and intellectual freedom that characterized the age of Pericles. It would be pleasant to think of the Athenians of this period enjoying the beauty of these temples that so wonderfully express the mood of the age. But such was not the case. The Parthenon, the first of the Acropolis structures to be completed, was not finished until 432, a scant year before the outbreak of the Peloponnesian War that ultimately brought Athens to her knees. By 432 the old civic-religious enthusiasm was already waning. For centuries after, Greek art would be a living, creative thing; indeed, some of its most illustrious masterpieces were products of these later centuries. But the balanced, confident spirit of Periclean Athens—the spirit that informed the works of Sophocles and Phidias and inspired the Parthenon—could never quite be recovered.

The Hellenistic Age

3

Alexander The Great (336–323 B.C.)

The decline of the polis in the fourth century culminated, as we have seen, in the triumphs of King Philip and the subordination of Greece to the power of Macedon. In 336 B.C., barely two years after his climactic victory over Athens and Thebes, Philip of Macedon was murdered as a consequence of a petty palace intrigue and was succeeded by his son, Alexander, later to be called "the Great." In his final months Philip had been preparing a large-scale attack against the Persian Empire, hoping to transform the grudging obedience of the Greek city-states into enthusiastic support by leading a great Pan-Hellenic crusade against the traditional enemy of Hellas. Alexander, during a dazzling reign of thirteen years, exceeded his father's most fantastic dreams, leading his all-conquering armies from Greece to India and redirecting the course of the ancient world.

Although he was only twenty when he inherited the throne, Alexander possessed in the fullest measure that combination of physical attractiveness, athletic prowess, and intellectual distinction which had always been the Greek ideal. He had a godly countenance, the physique of an Olympic athlete, and a penetrating, imaginative mind. He was a magnetic leader who inspired intense loyalty and admiration among his followers; a brilliant general who adapted his tactics and strategy to the most varied circumstances and won for himself a reputation of invincibility; and an ardent champion of Hellenic culture and the Greek way of life. He was the product of two master teachers: Aristotle, the master philosopher and universal intellect, and King Philip himself, the greatest general and most adroit political opportunist of the age. Alexander's turn of mind is symbolized by the two objects that he always kept beneath his pillow: the *Iliad* and a dagger.

At first the Greek city-states were restive under Alexander's rule. He quelled their revolts with merciless efficiency, destroying rebellious Thebes and frightening the rest into submission. But there was real enthusiasm for his campaign against the Persian Empire, and in time, as one victory followed another, Alexander came to be regarded as a national hero—the champion of Greece against the barbarian. In the spring of 334 B.C. he led a Greco-Macedonian army of some 40,000 men across the Dardanelles into Asia Minor. During the next three and one-half years he won a series of stunning victories over the aged and ramshackle Persian Empire, freeing the Ionian cities from Persian control and conquering the Persian provinces of Syria and Egypt. Then, striking deep into the heart of the empire, Alexander won a decisive victory over the unwieldy Persian army near Arbela on the Tigris in 331. The triumph at Arbela enabled Alexander to seize the vast imperial treasure, ascend the imperial throne, and bring an end to the dynasty of ancient Persia.

This was a glorious moment for the Greeks. The foe that had so long troubled Hellas was conquered. More than that, the ancient Near East was now under Greek control, open to the bracing influence of Greek enterprise, Greek culture and Greek rationalism. Alexander's conquest of Persia set the stage for a new epoch—a period known as the *Hellenistic Age* as distinct from the previous *Classical Age*. The Greeks were now the masters of the ancient world, and under their rule a great cosmopolitan culture developed, distinctly Greek in tradition yet transmuted by the influence of the subject oriental civilizations and by the spacious new environment in which the Greeks now lived.

The Hellenization of the Near East was stimulated by Alexander's policy of founding cities in the wake of his conquests and filling them with Greek settlers. These communities, although intended chiefly as military and commercial bases, became islands of Greek culture which were often able to exert a powerful influence on the surrounding area. Most of them were named, immodestly, after their founder. The greatest of them by far was Alexandria founded near the mouth of the Nile. Alexandria quickly outstripped the cities of Greece itself to become the great commercial center of the Hellenistic world, and before long it had developed a cultural and intellectual life that put contemporary Athens to shame.

No sooner had he ascended the throne of Persia than Alexander began preparations for further campaigns. The final seven years of his life were occupied in conquering the easternmost provinces of Persia and pushing on into India, impelled by an insatiable thirst for conquest and by the lure of undiscovered lands. His spirit and ingenuity were taxed to the utmost by the variety of difficulties that he encountered: the rugged mountains of Afghanistan, the hostile stretches of the Indus Valley, fierce armies equipped with hundreds of elephants. At length his own army, its endurance exhausted, refused to go further. Alexander returned to central Persia in 323 where, in the midst of organizing his immense empire, he fell ill and died, perhaps of malaria, at the age of thirty-two.

The empire of Alexander was the greatest that the world had ever seen—more extensive even than the Persian Empire. Wherever he went Alexander adapted himself to the customs of the land. He ruled Egypt as a divine pharaoh and Persia as an oriental despot, demanding that his subjects prostrate themselves in his presence. (His Greek followers objected vigorously to this.) He married the daughter of the last Persian emperor and urged his countrymen to follow his example by taking wives from among the Persian aristocracy. His goal was nothing less than a homogeneous Greco-Oriental empire—a fusion of east and west. To what extent this policy was the product of deliberate calculation, to what extent a consequence of his intoxication with the splendors of the ancient

Alexander the Great.   (Marburg/Art Reference Bureau)

Orient will never be known. But the project was scarcely underway when Alexander died, leaving behind him an overwhelming sense of loss and bewilderment and a vast state that nobody but a second Alexander could have held together.

The Successor States

The empire was divided among the able and ambitious generals of Alexander's staff who founded a series of Macedonian dynasties that ruled Greece and most of the ancient Near East until the Roman conquests of the second and first centuries B.C. There was great conflict over the division of the spoils, and for several decades after Alexander's death the political situation remained fluid. But in broad outline the succession went as follows: Ptolemy, one of Alexander's ablest generals, ruled Egypt, establishing the Ptolemaic dynasty that

lasted until a Roman army deposed Cleopatra, the last of the Ptolemies, in 30 B.C. From Alexandria, their magnificent capital, the Ptolemies ruled with all the pomp and severity of the most powerful pharaohs, enriching themselves by merciless exploitation of the peasantry and suppressing all political activities, even among the multitudes of Greeks in Alexandria. The great metropolitan capital, with its imposing public buildings, its superb library and museum, its far-flung commerce, and its million inhabitants was the wonder of the age, but elsewhere Egypt remained essentially unchanged except for a growing hostility toward the uncompromising authoritarianism of the Greek regime.

Northern Syria and most of the remaining provinces of the old Persian Empire fell to another of Alexander's generals, Seleucus, who founded the Seleucid dynasty. The kingdom of the Seleucids was far more heterogeneous and loosely organized than that of the Ptolemies, and as time went on certain of the more self-conscious Near Eastern peoples began to rebel against the Seleucid policy of Hellenization. This was particularly true of the Persians and Jews who had each produced powerful transcendental religions and resented bitterly the influx of Greek religious thought. Farther to the east, the more remote provinces of the Persian Empire gradually fell away from Seleucid control. The center of Seleucid power was the great city of Antioch in northern Syria which was second only to Alexandria in population, wealth, and opulence.

The third important successor state, Macedon, passed into the hands or a dynasty known as the Antigonids whose authority over the Greek cities to the south was never very firm and whose power was usually inferior to that of the Ptolemies and Seleucids. A number of smaller states also developed out of the wreckage of Alexander's empire, but the three dominant successor kingdoms were Antigonid Greece, Seleucid Asia, and Ptolemaic Egypt.

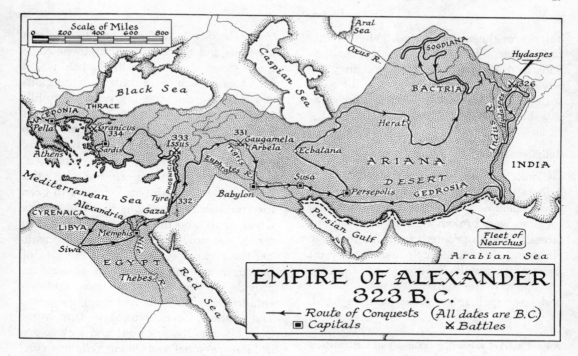

Scale of Miles
0   200   400   600   800

EMPIRE OF ALEXANDER
323 B.C.
← Route of Conquests (All dates are B.C.)
■ Capitals   × Battles

The Change in Mood

These huge political agglomerations now replaced the small city-states as the typical units of the Greek world. The new environment provided vast opportunities and encouraged a sense of cosmopolitanism that contrasts with the provincialism of the polis. This was a prosperous age, an age of vigorous and profitable business activity and successful careers in commerce and banking. The good life was reserved, however, to the fortunate few. Slavery continued, even increased, and the peasants and urban commoners were kept at an economic level of bare subsistence. The typical agrarian unit was no longer the small or middle-sized farm but the large plantation worked by slaves.

The city-states in Greece itself retained throughout the new age a portion of their earlier autonomy. Old civic institutions continued to function, and citizens still had a voice in domestic politics. But the Greek peninsula was now an economic backwater, and cities like Athens and Thebes were overshadowed by the new superstates. Ambitious Greeks were lured by opportunity far from their homeland, as they had once been lured to imperial Athens. No longer involved in political affairs or in the intense life of a free community, the overseas Greek found himself adrift in a wide and bewildering world over which he had no control. The cosmopolitanism of the Hellenistic age was accompanied by a sense of estrangement and alienation, of uncertainty, loneliness, and impotence. The trend toward extreme individualism, professionalism, and specialization which we have already observed in the fourth century was enormously accelerated. The impulse toward greater realism and individualism in sculpture was pushed to its limits, and many Hellenistic sculptors turned to portraying the bizarre and the grotesque—ugliness, deformity, agony, and old age—sometimes with exceedingly effective results. The civic consciousness of the comic playwright Aristophanes in the fifth century gave way to the highly individualized and superficial realism of the Hellenistic drawing-room comedy and bedroom farce. The Hellenistic Age produced superb works of art, but they lacked the serenity and balance of the earlier period. Whether this fact detracts from their artistic merit or adds to it is a matter of taste, but they are obviously products of a radically different society—still brilliant, still intensely creative, but anchorless.

Religion and Ethics

Hellenic religion with its traditional civic orientation was all but transformed in this new, kaleidoscopic age. Old bonds and old loyalties were broken as many adventurous Greeks were uprooted from their home cities and thrown on their own. The result ment or personal salvation rather than involvement in the community. Individualism and cosmopolitanism went hand in hand,

An old market woman, an example of Hellenistic realism.   (The Metropolitan Museum of Art, Rogers Fund, 1909)

for as the Greek abdicated spiritually from the polis and retired into himself, he came was a mood of intense individualism which found expression in a variety of religious and ethical ideas stressing personal fulfill- to regard all humanity as a multitude of individuals—a universal brotherhood in which intelligent Persians, Egyptians, and Jews were no worse than intelligent Greeks. The traditional contrast between Greek and barbarian faded, for it had been the free spirit of the polis that had set the Greek apart, and the polis, in its traditional sense, was now becoming an anachronism. Yet the concept of cosmopolis, the idea of human brotherhood, was too abstract to provide the sense of involvement and orientation that the polis had formerly given. The rootless Greek tended to turn away from his old Olympic gods and seek solace in more personal and potent religious concepts. Hellenistic religion is characterized by a withdrawal from active social participation—a search for sanctuary in a restless, uncertain world.

The Hellenistic age saw a vigorous revival of mystery and salvation cults such as Orphism and the worship of Dionysus and Demeter which had always lurked behind the Olympic foreground. And various Near Eastern mystery religions now became popular among the Greeks. Almost all of these were centered on the death and resurrection of a god and the promise of personal salvation. From Egypt came the cult of Osiris who died, was reborn, and now sat in judgment of the dead. From Asia Minor came a version of the ancient and widespread fertility cult of the Great Mother. From Persia, somewhat later, came the cult of Mithras, a variation of Zoroastrianism, which added to the traditional concept of a cosmic moral struggle between good and evil the idea of a savior-hero who redeemed mankind. Alongside these and other oriental cults came a revival of Babylonian astrology, of magic, witchcraft, and sorcery. Many ambitious men of the upper class were devoted to the goddess of

Fortune who rewarded talent and ambition and brought her worshipers material well-being. The Hellenistic world became a huge religious melting pot in which a single individual might be a devotee of a number of cults. Many thoughtful people adopted the idea of "syncretism," that is, the notion that the gods of different peoples are actually various manifestations of the same god—that Zeus, Osiris, even Yahweh, all symbolize a single divine spirit. (The more orthodox among the Jews found this doctrine abominable.) Religious beliefs and religious attitudes throughout the Hellenistic world were tending to become homogenized, thereby preparing the soil for the later triumph of Christianity.

Skeptics, Cynics, Stoics and Epicureans

Many Greeks of the post-Classical age turned neither to the old Orphic and Dionysian cults nor to the salvation cults of the Orient but sought to adapt elements of the Hellenic intellectual tradition to the new conditions. One group, the Skeptics, intensified the relativism of the Sophists by denying the possibility of any knowledge whatever, either of gods, man or nature. The human mind, they maintained, is incapable of apprehending reality (if, indeed, there is any such thing as "reality"), and all beliefs and statements of fact are equally unverifiable. Mirroring the profound uncertainty of the new age, the skeptics doubted everything and thus carried rationalism to its ultimate, self-destructive limit—doubting reason itself.

Another group, the Cynics, demonstrated in various forms of eccentric behavior their contempt for conventional piety and patriotism and their rebellion against the hypocrisy that they detected in the lives and attitudes of their contemporaries. Diogenes, the most famous of the Cynics, was something of a fourth-century hippie who sought to live with integrity in a world of phonies. He rejected all official and tradi-

tional religions, all participation in civic life, marriage, the public games, and the theater. He ridiculed the prestige that was associated with wealth, power, and reputation and honored instead the simple life of courage, reason and honesty—a life of virtue—which could best be attained by a rejection of civilization and a return to nature. The man of integrity, the wise and honest man, should live like a dog, without pretensions and uncluttered by worldly possessions. Indeed, the very word *cynic* originally meant *canine* or "doglike." So Diogenes wandered the streets begging for his food, a homeless but free man. His bedchamber was a gigantic pitcher outside a temple of the Great Mother; his latrine was the public street. He obeyed no laws, recognized no polis, and became next to Alexander, the most illustrious man of his age. He was a colorful symbol of the great Hellenistic withdrawal from the polis into the individual soul.

The same withdrawal is evident in the two religio-ethical systems that emerged in the fourth century and influenced human thought and conduct for centuries thereafter: Stoicism and Epicureanism. Both were philosophies of resignation that taught men to fortify their souls against the harshness of life. Zeno, the founder of the Stoic School, stressed, as the Cynics did, the vanity of worldly things and the supreme importance of individual virtue. Every man, whether statesman, artist, or peasant, should pursue his calling honestly and seriously. The significant thing, however, was not individual accomplishment but individual effort; such things as politics, art, and husbandry were ultimately valueless, yet in pursuing them as best he could the individual manifested his virtue. Since virtue was all-important, the good Stoic was immune to the vicissitudes of life. He might lose his property; he might even be imprisoned and tortured, but except by his own will he could not be deprived of his virtue which was his only really precious possession. By rejecting the world the Stoic created a citadel within his own soul. Out of this doctrine there emerged a sense not only of individualism but of cosmopolitanism; the idea of the polis faded before the wider (though vaguer) concept of human brotherhood.

Ultimately the Stoic emphasis on virtue was rooted in a lofty cosmic vision based on the Greek conception of a rational, orderly, purposeful universe. The harmonious movements of the stars and planets, the growth of complex plants from simple seeds, all pointed to the existence of a divine plan which was both intelligent and good. We humans were incapable of perceiving the details of the plan as it worked in our own lives, yet by living virtuously and doing our best we could cooperate with it. The God of the universe cared about mankind, and the stern nobility of Stoic ethics was tempered and humanized by this optimistic assurance.

Epicurus, whose school was Stoicism's great rival, differed from Zeno both in his concept of human ethics and in his vision of the universe. He taught that man should seek happiness rather than virtue. Yet happiness to the Epicureans was not the pursuit of sex, liquor, and euphoria, but rather a quiet, balanced life. The life of the drunkard is saddened by countless hangovers, the life of the philanderer by countless complications. Happiness was best achieved not by chasing pleasures but by living simply and unobtrusively, being kind and affectionate to one's friends, learning to endure pain when it comes, and avoiding needless fears. In short, good Epicureans did not differ noticeably from good Stoics in actual behavior, for virtue was the pathway to happiness. But the Epicureans rejected the optimistic Stoic doctrine of divine purpose. Epicurus followed the teachings of the atomists in viewing the universe not as a great hierarchy of cosmic spheres centering on the earth, but as a vast multiplicity of atoms much the same one place as another. Our world is not the handiwork of God, but a chance configuration. The gods, if they exist, care nothing for us, and we ought to draw from this fact the comforting conclusion that we need not fear them.

Epicureanism even more than Stoicism was a philosophy of withdrawal. It was a wise, compassionate teaching that sought to banish fear, curb passions, and dispel illusions. Its doctrine of happiness was too limited and too bland to stir the millions and convert empires, yet through the lofty epic poetry of the Roman writer Lucretius (98–53 B.C.), it made its impact on the intellectual life of Rome. Although never as popular as Stoicism, it gave solace and direction, during the remaining centuries of antiquity, to an influential minority of wise and sensitive men.

Hellenistic Science

In the Hellenistic age, Greek science reached maturity. The naive generalizations of the earlier period gave way to a rigorous and highly creative professionalism. Aristotle's salutary example was followed and improved on by the Hellenistic scientists who collected and sifted data with great thoroughness before framing their hypotheses.

Alexandria was the center of scientific thought in this age. Here the Ptolemies built and subsidized a great research center—the Museum of Alexandria—and collected a library of unprecedented size and diversity containing some half-million papyrus rolls. At Alexandria and elsewhere science and mathematics made rapid strides as Greek rationalism encountered the rich, amorphous heritage of Near Eastern astrology, medical lore, and practical mathematics. The fruitful medical investigations of Hippocrates' school were carried on and expanded by Hellenistic physicians, particularly in Alexandria. Their pioneer work in the dissection of human bodies enabled them to discover the nervous system, to learn a great deal about the brain, heart, and arteries, and to perform successful surgical operations. In mathematics, Euclid organized plane and solid geometry into a systematic, integrated body of knowledge. Archimedes of Syracuse did brilliant original work in both pure and applied mathematics, discovering specific gravity, experimenting successfully with levers and pulleys to lift tremendous weights, and coming very close to the invention of calculus.

The wide-ranging military campaigns of Alexander and the subsequent cultural interchange between large areas of the world led to a vast increase in Greek geographical knowledge. Eratosthenes, the head of the Alexandrian Library in the later third century, produced the most accurate and thorough world maps that had yet been made, complete with lines of longitude and latitude and climatic zones. He recognized that the earth was a sphere and was even able to determine its circumference with an error of less than 1 percent. He did this by measuring the altitude of the sun at different latitudes, calculating from this data the length of one degree of latitude on the earth's surface, and multiplying the result by 360 (degrees).

The same painstaking accuracy and dazzling ingenuity is evident in the work of the Hellenistic astronomers. Aristarchus of Samos suggested that the earth rotated daily on its axis and revolved yearly around the sun. This heliocentric hypothesis is a startling anticipation of modern astronomical conclusions, but Aristarchus' erroneous assumption that the earth's motion around the sun was uniform and circular rendered this system inaccurate. Its failure to explain the precise astronomical observations then being made at Alexandria, and its violation of the hallowed doctrine of an earth-centered universe, prevented its wide acceptance. Later the great Hellenistic astronomer Hipparchus developed a complex system of circles and subcircles centered on the earth which accounted exceedingly well for the observed motions of the heavenly bodies. Hipparchus' ingenious sytem, perfected by the Alexandrian astronomer Ptolemy in the second century A.D., represents antiquity's final word on the subject—a comprehensive geometrical model of the universe. It was fundamentally wrong yet it corresponded satisfactorily to the best observations of the day. And it should be remembered that a scientific hypothesis must be judged not by some absolute standard of rightness or wrongness but by its success in accounting for and predicting observed phenomena. By this criterion the Ptolemaic system stands as one of the impressive triumphs of Hellenistic thought.

The Hellenistic Legacy

Greek culture exerted a fundamental influence on the Roman Empire, the Byzantine and Muslim civilizations and medieval Western Europe, but it did so largely in its Hellenistic form. The conclusions of the Hellenistic philosophers and scholars tended to be accepted by the best minds of later ages, but the Hellenistic spirit of free inquiry and intellectual daring was not matched until the sixteenth and seventeenth centuries. There is something remarkably modern about the Hellenistic world with its confident scientists, its cosmopolitanism, its materialism, its religious diversity, its trend toward increasing specialization, its large-scale business activity and its sense of drift and disorientation. But the Hellenistic social conscience remained dormant, and Hellenistic economic organization, regardless of surface similarities, was vastly different from ours. Like all its Near Eastern predecessors, the Hellenistic economy was based on human slaves rather than machines (which are our modern slaves). It provided only a tiny fraction of the population with the benefits of its commercial prosperity. The great majority remained servile and illiterate.

Still, the upper classes throughout the Mediterranean world and the Near East were exposed to Greek culture and the Greek language, and the Greeks themselves were deeply influenced by Oriental thought. From Syria, Asia Minor, and the Nile Valley to Magna Graecia in the West, a common culture was developing with common ideas and common gods. The way was being paved for the political unification of the Mediterranean world under the authority of Rome, and its spiritual unification under the Christian Church. Alexander's dream of a homogeneous Greco-Oriental world was gradually coming into being. But if Alexander had foreseen the consequences of his work—the conquest of Hellas by an Italian city and an oriental faith—he might well have chosen to spend his days in seclusion.

GREEK CHRONOLOGY

All Dates B.C.

c.3000–1400:	Minoan civilization
c.1500–1120:	Mycenaean civilization
c.1200:	Trojan war
c.1200–1000:	Dorian invasions
c.1120–800:	"Dark Age"
c.750–550:	Era of colonization
c.650 ff.:	Rise of tyrants
c.594:	Solon reforms Athenian laws
c.582–507:	Pythagoras
561–527:	Pisistratus rules Athens
508:	Cleisthenes reforms Athenian laws
490–479:	Persian Wars
477:	Delian League established
c.460–429:	Era of Pericles
454:	Delian treasury moved to Athens
432:	Parthenon completed
431–404:	Peloponnesian War
469–399:	Socrates
427–347:	Plato
384–322:	Aristotle
359–336:	Reign of Philip of Macedon
338:	Battle of Chaeronea: Philip establishes mastery over Greece
336–323:	Reign of Alexander the Great
323 ff.:	The Hellenistic Age

SUGGESTED READINGS

The asterisk indicates a paperback edition.

Leonard Cottrell, *The Bull of Minos* (*New York: Grosset and Dunlap, 1958).

R. Higgins, *Minoan and Mycenaen Art* (*New York: Praeger, 1967).

P. MacKendrick, *The Greek Stones Speak* (*New York: Mentor, 1962).

H. J. Rose, *Handbook of Greek Mythology* (*New York: Dutton, 1958).

J. B. Bury, *A History of Greece* (New York: Macmillan, 3rd ed., rev. by R. Meiggs, 1951).

M. I. Finley, *The Ancient Greeks* (*New York: Viking, 1963).

M. I. Finley, ed. and trans., *Greek Historians* (*New York: Viking, 1959).

H. D. F. Kitto, *The Greeks* (*Baltimore, Md.: Penguin Books, 1957).

F. J. Frost, *Democracy and the Athenians* (*New York: Wiley, 1969).

Thucydides, *The History of the Peloponnesian War*, trans. by Richard Crawley (*New York: Modern Library, 1961).

W. H. Auden, *The Portable Greek Reader* (*New York: Viking, 1948).

Scott Buchanan, ed., trans. by B. Jowett, *The Portable Plato.* (*New York: Viking, 1948).

F. M. Cornford, *From Religion to Philosophy* (*New York: Harper, 1957).

G. M. Richter, *Handbook of Greek Art* (*New York: Phaidon, 1960).

H. J. Rose, *Handbook of Greek Literature* (*New York: Dutton, 1964).

Bruno Snell, *The Discovery of the Mind* (*New York: Harper, 1953).

Max Cary, *A History of the Greek World from 323 to 146 B.C.* (London: Methuen, 2nd ed., 1951).

B. Farrington, *Greek Science* (*Baltimore, Md.: Penguin Books, 1961).

W. W. Tarn, *Hellenistic Civilisation*, rev. by W. W. Tarn and G. T. Griffith (*Cleveland: Meridian, 1952).

Ulrich Wilcken, *Alexander the Great* (*New York: Norton, 1967).

Chester G. Starr, *The Ancient Greeks* (New York: Oxford, 1971).

Part 2 The Legacy of Rome

■ ■ ■ ■

4

The Rise of Rome: Kingdom, Republic, Empire

The rise of Rome from an inconsequential central-Italian village to the mastery of the ancient Mediterranean world is one of history's supreme success stories. The process was slow as compared with the dazzling imperialistic careers of Persia and Macedon, but it was far more lasting. There was nothing meteoric about the serious, hard-headed Romans—they built slowly and well. Their great military virtue was not tactical brilliance but stubborn endurance. They lost battles but from their beginnings to the great days of the Empire they never lost a war. Since it was they who ultimately provided the ancient world with a viable, encompassing political framework, students of history have always been fascinated by the development of Roman political institutions. Rome's greatest contributions were in the realm of law, government, and imperial organization. In her grasp of political realities lay the secret of her triumphant career.

Republican Rome

Had Alexander lived to middle age instead of dying at thirty-two he might well have led his conquering armies westward into Italy, Sicily and North Africa. Here he would have encountered three vigorous cultures: Carthage, the city-states of Magna Graecia, and the rapidly-expanding republic of Rome. Carthage was originally a Phoenician commercial colony but its strategic location on the North African coast, just south of Sicily, gave it a stranglehold on the western Mediterranean. It soon developed an extensive commercial empire of its own and far outstripped the Phoenician homeland in power and wealth. Carthage established a number of commercial bases in western Sicily which brought her face-to-face with the Greek city-states that dominated the eastern sections of the island.

The Greek cities of Sicily and southern Italy, known collectively as Magna Graecia, were products of the age of Greek colonization in the eighth and seventh centuries. Their political evolution ran parallel to that of the city-states in Greece. They experienced the same violent struggles between aristocratic, oligarchic, and democratic factions and the same intense cultural creativity. And like Old Greece, Magna Graecia was tormented by incessant intercity warfare. By Alexander's time the Sicilian polis of Syracuse had long been the leading power of the area, but the smaller polises guarded their independence jealously, and real unification was delayed until the Roman conquests of the third century brought these Greek cities under the sway of a common master.

Early Rome

The beginnings of Roman history are obscure. It seems likely that by about 750 B.C. settlers were living in huts on the Palatine Hill near the Tiber River. Gradually, several neighboring hills became inhabited, and around 600 these various settlements joined together to form the city-state of Rome. The strategic position of this cluster of hills, 15 miles inland on one of Italy's few navigable rivers, was of enor-

A Chimera, a fine Etruscan bronze.   (Alinari/Art Reference Bureau)

mous importance to Rome's future growth. Ancient ocean-going ships could sail up the Tiber to Rome but no farther, and Rome was the lowest point at which the river could be bridged easily. Hence Rome was a key river-crossing and road junction and also, at least potentially, a seaport. It was at the northern limit of a fertile agricultural district known as Latium whose rustic inhabitants, the Latins, gave their name to the Latin language. Immediately north of Rome lay the district of Etruria (the modern Tuscany) whose highly civilized inhabitants, the Etruscans, shaped the culture of the earliest Romans.

The Etruscan ruling class may have migrated to Etruria from Asia Minor around 800 B.C. bringing with it into central Italy important elements of the rich cultural heritage of the eastern Mediterranean and the Near East. The Etruscans borrowed heavily from the Greeks. Their art, their city-state political structure, and their alphabet, were all Hellenic in inspiration, but they adapted these cultural ingredients to their own needs and created out of them a vivacious, pleasure-loving civilization of considerable originality. It was in Etruscan form that Greek civilization made its first impact on Rome. The Romans adopted the Greek alphabet in its Etruscan version and perhaps through Etruscan inspiration they organized themselves into a city-state, thereby gaining an inestimable advantage over the numerous half-civilized tribes in the region between Etruria and Magna Graecia. During much of the sixth century, Rome was ruled by kings of Etruscan background whose talented and aggressive leadership made the Romans an important power among the peoples of Latium. The community grew in strength and wealth, and an impressive temple to the Roman god Jupiter was built in Etruscan style atop one of the hills. Rome was becoming a city in fact as well as in name.

About 509 B.C. the Roman aristocracy succeeded in overthrowing its Etruscan king, transforming Rome from a monarchy into an aristocratic republic. The king was replaced by two magistrates known as consuls who were elected annually by an aristocratic Senate and who governed with its advice. The consuls exercised their authority in the name of the Roman people but in the interests of the upper classes. The governing elite was composed of wealthy landowners known as patricians who defended their prerogatives zealously against the encroachments of the common people— the plebeians or plebs. Plebeian-patrician intermarriage was strictly prohibited, and for a time the plebeians were almost entirely without political rights.

But step by step plebeians improved their condition and came to play a significant role in the government. They began by organizing themselves into a deliberative body that later took the form of an important political organ known as the Tribal Assembly. They elected representatives called tribunes to be their spokesmen and represent their interests before the patrician-controlled city government. The tribunes acquired the remarkable power of vetoing anti-plebeian measures issuing from any organ of government, and anyone violating the sanctity of a tribune's person was to be punished by death. Under the leadership of their tribunes the plebeians were able to act as a unit and to make their strength felt. On at least one occasion they seceded as a body from the Roman state, leaving the patrician governors with nobody to govern and the patrician army officers with no troops to lead.

In about 450 B.C. the Romans took the important step of committing their legal customs to writing. The result was Rome's first law code—the Twelve Tables. By later standards these laws were harsh (defaulting debtors, for example, suffered capital punishment or were delivered up for sale abroad), but they had the effect of protecting individual plebeians from the capricious authority of the patrician consuls.

The Twelve Tables are exceedingly significant in Roman constitutional development, constituting as they do the first monument in the evolution of Roman law.

Having gained a measure of legal protection, the plebeians turned to the problem of land distribution and forced the government to grant them additional farms out of its own estates and from the territories of newly-conquered peoples. Gradually the Tribal Assembly of the plebeians acquired the power to initiate legislation and thereby came to play an important part in Roman government. Intermarriage was now allowed between the two classes, and a law of 367 B.C. opened the consulship itself to the plebeians. At the same time, or shortly afterward, it was stipulated that at least one of the two consuls be a plebeian. In the years that followed, plebeians became eligible for all offices of state. Collectively, these measures went far toward transforming Rome into a nominal democracy. This transformation was completed in 287 B.C. when legislation issuing from the Tribal Assembly acquired the force of law without the necessity of being ratified by the aristocratic Senate. The law was now, at least theoretically, in the hands of the people.

In the interest of simplicity and brevity we have not been able to do justice to the extreme complexity of Roman republican government. It included numerous magistrates with various functions and, at one time or another, several different assemblies. The Tribal Assembly, for example, shared power with another important public body: the Centuriate Assembly. Both were made up of the total Roman citizenry, plebeian and patrician alike, but each had its own specific power and function. Moreover, these two Assemblies differed significantly in organization. The Tribal Assembly, the more democratic of the two, was based on tribal or residential districts known as wards. Each ward had one vote, and the poorer rural wards outnumbered the urban ones. But since the patrician wards had the privilege of voting first, most matters had been decided by the time the plebeian wards cast their votes. By this means the patricians were able to limit plebeian political power within the nominally democratic framework.

The Centuriate Assembly, patterned on the organization of the Roman army, was divided into groups known as "centuries." The number of centuries allotted to each class depended on the number of men that class supplied to the army, and since wealth was the basis of Roman military service, the Centuriate Assembly was dominated by the wealthy. Empowered to elect Rome's chief magistrates and to vote on questions of war and peace, the Centuriate Assembly remained powerful throughout the later years of the Republic. With its wealth-based organization, it further compromised the so-called "democratic" regime that was established in 287.

Roman democracy after 287 was more apparent than real. The domination of the patricians was fading, but it was giving way to a more subtle domination by a wealthy oligarchy of leading plebeian and patrician families. For during the fifth and fourth centuries a number of plebeians had accumulated extensive estates, and many of them now rivaled the patricians in wealth. By being elected to magistracies, many wealthy plebeians gained admission into the Senate which, by the third century, had ceased to be a patrician preserve. Indeed, by 287 the old division between patrician It was replaced by a new division between the poor and the wealthy.* Since more and more wealthy plebeians were gaining admission into the Senate, it is conventional among historians to term the wealthy landholders of the later Republic the "senatorial aristocracy."

---

* Women remained without political rights. And at a social level beneath that of the free poor there existed, as in all ancient societies, a substantial slave class.

The complex machinery of Roman republican government offered many opportunities for the new oligarchy to retain in practice the control that in theory belonged to all the freemen of Rome. By means of political manipulation and patronage, the wealthy made their influence felt in the Tribal Assembly. They had a preponderant voice in the Centuriate Assembly, and they dominated the Senate—which lacked direct legislative power but retained enormous influence and prestige. In short, Rome in 287 was only a paper democracy. In reality, it was a plutocracy—a government of wealthy males—whose policies were controlled by the senatorial aristocracy.

Nevertheless the political realism of the Romans is well illustrated by the fact that the sweeping constitutional changes that took place between the fall of the Etruscan monarchy in 509 B.C. and the legislative supremacy of the Tribal Assembly in 287 B.C. occurred without major insurrections or excessive bloodshed. During these years much Roman blood was spilled on the battlefield but comparatively little on the city's streets. The willingness to settle internal conflicts by compromise—the ability of the patricians to bend before the winds of social change—preserved in Rome a sense of cohesiveness and a spirit of civic commitment without which its conquests would have been inconceivable.

The Career of Conquest

Civic commitment was a hallmark of the early Roman. Devoted to the numerous gods of city, field, and hearth, he was hard-working, respectful of tradition, obedient to civil and military authority, and dedicated to the welfare of the state. The backbone of Old Rome was the small, independent farmer who worked long and hard to raise crops from his fields and remained always vigilant against raids by tribesmen from the surrounding hills. To men such as these life was intensely serious. Their stern sobriety and rustic virtues were exaggerated by Roman moralists looking back nostalgically from a later and more luxurious age, but there can be little doubt that the tenacious spirit and astonishing military success of early republican Rome owed much to the discipline and steadfastness of these citizen-farmers. As triumph followed triumph, as the booty of war flowed into Rome from far and wide, the character of her citizenry inevitably suffered. One of the great tragic themes of Roman history is the gradual erosion of social morality by wealth and power—and by the gradual expansion of huge slave-operated estates at the expense of the small farmer. But long before this process was complete the empire had been won.

The expulsion of the last Etruscan king in 509 B.C. was followed by a period of retrenchment during which the Romans fought for their lives against the attacks of neighboring tribes. In time an alliance was formed between Rome and the communities of Latium in which Rome gradually

assumed the role of senior partner. Hostile tribes were subdued after long and agonizing effort, and shortly after 400 B.C. the Etruscan cities began to fall, one by one, under Roman control. The Romans were usually generous with the Italian peoples whom they conquered, allowing them a good measure of internal self-government, and were therefore generally successful in retaining their allegiance. In time, if a conquered people proved loyal, they might hope to be granted Roman citizenship. In this generous fashion Rome was able to construct an empire far more cohesive and durable than that of Periclean Athens. (Neither Pericles nor any of his contemporaries could have conceived of granting citizenship to non-Atticans.) Gradually the Roman conquests gained momentum. Battles were often lost—Rome itself was sacked in 387 B.C. by an army of Gauls from the north—but the Romans brushed off their defeats and pressed on. By 265 B.C. all Italy south of the Po Valley was under

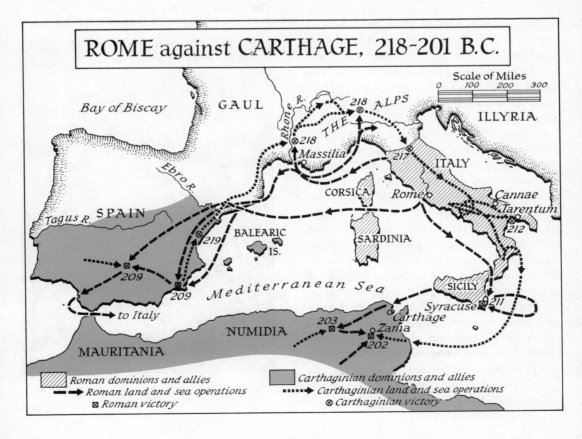

ROME against CARTHAGE, 218-201 B.C.

Roman dominions and allies
→ *Roman land and sea operations*
⊗ *Roman victory*

Carthaginian dominions and allies
······▶ *Carthaginian land and sea operations*
⊗ *Carthaginian victory*

their control. Etruscan power had collapsed, and even the Italian cities of Magna Graecia acknowledged Roman supremacy. Now, midway through the third century, Rome took its place alongside Carthage and the three great Hellenistic successor states as one of the leading powers of the Mediterranean world.

Carthage and Rome stood face to face, and in 264 B.C. these two great western powers became locked in the first of three savage conflicts known as the Punic Wars (after *Poenus*, the Latin word for Phoenician or Carthaginian). Rome was now forced to build a navy and take to the sea. The wars, especially the first two, were long and bitter. Rome lost numerous battles, scores of ships, and warriors and seamen by the hundreds of thousands. During the Second Punic War (218 to 201 B.C.) the armies of the masterly Carthaginian general Hannibal swept back and forth across Italy winning victory after victory, and only the dogged determination of the Romans and the loyalty of their subject-allies saved the state from extinction. But the Romans hung on, always managing to win the last battle. At the conclusion of the Third Punic War in 146 B.C. Carthage was in ruins and its far-flung territories in Africa, Sicily, and Spain were in Roman hands.

In the meantime Rome was drawn almost inadvertently into the rivalries among the Hellenistic kingdoms of the eastern Mediterranean. Ptolemaic Egypt, Seleucid Asia, Antigonid Macedon, and the several smaller Greek states had long been at one another's throats; Rome's victories over Carthage increased its power to the point where it was stronger than any of them. Greek states frequently sought Roman aid against their enemies, and more often than not the Romans gave the requested support in order to maintain the balance of power in the east and to prevent any one Greek kingdom from becoming dangerously strong. Rome entered the Greek world more as a pacifier than as a conqueror, but eventually it tired of its endless task as referee and remained to rule. During the second century almost all the Hellenistic world fell either directly or indirectly under Roman control. Rome won a decisive victory over the Seleucids in 189 B.C.; it conquered Macedon in 168 B.C.; in 146 it demolished the ancient Peloponnesian city of Corinth and transformed Greece into a Roman province under the direct authority of a governor appointed by the Roman state. The remaining Hellenistic kingdoms were now completely overshadowed and had no choice but to bow to Rome's leadership. Gradually they too became provinces.

Rome followed no blueprint for conquest—indeed many of its leaders were isolationists who would have preferred to remain aloof from the Greek east—but the political conditions of the Hellenistic states

Two Italian warriors carrying a dead comrade.   (Alinari/Art Reference Bureau)

exerted a magnetic attraction that was irresistible. As the second century drew toward its close, Rome was the master of the Mediterranean world. There now arose the baffling problem of adapting a government designed to rule a city-state to the needs of an empire.

Social and Political Changes   (264–146 B.C.)

The years of the three Punic Wars witnessed a transformation in the structure and spirit of Rome itself. These changes can be attributed partly to the intoxicating effect of unimagined wealth and military success that gradually undermined the old civic virtue and encouraged a mood of arrogance and materialism. More specifically, as Rome was conquering the Greek world, it was falling increasingly under the influence of Hellenistic culture. Later Roman writers such as Cato and Sallust lamented that Roman soldiers were corrupted by the luxuries of eastern Mediterranean lands. Ultimately, Greece was perhaps the victor after all. The full tide of Hellenistic skepticism and individualism, which had earlier done so much to dissolve the Greek polis, now began its corrosive work on Roman conservatism and civic dedication. As in Greece, the effects of this process were both good and bad. What Rome lost in civic virtue it gained in cultural and intellectual depth, for prior to its Hellenization, Rome was almost totally lacking in high culture. The Stoic notion of universal brotherhood was a singularly appropriate philosophy for a great empire, and it was a fortunate thing for the conquered peoples that in later years so many Roman statesmen became Stoics. But with Greek art, literature, and learning came the disquieting Hellenistic feeling of drift and alienation, aggravated by the importation of Hellenistic agricultural techniques.

The great Hellenistic successor states had emphasized the large plantation over the small independent farm, and now, as the conquests brought vast wealth and hordes of slaves into the hands of the Roman upper classes, most of central and southern Italy was converted into huge farms known as *latifundia*, worked by slaves and operated according to the latest Hellenistic techniques of large-scale scientific farming. Where the small farms had produced grain, the *latifundia* concentrated on the more lucrative production of wine and olive oil or the raising of sheep. The small farmers, whose energy and devotion had built the Roman Empire, were subjected to such heavy military demands that they found it increasingly difficult to maintain their farms. Many sold out to the *latifundia* owners and flocked into the cities, especially Rome itself, where they were joined by masses of penniless immigrants from the provinces and transformed into a chronically unemployed, irresponsible mob. In later years their riots terrorized the government. Their hunger and boredom eventually gave rise to the custom of subsidized food and free entertainment of an increasingly sadistic sort—"bread and circuses."

While Rome was engaged in its struggle with Carthage, important changes were occurring in the social structure of the Roman ruling elite. With the acceleration of commerce, a new class of businessmen and public contractors was developing that in time acquired such wealth as to rival the landed senatorial aristocracy. This new class came to be known as the equestrian order because the wealth of its members enabled them to serve in the Roman army as cavalry rather than infantry. The equestrian class was effectively excluded from the Senate. Fundamentally apolitical except in instances when its own interests were at stake, it was content to share with the senatorial aristocracy the rising living standards that were coming into Rome with military triumphs and increased contact with the Hellenistic world. As the equestrians and landed nobility came to

The Capitoline wolf symbol of
Rome.   (Alinari/Art Reference Bureau)

live in increasing luxury, the gap between rich and poor steadily widened, and the pressures of social unrest began to threaten the traditional stability of Roman civilization.

Meanwhile the Roman government, which had earlier acted with restraint toward its subject-allies in Italy, was proving itself incapable of governing justly its newly acquired overseas territories. Most of Rome's non-Italian holdings were organized as provinces ruled by aristocratic Roman governors and exploited by Roman tax gatherers. Infected with the selfishness and greed of Hellenistic individualism at its worst, governor and tax gatherer often worked in cruel partnership to bleed the provinces for personal advantage. The grossest kinds of official corruption were tolerated by the Roman courts of law whose aristocratic judges hesitated to condemn dishonest officials of their own class for the sake of oppressed but alien provincials. Indeed, some provincial governors made it a practice to set aside a portion of their booty to bribe the courts.

Violence and Revolution:
The Last Century of the Republic

The deep-seated problems that afflicted Rome brought about a century-long period of violence and unrest, between 133 and 30 B.C., which resulted ultimately in the downfall of the Republic and the advent of a new imperial government. The first steps toward revolution were taken by two aristocratic reformers, the brothers Tiberius and Gaius Gracchus, who advocated a series of popular reform measures and thereby built up a powerful faction among the Roman commoners who were struggling against the entrenched aristocracy of wealth. Tiberius Gracchus served as tribune in 133 B.C., and Gaius held the same office a decade later. The two Gracchi were deeply concerned with the ominous course of the Republic. Both recognized that the decline in able recruits for the Roman army and the deterioration of morale among the citizenry were caused by the virtual elimination of the small farm from central Italy. Their solution was to create out of the vast public lands owned by the Roman state a large number of new farms for the dispossessed. This was a courageous and compassionate program, but the virtuous Roman farmer of yesteryear could not be conjured back into existence at this late moment. As it happened, most of the public lands had long before fallen under the effective control of powerful members of the senatorial aristocracy. These wealthy men, long accustomed to farming state lands for their own profit, reacted frigidly to the proposal that they should now give up portions of these lands so that the state might create small farms for the impoverished. In the political holocaust that followed, both Gracchi were murdered—Tiberius in 133, Gaius in 121. The senatorial aristocracy demonstrated that, despite past concessions, it was still in control. But it also betrayed its political and moral bankruptcy. Violence had been introduced into Roman political affairs, and the whirlwind now unleased was to buffet the Republic for a century and finally demolish it.

For a generation the lower classes continued to press for the Gracchan reforms, and the senatorial aristocracy found itself pitted not only against the masses but

THE RISE OF ROME: KINGDOM, REPUBLIC, EMPIRE

sometimes against the equestrian order as well. But the great political fact of the last republican century was the rise of individual adventurers who sought to use successful military careers as springboards to political power. During the decade of the eighties, two able military commanders, Marius and Sulla, contended against one another for political supremacy. Marius drew much of his support from the lesser classes, whereas Sulla tended to ally with the wealthier and more established, but both were motivated strongly by personal ambition. In 106 B.C. Marius had taken the portentous step of abolishing the property qualification for military service and recruiting volunteers from the poorest classes. Prior to Marius' reform, the resources of Roman military manpower had been declining alarmingly, but now the jobless masses thronged into the legions. Military service became, for many, the avenue to economic security, since soldiers of a successful and politically influential general could often expect to receive on retirement a gift of land from the Senate. The army began to acquire a more professional outlook than before, and soldiers came to identify themselves with their commanders rather than with the state. The opportunities for a ruthless and ambitious general with a loyal army at his back were limitless. But Marius was unwilling to go so far as to seize and overthrow the government. The more ruthless Sulla had no such scruples. In 83 B.C. he marched on Rome with his own devoted legions and, in the following year, made himself dictator. Once in power, he purged his enemies and proscribed a number of wealthy citizens, enriching himself from their confiscated fortunes. But Sulla had no intention of holding power indefinitely. A conservative at heart, he employed his dictatorial prerogatives to establish a series of laws that confirmed and strengthened the power of the inept Senate, then retired to affluent private life on his country estate

in Campania, leaving the Republic to stagger on.

In the decade of the sixties, the great senatorial orator Cicero strove desperately to unite senators and equestrians against the growing threat of the generals and the riotous urban masses. Cicero's consummate mastery of Latin style, both in his orations and in his writings, earned him a lofty position in the field of Roman literature, but his political talents proved inadequate to the task of saving the Republic. His dream of reconciling the interests of senators and equestrians was shattered by the selfishness of each, and his efforts to perpetuate the traditional supremacy of the Senate were doomed by the Senate's own incapacity, by the smoldering unrest of the city mobs, and by the ambition of the military commanders. It was Cicero's misfortune to be a conservative in a epoch of revolutionary turbulence —a statesman in an age of generals.

The Republic was now approaching its final days in an atmosphere of chaos and naked force. The dominant political figures of Cicero's generation were military commanders such as Pompey and Julius Caesar, who bid against one another for the backing of the lower classes, seeking to convert mob support into political supremacy. Characteristically, the three great men of their age, Pompey, Cicero, and Caesar, all met violent deaths. The utter failure of republican government was now manifest, and the entire imperial structure seemed on the verge of collapse. As it turned out, however, Rome was to emerge from her crisis transformed and strengthened, and her empire was to endure for another 500 years.

CHRONOLOGY
OF THE ROMAN REPUBLIC
All Dates B.C.

753:	Traditional date for Rome's founding
c.616–509:	Etruscan kings rule Rome

c.450:	Twelve Tables
367:	Plebeians eligible for consulship
287:	Loss of Senate's veto power over Tribal Assembly legislation Rome becomes a paper democracy
265:	Rome controls all Italy south of the Po
264–241:	First Punic War
218–201:	Second Punic War
149–146:	Third Punic War
146:	Macedonia becomes Roman province
133:	Tribunate of Tiberius Gracchus
123–2:	Tribunate of Gaius Gracchus
121:	Gaius Gracchus killed
106:	Marius reorganizes military recruitment
83–80:	Sulla reestablishes republican constitution
60–44:	Caesar a dominant force in Roman politics
43:	Cicero killed

Julius Caesar and Augustus

The new order, which saved Rome from the agonies of the late Republic and brought a long era of peace and stability to the Mediterranean world, was chiefly the handiwork of two men: Julius Caesar and his grandnephew, Octavian, later called Augustus. Julius Caesar was a man of many talents—a superb general, a brilliant and realistic politician, an inspiring leader, and a distinguished man of letters whose lucid and forthright *Commentaries on the Gallic Wars* was a significant contribution to the great literary surge of the late Republic. Above all, Caesar was a man of reason who could probe to the heart of any problem, work out a logical, practical solution, and then carry his plan to realization.

Caesar managed to ride the whirlwind of violence and ruthless ambition that was shattering Roman society during the mid-first century B.C. His political intuition and unswerving faith in himself and his star

catapulted him to increasingly important political and military offices during the turbulent sixties. Opposed and distrusted by the conservative Senate led by the great orator Cicero, he allied himself with Pompey, a talented, disgruntled general, and Crassus, an ambitious millionaire. These three formed an extralegal coalition of political bosses, known to later historians as the "First Triumvirate," which succeeded in dominating the Roman state.

Leaving Italy in the hands of his two colleagues, Caesar spent most of the following decade (58–50 B.C.) in Gaul leading his army on a spectacular series of campaigns that resulted in the conquest of what is now France and Belgium and established

Caesar the Dictator.   (Anderson/Art Reference Bureau)

his reputation as one of history's consummate military scientists. Caesar's conquest of Gaul pushed the influence of Rome far northward from the Mediterranean into the heartland of western Europe. The historical consequences of his victories were immense, for in the centuries that followed, Gaul was thoroughly Romanized. The Roman influence survived the later barbarian invasions to give medieval and modern France a romance tongue* and to provide Western Europe with an enduring Greco-Roman cultural heritage.

While Ceasar was winning his triumphs in Gaul his interests in Italy were suffering. His advocacy of land redistribution and of other policies dear to the hearts of the lower classes earned him the hostility of the Senate, and his spectacular military success threatened to thwart Pompey's own ambition to be first among Romans. Out of their common fear of Caesar, Pompey and the Senate now joined forces, and in 49 B.C. Caesar was declared a public enemy. His career at stake, Caesar defied the Roman constitution by leading his own loyal army into Italy. In a series of dazzling campaigns during 49 and 48 B.C., he defeated Pompey and the hostile members of the Senate. Pompey fled to Egypt and was murdered there, and the Senate had no choice but to come to terms with the man who now towered unchallenged over Rome.

Caesar was a magnanimous victor. He restored his senatorial opponents to their former positions and ordered the execution of Pompey's murderer. He could afford to be generous; he was now the unquestioned master of the state. The Republic had traditionally, in time of grave crisis, concentrated all power in the hands of a dictator who was permitted to exercise his virtually unlimited jurisdiction for six months only. Caesar assumed the office of dictator and held it year after year. Ultimately he forced the Senate to grant him the dictatorship for

life. He also acquired the personal inviolability of the tribune and assumed several other key republican offices. Besides all these, he retained the title of *pontifex maximus* (supreme pontiff or chief priest of the civic religion), which he had held for some years. In 44 B.C. he was more-or-less deified: a temple was dedicated to his genius—the spirit of his family or clan—and the month of July was named in his honor. Most of the political institutions of the Republic survived, but they were now under his thumb. He controlled the appointment of magistrates, manipulated the assemblies, and overawed the Senate. The whole Roman electorate had become his clients.

Caesar used his power to reform the Republic along logical, realistic lines. The magnitude of his reforms defies description. He introduced a radically new calendar that, with one minor adjustment, is in almost universal use today. He organized numerous distant colonies that drained off a considerable number of Rome's unemployed masses, and halved the Roman bread dole. He did much to reform and rationalize Italian and provincial government and to purge the republican administration of its abuses. In short, he was the model of what would much later be called an "enlightened despot." Some historians have supposed that Caesar was aiming at a monarchy along Hellenistic lines, but it is more accurate to view him as a supremely talented Roman applying his intellect to the rational solution of Roman problems.

Caesar's remarkable success attests to the creative power of the human mind. His ultimate failure, however, suggests that in human affairs reason is not always enough —that the ingrained historical traditions of a people will resist the surgery of even the most skillful rationalist reformer. Caesar's reforms were immensely beneficial to the people of the Empire, but he went too far too fast. His disregard for republican institutions was too cavalier, and his assumption of the dictatorship for life alarmed

* i.e., a language derived from Latin.

powerful elements in the Senate. On the Ides of March (March 15), 44 B.C., he was stabbed to death at a Senate meeting by a group of conservative senatorial conspirators led by Brutus and Cassius. As they rushed from the Senate the assassins shouted, "Tyranny is dead!" They were wrong: it was the Republic that was dead, and Rome now had only the choice between one-man rule and anarchy. By killing Caesar, they had given up the former for the latter.

Caesar's assassination resulted in fourteen more years of civil strife during which the conservative party of Brutus and Cassius struggled against would-be heirs to Caesar's power while the heirs struggled against one another. In the complex maneuvers of this civil war some of the most famous figures in ancient history played out their roles. Mark Antony, Caesar's trusted lieutenant, defeated Brutus and Cassius in battle, and both committed suicide. The golden tongued Cicero, Rome's supreme literary craftsman, was murdered for his hostility to Antony. And when the fortunes of war turned against them, Antony and his exotic wife, Queen Cleopatra of Egypt, took their own lives. The ultimate victor in these struggles was a young man who had been almost unknown at the time of Caesar's death. Octavian, the later Augustus, Caesar's grandnephew and adopted son, had woven his way through the era of strife with matchless skill. A young man of eighteen when Caesar died, Octavian proved to the world that he was in truth Caesar's heir. For although inferior to Caesar in generalship and perhaps also in sheer intellectual strength, Octavian was Caesar's superior as a realistic, practical politician. During his long, illustrious reign Octavian completed the transformation of the Roman state from republic to empire. But his reforms were more traditionalist in spirit than Caesar's, and he succeeded— where Caesar had failed—in winning the Senate's respect. He reformed the Romans and made them like it.

The Augustan Age

In 31 B.C. Octavian's forces crushed those of Antony and Cleopatra at Actium. A year later Octavian entered Alexandria as master of the Mediterranean world. He was then the same age as Alexander at the time of his death, and it might be supposed that the two world-conquerors, both young, brilliant, and handsome, had much in common. But Octavian refused to visit Alexander's tomb in Alexandria, observing, so it was said, that true greatness lies not in conquest but in reconstruction. It is appropriate, therefore, that Octavian's immense historical reputation lies not in his military victories—which were won by his generals rather than himself—but in his accomplishments as peacemaker and architect of the Roman Empire.

The reformation of Rome, completed by Octavian, gave the Mediterranean world two centuries of almost uninterrupted peace and prosperity during which classical culture developed and spread to the outermost reaches of the Empire. This unprecedented achievement caused men, in the turbulent centuries that followed, to look back longingly at the almost legendary epoch of the "Roman Peace." Octavian accomplished the seemingly impossible task of reconciling the need for one-man rule with the republican traditions of Old Rome. He preserved the Senate; indeed, increased its prestige. He retained the elected republican magistracies. He made no attempt to revive the office of dictator, for he preferred to manipulate the government in more subtle ways. He controlled the army and, like Caesar, he concentrated various key republican offices and powers in his own person—*pontifex maximus*, consul, the authority of the tribunes, and others. In 27 B.C. he was given the novel name of Augustus, a term that carried with it no specific power, but had a connotation of reverence—almost holiness. And like Caesar he was honored by having a month (August) named in his honor. It is characteristic of his philosophy of government,

The Emperor Augustus.   (The Vatican Museum)

torate was incapable of governing the Empire, and a democratic empire with universal suffrage was inconceivable. Roman liberty was the single great casualty of the Principate, but its loss was rendered almost painless by the political deftness of the first *princeps*. In its place Augustus provided peace, security, prosperity, and justice. The administration of the provinces was now closely regulated by the *princeps*, and the gross corruption and exploitation of the late Republic were reduced. In Rome itself an efficient imperial bureaucracy developed which was responsible to the *princeps* alone. Although class distinction remained strong, it was now possible for an able man from one of the lower classes to rise in the government service, and men with literary and artistic gifts were sought out and supported by Augustus as a matter of policy.

The stable new regime, the promise of enduring peace, the policy of "careers open to talent," and the leadership of Augustus himself combined to evoke a surge of optimism, patriotism, and creative originality. In the field of arts and letters the "Augustan Age" is the climax of Roman creative genius, surpassing even the literary brilliance of the troubled late Republic of which Cicero stands as the supreme example. Under Augustus, Roman artists and poets achieved a powerful synthesis of Greek and Roman elements. Roman architecture was obviously modeled on the Greek, but it just as obviously expressed a distinctively Roman spirit. Roman temples rose higher than those of classical Greece and conveyed a feeling that was less serene—more imposing and dynamic. Augustan poetry—the urbane and faultless lyrics of Horace, the worldly, erotic verses of Ovid, the majestic cadences of Virgil—employed Greek models and ideas in original and characteristically Roman ways. Rome's supreme poem, Virgil's *Aeneid*, was cast in the epic form of Homer and dealt, as Homer's *Odyssey* did, with the voyage of an important figure in the Trojan

however, that Augustus preferred the relatively modest title of *princeps* or "first citizen." He was the leading Roman—nothing more. He lived relatively modestly, associated freely with his fellow citizens, revered the dignity of the Senate, and dressed and ate simply. It has been said that the Roman Principate (the government of the princeps) was the mirror opposite of the government of modern England: the former, a monarchy with republican trappings: the latter a republic with monarchical trappings. But if the Principate was at heart a monarchy, it was by no means an arbitrary one. Augustus ruled with a keen sensitivity toward popular and senatorial opinion and a respect for traditions.

Still, Augustus was the true master of Rome. The nature of the Empire was such that the liberty of the old Republic simply could not be preserved. The Roman elec-

Augustan art and propaganda, a detail from the Altar of Peace, symbolizing the fertility of Italy. (Alinari/Art Reference Bureau)

War. But Aeneas, Virgil's hero, was also the legendary founder of Rome, and the poem is shot through with patriotic prophecies regarding the great destiny of the state which Aeneas was to found. Indeed, some readers have seen in Aeneas a symbol of Augustus himself. The *Aeneid* also contains a compassionate humanitarian strain lacking in Homer but evident in the enlightened policies of Augustus and his successors—especially the emperors of the second century. Above all, there is the feeling of hope that the Roman people—founded by Aeneas, and now led by the great peacemaker Augustus—have at last fulfilled their mission to bring enduring concord and justice to the long-tormented world:

But Rome! 'tis thine alone, with awful sway,
To rule mankind, and make the world obey,
Disposing peace and war thine own majestic
   way

To tame the proud, the fetter'd slave to free:
These are imperial arts, and worthy thee.*

Imperial Leadership after Augustus

Augustus died at the age of 76 in A.D. 14. During the decades following his death, the Principate grew steadily more centralized and more efficient. The imperial bureaucracy expanded, the provinces were reasonably well governed, taxes were relatively light and intelligently assessed, the law became increasingly more humane, and the far-flung inhabitants of the Empire enjoyed unprecedented peace and prosperity. It is a tribute to Augustus's wisdom that the system that he created was sturdy enough to endure and flourish despite the relative incapacity of many of his imperial successors. The abilities of the first-century emperors

* Aeneid, Book VI (tr. John Dryden). Rome did not, in fact, bring an end to ancient slavery.

ranged from uninspired competence to downright madness, descending on occasion to the vain-glorious absurdity of a Nero or the grotesque lunacy of a Caligula, who wallowed in the pleasure of watching his prisoners being tortured to death. Caligula is reported to have allowed his favorite horse to dine at the imperial table during formal state dinners, consuming the finest food and wines from jeweled dishes and goblets. At Caligula's death he was on the point of raising the beast to the office of consul. Caligula and Nero were autocrats of the worst type, and both were removed violently from power. On the whole, however, the emperors of the early Principate retained the traditional "constitutional" attitudes exemplified by Augustus himself.

The second century A.D. witnessed a dramatic improvement in the quality of imperial leadership. Rome's rulers between A.D. 96 and 180 have been called the "five good emperors." One nineteenth-century historian described them in these words: "For eighty-four years a series of sovereigns, the best, the wisest and the most statesmanlike that the world has ever seen —Nerva, Trajan, Hadrian, Antoninus, Marcus Aurelius—sat upon the throne of the world."* And although more recent historians would look askance at such sweeping praise, there can be no question but that the "five good emperors" were sovereigns of rare ability.

The high level of imperial leadership that characterized this era can be attributed largely to the temporary solving of one of the knottiest dilemmas in the whole imperial system—the problem of succession. In theory the Senate chose the *princeps*, but in fact the succession usually fell to a close relative of the previous emperor and was often arranged by the emperor in advance. Too often this hereditary principle allowed the Empire to fall into the hands of an unworthy ruler; occasionally a disputed succession was settled by violence and even civil war. But none of the great second-century emperors—Trajan, Hadrian, Antoninus Pius, or Marcus Aurelius—came to power by normal hereditary succession. In each case, the previous emperor *adopted* as his son and successor a younger man of outstanding ability. The policy of adoption worked well for a time, but it did not represent a deliberate rejection of the hereditary succession principle. It was simply a consequence of the fact that none of the "five good emperors" had a son except Marcus Aurelius—the last of them. Marcus followed the hereditary principle—which had never consciously been abandoned— and chose his own son, the incompetent Commodus, as his heir. With the disastrous reign of Commodus (A.D. 180–192) the great age of imperial rule came to an end. It was followed by a century of military despotism, assassinations, economic and administrative breakdown, cultural decay, and civil strife which almost brought an end to the Roman state.

The Emperor Hadrian. (Anderson/Art Reference Bureau)

* Thomas Hodgkin, *The Dynasty of Theodosius* (Oxford, 1889), p. 18.

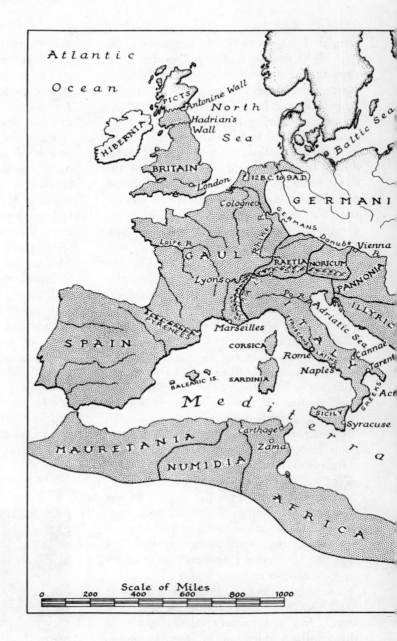

The Empire under the Principate

Before moving into the troubled third century, let us look briefly at the condition of the Empire at its height. During the two centuries from the rise of Augustus to the death of Marcus Aurelius (31 B.C.–A.D. 180), the Empire expanded gradually to include a vast area from the Euphrates to the Atlantic—from the Sahara to the Danube,

the Rhine, and the Cheviot Hills of northern Britain. A considerable amount of territory was added to the Empire under Augustus, and several later emperors, notably Trajan, made impressive conquests. But most of the emperors were content to guard the frontiers and preserve what had earlier been won.

The burden of defending the far-flung

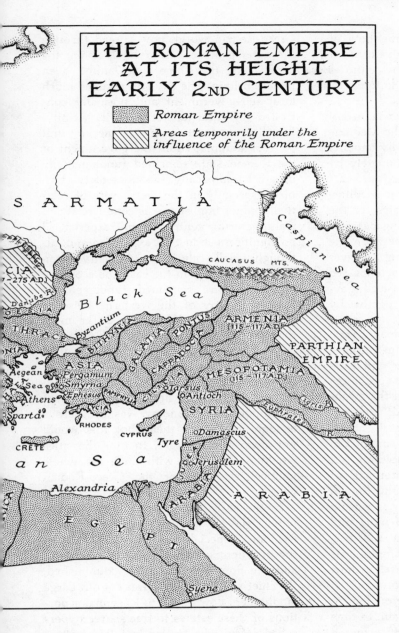

THE ROMAN EMPIRE AT ITS HEIGHT EARLY 2ND CENTURY

▓ Roman Empire

▨ Areas temporarily under the influence of the Roman Empire

frontiers rested on an army of some 300,-000 to 500,000 men, organized on principles laid down by Augustus. Infantry legions manned by Roman citizens on long-term enlistments were supplemented by auxiliary forces, both infantry and light cavalry, made up of non-Romans who were granted citizenship at the end of their extended terms of service. The army was concentrated along the frontiers except for the small, privileged praetorian guard that served the emperor in Rome itself. A high degree of mobility was insured by the superb system of roads which connected the city of Rome with its most remote provinces. Paved with stones fitted closely together, these roads were nearly as eternal as the city they served. Although built for military reasons, they eased the flow of commerce as well as the movement of troops and remained in use many centuries after the Roman Peace was shattered by anarchy and barbarian invasions.

The Empire's greatest commercial artery was not built of stone; it was the Mediterranean, completely surrounded by imperial territory and referred to affectionately by the Romans as *Mare Nostrum*—"our sea." Strong Roman fleets patrolled the Mediterranean and kept it free of pirates for the first time in antiquity, permitting peaceful shipping to move unimpeded between the many ports of the Empire. Now as never before, the immense territories encompassed by the Roman frontiers were well governed, well policed, and bound together by roads and protected seaways.

Under the aegis of the Roman Peace, commercial prosperity, Roman institutions, and classical culture spread far and wide across the Empire. As distant provinces became increasingly Romanized the meaning of the words "Rome" and "Roman" gradually changed. By the time of Augustus these terms were no longer confined to the imperial city and its inhabitants but had come to embrace the greater part of Italy. Now, as the decades of the Roman Peace followed one another, citizenship was progressively extended to more and more provincials until finally, in A.D. 212, every free inhabitant of the Empire was made a citizen. Emperors themselves now tended, as often as not, to be provincials: the great second-century emperor Trajan, for example, was a native of Spain. In time the terms "Rome" and "Roman" acquired a universal connotation: a Greek monarch in Constantinople, a Frankish monarch at Aachen, a Saxon monarch in Germany, a Hapsburg in Vienna could, in later centuries, all refer to themselves as "Roman emperors."

The most conspicuous effect of this process of diffusion was the urbanization of the entire Empire. The city-state, the characteristic political phenomenon of the Greco-Roman world, now spread through the outer provinces—into Gaul, Spain, the lands along the Rhine and Danube, even remote Britain. The city still retained much local self-government and normally controlled the rural territories in its vicinity. In other words, the city was the key unit of local administration—the government of the Roman state remained fundamentally urban. Paradoxically, the cities of the Empire, especially in the west, were of relatively minor importance as commercial and manufacturing centers. Rome experienced no significant industrial expansion and, although small-scale urban industry often flourished, chiefly in the east, the economy of the Empire remained fundamentally agrarian. Many of the western cities—including Rome itself—consumed far more than they produced and acted as parasites on the imperial economy. Basically they were administrative and military centers whose mercantile significance was secondary. During the first two centuries of the Empire the economy was prosperous enough to support them, but this would not always be the case. In time the cities would decline, and with them the whole political structure of the Greco-Roman world.

In the early Empire, as in the late Republic, slaves played a crucial role in the economy, especially in agriculture. But as the frontiers gradually ceased to expand and the flow of war captives diminished, the chief source of slaves was cut off. Large landholders now began to lease major portions of these estates to free sharecroppers called *coloni* who tended to fall more and more under the control of their landlords and sank slowly to a semiservile status akin to that of the medieval serfs. The *coloni*, like the impoverished masses who continued to crowd the larger cities, enjoyed little of the buoyant prosperity of the Principate. The age of the "five good emperors" was, by ancient standards, an epoch of material well-being, but it would be absurd to compare it to the abundance of the advanced industrial states of today. Roman society always included, beneath its veneer, a vast, wretched substratum of half-starved peasants and paupers.

The condition of the lower classes would have been still worse but for the humane policies of the imperial government. It was especially among the great second-century emperors that Stoic attitudes of human brotherhood, compassion, and social and political responsibility took hold. Unlike Caligula and Nero, who used their power to indulge their bizarre whims, emperors such as Hadrian and Marcus Aurelius viewed their authority as a trust, a responsibility to govern in the interests of the people whether rich or poor. The Empire of the second century is ornamented by its social conscience no less than by its leadership in military and administrative affairs.

The Silver Age

The cultural epoch from approximately the death of Augustus to the death of Marcus Aurelius is known as the Silver Age. Less illustrious than the golden Augustan Age, it nevertheless produced literary, intellectual, and artistic accomplishments of the first order. Some observers have seen in Silver Age writers such as the Stoic playwright Seneca, the satirist Lucian, and the biographer Plutarch, a decline in creative genius. They have stressed the stale conformity of second-century Roman art and literature resulting from the absence of genuine freedom, the "homogenization" of culture, and the dullness of peace and security. Such judgments are necessarily relative, and many sensitive spirits through the centuries have viewed writers of the Silver Age with enormous admiration.

Whatever one may think of the originality and excellence of Silver Age literature, there can be no question but that culture and learning spread outward and downward. Remote provincial cities built temples and baths, theaters and triumphal arches in the Roman style. Libraries and schools were scattered abundantly across the Empire, and the extent of urban literacy is demonstrated by the many irreverent and obscene scribbling and campaign slogans discovered by modern excavators on the buildings of Pompeii, buried and preserved by the eruption of Vesuvius in A.D. 79.

Alexandria, the Hellenistic metropolis, retained its commercial and intellectual importance throughout the age of the Principate, producing some of the most brilliant early Christian theologians as well as several distinguished scientists who developed and synthesized the achievements of earlier Hellenistic science. Greek and Hellenistic astronomical thought, for example, was developed into a sophisticated and comprehensive model of the universe by Ptolemy of Alexandria (d. about A.D. 180) who expanded the work of his predecessors into a geocentric world-system that accounted, with remarkable precision, for the observed motions of the sun, moon, and planets among the stars.* Ptolemy also wrote the most complete geography of antiquity, and Galen (A.D. 131–201), a great medical scientist from Hellenistic Pergamum, produced a series of works on biology and medicine that dominated these fields for more than a thousand years. The *Meditations* of Marcus Aurelius, the last of the "five good emperors," is a moving expression of the Stoic philosophy that deepened and humanized so much of the best thought of the era. In literature and art, science and philosophy, the Silver Age produced an effortless synthesis of Greek and Roman traditions. The rich legacies of Greece, Rome, and the ancient Orient were summarized and fused into a coherent whole.

Roman Law

Of all the achievements of this epoch perhaps the most far-reaching—certainly the most distinctively Roman—was the devel-

* See above, page 00.

opment of imperial law. The rigid code of the Twelve Tables was gradually broadened and humanized by the magistrates of the later Republic and early Empire, by the great legists of the second and third centuries A.D., and by the enlightened intervention of the emperors themselves. As the Romans became acquainted with more and more peoples, each with its unique set of laws and customs, they gradually emancipated themselves from the peculiarities of their own law and strove to replace it by a body of fundamental principles drawn from the laws of all people. The *Jus Gentium* or "law of peoples" slowly transformed the Roman code into a legal system suitable to a vast, heterogeneous empire.

The evolution of Roman law into a universal system of jurisprudence owed something also to the Greek concept of the *Jus Naturale*—the "law of nature"—which has played a prominent role in the history of Western thought. More abstract than the *Jus Gentium*, the "law of nature" or "natural law" is based on the belief that in a divinely ordered world there are certain universal norms of human behavior which all people tend to follow, regardless of their own individual customs and traditions. These norms, based on considerations of political and social justice, served to rationalize and humanize the law of the Empire and to provide it with a sturdy philosophical foundation. Accordingly, Roman law, a product of the Latin practical political genius influenced by Greek speculative thought, gave substance to the Augustan ideal of justice. Codified at enormous effort by the sixth-century emperor Justinian, it has become a crucial part of the Western heritage—the basis of many legal systems to this day in Europe and its former colonies.

■ ■ ■ ■ ■
5
Rome and Jerusalem

Roman Religion

Roman religion is immensely complex, for the Romans not only recognized many gods but had numerous separate cults. Like the Greek city-states, Rome had its official civic deities—Jupiter and Juno, Minerva and Mars, and many others, who by the later Republic had become identified with parallel gods of the Greek Olympic religion. The Roman Jupiter was the Greek Zeus, the Roman Minerva was the Greek Athena, and so on. Besides these Roman state deities there were the innumerable local gods of the myriad cities and districts of the Empire. And in Rome itself as well as throughout the Empire there were countless unofficial cults that normally enjoyed the toleration of the Roman state. None of these pagan cults was exclusive; none claimed a monopoly on truth, and a single individual might without compromise associate himself with several of them.

With the coming of the Principate an important new element was added to the state religion: the cult of the emperor. Augustus, like Julius Caesar, had been honored by the deification and worship of his "Genius," and both Augustus and his successors (with a few notorious exceptions) were deified by the Senate after their deaths. In those provinces where god-kings were traditional, the *princeps* was viewed as a deity while still alive, and it soon became customary for Romans and provincials alike to participate in formal religious observances to the deified emperors as well as to the major deities of the city of Rome. These observances were at heart more patriotic than religious. They were useful in encouraging the allegiance of diverse peoples and, in accordance with religious attitudes of the day, few objected to the addition of a handful of new deities to the divine crowd that they already worshiped. To the Jews, and later the Christians, these religio-patriotic observances were another matter, for the "jealous" God of the Jews permitted the worship of no other. But Rome recognized the Jews as a people apart and usually excused them from participation in the official cults. The Christians on the other hand, suffered gravely from their refusal to worship the emperors and gods of Rome. To the Romans such intransigence savored of both atheism and treason. It is no accident that Christianity alone of all the religions of the Empire was the object of serious Roman persecution.

The Mystery Cults

The centuries after Augustus witnessed a slow but fundamental shift in Roman religious attitudes, from the veneration of the traditional gods of household, clan, and city to the worship of transcendental deities imported from the Near East. The gods of Old Rome, like those of the Greek Olympus, had safeguarded the welfare of social and political groups; the new gods offered instead the hope of individual redemption, salvation, and eternal life. As the Roman imperial age progressed, the allegiance of the people slowly shifted from Jupiter and Minerva to the Egyptian Isis, the Persian Mithras, the Phrygian Great Mother, the Syrian Sun god, and other exotic deities who offered solace and eternal joy to people for whom the world was not enough—even the world of the Roman Peace.

This surge of mysticism was actually a

The god Mithras sacrifices the heavenly bull. (Alinari/Art Reference Bureau)

continuation and expansion of a trend we have already observed among the Hellenistic Greeks. The same forces that had encouraged the widespread rootlessness and disorientation of the Hellenistic world were now at work throughout the Roman Empire: cosmopolitanism, gradually increasing autocracy and, among the underprivileged masses, grinding poverty and loss of hope. The shift from civic god to savior god, from this world to the next, constitutes a profound transformation in mood— a repudiation of traditional Greco-Roman humanism. As the peace of the second century gave way to the anarchy of the third, the high hopes of classical humanism—the dream of a rational universe, an ideal republic, a good life—were beginning to seem like cruel illusions, and the movement toward the mystery cults gained enormous momentum.

The Emergence of Christianity

Two fundamental trends characterized religious development in the Roman Empire: the growing impulse toward mysticism that we have just examined, and the interpenetration and fusion of doctrines and practices between one cult and another—a process known as *syncretism*. The syncretic quality of Christianity itself has often been observed, for in numerous instances its beliefs and rituals were similar to those of earlier religions. Obviously, Christianity drew heavily from Judaism—nearly all the earliest Christians were Jews—but it was also anticipated in various particulars by Persian Zoroastrianism and Mithraism, the Isis-Osiris cult of Egypt, the Greek mysteries of Dionysus and Demeter, and even Stoicism. Many Christian doctrines had long pre-Christian histories: the concept of death and resurrection, the sacramental meal, baptism, personal salvation, and the brotherhood of man under the fatherhood of God, to name but a few. Yet Christianity was far more than a new configuration of old ideas, and it would be misleading to think of it as merely another of the oriental mystery religions. It differed from them above all in two basic ways: (1) its god was the God of the Hebrews, unique in all antiquity in his claims to exclusiveness and omnipotence, and now released by Christianity from his association with a specific chosen people and universalized as the God of all mankind; (2) Christianity's founder and Savior was a vivid historic personality, Jesus, beside whom such mythical idealizations as Mithras or Isis must have seemed tepid and diffuse.

Jesus, a younger contemporary of Augustus, was a figure in the Hebrew prophetic tradition whose life and teachings show little if any Greek influence. He is depicted in the Gospels as a warm, attractive, magnetic leader who miraculously healed the sick, raised the dead, and stilled the winds. His miracles were seen as credentials of the divine authority with which he claimed to speak. His ministry was chiefly to the poor and outcast, and in Christianity's early decades it was these classes that accepted the faith most readily. He preached a doctrine of love, compassion, and humility. Like the prophets he scorned empty formalism in religion and stressed the sober, unprepossessing life of generosity toward both friend and enemy and devotion to God. He does not seem to have objected to ritual as such, but only to ritual infected with pride and complacency and divorced from charity and upright conduct. His severe criticism of the moral shortcomings of the established Jewish priesthoods, combined apparently with his claims to speak with divine authority, resulted in his crucifixion as a subversive.

According to the Gospels, Jesus's greatest miracle was his resurrection—his return to life three days after he died on the Cross. He is said to have remained on earth for a short period thereafter, giving solace and inspiration to his disciples, and then to have "ascended" into heaven with the promise that he would return in glory to judge all souls and bring the world to an end. The first generations of Christians expected this second coming to occur quickly, and it is perhaps for that reason among others that formal organization was not stressed in the primitive church.

The early Christians not only accepted Christ's ethical precepts but worshiped Christ himself as the divine incarnation of the omnipotent God. The Christ of the Gospels distinguishes repeatedly between himself—"the Son of Man"—and God—"the Father"—but he also makes the statement, "I and the Father are One," and he enjoins his disciples to baptize all persons "in the Name of the Father and the Son and the Holy Spirit." Hence, Christianity became committed to the difficult and sophisticated notion of a triune Godhead with Christ as the "Son" or "Second Person" in a Trinity that was nevertheless one God. The doctrine of the Trinity gave Christianity the unique advantage of a single, infinite, philosophically respectable god who could be worshiped and adored in the person of the charismatic, lovable, tragic Jesus. The Christian deity was both transcendent and concrete.

The Early Church

The first generation of Christianity witnessed the beginning of a deeply significant development whereby the Judeo-Christian heritage was modified and enriched through contact with the main currents of Greco-Roman culture. Christ's own apostles were no more influenced by Hellenism than their Master, and some of them sought to keep Christianity strictly within the ritualistic framework of Judaism. But St. Paul, a Hellenized Jew and early convert, succeeded in orienting the church according to his own vision of a universal brotherhood, free of the strict Jewish dietary laws and the requirement of circumcision (which were bound to discourage the conversion of non-Jews), open to all people everywhere who would accept Jesus as God and Savior—and open also to the bracing winds of Hellenistic thought. St. Paul traveled far and wide across the Empire preaching the message of Christ as he interpreted it, winning converts, and establishing Christian communities in many towns and cities of the Mediterranean world. Other Christian missionaries, among them St. Peter and his fellow apostles who had been Christ's immediate followers, devoted their lives as St. Paul did to traveling, preaching and organizing—often at the cost of ridicule and persecution. Tradition has it that St. Paul and all the apostles died as martyrs. Their work was tremendously fruitful, for by the end of the apostolic generation Christianity had become a ponderable force among the underprivileged masses of Italy and the East. Within another century the new religion had spread throughout the greater part of the Empire.

From the first, the Christians regularly engaged in a sacramental meal which came to be called the "eucharist" or "holy communion" and was viewed as an indispensable avenue of divine grace through which the Christian was infused with the spirit of Christ. By means of another important sacrament, baptism, the postulant was initiated into the brotherhood of the church, had his sins forgiven by God, and received the grace of the Holy Spirit. A person could be baptized only once, and baptized persons alone could consider themselves true Christians, but in the early church baptism was frequently delayed until adulthood. Many unbaptized persons were therefore associated with the Christian communities without being Christians in the full sense of the word.

As Christian historical documents become more common, in the second and third centuries A.D., the organization of the church begins to emerge more sharply than before. The documents of this period disclose an important distinction between the clergy, who govern the church and administer the sacraments, and the laymen, who play a more passive role. The clergy itself was divided into several ranks, the most important of which were the bishops, who served as rulers and pastors over the various urban communities, and the priests, who led the services and administered the sacraments under the jurisdiction of the bishops. And the bishops themselves were of various degrees of eminence. Above the common bishops were the metropolitans or archbishops who resided in cities of special importance and exercised control over an extensive surrounding area. At the top of the hierarchy were the bishops of the three or four greatest cities of the Empire—Rome, Alexandria, Antioch, and later Constantinople—who were known as patriarchs and who enjoyed a spiritual hegemony (often more theoretical than real) over vast areas of the Mediterranean world.* As time went on, the bishop of Rome—the pope—came to be regarded more and more as the highest of the patriarchs, but the actual establishment of papal authority over even the Western church was to require the efforts of many centuries.

Christianity and Hellenism

Medieval and modern Christian theology is a product of both the Hebrew and the Greek traditions. The synthesis of these two intellectual worlds began not among the Christians but among the Jews themselves, especially those who had migrated in large numbers to Alexandria. Here Jewish scholars—in particular a religious philosopher of the early first century A.D. named Philo Judaeus—worked toward the reconciliation of Jewish revelation and Greek philosophy. Drawing heavily from Aristotle, the Stoics, and particularly Plato, Philo developed a symbolic interpretation

---

* For a time there was also a patriarch of Jerusalem.

of the Old Testament that was to influence Christian thought across the centuries.

Following many of the fruitful leads of Philo, Christian theologians strove to demonstrate that their religion was more than merely an immensely appealing myth—that it could hold its own in the highest intellectual circles. The Savior Christ, for example, as true God and true man, constituted a unique synthesis of the material and spiritual worlds. In Greek terms, Christ reconciled Plato's dualism, for Christ was at once a particular person and an archetype. Christianity differed from most of the Near Eastern mystery religions—especially those emanating from Persia—in its refusal to reject the material world. Matter could not be evil of itself, for it was the handiwork of God; the human body could not be wholly corrupt, for Christ himself was a human in the fullest sense. Christianity was therefore not so radically at odds with Greek humanism as, say, Mithraism—although its concept of sin and its doctrine of the fall of man through the disobedience of Adam were obviously far removed from the traditional humanistic viewpoint of the Greeks.

The fusion of matter and spirit, so fundamental to orthodox Christianity, did not escape challenge among the early Christians. Once the expectation of an immediate second coming began to fade, many Christians began to examine their faith more philosophically than before and to raise difficult questions about the nature of Christ and the Trinity. A diversity of opinions emerged, some of which seemed so inconsistent with the majority view that they were condemned as heresies. As questions were raised and orthodox solutions agreed on, the Christian faith became increasingly precise and increasingly elaborate. The early heresies sought to simplify the nature of Christ and the Trinity. One group, known as the Gnostics, interpreted Christ in the light of the Persian notion that matter was evil. They insisted that Christ was not really human—only a divine phantom—that a good God could not assume a physical body. Others maintained that Christ was not fully divine—not an equal member of the triune Godhead. The latter position was taken up by the fourth-century Arians, whom we shall meet later in this chapter. The orthodox position lay midway between these two views: Christ was fully human and fully divine—a co-equal member of the Holy Trinity. He had become incarnate in human form at a particular moment in time, and walked the earth, taught, suffered, and died, as the man Jesus. Thus the synthesis of matter and spirit was strictly preserved, and Christ remained the bridge between the two worlds.

The Christian apologists—the defenders of orthodoxy against pagan attacks from without and heterodox attacks from within—played a crucial role in formulating and elaborating Christian doctrine, coping with problems that had not even occurred to the apostolic generation. It is of the highest significance that a great many serious Christian thinkers worked within the framework of the Greek philosophical tradition. This is especially true of the greatest of them, the Alexandrian theologian Origen (d. 254) who created a coherent, all-inclusive Christian philosophical system on Platonic foundations. Origen was one of the foremost thinkers of his age and is widely regarded as one of the supreme minds in the entire history of the church. His religious system did not win over the pagan intellectual world at a blow—indeed, several of his conclusions were rejected by later Christian orthodoxy—but he and other Christian theologians succeeded in making Christianity meaningful and intellectually attractive to men whose thinking was cast in the Greco-Roman philosophical mold. The greatest of the Greek philosophers, so these Christian writers said, had been led toward truth by the subconscious inspiration of the Christian God.

Christianity and the Empire

At the very time that Christian theology was being Hellenized, pagan thought itself was shifting increasingly toward other-worldliness. Origen's greatest pagan contemporary was the Neoplatonist Plotinus. Indeed, the two had even been schoolmates for a time. One of the deepest and subtlest minds of the age, Plotinus popularized the doctrine of a single god, infinite and beyond reasoning, unknowable and unapproachable except through an ecstatic trance. Plotinus taught that God was the source of reality and existence. All being, both physical and spiritual, radiated outward from him like concentric ripples in a pool. The Neoplatonists taught that the gods of the pagan cults were all symbols of the one unknowable god and that each pagan cult therefore had validity.

The growth of a transcendental outlook throughout the ancient world created an atmosphere highly nourishing to a salvation religion such as Christianity. The Christian viewpoint was becoming increasingly in tune with the times; it appealed to an age hungry for a profound and consoling doctrine of personal redemption. Yet its triumph was by no means assured, for it faced other salvation religions such as Mithraism and the Isis cult—and traditional Greco-Roman paganism in its new other-worldly, Neoplatonic guise. Against these rivals Christianity could offer the immense appeal of the historic Jesus, the ever-increasing profundity of its theology, the infinite majesty of its God, and the compassion and universalism of its message preserved and dramatized in its canonical books—the Old and New Testaments. Few social groups were immune to its attraction. The poor, humble, and underprivileged made up the bulk of its early converts, and it was to them that Jesus directed much of his message. Thoughtful men were drawn by its Hellenized theology, men of feeling were captivated by its mysticism, and men of affairs were at-tracted by the ever-increasing effectiveness of its administrative hierarchy. For in administration no less than in theology the church was learning from the Greco-Roman world.

Before the collapse of the Roman Empire in the West, Christianity had absorbed and turned to its own purposes much of Rome's heritage in political organization and law, carrying on the Roman administrative and legal tradition into the medieval and modern world. Roman civil law was paralleled by the canon law of the church. The secular leadership of the Roman Empire gave way to the spiritual leadership of the Roman pope, who assumed the old republican and imperial title of *pontifex maximus*—supreme pontiff—and preserved much of the imperial ceremonial of the later Empire. As imperial governors and local officials gradually disappeared in the west, their traditions were carried on, in a new spiritual dimension, by metropolitans and bishops. Indeed, the *diocese*, the traditional unit of a bishop's jurisdiction, was originally an imperial administrative district. In this organizational sense, the medieval church has been described as a ghost of the Roman Empire. Yet it was far more than that. For the church reached its people as Rome never had, giving the impoverished masses a sense of participation and involvement that the Empire had failed to provide.

From the beginning the Christians of the Empire were a people apart, convinced that they alone possessed the truth and that the truth would one day triumph, eager to win new converts to their faith, uncompromising in their rejection of all other religions, willing to learn from the pagan world but unwilling ever to submit to it. Their stark seriousness of purpose, their cohesiveness (which doubtless appeared to their enemies as conspiratorial), their sense of destiny, and their refusal to worship the state gods proved exceedingly aggravating to their pagan contemporaries. Consequently, the Christians were often objects of suspicion, hatred, and persecution. The emperors themselves followed a rather inconsistent policy toward them. Violent persecutions, such as those under Nero and Marcus Aurelius, alternated with long periods of inaction. On the whole, the church throve on the blood of its martyrs; the persecutions were neither sufficiently ruthless nor sufficiently lengthy to come near wiping out the entire Christian community.

Most of the emperors, if they persecuted Christians at all, did so reluctantly. The "good emperor" Trajan instructed a provincial governor neither to seek Christians out nor to heed anonymous accusations. (Such a procedure, Trajan observed, is inconsistent with "the spirit of the age.") Only if a man should be denounced as a Christian, tried and found guilty, and then should persist in his refusal to worship the imperial gods, was he to be punished. One can admire the Christian who would face death rather than worship false gods, but one can also sympathize with emperors such as Trajan who hesitated to apply their traditional policy of religious toleration to a people who seemed bent on subverting the Empire and its gods.

The persecutions of the first and second centuries, although occasionally severe, tended to be limited in scope to specific local areas. The great empire-wide persecutions of the third and early fourth centuries were products of the crisis that Roman civilization was then undergoing. The greatest imperial persecution—and the last—occurred at the opening of the fourth century under the Emperor Diocletian. By then Christianity was too strong to be destroyed, and the failure of Diocletian's persecution must have made it evident that the Empire had no choice but to accommodate itself to the church. A decade after the outbreak of this last persecution, Constantine, the first Christian emperor, undertook a dramatic reversal of religious policy. Thereafter the Empire endorsed Christianity rather than fighting it, and by the close of the fourth century the majority of the urban inhabitants of the Empire had been brought into the Christian fold. Rome and Jerusalem had come to terms at last.

The Beginnings of Imperial Decline: The Third Century

The turbulent third century—the era of Origen and Plotinus—brought catastrophic changes to the Roman Empire. The age of the "five good emperors" (A.D. 96–180) was followed by a hundred troubled years during which anarchy alternated with military despotism. The army, now fully conscious of its strength, made and unmade emperors. One military group fought against another for control of the imperial title—a man might be a general one day, emperor the next, and dead the third. No less than 19 emperors reigned during the calamitous half-century between 235 and 285, not to mention innumerable usurpers and pretenders whose plots and machinations contributed to the general chaos. In this 50-year period every emperor save one died violently—either by assassination or in battle. The Silver Age had given way to what one contemporary historian describes as an age "of iron and rust."

A crucial factor in the chaos of the third century was the problem of the imperial succession. All too often, a competent emperor would be followed by an incompetent son. As the power of the army increased and military rebellions became commonplace, the imperial succession came more and more to depend on the whim of the troops. Perhaps the most successful emperor of the period, Septimius Severus (193–211), maintained his power by expanding and pampering the army, opening its highest offices to every class, and broadening its recruitment. A military career was now the logical avenue to high civil office, and the bureaucracy began to display an increasingly military cast of mind. The old ideals of Republic and Principate were less and less meaningful to the new governing class, many of whom rose from the lower orders of society through successful army careers to positions of high political responsibility. These new administrators were often men of strength and ability, but they were not the sort who could be expected to cherish the old Roman political traditions. Septimus Severus increased imperial taxes to fatten his treasury and appease his troops. Soldiers prospered at the expense of an increasingly impoverished civilian population as the Empire drifted more and more toward military absolutism. Septimius' dying words to his sons are characteristic of his reign and his times: "Enrich the soldiers and scorn the world."

But Rome's troubles in the third century cannot be ascribed entirely to the problem of imperial succession. As early as the reign of Marcus Aurelius (161–180) the Empire had been struck by a devastating plague that lingered on for a generation and by an ominous irruption of Germanic barbarians who spilled across the Rhine-Danube frontier as far as Italy itself. Marcus Aurelius, the philosopher-emperor, was obliged to spend the greater part of his reign campaigning against the invaders, and it was only at enormous effort that he was able to drive them out of the Empire. During the third century the Germans attacked repeatedly, penetrating the frontiers time and again, forcing the cities of the Empire to erect protective walls, and threatening for a time to submerge the state under a barbarian flood. And the Germanic onslaught was accompanied by attacks from the east by the recently reconstituted Persian Empire led by the able kings of its new Sassanid dynasty (226–651 A.D.).

Rome's crucial problems, however, were internal ones. During the third century, political disintegration was accompanied by social and economic breakdown. The ever-rising fiscal demands of the mushrooming bureaucracy and the insatiable army placed an intolerable burden on the inhabitants of town and country alike. Peasants fled from their fields to escape the hated tax collec-

tor, and the urban middle classes became shrunken and demoralized. The self-governing town, the bedrock of imperial administration and, indeed, of Greco-Roman civilization itself, was beginning to experience serious financial difficulties, and as one city after another turned to the emperor for financial aid, civic autonomy declined. These problems arose partly from the parasitical nature of many of the Roman cities, partly from rising imperial taxes, and partly from the economic stagnation that was slowly gripping the Empire. Long before the death of Marcus Aurelius, Rome had abandoned its career of conquest in favor of a defensive policy of consolidation. The flow of booty from conquered lands had ceased, and the Empire as a whole was thrown back on its own resources and forced to become economically self-sufficient. For a while all seemed well, but as administrative and military expenses mounted without a corresponding growth in commerce and industry, the imperial economy began to suffer. The army, once a source of riches from conquered lands, was now an unproductive encumbrance.

By the third century, if not before, the Roman economy was shrinking. Plagues, hunger, and a sense of hopelessness resulted in a gradual decline in population. At the very time when imperial expenses and imperial taxes were rising, the tax base was contracting. Prosperity gave way to depression and desperation, and the flight of peasants from their farms was accompanied by the flight of the savagely-taxed middle classes from their cities. The Empire was now clogged with beggars and bandits, and those who remained at their jobs were taxed all the more heavily. It was the western half of the Empire that suffered most. What industry there was had always been centered in the East, and money was gradually flowing eastward to productive centers in Syria and Asia Minor and beyond, to pay for luxury goods, some of which came from outside the Empire altogether—from Persia, India, and China. In short, the Empire as a whole, and the western Empire especially, suffered from an unfavorable balance of trade that resulted in a steady reduction in Rome's supply of precious metals.

The increasingly desperate financial circumstances of the third-century Empire forced the emperors to experiment in the devaluation of coinage—adulterating the precious metals in their coins with baser metals. This policy provided only temporary relief. In the long run, it resulted in runaway inflation that further undermined the economy. Between A.D. 256 and 280 the cost of living rose 1000 percent.

The third-century anarchy reached its climax during the 260s. By then the Roman economy was virtually in ruins. Barbarian armies were rampaging across the frontiers. Gaul and Britain in the west and a large district in the east had broken loose from imperial control and were pursuing independent courses. The population was speedily shrinking, and countless cities were in an advanced state of decay. Rome's demise seemed imminent. As it turned out, however, the Empire was saved by the tremendous efforts of a series of stern leaders who rose to power in the later third century. The Roman state survived in the west for another two centuries and in the east for more than a millennium. But the agonies of the third century left an indelible mark on the reformed Empire. The new imperial structure that brought order out of chaos was profoundly different from the government of the Principate: it was a naked autocracy of the most thoroughgoing sort.

The Reforms of Diocletian

Even at the height of the anarchy there were emperors who strove desperately to defend the Roman state. After A.D. 268 a series of able, rough-hewn emperor-generals from the Danubian provinces managed to turn the tide, restoring the frontiers, smashing the invading armies of Germanic barbarians and Persians, and recovering the alienated provinces in Gaul and the East. At the same time measures were undertaken to arrest the social and economic decay that was debilitating the Empire. These policies were expanded and brought to fruition by Diocletian (284–305) and Constantine (306–337) to whom belong the credit—and responsibility—for reconstituting the Empire along authoritarian lines. No longer merely a *princeps*, the emperor was now *dominus et deus*—lord and god—and it is appropriate that the new despotic regime that replaced the Principate should be called the "Dominate."

In the days of Augustus it had been necessary, so as not to offend republican sensibilities, to disguise the power of the emperor. In Diocletian's day the imperial title had for so long been dishonored and abused that it was necessary to exalt it. Diocletian and his successors glorified the office in every way imaginable. The emperor became a lofty, remote, unapproachable figure clothed in magnificent garments, a diadem on his head. An elaborate court ceremonial was introduced, somewhat similar to that of Persia, which included the custom of prostration in the emperor's sacred presence.

Diocletian's most immediate task was to bring to a close the turbulent era of short-lived "barracks emperors" and military usurpers. In order to stabilize the succession and share the ever-growing burden of governing the Empire, he decreed that there would thenceforth be two emperors—one in the east, the other in the west—who would work together harmoniously for the welfare and defense of the state. Each of the two would be known by the title *Augustus*, and each would adopt a younger colleague—with the title *Caesar*—to share his rule and ultimately to succeed him. The Empire was now divided into four parts, each supervised by an Augustus or a Caesar. Well aware of the increasing importance of the eastern over the western half of the Empire, Diocletian made his capital in the east and did not set foot in Rome until the close of his reign. A usurper would now, presumably, be faced with the perplexing task of overcoming four widely-scattered personages instead of one. The chances of military usurpation were further reduced by Diocletian's rigorous separation of civil and military authority. The army was considerably enlarged, chiefly by the incorporation of barbarian forces who now assumed much of the burden of guarding the frontiers, but it was organized in such a way that the emperor (or emperors) could control it far more effectively than before.

Imperial control was the keynote of this new, centralized regime. The Senate was now merely ornamental, and the emperor ruled through his obedient and ever-expanding bureaucracy—issuing edict after edict to regulate, systematize, and regiment the state. The shortage of money was circumvented by a new land tax to be collected in kind (that is, goods), and the widespread flight from productive labor was reduced by new laws freezing peasants, craftsmen, and businessmen to their jobs. A system of hereditary social orders quickly developed; sons were required by law to take up the careers and tax burdens of their fathers. Peasants were bound to the land, city dwellers to their urban professions. Workers in the mines and quarries were literally branded. The system was more theoretical than real, for these measures were difficult to enforce, and a degree of social mobility remained. Nevertheless, the Dominate was a relatively regimented society. Economic collapse was temporarily averted, but at the cost of social petrification and loss of hope. The once-autonomous cities now lay under the iron hand of the imperial government. Commitment to the Empire was rapidly waning among the tax-ridden urban commercial elite, who had formerly been among its most enthusiastic supporters but were now (as one historian has put it) condemned for life to the Chamber of Commerce.

It was Diocletian's mission to save the Empire whatever the cost, and it may well be that authoritarian measures were the only ones possible under the circumstances. For every problem Diocletian offered a solution—often autocratic and heavy-handed, but a solution nevertheless. A thoroughgoing currency reform had retarded inflation but had not stopped it altogether, so Diocletian issued an edict fixing the prices of most commodities by law. To the growing challenge of Christianity, Diocletian responded, regretfully, by inaugurating a persecution of unprecedented severity. As it turned out, neither the imperial price controls nor the imperial persecution achieved their purposes, but the very fact that they were attempted illustrates the lengths to which the Emperor would go in his effort to preserve by force the unity and stability of the state.

The division of the Empire among the two Augustuses and the two adopted Caesars worked satisfactorily only so long as Diocletian himself was in command. Once his hand was removed, a struggle for power brought renewed civil strife. The principle of adoption, which the sonless Diocletian had revived without serious difficulty, was challenged by the sons of his successors. The era of chaos ran from the end of Diocletian's reign in 305 to the victory of Constantine over the last of his rivals in 312 at the battle of the Milvian Bridge near Rome.

The Reign of Constantine (A.D. 306-337)

Constantine's triumph at the Milvian Bridge marked the return of political stability and the consummation of Diocletian's economic and political reforms. Diocletian's policy of freezing occupations and making them hereditary was tightened by Constantine in an edict of A.D. 332. Imperial ceremonial was further elaborated, and authoritarianism grew. In certain respects, however, Constantine's policies took radical new directions. In place of the abortive principle of adoption, Constantine founded an imperial dynasty of his own. For a time he shared his authority with an imperial colleague (his brother-in-law), but in 324 he conquered him and thereafter ruled alone. Nevertheless, the joint rule of an eastern and a western emperor became common in the years after Constantine's death, and he himself contributed to the division of the Empire by building the magnificent eastern capital of Constantinople on the site of the ancient Greek colony of Byzantium.

Constantinople was a second Rome. It had its own senate, its own imposing temples, palaces, and public buildings, and its own hungry proletariat fed by the bread dole and diverted by chariot races in its enormous Hippodrome. A few decades after its foundation it even acquired its own Christian patriarch. Constantine plundered the Greco-Roman world of its artistic treasures to adorn his new city and lavished his vast resources on its construction. Founded in A.D. 330, Constantinople was to remain the capital of the Eastern Empire for well over a thousand years, impregnable behind its great walls, protected on three sides by the sea, perpetually renewing itself through its control of the rich commerce flowing between the Black Sea and the Mediterranean. The age-long survival of the Eastern Empire owes much to the superb strategic location of its capital, which dominated the straits between these two seas.

Even more momentous than the building of Constantinople was Constantine's conversion to Christianity and his reversal of imperial policy toward the church. Although he put off baptism until his dying moments, Constantine had been committed to Christianity ever since his triumph in 312. From that time onward he issued a continuous series of pro-Christian edicts insuring full toleration, legalizing bequests

to the church (which accumulated prodigiously over the subsequent centuries), and granting a variety of other privileges. Christianity was now an official religion of the Empire. It was not yet *the* official religion, but it would become so before the fourth century was ended.

Several explanations have been offered for Constantine's conversion. He has been portrayed as an irreligious political schemer bent on harnessing the vitality of the church to the failing state. But there seems no reason to doubt that, in fact, his conversion was sincere if somewhat superficial. Strictly speaking, there were no irreligious men in the fourth century.

The Christian Empire

The respite gained by Diocletian's reforms and the subsequent conversion of Constantine made it possible for the church to develop rapidly under the benevolent protec-

The Emperor Constantine, a fragment of the colossal statue.   (Alinari/Art Reference Bureau)

tion of the Empire. The years between Constantine's victory at the Milvian Bridge in 312 and the final suppression of the Western Empire in 476 were momentous ones in the evolution of Christianity. For one thing, the fourth century witnessed mass conversions to the Christian fold. Perhaps 10 percent of the inhabitants of the Western Empire were Christians in 312 (in the east the figure would be considerably higher) whereas by the century's end the now respectable Christians were in the majority. But, as is so often the case, triumph evoked internal dissension, and the fourth century witnessed a violent struggle between orthodoxy and heresy. Here, too, the Christian emperors played a determining role, and it was with strong imperial support that the greatest of the fourth-century heresies, Arianism, was at length suppressed within the Empire.

The Arians maintained that the purity of Christian monotheism was compromised by the orthodox doctrine of the Trinity. Their solution to this conflict was the doctrine that God the Father was the only true god—that Christ the Son was not fully divine. The orthodox Trinitarians regarded this doctrine as subversive to one of their most fundamental beliefs: the equality and codivinity of Father, Son, and Holy Spirit. Constantine sought to heal the Arian-Trinitarian dispute by summoning an ecumenical (universal) council of Christian bishops at Nicaea in A.D. 325. He had no strong convictions himself, but the advocates of the Trinitarian position managed to win his support. With imperial backing, a strongly anti-Arian creed was adopted almost unanimously. The three divine Persons of the Trinity were declared equal: Jesus Christ was "of one substance with the Father."

But Constantine was no theologian. In after years he vacillated, sometimes favoring Arians, sometimes condemning them, and the same ambiguity characterized imperial policy throughout the greater part of the fourth century. Indeed, one of Constantine's fourth-century successors, Julian "the Apostate" reverted to paganism. At length, however, the uncompromisingly orthodox Theodosius I came to the throne (378–395) and broke the power of the Arians by condemning and proscribing them. It was under Theodosius and his successors that Christianity became the one legal religion of the Empire. Paganism itself was now banned and persecuted and quickly disappeared as an organized force.

Orthodox Christianity now dominated the Empire, but its triumph, won with the aid of political force, was far from complete. For one thing, the mass conversions of the fourth century tended to be superficial—even nominal. Conversion to Christianity was the path of least resistance, and the new converts were on the whole a far cry from the earlier society of saints and martyrs. It was at this time that many ardent Christians, discontented with mere membership in a respectable, work-a-day church, began taking to the desert as hermits or flocking into monastic communities.

Moreover, the imperial program of enforced orthodoxy proved difficult to carry out. Old heresies lingered on and vigorous new ones arose in the fifth century and thereafter. Even Arianism survived, not among the citizens of the Empire, but among the Germanic barbarians. For during the mid-fourth century, at a time when Arianism was still strong in the Empire, large numbers of barbarians had been converted to Christianity in its Arian form, and the Trinitarian policies of Theodosius I had no effect on them whatever. Accordingly, when the barbarians ultimately formed their kingdoms on the ruins of the Western Empire, most of them were separated from their Old-Roman subjects not only by language and custom but by a deep religious chasm as well.

Finally, by accepting imperial support against paganism and heresy, the church sacrificed much of its earlier independence.

The Christians of Constantine's day were so overwhelmed by the emperor's conversion that they tended to glorify him excessively. As a Christian, Constantine could no longer claim divinity, but contemporary Christian writers such as the historian Eusebius allowed him a status that was almost quasi-divine. To Eusebius and his contemporaires, Constantine was the thirteenth apostle; his office was commissioned by God; he was above the church. His commanding position in ecclesiastical affairs is illustrated by his domination of the Council of Nicaea, and the ups and downs of Arianism in the following decades depended largely on the whims of his successors. In the east, this glorification of the imperial office ripened into the doctrine known as *caesaropapism*—that the emperor is the real master of both church and state, that he is both caesar and pope—and caesaropapism remained a dominant theme in the Eastern or Byzantine Empire throughout its long history. Church and state tended to merge under the sacred authority of the emperor. Indeed, the Christianization and sanctification of the imperial office were potent forces in winning for the eastern emperors the allegiance and commitment of the masses of their Christian subjects. Religious loyalty to the Christian emperor provided indispensable nourishment to the East Roman state over the ensuing centuries. Conversely, widespread hostility toward imperial orthodoxy in districts dominated by heretical groups resulted in the alienation and eventual loss to the Byzantine Empire of several of its fairest provinces.

Caesaropapism was far less influential in the west, for as the fifth century dawned the Western Empire was visibly failing. Western churchmen were beginning to realize that Christian civilization was not irrevocably bound to the fortunes of Rome. Gradually the Western church began to assert its independence of state control—with the result that church and state in medieval Western Europe were often at odds and never fused.

The Doctors of the Latin Church

During the later fourth and early fifth centuries, at a time when the Christianization of the Roman state was far advanced but before the Western Empire had lost all its vitality, the long-developing synthesis of Judeo-Christian and Greco-Roman culture reached its climax in the west with the work of three gifted scholar-saints: Ambrose, Jerome, and Augustine. These men came to be regarded as "Doctors of the Latin Church," for their writings deeply influenced medieval thought. Each of the three was thoroughly trained in the Greco-Roman intellectual tradition; each devoted his learning and his life to the service of Christianity; each was at once an intellectual and a man of affairs.

Ambrose (c. 340–397) was bishop of Milan, which by the later fourth century had replaced Rome as the western imperial capital. He was famed for his eloquence and administrative skill, for his vigor in defending Trinitarian orthodoxy against Arianism, and for the ease and mastery with which he adapted the literary traditions of Cicero and Virgil and the philosophy of Plato to his own Christian purposes. Above all, he was the first churchman to assert that in the realm of morality the emperor himself is accountable to the Christian priesthood. When the powerful Emperor Theodosius I massacred the inhabitants of rebellious Thessalonica, Ambrose barred him from the Church of Milan until he had formally and publicly repented. Ambrose's bold stand and Theodosius' submission constituted a stunning setback for the principle of caesaropapism and a prelude to the long struggle between church and state in the Christian west.

Jerome (c. 340–420) was a masterly scholar and a restless, inquisitive reformer with a touch of acid in his personality. He once remarked to an opponent, "You have the will to lie, good sir, but not the skill to lie." Wandering far and wide through the Empire, he founded a monastery in Bethlehem where he set his monks to work copying manuscripts, thereby instituting a custom that throughout the Middle Ages preserved the tradition of Latin letters and transmitted it to the modern world. Like other Christian thinkers he feared that his love of pagan literature might dilute his Christian fervor, and he tells of a dream in which Jesus banished him from heaven with the words, "Thou art a Ciceronian, not a Christian." But in the end he managed to reconcile pagan culture and Christian faith by using the former only in the service of the latter. His greatest contribution to Christian thought was in the field of biblical translation and commentary—above all, in his scholarly translation of the Scriptures from Hebrew and Greek into Latin. Jerome's Latin Vulgate Bible has been used ever since by Roman Catholics and has served as the basis of innumerable translations into modern languages. (English-speaking Catholics use the Douay translation of Jerome's Vulgate.) It was an achievement of incalculable significance to Western Civilization.

The most profound of the Latin Doctors was Augustine (354–430), who spent his final 40 years as bishop of the North African city of Hippo. Like Jerome, Augustine worried about the dangers of pagan culture to the Christian soul, finally concluding, much as Jerome did, that Greco-Roman learning, although not to be enjoyed for its own sake, might properly be used to elucidate the Faith. Augustine was the chief architect of medieval theology. Even more than his contemporaries he succeeded in fusing Christian doctrine with Greek thought—especially the philosophy of Plato and the Neoplatonists. It has been said that Augustine baptized Plato. As a Platonist he stressed the importance of ideas or archetypes over tangible things, but instead of locating his archetypes in the abstract Platonic "heaven" he placed them in the mind of God. The human mind had access to the archetypes through an act of God which Augustine called "divine illumination."

As a bishop, Augustine was occupied with the day-to-day cares of his diocese and his flock. His contribution to religious thought arises not from the dispassionate working-out of an abstract system of theology but rather from his responses to the burning issues of the moment. His thought is a fascinating mixture of profundity and immediacy—of the abstract and the human. His *Confessions*, the first psychologically sensitive autobiography ever written, tells of his own spiritual journey through various pagan and heretical cults to Christian orthodoxy. Implicit in this book is the hope that others as misguided as he once was might also be led by God's grace to the truth in Christ.

Against the several heretical doctrines that threatened Christian orthodoxy in his day Augustine wrote clearly and persuasively on the nature of the Trinity, the problem of evil in a world created by God, the special character of the Christian priesthood, and the nature of free will and predestination. His most influential work, the *City of God*, was prompted by a barbarian sack of Rome in A.D. 410, which the pagans ascribed to Rome's desertion of her old gods. Augustine responded by developing a Christian theory of history which interpreted human development not in political or economic terms but in moral terms. As the first Christian philosopher of history, Augustine drew heavily on the historical insights of the ancient Hebrews. Like the Hebrew prophets of old, he asserted that kingdoms and empires rose and fell according to a divine plan, but he insisted that this plan lay forever beyond human comprehension. Augustine rejected the theory, common in antiquity, that history was an endless series of cycles, arguing on the contrary that history was moving toward a divinely appointed goal.

This linear view of history set something of a precedent for the modern secular concept of historical progress. Augustine also rejected the Hebrew notion of tribal salvation, putting in its place the Christian notion of *individual* salvation. The ultimate units of history were not tribes and empires but individual immortal souls.

The salvation of souls, Augustine stated, depends not on the fortunes of Rome but on the grace of God. Christ is not dependent on Caesar. And if we look at history from the moral standpoint—from the standpoint of souls—we see not the clash of armies or the rivalry of states but a far more fundamental struggle between good and evil which has raged through history and which rages even now within each soul. Humanity is divided into two classes: those who live in God's grace and those who do not. The former belong to what Augustine called the "City of God," the latter to the "Earthly City." The members of the two cities are hopelessly intermixed in this world, but they will be separated at death by eternal salvation or damnation. It is from this transcendental standpoint, Augustine believed, that the Christian must view history. Only God could know what effect Rome's decline would have on the City of God. Perhaps the effect would be beneficial, perhaps even irrelevant.

Augustine is one of the two or three seminal minds in Christian history. His Christian Platonism governed medieval theology down into the twelfth century and remains influential in Christian thought today. His emphasis on the special sacramental power inherent in the priestly office remains a keystone of Catholic theology. His emphasis on divine grace and predestination, although softened considerably by the medieval church, reemerged in the sixteenth century to dominate early Protestant doctrine. And his theory of the two cities, although often in simplified form, had an enormous influence on Western historical and political thought over the next millennium.

Ambrose, Jerome, and Augustine were at once synthesizers and innovators. The last great minds of the Western Empire, they operated at a level of intellectual sophistication that the Christian West would not reach again for 700 years. The strength of the classical tradition that underlies medieval Christianity and Western civilization owes much to the fact that these men, and others like them, found it possible to be both Christians and Ciceronians.

6
The Waning of the Western Empire

"Decline and Fall"

The catastrophe of Rome's decline and fall has always fascinated historians, for it involves not only the collapse of mankind's most impressive and enduring universal state but also the demise of Greco-Roman civilization itself. The reasons are far too complex to be explained satisfactorily by any single cause: Christianity, disease, slavery, lead poisoning, soil exhaustion, or any of the other "master-keys" that have been proposed from time to time. One must always bear in mind that the Roman Empire "fell" only in the west. It endured in the east, although there, too, Greco-Roman civilization was significantly changed. The civilization of the Eastern Empire during the medieval centuries is normally described not as "Roman" or even "Greco-Roman" but as "Byzantine," and the change in name betokens a profound alteration in mood. In other words, Greco-Roman culture was gradually transformed in both east and west, but its transformation in the west was accompanied by the dismemberment of the Roman state whereas its transformation in the east occurred despite an underlying political continuity in which emperor followed emperor in more-or-less unbroken succession.

In the west, then, we are faced with two separate phenomena—political breakdown and cultural transformation. The political collapse culminated in the deposition of the last western emperor in A.D. 476, but the true period of crisis was the chaotic third century. The recovery under Diocletian and Constantine was only partial and temporary: the impending death of the body politic was delayed, but the disease remained uncured. The impoverished masses in town and countryside had never participated meaningfully in Roman civilization, and the third-century anarchy resulted in the spiritual disengagement of the middle classes as well. Initiative and commitment ebbed in the atmosphere of economic and political upheaval and were stifled by the autocracy that followed. Fourth-century

Rome was an authoritarian, highly centralized state that robbed its subjects of their independence and watched over them through a network of informers and secret agents. The collapse of such a state cannot be regarded as an unmitigated disaster; to many it must have seemed a blessing.

The west had always been poorer and less urbanized than the east, and its economy, badly shaken by the political chaos of the third century, began to break down under the growing burden of imperial government and the defense of hard-pressed frontiers. Perhaps the fatal flaw in the western economy was its inability to compensate for the cessation of imperial expansion by more intensive internal development. There was no large-scale industry, no mass production; the majority of the population was far too poor to provide a mass market. Industrial production was inefficient, and technology progressed at a snail's pace. The economy remained fundamentally agrarian, and farming techniques advanced little during the centuries of the Empire. The Roman plow was rudimentary and inefficient; windmills were unknown and water mills exceptional. The horse could not be used as a draught animal because the Roman harness crossed the horse's windpipe and tended to strangle him under a heavy load. Consequently, Roman agriculture was based on the less efficient oxen and on the muscles of slaves and *coloni.*

Economic exhaustion brought with it the twin evils of population decline and growing poverty. At the very time that the manpower shortage was becoming acute and impoverishment was paralyzing the middle classes, the army and bureaucracy were expanding to unprecedented size and the expenses of government were soaring. One result of these processes was the deurbanization of the west. By the fifth century the once vigorous cities were becoming ghosts of their former selves, drained of their wealth and much of their population. Only the small class of great landowners managed to prosper in the economic atmosphere of the late Western Empire, and these men now abandoned their town houses, withdrew from civic affairs, and retired to their estates where they often assembled sizable private armies and defied the tax collector. The aristocracy, having now fled the city, would remain an agrarian class for the next thousand years. The rural nobility of the Middle Ages had come into being.

The decline of the city was fatal to the urbanized administrative structure of the Western Empire. More than that, it brought an end to the urban-oriented culture of Greco-Roman antiquity. The civilization of Athens, Alexandria, and Rome could not survive in the fields. It is in the decay of urban society that we find the crucial connecting link between political collapse and cultural transformation. In a very real sense Greco-Roman culture was dead long before the final demise of the Western Empire, and the deposition of the last emperor in 476 was merely the faint postscript to a process that had been completed long before. By then the cities were moribund; the rational, humanist outlook had given way completely to transcendentalism and mysticism; the army and even the civil government had become barbarized as the desperate emperors, faced with a growing shortage of manpower and resources, turned more and more to Germanic peoples to defend their frontiers and preserve order in their state. In the end, barbarians abounded in the army, entire tribes were hired to defend the frontiers, and Germanic military leaders came to hold positions of high authority in the Western Empire. Survival had come to depend on the success of half-hearted Germanic defenders against plunder-hungry Germanic invaders.

Despite the deurbanization, the mysticism, and the barbarism of the late Empire, it is nevertheless true that in a certain sense the Greco-Roman tradition never died in the west. It exerted a profound influence, as we have seen, on the Doctors of the

Latin Church and, through them, on the mind of the Middle Ages. It was the basis of repeated cultural revivals, great and small, down through the centuries. And if in one sense the Roman state was dead long before the line of western emperors ended in 476, in another sense it survived long thereafter—in the ecclesiastical organization of the Roman Catholic Church and in the medieval Holy Roman Empire. Roman law endured to inspire Western jurisprudence; the Latin tongue remained the language of educated Europeans for more than a millennium while evolving in the lower levels of society into the Romance languages: Italian, French, Spanish, Portuguese, and Rumanian. In countless forms the rich legacy of classical antiquity was passed on to the Middle Ages. Europeans for centuries to come would be nourished by Greek thought and haunted by the memory of Rome.

The Germanic Peoples

Medieval civilization owed much to its Greco-Roman heritage, but it drew sustenance also from the Judaeo-Christian and the Germanic cultural traditions. We have already observed the fusion of Greco-Roman and Christian culture in the Roman Empire, culminating in the work of Ambrose, Jerome, and Augustine. By the fifth century the fusion of these two traditions was essentially complete, but their integration with Germanic culture had only begun. Throughout the turbulent centuries of the Early Middle Ages the Greco-Roman-Christian tradition was preserved by the Church, whereas the Germanic tradition dominated the political and military organization of the barbarian states which established themselves on the carcass of the Western Empire. The Germanic invaders soon became at least nominal Christians, but for centuries a cultural gulf remained between the Church, with its Greco-Roman-Christian heritage, and the Germanic kingdoms with their primitive war-ori-

ented culture. The Church of the Early Middle Ages was able to preserve ancient culture only in a simplified and debased form, for as time went on ecclesiastical leaders and aristocratic laymen came more and more to be drawn from the same social milieu. Still, it remained the great task of the early medieval Church to civilize and Christianize the Germanic peoples. In the end the Classical-Christian-Germanic synthesis was achieved and a new Western European civilization came into being.

Most of the tribes that invaded the Western Empire seem to have come originally from the Scandinavian area, the homeland of the later Vikings. Gradually they migrated into Eastern and Southeastern Europe and began to press against the Rhine and Danube frontiers. It is hazardous to make broad generalizations regarding their culture and institutions, for customs varied considerably from tribe to tribe. The Franks, the Angles, and the Saxons, for example, were agrarian peoples whose movements were slow, but who, once settled, were difficult to displace. Little influenced by Roman civilization they came into the empire as heathens. The Visigoths, Ostrogoths, and Vandals, on the other hand, were far more mobile. All three had absorbed Roman culture to some degree before they crossed the frontiers, and all had been converted in the fourth century to Arian Christianity.

A good contemporary account of early Germanic institutions is to be found in a short book entitled *Germania* written by the Roman historian Tacitus in A.D. 98. This work is not entirely trustworthy; it is a morality piece written with the intention of criticizing the "degeneracy" of the Romans by comparing them unfavorably with the simple and upright barbarians. Nevertheless, it is an invaluable source of information on early Germanic customs and institutions. We can certainly accept Tacitus' description of the Germans as large men with reddish-blond hair and blue eyes, living in simple villages, but his eulogy of their virtue and chastity is a gross exaggeration. On the whole they appear to have been drunks, liars, and lechers, whose vices were certainly no less numerous than those of the Romans, only cruder. Their standards of personal hygiene are suggested by the observation of a fifth-century Roman gentleman: "Happy the nose that cannot smell a barbarian."*

Although the Germans used iron tools and weapons, their social and economic organization was in many ways reminiscent of the Neolithic culture stage. Their chief activities were tending crops or herds and fighting wars. The key social unit within the tribe had traditionally been the kindred group or clan, which protected the welfare of its members by means of the blood feud. When a man was killed, his clan was bound to avenge his death by conducting a feud —declaring war, as it were—against the killer and his clan. In the boisterous atmosphere of the tribe, killings were only too common, and in order to keep the social fabric from being torn asunder by blood feuds it became customary for the tribe to establish a *wergeld*, a sum of money that the killer might pay to the relatives of his victim to appease their vengeance. Wergeld schedules became quite elaborate, the amount of money to be paid by the killer varying in accordance with the social status of his victim. Smaller wergelds were established for lesser injuries such as the cutting off of a victim's arm, leg, thumb, or finger. There was no guarantee, however, that the man who did the killing or maiming would agree to pay the wergeld, or that the victim or his clan would agree to accept it. In spite of the wergeld system, blood feuds continued far into the Middle Ages.

The ties of kinship were strong among the early Germans, but they were rivaled by those of another social unit, the war

band or *comitatus*. Kinship played no part in this institution; it consisted rather of a group of warriors bound together by their loyalty to a chief or king. The comitatus was a kind of military brotherhood based on honor, fidelity, courage, and mutual respect between the leader and his men. In warfare the leader was expected to excel his men in courage and prowess, and should the leader be killed, his men were honor-bound to fight to the death even if their cause should appear hopeless. The heroic virtues of the comitatus persisted throughout the Early Middle Ages as the characteristic ideology of the European warrior nobility.

The comitatus and the clan were subdivisions of a larger unit, the tribe, whose members were bound together by their allegiance to a king and by their recognition of a body of customary law. Germanic law was arbitrary and childish compared with the majestic legal edifice of Rome. Procedural formalities were all important, and guilt or innocence was often determined by requiring the accused to grasp a bar of red-hot iron or to plunge his hand into a cauldron of boiling water. Nevertheless, throughout the Early Middle Ages the legal structure of the Western European states tended to be Germanic rather than Roman. It was not until the twelfth century that Roman law was revived in the West and began to make its influence felt once again. In the meantime, Germanic law, for all its crudeness, implanted one singularly fruitful idea in the Western mind: that law was a product not of the royal will but of the immemorial customs of the people. And if law could not be altered by the king, then royal authority could not be absolute. In the Early Middle Ages a number of Germanic kings had the customs of their people put into writing, but they rarely claimed the power to legislate on their own.

The centuries immediately preceding the invasions witnessed the development of relatively stable royal dynasties among many of the Germanic tribes. Perhaps an

* The authors, some of whose best friends are of Frankish and Anglo-Saxon descent, disclaim any sort of ethnic bias. The crudeness of the barbarians was due entirely to their lack of social and educational opportunities.

unusually gifted warrior with a particularly large comitatus might start such a dynasty, but before many generations had gone by the kings were claiming descent from some divine ancestor. When a king died, the assembly of the tribe chose as his successor the ablest member of his family. This might or might not be his eldest son, for the tribal assembly was given considerable latitude in its power to elect. The customs of election persisted in most Germanic kingdoms far into the Middle Ages. Its chief consequence during the fifth-century invasions was to insure that the barbarian tribes were normally led by clever, battle-worthy kings or chieftains at a time when the Western Empire was ruled by weaklings and fools.

Historians of previous centuries made much of the fact that certain Germanic institutions seemed to contain the seeds of constitutionalism and popular sovereignty. Democracy, so it was said, had its genesis in the forests of Germany. It should be obvious, however, that the veneration of a customary "law of the folk" or the political prominence of a tribal assembly is not uniquely Germanic but is common to many primitive peoples. The noteworthy thing about these institutions is not their existence among the Germanic barbarians but their endurance and development in the centuries that followed.

The Barbarian Invasions

The Germanic peoples had long been a threat to the Empire. They had defeated a Roman army in the reign of Augustus; they had probed deep into the Empire under Marcus Aurelius and again in the mid-third century. But until the later fourth century the Romans had always managed eventually to drive the invaders out or settle them under Roman rule. Beginning in the mid-370s, however, an exhausted Empire was confronted by renewed barbarian pressures of an unprecedented magnitude. Lured by the relative wealth, the good soil, and the sunny climate of the Mediterranean world, the barbarians tended to regard the Empire not as something to destroy but as something to enjoy. Their age-long yearning for the fair lands across the Roman frontier was suddenly transformed into an urgent need by the westward thrust of a tribe of Asian nomads known as the Huns. These fierce horsemen conquered one Germanic tribe after another and turned them into satellites. The Ostrogoths fell before their might and became a subject people. The other great Gothic tribe, the Visigoths, sought to avoid a similar fate by appealing for sanctuary behind the Roman Danube frontier. The Eastern Emperor Valens, a fervent Arian, sympathized with the Arian Visigoths, and in 376 they all crossed peacefully into the Empire.

There was trouble almost immediately. Corrupt imperial officials cheated and abused the Visigoths, and the hot-tempered tribesmen retaliated by going on a rampage. At length Emperor Valens himself took the field against them, but the Emperor's military incapacity cost him his army and his life at the battle of Adrianople in 378. Adrianople was a military debacle of the first order. Valens' successor, the able Theodosius I, managed to pacify the Visigoths but he could not expel them. When Theodosius died in 395 the Roman Empire was split between his two incompetent sons, and, as it happened, the eastern and western halves were never again rejoined. A vigorous new Visigothic leader named Alaric now led his people on a second campaign of pillage and destruction that threatened Italy itself. In 406 the desperate Western Empire recalled most of its troops from the Rhine frontier to block Alaric's advance, with the disastrous consequence that the Vandals and a number of other tribes swept across the unguarded Rhine into Gaul. Shortly thereafter the Roman legions abandoned distant Britain and the defenseless island was gradually overrun by Angles, Saxons, and Jutes. In 408 the only able general in the West was executed by the frantic, incompetent Emperor Honorius who then took refuge behind the marshes of Ravenna. The Visigoths entered Rome unopposed in 410 and Alaric permitted them to plunder the city for three days.

The sack of Rome had a devastating impact on imperial morale, but in historical perspective it appears as a mere incident in the disintegration of the Western Empire. The Visigoths soon left the city to its blundering emperor and turned northward into southern Gaul and Spain where they established a kingdom that endured until the Muslim conquests of the eighth century. Meanwhile other tribes were carving out kingdoms of their own. The Vandals swept through Gaul and Spain and across the Straits of Gibraltar into Africa. In 430, the very year of St. Augustine's death, they took his city of Hippo. A new Vandal kingdom arose in North Africa, centering on ancient Carthage. Almost immediately the Vandals began taking to the sea as buccaneers, devastating Mediterranean shipping and sacking one coastal city after another. Vandal piracy shattered the age-long peace of the Mediterranean and dealt a crippling blow to the waning commerce of the Western Empire.

Midway through the fifth century the Huns themselves moved against the west, led by their pitiless leader Attila, the "Scourge of God." Defeated by a Roman-Visigothic army in Gaul in 451, they returned the following year, hurling themselves toward Rome and leaving a path of devastation behind them. The western emperor abandoned Rome to Attila's mercies, but the Roman bishop, Pope Leo I, traveled northward from the city to negotiate with the Huns on the wild chance that they might be persuaded to turn back. Oddly enough, Pope Leo succeeded in his mission. Perhaps because the health of the Hunnish army was adversely affected by the Italian climate, perhaps because the majestic Pope Leo was able to overawe the superstitious Attila, the Huns retired from Italy. Shortly afterward Attila died, the Hunnish empire collapsed, and the Huns themselves vanished from history. They were not mourned.

In its final years the Western Empire, whose jurisdiction now scarcely extended beyond Italy, fell under the control of hardbitten military adventurers of Germanic birth. The emperors continued to reign for a time but their Germanic generals were the powers behind the throne. In 476 the barbarian general Odovacar, who saw no point in perpetuating the farce, deposed the last emperor, sent the imperial trappings to Constantinople, and asserted his sovereignty over Italy by confiscating a good deal of farmland for the use of his Germanic troops. Odovacar claimed to rule as an agent of the Eastern Empire but, in fact, he was on his own. A few years later the Ostrogoths, now free of Hunnish control and led by a skillful king named Theodoric, advanced into Italy, conquered Odovacar, and established a strong state of their own.

Theodoric ruled Italy from 493 to 526. More than any other barbarian king he appreciated and respected Roman culture, and in his kingdom the Arian Ostrogoths and the Orthodox Romans lived and worked together in relative harmony, repairing aqueducts, erecting impressive new buildings, and bringing a degree of prosperity to the long-troubled peninsula. The improved political and economic climate gave rise to a minor intellectual revival that contributed to the transmission of Greco-Roman culture into the middle ages. The philosopher Boethius, a high official in Theodoric's regime, produced philosophical works and translations which served as fundamental texts in western schools for the next 500 years. His *Consolation of Philosophy*, an interesting mixture of Platonism and Stoicism, was immensely popular throughout the Middle Ages. Theodoric's own secretary, Cassiodorus, was another scholar of considerable distinction. Cassiodorus spent his later years as abbot of a monastery and set his monks to the invaluable task of copying and preserving the great literary works of antiquity, both Christian and pagan.

During the years of Theodoric's beneficent rule in Ostrogothic Italy, another famous barbarian king, Clovis (481–511), was creating a Frankish kingdom in Gaul. Clovis was far less Romanized, far less enlightened, far crueler than Theodoric, but his kingdom proved to be the most enduring of all the barbarian successor states. The Franks were good farmers as well as good soldiers and they established deep roots in the soil of Gaul. Moreover, the Frankish regime was buttressed by the enthusiastic support of the Roman Catholic Church. For Clovis, who had been untouched by Arianism, was converted directly from heathenism to Catholic Christianity. He remained a brutal barbarian to the end, yet the church came to regard him as another Constantine—a defender of orthodoxy in a sea of Arianism. As the centuries went by, the royal name "Clovis" was softened to "Louis" and the "Franks" became the "French." And the friendship between the Frankish monarchy and the church developed into one of the great determining elements in European politics.

Europe in A.D. 500

As the sixth century dawned, the Western Empire was only a memory. In its place was a group of barbarian successor states that foreshadowed in certain respects the nations of modern Western Europe. Theodoric headed a tolerant and relatively enlightened Ostrogothic-Arian regime in Italy. The barbaric but orthodox Clovis was completing the Frankish conquest of Gaul. The Vandal monarchy, Arian in religion and increasingly corrupt and intolerant, lorded it over the restive population of North Africa. The Arian Visigoths were being driven out of Southern Gaul by the Franks, but their regime continued to dominate Spain for the next two centuries. And

the Angles and Saxons were in the process of establishing a group of small heathen kingdoms in Britain that would one day coalesce into "Angleland" or England.

At the very time that the Germanic kingdoms were establishing themselves in the West, the Roman papacy was beginning to play an important independent role in European society. We have seen how the great mid-fifth century pope, Leo I (440–461), assumed the task of protecting the city of Rome from the Huns, thereby winning for himself the moral leadership of Italy. Leo and his successors declared that the papacy was the highest authority in the Church, and, following the example of St. Ambrose, they insisted on the supremacy of Church over state in spiritual matters. In proclaiming its doctrines of papal supremacy in the Church and ecclesiastical independence from state control, the papacy was hurling a direct challenge at Byzantine Caesaropapism. In the fifth century these papal doctrines remained little more than words, but they were to result in an ever-widening gulf between the Eastern and Western Church. More than that, they constituted the opening phase of the prolonged medieval struggle between the rival claims of Church and state. The mighty papacy of the High Middle Ages was yet many centuries away, but it was already foreshadowed in the bold independence of Leo I. The Western Empire was dead, but eternal Rome still claimed the allegiance of the world.

CHRONOLOGY OF THE ROMAN EMPIRE

44 B.C.:	Assassination of Julius Ceasar
31 B.C.–A.D. 14:	Reign of Augustus
96–180:	The age of the great second-century emperors
235–284:	Height of the anarchy
185–254:	Origen
205–270:	Plotinus
284–305:	Reign of Diocletian
306–337:	Reign of Constantine

EUROPE AT CLOVIS'S DEATH
A.D. 511

325:	Founding of Constantinople
330:	Council of Nicaea
354–430:	St. Augustine of Hippo
376:	Visigoths cross Danube
378:	Battle of Adrianople
378–395:	Reign of Theodosius I
395:	Final division of Eastern and Western Empires
410:	Alaric sacks Rome
430:	Vandals capture Hippo
440–461:	Pontificate of Leo I
451–452:	Huns invade Western Europe
476:	Last Western emperor deposed by Odovacar
493–526:	Theodoric the Ostrogoth rules Italy
481–511:	Clovis rules Franks, conquers Gaul

SUGGESTED READINGS

The asterisk indicates a paperback edition.

Michael Grant, *The World of Rome* (*New York: Mentor, 1960).

N. Lewis and M. Reinhold, *Roman Civilization* (*2 vols. New York: Harper, 1955).

M. Rostovtzeff, *Rome* (*New York: Oxford Galaxy, 1928).

T. W. Africa, *Rome of the Caesars* (*New York: Wiley, 1965).

H. Mattingly, *Roman Imperial Civilization* (*Garden City: Anchor, 1923).

Theodor Mommsen, *The History of Rome* (*New York: Meridian, 1963).

H. H. Scullard, *From the Gracchi to Nero* (*New York: Praeger, 1959).

Ronald Syme, *The Roman Revolution* (*Fair Lawn: Oxford, 1959).

R. Bultmann, *Primitive Christianity in its Contemporary Setting* (*New York: Meridian, 1956).

C. N. Cochrane, *Christianity and Classical Culture* (*Fair Lawn: Oxford, 1944).

F. Cumont, *Oriental Religions in Roman Paganism* (*New York: Dover, 1956).

Michael Gough, *The Early Christians* (New York: Praeger, 1961).

K. S. Latourette, *A History of Christianity*

(New York: Harper, 1953).

H. O. Taylor, *The Emergence of Christian Culture in the West* (*New York: Harper, 1958).

J. B. Bury, *History of the Later Roman Empire* (*2 Vols. New York: Dover, 1928).

B. Davenport, ed., *The Portable Roman Reader* (*New York: Viking, 1951).

Samuel, Dill, *Roman Society in the Last Century of the Western Empire* (*New York: Meridian, 1899).

Edward Gibbon, *The Triumph of Christendom in the Roman Empire* (*New York: Harper, 1932).

Chapters XV to XX from Gibbon's masterpiece, The Decline and Fall of the Roman Empire. *The entire work is available in a three-volume Modern Library edition.*

Gregory of Tours, *History of the Franks,* trans. by E. Brehaut (*New York: Norton, 1969).

A. H. M. Jones, *The Later Roman Empire* (3 vols. Oxford: Blackwell's, 1964).

F. Lot, *The End of the Ancient World and the Beginnings of the Middle Ages.* (*New York: Harper, 1931).

Chester G. Starr, *The Ancient Romans* (*New York: Oxford Press, 1971).

Part 3
The Early Middle Ages: The Genesis of Western Civilization

7

Byzantine, Islam, and Western Christendom

Medieval Western Eurasia: a General View

In A.D. 500 the western portion of the Eurasian land mass contained two great civilized powers: the Eastern Roman or "Byzantine" Empire centered on Constantinople and, to its east, the Persian Empire under the rule of the Sassanid dynasty. During the centuries that followed, two other civilizations arose—Western Christendom and Islam. In the seventh century Islam conquered and absorbed Sassanid Persia, and the Eastern Roman Empire had to fight for its life against this explosive new threat from the Arabian Desert. But the Eastern Roman Empire stood its ground against the full force of youthful, militant Islam. Important Byzantine provinces were lost permanently to the Arabs, but Byzantium survived as an empire and a civilization for another 800 years. And as Islam and Byzantium struggled with one another, the civilization of Western Christendom was gradually painfully arising among the former western provinces of the Roman Empire. In 800 the Frankish monarch Charlemagne was crowned Roman Emperor in the West, thereby endowing this new civilization with the dignity and prestige of the ancient imperial title. By 800 the three great civilizations of medieval Western Eurasia—Islam, Byzantium, and Western Christendom—were firmly rooted. For the remainder of the Middle Ages these would continue to dominate Europe, North Africa, and the Middle East.

It was not until the eleventh century, however, that Western Christendom began to achieve sufficient political stability, economic well-being, and creative power to rival Byzantium and Islam. From A.D. 500 to about 1050, Western Christendom was an underdeveloped society struggling for its survival against invaders—and against its own poverty and ignorance. It was in no sense comparable to the civilizations of the Byzantines and Arabs. It commands our attention less for its military, political, intellectual, and artistic achievements than

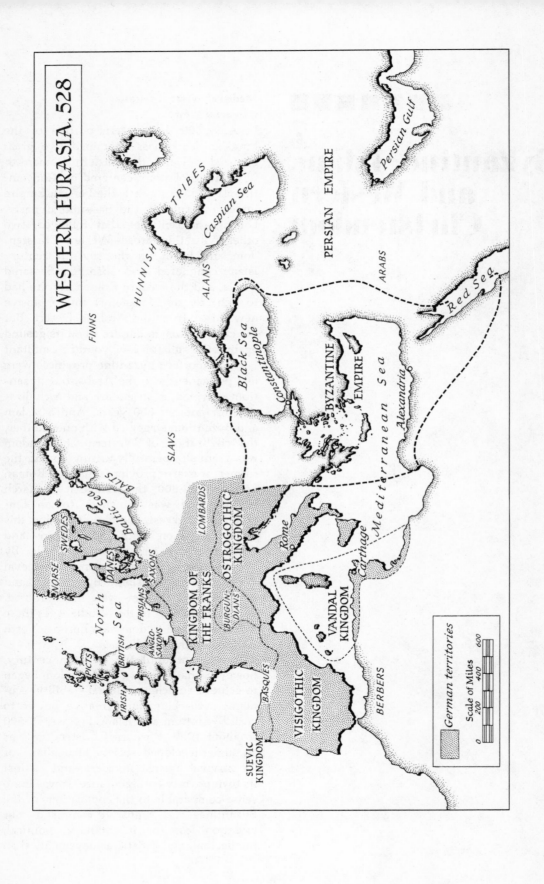

WESTERN EURASIA, 528

FINNS

HUNNISH
TRIBES

Caspian Sea

ALANS

PERSIAN EMPIRE

Persian Gulf

ARABS

Red Sea

SLAVS

Black Sea

Constantinople

BYZANTINE
EMPIRE

Mediterranean Sea

Alexandria

NORSE

SWEDES

BALTS

Baltic Sea

DANES

FRISIANS

SAXONS

ANGLO-SAXONS

PICTS

BRITISH

IRISH

North Sea

LOMBARDS

KINGDOM OF
THE FRANKS

BURGUN-
DIANS

OSTROGOTHIC
KINGDOM

Rome

VANDAL
KINGDOM

Carthage

BERBERS

BASQUES

SUEVIC
KINGDOM

VISIGOTHIC
KINGDOM

German territories

Scale of Miles
0   200   400   600

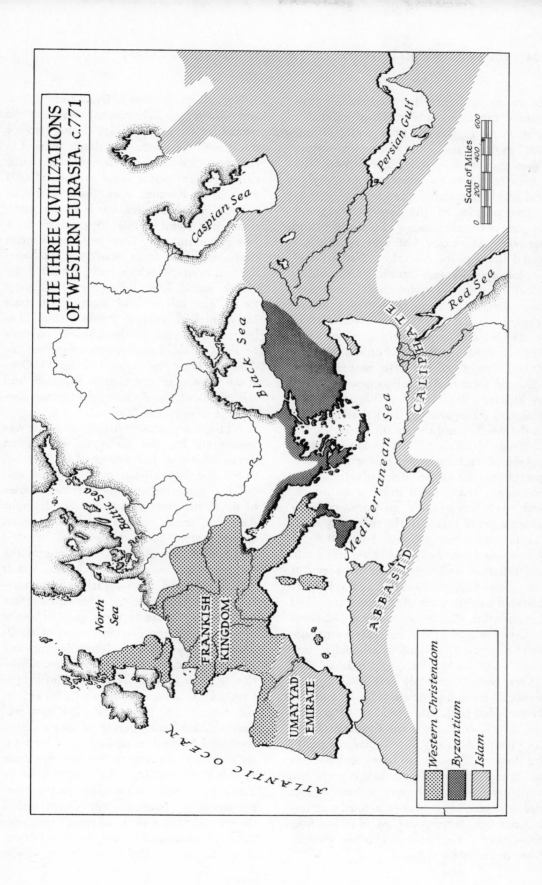

THE THREE CIVILIZATIONS
OF WESTERN EURASIA, c.771

Scale of Miles
0   200   400   600

Caspian Sea

Persian Gulf

Red Sea

CALIPHATE

Black Sea

Mediterranean Sea

ABBASID

Baltic Sea

North Sea

FRANKISH
KINGDOM

UMAYYAD
EMIRATE

ATLANTIC OCEAN

Western Christendom

Byzantium

Islam

for its success in creating the beginnings of certain institutions and habits of mind that contributed to the rise of a great civilization in twelfth- and thirteenth-century Western Europe—a civilization that, later on, extended its power techniques, styles, and ideologies across the globe.

The peoples of the three civilizations fought not only among themselves and between each other but also against external nomadic or seafaring "barbarians." Germanic, Viking, Berber, and Slavic tribes were an incessant threat, and even more dangerous were the Altaic invaders from Central Asia who came westward in recurring waves for nearly a millennium. The Huns, who had preyed on the faltering Roman Empire of the fifth century, were followed westward in subsequent centuries by kindred Altaic peoples: Bulgars, Avars, Magyars (Hungarians), Turks, and finally, in the twelfth and thirteenth centuries, the dreaded Mongols. These Asian invaders possessed ruthlessly efficient military organizations based on light cavalry. Their nomadism made them difficult to attack, and their remarkable military mobility posed a grave threat to the sedentary civilizations that they assailed. Some of these Altaic people were eventually absorbed into the religious and cultural frameworks of the defending civilizations. The Bulgars adopted Eastern Orthodox Christianity and submitted to the patriarch and the emperor in Constantinople; the Magyars eventually were converted to Roman Catholicism, and their king became a papal vassal. The Avars were ultimately annihilated as a political force by Charlemagne; and the Huns faded back into the East. After 1050 the Seljuk Turks (and the Ottoman Turks four centuries later) were to assume political control of much of Islam and become militant Muslims. But whether repelled, assimilated, or destroyed, these Altaic peoples were for centuries a source of turbulence and terror, and on occasion they threatened the very survival of the civilizations of Europe and Asia.

The cultural sources of Byzantium, Islam, and Western Christendom were by no means limited to the classical and Hebrew traditions. Western Christendom was a fusion of classical, Christian, and Germanic culture; Islam was at least as oriental as it was Greco-Roman, and the culture of Islamic Baghdad owed much to the traditions of ancient Persia; Byzantium drew inspiration not only from its Greco-Roman past but also from the Ancient-Near-Eastern heritage, which had permeated the Greek world long before, in Hellenistic times. The solemn and magnificent court ceremonial of ancient Persia, which was borrowed in part by the Roman emperors of the late third and fourth centuries, influenced both the imperial rites of Constantinople over the next millennium and the rituals of the Roman papacy that continue to the present day.

Again, late-Roman religious thought was influenced by the concepts of Persian Zoroastrianism. The universal conflict between the Zoroastrian gods of good and evil was projected into the world as a series of dualisms: good versus evil, light versus darkness, truth versus falsehood, spirit versus matter. Spirit-matter dualism is to be found in the religious traditions of the Hebrews and even of the Greeks, but it was manifested most clearly and powerfully in Persian thought. Dualism became the dominant note in three great religious movements of the Roman Empire—Gnosticism, Mithraism, and Manichaeism—and through these movements it affected Christianity itself. There were many influential Christian Gnostics in the early history of the church; St. Augustine of Hippo had been a Manichaean before he was a Christian; and Mithraism was one of Christianity's chief rivals among the mystery cults of the third century. Christian orthodoxy consistently resisted the more extreme implications of dualism. Yet Christianity's distinctive vision of a universal synthesis between spirit and matter, soul and body, was modified in the early church, under dualistic influences, into an attitude of re-nunciation and withdrawal from the world. God had created the earth, and He had dignified the human body by assuming it unto himself in the incarnate Christ. Yet early Christians, living in a religious atmos-phere profoundly affected by the dualistic viewpoint—and in an age of great political and cultural upheaval—tended to renounce the body and flee the world.

Byzantium

By about A.D. 500 the former western provinces of the Roman Empire had be-come a cluster of political fragments ruled by Germanic tribes, but the Eastern Roman emperors, with their capital at Constanti-nople, retained control of an immense, crescent-shaped empire girdling the eastern Mediterranean from the Balkans through Asia Minor, Syria, and Palestine, to Egypt. The last western emperor was deposed in 476, and the western provinces had by then been lost, but since the reign of Diocletian (284–305) the policital power of the Roman Empire had been concentrated in the East. During the fourth and fifth centuries the Empire changed internally and contracted geographically, yet it sur-vived as an apparently indestructible state and, centered on Constantine's eastern capital, it lived on for another millennium.

Nevertheless, the culture of classical antiquity was gradually transformed in the East, just as in the West, even though the line of eastern emperors continued without significant interruption from the time of Diocletian to 1453. Historians recognize this cultural transformation by giving a new name to the Eastern Roman Empire from about the sixth century onward. It is called the Byzantine Empire, after the ancient Greek town of Byzantium on whose site Constantinople was built. But the cul-tural change was exceedingly gradual, and one might equally well argue that the era of most significant transition was the third

and fourth centuries rather than the sixth.

Byzantine civilization was built on a fusion of three ingredients: Roman govern-ment, Christian religion, and Greco-Oriental culture. From Rome, and most particularly from the authoritarian empire of Diocletian and Constantine, Byzantium inherited its autocracy, its administrative system, and its fusion of religious and political power that has been termed caesaropapism. The celebrated Byzantine emperor Justinian (527–565) sent his armies westward to bring Italy and North Africa back under imperial control, and although these conquests were both expen-sive and short-lived, they testify to Justin-ian's dream of reviving the Roman Empire of old. This same concern for the Roman past impelled Justinian to set a group of talented Byzantine lawyers at the task of assembling the huge mass of legal pre-cedents, judicial opinions, and imperial edicts that constituted the age-long legacy of Roman law. These materials were arranged into a huge, systematic collection known as the *Corpus Juris Civilis*—the "body of civil law." Justinian's *Corpus* not only became the basis of all future Byzan-tine jurisprudence but also served as the vehicle in which Roman law returned to Western Europe in the twelfth century to challenge the traditional domination of Germanic legal custom. The appearance of the *Corpus Juris Civilis* in the medieval West was of incalculable importance to the development of rational legal systems in the European states. Its effect is still evi-dent in the legal codes of modern nations.

The prevailing Byzantine mood, like the mood of the fourth- and fifth-century em-pire, was one of defense—of self-preserva-tion. To the Byzantines, their state was the ark of civilization in an ocean of bar-barism—the political embodiment of the Christian faith—and as such it had to be preserved at all costs. The virtues appropri-ate to such a state were entrenchment, not conquest; caution, not daring. If Justinian is the most famous of the long line of

Byzantine emperors, he is also the least typical.

The Byzantine Legacy

Throughout the Middle Ages, Constantinople remained Europe's eastern bastion against the Muslims. Its impregnable walls protected not only the Byzantine Empire but Western Europe too from the ravages of Asiatic invaders. And the West was indebted to Byzantium for far more than its soldiers and its walls. The Eastern Empire served Western Europe and the world as a custodian of classical culture. The writings of Greek philosphers, for example, were with a few exceptions unknown in the early medieval West but were preserved and studied in Constantinople. The Byzantines systematized and perpetuated the Roman legal heritage. Byzantine art influenced the work of medieval and Renaissance architects and painters. Byzantine missionaries Christianized and civilized the Slavs and laid the political and theological foundation for Czarist Russia. Indeed, when Constantinople fell in 1453, Moscow became the third Rome: its rulers assumed the Byzantine mantle as Caesars or Czars, lording it over both Church and state just as their Byzantine predecessors had. It has even been suggested that the present rulers of Russia, with their control of both the State and the Communist ideological apparatus, are carrying on the tradition of Byzantine caesaropapism in a secularized form.

Yet the Byzantine achievement had its limitations. Byzantium remained an autocracy to the end, and its creative genius was often inhibited by its profound conservatism. For much of its long history it was a society under siege, and so much of its energy was devoted to its own survival that little was left for social, political, or technological experimentation or bold philosophical speculation. It performed the priceless service of preserving the thought and letters of Greco-Roman antiquity, but perhaps its classical heritage was also a kind of burden; perhaps the Byzantines were so awed by the achievements of their Greco-Roman forebears that they were hesitant to strike out in new directions. In this sense the Byzantines were prisoners of their own past. The sophistication of Constantinople stands in sharp contrast to the ignorance and barbarism of the early medieval West, but the West, for all its barbarism, had the inestimable advantages of a fresh start. Its relapse into intellectual twilight and semi-savagery resulted ultimately in its liberation from the dead hand of the past. The spirit of Greco-Roman antiquity inspired and enriched Western Christendom but did not shackle it.

Islam

Each of Rome's three "heirs"—Byzantium, Islam, and Western Christendom—has affected world history down to the present day. The impact of Western Christendom on today's world is obvious enough. Byzantium shaped the future of Russia and the Balkans. Islam remains a distinctive culture and a living religion extending across an immense area in South Asia, the Middle East, and North Africa—from the East Indies to Pakistan to the Arab world of southwest Asia and Mediterranean Africa. This vast Islamic belt was created by a militant, compelling religion that burst into the world in seventh-century Africa.

The new faith was called "Islam" (the Arabic word for "surrender"). Created by the Arab prophet Mohammed out of Christian, Hebrew, and Zoroastrian elements, it was centered on the worship of the omnipotent God of the Hebrews, whom the Muslims called Allah. Mohammed did not claim divinity for himself; rather, he claimed to be the last and greatest of a long line of prophets running back through Jesus to the Hebrew prophets of old. There was no trinity; Allah was, in the purest sense, One God. Thus, the central dogma of the Islamic faith declares, "There is no god but Allah, and Mohammed is His prophet."

Islam respected the Old and New Testaments and was relatively tolerant toward Jews and Christians—the "people of the book." But the Muslims had a book of their own, the Koran, which superseded its predecessors and was believed to contain the pure essence of divine revelation. The Koran is the comprehensive body of Mohammed's writings, the bedrock of the Islamic faith: "All men in jinn in collaboration," so it is said, "could not produce its like." Muslims regard it as the word of Allah dictated to Mohammed by the angel Gabriel from an original "uncreated" book located in heaven. Accordingly, its divine inspiration and authority extend not only to its precepts but also to its every letter (of which there are 323,621). Thus it loses its authority when translated into another language. Every good Muslim must read the Koran in its original Arabic. As Islam spread, the Arabic language necessarily spread with it.

Mohammed's religion spread outward from Arabia with remarkable speed. During the hundred years following the Prophet's death in 632, Islamic armies shattered the Christian domination of the Mediterranean, destroyed the Persian Empire, seized Byzantium's richest provinces and nearly took Constantinople, Far to the west, the Muslims swept across North Africa, crossed into Visigothic Spain and conquered it, and pressed deeply into France until they were turned back by the Frankish Christian leader, Charles Martel, in 732, on a battlefield between Tours and Poitiers.

The vast territories that the Arabs conquered were united by a common tongue, a common faith, and a common culture. The untutored Arab from the desert became the cultural heir of Greece, Rome, Persia, and India, and within less than two centuries after Mohammed's death Islamic culture had reached the level of a mature, sophisticated civilization. Its swift rise was a consequence of the Arabs' success in absorbing the great civilized traditions of their conquered peoples and of employing these traditions in a cultural synthesis both new and unique. Islam borrowed, but never without digesting. What it drew from other civilizations it transmuted and made its own.

During his lifetime Mohammed had become both the religious leader and the political leader of Arabia. And the fusion of religion and politics that he created remained a fundamental characteristic of Islamic society for centuries thereafter. There was no Muslim priesthood; there was no Muslim "church" apart from the Islamic state itself. Mohammed's political successors, the caliphs, were defenders of the faith and guardians of the faithful. The creative tension between church and state, which was to provoke such violence and such creativity in medieval Western Europe, was quite unknown in the Muslim world.

The Islamic Impact

And yet the world of Islam was deeply creative. From Cordova in Spain to Baghdad in Iraq and far to the east, Muslim scholars and artists developed the legacies of past civilizations. Architects molded Greco-Roman forms into a brilliant, distinctive new style. Philosophers studied and elaborated the writings of Plato and Aristotle, despite the hostility of narrowly orthodox Islamic theologians. Physicians expanded the ancient medical doctrines of Galen and his Greek predecessors, describing new symptoms and identifying new curative drugs. Astronomers tightened the geocentric system of Ptolemy, preparing accurate tables of planetary motions, and giving Arabic names to the stars—names such as Altair, Deneb, and Aldebaran—which are still used. The renowned astronomer poet of eleventh-century Persia, Omar Khayyam, devised a calendar of singular accuracy. Muslim mathematicians borrowed

Mausoleum of the Sassinids, Bukhasa, Central Asia, tenth century.   (Roger-Viollet, Paris)

creatively from both Greece and India. From the Greeks they learned geometry and trigonometry, and from the Hindus they appropriated the so-called Arabic numerals, the zero, and algebra, which were ultimately passed on to the West to revolutionize European mathematics.

The Arab conquests during the century after Mohammed changed the historical course of North Africa and Southwest Asia decisively and permanently. The Arabs conquered their vast territories thrice over: with their armies, their faith, and their language. In the end, the term "Arab" applied to every Muslim from Morocco to Iraq, regardless of his ethnic background. Within its encompassing religious and linguistic framework, Arab culture provided a new stimulus and a new orientation to the long-civilized peoples of former empires. With its manifold ingredients, the rich Islamic heritage would one day provide invaluable nourishment to the voracious mind of the twelfth and thirteenth-century West. Later, Islamic armies would bring Byzantium to an end and make Constantinople a Muslim city. Later still, in the sixteenth and seventeenth centuries, they would be at the gates of Vienna. Only in

the nineteenth century did Islam become clearly subordinate to the West militarily and politically. And today there are clear signs that this subordination is ending.

WESTERN CHRISTENDOM

During the half millennium following A.D. 500, while Byzantium struggled to preserve its territory and culture, and while Islamic civilization rose and flowered, Western Europe underwent an agonizing process of decline and rebirth. Classical civilization collapsed almost totally, and on its ruins there arose, slowly, the new civilization of Western Christendom.

Although many Roman towns survived in the barbarian West, as the headquarters of important bishoprics and the sites of cathedral churches,* they played a drastically reduced role in the economy of the new Germanic states. The important economic centers of the age were the monastery, the peasant village, and the great farm or villa owned by some wealthy Roman or Germanic aristocrat and divided into small plots worked by semifree tenant farmers. A small-scale international luxury trade persisted, but by and large the sixth and seventh centuries were characterized by economic localism. Small agrarian communities produced most of their own needs and were very nearly self-sufficient.

Except in Britain and the western Rhineland, the Germanic invaders were gradually absorbed by the more numerous native populations. Among the Franks, Visigoths, and Burgundians, the free farmers often sank to the level of semi-servile *coloni* within a few generations. The Germanic warrior nobility was to retain its separate identity much longer, especially in Italy, where a Germanic tribe known as the Lom-

---

* Technically, the term *cathedral* denotes the seat of a bishopric—literally, the bishop's throne. A church, whether large or small, is a "cathedral" if it serves as a bishop's headquarters.

bards held sway from the late sixth to the late eighth century. Even after the old and new upper classes became fused through intermarriage, the aggressive, rough-and-ready values of the Germanic aristocracy prevailed.

The barbarian kings, with the exception of the Ostrogoth, Theodoric, in Italy (493–526), proved incapable of carrying on the Roman administrative traditions they inherited. The Roman tax system broke down almost completely, the privilege of minting coins fell into private hands, and the power and wealth of the government declined accordingly. The Germanic kings lacked any conception of responsible government and regarded their kingdoms as private estates to be exploited or alienated according to their whims. They made reckless gifts of land and political authority to the nobility and the church and used what was left for their own personal enrichment. They managed to combine the worst features of anarchy and tyranny.

Since the Germanic kings were doing nothing to enhance the economy or ameliorate the general improverishment, the Church strove to fill the vacuum. It dispensed charity, offered eternal salvation to the poor, and glamorized the virtue of resignation. But even the Church was ill-equipped to cope with the chaos of the barbarian West. The Roman popes claimed leadership over the Church yet seldom asserted real power beyond central Italy. Elsewhere ecclesiastical organization was confined largely to the almost deserted towns and the walled monasteries. Only gradually were rural parishes organized to meet the needs of the countryside, and not until the eighth century did they become common. Until then a peasant was fortunate if he saw a priest once a year. The monarchy and the Church, the two greatest landholders in the barbarian kingdoms, were better known among the peasantry as acquisitive landlords than as fountains of justice and divine grace. The countryside was politically and spiritually adrift, and peasant life was harsh, brutish, and short.

Monasticism and Early Medieval Culture

What little high culture there was in the Early Middle Ages was centered in the monasteries. Ireland had been won for Christianity by St. Patrick in the fifth century, and, by about 600, Irish monasteries had developed a richly creative Celtic-Christian culture. Irish scholars were studying both Greek and Latin literature at a time when Greek was unknown elsewhere in the West. Irish artists were producing superb sculptured crosses and illuminated manuscripts in the flowing, curvilinear Celtic style. Irish Christianity, isolated from the continental Church by the pagan Anglo-Saxon kingdoms, developed its own distinctive organization and spirit, centered on the monastery rather than the diocese. Irish monks were famous for their learning, the austere severity of their lives, and the vast scope of their missionary activities. They converted large portions of Scotland to their own form of Christianity and by the early 600s were doing missionary work on the continent itself.

Meanwhile a very different kind of monastic order, spreading northward from Italy, was making a deep impact on the life of dark-age Europe. This movement was organized in the early sixth century by St. Benedict of Nursia (c. 480–c. 544), a contemporary of Justinian. St. Benedict founded the great monastery of Monte Cassino, between Rome and Naples, and framed a rule of monastic life that inspired and energized the medieval Church. Pope Gregory the Great (590–604) described the Benedictine Rule as "conspicuous for its discretion." Rejecting the harsh asceticism of earlier Christian monasticism, it provided for a busy, closely regulated life, simple but not austere. Benedictine monks were decently clothed, adequately fed, and seldom left to their own devices. Theirs was a life dedicated to God and to the quest for personal sanctity, guided by the obligations of chastity, poverty, and obedience to the abbot. Yet it was also a life that was available to any dedicated Christian, not merely to the spiritual hero. Its ideals were service and prayer under moderate, compassionate leadership.

In the two centuries after St. Benedict's death his order spread throughout Western Christendom. The result was not a vast, hierarchial monastic organization, but rather hundreds of individual, autonomous monasteries sharing a single rule and way of life. Benedict had pictured his monasteries as spiritual sanctuaries into which pious men might withdraw from the world, but the chaotic, illiterate society of the barbarian west, desperately in need of the discipline and learning of the Benedictines, could not permit them to renounce secular affairs.

The Benedictines had an enormous impact on the world they had sought to abandon. Their schools produced the majority of literate Europeans during the Early Middle Ages. They served as a vital cultural link with the classical past, transcribing and preserving the writings of Latin antiquity. They spearheaded the penetration of Christianity into pagan England at the end of the sixth century, into Germany two centuries later, and, in the tenth century, into Scandinavia, Poland, and Hungary. They served as scribes and advisers to kings and were drafted into high ecclesiastical offices. As recipients of gifts of land from pious donors over many generations, they held and managed vast estates that became models of intelligent agricultural management and technological innovation. As islands of peace, security, and learning in an ocean of barbarism, the Benedictine monasteries became the spiritual and intellectual centers of the developing Classical-Christian-Germanic synthesis that underlay European civilization. In short, Benedictine monasticism was the supreme civilizing influence in the barbarian West.

Pope Gregory the Great

The Benedictines carried out their great civilizing mission with the enthusiastic and invaluable support of the papacy. The alliance between these two institutions was consummated by the monk-pope, Gregory the Great, who recognized immediately how effective the Benedictines might be in spreading the Catholic faith and extending papal leadership far and wide across Christendom.

Pope Gregory was an important early-medieval scholar—a popularizer of Augustinian thoughts. But his theology, although highly influential in subsequent centuries, failed to rise much above the intellectual level of his age. His real genius lay in his keen understanding of human nature and his ability as an administrator and organizer. His *Pastoral Care*, a treatise on the duties and obligations of a bishop, is a masterpiece of practical wisdom and common sense. It answered a great need of the times and became one of the most widely read books in the Middle Ages.

Gregory loved the monastic life and ascended the papal throne with genuine regret. On hearing of his election he went into hiding and had to be dragged into the Roman basilica of St. Peter's to be consecrated. But once resigned to his new responsibilities, Gregory devoted all his energy to the extension of papal authority. Following in the tradition of Pope Leo I. Gregory the Great believed fervently that the pope, as successor of St. Peter, was the rightful ruler of the Church. He reorganized the financial structure of the papal estates and used the increased revenues for charitable works to ameliorate the wretched poverty of his age. His integrity, wisdom, and administrative ability won for him an almost regal position in Rome and central Italy, towering over the contemporary

Lombards and Byzantines who were then struggling for control of the peninsula. The reform of the Frankish Church was beyond his immediate powers. But he set in motion a process that would one day bring both France and Germany into the papal fold when he dispatched a group of Benedictine monks to convert heathen England.

The Conversion of England

The mission to England was led by the Benedictine St. Augustine (not to be confused with the great theologian of an earlier day, St. Augustine of Hippo). In 597, Augustine and his followers arrived in the English kingdom of Kent and began their momentous work. England was then divided into a number of independent barbarian kingdoms of which Kent was momentarily the most powerful, and Augustine was assured a friendly reception by the fact that the king of Kent had a Christian wife. The conversion progressed speedily, and on Whitsunday, 597, the king and thousands of his subjects were baptized. The chief town of the realm, "Kent City" or Canterbury, became the headquarters of the new Church, and Augustine himself became Canterbury's first archbishop.

During the decades that followed, the fortunes of English Benedictine Christianity rose and fell with the varying fortunes of the barbarian kingdoms. Kent declined, and by the mid-60s political power had shifted to the northernmost of the Anglo-Saxon states, Northumbria. This remote outpost became the scene of a deeply significant encounter between the two great creative forces of the age: Irish-Celtic Christianity moving southward from its monasteries in Scotland, and Roman-Benedictine Christianity moving northward from Kent.

Although the two movements shared a common faith, they had different cultural backgrounds, different notions of monastic life and ecclesiastical organization, and even different systems for calculating the date of Easter. At stake was England's future relationship with the Continent and the papacy; a Celtic victory might well have resulted in the isolation of England from the main course of Western Christian development. But at the Synod of Whitby in 664, the king of Northumbria decided in favor of Roman-Benedictine Christianity, and papal influence in England was assured. Five years later, in 669, the papacy sent the scholarly Theodore of Tarsus to assume the archbishopric of Canterbury and reorganize the English Church into a coherent hierarchial system. As a consequence of Northumbria's conversion and Archbishop Theodore's tireless efforts, England, only a century out of heathenism, became Europe's most vigorous and creative Christian society.

The Irish-Benedictine encounter in sev-

Cross Page from the Lindisfarne Gospels (c. A. D. 700), illustrating the artistic illuminations typical of the Northumbrian Renaissance.   (The Trustees of the British Museum)

enth-century Northumbria produced a significant cultural surge known as the Northumbrian Renaissance. The two traditions influenced and inspired one another to such an extent that the evolving civilization of the barbarian West reached its pinnacle in this remote land. Boldly executed illuminated manuscripts in the Celtic curvilinear style, a new script, a vigorous vernacular epic poetry, an impressive architecture—all contributed to the luster of Northumbrian civilization in the late 600s and the early 700s. This Northumbrian Renaissance centered in the great monasteries founded by Irish and Benedictine missionaries, particularly in the Benedictine monastery of Jarrow. Here the supreme scholar of the age, St. Bede the Venerable, spent his life.

Bede entered Jarrow as a child and remained there until his death in 735. The greatest of his many works, the *Ecclesiastical History of England,* displays a keen critical sense far superior to that of Bede's medieval predecessors and contemporaries. The *Ecclesiastical History* is our chief source for early English history. It reflects a remarkable cultural breadth and a penetrating mind, and establishes Bede as the foremost Christian intellectual since Augustine.

By Bede's death in 735 the Northumbrian kings had lost their political hegemony, and Northumbrian culture was beginning to fade. But the tradition of learning was carried from England back to the Continent during the eighth century by a group of intrepid Anglo-Saxon Benedictine missionaries. In the 740s the English monk St. Boniface reformed the Church in Frankland, infusing it with Benedictine idealism and binding it more closely to the papacy. Pope Gregory had now been in his grave for 140 years, but his spirit was still at work. St. Boniface and other English missionaries founded new Benedictine monasteries among the Germans east of the Rhine and began the long and difficult task of Christianizing and civilizing these savage peoples, just as Augustine and his monks had once Christianized heathen Kent. By the later 700s the cultural center of Christendom had shifted southward again from England to the rapidly rising empire of the Frankish leader Charlemagne, whose career will be traced in the following chapter. Significantly, the leading scholar in Charlemagne's kingdom was Alcuin, a Benedictine from Northumbria.

The Church and Western Civilization

The barbarian West differed from the Byzantine and Islamic East in innumerable ways, the most obvious being its far lower level of civilization. But even more important is the fact that the Western Church was able to reject caesaropapism and to develop more or less independently of the state. Church and state often worked hand in hand, yet the two were never merged as they were in Byzantium, Islam, and most ancient civilizations. The early Christian West was marked by a profound dichotomy —a separation between cultural leadership, which was ecclesiastical and monastic, and political power, which was in the hands of the barbarian kings. This dualism underlay the fluidity and dynamism of Western culture. It produced a creative tension that tended toward change rather than crystallization, toward an uninterrupted series of cultural climaxes, and toward ever-new intellectual and spiritual configurations. The heroic warrior culture of the Germanic states and the classical-Christian culture of Church and monastery remained always in the process of fusion yet never completely fused. The interplay between these two worlds governed the development of medieval civilization.

8
Carolingian Europe and the New Invasions

The Rise of the Carolingians

Just as the new Europe was aroused spiritually by the wide-ranging Benedictines, it was united politically by the new Carolingian dynasty of Frankish monarchs.* The original Frankish dynasty—the Merovingians—had declined over the centuries since Clovis's days from bloodthirsty autocrats to crowned fools. Their policy of dividing royal authority and crown lands among all the sons of a deceased king further weakened Merovingian authority, and by the later 600s all real power had passed to the aristocracy. The greatest Frankish noble family at this time, the Carolingians, had risen to power in northeastern Frankland and had established a firm grip on the chief viceregal office in the kingdom. The Carolingians became hereditary "mayors of the palace" of the Merovingian kings. In reality they were, by the late 600s, the military and political master of Frankland, leading their own armed retainers against internal rivals and commanding the Frankish host against foreign enemies. So it was that Charles Martel (714–741), a masterful and ruthless Carolingian mayor of the palace, led the Franks to victory over the Muslims at Tours in 732. Charles Martel's son, Pepin the Short, won for his family the Frankish crown itself, and Pepin's son, Charlemagne, won an empire.

The Coronation of Pepin (751)

By about 750, the Carolingian mayor, Pepin the Short (741–768), had hopes of establishing his own dynasty on the Frankish throne in place of the incompetent Merovingians. But the Merovingian kings, for all their weaknesses, retained the enormous prestige that Germanic royal dynasties always enjoyed. If the Carolingians aspired to replace them, they would have

* The dynasty has been termed "Carolingian" by later historians, after its greatest ruler, Charlemagne (Latin: *Carolus Magnus*).

to call on the most potent spiritual sanction available to their age: papal consecration. As mayors of the palace, the Carolingians had supported the reforming activities of St. Boniface and his English Benedictine monks in Frankland and had thereby established a warm relationship with the Benedictine's great ally, the papacy. Now, seeking papal support for a dynastic revolution, Pepin the Short could reasonably expect a favorable response from Rome.

The popes, for their part, had been seeking a defender against the Byzantines and the aggressive Lombards who had long been contending for political supremacy in Italy. The Carolingians would have seemed strong candidates for the role of papal champion. And by the mid-eighth century the pope was in desperate need of such a champion. For the Lombards, although they had by now adopted trinitarian Christianity, were an ominous threat to papal independence. And by 750 they were on a rampage, threatening not only the Byzantine territories in Italy but the lands of the pope himself. The Byzantines seemed neither able nor inclined to protect the papacy. Over the years the Eastern and Western Churches had been drifting apart, and by 750 they were separated by major theological differences. If Pepin the Short needed the papacy, the papacy needed Pepin even more.

Hence, the alliance was struck. Pepin was anointed King of the Franks by the Pope's representative, St. Boniface, in 751 and by the pope himself three years later. Thus Pepin became a king not by mere force but by the supernatural potency of the royal anointing. The last of the Merovingians were packed off to a monastery, and shortly thereafter Pepin paid his debt by leading an army into Italy. Defeating the Lombards in battle he granted the pope a large territory around Rome. This "Donation of Pepin" had the immediate effect of relieving the papacy of the dangerous Lombard pressure. More important, the lands that the pope received from Pepin became the nucleus of the Papal States, which would dominate central Italy until the late nineteenth century.

Charlemagne (768–814)

Pepin, for all his accomplishments, was overshadowed by his far more celebrated son. Charles the Great, or Charlemagne, was a phenomenally gifted military commander, a statesmen of rare skill, a friend of learning, and a monarch possessed of a deep sense of responsibility for the welfare of his society. Like all successful rulers of his time, he was a warrior-king. He led his armies on yearly campaigns as a matter of course; the decision to be made each year was not whether to fight but whom to fight. Only gradually did Charlemagne develop a notion of Christian mission and a program of unifying and systematically expanding the Christian

West. At the behest of the papacy, he conquered Lombard Italy in 774 and incorporated it into his growing empire. He carved out at Muslim expense a "Spanish March" on the Iberian side of the Pyrenees, centered in Barcelona. He conquered and absorbed Bavaria, organizing its easternmost district into a forward defensive barrier against the Slavs. This East March or *Ostmark* became the nucleus of a new state later to be called Austria. Most important of all, he campaigned intermittently for more than 30 years in northern Germany against the pagan Saxons (772–804). By the early ninth century the Frankish control of Saxony was assured, and in subsequent decades, through the tireless work of Benedictine monks, the Saxons were thoroughly Christianized. A century and a half later, Christian Saxons were governing the most powerful and enlightened state in Europe.

Charlemagne's armies, by incorporating central Germany into the new civilization, had succeeded where the Roman emperors had failed. By 800, Charlemagne was the master of Western Christendom. Only a few small Christian kingdoms in the British Isles and northwestern Spain remained outside his jurisdiction. On Christmas Day, 800, his accomplishment was given formal recognition when the pope placed the imperial crown on his head and acclaimed him "Emperor of the Romans." From the standpoint of legal theory, this coronation reconstituted the Roman Empire in the West after an interregnum of 324 years.

But Carolingian Europe differed radically from the Western Roman Empire of old. It was a land without large cities, thoroughly agrarian in economic organization, with its culture centered on the monastery and cathedral rather than the forum. Although Charlemagne extended his authority into Italy, Spain, and Germany, his capital and his heart remained in northern Frankland. Thus, Carolingian Europe no longer faced the Mediterranean. The axis of western culture had shifted northward. And this

Contemporary bronze figure of Charlemagne.
(Cliché des Musees Nationaux)

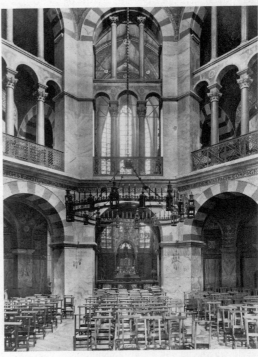

Charlemagne's palace church, Aachen, based on
San Vitale, Ravenna; the chandelier was added in
the twelfth century.   (Marburg/Art Reference
Bureau)

northward shift shaped Europe's development far into the future.

Agrarian Technology

The relative brightness of Charlemagne's age resulted from creative processes that had been at work during the preceding darker centuries. One of the most important of these processes was the development of a new agrarian technology that eventually increased the productivity of northern European farmlands well beyond the level of the old Roman Empire.

By the opening of the eighth century, the ineffective scratch plow of Roman times had been replaced in the northern districts of Western Europe by a heavy compound plow with wheels, colter, plowshare, and moldboard, which cut deeply into the soil, pulverized it, and turned it aside into ridges and furrows. This heavy plow—which may have been introduced from the Slavic lands in Eastern Europe—could be used in vast areas of rich, heavy soil where the Roman scratch plow was ineffective. It also accentuated the tendency toward dividing fields into long strips cultivated by the eight-ox teams the heavy plow required. Peasants now pooled their oxen and their labor in order to exploit the heavy plow, and in doing so they laid the foundation for the cooperative agricultural communities of medieval Europe, with their strong village councils regulating the division of labor and resources.

The coming of the heavy plow resulted in a significant change in the method of crop rotation. By the Carolingian age, much of northern Europe was beginning to adopt the three-field system in place of the two-field system characteristic of Roman times. Formerly, a typical farm had been divided into two fields, each of which, in turn, was planted one year and left fallow the next. This pattern continued in southern Europe throughout the Middle Ages. But the rich northern soils, newly opened by the heavy plow, did not require a full year's rest between crops. They were often divided now into three fields, each of which underwent a three-year cycle system of autumn planting, spring planting, and fallow. The three-field system increased food production significantly and brought unprecedented prosperity to northern Europe, perhaps contributing to the northward shift of the Carolingian era.

Meanwhile the water mill, which was used only occasionally in antiquity for grinding grain, had come into fairly widespread use on Carolingian farms. During the centuries following Charlemagne's death the water mill was put to new uses —to power the rising textile industry of the eleventh century and to drive trip hammers in forges. Thus, technological progress continued over the medieval centuries. By A.D. 1000 the coming of the horseshoe and a new, efficient horse collar —both apparently imported from Siberia or Central Asia—made possible the very gradual substitution of the horse for the less efficient ox on the richer north European farms. And in the twelfth century the windmill made its debut in the Euro-pean countryside. These post-Carolingian advances resulted in the greater productivity underlying the vital civilization of the twelfth and thirteenth centuries. Carolingian Europe profited from the earlier phase of this steady advance in agrarian technology.

Carolingian Renaissance

The significant intellectual revival known as the "Carolingian Renaissance" was largely a product of Charlemagne's concern for the welfare of the church and the perpetuation of Classical-Christian culture. Charlemagne assembled scholars from all over Europe. These Carolingian writers produced no lofty abstract thought, or original philosophical or theological systems, no institutions of higher learning. Rather, they sought to revive and preserve the rudiments of the Classical-Christian intellectual tradition. Under the leadership of the Englishman Alcuin of York they set about to rescue continental culture from the pit of ignorance into which it was sinking. Alcuin prepared an accurate new edition of the Bible, purged of the scribal errors that had crept into it over the centuries, thereby saving Western Christian culture from the confusion arising from the corruption of its fundamental text. Carolingian scholars also purified the church liturgy and encouraged the preaching of sermons. They carried further the monastic reforms begun in Frankland by earlier Benedictines and saw to it that every major monastery had a school. They developed a new, standardized script—the Carolingian minuscule—to replace the varied and sometimes illegible scripts previously employed. And throughout the realm, monks set about copying manuscripts on an unprecedented scale.

With the gradual disintegration of Western European unity after Charlemagne's death in 814, the momentary fusion of political and spiritual energies slowly dissolved, yet the intellectual revival continued. In ninth- and tenth-century monasteries and cathedrals (particularly those of the recently conquered German districts), documents continued to be copied and schools continued to function. By the eleventh century, Europe was ready to build soaring and original intellectual edifices on its sturdy Carolingian foundations.

CAROLINGIAN CHRONOLOGY

714–741:	Rule of Charles Martel
732:	Arabs defeated at Tours
741–768:	Rule of Pepin the Short
751:	Pepin crowned king of the Franks. Merovingian Dynasty ends
768–814:	Reign of Charlemagne
772–804:	Charlemagne's Saxon Wars
800:	Charlemagne crowned Roman Emperor
843:	Treaty of Verdun

The Carolingian Breakdown

The economic and cultural revival under Charlemagne was reversed after his death by an internal political breakdown and new invasions from without. During the ninth and tenth centuries Europe struggled grimly against the attacks of Hungarians (Magyars) from Central Asia, Saracens (Muslims) from North Africa, and Vikings from Scandinavia. In addition to these external pressures, the empire suffered an internal breakdown under Charlemagne's immediate successors. In the Treaty of Verdun (843) the empire was divided among his three grandsons, and the division became permanent. The three kingdoms created by the Treaty of Verdun foreshadowed the political division of later Western Europe. The East Frankish realm became the nucleus of modern Germany; the West Frankish realm evolved directly into the kingdom of France. The Middle Kingdom stretched northward from Italy through Burgundy, Alsace, Lorraine, and the Netherlands and included considerable parts of what are now western Germany and eastern France. Its territories soon became fragmented and were to be the source of disputes between France and Germany over the next millennium.

Saracens and Magyars

The Saracens of the ninth and tenth centuries, unlike their Muslim predecessors in the seventh and eighth, came as brigands rather than conquerors and settlers. From their pirate nests in Africa, Spain, and the Mediterranean islands they attacked shipping, plundered coastal cities, and sailed up rivers to carry their devastation far inland.

St. Peter giving symbols of authority to Pope Leo III and Charlemagne—the pallium to Leo III, the imperial standard to Charlemagne, Mosaic in St. John's Lateran, Rome.   (Alinari/Art Reference Bureau)

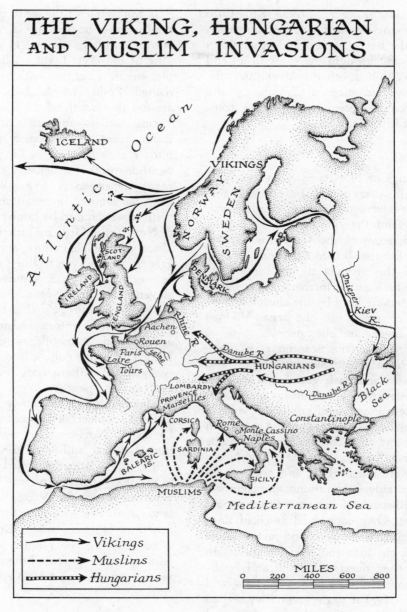

THE VIKING, HUNGARIAN AND MUSLIM INVASIONS

In 846 Saracen brigands raided Rome itself, and as late as 982 a Saracen force routed the army of King Otto II of Germany in southern Italy. But by then the raids were tapering off. Southern Europe, now bristling with fortifications, had learned to defend itself and was beginning to challenge Saracen dominion of the western Mediterranean.

The Hungarians (Magyars), fierce Altaic mounted nomads from the Asiatic steppes, settled in Hungary and, between the late 800s and 955, terrorized Germany and northern Italy. Hungarian raiding parties ranged far and wide, seeking defenseless settlements to plunder, avoiding fortified towns, and outriding and outmaneuvering the armies sent against them. But in time they became more sedentary, gave more attention to their farms, and lost much of their nomadic savagery. In 955, King Otto I of Germany crushed a large Hungarian army at the Battle of Lechfeld in southern Germany and brought the raids to an end at last. Within another half century the Hungarians had adopted Christianity and were becoming integrated into the community of Christian Europe.

The Vikings

The Vikings or Norsemen, were the most fearsome invaders of all. These redoubtable warrior-seafarers came from Scandinavia, the very land that had, centuries before, disgorged many of the Germanic barbarians into Europe. But to the ninth-century European—the product of countless Germanic-Celtic-Roman intermarriages, warlike still, but civilized by the church and by centuries of settled life—the pagan Vikings seemed a savage and alien people.

Then, as now, the Scandinavians were divided roughly into Swedes, Danes, and Norwegians, and each group had its own area of enterprise. The Danes concentrated on Northern France and England, the Norwegians on Scotland, Ireland, and the North Atlantic, and the Swedes on the Baltic shores and Russia. Yet the three Norse peoples were much alike, and one can regard their raids, explorations, and commercial activities as a single great international movement. They conquered much of England, terrorized France, and even sailed around Spain into the Mediterranean. In the East, they overran Finland and established a powerful state in Russia—the grand duchy of Kiev. Far to the west, they settled Iceland, discovered Greenland, and planted a short-lived colony on the coast of North America.

In the course of the tenth century, Christianity was beginning to penetrate the Norse world. In about 911 a Carolingian king of the West Franks, Charles the Simple, struck a bargain with a Viking leader named Rollo, whose band had settled around the mouth of the River Seine. The Viking settlers adopted Christianity, and Rollo swore his allegiance to Charles the Simple in return for the king's official recognition of the settlement as a legitimate royal dependency. Expanding gradually over subsequent generations, this Norse settlement came to be known as the duchy of Normandy. Little by little its inhabitants absorbed French culture and adopted the French tongue, yet retained much of their former vitality and wanderlust. By the eleventh century, Normandy was producing some of Europe's ablest knights, crusaders, administrators, and monks, and its armies and statebuilders were carrying French Christian culture into faraway lands —England, Southern Italy, Sicily, Antioch, and Muslim Spain.

Meanwhile, in Scandinavia itself centralized monarchies were developing in Denmark, Norway, and Sweden, and as their political authority grew, the Viking spirit was gradually tamed. Around the year 1000 Christianity was winning converts all across the Viking world. In Iceland, in Russia*—even in the kingdoms of Scandinavia itself—the ferocious Northmen were adopting the religion of the monks who had once so feared them. Scandinavia was becoming a part of Western European culture.

* Where the grand duke of Kiev adopted Byzantine Christianity in about 988.

9
Europe Survives the Siege

The invasions of the ninth and tenth centuries wrought notable changes in the political and social organization of Western Europe. Generally speaking, political authority tended to crumble into small, local units as cumbersome royal armies proved incapable of coping with the lightning raids. This was decidedly true in France, but less so in Germany where the monarchy, after a period of relative weakness, recovered spectacularly in the tenth century. In England, paradoxically, the hammer blows of the Danes ultimately led to the union of the several Anglo-Saxon states into a single English kingdom.

The Unification of England

In the late eighth century, on the eve of the Viking invasions, England was politically fragmented, as it had been ever since the Anglo-Saxon conquests. Its conversion to Christianity in the sixth and seventh centuries had produced a degree of ecclesiastical centralization but no political unity. Over the centuries, however, the smaller kingdoms had gradually been passing under the control of three larger ones—Northumbria in the north, Mercia in the midlands, and Wessex in the south. The Danish attacks of the ninth century destroyed the power of Wessex's rivals, clearing the field for the Wessex monarchy and thereby hastening the trend toward consolidation that was already underway.

King Alfred the Great

The Danes might well have conquered Wessex itself had it not been that at the moment of crisis a remarkable leader rose to the Wessex throne. Alfred the Great (871–899) did everything in his power to save his kingdom from the Vikings, fighting them, bribing them, constructing fortress-sanctuaries throughout the land, directing the building of an English fleet. And in the end, Wessex not only endured but expanded significantly under Alfred's

leadership. In the 880s a peace treaty between Alfred and the Danes gave Wessex most of southern and western England. The remainder of England—the "Danelaw"—remained hostile, but all non-Danish England was now united under King Alfred.

Like all successful leaders of the age Alfred was an exceedingly able warrior. But he was far more than that. He was a brilliant, imaginative organizer who systematized military recruitment and founded the English navy, seeing clearly that Christian Europe could not hope to drive back the Vikings without challenging them on the seas. He filled his land with fortresses which served both as defensive strongholds and as places of sanctuary for the agrarian population in time of war. And gradually, as the Danish tide was rolled back, new fortresses were built to secure the territories newly reconquered. Alfred clarified and rationalized the laws of his people, enforced them strictly, and ruled with an authority such as no Anglo-Saxon king had exercised before his time.

This remarkable monarch was also a scholar and a patron of learning. His intellectual environment was even less promising than Charlemagne's had been. The great days of Bede, Boniface, and Alcuin were far in the past, and by Alfred's time, Latin—the key to classical Christian culture —was almost unknown in England. Like Charlemagne, Alfred gathered scholars from far and wide—England, Wales, the Continent—and set them to work teaching Latin and translating Latin classics into the Anglo-Saxon language. Alfred himself participated in the work of translation, rendering such works as Boethius' *Consolation of Philosophy*, Pope Gregory's *Pastoral Care*, and Bede's *Ecclesiastical History* into the native tongue. In his translation of Boethius, Alfred added a wistful comment of his own: "In those days one never heard tell of ships armed for war." And in his preface to the *Pastoral Care* he alluded with nostalgia to the days "before everything was ravaged and burned, when England's churches overflowed with treasures and books." Alfred's intellectual revival even more than Charlemagne's, was a salvage operation rather than an outburst of originality. He was both modest and accurate when he described himself as one who wandered through a great forest collecting timber with which others could build.

Alfred's task of reconquest was carried on by his able successors in the first half of the tenth century. Midway through the century all England was in their hands, and the kings of Wessex had become the kings of England. Great numbers of Danish settlers still remained in northern and eastern England—the amalgamation of Danish and English customs required many generations —but the creative response of the Wessex kings to the Danish threat had transformed

and united the Anglo-Saxon world. Out of the agony of the invasions the English monarchy was born.

French Feudalism

In England the invasions stimulated the trend toward royal unification; in France they encouraged a shattering of political authority into small local units. This paradox can be explained in part by the fact that France, unlike England, was far too large for the Vikings to conquer. Although many of them settled in Normandy, the chief Norse threat to France came in the form of plundering expeditions rather than large conquering armies. Distances were too great, communications too primitive, and the national territorial army too unwieldy for the king to take the lead in defending his realm. Military responsibility descended to local lords who alone could hope to protect the countryside from the swift and terrible Viking assaults. The French Carolingians became increasingly powerless until at length, in 987, the crown passed to a new dynasty—the Capetians.* During the twelfth and thirteenth centuries the Capetian family produced some of France's most illustrious kings, but for the time being the new dynasty was as powerless as the old one. After 987, as before, the nobles overshadowed the king. About all one can say of the French monarchy in these dark years is that it survived.

The Viking Age witnessed the birth of feudalism in France. In a very real sense feudalism was a product of France's response to the invasions. Yet in another sense the Franks had long been drifting in a feudal direction. The roots of feudalism ran deep: one root was the honorable bond of fidelity and service of a warrior to his

* The decline of the later Carolingian kings of France and Germany is suggested by the various nicknames they received: Charles the Bald, Louis the Stammerer, Charles the Simple, Louis the Blind, Charles the Fat, Louis the Child, etc. One late Carolingian was called simply Boso.

lord, which characterized the lord-vassal relationship of late-Merovingian and early-Carolingian times, and the still earlier comitatus of the Germanic barbarians. Another root was the late-Roman and early-medieval concept of land-holding in return for certain services to the person who granted the land. An estate granted to a tenant in return for service was known as a *benefice*.

The Carolingians took an important step toward feudalism by joining the institutions of benefice and vassalage. There were several reasons for this step. For one thing money was in very short supply throughout the Early Middle Ages so that it was difficult for a ruler to support his soldiers with wages. Often the vassals of an important Frankish lord were fed and sheltered in his household. Indeed, the "household knight" persisted throughout the feudal age. But as their military importance grew these warrior-vassals exhibited an ever-increasing hunger for land. Their lords were therefore under considerable pressure to grant them estates—benefices—in return for their loyalty and service.

This tendency was associated with a shift in Frankish military tactics. In Merovingian times the Franks had fought chiefly with foot soldiers and light cavalry. Thereafter, heavy cavalry became increasingly important. By the tenth century the Frankish warrior *par excellence* was the armored, mounted knight. A warrior of this sort needed a fine mount, heavy armor and weapons, several attendants, and many years of training. Hence the tendency for a lord to support his knightly vassals by granting them estates in return for their service. The knight did not, of course, labor on his own fields; rather he administered them and collected dues, chiefly in kind from his peasants.

The Carolingian military vassal was typically a knight. As knightly tactics came more and more to dominate warfare the custom of vassalage spread widely. The great Frankish magnates of Charlemagne's time pledged their allegiance to their em-

peror and thereby recognized that they were his vassals and he their lord. Moreover, these royal vassals had vassals of their own who owed primary allegiance to their immediate lords rather than to the emperor. Charlemagne himself approved of this practice and encouraged the free men of his realm to become vassals of his magnates. In time of war these vassals of vassals (or subvassals) were expected to join their lords' contingents in the royal army. The centrifugal tendencies implicit in such an arrangement are obvious. Yet Charlemagne, lacking a civil service or adequate funds to hire a professional army of his own, was obliged to depend on this potentially unstable hierarchy of authority and allegiance.

With the removal of Charlemagne's commanding personality, and under the pressure of the invasions, the rickety hierarchy began to crumble into its component parts. Charlemagne's old territorial officials, the dukes, counts, and margraves, backed by their own vassals, tended increasingly to usurp royal rights, revenues, and prerogatives. They administered justice and collected taxes without regard for the royal will. In time, they built castles and assumed all responsibility for the defense of their districts. Nominally these feudal magnates remained vassals of the kings of France, but they soon became too powerful to be coerced by the crown. Their authority was limited chiefly by the independence of their own vassals who began to create subvassals or sub-subvassals of their own. At the height of the feudal age the lord-vassal relationship might run down through some ten or twenty levels; there was scarcely a vassal to be found who was not the lord of some still lower vassal.

The ultimate consequences of these developments have been described as "feudal anarchy." In a sense the term is well chosen, but it should not mislead us into thinking of feudalism simply as a "bad thing." Given the instability of the Carolingian Empire and the desperate plight of

France in the Viking era, feudalism emerges as a realistic accommodation to the hard facts of the age. It should never be forgotten that whereas Roman Europe succumbed to barbarian invasions, Feudal Europe survived its invaders and ultimately absorbed them.

French feudalism reached its height in the tenth and eleventh centuries. Its key institution was the military benefice, the estate granted by a lord to his vassal in return for allegiance and service—primarily knightly military service. This military benefice was commonly known as a *fief* (rhyming with beef).* It was a logical response to the desperate requirements of local defense, the perpetuation of at least some degree of political authority, and the scarcity of money which necessitated paying for service in land rather than wages. A great lord would grant an estate—a fief— to his vassal. The vassal might then grant a part of the estate—another fief—to a vassal of his own. And so on and on, down and down, the process of enfeoffment went. The result was a hierarchically organized landed knightly aristocracy. Each knight gave homage and fealty—that is, the pledge of his personal allegiance—to his immediate lord; each lived off the labor and dues of a dependent peasantry which tilled the fields that his fief embraced; each administered a court and dispensed justice to those below him.

Such were the essential ingredients of feudalism. The term is extremely difficult to define and has been frequently abused and misunderstood. If we wish to put the whole institution in a nutshell we can do no better than repeat the description of medieval feudalism's greatest modern scholar, the French historian Marc Bloch:

A subject peasantry; widespread use of the service tenement (that is, the fief) instead of a salary, which was out of the question; the supremacy of a class of specialized warriors;

* The Latin word for "fief" is *feudum*. Hence, our modern term, "feudalism"—a system based on the *feudum* or fief.

ties of obedience and protection which bind man to man and, within the warrior class, assume the distinctive form called vassalage; fragmentation of authority—leading inevitably to disorder; and in the midst of all this, the survival of other forms of association, family and state . . . —such then seem to be the fundamental features of European feudalism.*

With this description in mind it may be helpful to emphasize some of the things that feudalism was not. It was not, for one thing, a universal and symmetrical system. Born in northern France in the Viking age it spread across Europe, taking on many different forms as it expanded into other lands. In northern France itself it varied widely from one region to another. It by no means encompassed all the land, for even at its height many landowners owed no feudal obligations and had no feudal ties. The feudal hierarchy or feudal "pyramid" was riddled with ambiguities: a single vassal might hold several fiefs from several lords; a lord might receive a fief from his own vassal, thereby putting himself in the extraordinary position of being his vassal's vassal. The degree of confusion possible in feudalism can best be appreciated by examining a typical document of the age:

I, John of Toul, affirm that I am the vassal of the Lady Beatrice, countess of Troyes, and of her son Theobald, count of Champagne, against every creature living or dead, excepting my allegiance to Lord Enjourand of Coucy, Lord John of Arcis, and the count of Grandpré. If it should happen that the count of Grandpré should be at war with the countess and count of Champagne in his own quarrel, I will aid the count of Grandpré in my own person and will aid the count and countess of Champagne by sending them the knights whose services I owe them from the fief which I hold of them.

So much for feudal order.

Feudalism was not, in its heyday, associated with the romantic knight errant, the

* Bloch, *Feudal Society, II,* 446.

many-turreted castle, or the lady fair. The knight of the ninth, tenth, and eleventh centuries was a rough-hewn warrior. His armor was simple, his horse was tough, his castle was a crude wooden tower atop an earthen mound, and his lady fair was any available wench. Chivalry developed after a time, to be sure, but not until the foundations of the old feudal order were being eroded by the revival of commerce and a money economy, and by stronger monarchies. Only then did the knight seek to disguise his declining usefulness by turning to elaborate shining armor, lace and ruffles, courtly phrases, and wedding-cake castles.

Feudalism was not entirely military. The vassal owed his lord not only his military service but a variety of additional obligations as well. Among these were the duty to join his lord's retinue on tours of the countryside; to serve, when summoned, in his lord's court of justice; to feed, house, and entertain his lord and his lord's retinue on their all-too-frequent visits; to give money to his lord on a variety of specified occasions; to contribute to his lord's ransom should he be captured in battle. Early in its history the fief became hereditary. The lord, however, retained the right to confiscate it should his vassal die without heirs, to supervise and exploit it during a minority, and to exercise a power of veto over the marriage of a female fief-holder. In return for such rights as these the lord was obliged to protect and uphold the interests of his vassals. The very essence of feudalism was the notion of reciprocal rights and obligations. Consequently the feudal outlook played a key role in steering medieval Europe away from autocracy.

Feudalism was both a military system and a political system. With military responsibility went political power. As the kings of West Frankland demonstrated an ever-increasing incapacity to cope with the invasions or keep peace in the countryside, sovereignty tended to descend to the level of the greater feudal lords. Although nom-inally royal vassals, these magnates were in effect powers unto themselves, ruling their own territories without royal interference and maintaining their own courts and administrative systems as well as their own armies. In the days of the Viking raids many of these magnates had extreme difficulty in controlling their own turbulent vassals; feudal tenants several steps down in the pyramid were often able to behave as though they had no real superiors. Subvassals with their own courts and armies were frequently in a position to defy their lords. It is difficult therefore to identify the real locus of political power in early feudal France. Sovereignty was spread up and down the aristocratic hierachy, and a lord's real power depended upon his military prowess, his ambition, and the firmness of his leadership.

The feudal chaos of the ninth and tenth centuries, with its extreme fragmentation of sovereignty and its incessant private wars, gradually yielded to a more orderly regime as dukes and counts consolidated their authority over large districts such as Anjou, Normandy, and Flanders. In the eleventh and twelfth centuries royal governments grew stronger, yet the feudal lords remained powerful, drawing their strength from their fiefs. Their prerogatives, and their contractual relationship with the monarchy, gave them a degree of autonomy that was based on both legal theory and political reality. Often they cooperated with the monarchy in governing society, but at times they acted, in their own interest, to curb the autocratic impulses of an ambitious king. Like the church, the feudal aristocracy helped to shield medieval Western Europe from the royal absolutism common to most civilizations. The politics of high-medieval Christendom were marked not by the unchallenged rule of priest-kings but by the ever-changing power relationships and creative tensions between monarchy, landed aristocracy, and international church.

THE HOLY ROMAN EMPIRE IN 962

North Sea

Baltic Sea

K. OF DEN.

SLAVS

FRISIA

SAXONY

Rhine R.

Elbe R.

LORRAINE

FRANCONIA

BOHEMIA

FRANCE

Lechfeld

Danube R.

SWABIA

BAVARIA

CARINTHIA   HUNGARIANS

KINGDOM OF BURGUNDY

Rhone R.

K D M.   OF   ITALY

Venice

KDM. OF CROATIA

SERVIA

CORSICA

Rome

BENEVENTO

APULIA

SARDINIA

CALABRIA

SICILY

0   100   200   300 MILES

The Holy Roman Empire
The Five Stem Duchies

The Decline and Revival of the German Monarchy

East Frankland—which evolved directly into the kingdom of Germany—was attacked first by the Vikings and later by Hungarian horsemen of the east. The late-Carolingian kings of Germany—the successors of Charlemagne's grandson who had gained East Frankland in 843 at the Treaty of Verdun—proved incapable of coping with the Hungarian raids. As in France, real authority descended to the great magnates of the realm. Since much of Germany had been only recently incorporated into Western Christendom, the tribal consciousness of Saxons, Bavarians, and Swabians was still strong, and when the kings faltered, it was dukes of these "tribal duchies" who seized power.

The German Carolingian line ended in 911, and within a few years the dukes of Saxony had established a new royal dynasty. It was under the Saxon dynasty, and particularly under its greatest representative, Otto I, that the particularistic trend was reversed and the king won supremacy.

Otto I—"the Great" (936–973)—based his power on three significant achievements. First, he defended Germany against the Hungarians and crushed them militarily at the Battle of Lechfeld (955), thus opening Germany's eastern frontier to gradual eastward penetration by German-Christian culture. Second, he established royal supremacy over the other tribal duchies, putting down rebellions and recovering royal rights and revenues. And third, he extended German royal control into the crumbling unstable Middle Kingdom that had been created by the Treaty of Verdun in 843 and had begun to disintegrate soon afterward. The dukes of Swabia and Bavaria had notions of seizing the Burgundian and Italian portions of this defunct state. Otto the Great, anxious to forestall them, led his own armies into Italy and, in 962, was crowned Roman emperor by the pope.

It is the coronation of Otto I in 962, rather than the coronation of Charlemagne in 800, that marks the true genesis of the medieval Holy Roman Empire. Otto's empire differed from Charlemagne's chiefly in the fact that it was German, or German-Italian—not a universal empire as Charlemagne's had pretended to be. Otto and his imperial successors exercised no jurisdiction over France nor the remainder of Western Christendom. The medieval Holy Roman Empire had its roots deep in the soil of Germany, and most of the emperors subordinated imperial interests to those of the German monarchy.

Otto and his heirs were never very successful in ruling Italy, but in Germany the emperor was supreme. The great magnates were, for the most part, his obedient vassals. The church was in his power, and he controlled the important ecclesiastical appointments, handpicking his great bishops and abbots and using them as his trusted lieutenants in the royal administration. After 962 the German monarchy was even moderately successful in appointing popes. The emperor was regarded as *rex et sacerdos*, king and priest, sanctified by the holy anointing at his coronation. He was the vicar of God, the living symbol of Christ the King, the "natural" leader of the imperial church. There would come a time when the church, under papal leadership, would rebel against this imperial system and ideology, but in Otto the Great's age the time was still far-off.

Otto's remarkable reign gave rise to an intellectual revival that flowered under his two successors, Otto II (973–983) and Otto III (983–1002). This "Ottonian Renaissance" produced talented artists and a group of able administrators and scholars, the most brilliant of whom was Gerbert of Aurillac—later Pope Sylvester II (d. 1003).

The Ottonian crown, tenth century. (Kunsthistorisches Museum, Vienna)

Gerbert visited Spain and returned with a good grasp of Islamic science. The Arab intellectual legacy was beginning to filter into Western Christendom at last. A master of classical literature, logic, mathematics, and science, Gerbert astonished his age by teaching the Greco–Arab doctrine that the earth was spherical. Rumors circulated that he was a wizard in league with the devil, but the rumors were dampened by his elevation to the papacy. Gerbert was no wizard. Rather, he was a herald of the intellectual awakening that Europe was about to undergo—a harbinger of the High Middle Ages.

Europe on the Eve of the High Middle Ages

By 1050 both England and Germany were relatively stable, well-organized kingdoms. The French monarchy remained weak, but its hour was approaching, and meanwhile French feudal principalities such as Normandy, Flanders, and Anjou were achieving political cohesion. Warfare was still endemic, but it was beginning to lessen as Europe advanced toward political stability. Above all, the invasions were over—the siege had ended—and Western Europe would remain untroubled by outside invaders for the next millennium. Hungary and the Scandinavian world were being absorbed into Christendom, and Islam was by now on the defensive.

Throughout Western Christendom, food production continued to rise with the gradual improvements in agricultural technology and the slowly increasing pacification of the countryside. Beneath the level of the ecclesiastical, political, and military aristocracy, 80 to 90 percent of the population continued to labor on the land. Agrarian organization was almost infinitely diverse: medieval agricultural units ranged from small independent farms to large manors divided between the peasants' fields and the lord's demesne fields.* The peasants themselves varied from slaves to freemen, although slaves were sharply declining in number between the ninth and eleventh centuries and the majority of peasants—the serfs or villains—were neither completely free nor completely enslaved. Like the old Roman *coloni*, they were bound to their land. They owed their manorial lord various dues, chiefly in crops, and were normally expected to labor for a certain number of days per week on their lord's fields. But they were not slaves—they could neither be sold nor be deprived of their hereditary fields. After paying manorial dues, they could keep the remaining produce of their lands, and an efficient serf with good land might hope to prosper. Although hardly affluent, they appear to have been distinctly better off than the peasantry of the ancient civilizations and of medieval Byzantium and Islam. Western Europe was developing into the first major nonslave civilization in human history.

By the mid-eleventh century Western Christendom was beginning to draw abreast of its two neighboring civilizations in political power and in intellectual and cultural vitality. Byzantium and Islam, having dominated Western Eurasia and North Africa during the early middle ages, were both entering periods of political turbulence and decline. But in Western Europe agricultural productivity was increasing, the population was expanding, commerce was quickening, political cohesion was growing, great Romanesque churches were rising, minds were awakening. In the church an impulse toward renewal was galvanizing the spiritual life of the west. Reform monasteries were spreading across the land, and the papacy was about to emerge from its long

* Manorialism, which regulated the peasants lives and their relations with their lords, should not be confused with feudalism, which regulated the relations of the nobles with their king and among themselves.

passivity to challenge the traditional secular dominion over the Church. Western Christendom was on the threshold of an immense creative surge.

CHRONOLOGY OF THE AGE OF SIEGE AND ITS AFTERMATH

England

c.787:	First Danish raid
871–899:	Reign of Alfred
c.954:	Reconquest of Danelaw completed

France

814:	Charlemagne's death
843:	Treaty of Verdun
c.911:	Duchy of Normandy established
987:	Capetians replace Carolingians as Kings of France

Germany

814:	Charlemagne's death
843:	Treaty of Verdun
936–973:	Reign of Otto the Great
955:	Otto defeats Hungarians at Lechfeld
962:	Otto crowned Roman Emperor
973–983:	Reign of Otto II
983–1002:	Reign of Otto III
1003:	Gerbert of Aurillac dies

SUGGESTED READINGS

The asterisk indicates a paperback edition.

John W. Barker, *Justinian and the Later Roman Empire* (Madison, Wisc.: University of Wisconsin Press, 1966).

J. M. Hussey, *The Byzantine World* (*New York: Harper and Row, 1961).

G. Ostrogorsky, *History of the Byzantine State* (New Brunswick, N.J.: Rutgers University Press, rev. ed., 1969).

A. J. Arberry, ed., *Aspects of Islamic Civilization* (*Ann Arbor, Mich.: Ann Arbor Paperbacks, 1957).

N. J. Dawood, trans. *The Thousand and One Nights* (*Baltimore, Md.: Penguin Books, 1954).

H. A. R. Gibb, *Mohammedanism: An Historical Survey* (*New York: Oxford University Press, 2nd ed., 1953).

Gustave E. von Grunebaum, *Medieval Islam* (*Chicago: Phoenix Books, 2nd ed., 1961).

P. K. Hitti, *History of the Arabs* (*New York: St. Martin's Press, 6th ed., 1958).

Marc Bloch, *Feudal Society*, trans. by L. A. Manyon (*Chicago: University of Chicago Press, 1961. 2 Vols.).

Marc Bloch, *French Rural History*, trans. by J. Sondheimer (Berkeley and Los Angeles: University of California Press, 1966).

Jacques Boussard, *The Civilization of Charlemagne*, trans. by Frances Partridge. (*New York: World University Library, 1968).

Christopher Dawson, *The Making of Europe* (*New York: Meridian, 1946).

Einhard, *Life of Charlemagne*, trans. by S. E. Turner (*Ann Arbor, Mich.: Ann Arbor Paperbacks, 1960).

F. L. Ganshof, *Feudalism*, trans. by P. Grierson (*New York: Harper and Row, 2nd ed., 1961).

M. L. W. Laistner, *Thought and Letters in Western Europe*, A.D. 500–900. (*London: Methuen, 2nd ed., 1955).

Robert Latouche, *The Birth of Western Economy*, trans. by E. M. Wilkinson (*New York: Barnes and Noble, 1961).

H. R. Loyn, *Anglo-Saxon England and the Norman Conquest* (New York: St. Martin's Press, 1963).

P. H. Sawyer, *The Age of the Vikings* (New York: St. Martin's Press, 1962).

Lynn White, jr., *Medieval Technology and Social Change* (*New York: Oxford University Press, 1962).

Part 4 The High Middle Ages: The First Flowering of European Culture

10
Economic Revolution and New Frontiers

The High Middle Ages: 1050–1300

History, it has often been said, is a seamless web. But the human mind can only cope with the flow of historical reality by dividing it into arbitrary chronological units —forcing it into compartments of the historian's own making. In this sense every historical "period" is a kind of falsehood— an affront to the continuity of human development. Yet unless we concoct historical epochs, unless we invent ages, unless we force the past into some relatively tidy chronological framework, we cannot make history intelligible to the human mind. Thus the historian speaks of "Classical Antiquity," "The Early Middle Ages," "The Renaissance," and the like. These are all historical lies, to be sure, but they are necessary lies—white lies—without which the past would have little meaning. It is possible, of course, to subdivide the past into totally different eras than the traditional ones (for example, "Europe in the Making: A. D. 250–1100," "Pre-Industrial Europe: 1100–1789"). But we cannot do without eras altogether; nor should we ever forget that they are inventions of our own.

The term *High Middle Ages* has been applied to the great cultural surge of the later eleventh, twelfth, and thirteenth centuries. The surge did not occur everywhere in Western Christendom at a single moment. Its coming was gradual and uneven. Ever since the ebbing of the Viking, Hungarian, and Saracen invasions, many decades prior to 1050, Western Europe had been pulsing with new creative energy. But, broadly speaking, the scope and intensity of the revival did not become evident until after the mid-eleventh century. By the century's end, Europe's lively commerce and bustling towns, her intellectual vigor and growing political cohesion, her military expansion and her heightened religious enthusiasm left no doubt that potent new forces were at work—that Western Christendom had at last become a mature civilization.

The causes of an immense culture awakening such as occurred in the High Middle Ages are varied and obscure. One essential element was the ending of the invasions and the increasing political stability that followed. We know that in the eleventh century Europe's population was beginning to rise sharply and that its food production was growing. Whether increased productivity led to increased population or vice versa is difficult to say, but productivity could not have risen as it did without the improvements in agrarian technology that had occurred during the preceding centuries.

The Growth of Towns

The growth in productivity and population was accompanied by a significant commercial revival and a general reawakening of urban life. And the new towns, in turn, became the centers of a reinvigorated culture. The frequent human contacts arising from town life stimulated thought and art. The cathedral and the university, two of the supreme achievements of high-medieval culture, were both urban phenomena; the Franciscan order, the most dynamic religious institution of the age, devoted itself primarily to urban evangelism. Yet the towns were also, and above all, centers of commercial and industrial enterprise. The high-medieval economy remained fundamentally agrarian, but the towns were the great economic and cultural catalysts of the era.

The new towns, unlike the administrative-military towns of the Western Roman Empire or the episcopal towns of the Early Middle Ages, were economically self-supporting. Instead of depending on the labor and taxes of the countryside, the towns lived off the fruits of their own merchant and industrial activities. Small, foul, disease-ridden, and often torn by internal conflict, they were Western Europe's first cities in the modern sense.

The growth of the towns corresponded to the general upsurge of commerce. Sometimes the towns originated as suburbs of older cathedral towns, sometimes as trading posts outside the walls of castles. By 1100 they were springing up all over Europe, but they were concentrated most densely in Flanders and northern Italy, where the opportunities of international commerce were first exploited.

The greatest Italian city of the age was Venice, long a Byzantine dependency but by this time an independent commercial republic that carried on a lucrative trade with Constantinople and the East. Other Italian coastal towns—Genoa, Pisa, and Amalfi—soon followed Venice into the profitable markets of the eastern Mediterranean, and their commerce brought vigorous new life to inland towns such as Florence and Milan. The Muslims were all but driven from the seas, and Italian merchants dominated the Mediterranean.

The Flemish towns grew rich from the commerce of the North, trading with northern France and the British Isles, the Rhineland, and the Baltic coast. Both they and the northern Italian towns became manufacturing as well as commercial centers, producing woolen cloth in large quantities. Textile production developed into the major manufacturing enterprise of the age. As the twelfth and thirteenth centuries progressed, towns were rising and prospering in England, France, and Germany. While the Germans were pushing eastward along the Baltic shore, the thriving towns of old Germany were sending out numerous commercial colonies into the new territories—colonies which themselves became important towns. The North German towns, working collectively, came in time to dominate the Baltic trade and developed far-flung commercial links that stretched from Western Europe into Russia. Eventually, these towns formed themselves into an interurban confederation known as the Hanseatic League, establishing commercial colonies in such western cities as Bruges and London. Even before the advent of the

German Hanseatic League, the towns of northern Italy had organized for mutual protection into a Lombard League.

This tendency toward confederation illustrates the townsmen's need to combine forces against the repression of the old order. The Lombard League struggled for independence from the Holy Roman Empire. And, on a smaller scale, a great many towns had to fight for their autonomy against the monarchs, bishops, or feudal lords on whose lands the town had risen. Only by collective action could the town merchants win the privileges essential to their new vocation: personal freedom from servile status, freedom of movement, freedom from inordinate tolls at every bridge or feudal boundary; the right to own property in the town, to be judged by the town court, to execute commercial contracts, and to buy and sell freely. Collective action expressed itself through tightly regulated merchant guilds, and during the twelfth and thirteenth centuries a number of lords, either through farsightedness or through coercion—or for a price—were issuing town charters that guaranteed many of these rights. Indeed, some lords began founding and chartering new towns on their own initiative.

The charters tended to transform the towns into semiautonomous political and legal entities, each with its own government, its own court, its own tax-collecting agencies, and its own laws. Taxes continued to be paid to the lords in most cases, but they were paid collectively rather than individually.

Within the towns themselves, class distinctions were sharpening. The guilds, composed of merchants who engaged in long-distance trade, tended to dominate, and the craftsmen were, at least at first, in a subordinate status. Before long, however, craftsmen were making their weight felt by combining into various craft guilds. As time progressed, an urban working class grew increasingly numerous, and as conflicts between townsmen and their external

lords gradually eased, class conflicts among townsmen grew increasingly severe.

Yet throughout the greater part of the High Middle Ages the towns were avenues to personal freedom and commerical success, astir with new life and bursting with energy. The wealth that they produced was beginning to transform the European economy. Feudalism changed as kings and lords acquired the wealth necessary to replace landed knights with mercenaries in their armies and to replace feudal magnates with professional judges and bureaucrats in their courts and administration. The feudal aristocracy remained strong, but the traditional feudal concept of service in return for land tenure was dissolving.

Agrarian life, too, was changing. Capital and labor were now available to carve out extensive new farm sites from forest and marsh. The great primeval forests of northern Europe were reduced to scattered woods, swamps and marshes were drained, and vast new territories were opened to cultivation. Agricultural surpluses could now be sold to townsmen and thereby converted into cash. Slavery all but vanished, and serfs were freed on a large scale. With the opening of new lands, a competition developed for peasant settlers, and peasant communities were often granted the status and privileges of chartered communes. High-medievel Europe was a buoyant, prosperous society—a society in process of change and growth, which expanded inwardly through the clearing of forest and swamp, and outwardly through the conquest and settlement of vast new territories.

Territorial Expansion

The open, expanding frontier is one of the most characteristic aspects of Europe in the High Middle Ages. Considerable areas of the Arab, Byzantine, and Slavic worlds were incorporated within the ballooning boundaries of Western Christendom, intensifying Europe's spirit of enterprise and adding wealth to its flourishing economy.

Western Christendom had been expanding ever since 732, and since about 1000 it had pushed far to the north and east through the conversion of regions such as Scandinavia, Hungary, Bohemia, and Poland. North of the Balkans and west of Russia, most Slavic peoples accepted Catholic Christianity rather than Byzantine Orthodoxy. Indeed, Hungary, Bohemia, and Poland, at one time or another, all acknowledged the political lordship of the pope.

During the High Middle Ages, the population boom produced multitudes of landless aristocratic younger sons who sought land and glory on Christendom's frontiers. The church, always eager for new converts, supported them. The townsmen, seeking ever larger fields for commercial enterprise, encouraged and sometimes financed them.

And the proliferating peasantry served as a potential labor force for the newly conquered lands.

Reconquest of Spain

Thus it was that knightly adventurers from all over Christendom—and particularly from feudal France—streamed southward into Spain in the eleventh century to aid the Iberian Christian kingdoms in their struggle with Islam. The great Muslim caliphate of Cordova had disintegrated after 1002 into small, warring fragments, and the Christians seized the opportunity. Often the reconquest was delayed by wars among the Christian kingdoms themselves. But at length, in 1085, the Christian kingdom of Castile captured the great Muslim city of Toledo, which thenceforth became a crucial contact point between Islamic and

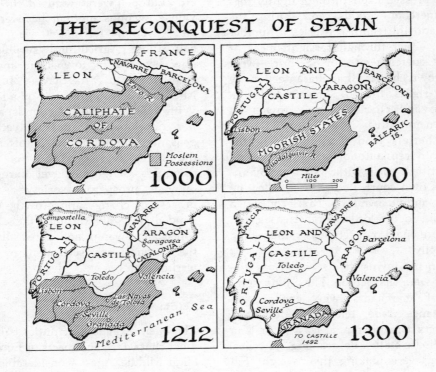

Christian culture. Here, numerous Arabic scientific and philosophical works were translated into Latin and then disseminated throughout Europe to challenge and invigorate the Western mind.

Early in the twelfth century the Christian Kingdom of Aragon, contesting Castile's supremacy, took the offensive against the Moors.* In 1140 Aragon strengthened itself by uniting with Catalonia—the wealthy state around Barcelona which had once been Charlemagne's Spanish March. But further inter-Christian warfare delayed the reconquest until 1212, when Pope Innocent III proclaimed a crusade against the Moors. Advancing from Toledo with a pan-Iberian army, the king of Castile won a decisive victory at Las Navas de Tolosa, permanently crippling Moorish power. Cordova fell to a Castile in 1236, and by the 1260s the Moors were confined to the small southern Kingdom of Granada, where they remained until 1492. Castile now dominated central Spain, and Christian peasants were imported en mass to resettle the conquired lands. Aragon, meanwhile, occupied the Muslim islands of the western Mediterranean and won a powerful maritime empire. Thus, the High Middle Ages witnessed the Christianization of nearly all the Iberian Peninsula and its division into two strong Christian kingdoms and several weaker ones.

Southern Italy and Sicily

Probably the most vigorous and militant force in Europe's eleventh-century awakening was the warrior-aristocracy of Normandy—largely Viking in ancestry but now thoroughly adapted to French culture. These Norman knights—French in tongue, Christian in faith, feudal in social organization—plied their arms across the length and breadth of Europe in the reconquest of

---

* By then most of Muslim Spain was ruled by North African Berbers who, having also conquered Morocco, were called Moors in Europe.

Spain, on the Crusades to the Holy Land, on the battlefields of England and France, and in southern Italy and Sicily. Normandy itself was growing in prosperity and political centralization, and an ever-increasing population pressure drove the greedy and adventurous Norman warriors far and wide on distant enterprises.

During the course of the eleventh century the Normans became masters of southern Italy and Sicily. They came first as mercenaries to serve in the chaotic south-Italian political struggles between Byzantine coastal cities, Lombard principalities, and rising seaport republics such as Naples and Amalfi. Within a few decades the Normans had overthrown their paymasters. By the close of the eleventh century they had won southern Italy for themselves and had conquered Muslim Sicily as well. And in 1130, the Norman leader Roger the Great (d. 1154) fused Sicily and southern Italy into a single kingdom and became its first king.

Roger the Great and his successors ruled firmly but tolerantly over the kingdom of Sicily and southern Italy, with its variety of peoples, faiths, customs, and tongues. Here, a synthesis was achieved of Byzantine, Islamic, Lombard, and northern French cultural traditions, and a highly effective political structure was created out of the Byzantine and Islamic administrative machinery that the Normans inherited and shaped. The Sicilian capital of Palermo, with its superb harbor and bustling international commerce, its impressive palace and luxurious villas, was known as the city of the threefold tongue. Islamic, Byzantine, and Western scholars worked under royal patronage, providing Western Christendom with Latin translations of Arabic and Greek texts, and doing important original work of their own. East and west met in Roger the Great's glittering, sundrenched realm, and worked creatively together to make his kingdom the most sophisticated state of its day.

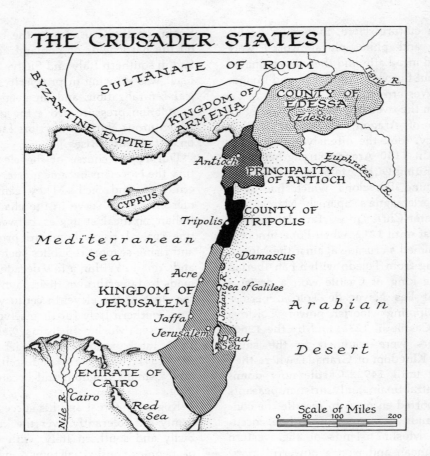

The Crusades

The Crusades to the Holy Land were the most self-conscious acts of Western Christian expansionism in the High Middle Ages, although not the most lasting. They arose in response to the conquests in the Near East of the recently Islamized Seljuk Turks and, in particular, a great Turkish victory over Byzantium at Manzikert (1071), which gave the Turks control of Anatolia. When Constantinople appealed to the West for help, Western Christendom, under the leadership of a reinvigorated papacy, responded emphatically.

The Crusades represented a fusion of three characteristic impulses of medieval man: sanctity, pugnacity, and greed. All three were essential. Without Christian idealism the Crusades would have been inconceivable, yet the pious dream of liber-

ating Jerusalem from the infidel was mightily reinforced by the lure of adventure, new lands, and riches. And to the Italian towns, which financed and provided transportation for many of the Crusades, the Near East offered alluring commercial opportunities.

Accordingly, when in 1095 Pope Urban II urged the European nobility to undertake a crusade to liberate the Holy Land, the response was overwhelming. A great international army—with a large contingent of knights from France, Normandy and Norman Sicily—poured into Syria and, in 1099, captured Jerusalem. A long strip of territory along the eastern Mediterranean, previously under Islamic rule, was now divided into four Crusader States, the chief of which was the Kingdom of Jerusalem. The king of Jerusalem was the theoretical feudal overlord of the four states, but he had trouble enforcing his authority outside his own realm. Indeed, the knightly settlers in the Holy Land were far too proud and independent for their own good, and from the beginning the Crusader States were torn by internal dissension.

Gradually, the Muslims recovered their strength and began the reconquest of their lost lands. Jerusalem fell to them in 1187, and though in later years such illustrious Christian monarchs as Richard the Lion-Hearted, Emperor Frederick Barbarossa, and St. Louis led crusading armies against the Muslims, the Crusader States continued to crumble. In 1291 they came to an end with the fall of Acre, the last Christian bridgehead on the Syrian coast.

For a time during the Crusading era Constaninople itself was ruled by western-ers. The Fourth Crusade (1202–1204) was diverted from Jerusalem to Constantinople by the greed of its Venetian financial back-ers. The Crusaders took the city by siege in 1204, succeeding where so many before them had failed, and a dynasty of western emperors ruled Constantinople for half a century, until a Byzantine dynasty replaced them in 1261.

The Crusades were more than merely a colorful failure. For nearly two centuries Christians ruled portions of the Holy Land. There, and in Constantinople, they broad-ened their perspectives by contacts with other cultures. Western merchants estab-lished footholds in Syria, vastly enlarging their role in international commerce and bringing wealth and vitality to the Italian cities. When the Crusades withdrew at last from the Holy Land, the Italian merchants remained.

Germanic Expansion in Eastern Europe

The High Middle Ages also witnessed the incorporation of vast areas of Eastern Eu-rope into the civilization of Western Chris-tendom. The Slavic peoples of the Balkans and Russia passed into the sphere of By-zantine Orthodox Christianity, but those north of the Balkans and west of Russia became Roman Catholics. The process of converting these peoples had begun in the tenth century when Otto the Great (936–973) defeated the Hungarians at Lechfeld and established his supremacy over the Slavic lands between the Elbe and Oder rivers. For a time thereafter, the dual proc-esses of Christianization and Germaniza-tion went hand in hand. But by the year 1000 the Slavs and Hungarians, while ac-cepting Catholic Christianity, were vigo-rously resisting German colonization and political suzerainty. Hungary, under its il-lustrious king, St. Stephen (997–1038), adopted Christianity and turned from no-madism to a settled agrarian society of the western type. But St. Stephen and his suc-cessors rejected German influences, submit-ting instead to a tenuous papal overlord-ship, and the same course was followed by the Catholic kings of Poland.

In the early twelfth century Germany began once again to expand its authority and commerce eastward in parnership with Christian evangelism. This new German eastward push—the *Drang nach Osten*—concentrated on the lands along the south-eastern shore of the Baltic Sea. It was not a product of active royal policy but, rather, a movement led by enterprising local aris-tocrats. They succeeded, over a long period running from about 1125 to 1350, in mov-ing the eastern boundary of Germany from the Elbe River past the Oder to the Vistula at Slavic expense. They consolidated their gains by building innumerable agrarian vil-lages and encouraging a massive eastward migration of German peasants. New towns were established that maintained close commercial ties with the older North Ger-man towns and that eventually joined with them in the Hanseatic League. The league itself, with its flourishing outposts to the east, was able to dominate the rich trade between Western Europe and the Baltic and

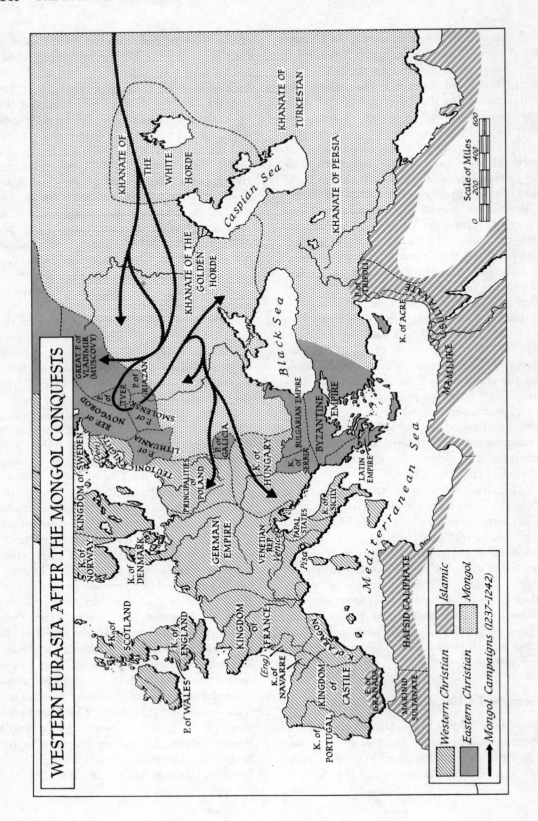

WESTERN EURASIA AFTER THE MONGOL CONQUESTS

Russia. Thus as the new lands were conquered, they were in large part Christianized and Germanized.

The later phases of the *Drang nach Osten* were spearheaded by the Teutonic Knights, a semimonastic German crusading order which transferred its activities from the Holy Land to northern Germany. The Teutonic Knights penetrated far northward into Lithuania, Latvia, and Estonia and even made an unsuccessful bid to conquer the Russian principality of Novgorod in 1242. During the fourteenth and fifteenth centuries, the Teutonic order was obliged to forfeit some of its conquests, yet much of the German expansion proved to be permanent.

By the late thirteenth century the great European expansion was drawing to an end. The internal frontiers of forest and swamp had by then been won, and the external frontiers were hardening, sometimes even receding as in the Holy Land. The German eastward push continued to the mid-fourteenth century, yet as early as the 1240s the Mongols swept out of Asia to seize most of Russia and for a brief, terrifying moment pierced into the heart of Catholic Central Europe.

The closing of the frontiers was accompanied by diminishing prosperity and a drying up of high medieval culture. The brilliant cultural achievements of the High Middle Ages were products of a buoyant, expanding, frontier society, fired by a powerful faith, driven by immense ambitions, and beguiled by a world in which, so it seemed, anything was possible. This world came to an end when the frontiers closed.

CHRONOLOGY OF THE EUROPEAN FRONTIER MOVEMENT

Spain

1002:	Breakup of Caliphate of Cordova
1085:	Capture of Toledo
1140:	Aragon unites with Catalonia
1212:	Great Christian victory at Las Navas de Tolosa
1236:	Castile takes Cordova
1260:	All Spain except Granada is under Christian rule

Sicily

1016:	Norman infiltration begins
1060-1091:	Sicily conquered
1130:	Coronation of Roger the Great
1154:	Death of Roger the Great

Holy Land

1095:	Calling of First Crusade
1099:	Crusaders take Jerusalem
1187:	Crusaders lose Jerusalem
1204:	Crusaders take Constantinople
1291:	Crusaders driven from Holy Land

11
The Politics of High-Medieval Europe

While the frontiers of Western Christendom were expanding, developments of the greatest historical significance were occuring in the Western European heartland. England and France evolved into centrally governed kingdoms on the road to nationhood. The papacy and the Holy Roman Empire, on the other hand, were locked in struggle. On the eve of their conflict, in 1050, Germany had the mightiest monarchy in Western Christendom, and the German king—or Holy Roman emperor—held the papacy in his palm. By 1300 the Holy Roman Empire was reduced to a specter of its former greatness, and the papacy, after 250 years of political prominence, was exhausted, battle-scarred, and on the brink of a prolonged decline.

The Papacy and the Holy Roman Emperors

The second half of the eleventh century was an epoch of religious awakening and reform. The Christianization of the European countryside had been proceeding steadily over the previous centuries, and a wave of religious enthusiasm was now sweeping through the new towns. Ever since the early tenth century, monastic reform had been surging through Europe, and a centralized network of reform monasteries known as the Congregation of Cluny had become, by the eleventh century, a potent agent of spiritual regeneration.

Despite papal claims of the spiritual authority of churchmen over laymen and popes over bishops, the papacy had long been weak, and the church of the mid-eleventh century remained under the firm control of the lay* aristocracy. This arrangement had become traditional and unquestioningly accepted, but to the bearers of the soaring new piety, a captive church

* The term "lay" means anyone not in holy orders; its opposite is "clerical."

The Holy Roman Emperor with orb and scepter:
manuscript illumination from the Gospel Book of
Otto III, A. D. 1000.   (Staatsbibliothek, Munich)

—well-fed, conservative, docile, and mildly
corrupt—was unacceptable. Pious Christians such as the monks of Cluny protested
against the widespread vices of clerical
marriage and simony (the purchasing of
church offices). And reformers of a still
more radical stance, including many of the
later-eleventh-century cardinals and popes,
went far beyond the limited protests of the
Cluniac monks. These radical reformers
demanded nothing less than overturning of
the lay-dominated social order. They insisted that churchmen must not be appointed by laymen but must be elected by
other churchmen in accordance with ecclesiastical law. The aristocracy, long accustomed to governing through loyal ecclesiastical subordinates, fought violently against
the new reformers. But despite this lay
hostility, the radicals gained control of the
Roman Synod of 1059 and issued two ringing decrees that, ultimately, shifted the
power structure of medieval Europe.

The Investiture Controversy

Striking out in behalf of ecclesiastical independence, the Synod of 1059 declared (1)
that thenceforth the pope would not be
appointed by emperors or Roman nobles
but would be elected by the cardinals, and
(2) that laymen would no longer invest
new churchmen with the symbols of their
offices. For when a layman invested a
bishop-elect with the symbolic ring and
pastoral staff, the implication was that the
bishop owed his office to his lay patron.
Henceforth, the church would be its own
master.

For nearly 250 years thereafter a powerful, independent papacy strove with considerable success to rule a centralized,
hierarchical church—to wrest ecclesiastical
appointments from lay control, to subordinate monarchs to its spiritual jurisdiction,
and to build a vast papal administration
adequate to the needs of an international
government. Throughout this era the papacy's chief antagonists were the Holy
Roman emperors, who struggled to keep
control of the imperial church and to extend their political authority deep into Italy.
Geographically, papacy and empire were
cheek to jowl; ideologically, they were
worlds apart.

During the long struggle, the empire employed military power against the papacy,
and the papacy replied with potent spiritual sanctions against the emperors—excommunicating them, declaring them deposed, even ordering the suspension of
church services (the *interdict*) throughout
their domains. There were, oftentimes, imperially supported antipopes and papally
supported anti-emperors. The papacy would
counter imperial force with the military
force of its own allies—the Sicilian Normans, the particularistic German princes,
or the North Italian towns. And, at times,
England and France were drawn into the
conflict, always on opposite sides.

The first great papal-imperial crisis occurred during the pontificate of the fiery reformer, Gregory VII (1073–1085). Pope Gregory reissued the lay-investiture ban and took steps to prevent imperial appointments to North Italian bishop. He was immediately challenged by the young emperor Henry IV (1056–1106). The crisis deepened as Gregory excommunicated Henry IV's advisers, Henry declared Gregory deposed, and Gregory declared Henry deposed and excommunicated. At this point many restive German princes, irritated by the ever-tightening imperial centralization, rose against their excommunicated sovereign and threatened to choose another monarch unless Henry IV obtained Gregory's forgiveness. So it was that in 1077 Henry crossed the Alps and stood penitent and barefoot in the snow before Gregory at the Tuscan castle of Canossa.

This ultimate act of royal humiliation was also an act of political expedience, for at Canossa Henry was forgiven and reinstated. He returned to Germany to rebuild his power, and once his throne was secure he resumed the struggle against papal reform. Amidst the thunder of armed clashes and renewed excommunications and depositions, Gregory VII died. But there were other popes who would fight, as Gregory had, for a papal monarchy over a free international church—for the supremacy of *ecclesia* over *imperium*. And there were other kings and emperors who, like Henry IV, would struggle grimly to retain their prerogatives over both laymen and churchmen within their dominions.

The Investiture Controversy itself was settled by compromise in 1122. The emperor yielded the right to invest churchmen, while retaining a real, if indirect, voice in their appointment. But the core of the church-state struggle remained untouched. The rival claims of monarchs who aspired to fuller sovereignty and of an international church that aspired to power

and independence within each state could not be reconciled.

Frederick Barbarossa, Innocent III, Frederick II

The conflict broke out anew in the reign of the great German emperor, Frederick Barbarossa (1152–1190), who sought to establish firm imperial control in northern Italy and met the fierce opposition of the papacy and the Lombard League of North Italian city-states. The struggle continued during the pontificate of Innocent III (1198–1216), the most powerful of all popes, who directed his astute diplomatic skills not only against recalcitrant emperors but against the kings of England and France as well. He forced King Philip Augustus of France to return to an abandoned first wife; he forced King John of England to accept an archbishop that John had not wanted; and, maneuvering shrewdly through the quicksand of German politics, he enforced his will in a disputed imperial succession.

The final phase of the struggle commenced just after Innocent III's death, when his youthful, handpicked emperor, Frederick II (1211–1250), defied the papacy and sought to bring all Italy under his rule. Frederick II matured into a brilliant, anticlerical skeptic, known to his admirers as *stupor mundi*—the Wonder of the World—and suspected by his enemies of being the incarnate antichrist. He inherited the Norman Kingdom of Sicily from his mother and Germany from his father. And it took all the skill of the papacy and the unremitting efforts of the North Italian cities to defeat his armies and thwart his ambitions. Shortly after Frederick II's death, the imperial office fell vacant and remained unoccupied for 19 years (1254–1273). At length, it passed to Rudolph of Hapsburg, through election by the German princes and with papal approval.

Consequences of the Papal-Imperial Struggle

By now the imperial office had lost its power. Two centuries of conflict had transformed Germany from a strongly governed state into a chaos of independent magnates. The ambitious princes had usurped imperial lands, revenues, and rights, until, by the late thirteenth century, they had become powers unto themselves. The papal policy of promoting internal dissension and of encouraging rival emperors from competing houses had destroyed the hereditary principle in Germany. The emperors were now elected by the chief princes, and a son succeeded his father only if the powerful princely electors approved. Thus, the papal-imperial conflict doomed Germany to centuries of disunity and political impotence in the affairs of Europe.

Italy suffered, too, for it was the chief papal-imperial battleground. Yet the North Italian cities, encouraged and supported by the papacy, won their independence from imperial authority and emerged from the conflict as independent communes. Cities like Milan, Florence, and Siena—once under imperial jurisdiction—were now autonomous city-states in which, by the late thirteenth century, a rich urban culture was brewing.

The papacy emerged victorious over the empire, yet it, too, lost much in the struggle. Pope Gregory VII had ridden the wave of the new popular piety and, by and large, the townsmen and monastic reformers had been with him. Innocent III, on the contrary, was no man of the people but an aristocratic canon lawyer who presided over an immense, complex papal administrative machine. He and his successors were highly skilled in the fields of law, diplomacy, and administration. They built a superb bureaucracy and they humbled monarchs. But gradually, almost imperceptibly, they lost touch with the religious aspirations of the common people. Basically, the power of the papacy rested on its spiritual prestige, and the flock of Christ would not always give its full allegiance to lawyers, tax-gatherers, and politicians. The high-medieval papacy was not a corrupt institution. Rather, it was the victim of its own impulse to enter dynamically into all human affairs. In the beginning it aspired to be a great spiritual force in the world; in the end it became worldly.

As the thirteenth century closed, the papacy was itself humbled, not by the weakened Holy Roman Empire but by the rising monarchies of England and France, whose kings taxed their churchmen against papal wishes and defied the fulminations of Rome. In 1303 French troops seized the proud, intransigent Pope Boniface VII, and a few years later a French Pope, Clement V, abandoned Rome and made his capital at Avignon, in the shadow of the French monarchy. The old medieval powers—papacy and empire—were, by the end of the High Middle Ages, giving way before the centralized kingdoms that would dominate early modern Europe.

CHRONOLOGY OF THE PAPAL-IMPERIAL CONFLICT

1056–1106:	Reign of Henry IV
1059:	Papal Election Decree
1073–1085:	Pontificate of Gregory VII
1075:	Gregory VII bans lay investiture
1076:	Gregory VII excommunicates and deposes Henry IV
1077:	Henry IV humbles himself at Canossa
1122:	Concordat of Worms
1152–1190:	Reign of Frederick I, "Barbarossa"
1198–1216:	Pontificate of Innocent III
1211–1250:	Reign of Frederick II
1254–1273:	Interregnum
1273–1291:	Reign of Rudolph of Hapsburg

1294–1303:   Pontificate of Boniface VIII
1303:   Boniface VIII humiliated at
              Anagni

England

England was already a unified monarchy by
the mid-eleventh century. In the course of
the High Middle Ages it became far more
tightly unified, far more sophisticated in its
laws and administration, and far richer and
more populous. In 1066 William, Duke of
Normandy, won a momentous victory at
Hastings and established a new royal
dynasty in England. William the Conqueror's new kingdom was unique in its
lucrative royal land tax—the danegeld*—and
in its well-functioning system of local
courts. The Conqueror further centralized
his power by adding significantly to the
royal estates and by granting extensive
lands as military fiefs to loyal Norman
vassals who usually respected the royal
authority. William I's great land survey of
1086, recorded in *Domesday Book*, illustrates both the administrative precocity of
his government and its claim to ultimate
jurisdiction over all of England's lands and
people.

The process of political consolidation
gathered momentum under William I's
twelfth-century successors, particularly
Henry I (1100–1135) and Henry II (1154–
1189). Henry I, for example, developed a
remarkable royal accounting bureau—the
Exchequer—which processed the revenues
collected by the royal representatives in the
shires—the sheriffs ("shire reeves"). And
under Henry II, significant steps were taken
toward the development of a common law,
under the jurisdiction of royal courts, to
supersede the various and complex jurisdictions of local and feudal courts. Generally
speaking, legal actions relating to the all-
important subject of land tenure passed

* This tax had originated long before the Norman
Conquest as a source of royal revenue for buying
off the invading Danes. In time the Danish threat
ceased, but the tax did not. Taxes seldom do.

under royal jurisdiction in Henry II's reign.
The political unification of England by the
Anglo-Saxon kings beginning in the late
ninth century was now being paralleled by
a legal unification under the expanding
jurisdiction of the twelfth-century royal
courts.

The era also witnessed the dynastic fusion of England with portions of northern
France. The effect of William's conquest
in 1066 was the formation of an Anglo-
Norman state, and, as a result of successive
royal marriages, Henry II ruled not only
England and Normandy but Anjou, Aquitaine, and other French principalities as
well. This immense constellation of territories—known as the "Angevin Empire"—
remained intact for half a century (1154–
1204), dwarfing the domains of the French
crown. At length, King Philip Augustus
of France seized the northern French districts of the Angevin Empire from the unlucky King John of England (1199–1216).
Thenceforth, for more than a century,
English royal jurisdiction was limited
mainly to the British Isles. John made important advances in Ireland and, late in the
thirteenth century, Edward I (1272–1307)
conquered Wales. But not until the 1330s
and 1340s, with the opening of the Hundred Years' War, did an English king once
again lead his armies into northern France.

During the thirteenth century the English
central administration continued to increase
in refinement and scope. Royal authority
over lands and law, which had been advanced so promisingly under Henry II,
reached its climax in Edward I's reign. The
central government was now issuing
statutes binding on all Englishmen, and the
common law was carried everywhere by a
powerful system of fixed and itinerant
royal courts. Full administrative records
were being maintained, and the simple
Exchequer of Henry I's day had evolved
into a complex and highly efficient machine, drawing large revenues from the
prosperous manors and bustling towns of
thirteenth-century England.

THE ANGEVIN EMPIRE, 1154

Legend:
- Angevin Empire in 1154
- Capetian Domain

Scale of Miles
0   50   100   150   200

The Rise of Parliament

But the steady growth of the thirteenth-century royal administration gave rise to a concurrent trend toward limiting the powers of the king himself: *Magna Carta* (1215) and the rise of Parliament in the later thirteenth century are the chief monuments in this trend, and both were rooted in the earlier feudal order.

England, like other medieval kingdoms, was a feudal monarchy dominated by the lord-king and his aristocratic vassals. Since the traditional feudal relationship of lord and vassal was a relationship of *mutual* rights and obligations, a monarchy arising out of such a system tended to be limited rather than absolute. The king was always bound by customs—feudal, regional and national—and arbitrary royal taxes or directives were always resisted.

Thus, *Magna Carta* (or the Great Charter), the reputed keystone of England's "government under the law," was a profoundly feudal document which limited royal exploitation of feudal and customary rights in a variety of specific ways. It was, indeed, a product of baronial resistance to the centralizing policies of the monarchy—designed to strengthen and make more specific the traditional safeguards of the lord-vassal relationship against an ambitious king who had exceeded the customary limits of his lordship.

The English baronage undertook several major rebellions during the thirteenth century—not with the purpose of weakening the royal administration but, rather, with the purpose of sharing in its control. The monarchy, forced to recognize these essentially conservative demands of its feudal magnates, gradually transformed the great baronial royal council—the *curia regis*—into Parliament. By the reign of Edward I, late in the century, the power struggle had been largely resolved. When the king issued his statutes, or proclaimed new unprecedented taxes, or made unusual military demands on his subjects, he now did so "in parliament"—with the consent of the great barons of the realm sitting with him in council. Indeed, the soaring prosperity of town and countryside resulted in the inclusion in royal parliaments of representative townsmen and members of the rural gentry —the "knights of the shire." The composition of Edward I's parliaments varied, but by the close of the thirteenth century they were coming increasingly to include all three classes—barons, shire knights, and townsmen (with bishops and abbots meeting separately in ecclesiastical "convocations)". In the course of the fourteenth century the townsmen and shire gentry split off into a separate House of Commons, which gradually, during the fourteenth century, gained control of the royal purse strings.

High-medieval England did not invent constitutional monarchy. Similar constitutional developments were occurring in France, the Spanish kingdoms, the German principalities, and elsewhere. And, as in England, they always evolved out of old Germanic and feudal notions that held custom superior to king and upheld the rights of vassals with respect to their lords. In England alone, however, do we find the evolution from feudalism to constitutionalism occurring as a continuous process down to modern times.

France

The French monarchy began the High Middle Ages far weaker than its English counterpart and ended far less restricted by national customs and national assemblies. The Capetian dynasty, which had gained the weak French throne in 987, remained, at the time of the Norman Conquest, limited to an uneasy jurisdiction over the diminutive *Île de France* around Paris and Orleans. To realize the immense potential of their royal title, the Capetians had three tasks before them: (1) to master and pacify their turbulent barons in the Ile de France itself, (2) to expand their political and economic base by bringing additional territories under direct royal authority, and (3) to make their lordship over the feudal duchies and counties of France a reality rather than a mere formality.

During the twelfth and thirteenth centuries a series of remarkable Capetian kings pursued and achieved these goals. Their success was so complete that by the opening of the fourteenth century, the Capetians controlled all France, either directly or through obedient vassals. They had developed by this time a sophisticated royal bureaucracy almost as efficient as England's and far more single-mindedly devoted to the interests of the king. The Capetians followed no set formula. Instead, their success depended on a combination of luck and ingenuity—on their clever exploi-

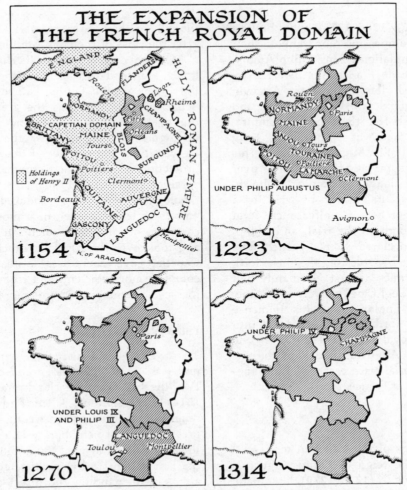

THE EXPANSION OF
THE FRENCH ROYAL DOMAIN

tation of the powers that, potentially, they had aways possessed as kings and feudal overlords. They succeeded in avoiding the family squabbles that had, at times, divided Germany and England. Whereas Germany exhausted herself in struggles with the papacy, and even England was torn at times by church-state conflicts, the Capetians maintained relatively good relations with the Church. They had the enormous good fortune of an unbroken sequence of direct male heirs from 987 to 1328. Above all, they seldom overreached themselves. They avoided grandiose schemes, preferring to pursue modest, realistic goals. They extended their power gradually and cautiously by favorable marriages, by confiscating the fiefs of vassals who died without heirs, and by dispossess-

ing vassals who violated their feudal obligations to the monarchy. Yet they had no desire to absorb all the territories of their vassals. Rather they sought to build a kingdom with a substantial core of royal domain lands surrounded by the fiefs of loyal, obedient magnates.

The Early Capetians Kings

In the period beginning about 1060 and lasting until about 1180, the Capetians succeeded in taming the Ile de France and in bringing some of their powerful vassals into a condition of increased dependency. The years between 1180 and 1314 were dominated by the rule of three great Capetian kings—Philip II "Augustus" (1180–1223), St. Louis IX (1226–1270), and Philip

IV "the Fair" (1285–1314)—who built a powerful, encompassing monarchy on their ancestors' foundations. King Philip Augustus, whose Île de France was dwarfed by the vast French dominions of the Angevin kings of England, worked shrewdly and tirelessly to shatter the Angevin Empire. His success came, at last, during King John's reign. Philip Augustus, utilizing his position as supreme feudal lord over John's French lands, summoned John to his feudal court in Paris to be tried for a relatively minor act of malfeasance. John refused to submit to the trial, and Philip, accordingly, declared John's French fiefs forfeited. In the role of the just lord, Philip sent armies against Normandy and Anjou. John fought ineffectively for a time, then fled to England, and his immense dominions in northern France passed into the French royal domain (1204). In one stroke, Philip Augustus had won the extensive territorial base essential for Capetian control over France.

St. Louis

The golden age of the Capetian monarchy occurred in the reign of Philip Augustus' grandson, Louis IX (1226–1270), later made a saint. Louis was a strong, pious king who ruled France wisely and firmly, winning invaluable prestige for the crown through his crusades and charities while his devoted royal officials worked unremittingly to extend the king's power. Capetian officials, unlike their English counterparts, were drawn largely from among ambitious townsmen and university graduates—men lacking strong local roots, utterly devoted to the royal interest. The fusion of local and royal interests, evident in the English administration in general, and the English Parliament in particular, failed to develop in France. Rebellion became the chief instrument of the French nobility for curbing royal power. Thus the potentialities for both royal absolutism and anarchy were present in thirteenth-century France, al-

though neither threat materialized until after the close of the High Middle Ages.

Medieval culture reached its climax in St. Louis' France. Town life flourished, and in the towns superb Gothic cathedrals were being erected. This was the great age of the medieval universities, and the most distinguished university of the age, the University of Paris, enjoyed the favor and protection of the French crown. The universities produced brilliant and subtle theologians; they also produced learned, ambitious lawyers—men of a more secular cast who devoted their talents to the king and took over the royal bureaucracy. The Capetian government became steadily more complex, more efficient, and from the aristocracy's standpoint, more oppressive.

Philip IV, "the Fair"

These trends reached their culmination under St. Louis' ruthless grandson, Philip IV, "the Fair" or "the Handsome" (1285–1314)—a mysterious, silent figure whose reign was marked by unceasing royal aggression against neighboring lands, against the papacy, and against the nobility. Philip the Fair sought to bypass the feudal hierarchy by demanding the direct allegiance of all Frenchmen. Royalist doctrine, anticipating the goals of later French monarchs, proclaimed the king supreme in France and France supreme in Europe. And in Philip the Fair's reign the doctrine came close to realization. The papacy was humbled. The wealthy crusading order of Knights Templars was looted and destroyed to fatten the royal purse. And France began to expand eastward at the expense of the weakened Holy Roman Empire. In 1302 the French Estates General was summoned for the first time, for reasons akin to those that prompted the development of the English Parliament. But, owing in part to the chasm between king and nobility, in part to the ingrained localism of rural France, the medieval Estates General lacked Parliament's potential for creative development as a vital organ of the central government. The Capetians had made the king supreme in France and, in so doing, had taken the initial steps along the road from feudal monarchy to absolutism.

CHRONOLOGY OF THE ENGLISH AND FRENCH MONARCHIES IN THE HIGH MIDDLE AGES

England

1066:	Norman Conquest of England
1066–1087:	Reign of William the Conqueror
1100–1135:	Reign of Henry I
1154–1189:	Reign of Henry II
1189–1199:	Reign of Richard the Lion-Hearted
1199–1216:	Reign of John
1203–1204:	Loss of Normandy
1215:	Magna Carta
1272–1307:	Reign of Edward I

France

987–1328:	Rule of the Capetian Dynasty
1180–1223:	Reign of Philip II, "Augustus"
1226–1270:	Reign of St. Louis IX
1285–1314:	Reign of Philip IV, "the Fair"

12
New Dimensions in Medieval Christianity

The Church in the Middle Ages

Although the Middle Ages witnessed the beginnings of European nationhood, it was not until much later that nationalism began to play an important role in the European mind. In the twelfth and thirteenth centuries the majority of Europeans were still intensely local in their outlook, only vaguely aware of what was going on beyond their immediate surroundings. But alongside their localism was an element of cosmopolitanism—a consciousness of belonging to the great international commonwealth of Western Christendom, fragmented politically, but united culturally and spiritually by the Church. Paradoxically, high medieval Europe was at once more localized and more internationalized than the Europe of modern times.

The Church in the High Middle Ages was a powerful unifying influence. It had made notable progress since the half-heathen pre-Carolingian era. A flourishing parish system had by now spread across the European countryside to bring the sacraments and a modicum of Christian instruction to the peasantry. New bishoprics and archbishoprics were formed, and old ones were becoming steadily more active. The papacy never completely succeeded in breaking the control of kings and secular lords over their local bishops, but in the wake of the Investiture Controversy it exercised a very real control over the European episcopacy, and the growing efficiency of the papal bureaucracy evoked the envy and imitation of the rising royal governments.

The buoyancy of high medieval Europe is nowhere more evident than in the accelerating impact of Christian piety on European society. The seven sacraments of the Church introduced a significant religious dimension into the life of the typical European layman: His birth was sanctified by the sacrament of *baptism* in which he was cleansed of the taint of original sin and initiated into the Christian fellowship. At puberty he received the sacrament of *con-firmation,* which reasserted his member-bership in the Church and gave him the additional grace to cope with the problems of adulthood. His wedding was dignified by the sacrament of *marriage.* If he chose the calling of the ministry, he was spiritu-ally transformed into a priest by the sacra-ment of *holy orders.* At his death he re-ceived the sacrament of *extreme unction,* which prepared his soul for its journey into the next world. And throughout his life he could receive forgiveness from the damning consequences of mortal sin by re-penting his past transgressions and humbly receiving the comforting sacrament of *pen-ance.* Finally, he might partake regularly of the central sacrament of the Church—the *eucharist*—receiving the body of Christ into his own body by consuming the eu-charistic bread.* Thus the Church, through its seven sacraments, brought God's grace to all Christians, great and humble, at every critical juncture of their lives. The sacramental system, which only assumed final form in the High Middle Ages, was a source of immense comfort and reassur-ance: it brought hope of salvation not simply to the saintly elite but to the sinful majority; it made communion with God not merely the elusive goal of a few mys-tics but the periodic experience of all be-lievers. And, of course, it established the Church as the essential intermediary be-tween God and man.

The ever-increasing scope of the Church, together with the rising vigor of the new age, resulted in a deepening of popular piety throughout Europe. The High Mid-dle Ages witnessed a profound shift in religious attitude from the awe and mys-tery characteristic of earlier Christianity to a new emotionalism and dynamism. This

shift is evident in ecclesiastical architec-ture, as the stolid, earthbound Romanesque style gave way in the later twelfth century to the tense, upward-reaching Gothic. A parallel change is evident in devotional practices as the divine Christ sitting in judgment gave way to the tragic figure of the human Christ suffering on the Cross for man's sins. And it was in the High Middle Ages that the Virgin Mary came into her own as the compassionate inter-cessor for hopelessly lost souls. No matter how sinful a person might be, he could be redeemed if only he won the sympathy of Mary, for what son could refuse the peti-tion of his mother? Indeed, a legend of the age told of the devil complaining to God that the soft-hearted Queen of Heaven was cheating Hell of its most promising candidates. The God of Justice became the merciful, suffering God who died in agony to atone for the sins of men and to bring them to everlasting life.

Like all human institutions, the medieval Church fell far short of its ideals. Corrupt churchmen were in evidence throughout the age, and certain historians have de-lighted in cataloguing instances of lar-cenous bishops, gluttonous priests, and licentious nuns. But cases such as these were exceptional. The great shortcoming of the medieval Church was not gross cor-ruption but rather a creeping complacency which resulted sometimes in a shallow, mechanical attitude toward the Christian religious life. The medieval Church had more than its share of saints, but among the rank and file of the clergy the profund-ity of the Faith was often lost in the day-to-day affairs of the pastoral office and the management of far-flung estates.

The Crisis in Benedictinism

The drift toward complacency was a recur-ring problem in Christian monasticism—as in all human institutions. Again and again, the lofty idealism of a monastic reform movement was eroded and transformed by

---

* Until the High Middle Ages, Christian laymen had traditionally received the body and blood of Christ by eating consecrated bread and drinking consecrated wine from a common cup. In the course of the twelfth century, partly for hygienic reason, the drinking of the eucharistic wine was limited to the officiating clergy.

time and success until, at length, new reform movements arose in protest against
the growing worldliness of the old ones.
This cycle has been repeated countless
times. Indeed, the sixth-century Benedictine movement was itself a protest against
the excesses and inadequacies of earlier
monasticism. St. Benedict had regarded his
new order as a means of withdrawing
from the world and devoting full time to
communion with God. But Benedictinism,
despite Benedict's ideal, quickly became
involved in teaching, evangelism, and ecclesiastical reform, and by the tenth and
eleventh centuries the whole Benedictine
movement had become deeply involved in
worldly affairs. Benedictine monasteries
controlled vast estates, supplied contingents of knights in their service to feudal
armies, and worked closely with secular
princes in affairs of state. Early in the
tenth century the Cluniac movement,
which was itself Benedictine in spirit and
rule, arose as a protest against the worldliness and complacency of contemporary
Benedictine monasticism. But by the later
eleventh century the Congregation of
Cluny had come to terms with the secular
establishment and was beginning to display traces of the very complacency
against which it had originally rebelled.
Prosperous, respected, and secure, Cluny
was too content with its majestic abbeys
and priories, its elaborate liturgical program, and its bounteous fields to throw its
full support behind the radical transformation of Christian society for which Pope
Gregory VII was struggling.

The aims of Gregory VII were almost
exactly the opposite of St. Benedict's, for
whereas Benedict had sought to create
monastic sanctuaries in which Christians
might retire from the world, Gregory VII
endeavored to sanctify society itself. His
goal was not *withdrawal* but *conversion*.
Rather than making Christians safe from
the world, he would make the world safe
for Christianity. During the Investiture
Controversy and its aftermath, these two
contrary tendencies—withdrawal and conversion—both had a profound impact on
monastic reform.

In the opening decades of the High
Middle Ages the Benedictine movement
was showing signs of exhaustion. During
the long, troubled centuries of the Early
Middle Ages, Benedictine teachers and
missionaries, scribes and political advisers,
had provided indispensable services to society. Benedictine monasteries had served
as the spiritual and cultural foci of Christendom. But in the eleventh and twelfth
centuries, the Benedictines saw their peda-
gogical monopoly broken by the rising
cathedral schools and universities of the
new towns. These urban schools produced
increasing numbers of well-trained scholars who gradually superseded the Benedictine monks as scribes and advisers to
princes. In other words, the great urbaniz-
ing impulse of the High Middle Ages drastically diminished the traditional Benedictine contribution to the functioning of
society.

Still, the Benedictines retained their
great landed wealth. The Benedictine monastery was scarcely the sanctuary from
worldly concerns that St. Benedict had
planned. Nor was it any longer the vital
force it had once been in Christianizing
the world. Twelfth-century Benedictinism
followed neither the path of withdrawal
nor the path of conversion, and even in the
arena of secular affairs it was losing its
grip. The Benedictine life was beginning
to appear tarnished and unappealing to
sensitive religious spirits caught up in the
soaring piety of the new age.

The New Monasticism

The monastic revolt against Benedictinism
followed the two divergent roads of uncompromising withdrawal from society
and ardent participation in the Christianization of society. The impulse toward
withdrawal pervaded the Carthusian order
which arose in eastern France in the later

eleventh century and spread across Christendom in the twelfth. Isolated from the outside world, the Carthusians lived in small groups, worshipping together in communal chapels but otherwise living as hermits in individual cells. This austere order exists to this day and, unlike most monastic movements, its severe spirituality has seldom waned. Yet even in the spiritually charged atmosphere of the twelfth century it was a small movement, offering a way of life for only a minority of heroically holy men. Too ascetic for the average Christian, the Carthusian order was much admired but seldom joined.

The greatest monastic movement of the twelfth century, the Cistercian order, managed for a time to be both austere and popular. The mother house of this order, Citeaux, was established in 1098 on a wild, remote site in eastern France. The Cistercian order grew very slowly at first, then gradually acquired momentum. In 1115 it had 4 daughter houses; by the end of the century it had 500.

The spectacular success of the Cistercians demonstrates the immense appeal of the idea of withdrawal to the Christians of the twelfth century. Like Citeaux, the daughter houses were deliberately built in remote wilderness areas. The abbeys themselves were stark and austere, in dramatic contrast to the elaborate Cluniac architecture and sculpture. Cistercian life was austere, too—less severe than that of the Carthusians but far more so than that of the Cluniacs. The Cistercians sought to resurrect the strict, simple life of primitive Benedictinism, but in fact they were stricter than Benedict himself. The lands surrounding their wilderness abbeys were cleared and tilled by Cistercian monks and lay brothers, rather than by the ordinary serfs who worked the Benedictines' Fields. The numerous Cistercian houses were bound together tightly, not by the authority of a central abbot as at Cluny but by an annual council of all Cistercian abbots meeting at Citeaux. Without such central-

ized control it is unlikely that the individual houses could have clung for long to the harsh, ascetic ideals on which the order was founded.

The key figure in the twelfth-century Cistercianism was St. Bernard, who joined the community of Citeaux in 1112 and three years later became the founder and abbot of Clairvaux, one of Citeaux's earliest daughter houses. St. Bernard of Clairvaux was the leading Christian of his age—a profound mystic, a brilliant religious orator, and a crucial figure in the meteoric rise of the Cistercian order. His moral influence was so immense that he became Europe's leading arbiter of political and ecclesiastical disputes. He persuaded the king of France and the Holy Roman emperor to participate in the Second Crusade. He persuaded Christendom to accept his candidate in a hotly disputed papal election in 1130. On one occasion he even succeeded in reconciling the two great warring families of Germany, the Welfs and Hohenstaufens. He rebuked the pope himself: "Remember, first of all, that the Holy Roman Church, over which you hold sway, is the mother of churches, not their sovereign mistress—that you yourself are not the lord of bishops but one among them. . . ." And he took an uncompromising stand against one of the rising movements of his day: the intoxicating dream of reconciling the Catholic faith with human reason, which was spearheaded by the brilliant twelfth-century philosopher, Peter Abelard. In the long run Bernard failed to halt the reconciliation of faith with reason, but he succeeded in making life miserable for the unfortunate Abelard and in securing the official condemnation of certain of Abelard's teaching (see pp. 171–172).

Bernard's career demonstrates vividly the essential paradox of Cistercianism. For although the Cistercians strove to dissociate themselves from the world, Bernard was drawn inexorably into the vortex of secular affairs. Indeed, as the twelfth century progressed, the entire Cistercian movement became increasingly worldly. Like the later Puritans, the Cistercians discovered that their twin virtues of austere living and hard work resulted in an embarrassing accumulation of wealth and a concomitant corrosion of their spiritual simplicity. Their efforts to clear fields around their remote abbeys placed them in the vanguard of the internal frontier movement. They became pioneers in scientific farming and introduced notable improvements in the breeding of horses, cattle, and sheep. The English Cistercians became the great wool producers of the realm. Altogether the Cistercians exerted a powerful, progressive influence on European husbandry and came to play a prominent role in the European economy. Economic success brought ever-increasing wealth to the order. Cistercian abbey churches became steadily more elaborate and opulent, and the primitive austerity of Cistercian life was progressively relaxed. In later years there appeared new offshoots, such as the Trappists, which returned to the strict observance of original Cistercianism.

The Cistercians had endeavored to withdraw from the world, but despite their goal they became a powerful force in twelfth-century Europe. At roughly the same time, other orders were being established with the deliberate aim of participating actively in society and working toward its regeneration. The Augustinian Canons, for example, submitted to the rigor of a monastic rule, yet carried on normal ecclesiastical duties in the world, serving in parish churches and cathedrals, and staffing the hospitals that were being built just then in great numbers all across Europe. The fusion of monastic discipline and worldly activity culminated in the twelfth-century Crusading orders—the Knights Templars, the Knights Hospitallers, the Teutonic Knights, and similar groups whose ideal was a synthesis of the monastic and the military life for the purpose of expanding the political frontiers of Western Christen-

dom. These and other efforts to direct the spiritual vigor of monastic life toward the Christianization of society typify the bold visions and lofty hopes of the new, emotionally charged religiosity that animated twelfth-century Europe.

Heresies and the Inquisition

The new surge of popular piety also raised serious problems for the Church and society, for it resulted in a flood of criticism against churchmen. It was not that churchmen had grown worse, but rather that laymen had begun to judge them by more rigorous standards. Popular dissatisfaction toward the work-a-day Church manifested itself in part in the rush toward the austere twelfth-century monastic orders. Yet the majority of Christians could not become monks, and for them, certain new heretical doctrines began to exert a powerful appeal.

The heresies of the High Middle Ages flourished particularly in the rising towns of southern Europe. The eleventh-century urban revolution had caught the Church unprepared; whereas the new towns were the real centers of the burgeoning lay piety, the Church, with its roots in the older agrarian feudal order, seemed unable to minister effectively to the vigorous and widely literate new burgher class. Too often the urban bishops appeared as political oppressors and enemies of burghal independence rather than inspiring spiritual directors. Too often the Church failed to understand the townsmen's problems and aspirations or to anticipate their growing suspicion of ecclesiastical wealth and power. Although the vast majority of medieval townsmen remained loyal to the Church, a troublesome minority, particularly in the south, turned to new, anticlerical sects. In their denunciation of ecclesiastical wealth, these sects were doing nothing more than St. Bernard and the Cistercians had done. But many of the anticlerical sects crossed the boundary between orthodox reformism and heresy by preaching without episcopal or papal approval; far more important, they denied the exclusive right of the priesthood to perform sacraments.

One such sect, the Waldensians, was founded by a merchant of Lyons named Peter Waldo who *c.* 1173 gave all his possessions to the poor and took up a life of apostolic poverty. At first he and his followers worked within the bounds of orthodoxy, but gradually their flamboyant anticlericalism and their denial of special priestly powers earned them the condemnation of the Church. Similar groups, some orthodox, some heretical, arose in the communes of Lombardy and were known as the *Humiliati.* These groups proved exceedingly troublesome and embarrassing to the local ecclesiastical hierarchies, but generally they escaped downright condemnation unless they themselves took the step of denying the authority of the Church. Many did take that step, however, and by the thirteenth century heretical, anticlerical sects were spreading across nothern Italy and southern France, and even into Spain and Germany.

The most popular and dangerous heresy in southern France was sponsored by a group known as the *Cathari* (the pure) or the Albigensians, after the town of Albi, where they were particularly strong. The Albigensians represented a fusion of two traditions, (1) the anticlerical protest against ecclesiastical wealth and power and (2) an exotic theology derived originally from Persian dualism. The Albigensians recognized two gods—the god of good who reigned over the universe of the spirit and the god of evil who ruled the world of matter. The Old-Testament God, as creator of the material universe, was their god of evil; Christ, who was believed to have been a purely spiritual being with a phantom body, was the god of good. Albigensian morality stressed a vigorous rejection of all material things—of physical appetites, wealth, worldly vanities, and sexual inter-

course—in the hope of one day escaping from the prison of the body and ascending to the realm of pure spirit. In reality this severe ethic was practiced only by a small elite the rank and file ate well, begat children, and participated only vicariously in the rejection of the material world—by criticizing affluence of the Church. Indeed, their opponents accused them of gross licentiousness, and it does seem to be true that certain Provençal noblemen were attracted to the new teaching by the opportunity of appropriating Church property in good conscience.

However this may be, Albigensianism was spreading rapidly as the thirteenth century dawned and was becoming an ominous threat to the unity of Christendom and the authority of the Church. Pope Innocent III, recognizing the gravity of the situation, tried with every means in his power to eradicate Albigensianism. At length, in 1208, he summoned a crusade against European Christians. The Albigensian Crusade was a ruthless, savage affair which succeeded in its purpose but only at the cost of ravaging the vibrant civilization of southern France. The French monarchy intervened in the crusade's final stages and thereby extended its sway to the Mediterranean. The Albigensian Crusade was an important event in the development of French royal power, and it succeeded in reversing the trend toward heresy in southern Europe. It also disclosed the brutality of which the Church was capable when sufficiently threatened.

In the years of the Albigensian Crusade, there emerged an instittuion that will always stand as a grim symbol of the medieval Church at its worst—the Inquisition. The Christian persecution of heretics dates from the later fourth century, but it was not until the High Middle Ages that heterodox views presented a serious problem to European society. Traditionally, the problem of converting or punishing heretics was handled at the local level, but in 1223 the papacy established a permanent central tribunal for the purpose of standardizing procedures and increasing efficiency in the suppression of heresies. The methods of the Inquisition included the use of torture, secret testimony, conviction on the testimony of only two witnesses, the denial of legal counsel to the accused, and other procedures offensive to the Anglo-American legal tradition but not especially remarkable by standards of the times. Indeed, many of these procedures—including torture—were drawn from the customs of Roman law. In defense of the Inquisition it might be said that convicted heretics might escape death by renouncing their "errors," and that far from establishing a reign of terror, the Inquisition often seems to have enjoyed popular support.

Some historians have adduced other arguments in an attempt to defend an indefensible institution. Let us say here merely that the Christian Faith was far more important to the people of medieval Europe than national allegiance—that the medieval Church, with its elaborate charitable activities, its hospitals and universities, and its other social services, performed many of the functions of the modern state, and that therefore medieval heresy is more or less analogous to modern treason. To the medieval Christian, heresy was a hateful, repugnant thing, an insult to Christ, and a source of contamination to others. Today, when political and economic doctrines are more important to most people than religious creeds, the closest parallel to medieval Waldensianism or Albigensianism is to be found in the Communist and Nazi parties in modern America. In examining popular opposition toward extremist groups such as these, perhaps we can gain an inkling of the state of mind that produced the medieval Inquisition.

Mendicantism

The thirteenth century found an answer to the heretical drift in urban piety which was far more compassionate and effective than the Inquisition. In the opening decades of the century two radically new orders emerged—the Dominican and the Franciscan—which were devoted to a life of poverty, preaching and charitable deeds. Rejecting the life of the cloister, they dedicated themselves to religious work in the world, particularly in the towns. Benedictines and Cistercians had traditionally taken vows of personal poverty, but the monastic orders themselves could and did acquire great corporate wealth. The Dominicans and Franciscans, on the contrary, were pledged to both personal and corporate poverty and were therefore known as mendicants (beggars). Capturing the imagination of thirteenth-century Christendom, they drained urban heterodoxy of much of its former support by demonstrating to the townsmen of Europe that Christian orthodoxy could be both relevant and compelling.

St. Dominic (1170–1221), a Spaniard who had preached in southern France against the Albigensians, conceived the idea of an order of men trained as theologians and preachers, dedicated to poverty and the simple life, and to winning over heretics through argument, oratory, and example. Sanctioned by the papacy in 1216, the Dominicans expanded swiftly and, by midcentury, had spread across Christendom. The order produced some of the greatest philosophers and theologians of the age, including St. Thomas Aquinas. Dominicans also participated actively in the Inquisition, but their most effective work was done through persuasion rather than force. In time, the ideal of corporate poverty was dropped; the Dominicans came to recognize the great truth that full-time scholars and teachers could not beg or do odd jobs or be in doubt as to the source of their next meal. But long after their original mendicant ideals were modified, the Dominicans remained faithful to their mission of championing orthodoxy by word and pen.

Dominic's remarkable achievement was

overshadowed by that of his contemporary, St. Francis (c. 1182–1226), a warm and appealing man who is widely regarded as Christianity's greatest saint. Francis was a true product of the urban revolution. He was the son of a wealthy cloth merchant of Assisi, a northern Italian town with an influential Albigensian minority. After a boisterous but harmless adolescence, he underwent a profound conversion, lived in solitude for a brief time, and then returned to human society with a firm dedication to give up all worldly goods and to devote his life to the service of the poor and diseased. Francis was firm, but he was anything but grim. Indeed, it was his joyousness no less than his deep sanctity that captivated his age. As disciples flocked to his side, he wrote a simple rule for them based on the imitation of Christ through charitable activity in the world, total dedication to the work of God, and the absolute rejection of worldly goods. In 1210 he appealed to Pope Innocent III for approval of his rule, and that mightiest of all popes, with some misgivings, authorized the new order. In the years that followed, the Franciscan order expanded phenomenally. The irresistably attractive personality of Francis himself was doubtless a crucial factor in his order's popularity, but it also owed much to the fact that Franciscan ideals appealed with remarkable effectiveness to the highest religious aspirations of the age. Urban heresy lost its allure as the cheerful, devoted Franciscans began to pour into Europe's cities, preaching in the crowded streets and setting a living example of Christian sanctity.

Pious men of other times have fled the world, the Albigensians renounced it as the epitome of evil. But Francis embraced it joyfully as the handiwork of God. In his "Song of Brother Sun," he expressed poetically his holy communion to the physical universe:

Praise to Thee, my Lord, for all Thy creatures,
Above all Brother Sun
Who brings us the day, and lends us his light;

Beautiful is he, radiant with great splendor,
And speaks to us of Thee, O most high.

Praise to Thee, my Lord, for Sister Moon and for the stars;
In heaven Thou hast set them, clear and precious and fair.

Praise to Thee, my Lord, for Brother Wind,
For air and clouds, for calm and all weather
By which Thou supportest life in all Thy creatures.

Praise to Thee, my Lord, for Sister Water
Which is so helpful and humble, precious and pure.

Praise to Thee, my Lord, for Brother Fire,
By whom Thou lightest up the night.
And fair is he, and gay and mighty and strong.

Praise to Thee, my Lord, for our sister, Mother Earth,
Who sustains and directs us,
And brings forth varied fruits, and plants and flowers bright. . . .

Praise and bless my Lord, and give Him thanks,
And serve Him with great humility.

Early Franciscanism was too good to last. As the order expanded it outgrew its primitive ideals, and even before Francis' death in 1226, the papacy was obliged to authorize a more elaborate and practical rule for his order. In time Franciscan friars began devoting themselves to scholarship and took their places alongside the Dominicans in Europe's universities. Indeed, Franciscan scholars such as Roger Bacon in thirteenth-century England played a central role in the revival of scientific investigation, and the minister general of the Franciscan order in the later thirteenth century, St. Bonaventure, was one of the most illustrious theologians of the age. The very weight and complexity of the Franciscan organization forced it to compromise its original ideal of corporate poverty. Although it neither acquired nor sought the immense landed wealth of the Benedictines or Cistercians, it soon possessed sufficient means to sustain its members. In time, therefore, the Franciscans followed the course of earlier orders: their primitive simplicity and enthusiasm were exhausted by time and attenuated by popularity and success. A splinter group known as the "Spiritual Franciscans" sought to preserve the apostolic poverty and artless idealism of Francis himself, but the majority of Franciscans were willing to meet reality halfway. They continued to serve society, but by the end of the thirteenth century they had ceased to inspire it.

The pattern of religious reform in the High Middle Ages is one of rhythmic ebb and flow. A reform movement is launched with high enthusiasm and lofty purpose, it galvanizes society for a time, then succumbs gradually to complacency and gives way to a new and different wave of reform. But with the passing of the High Middle Ages one can detect a gradual waning of spiritual vigor. Until the Protestant Reformation, no new religious order attained the immense popularity and social impact of thirteenth-century Franciscanism. Popular piety remained strong, particularly in northern Europe, where succeeding centuries witnessed a significant surge of mysticism. But in the south a more secular attitude was slowly beginning to emerge. Young men no longer flocked into monastic orders; soldiers no longer rushed to Crusades; papal excommunications no longer wrought their former terror. The electrifying appeal of a St. Bernard, a St. Dominic, and a St. Francis was a phenomenon peculiar to their age. By the fourteenth century, their age was passing.

CHRONOLOGY OF HIGH MEDIEVAL MONASTICISM AND HETERODOXY

910:	Founding of Cluny
1084:	Establishment of Carthusian order
1098:	Establishment of Citeaux
1112–1153:	Career of St. Bernard of Clairvaux as a Cistercian
1128:	Original rule of Knights Templars
1173:	Beginning of Waldensian sect
1208:	Innocent III calls Albigensian Crusade
1210:	Innocent III authorizes Franciscan order
1216:	Dominican Rule sanctioned by papacy
1226:	Death of St. Francis
1233:	Inquisition established

13
Thought, Letters, and the Arts

The Dynamics of High Medieval Culture

Thirteenth-century Paris has been described as the Athens of medieval Europe. It is true, of course, that a vast cultural gulf separates the golden age of Periclean Athens from the golden age of thirteenth-century France, but it is also true that these two golden ages had something in common. Both developed within the framework of traditional beliefs and customs which had long existed but were being challenged and transformed by powerful new forces. The social-religious world of the Early Middle Ages, like the social-religious world of the early Greek polis, was parochial and rather tradition-bound. As the two cultures passed into their golden ages, the values of the past were being challenged by new intellectual currents, and the old economic patterns were breaking down before a sharp intensification of commercial activity. Yet, for a time, these dynamic new forces resulted in a heightened cultural expression of the old values. The Parthenon, dedicated to the venerable civic goddess Athena, and the awesome Gothic cathedral of Paris dedicated to Notre Dame (Our Lady), are both products of a new creativity harnessed to the service of an older ideology. In the long run, the new creative impulses would prove subversive to the old ideologies, but for a time, both ancient Greece and medieval Europe achieved an elusive equilibrium between old and new. The results, in both cases, were spectacular.

Thus twelfth- and thirteenth-century Europe succeeded, by and large, by keeping its vibrant and audacious culture within the bounds of traditional Catholic Christianity. And the Christian world view gave form and orientation to the new creativity. Despite the intense dynamism of the period, it can still be called, with some semblance of accuracy, an Age of Faith.

Europe in the High Middle Ages underwent a profound artistic and intellectual awakening which affected almost every imaginable form of expression. Significant creative work was done in literature, architecture, sculpture, law, philosophy, political theory, and even science. By the close of the period, the foundations of the Western cultural traditions were firmly established. The pages that follow will provide only a glimpse at a few of the remarkable cultural achievements of this fertile era.

Literature

The literature of the High Middle Ages was abundant and richly varied. Poetry was written both in the traditional Latin—the universal scholarly language of medieval Europe—and in the vernacular languages of ordinary speech that had long been evolving in the various districts of Christendom. Traditional Christian piety found expression in a series of somber and majestic Latin hymns, whose mood is illustrated (through the clouded glass of translation) by these excerpts from "Jerusalem the Golden":

The world is very evil, the times are waxing late.
Be sober and keep vigil; the judge is at the gate. . . .
Brief life is here our portion; brief sorrow, short-lived care.
The life that knows no ending, the tearless life, is there. . . .
Jersalem the Golden, with milk and honey blessed,
Beneath thy contemplation sink heart and voice oppressed.
I know not, O I know not, what social joys are there,
What radiancy of glory, what light beyond compare.

At the opposite end of the spectrum of medieval Latin literature one encounters poetry of quite a different sort, composed by young, wandering scholars and aging perpetual-undergraduate types. The deliberate sensuality and blasphemy of their poems are expressions of student rebelliousness against the ascetic ideals of their elders:

For on this my heart is set, when the hour is neigh me,
Let me in the tavern die, with a tankard by me,
While the angels, looking down, joyously sing o'er me . . . etc.

One of these wandering-scholar poems is an elaborate and impudent expansion of the Apostles' Creed. The phrase from the Creed, "I believe in the Holy Ghost, the Holy [Catholic] Church . . . " is embroidered as follows:

I believe in wine that's fair to see,
And in the tavern of my host
More than in the Holy Ghost
The tavern will my sweetheart be,
And the Holy Church is not for me.*

These sentiments should not be regarded as indicative of a sweeping trend toward agnosticism. Rather, they are distinctively medieval expressions of the irreverent student radicalism that most ages know.

For all its originality, the Latin poetry of the High Middle Ages was overshadowed both in quantity and in variety of expression by vernacular poetry. The drift toward emotionalism, which we have already noted in medieval piety, was closely paralleled by the evolution of vernacular literature from the martial epics of the eleventh century to the delicate and sensitive romances of the thirteenth. Influenced by the sophisticated romanticism of the southern troubadour tradition, the bellicose spirit of northern France gradually softened.

In the eleventh and early twelfth centuries, heroic epics known as *Chansons de Geste* (Songs of Great Deeds) were enormously popular among the feudal nobility of nothern France. Many of these *Chansons* were exaggerated accounts of events surrounding the reign of Charlemagne. The most famous of all of the *Chansons de Geste*, the *Song of Roland*, told of a heroic and bloody battle between a hoard of

* Our italics.

Moslems and the detached rearguard of Charlemagne's army as it was withdrawing from Spain. Like old-fashioned Westerns, the *Chansons de Geste* were packed with action, and their heroes tended to steer clear of sentimental entanglements with women. Warlike prowess, courage, and loyalty to one's lord and fellows-in-arms were the virtues stressed in these heroic epics. The battle descriptions were characterized by gory realism:

He sees his bowels gush forth out of his side
And on his brow the brain laid bare to sight.

In short, the *Chansons de Geste* were mirrors of the rough, warrior ethos of eleventh-century feudal knighthood.

During the middle and later twelfth century the martial spirit of northern French literature was gradually transformed by the influx of the romantic troubadour tradition of southern France. In Provence, Toulouse, and Aquitaine, a rich and colorful culture had been developing in the eleventh and twelfth centuries; out of this vivacious society came a lyric poetry of remarkable sensitivity and enduring value. The lyric poets of the south were known as *troubadours*. Most were court minstrels, but some, including a duke of Aquitaine himself, were members of the upper nobility. Their poems were far more intimate and personal than the *Chansons de Geste* and placed much greater emphasis on romantic love. The delicacy and romanticism of the troubadour lyrics betoken a more genteel and sophisticated nobility than that of the feudal north—a nobility that preferred songs of love to songs of war. Indeed, medieval southern France was the source of the entire romantic-love tradition of Western Civilization, with its idealization of women, its emphasis on male gallantry and courtesy, and its impulse to embroider relations between man and woman with potent emotional overtones of eternal oneness, undying devotion, idealization, agony, and ecstasy:

I die of wounds from blissful blows,

And love's cruel stings dry out my flesh,
My health is lost, my vigor goes,
And nothing can my soul refresh.
I never knew so sad a plight,
It should not be, it is not right. . . .

I'll never hold her near to me
My ardent joy she'll ever spurn,
In her good grace I cannot be,
Nor even hope, but only yearn.
She tells me nothing, false or true,
And neither will she ever do.

The author of these lines, Jaufré Rudel (mid-twelfth century), unhappily and hopelessly in love, finds consolation in his talent as a poet, of which he has an exceedingly high opinion. The song from which the lines above are taken concludes on an optimistic note:

Make no mistake, my song is fair,
With fitting words and apt design.
My messenger would never dare
To cut it short or change a line. . . .
My song is fair, my song is good,
'Twill bring delight, as well it should.

The Romance

Midway through the twelfth century, the southern tradition of courtly love began to spread to the courts of northern France and, soon after, into England and Germany. As its influence grew, the northern knights discovered that more was expected of them than loyalty to their lords and a life of carefree slaughter. They were now expected to be gentlemen as well—to be courtly in manner and urbane in speech, to exhibit delicate and refined behavior in feminine company, and to idolize some noble lady. Such, briefly, were the ideals of courtly love. Their impact on the actual behavior of knights was distinctly limited, but their effect on the literature of Northern Europe was revolutionary. Out of the convergence of vernacular epic and vernacular lyric, there emerged a new poetic form known as the romance.

Like the *Chanson de Geste*, the romance

was a long narrative poem, but like the southern lyric, it was sentimental and imaginative. It was commonly based on some theme from the remote past: the Trojan War, Alexander the Great, and, above all, King Arthur—the half-legendary sixth-century British king. Arthur was transformed from a misty figure of Welsh legend into an idealized twelfth-century monarch surrounded by charming ladies and chivalrous knights. His court at Camelot, as described by the great French poet, Chrétien de Troyes, was a center of romantic love and refined religious sensitivity where knights worshipped their ladies, went on daring quests, and played out their chivalrous roles in a world of magic and fantasy.

In the *Chanson de Geste* the great moral imperative was loyalty to one's lord: in the romance, as in the southern lyric, it was love for one's lady. From *The Song of Roland* came the words:

Men must face great privation for their lord,
Must suffer cold for him, and searing heat,
And must endure sharp wounds and loss of blood.

But from the southern French lyric poetess Beatriz de Dia (*c.* 1160) came sentiments of a radically different sort:

My heart is filled with passion's fire.
My well-loved knight, I grant thee grace,
To hold me in my husband's place,
And do the things I so desire.

Several northern romances portray the old and new values in direct conflict. An important theme in both the Arthurian romances and the twelfth-century romance of *Tristan and Iseult* is a love affair between a vassal and his lord's wife. Love and feudal loyalty stand face to face, and love wins out. Tristan loves Iseult, the wife of his lord, King Mark of Cornwall. King Arthur's beloved knight Lancelot loves Arthur's wife, Guinevere. In both stories the lovers are ruined by their love, yet love they must—they have no choice—and al-

though the conduct of Tristan and Lancelot would have been regarded by earlier feudal standards as nothing less than treason, both men are presented sympathetically in the romances. Love destroys the lovers in the end, yet their destruction is itself romantic—even glorious. Tristan and Iseult lay dead side by side, and in their very death their love achieved its deepest consummation.

Alongside the theme of love in the medieval romances, and standing in sharp contrast to it, is the theme of Christian purity and dedication. The rough-hewn knight of old, having been taught to be courteous and loving, was now taught to be holy. Lancelot was trapped in the meshes of a lawless love, but his son, Galahad, became the prototype of the Christian knight—pure, holy, and chaste. And Perceval, another knight of the Arthurian circle, quested not for a lost loved one but for the Holy Grail of Christ's Last Supper.

The romance flourished in twelfth- and thirteenth-century France and among the French-speaking nobility of England. It was also a crucial element in the evolution of German vernacular literature. The German poets—known as *minnesingers*—were influenced by the French lyric and romance but developed these literary forms along highly original lines. The *minnesingers* produced their own deeply sensitive and mystical versions of the Arthurian stories, which, in their exalted symbolism and profundity of emotion, surpass even the works of Chrétian de Troyes and his French contemporaries.

Vernacular poetry came late to Italy, but in the works of Dante (d. 1321) it achieved its loftiest expression. Dante's *Divine Comedy*, written in the Tuscan vernacular, is a magnificent synthesis of medieval literature and medieval thought. Rich in allegory and symbolism, it tells of Dante's own journey through hell, purgatory, and paradise to the very presence of God himself. This device allows Dante to make devastating comments on past and contemporary history by placing all those of whom he disapproved—from local politicians to popes—in various levels of hell. Virgil, the archetype of ancient rationalism, is Dante's guide through hell and purgatory; the lady Beatrice, a symbol of purified love, guides him through the celestial spheres of paradise; and St. Bernard, the epitome of medieval sanctity, leads him to the threshold of Almighty God. Having traversed the entire cosmos of medieval thought, Dante ends his journey, and his poem, alone in the divine presence:

Eternal Light, thou in thyself alone
Abidest, and alone thine essence knows,
And loves, and smiles, self-knowing and
self-known. . . .
Here power failed to the high fantasy,
But my desire and will were turned—as one—
And as a wheel that turneth evenly,
By Holy Love, that moves the stars and sun.

Architecture: From Romanesque to Gothic

The High Middle Ages are one of the great epochs in the history of Western architecture. Stone churches, large and small, were built in prodigious numbers: In France alone, more stone was quarried during the High Middle Ages than by the pyramid and temple builders of ancient Egypt throughout its three-thousand-year history. Yet the real achievement of the medieval architects lay not in the immense scope of their activities but in the splendid originality of their aesthetic vision. Two great architectural styles dominated the age

(a) Barrel vault. (b) Cross vault

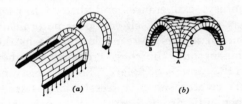

(a)   *(b)*

—the Romanesque style evolved in the eleventh-century, rose to maturity in the early twelfth, and during the latter half of the twelfth century gave way gradually to the Gothic style. From about 1150 to 1300 the greatest of the medieval Gothic cathedrals was built. Thereafter, the Gothic style became increasingly elaborate, basic structural innovation gave way to opulent decoration. But during the High Middle Ages it constituted one of humanity's most audacious and successful architectural experiments.

High medieval architecture was deeply affected by two of the basic cultural trends of the period. First of all, the great cathedrals were products of the urban revolution and the rise of intense urban piety. Second, the evolution from Romanesque to Gothic closely parallels the shift which we have already observed in literature and piety toward emotional sensitivity and romanticism. Romanesque architecture, although characterized by an exceeding diversity of expression, tended in general toward the solemnity of earlier Christian piety and the sturdy power of the *Chansons de Geste*. Gothic architecture, on the other hand, is dramatic, upward-reaching, and structurally sophisticated.

The development from Romanesque to Gothic can be understood as an evolution in the principles of structural engineering The key architectural ingredient in the Romanesque churches was the round arch. Romanesque roof design was based on the various elaborations of the round arch, such as the barrel vault and the cross vault (see Figures (*a*) and (*b*)). These heavy stone roofs required thick supporting walls; windows were necessarily few and small. A church in the fully developed Romanesque style conveys a powerful feeling of unity and earthbound solidity. Its massive arches, vaults, and walls, and its somber, shadowy interior give the illusion of mystery and otherworldliness, yet suggest at the same time the steadfast might of the universal Church.

During the first half of the twelfth century new structural elements began to be employed in the building of Romanesque churches: first were ribs of stone that ran along the edges of the arched cross vaults and helped to support them; next were pointed arches that permitted greater flexibility and height in the vaulting. By mid-century these novel features—ribbed vault and pointed arch—were providing the basis for an entirely new style of architecture, no longer Romanesque but Gothic. They were employed with such effect by Abbot Suger in his new abbey church of Saint-Denis near Paris, around 1140, that Saint-Denis is often regarded as the first true Gothic church.

French Gothic churches of the late twelfth century—such as Notre Dame de Paris—disclose the development of ribbed vault and pointed arch into a powerful and coherent new style. But not until the thirteenth century were the full potentialities of Gothic architecture realized. The discovery of the ribbed vault and pointed arch, and of a third Gothic structural element—the flying buttress—made it possible to support weights and stresses in a totally new way. The traditional building, a roof supported by walls, was transformed into a radically new kind of building—a skeleton—in which the stone vault rested not on walls but on slender columns and graceful exterior supports. The wall became structurally superfluous, and the vast areas between the supporting columns could be filled with glass. Concurrent with this architectural revolution was the development, in twelfth- and thirteenth-century Europe, of the art of stained glass making. The colored windows created in these centuries, with episodes from the Bible and religious legend depicted in shimmering blues and glowing reds, have never been equalled.

During the first half of the thirteenth century all the structural possibilities of the Gothic skeleton design were fully exploited. In the towns of central and north-

Gothic architecture; west facade of Amiens Cathedral, France, thirteenth century. (French Embassy Press and Information Division)

ern France there now rose churches of delicate, soaring stone, with walls of lustrous glass. Never before in history had windows been so immense or buildings so lofty; and never since has European architecture been at once so assured and so daringly original.

Gothic sculpture, like Romanesque, was intimately related to architecture, yet the two styles differed markedly. Romanesque fantasy, exuberance, and distortion gave way to a serene, self-confident naturalism. Human figures were no longer, as in the Romanesque churches, crowded together on the capitals of pillars. The Gothic sculptors created the first freestanding statues since antiquity and arranged them in long rows across the cathedral exteriors. Saints, prophets, kings, and angels, Christ and the Virgin, were depicted as tall, slender figures, calm yet warmly human—or as beautiful young women, placid and often smiling. The greatest Gothic churches of thirteenth century France—Bourges, Chartres, Amiens, Reims, Sainte-Chapelle—are superb syntheses of many separate arts. Their interiors convey a striking illusion of graceful stone vaulting springing up from walls of luminous colored glass. The pictures in the glass, the sculpture, and the architecture of the buildings themselves, became a single, majestic setting for the greatest of all medieval dramas—the reenactment of Christ's redemption of mankind in the Mass. Here, all the arts of the Middle Ages were directed to a single end: the expression and illumination of a deep, vital faith.

The Rise of Universities

Like the Gothic cathedral, the university was a product of the medieval town. The urban revolution of the eleventh and twelfth centuries brought about the decline of the old monastic schools which had done so much to preserve culture over the previous centuries. They were superseded north of the Alps by cathedral schools located in the rising towns, and in Italy by semi-secular municipal schools. Both the cathedral schools and the municipal schools had long existed, but it was only in the eleventh century that they arose to great prominence. Many of these schools now became centers of higher learning of a sort that Europe had not known for centuries. Their enrollments increased steadily and their faculties grew until, in the twelfth century, some of them evolved into universities.

In the Middle Ages, *university* was an exceedingly vague term. A university was simply a group of persons associated for any purpose. The word was commonly applied to the merchant guilds and craft guilds of the rising towns. A guild or university of students and scholars engaged

Gothic sculpture: Apostle's head, from the Cathedral of Sens, France, c. 1190-1200. (Courtesy Cathedral of Sens, France)

in the pursuit of higher learning was given the more specific name, *stadium generale*. When we speak of the medieval university, therefore, we are referring to an institution that would have been called a *stadium generale* by a man of the thirteenth century. It differed from lesser schools in three significant respects. (1) The *stadium generale* was open to students from many lands, not simply those from the surrounding district; (2) the *stadium generale* was a large school with a number of teachers rather than merely one omnicompetent master; (3) the *stadium generale* offered both elementary and advanced curricula. It offered a basic program of instruction in the traditional "seven liberal arts"—astronomy, geometry, arithmetic, music, grammar, rhetoric, and dialectic— and also instruction in one or more of the "higher" disciplines—theology, law, and medicine. Upon the successful completion of his liberal arts curriculum, the student could apply for a license to teach, but he might also wish to continue his studies by specializing in medicine, theology, or—most popular of all—civil or canon law. Legal training offered as its reward the promise of a lucrative administrative career in royal government or the Church.

Fundamentally, the medieval university was neither a campus nor a complex of buildings, but a *guild*—a privileged corporation of teachers, or sometimes of students. With its classes normally held in rented rooms, it was a highly mobile institution, and on more than one occasion when a university was dissatisfied with local conditions it won important concessions from the townsmen simply by threatening to move elsewhere.

In the thirteenth century, flourishing, universities were to be found at Paris, Bologna, Naples, Montpelier, Oxford, Cambridge, and elsewhere. Paris, Oxford, and a number of others were dominated by guilds of instructors in the liberal arts. Bologna, on the other hand, was governed by a guild of students who managed to reduce the exorbitant local prices of food and lodgings by threatening to move collectively to another town. The student guild of Bologna established in this Golden Age of student government, professors were given such outrageous requirements as having to begin and end their classes on time and to cover the prescribed curriculum. It is important to point out, however, that Bologna specialized in legal studies and that its pupils were older professional students for the most part—men who had completed their liberal arts curriculum and were determined to secure sufficient training for successful careers in law.

The students of the medieval universities were, on the whole, rowdy and exuberant, imaginative in their pranks, and hostile toward the surrounding towns. Thus the history of the medieval universities is punctuated by frequent town-gown riots. New students were hazed unmercifully; unpopular professors were hissed, shouted down, and even pelted with stones. Most of the students were of relatively humble origin—from the towns or the ranks of the lesser nobility—but they were willing to spend their student days in abject poverty if necessary in order to acquire the new knowledge and prepare themselves for the rich social and economic rewards that awaited many graduates.

Despite the enormous difference between medieval and modern university life, it should be clear that the modern university is a direct outgrowth of the institution that came into being in high medieval Europe. We owe to the medieval university the concept of a formal teaching license, the custom—unknown to antiquity—of group instruction, the idea of academic degrees, the notion of a liberal arts curriculum, the tradition of professors and students dressing in clerical garb (caps and gowns) on commencement day, and numerous other customs of university life. Even the letters written by medieval students to their parents or guardians have a curiously modern ring:

This is to inform you that I am studying at Oxford with the greatest diligence, but the matter of money stands greatly in the way of my promotion, as it is now two months since I have spent the last of what you sent me. The city is expensive and makes demands; I have to rent lodgings, buy necessities, and provide for many other things which I cannot now specify. [A fuller elaboration here would have been illuminating.] Wherefore I respectfully beg your paternity that by the prompting of divine pity you may assist me, so that I can complete what I have well begun. For you must know that without Ceres and Bacchus, Apollo grows cold.

Medicine and Law

The chief medical school of medieval Europe was the University of Salerno in southern Italy. Here, in a land of vigorous cultural intermingling, scholars were able to draw from the medical heritage of Islam and Byzantium. In general, medieval medical scholarship was a bizarre medley of cautious observation, common sense, and gross superstition. In one instance we encounter the advice that a person should eat and drink in moderation, but we are also instructed that onions will cure baldness, that the urine of a dog is an admirable cure for warts, and that all one must do to prevent a woman from conceiving is to bind her head with a red ribbon. Yet in the midst of this nonsense, important progress was being made in medical science. The writings of the great second-century scientist Galen, which constituted a synthesis of classical medical knowledge, were studied and digested, as were the important works of Arab students of medicine. And to this invaluable body of knowledge European scholars were now making their own original contributions on such subjects as the curative properties of plants and the anatomy of the human body. It is probable that both animal and human dissections were performed by the scholars of twelfth-century Salerno. These doctors, their crude and primitive methods notwithstanding, were laying the foundations on which Western European medical science was to rise.

Medieval legal scholarship addressed itself to two distinct bodies of material— canon law and civil law. The study of canon law or church law was enormously stimulated by the Investiture Controversy and subsequent church-state struggles. Drawing their precedents from the Bible, from the writings of the Latin Church Fathers, and from papal and conciliar decrees, the canon lawyers of Bologna and elsewhere elaborated difficult points of law, struggled to reconcile discordant canons, and assembled a series of great canonical collections. Many canon lawyers were enthusiastic supporters of the papal cause and devoted their scholarship to the task of providing a powerful legal foundation for the sweeping claims of the twelfth- and

thirteenth-century papacy. Indeed, as we have seen, many of the popes were themselves canon lawyers.

Civil lawyers, on the other hand, tended to exalt the emperor and the kings under whom so many of them served. The science of civil law was built on the framework of Justinian's *Corpus Juris Civilis* (see p. 105), which was first studied seriously in the West in late-eleventh-century Bologna. Roman law appealed to the legal scholars of the High Middle Ages as a uniquely comprehensive and rational body of jurisprudence. Although it contained a strong element of constitutionalism, it inherited from Justinian's age a tendency toward imperial absolutism which was put to effective use by the court lawyers of the rising monarchies. Roman law became the basis of most of the legal systems of continental Europe, where it served to make government at once more systematic and more autocratic. Thus the civil lawyers played a significant role in the evolution of France from the limited Germanic monarchy of the earlier Capetians toward the absolutism of later times. And the development and durability of a parliamentary regime in England owed much to the fact that a strong monarchy, based on the principles of Germanic law, was already well established before Europe felt the full impact of the Roman law revival.

Major Issues in Medieval Philosophy

It is only to be expected that an age that witnessed such sweeping economic and political developments and such vigorous creativity in religious and artistic expression would also achieve notable success in the realm of abstract thought. Medieval philosophy is exceedingly variegated and is marked by boundless curiosity and heated controversy. Among the diverse investigations and conflicting opinions of the medieval thinkers, three central issues deserve particular attention: (1) the degree of interrelationship between faith and reason, (2) the relative merits of the Platonic-Augustinian and the Aristotelian intellectual traditions, and (3) the reality of the Platonic archetypes or "universals."

The issue of faith versus reason was perhaps the most far-reaching of the three. Ever since Tertullian in the third century, there had been Christians who insisted that God so transcended reason that any attempt to approach Him through logic was not only useless but blasphemous. It was the mystic who knew God, not the theologian. Against this view, medieval philosophers such as Anselm and Thomas Aquinas maintained that faith and reason were dual avenues to truth, that they often led to the same conclusions, and that in no case were their conclusions contradictory.

The conflict between the systems of thought of Plato-Augustine and Aristotle did not emerge clearly until the thirteenth century when the full body of Aristotle's writings came into the West in Latin translations from Greek and Arabic. Until then most efforts at applying reason to faith were based on the Platonic traditions transmuted and transmitted by Augstine into the medieval West. Many philosophers of the more conservative type were deeply suspicious of the newly recovered Aristotelian writings, regarding them as pagan in viewpoint and dangerous to the Faith. Others, such as St. Thomas Aquinas, were much too devoted to the goal of reconciling faith and reason to ignore the works of a man whom they regarded as antiquity's greatest philosopher. St. Thomas sought to Christianize Aristotle as Augustine had Christianized Plato. In the middle decades of the thirteenth century, as high medieval philosophy was reaching its climax, the Platonic and Aristotelian traditions flourished side by side, and in the works of certain English thinkers of the age they achieved a singularly fruitful fusion.

The contest between medieval Platonism-Augustinianism and medieval Aristotelianism carried the seeds of still another controversy: the problem of archetypes or universals. Plato had taught that terms such as "dog," "man," or "cat" not only described certain creatures but also had reality in themselves—that individual cats are imperfect reflections of a model cat, an archetypal or universal cat. Again, we call certain acts "good" because they partake of a universal good which exists in heaven. In short, these universals—cat, dog, beauty, goodness, etc.—exist apart from the multitude of individual cats, dogs, and beautiful and good things in this world. And the person who seeks knowledge ought to meditate on these universals rather than study the world of phenomena in which they are reflected only imperfectly. St. Augustine accepted Plato's theory of universals with one amendment: that the archetypes existed in the mind of God rather than in some abstract realm, and that God put a knowledge of universals directly into our minds by a process which Augustine called "divine illumination." Both Plato and Augustine agreed that the universal existed apart from the particular and, indeed, that the universal was *more real* than the particular. In the High Middle Ages those who followed the Platonic-Augustinian approach to the universals were known as *realists*—they believed that universals were real.

The Aristotelian tradition brought with it another viewpoint on universals: that they existed, to be sure, but only in the particular—only by studying particular things in the world of phenomena could men gain knowledge of universals. The universals were real, but in a sense less real than Plato and Augustine believed. Accordingly, medieval philosophers who inclined toward the Aristotelian position have been called *moderate realists*.

But medieval philosophers were by no means confined to a choice between these two positions. Several worked out subtle solutions of their own. As early as the eleventh century the philosopher Roscellinus declared that universals were not real at all. They were mere names that humans gave to arbitrary classes of individual things. Reality was not to be found in universals but rather in the multiplicity and variety of objects which we can see, touch, and smell in the world around us. Those who followed Roscellinus in this view were known as *nomilists*—for them the universals were *nomina*, the Latin for "names." Nominalism lurked in the intellectual background during the twelfth and thirteenth centuries but was revived in the fourteenth. Many churchmen regarded it as a dangerous doctrine, for its emphasis on the particular over the general or universal seemed to suggest that the Catholic Church was not, as good churchmen believed, a single universal body but rather a vast accumulation of individual believers.

Having examined briefly three important issues of high medieval philosophy—reason versus revelation, Plato-Augustine versus Aristotle, and the problem of universals— we shall now see how these issues developed in the minds of individual philosophers between the eleventh and fourteenth centuries.

St. Anselm

The philosophers of this period were known as "scholastics" because nearly all of them were connected with schools— monastic schools, or universities. They first appeared in the later eleventh century as a product of the reawakening that Europe was just then beginning to undergo. The first great figure in scholastic philosophy was St. Anselm, an Italian who taught for many years in the vigorous monastic school of Bec in Normandy. In time he was appointed abbot of Bec, and in the 1090s he became archbishop of Canterbury. As archbishop he struggled vigorously against the Norman kings of England over the issue of lay investiture, and shortly after agreeing to a compromise settlement of the contro-

versy he died in 1109. During his eventful career he found time to think and write profoundly on such subjects as the atonement of mankind through Christ's crucifixion, the possibility of a rational proof of God, and the relationship between faith and reason. Anselm stood solidly in the Platonic-Augustinian tradition and was singularly important in the development of medieval thought because of his confidence that reason was not compatible with faith. He taught that faith must precede reason but that reason could serve to illuminate faith. His emphasis on reason, employed within the framework of a firm Christian conviction, set the stage for the significant philosophical development of the following generations, and his keen analytical mind made him the most notable Western philosopher since Augustine. With Anselm, Western Christendom regained at last the intellectual level of the fourth-century Latin Fathers.

Peter Abelard

The twelfth-century philosophers, intoxicated by the seemingly limitless possibilities of reason and logic, advanced boldly across new intellectual frontiers at the very time when their contemporaries were pushing forward the geographical frontiers of Europe. The most brilliant and audacious of these twelfth-century Christian rationalists was Peter Abelard (1079–1142), an immensely popular teacher, dazzling and egotistical, whose meteoric career ended in tragedy and defeat.

Abelard is perhaps best known for his love affair with the young Heloise, an affair that ended with Abelard's castration at the hands of thugs hired by Heloise's enraged uncle. The lovers were then separated permanently, both taking monastic vows, and in later years Abelard wrote regretfully of the affair in his autobiographical *History of My Calamities*. There followed a touching correspondence between the two lovers in which Heloise, now an abbess, confessed her enduring love and Abelard, writing almost as a father confessor, offered her spiritual consolation but nothing more. Abelard's autobiography and the correspondence with Heloise survive to this day, providing modern students with a singularly intimate and tender picture of romance and pathos in a society far removed from our own.*

Abelard was the supreme logician of the twelfth century. Writing several decades prior to the great influx of Aristotelian thought in Latin translation, he anticipated Aristotle's position on the question of universals by advocating a theory of moderate realism. Universals, Abelard believed, had no separate existence but were derived from particular things by a process of abstraction. In a famous work entitled *Sic et Non (Yes and No)*, Abelard collected opinions from the Bible, the Latin Fathers, the councils of the Church, and the decrees of the papacy on a great variety of theological issues, demonstrating that these hallowed authorities very often disagreed on important religious matters. Others before Abelard had collected authoritative opinions on various legal and theological issues but never so thoroughly or systematically. Abelard, in his *Sic et Non*, employed a method of inquiry that was developed and perfected by canon lawyers and philosophers over the next several generations. But his successors sought to reconcile the contradictions and arrive at conclusions, whereas Abelard left many of the issues unresolved and thereby earned the enmity of his conservative contemporaries. Abelard was a devoted Christian, if something of an intellectual show-off, but many regarded him as a dangerous skeptic. Thus he left himself open to bitter attacks by men such as St. Bernard who were deeply hostile to his merger of faith and reason. The brilliant

teacher was hounded from one place to another and finally condemned for hersey in 1141. He died at Cluny, on his way to Rome to appeal the condemnation.

The New Translations of Aristotle

But twelfth-century rationalism was far more than a one-man affair, and the persecution of Abelard failed to halt its growth. In the later twelfth and early thirteenth centuries the movement was powerfully reinforced by the arrival of vast quantities of Greek and Arabic writings in Latin translation. Significant portions of the philosophical and scientific legacy of ancient Greece now became available to European scholars. Above all, the full Aristotelian corpus now came into the West through the labors of translators in Spain and Sicily.

These translations were by no means fortuitous. They came in answer to a deep hunger on the part of Western thinkers for a fuller knowledge of the classical heritage in philosophy and science. Still, the introduction of certain new Aristotelian works created a profound intellectual crisis in Christendom, for they contained implications which seemed hostile to the Faith. The apparent incompatibility between these new Aristotelian writings and Christianity was heightened by the fact that they came into the West accompanied by the commentaries of a great heterodox Spanish Muslim philosopher, Averroes. This brilliant skeptic emphasized Aristotle's doctrine that the world had always existed and was therefore uncreated. He also interpreted Aristotle in such a way as to deny personal immortality. Averroes reconciled these views with orthodox Islam by a curious intellectual device known as the "doctrine of the twofold truth." He maintained that certain things could be true philosophically yet false from the standpoint of revealed religion. The importation of this twofold-truth doctrine into the West had two important consequences, (1) the development of a group of "Latin Averroists," who insisted on the

---

* The entire correspondence has recently been branded as a forgery of the late-twelfth and thirteen centuries. Is nothing sacred to the modern revisionist historian?

philosophical validity of Aristotle's hetero-dox opinions yet defended the Christian Faith as ultimately true, even though at variance with reason, and (2) the condemnation of certain of Aristotle's writings by the Church.

Thomas Aquinas

Against this background there emerged in the mid-thirteenth century a bold group of men dedicated to the reconciliation of reason and faith and therefore to the fusion of Aristotle and Christianity. They sought to confound the Latin Averroists by demonstrating that reason and revelation pointed to one truth, not two. The greatest figures in this tradition were the German philosopher Albertus Magnus (Albert the Great) and his remarkable Norman-Italian pupil, Thomas Aquinas. Both men were Dominicans; both taught at the University of Paris, concurrently with the great Franciscan philosopher Bonaventure who was the thirteenth century's greatest exponent of the Platonic-Augustinian tradition. The confluence of men such as these made mid-thirteenth century Paris one of history's most notable intellectual centers.

St. Thomas Aquinas created medieval Europe's consummate synthesis of reason and revelation. In his immense *Summa Theologica*, St. Thomas explored all the great questions of philosophy and theology, political science and morality, using Aristotle's logical method and Aristotle's categories of thought but arriving at conclusions that were in complete harmony with the Christian Faith. A moderate realist on the problem of universals, St. Thomas reasoned from sense experience rather than divine illumination. Like Abelard, he assembled every possible argument, pro and con, on every subject that he discussed, but unlike Abelard, he drew conclusions. Few philosophers before or since have been so generous in presenting and exploring opinions contrary to their own, and none has been so systematic and exhaustive. St.

Thomas created a vast, unified intellectual system, ranging from God to the natural world, logically supported at every step. As the Gothic cathedral was the artistic embodiment of the high medieval world, so the philosophy of Aquinas was its supreme intellectual expression. It is not without reason that the *Summa Theologica* has been called a cathedral of thought.

To this day there are those who subscribe essentially to the philosophy of Aquinas. On the other hand, many of his own thirteenth-century contemporaries rejected it in whole or in part. Franciscan intellectuals such as Bonaventure were particularly suspicious of the *tour de force* of this gifted Dominican. In England a profoundly un-Thomistic point of view was gradually emerging in the thirteenth century—a point of view that combined the mathematical tradition of Plato with the experimental tradition of Aristotle and directed them toward the investigation of the physical world.

Science

It was in thirteenth-century England that Western European science was born. The great English scholar Robert Grosseteste (d. 1253) was on intimate terms with Neoplatonic philosophy, Aristotelian physics, and the rich scientific legacy of Islam. He pioneered in the development of scientific method by outlining a procedure of observation, hypothesis, and experiment, and by urging the use of mathematical analysis whenever possible. Like other pioneers, Grosseteste followed many false paths—his explanations of such phenomena as colors, heat, and rainbows, were rejected in later centuries—but the experimental methods which he advocated were developed by his successors into a powerful intellectual tool. Grosseteste's disciple, the Franciscan Roger Bacon (*c.* 1214–1294), produced a fascinating body of scientific sense and nonsense. Roger Bacon was more an advocate of experimental science than a consistent practitioner of it, but at his best he was almost prophetic:

Experimental science controls the conclusions of all other sciences. It reveals truths which reasoning from general principles [the method of Abelard and St. Thomas] would never have discovered. Finally, it starts us on the way to marvelous inventions which will change the face of the world.

Hence the intense intellectual activity of the thirteenth century produced both the supreme synthesis of Christian rationalism and the genesis of a new method of scientific inquiry. In the realm of thought, as in so many other areas, the thirteenth century was both synthetic and creative. As the century drew to its close the intellectual synthesis of St. Thomas was being eroded by the doubts of his successors, who began to suspect that in seeking to reconcile reason and revelation he was attempting the impossible. Subsequent philosophers tended more and more to separate the two realms, some of them reverting to the Averroistic notion of the "twofold truth." Universal systems such as that of St. Thomas have seldom been lasting, but for a few brief years Thomas represented, for many, the perfect merger of intellect and belief—of mind and soul. As such, it takes its place alongside the Gothic cathedral, the *Divine Comedy* of Dante, and the piety of St. Francis as a supreme and mature expression of the dynamic resurgence of high medieval Europe.

The world of the High Middle Ages is described in some outworn textbooks as stagnant, gloomy, and monolithic. At the other extreme, it has been portrayed as an ideally constituted society, free of modern fears and tensions, where men of all classes could live happily and creatively. In reality, it was an age of vitality, of striking contrasts, of dark fears and high hopes, of poverty that was often brutal yet gradually diminishing. Above all, it was an age in which Europeans awoke to the rich variety of possibilities that lay before them. A thir-

teenth-century poet, in his celebration of springtime, captured perfectly the spirit of this rewakening.

The earth's ablaze again
With lustrous flowers
The fields are green again
The shadows deep.
Woods are in leaf again
And all the world
Is filled with joy again.
This long-dead land
Now flames with life again.
The passions surge,
Love is reborn,
And beauty wakes from sleep.

SUGGESTED READINGS

The asterisk indicates a paperback edition.

R. W. Southern, *The Making of the Middle Ages* (*New Haven: Yale University Press, 1953).

Steven Runciman, *A History of the Crusades* (3 Vols. New York: Harper, 1951–1954).

Gerd Tellenbach, *Church, State and Christian Society at the Time of the Investiture Contest* (Oxford Basil Blackwell, 1940).

Geoffrey Barraclough, *The Medieval Papacy* (*New York: Harcourt, Brace, Jovanovich, 1968).

David Douglas, *William the Conqueror* (*Berkeley, University of California Press, 1964).

C. W. Hollister, *The Making of England, 55 B.C.–A.D. 1399* (*Boston: D. C. Heath, 2nd ed., 1971).

Robert Fawtier, *The Capetian Kings of France* (*New York: St. Martin's Press, 1960).

David, Knowles, *The Evolution of Medieval Thought* (*New York: Vintage, 1964).

Jean Leclercq, *The Love of Learning and the Desire for God* (*New York: Mentor, 1962). *A short study of monasticism.*

Christopher Brooke, *The Structure of Medieval Society* (*New York: McGraw-Hill, 1971).

Robert Henri Bautier, *The Economic Development of Medieval Europe* (*New York: Harcourt & Brace Jovanovich, 1971).

Robert S. Lopez, *The Commercial Revolution of the Middle Ages, 950–1350* (*Englewood Cliffs, N.J.: Prentice-Hall, 1971).

John W. Baldwin, *The Scholastic Culture of the Middle Ages, 1000–1300* (*Lexington, Mass.: D. C. Heath, 1971).

Jeffrey B. Russell, *A History of Medieval Christianity: Prophecy and Order* (*New York: Thomas Y. Crowell, 1968).

Bennett D. Hill, *Church and State in the Middle Ages* (*New York: Wiley, 1970).

John C. Moore, *Love in Twelfth-Century France* (*Philadelphia: University of Pennsylvania Press, 1972).

Gordon Leff, *Medieval Thought* (*Baltimore, Md.: Penguin, 1958).

C. W. Hollister, *The Twelfth-Century Renaissance* (*New York: Wiley, 1969).

C. H. Haskins, *The Rise of the Universities* (*Ithaca, N.Y.: Cornell University Press, 1957).

C. H. Haskins, *The Renaissance of the Twelfth Century* (*New York: Meridian Books, 1957).

Erwin Panofsky, *Gothic Architecture and Scholasticism* (*New York: Meridian Books, 1957).

C. H. McIlwain, *The Growth of Political Thought in the West* (New York: Macmillan, 1932).

Walter Ullmann, *A History of Political Thought: The Middle Ages* (*Baltimore, Md.: Penguin, 1965).

Villehardouin and Joinville, *Memoirs of the Crusades*, trans. by Sir Frank Marzials (London: Everyman, 1908).

Part 5
Late-Medieval and Renaissance Europe: The Ordeal of Transition

14
Church and State in the Fourteenth and Fifteenth Centuries

The fourteenth and fifteenth centuries are the despair of teachers, students, and textbook writers. We are almost tempted to suggest skipping this section altogether. But confusing as they are, the developments that occurred during the centuries between the High Middle Ages and the Reformation have shaped the future of Europe and the world. Among the discoveries of that era are printing, perspective, gunpowder, and North America. It was an age of plague, doubt, and invention —of decay and rebirth. When we call it "late-medieval and Renaissance Europe" we do not mean to imply that the exhaustion of medieval culture was followed by a Renaissance. The great difficulty is that both were going on at the same time. And historians have been notoriously unsuccessful in deciding whether to weep at the decay, revel in the process of crisis and change, or applaud the Renaissance. This indecision emerges in the contrasting titles of the two greatest books on the period: Jacob Burckhardt's *Civilization of the Renaissance in Italy* and John Huizinga's *Waning of the Middle Ages*.

Both books deal with the same age, but from vastly different perspectives. It may be of some help to realize that Huizinga was writing about France and the Netherlands whereas Burckhardt was concerned with Italy. And it is true that the phenomenon we call "the Renaissance" was in large measure an *Italian* Renaissance, which occurred while the rest of Europe was struggling through the crises of the Late Middle Ages. But the late-medieval economic depression afflicted Italy and northern Europe alike, and so did the late-medieval plague. Renaissance Italy was economically troubled, pestilential, and war-torn. Only a tiny elite of nobles, artists, and intellectuals had any idea that a Renaissance was going on. The majority of Italians were enduring the same hard times that most other Europeans were undergoing. And conversely, Renaissance ideas and styles were seeping into the

North; early in the sixteenth century, for example, Italian Renaissance humanism was inspiring northern humanists like Erasmus of Rotterdam and the Englishman Thomas More.

Thus the "Late Middle Ages" and the "Renaissance" are concurrent, interwoven aspects of a single era. This chapter, and the next, will focus primarily on northern Europe, whereas Chapter 16—"The Culture of the Renaissance," will be concerned chiefly (but not exclusively) with Italy. Having read them all, the reader may find himself still at a loss to encapsulate the era in a handful of apt generalizations. Anyone who thinks he can do so is either a genius or a fool. For the rest of us, there will always remain a touch of bewilderment as we approach this ambiguous, deeply complex age of ends and beginnings, hope and despair, suffering and growth.

The Decline of the High-Medieval Synthesis

Like most eras of transition, the fourteenth and fifteenth centuries were violent and unsettled, marked by a gradual ebbing of the self-confidence on which the high-medieval synthesis had rested. Prosperity gave way to sporadic depression, optimism to disillusionment, and the thirteenth-century dream of fusing the worlds of matter and spirit came to an end. Social behavior ran to extremes—to rebellion, sensualism, flagellation, cynicism, and witchcraft. Powerful creative forces were at work in these centuries, but they were less evident to most contemporary observers than the forces of disintegration and decay. The shrinking of Europe's economy, population, and territorial frontiers was accompanied by a mood of pessimism and claustrophobia, exploding periodically into frenzied enthusiasm or blind rage. The literature and art of the period express a preoccupation with fantasy, eccentricity, and death. England and France were torn by war, and both were ruled for a time by madmen. The Black

Death struck Europe in the mid-fourteenth century and returned periodically to darken men's spirits and disrupt society.

These varied symptoms of social neurosis were associated with a gradual shift in Western Europe's political orientation—from a Christian commonwealth to a constellation of territorial states. The Roman Catholic Church fared badly during the Late Middle Ages. The western kingdoms were racked by civil and external war and, at times, by a near-breakdown of royal government. Yet during the final half-century of the period (c. 1450–1500) strong monarchies emerged in England, France, and Spain. These three states were destined to dominate Western European politics far into the future. By 1500 the monarchy was beginning to replace the Church as the object of men's highest allegiance. The pope had become mired in local Italian politics, and medieval Christian internationalism was breaking up into sovereign fragments.

Church and State in the Late Middle Ages

The late-medieval evolution from Christendom toward nationhood was not so much a transformation as a shift in balance. Even during the High Middle Ages the ideal of a Christian commonwealth, guided by pope and clergy, had never been fulfilled. At best, popes could win momentary political victories over kings and could achieve an uneasy equilibrium between royal and clerical authority within the European kingdoms. And by the end of the thirteenth century the balance was already tipping in favor of monarchs such as Edward I of England and Philip the Fair of France. Two centuries later, in 1500, the papacy was far weaker as an international force and the monarchies stronger, but "nationhood," by any strict definition, had not yet come. Still, papal authority over the churches within the various kingdoms, which had been a significant reality in the High Middle Ages, was becoming tenuous by 1500. The princely electors of Germany had long before denied the papacy any role in imperial elections or coronations, and papal influence in the appointment of French, English, and Spanish prelates had ebbed. More important still, the Late Middle Ages witnessed a collapse of papal spiritual prestige and a widening chasm between Christian piety and the organized church.

Christianity did not decline noticeably during this period; it merely became less ecclesiastical. The powerful movement of lay piety, which had been drifting away from papal leadership all through the High Middle Ages, now became increasingly hostile to ecclesiastical wealth and privilege, increasingly individualistic, and increasingly mystical. The wave of mysticism that swept across late-medieval Europe was not, for the most part, openly heretical. But by stressing the spiritual relationship between the individual and God the mystics tended to deemphasize the role of the ordained clergy and the sacraments as channels of divine grace. The mystic, although he believed in the efficacy of the Holy Eucharist, devoted himself chiefly to the direct mystical apprehension of God, for which no clerical hierarchy, no popes, and no sacraments were needed.

Mystics and Reformers

Mysticism had always been an element in Christian devotional life, and it was well known to the High Middle Ages. But with the breakdown of the high-medieval synthesis, and with the growth of complacency and corruption within the church, mysticism became, for the first time, a large-scale movement among the laity. Early in the fourteenth century, the great Dominican mystic, Meister Eckhardt (d. 1327), taught that man's true goal is utter separation from the world of the senses and absorption into the Divine Unknown. Eckhardt had many followers, and as the century progressed, several large mystical

brotherhoods took form. The greatest of them, the Brethren of the Common Life, was founded about 1375 by the Flemish lay preacher Gerard Groot, a student of one of Eckhart's disciples. The Brethren of the Common Life devoted themselves to simple lives of preaching, teaching, and charitable works. Their popularity in fifteenth-century Northern Europe approached that of the Franciscans two centuries before, but the Brethren, unlike the Franciscans, took no lifetime vows. Their schools were among the finest in Europe and produced some of the leading mystics, humanists, and reformers of the fifteenth and sixteenth centuries. Erasmus and Luther were both products of the Brethren's schools, as was Thomas à Kempis (d. 1471) whose *Imitation of Christ* stands as the supreme literary expression of late-medieval mysticism.* The *Imitation of Christ* typifies the mystical outlook in its emphasis on adoration over speculation, inner spiritual purity over external "good works," and direct experience of God over the sacramental avenues of divine grace. The *Imitation* remained well within the bounds of Catholic orthodoxy, yet it contained ideas that had great appeal to the sixteenth-century Protestant reformers. The emphasis on individual piety, common to all the mystics, tended to erode the medieval Christian commonwealth by transforming the Catholic church into a multitude of individual souls, each groping his way toward salvation alone.

This element of Christian individualism was carried at times to the point of outright heresy. John Wycliffe (d. 1384), a professor at Oxford, anticipated the later Protestants by placing the authority of Scriptures over the pronouncements of popes and councils. Extending the implications of contemporary mysticism to their limit, Wycliffe stressed the individual's inner journey toward God, questioned the real presence of Christ in the Holy Eu-

---

* Although most scholars attribute *The Imitation of Christ* to Thomas à Kempis, the attribution is not certain.

charist, deemphasized the entire sacramental system, and spoke out strongly against ecclesiastical wealth. This last protest had been implicit in the thirteenth-century Franciscan movement, although St. Francis had shown his devotion to apostolic poverty by living it rather than forcing it on others. The compromises of later Franciscanism on the matter of property had given rise to a zealous splinter group— the "Spiritual Franciscans"—whose insistence on universal ecclesiastical poverty had made them anticlerical and antipapal. John XXII (1316–1334), the shrewd Avignonese "financier-pope," had been obliged in 1323 to denounce the doctrine of apostolic poverty as heretical. And Wycliffe, more than half a century later, was stripped of his professorship and convicted of heresy. Owing to his powerful friends at court, and to unpopularity of the papacy in fourteenth-century England, he was permitted to die peacefully, but his followers, the Lollards, were hunted down. Their fate is suggested by the title of a parliamentary act of 1401: "The Statute on the Burning of Heretics."

English Lollardy represented an extreme expression of a growing discontent with the official Church. Wycliffe's doctrines spread to faraway Bohemia where they were taken up by the reformer John Hus. The Hussites used Wycliffe's anticlericalism as a weapon in the struggle for Czech independence from German political and cultural influence. John Hus was burned at the stake at the Council of Constance in 1415, but his followers survived into the Reformation era as a dissident national group. Both Wycliffe and Hus represented, in their opposition to the organized international church, a reconciliation of personal religious faith with the idea of national sovereignty. If Christianity was to be an individual affair, then the political claims of popes and prelates were meritless, and secular rulers might govern without ecclesiastical interference. Thus the radical thrust of late-medieval Christianity, by its very anticlericalism,

tended to support the growing concept of secular sovereignty. Ardent religious spirits such as John Hus—and Joan of Arc, burned as a heretic in 1431—could fuse Christian mysticism with the beginnings of patriotism.

Crisis of the Papacy: The Schism and the Conciliar Movement

The mystics and reformers, implicitly or explicitly, rejected the pope as the mediator between God and the Christian community. Actually, the late-medieval papacy did little to merit the awesome responsibility of mediator. Under pressure from King Philip the Fair the papacy had moved to Avignon, on the Rhone River, officially outside the domains of France yet always in their shadow. There a series of French popes ruled from 1309 to 1376. The Avignon popes were subservient to the French crown only to a degree. They were capable of independent action, particularly when France had weak rulers, but their very location suggested to non-Frenchmen that they were no longer an impartial international force. Until 1376 attempts to return the papacy to Rome were foiled by the insecurity and violent factionalism of the holy city. Meanwhile the Avignon popes carried the thirteenth-century trend toward administrative and fiscal efficiency to its ultimate degree. Englishmen and Germans resented paying high taxes to an apparent tool of the French crown. And the immense bureaucracy of papal Avignon could hardly be expected to inspire mystics and reformers. As one contemporary observed, the pope's proper role was to shepherd Christ's flock, not to fleece it.

In 1376, Pope Gregory XI finally moved the Holy See from Avignon back to Rome. Chagrined by the turbulent conditions he encountered there, he made plans to return to France, but died in 1378 before he could carry them out. Urged on by a Roman mob, the cardinals—most of whom were homesick Frenchmen—grudgingly elected an Italian to the papal throne. The new pope, Urban VI, had previously been a colorless functionary in the ecclesiastical establishment. Now to everyone's surprise, he became a zealous reformer and began taking steps to reduce the cardinals' revenues and influence. The French cardinals fled Rome, cancelled their previous election on the grounds of mob intimidation, and elected a French pope who returned with them to Avignon. Back in Rome, Urban VI appointed new cardinals, and for the next 37 years the Universal Church was torn by schism. When the rival popes died, their cardinals elected rival successors. Excommunications were hurled to-and-fro between Rome and Avignon, and the states of Europe chose their sides according to their interests. France and its allies supported Avignon, England and the Holy Roman Empire backed Rome, and the Italian states shifted from one side to the other as it suited their purposes. Papal prestige was falling in ruin, yet in the face of age-long papal claims to absolute spiritual authority, there seemed no power on earth that could claim to arbitrate between two rival popes. The church was at an impasse.

As the schism dragged on, increasing numbers of Christians became convinced that the only solution was the convening of a general church council. Both popes argued that councils were inferior to them and could not judge them, and Christians were perplexed as to who, if not the popes, had the authority to summon a council. At length the cardinals themselves, in both camps, called a council to meet in Pisa. There, in 1409, a group of 500 prelates deposed both popes and elected a new one. Since neither pope recognized the conciliar depositions, the effect of the Council of Pisa was to transform a two-way schism into a three-way schism. The situation was not only scandalous but ludicrous.

At length the Holy Roman emperor, drawing on the ancient precedent of the Emperor Constantine, summoned the prelates of Europe to the Council of Constance (1415–1418). Here, at last, the depositions of all three popes were voted and enforced, and the schism was healed by the election of a conciliar pope, Martin V (1417–1431).

To many thoughtful Christians the healing of the schism was not enough. The papacy stood discredited, and it was argued that future popes should be guided by general councils meeting regularly and automatically. The role of councils and assemblies was familiar enough to contemporary secular governments. Why should not the church, too, be governed "constitutionally"? Such views were being urged by political philosophers such as Marsilius of Padua in the fourteenth century and Nicolas of Cusa in the fifteenth, and they were widely accepted among the prelates at Constance. That these delegates were essentially conservative is suggested by their decision to burn John Hus, who came to Constance with an imperial promise of safe conduct. Yet the Council of Constance made a genuine effort to reform the constitution of the church along conciliar lines. The delegates affirmed, against papal objection, the ultimate authority of councils in matters of doctrine and reform, and they decreed that thenceforth general councils would convene at regular intervals.

These broad principles, together with a number of specific reforms voted by the Council of Constance, met with firm opposition from Pope Martin V and his successors, who insisted on absolute papal supremacy. The popes reluctantly summoned a council in 1423 and another in 1431, but worked to make them ineffective. The last of the important medieval councils, the Council of Basel (1431–1449), drifted gradually into open schism with the recalcitrant papacy and petered out ingloriously in 1449. By then Europe's enthusiasm for conciliarism was waning; the conciliar movement died, and a single pope ruled unopposed once more in Rome.

The men who sat on the papal throne between the dissolution of Basel (1449) and the beginning of the Protestant Reformation (1517) were radically different from their high-medieval predecessors. Abandoning much of their former jurisdiction over the international Church, they devoted themselves to the beguiling culture and bitter local politics of Renaissance Italy. By now the popes were normally Italians, and so they would remain on into the future. Struggling to strengthen their hold on the Papal States, maneuvering through the shifting sands of Italian diplomacy, they conceded to northern monarchs an extensive degree of control over Church and clergy in return for a formal recognition of papal authority and an agreed division of church revenues between pope and king.

CHRONOLOGY OF THE LATE-MEDIEVAL CHURCH

1309–1378:	Avignon Papacy
1305–1314:	Pontificate of Clement V
1316–1334:	Pontificate of John XXII
1327:	Death of Master Eckhart
1370–1378:	Pontificate of Gregory XI; Return to Rome
1372:	Wycliffe attacks papal domination of the Church
1378–1417:	The Great Schism
1409:	Council of Pisa fails to heal Schism
1414–1449:	Era of Conciliarism
1414–1418:	Council of Constance heals Schism, burns John Hus
1417–1431:	Pontificate of Martin V
1431–1449:	Council of Basel

The Rise of the State

The shift in emphasis from international Catholicism toward secular sovereignty was ably and forcefully expressed in Marsilius of Padua's important treatise, the *Defensor Pacis* (1324). Here the dilemma of conflicting sovereign jurisdictions, secular and ecclesiastical, was resolved uncompromisingly in favor of the state. The Church, Marsilius argued, should be stripped of political authority, and the state should

wield sovereign power over all its subjects, lay and clerical alike. Thus the Church, united in faith, would be divided politically into dozens of state churches obedient to their secular rulers and not to the pope. In its glorification of the sovereign state, the *Defensor Pacis* foreshadowed the evolution of late-medieval and early-modern politics.

It was only after 1450, however, that the western monarchies were able to assert their authority with any consistency over the particularistic nobility. During the period from the early-fourteenth to the mid-fifteenth century, the high-medieval trend toward royal centralization seemed to have reversed itself. The major Iberian powers—Aragon, Castile, and Portugal—were tormented by sporadic internal upheavals and made no progress toward reducing Granada, the remaining Islamic enclave in the peninsula. For most of the period, England and France were involved in the Hundred Years' War (1337–1453), which drove England to the brink of bankruptcy and ravaged the French countryside and population.

England: The Growth of Parliament and the Hundred Years' War

Nevertheless, the unwritten English "constitution" developed significantly during these years. In the course of the fourteenth century, Parliament changed from a body that met occasionally to a permanent institution and split into Lords and Commons. The House of Commons, consisting of representative townsmen and shire knights, bargained with a monarchy hard pressed by the expenses of the Hundred Years' War. Commons traded its fiscal support for important political concessions, and by the century's end it had gained the privilege of approving or disapproving all taxation not sanctioned by custom. With control of the royal purse strings secured, Commons then won the power to legislate. Adopting the motto, "redress before supply," it refused to pass financial grants until the king had approved its petitions, and in the end, Commons petitions acquired the force of law.

Without belittling these constitutional advances, one must recognize that the late-medieval Commons was largely controlled by the force or manipulation of powerful aristocrats. Elections could be rigged; representatives could be bribed or overawed. And although Parliament deposed two English kings in the fourteenth century—Edward II in 1327 and Richard II in 1399—in both instances it was simply ratifying the results of aristocratic power struggles. It is significant that such parliamentary ratification should seem necessary to the nobility, but one must not conclude that Parliament had yet become an independent agent. Symbolically, it represented the will of the English community; actually it remained vulnerable to aristocratic force and tended to affirm decisions already made in castles or on battlefields.

The Hundred Years' War, which proved such a stimulus to the growth of parliamentary privileges, also constituted a serious drain on English wealth and lives. Beginning in 1337, the war dragged on fitfully for 116 years with periods of savage warfare alternating with prolonged periods of truce. Broadly speaking, the conflict was a continuation of the Anglo-French rivalry that dated from the Norman Conquest. Since 1066 England and France had battled

on numerous occasions. In 1204 the Capetian crown had won the extensive northern French territories of the Angevin Empire. Normandy, Anjou, and surrounding lands had fallen more or less permanently into French royal hands, but the English kings retained a tenuous lordship over Gascony in the southwest. The English Gascon claim, cemented by a brisk commerce in Bordeaux wine and English cloth, gave rise to an expensive but inconclusive war (1294–1303) between Philip the Fair of France and Edward I of England. Competing English and French claims to jurisdiction in Gascony constituted one of several causes for the resumption of hostilities in 1337.

Another cause of the Hundred Years' War was the Anglo-French diplomatic struggle for control of Flanders, which France needed to round out its territories and which England needed to secure its profitable wool trade. Tension mounted in 1328 when, on the death of the last French Capetian King, Edward III of England (1327–1377) laid claim to the throne of France. Edward III's mother was a daughter of Philip the Fair, but the French nobility, refusing to be governed by an English monarch, revived the ancient custom that the succession could not pass through a female. Accordingly, they chose Philip VI (1328–1350), the first king of the long-lived Valois dynasty. Edward III accepted the decision at first, but in 1337, when other reasons prompted him to take

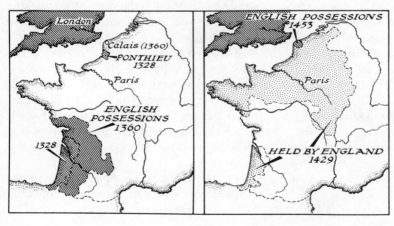

up arms, he renewed his claim and titled himself king of France and England.

None of these causes can be considered decisive, and war might yet have been avoided, but Edward III and Philip VI were chivalric, high-spirited romantics longing for heroic clashes of arms. The same spirit infected the nobility on both sides, although the French knights lost their ardor when English longbowmen won smashing victories at Crécy (1346) and Poitiers (1356). The English revered Edward III so long as English arms were victorious, but they deposed his successor, Richard II (1377–1399), who showed no interest in fighting Frenchmen. Henry V (1413–1422) revived hostilities and gained the adulation of his subjects by winning a momentous victory over the French at Agincourt in 1415. But Henry V's early death, and the subsequent career of Joan of Arc (see p. 187), turned the tide of war against the English. By 1453, when the long struggle ended at last, England had lost all of France except the port of Calais. The centuries-long process of Anglo-French disentanglement was completed, and Joan of Arc's vision was realized: her dauphin (crown prince) ruled France unopposed as King Charles VII.

The Hundred Years' War had been over for scarcely two years when England entered an era of civil strife between the rival houses of York and Lancaster, both claiming the throne. The Wars of the Roses, which raged off and on between the years 1455 and 1485, were the medieval English nobility's last orgy of violence. Weary of endless bloodshed, ordinary Englishmen longed for firm royal governance. They achieved it, to a degree, in the reign of the Yorkist Edward IV (1461–1483). And after a final burst of warfare, strong monarchy came permanently to England with the accession of the first Tudor king, that crafty, treacherous miser, Henry VII (1485–1509). Both Edward IV and Henry VII sought peace, a full treasury, and effective government, and by the late fifteenth century these goals were coming within reach. The economy was reviving, many of the more troublesome nobles had perished in the Wars of the Roses, and most Englishmen were willing to exchange violent independence for obedience and peace. All that was needed now was strong royal leadership, and that was supplied in full measure by the willful, determined Tudors.

France

The Hundred Years' War was a far greater trial to France than to England. All the fighting took place on French soil, and mercenary companies continually pillaged the French countryside. King John the Good (1350–1364)—a very bad king indeed —was powerless to cope with the English or bring order to a demoralized, plague-ridden land. In 1356, a decade after the French military debacle at Crecy and eight years after the onset of the Black Death (see p. 194). France was stunned by a crushing defeat at Poitiers. French nobles fell in great numbers, and King John himself was taken prisoner by the English.

The Estates General, meeting in Paris under the leadership of a dynamic Parisian cloth merchant, Etienne Marcel, momentarily assumed the reins of government. In 1357 they forced King John's son, the young Dauphin Charles, to issue a radical constitutional statute known as the "Great Ordinance." This statute embodied the demands of the bourgeois-dominated Estates General to join with the monarchy in the governance of France. The Estates General were thenceforth to meet on regular occasions and to supervise the royal finances, courts, and administration through a small standing committee. The Dauphin Charles, deeply hostile to this infringement of royal authority, submitted for a time, then fled Paris to gather royalist support in the countryside.

By 1358 the horrors of plague, depression, and mercenary marauders had goaded the French peasantry into open revolt. The

Jacquerie—as the rebellious peasants were called—lacked coherent goals and effective leaders, but they managed for a time to terrorize rural France. On one occasion they are reported to have forced an aristocratic wife to eat her roasted husband, after which they raped and murdered her. But within a few months the aristocracy and urban elites succeeded in crushing the Jacquerie with a savagery worthy of the rebels themselves. The peasants' rebellion of 1358 evoked a widespread longing for order and a return to the ways of old. This conservative backlash resulted in a surge of royalism which doomed Etienne Marcel's constitutional movement in Paris. Marcel himself was murdered in midsummer, 1358, and the Dauphin Charles returned to the city in triumph.

The Great Ordinance of 1357 became a dead letter after Marcel's fall, and in later centuries the Estates General met less and less frequently. The Dauphin Charles, who became the able King Charles V (1364–1380), instituted new tax measures that largely freed the monarchy from its financial dependence on assemblies and made it potentially the richest in Europe. The Estates General, unlike the English Parliament, failed to become an integral part of the government, and French kings reverted more and more to their high-medieval practice of dealing with their subjects through local assemblies. There were "Parlements" in France—outgrowths of the central and regional courts—but their functions remained largely judicial; they did not deliberate on the granting of taxes, and they did not legislate. French national cohesion continued to lag behind that of England primarily because France was much larger, more populous, and culturally diverse. During the Late Middle Ages its great dukes still ruled whole provinces with little interference from Paris. In the absence of an articulate national parliament the only voice that could claim to speak for all the French people was the voice of their king.

Charles V succeeded in turning the tide

of war by avoiding pitched battles. His armies harassed the English unceasingly and forced them, little by little, to draw back. By Charles' death the French monarchy was recovering, and the English, reduced to small outposts around Bordeaux and Calais, virtually abandoned the war for a generation.

But Charles V was succeeded by the incompetent Charles VI (1380–1422)—"Charles the Mad"—who grew from a weak child into a periodically insane adult. His reign was marked by a bloody rivalry between the houses of Burgundy and Orléans. The Duke of Orléans was Charles the Mad's brother, the Duke of Burgundy his uncle. In Capetian times, such powerful fief-holding members of the royal family had usually cooperated with the king, but now, with a madman on the throne, Burgundy and Orléans struggled for control of the kingdom. In the course of the fifteenth century, the Orléanist faction became identified with the cause of the Valois monarchy, and Burgundy evolved into a powerful independent state between France and Germany. But at the time of Charles the Mad all was uncertain.

With France ravaged once again by murder and civil strife, King Henry V of England resumed the Hundred Years' War and, in 1415, won his overwhelming victory at Agincourt. The Burgundians then joined the English, and Charles the Mad was forced to make Henry V his heir. But both kings died in 1422, and while Charles the Mad's son, Charles VII (1422–1461), carried on a halfhearted resistance, the Burgundians and English divided northern France between them and prepared to crush the remaining power of the Valois monarchy.

At the nadir of his fortunes, Charles VII, as yet uncrowned, accepted in desperation the military services of the peasant visionary, Joan of Arc. Joan's victory at Orléans, her insistence on Charles' coronation in Reims, and her capture and death at the stake in 1431 have become legendary. The spirit that she kindled raised French hopes, and in the two decades following her death Charles VII's armies went from victory to victory. The conquest of France had always been beyond English resources, and English successes in the Hundred Years' War had been mainly a product of wretched French leadership and paralyzing internal division. Now, as the war drew at last to a successful close, Charles VII could devote himself to the rebuilding of the royal government. He was supported in his task by secure tax revenues, a standing army, and the steady development of effective administrative institutions.

Centralization was carried still further by Louis XI (1461–1483), known as the "Spider King"—a name befitting both his appearance and his policies. Son and heir of Charles VII (whom he despised), Louis XI wove webs about his various rivals, removing them by murder, beheadings, and treachery. The Burgundian threat dissolved in 1477 when the last duke of Burgundy died fighting Louis' Swiss allies, and the Spider King swiftly confiscated the entire duchy. Plotting his way through a labyrinth of shifting alliances and loyalties, he advanced significantly toward the goals of French unification and Valois absolutism.

By 1500 the French monarchy was ruling through a central administration of middle-class professional bureaucrats. The nobility was pampered but apparently tamed, the towns were flourishing, and new royal armies were carrying the dynastic claims of the Valois kings into foreign lands.

CHRONOLOGY OF LATE-MEDIEVAL ENGLAND AND FRANCE

England

1307–1327:	Reign of Edward II
1327–1377:	Reign of Edward III
1337–1453:	Hundred Years' War
1346:	Battle of Crécy
1348–1349:	Black Death
1356:	Battle of Poitiers
1377–1399:	Reign of Richard II
1381:	Peasants' Revolt
1413–1422:	Reign of Henry V
1415:	Battle of Agincourt
1455–1485:	Wars of the Roses
1461–1483:	Reign of Edward IV
1485–1509:	Reign of Henry VII. Beginning of Tudor Dynasty

France

1328–1589:	Valois Dynasty
1328–1350:	Reign of Philip VI
1337–1453:	Hundred Years' War
1346:	Battle of Crécy
1348–1349:	Black Death
1350–1364:	Reign of John the Good
1356:	Battle of Poitiers
1357:	The Great Ordinance
1358:	Jacquerie Rebellion
1364–1380:	Reign of Charles V
1380–1422:	Reign of Charles VI, "the Mad"
1415:	Battle of Agincourt
1422–1461:	Reign of Charles VII
1429–1431:	Career of Joan of Arc
1461–1483:	Reign of Louis XI

Spain

The course of Spanish history in the Late Middle Ages runs parallel to that of England and France, with generations of internal turmoil giving way in the later fifteenth century to political coherence and ruthless royal consolidation. As the high-medieval *Reconquista* slowed to a halt around 1270, the Iberian Peninsula contained two strong Christian kingdoms— Castile and Aragon—the weaker Christian kingdom of Portugal along the western coast, and Muslim Granada in the extreme south. Aragon, smaller than Castile, was more highly urbanized and far more imperialistic. During the thirteenth and fourteenth centuries its kings conquered the Islamic Mediterranean islands of Majorca, Minorca, Sardinia, and Sicily. The old Norman kingdom of Sicily (including southern

Italy) had passed, after the death of Emperor Frederic II, to a junior member of the French Capetian house. The Sicilians, rebelling against French control in 1282, invited King Peter III of Aragon to be their monarch, and after a savage twenty-year struggle—the War of the Sicilian Vespers—the kingdom was divided in two. Aragon thenceforth ruled the island of Sicily while, on the Italian mainland, a "Kingdom of Naples" remained under the control of the French dynasty. The two kingdoms, Sicily and Naples, were reunited in 1435 under an Aragonese king, but for long years thereafter southern Italy and Sicily remained a source of antagonism between Spain and France.

Aragon and Castile were both plagued by civil turbulence during the Late Middle Ages. Aragonese kings strove with only limited success to placate the nobility and townsmen by granting significant concessions to the Cortes—the regional representative assemblies. A prolonged revolt by the mercantile class in the Aragonese province of Catalonia was put down in 1472 only with the greatest difficulty. Castile, in the meantime, was torn by constant aristocratic uprisings and disputed royal successions. Peace and strong government came within reach at last when Ferdinand of Aragon married Isabella of Castile in 1469. Isabella inherited her throne in 1474; Ferdinand inherited his in 1479. And thereafter, despite the continuation of regional Cortes, tribunals, and customs, an efficient central administration governed the two realms and eventually transformed them into the Kingdom of Spain.

In 1492, Columbus' voyage to America opened the great age of the Spanish global empire. And in the same year, Spain completed the long-delayed *Reconquista* by conquering Muslim Granada. Working grimly toward the enforcement of obedience, unity, and orthodoxy, the Spanish monarchy presented its Muslim and Jewish subjects with the choice of conversion or banishment, and the consequent Jewish exodus drained the kingdom of valuable mercantile and intellectual talent. The Catholic Inquisition became a tool of the state and, as an instrument of both political and doctrinal conformity, it brought the

SPAIN AT THE TIME OF FERDINAND AND ISABELLA

crown not only religious unity but lucrative revenues as well. The nobility was persuaded that its best interests lay in supporting the monarchy rather than in opposing it, and regional separation was curbed. With unity established and with the immense wealth of the New World soon to be pouring in, Spain in 1500 was entering a period of rich cultural expression and international power.

The wealth of Spain and Portugal in the sixteenth century was to result from their strategic location in the extreme west of Europe, facing the Atlantic. The first Atlantic explorations had been pioneered by Italian seamen of the High Middle Ages who could draw on their experience in Mediterranean commerce. But by the mid-fifteenth century the Canaries, Madeiras, Azores, and Cape Verde islands had all passed into Spanish or Portugese hands, and Portugese ships were exploring and trading down the west coast of Africa. The climax of all these ventures came in the 1490s, when Spanish ships reached America and Portugese ships (in 1497–1499) sailed around Africa to India. The subsequent Spanish Golden Age would be financed by American silver, while the Portugese trade route to the Orient short-circuited the traditional overland routes, enriching Portugal beyond all dreams, and depressing the once-flourishing commerce of the Ottoman Empire and Renaissance Italy. Europe's global career was underway, and Spain and Portugal, whose enterprise began it all, were its first beneficiaries.*

Germany

Late medieval Germany and Italy suffered from much the same sort of regional particularism that afflicted England, France, and the Iberian Peninsula, but the late fifteenth century brought no corresponding

* The voyages of discovery are discussed more fully below, pp. 220 ff.

trend toward centralization. Both lands passed into the modern era divided internally and incapable of competing with the western monarchies. The weak elective Holy Roman Empire that emerged in Germany from the papal-imperial struggles of the High Middle Ages was given formal sanction in the Golden Bull of 1356. The Bull excluded any papal role in the imperial appointment or coronation, leaving the choice of succession to the majority vote of seven great German princes. These "electors" included the archbishops of Mainz, Trier, and Cologne, the Count Palatine of the Rhine, the Duke of Saxony, the Margrave of Brandenburg, and the King of Bohemia. The electoral states themselves remained relatively stable, as did other large German principalities such as the Hapsburg duchy of Austria, but the empire itself became powerless. Germany in 1500 was a jigsaw puzzle of more than 100 principalities—fiefs, ecclesiastical city-states, free cities, counties, and duchies —their boundaries shifting periodically through war, marriage, and inheritance. Imperial authority in Italian politics was as dead as papal authority in imperial elections. Germany and Italy were disengaged at last, but both continued to suffer the political disintegration that resulted from their former entanglement.

Eastern Europe

Eastern Europe was, in general, no more successful than Germany and Italy in achieving political cohesion. Poland, Lithuania, and Hungary (as well as the Scandinavian states to the north) were all afflicted by aristocratic turbulence and dynastic quarrels. The Teutonic Knights were humbled by Slavic armies and internal rebellions, and the kingdoms of Serbia and Bulgaria were overwhelmed by the Ottoman Turks. Only the Russians and Ottomans were able to build strong states, and both, by 1500, were uncompromisingly autocratic.

Beginning in 1386, Poland united for a time with rapidly expanding Lithuania, and the Polish-Lithuanian state became the largest political unit in Europe. It was also, very possibly, the worst governed. Under the Lithuanian warrior-prince Jagiello (1377–1434), who converted to Catholicism when he accepted the Polish crown, the dual state routed the Teutonic Knights at the decisive battle of Tannenberg (1410). But even under Jagiello, Poland-Lithuania had no real central government; its nobles would cooperate with their ruler only against the hated Germans, and even then only momentarily. Stretching all the way from the Black Sea to the Baltic, incorporating many of the former lands of the Teutonic Order and most of the old state of Kievan Russia, Poland-Lithuania lacked the skilled administrators and political institutions necessary to govern its vast territories. Its nobles were virtually all-powerful, and its peasantry was slipping toward serfdom. Its political impotence guaranteed that no strong state would emerge between Germany and Russia during Europe's early modern centuries.

Modern Russia evolved gradually out of the Muscovite principality that had managed to survive and expand during the centuries of Mongol domination. The Grand Princes of Moscow extended their influence in northern Russia by collaborating with their Mongol Khans and winning the support of the Orthodox Church. They were appointed sole collectors of the Mongol tribute, and on occasion they helped the Mongols crush the rebellions of other Russian princes. Moscow became the headquarters of Russian Orthodox Christianity, and when the Turks took Constantinople in 1453, Moscow, the "Third Rome," claimed spiritual sovereignty over the Orthodox Slavic world. At first the Muscovite princes strengthened their position with the full backing of the Mongol Khans, but toward the end of the fourteenth century Moscow began taking the lead in anti-Mongol resistance. At last, in

Saint Basil's Cathedral, Moscow, sixteenth century.   (PIX/Transworld Feature Syndicate)

1480, Ivan III, the Great, Grand Prince of Moscow and Czar of the Russians, repudiated Mongol authority altogether and abolished the tribute.

The Muscovite princes enjoyed a certain measure of popular support in their struggle against the Mongols, but their rule was autocratic to a degree worthy of Genghis Khan himself. Nascent republicanism in city-states such as Novgorod was crushed with the expansion of Muscovite authority. The Grand Princes were despots, inspired politically by Central Asia rather than by the West. Their state had no local nor national assemblies and no articulate middle class. Russia was eventually to acquire the material and organizational attributes of a great power, but the centuries of its Mongol isolation from the rest of Europe left their imprint.

The great outside threat to Eastern Europe came from the southeast, where the Ottoman Turks pressed into the Balkans from Asia Minor. These Altaic tribesmen, driven from their Central Asian homeland by the Mongols, came into Asia Minor first as mercenaries, then as conquerors. Adopt-

ing the Islamic faith, the Ottomans subjected the greater part of Asia Minor to
their rule and intermarried with the local
population. In 1354, bypassing the diminutive Byzantine Empire, they invaded
Europe. During the latter half of the fourteenth century they crushed Serbia and
Bulgaria and extended their dominion over
most of the Balkan Peninsula.

At the decisive battle of Varna (1444)
the Ottomans decimated a Christian crusading army and consolidated their hold on
southeastern Europe. After the great Ottoman victory at Varna, the storming of Constantinople in 1453 was little more than a
postscript. Yet all Europe recognized that
the Sultan Mohammed II, in conquering the
unconquerable city, had ended an era.

The Ottoman Empire continued to
threaten Europe for another two hundred
years. It endured until the twentieth century; as the Republic of Turkey it endures
still. Like the Muscovite princes, the Ottoman sultans were autocrats. Slaves served
in their administration and fought in their

armies alongside mounted noblemen of the
Ottoman landed aristocracy. While the sultans were living in splendor in the former
capital of Byzantium, their government was
insulating southeastern Europe from the
civilization of the West. And Western Europe, with its eastern trade routes blocked
by the Turks, set out into the Atlantic.

CHRONOLOGY OF LATE-MEDIEVAL CENTRAL AND EASTERN EUROPE

1237–1242:	Mongols invade Eastern Europe
1340:	Mongols control Russia
1354–1400:	Ottoman Turks conquer Balkans
1356:	Golden Bull increases powers of the seven imperial electors
1377–1434:	Jagiello rules Lithuania, unites it with Poland (1386)
1453:	Constantinople falls to the Turks
1462–1505:	Reign of Ivan III "the Great" who ends Russian tribute to Mongols (1480)

THE OTTOMAN ADVANCE

15
Economic and Cultural Change

The Late Medieval Economy

The shift from boom to depression came gradually and unevenly to Western Europe in the years around 1300. From the early fourteenth century through much of the fifteenth, a number of related trends—shrinking population, contracting markets, an end to the long process of land reclamation, and a creeping mood of pessimism and retrenchment—resulted in a general economic slump and a deepening of social antagonisms. These trends were far from universal. They tended to be less marked in northern Italy than elsewhere, and various localities north of the Alps, by profiting from favorable commercial situations or technological advances, became more prosperous than before. At a time when many English towns were declining, Coventry and certain others grew wealthy from the rise of woolen-cloth production. The Flemish town of Bruges remained throughout most of the Late Middle Ages a bustling center of commerce on the northern seas. Florence, with its large textile industry and its international banking, became the focal point of Italian Renaissance culture. In Florence and elsewhere, enterprising individuals and families grew wealthy from the profits of international commerce and banking. The Bardi, Peruzzi, and Medici were the great Florentine banking families, and they had their counterparts north of the Alps in such figures as Jacques Coeur of Bourges—financier of the fifteenth-century French monarchy—and the Fuggers of Augsburg, bankers of the Holy Roman emperors. But such great financiers as these were exceedingly insecure in the turbulent years of the Late Middle Ages. The Bardi and Peruzzi houses collapsed in the mid-fourteenth century, and Jacques Coeur was ruined by his royal debtor, King Charles VII. Even though some fortunes continued to grow, the total assets of late-medieval bankers fell considerably below those of their thirteenth-century predecessors. The success of families such as the Medicis and Fuggers illustrates the late-medieval tendency toward an increasingly unequal distribution of wealth. The other side of the picture is to be seen in intensified urban strife and peasants' rebellions.

The Black Death

The late-medieval depression began well before the coming of the Black Death (1348–1349). The fundamental trends of demographic and economic decline were not initiated by the plague, but they were enormously aggravated by it. Carried by fleas that infested black rats, the bubonic plague entered Europe along the trade routes from the East and spread with frightening speed. The death toll cannot be determined with any precision. The best estimate would probably be one-fourth to one-third of Europe's population. It seems likely that in many crowded towns more than half the inhabitants died, whereas isolated rural areas tended to be spared. Consequently, the most progressive, most enterprising, and best-trained Europeans were hit hardest. Few urban families can have been spared altogether. Survivors of the terrible years 1348 to 1349 were subjected to periodic recurrences of the plague, which returned to Europe repeatedly over the next three centuries. Fourteenth-century medical science was at a loss to explain the process of infection, while lack of sanitation in the towns encouraged its spread. Some fled their cities in panic, some gave way to religious frenzy, or debauchery, and some remained faithfully at their posts, hoping for divine protection against the pestilence. But none emerged unaffected from this monstrous eruption of suffering, grief, and death—this unspeakable catastrophe.

Town and Country

The towns of late-medieval Europe, confronted with shrinking markets and decreasing opportunities, lost their earlier social mobility and buoyancy. Privileged classes closed their ranks, the guilds guarded their monopolies, and heredity became the chief avenue to the status of the guild master. In their grim efforts to retain their share of declining markets, guilds struggled with one another, with the district nobility, and with the increasingly desperate urban proletariat, its class consciousness growing as its upward mobility was choked off. Few towns of late-medieval Europe escaped being torn by class violence. In 1378 Florence experienced the most severe workers' rebellion of the period.

The rich businessmen of the European towns usually managed to retain their privileged economic status in the face of lower-class pressure. They did so by allying with great magnates or kings, or, in Italy, by abdicating their political power to despots. The wealthy merchants and bankers were generally able, through political control or manipulation, to keep down wages despite the plague-induced labor shortage and to smash the resulting lower-class uprisings.

The rural nobility of Western Europe, like the urban upper class, managed to survive the turbulent socio-economic changes of the Late Middle Ages. Faced with a gradual shift from a barter to a money economy, the nobles were able, with some exceptions, to hold their extensive lands and preserve much of their wealth. They responded to the decline in grain prices by accelerating the high-medieval processes of leasing their own lands to peasants and commuting customary peasant services to fixed money payments. In this way, aristocratic incomes were protected against deflation so long as peasants could manage the agreed payments. And consequently, the peasants continued to rise in legal status from land-bound serfs to free tenant farmers until, by 1500, serfdom had almost disappeared from Western Europe. But the passing of serfdom was by no means accompanied by increased peasant prosperity. On the contrary, the declining population and the contracting grain market resulted in abandoned fields and a growing class of landless paupers. Some rural noblemen retained direct control of their land, hiring workers to farm it or converting it from grain crops to the more profitable wool growing.

In general, then, the peasant passed from his former manorial status (of customary payments in goods and labor services) to a new status based on cash; by 1500 he tended to be either a rent-paying tenant or a landless wage earner. And the nobleman dealt in receipts and expenditures rather than in the exploitation of customary services. These changes had begun in the High Middle Ages and were largely completed by 1500. At times of drastic population decline, as in the decades following the Black Death, the resulting labor shortage tended to force up wages, and the nobility fought this tendency either through collective conspiracy or through legislation. In England, for example, the Statutes of Laborers of 1351 and thereafter were aimed at freezing wages in the wake of the plague. They succeeded only to a point, and at a price of creating a deep sense of grievance among the peasantry, a feeling that contributed to the abortive English Peasants' Revolt of 1381. This confused and bloody uprising was merely one of a considerable number that terrorized late-medieval Europe. Like the Jacquerie rebellion in France, and like many similar peasant insurrections of the period, it bore witness to an unbalanced society in which classes struggled bitterly for their share of a declining wealth.

In Eastern Europe the peasant's lot was even worse than in the West, for the eastern nobility was reducing its peasantry to serfdom at the very time that western peasants were achieving legal freedom. The late-medieval landed nobility of both Eastern and Western Europe jealously guarded its privileges against peasantry and monarchy, and for a time, in both East and West, this nobility seemed to be reversing the high-medieval trend toward stronger royal government. With the exception of Russia, eastern monarchies made no real progress against their nobles, but by the later fifteenth century, western monarchies were beginning to curb the fractious independence of the landed aristocracy. The new Tudor monarchy in England tended to favor the mercantile class, but in Spain and France the nobility was rewarded for its political submissiveness by economic favoritism and privileged positions in the royal administration, the army, and the Church.

Thus, the western nobles evolved, during the High and Late Middle Ages, from robber barons into silk-clad courtiers. The traditional role of mounted knight in the feudal host was a thing of the past, for monarchs were now fighting with mercenaries, and footsoldiers were winning most of the major battles. Moreover, the increasing use of gunpowder was making knightly armor and knightly castles highly vulnerable. But while the feudal knight was vanishing from European armies, he was becoming ever more prominent in art, literature, and court ceremonial. The fifteenth century was an age of elaborate shining armor, fairy-tale castles, coats of arms, and extravagant tournaments. Knighthood, driven from the battlefield, took refuge in fantasy, and an age of ruthless political cynicism saw the full flowering of a romantic code of chivalric ethics. Behind this fanciful façade, the landed aristocracy retained its privileged position atop the social order.

The consolidation of royal authority in late-fifteenth-century Western Europe coincided with a general economic upsurge following a long recession. Europe's population in 1500 may well have been lower than in 1300, but it was increasing again. Commerce was quickening and towns were growing. Technological progress had never ceased, and now water-driven fulling mills were increasing wool production, while water-driven pumps were draining mines. With advances in mining technology, Europe was increasing its supply of silver and the various metals essential to its rising industries: iron, copper, alum, and tin. The development of artillery and movable-type printing depended not merely on the inventive idea but also on many generations of progress in the metallurgical arts. Furthermore, advances in ship design and navigation lay behind the Atlantic voyages that would soon bring a torrent of wealth into Western Europe. By 1500 the long economic crisis had passed; Europe had entered on an era of economic growth and world expansion that would far outstrip her earlier surge in the High Middle Ages.

Intellectual and Cultural Evolution

Printing and gunpowder were the two most spectacular technological innovations of the Late Middle Ages. Gunpowder came first, and by the fifteenth century cannons were being used with some effect in the Hundred Years' War, the Turkish conquests and, indeed, most of the military engagements of Europe. Printing from movable type was developed midway through the fifteenth century, and although its effect on European culture was immense, the full impact was not felt until after 1500.* Even among the "new men" of the Italian Renaissance, printed books were regarded as vulgar imitations of handwritten originals. This fact should warn us against viewing late-medieval Europe—and even Renaissance Italy—exclusively in terms of new beginnings. There was, to be sure, a strong sense of the new and "modern" among many creative Europeans of the period, but there was also a perpetuation of medieval ways, styles, and habits of thought. Often one encounters a sense of loss over the fading of medieval ideas and institutions, a conviction that civilization was declining. Some Renaissance writers were optimistic about the human condition, but others were not. The Italian humanist Aeneas Sylvius—later Pope Pius II (d. 1464)—could look at the Turkish threat and the strife among Christian states and conclude that there was nothing good

* See below, pp. 219–220.

in prospect. The generation living after 1500, aware of the voyages of exploration and of the growing prosperity and political consolidation, might well be hopeful of the future, but between 1300 and 1500 a gloom hung over much of Europe. The rise of modern civilization was less apparent than the decay of the Middle Ages.

Beneath the gloom one finds a sense of nervous unrest, a violent emotionalism that gives dramatic intensity to late-medieval works of art but robs them of the balanced serenity characteristic of the best thirteenth-century creations. Society was in a state of crisis. The practice of self-flagellation acquired wide popularity, and the Dance of Death became a favorite artistic theme. In an era of depression, plague, and disorder, the high-medieval synthesis could no longer hold together. Unity was giving way to diversity.

Philosophy

The breakdown of hierarchy and order expressed itself in a hundred ways—in the intensifying conflict between class and class, in the architectural shift from organic unity to flamboyant decoration, in the divorce between knightly function and chivalric fantasy, in the evolution from Christian commonwealth to territorial states, and in the disintegration of St. Thomas Aquinas' fusion of faith and reason. The medieval dream of a City of God on earth had achieved its supreme intellectual embodiment in Aquinas' hierarchical ordering and reconciliation of matter and spirit, body and soul, logic and revelation. The fading of that dream is nowhere more evident than in the attacks of fourteenth-century philosophers on the Thomist system.

St. Thomas' *Summa Theologica*, like the cathedral of Chartres, unifies religious aspiration and logical order on the basis of an omnipotent God who is both loving and rational. The fourteenth-century attack on this reconciliation was founded on two related propositions. (1) To ascribe rationality to God is to limit his omnipotence by the finite rules of human logic. Thus, the Thomist God of reason gave way to a God of will, and the high-medieval notion of a logical divine order was eroded. (2) Human reason, therefore, can tell us nothing of God; logic and Christian belief inhabit two separate, sealed worlds.

The first steps toward this concept of a willful, incomprehensible God were taken by the Oxford Franciscan, Duns Scotus (d. 1308), who produced a detailed critique of St. Thomas' theory of knowledge. Duns Scotus did not reject the possibility of elucidating revealed truth through reason, but he was more cautious in his use of logic than Aquinas had been. Whereas St. Thomas is called "The Angelic Doctor," Duns Scotus is called "The Subtle Doctor," and the extreme complexity of his thought prompted men in subsequent generations to describe anyone who bothered to follow Duns' arguments as a "dunce." The sobriquet is unfair, for Duns Scotus is an important and original figure in the development of late scholasticism. Yet one is tempted to draw a parallel between the intricacies of his intellectual system and the decorative elaborations of late-Gothic churches. A Christian rationalist of the most subtle kind, he nevertheless made the first move toward dismantling the Thomist synthesis and withdrawing reason from the realm of religion.

William of Ockham

Another Oxford Franciscan, William of Ockham (d. 1349), attacked the Thomist synthesis on all fronts. Ockham was a nominalist; he argued that the platonic archetypes were not realities but merely names. And thus he saw the world as a countless multitude of individual, concrete things, lumped together by the fallible human intellect into classes and categories of our own making. Ockham argued further that God and Christian doctrine, utterly undemonstrable, must be accepted on faith alone,

and that human reason must be limited to the realm of observable phenomena. In this unpredictable world of an unpredictable Creator, one can reason only about things that one can see or directly experience. With this radical empiricism Ockham ruled out all metaphysical speculations, all rational arguments from an observable diversity of things to an underlying unity of things. And out of this great separation of reason and faith came two characteristic expressions of late-medieval thought: the scientific manipulation of material facts, and pietistic mysticism untouched by logic. In Ockham and many of his followers, one finds empiricism and mysticism side by side. For since the two worlds never touched, they were in no way contradictory. An intelligent Christian could keep one foot in each of them.

The Ockhamist philosophy served as an appropriate foundation for both late-medieval mysticism and late-medieval science. Some mystics, indeed, regarded themselves as empiricists. For the empiricist is a person who accepts only those things that he experiences, and the mystic, abandoning the effort to *understand* God, strove to *experience* him. Science, on the other hand, was now freed of its theological underpinnings and could proceed on its own. Nicholas Oresme, a teacher at the University of Paris in the fourteenth century, attacked the Aristotelian theory of motion and proposed a rotating earth as a possible explanation for the apparent daily movement of the sun and stars across the sky. Oresme's theories probably owed more to thirteenth-century scientists such as Robert Grosseteste than to Ockham, but his willingness to tinker with the traditional explanations of the physical structure of God's universe is characteristic of an age in which scientific speculation was being severed from revealed truth.

Many late-medieval philosophers rejected Ockham's criticism and remained Thomists. But owing to the very comprehensiveness of Aquinas' achievement, his successors were reduced to detailed elaboration or minor repair work. Faced with a choice between the tedious niggling of late Thomism and the drastic limitations imposed by Ockham on the scope of philosophical inquiry, many of Europe's finest minds shunned the great philosophical issues altogether for the more promising fields of science, mathematics, and classical learning.* When the philosopher John Gerson (d. 1429), chancellor of the University of Paris, spoke out in his lectures against "vain curiosity in the matter of faith," the collapse of the faith-reason synthesis was all but complete.

Art and Literature

The evolution from high-medieval synthesis to late-medieval diversity, so evident in philosophy, also occurred in literature and the arts. The Gothic churches of late-medieval Europe were adorned with increasingly elaborate sculptural decoration; artists depicted man and nature in marvelous, naturalistic detail. Stone vines twined lifelike around the choir screens and capitals of columns; Flemish painters approached the intricate realism of a color photograph.* In this atmosphere of artistic nominalism the detail became as important as the whole.

In literature, the medieval romance lost its inspiration and became a sentimentalized, formalized bore. Late-medieval writers could achieve vitality only by turning from warmed-over chivalry to graphic realism. Geoffrey Chaucer (d. 1400), in his *Canterbury Tales*, combines rare psychological insight with a skill in descriptive characterization worthy of the Flemish painters or the late-Gothic stone carvers. Chaucer describes one of his Canterbury pilgrims, a corrupt friar, in these words:

Highly beloved and intimate was he
With country folk wherever he might be,
And worthy city women with possessions;
For he was qualified to hear confessions,
Or so he said, with more than priestly scope;
He had a special license from the pope.
Sweetly he heard his penitents at shrift
With pleasant absolution, for a gift.

And François Villon (d. 1463), a brawling Parisian vagabond, expressed in his poems an anguished, sometimes brutal realism that captures the late-medieval mood of insecurity and plague:

Death makes one shudder and turn pale,
Pinches his nose, distends his veins,
Swells out his throat, his members fail,
Tendons and nerves grow hard with strains.

To Villon, writing in a society of sharp class distinctions, death was the great democrat:

I know this well, that rich and poor,
Fools, sages, laymen, friars in cowl,
Large-hearted lords and each mean boor,
Little and great and fair and foul,
Ladies in lace, who smile or scowl,
From whatsoever stock they stem,
Hatted or hooded, prone to prowl,
Death seizes every one of them.

---

* The revival of classicism in the Italian Renaissance will be discussed in the next chapter.

* See below, pp. 206–209.

16
The Culture of the Renaissance

Death was close at hand in the fourteenth and fifteenth centuries, and few could ignore it. But from the same period there rose a vision of rebirth—or renaissance. This new, more hopeful perspective first emerged in Italy, where it produced a richly expressive culture of writers, artists, and nobles. By the sixteenth century it was spreading into the North. The Renaissance is usually treated as an historical period, but it was actually more a phenomenon than an era. As such, it overlapped the Late Middle Ages and the Reformation alike, affecting them both. When François Villon was roaming the streets of fifteenth-century Paris and writing of death, Florence was teeming with Renaissance artists and writers. And when, generations later, Luther was bringing the Reformation to Germany, the Renaissance humanist Erasmus of Rotterdam was berating him for shattering the unity of Catholic Europe.

Thus the common use of the term Renaissance to mean the cultural developments in Europe from the fourteenth to the sixteenth centuries is hazardous. For one thing, the word does not fit the facts very closely and, for another, it distinguishes one period too sharply from another. The word is too small and neat for the period. Coined by the Italian artist and art historian Vasari to applaud the return of classical excellence—*rinascita* means a rebirth—the term was taken up by later French historians and given a more general application. This was unfortunate, for even within the limited ambit of art and architecture the idea of a sudden rebirth was partly a myth and a delusion. But the concept has won security of tenure by long usage and cannot be dislodged. Because it seems to lend special glamor to a particular time span and to play favorites with eras, it has offended some sensibilities. Historians have seen a Renaissance in the twelfth and thirteenth centuries, and they see maturer expressions of fifteenth-century trends in the sixteenth and seventeenth centuries. This is not surprising, for Clio, the muse of history, knows no periods.

In the past, when history was conceived of primarily as cultural and political history, and when historians took the humanists' notion of their own originality at face value, it was possible for some scholars to reduce Renaissance culture to a few quintessentials: the rediscovery of man and the world; a renewed sense of joy in life; asceticism and symbolism giving way to sensuousness and naturalism; and experimentation in the pursuit of knowledge displacing traditionalism and obscurantism.

To a degree, all of these formulas are correct, but they emphasize change at the expense of continuity. "Restless youth and crabbed age" do always live together, and new departures were shaped by old concerns and only gradually replaced them. In architecture the concept of a Renaissance veils the wonderful resilience of Gothic style in northern Europe. In England, for instance, there remain majestic monuments of Perpendicular Gothic from the sixteenth century, including the ethereal splendor of King's College Chapel, Cambridge, the fabric of which (but for windows, choir screen, and organ) was completed in 1515.* Often Renaissance historians underestimated the change and vitality of the Middle Ages, and naïvely equated the novel features of the Renaissance with the good, and the rest as husk that had to be outgrown before the world could come of age. Some scholars disenchanted with the holocausts of modern Europe, have been less sanguine about the Renaissance. From the outset, they accept the period as a complex one, full of ambivalences; a period with a checkered moral legacy.

The previous chapters suggested that the unifying forces of the High Middle Ages were seriously weakened in the fourteenth and fifteenth centuries and that new movements and institutions were bringing in-

* See below, page 207.

ternal wars and social dislocation in their trains. At the same time, retrenchment and the specter of Ottoman invasion cast a gloom which makes the achievement of Renaissance humanists all the more remarkable, almost perverse. They remained optimistic about human nature and the possibilities of human reason, despite much of the evidence. They offered a set of secular and cultural values that threatened to replace the power of the papacy as a unifying factor until the Reformation sundered Europe spiritually forever. Above all, they generated and disseminated an enthusiasm for "new learning" which, in spirit if not in form, is still alive.

The Setting

As the old sense of medieval universalism was departing, in its stead had grown a new awareness of diversity: there were new focuses for popular allegiance. North of the Alps, the nation-state was becoming the focus of strong loyalties: France and England were born as nations in the travail of the Hundred Years War. But the birthplace of the Renaissance was Italy, which emerged from the High Middle Ages as a checkerboard of small principalities and city-states. For some generations thereafter, the stronger Italian cities managed to maintain a measure of independence but, by a process of large eating small, only seven major states existed by the end of the fifteenth century. The Kingdom of Naples, long disputed territory between the Houses of Anjou and Aragon, finally fell to Aragon in 1435, and Aragon also controlled Sicily. Spain thus came to control the southern half of the peninsula. Acting as a buffer between the feudal south and the commercial north, the papal states joined Adriatic Sea to Mediterranean. This loose conglomeration of cities and principalities was jostled from the north by the Duchy of Ferrara and the Republics of Florence and Siena. These, with the Duchies of Mantua and

Modena, were the smaller principalities, Florence being dominant among them. All were flanked to the north by the larger holdings of the dukes of Savoy, by Milan, and by the Venetian Republic.

It was in the north of Italy, among the furious world of little states that the Renaissance first flourished. The northern states were neither feudal nor puppets; they were independent. Many of them were republics while others, like Milan, fell under the rule of a single, all-powerful dynasty. Since 1311 Milan had been ruled by despots of the Visconti family, whose male line died out in 1447. Sovereignty then reverted to the republic, until an upstart mercenary captain, Francesco Sforza, made himself duke of Milan by starving the city into submission. Similarly, Ferrara was governed by the Este family, and Mantua by the Gonzagas.

Florence, Venice, and Siena were the outstanding republics, but a Renaissance republic should not be confused with a democracy. Siena was an oligarchy, while in Florence the Medici family, by virtue of their wealth from banking and their constitutional astuteness, managed to dominate the city's Councils. Venice, though it boasted a complex constitution of checks and balances, never pretended to be anything other than a mercantile oligarchy.

The first manifestations of the Renaissance are generally acknowledged to be Florentine. During the consolidation of the republican oligarchy, after the early 1380s, Florence found itself encircled and isolated by the conquests of the duke of Milan. This threat distilled among Florentines an awareness both of their political danger and of the virtues that their republican system embodied. Its origins could be traced back to the ancient communes of Italy before the rise of the Roman Empire. By exploring their special heritage, Florentines generated public pride and self-consciousness, and came to value and extol civic-mindedness in all pursuits, whether art or commerce,

scholarship or government. In time, these attitudes spread far beyond Florence itself.

Venice had always been more stable than the other Italian states; and though this stability was often credited to her constitution, it owed more to the uniform seafaring interests of her peoples and to the relatively invulnerable position of the island capital. On the mainland, not only was state pitted against state but also class against class. Lesser guilds clamored for power against greater guilds and, cutting through all these squabbles, Guelphs campaigned against Ghibellines. Ghibellines were those who favored and relied on the old Imperial connection, and Guelphs were those who were opposed to that link and who looked to the papacy for support. Northern Italy offered the stimulating prospect of endless turmoil and incessant commotion.

If this lusty independence was a breeding ground of the Renaissance, it is also true that the Renaissance was an urban phenomenon. The bustle of the city included the busy hum of commerce. While it is true that the middle class was proliferating, the period was one of considerable dislocation, of closing frontiers, and of limited resources. Some bourgeois were declining, particularly those whose fortunes were tied up in the woolen guilds. Indeed, guilds of all kinds, throughout Europe, were slowly losing influence in society at large as they lost control of their own members. Throughout the period the guilds fought a defensive battle to supervise the standards of production and to oversee wages, prices, and the conditions of apprenticeship. A market system and market values were making breaches through their older restrictive practices. Individual and joint stock ventures had become the high roads to wealth traveled by a minority. Banking, trading, the exploitation of mines and forests, the holding of a concession here and a monopoly there, all these were still fields of promise provided that one streamlined operations and supervised every detail of business with the utmost rigor—in the style of a Jacob Fugger. Even so, a fabulous fortune could be dissipated by bad luck or political miscalculation.

Renaissance Humanism

During the Renaissance, art, letters, philosophy, science, and music freed themselves increasingly from the tutelage of the church, matching the steady growth (from the thirteenth century) of court and individual lay patronage. Indeed, the church found itself drawn willy-nilly into the wake of new intellectual fashions that it had not prescribed. The spectacle of Gregory VII at Canossa (in 1077) with Emperor Henry IV standing humbly in the snow begging him for forgiveness was quite different from that of Julius II (in 1506) hoping that Michelangelo would not leave Rome after a tiff. Speculation and scholarship had once been the virtual monopoly of the Church; now popes and bishops were patron-pupils of the Renaissance. Laymen crowded clergy at the fountains of knowledge and the Renaissance saw the quickening of a process that is still occurring: the laicization of culture.

This bold departure—the founding and development of a nonclerical intellectual aristocracy—was fortified by the authority of the past, especially in Italy where the remains of ancient Rome were still to be seen. The classical (sometimes misleadingly called the pagan) revival was a primary and original impetus for changes in intellectual manners, and it remained a constant influence throughout this period. Antiquity gave legitimacy to the secular pursuits of the Renaissance. It offered a treasury of literature, art, architecture, jurisprudence, philosophy, and science—all of which, to the Renaissance mind, had been inadequately appreciated in the past. The Renaissance was, indeed, unfair to the Middle Ages; it overestimated its own achievement and un-

derestimated the fervor and vitality of the earlier period. It scoffed at medieval enslavement to tradition but, in abandoning one authority, the Renaissance was quick to substitute another; the distant past was venerated because its prestige shed security on the secular invasion of hidden mysteries. As a layman venturing to write a cosmic epic—The Divine Comedy—Dante (1265–1321) was comforted by the companionship of Virgil in his journey through the medieval cosmos. Yet antiquity was more than a brace and a touchstone of legitimacy. It was an ideal, a source of inspiration, and sometimes an obstruction. Possibly Leonardo da Vinci (1452–1519) might have discovered the circulation of the blood if Galen's theory of invisible pores in the wall of the heart had not inhibited him.

The rediscovery of classical Latin style and its imitation were preconditions of Renaissance success. The flexible and living language known as medieval Latin fell into disrepute, and pure classical Latin became the universal language of Renaissance humanism. In elegance and precision, classical Latin well suited the courtly patronage that sustained the humanists.

The consideration of antiquity also encouraged the use of vernacular, since Latin and Greek, in their day, had been vulgar tongues. Actually, vernacular literature had flourished in the High Middle Ages; the humanists carried on the tradition and channeled it into new literary forms, dignifying local Italian dialects by employing them in their finest works. Dante, Petrarch (1304–1374), and Boccaccio (1313–1375), devout classicists as they were, helped to make their native Tuscan the language of Italy by giving it shape and beauty. The use of vernacular also accompanied the growing sense of national identity north of the Alps. Thus the patriot-heretic Wycliffe (about 1320–1384), wrote vigorous and balanced English prose, which Chaucer (about 1340–1400) simplified and smoothed in preparation for the splendor of the Elizabethan era. In France, Rabelais (about 1495–1553) followed in the footsteps of irreverent troubadours and poets who sang and rhymed in vernacular; and Cervantes (1547–1616) performed a similar service for Spain when he wrote his vernacular masterpiece, *Don Quixote.*

In the short run the revival of classical Latin served the humanists' elitist purpose well enough, but in the long run it is clear that they killed a vital, living language in order to revive a dead thing. In patronizing the vernacular tongues, however, the Renaissance contributed to the mass national literacy and the mass secular culture that is now in being.

Strictly speaking, humanists were scholars of the classics. But in the broader, Ciceronian sense, *humanitas* meant a literary refinement and a mental cultivation that went far beyond mere academic discipline. In the fullest sense it amounted to an attitude toward life, to a fresh view of man's place in the cosmos, and to a substantial reassessment of his scale of values. Whereas the saint, the ascetic, or the chivalrous knight formerly had been ideal types, now homage was paid to the prince and his courtly following. *The Book of the Courtier,* by Castiglione (1478–1529), idealized the man of affairs with a quiverfull of accomplishments, devoted to his prince. This courtier was expected to have mastered etiquette and the classics. He should possess every grace; he should spice every conversation with wit and should give honest counsel to the prince under the spur of his strong sense of civic duty. He was also expected to be a hardy warrior. Few men approximated this ideal. Michelangelo (1475–1564) was no courtier; Leonardo was too preoccupied with his experiments to be a man of affairs. The many-sided Italian artist Benvenuto Cellini (1500–1571) was half genius and half undisciplined adolescent, and Sir Walter Raleigh (about 1552–1618) the Elizabethan sea-dog and courtier, was deficient in emotional balance though not in talents. If no one was perfect, there were plenty of men who were jacks of many trades and masters of them, too. The specialization of functions, characteristic of both modern and medieval society, did not exist among the urban elite of Renaissance Italy, and distrust between the humanities and science was not yet abroad.

So persuasive was the ideal of "the Renaissance man" that new schools sprang up exemplifying a novel philosophy of education. Vittorini da Feltre (1378–1446) hoped to produce able, graceful, cultivated dilettanti by steeping them in an all-round curriculum centered on the classics. In general, Western European education followed that pattern until this century, and the ideal of the good "all-rounder" still has currency in English private schools and American liberal arts colleges.

The self-conscious cultivation of the classics led the humanists to an awareness of history. At first they were obsessed with fame—fame of the past and fame of the self. Among early humanists, Boccaccio wrote of the fame (and also, rather lovingly, of the infamy) of ancient women. Petrarch addressed moving epistles to posterity. After all, had not the Roman poet, Horace, predicted that he would grow great in the praise of posterity? Giorgio Vasari (1511–1574) was sufficiently aware of posterity to leave us his *Lives of the Painters, Sculptors and Architects,* which included a long sketch of himself. It was only a short step from an appreciation of one's own and others' lasting glory to a sense of history.

For the first time since antiquity, observers of affairs began to write rigorously critical secular history. Phillip de Commynes (about 1447–1511), the Flemish adviser to the French "Spider King," Louis XI, was the earliest to use his intimate knowledge of royal policy to describe and analyze in detail the crucial reign that consolidated France in the aftermath of the

Hundred Years War. Guicciardini (1483–1540) and Machiavelli (1469–1527), both Florentines, carried Commynes' secular beginning still further in their histories of Florence.

If Guicciardini was pessimistic, Machiavelli plumbed the very depths of cynicism. His *Prince* was an amoral handbook on how to succeed in political business. One historian reads it as a satire; others view it as the last resort of a republican patriot whose hopes of a united Italy were threatened by foreign warriors. Yet another resolves the incompatibility between *The Prince* and Machiavelli's avowed republicanism by reference to his cyclical theory of constitutional change, drawn from the ancient Roman writer, Polybius. The anarchy that was then current could only be followed by rule of a single person. This would fit *The Prince* into a theory of historical inevitability where the causes of change lie—barring accidents or fate—in the nature of man and political society. Whatever the case, Machiavelli's secular analyses, so naked and unashamed, shocked contemporaries. With Machiavelli, the study of politics as well as history shed their religious coverings, and politics became an autonomous and self-justifying art.

Part and parcel of the secular historical method was a critical approach to sources. This had long been an important aspect of the humanists' work in gathering and collating manuscripts, and one of them, Lorenzo Valla (about 1407–1457), won a resounding victory for source criticism by proving that the anachronisms in the Donation of Constantine rendered it impossible that it could have been written in the fourth century A.D. The papacy's claim to dominion over surrounding lands by gift of the Emperor Constantine was based on a fraud.* Not that the revelation altered

the political realities at all, but the skill and cogency of Valla's demonstration eminently qualified it to be a model for subsequent analysis.

Some scholars believe that the humanists' critical approach to sources was their major lasting achievement. It was, of course, the beginning of the source and form criticism of today. But one can exaggerate the humanists' accomplishments. Although Erasmus (about 1466–1536) had a tenth-century manuscript to use for his Greek Testament, he made little use of it because it differed more than his other and later manuscripts did from St. Jerome's *Vulgate*. And when the humanist Beza translated the Bible in 1589, he had both a fifth- and a sixth-century manuscript, but he made little use of them because they differed widely from Erasmus' text! Still, if Renaissance criticism was less than thoroughgoing, it made, at least, a start.

Much of the critical work of the Renaissance was destructive; much of it took the form of satire. Erasmus learned that ridicule was as effective a method as argument in undermining rival positions, and in numerous works, most notably in the *Praise of Folly*, he slashed at the foibles and intellectual fads of past and present generations with a sharp quill. Lowly priests, monks, and friars were particularly the butt of humanist barbs, for these were the purveyors of outmoded values. They, too, were the most vulnerable objects of scorn, living close to the people and to mundane temptations yet professing purity and owning special privileges. From a humanist's point of view, they shared the defects of their ecclesiastical betters and lacked their virtues. They were often mercenary and corrupt and, in addition, were unlettered and contributed nothing to the cause of learning. One might gather from Boccaccio's *Decameron* that priests and friars were not to be trusted with women (married or unmarried) and that monasteries and nunneries were sinks of profligacy. The Renaissance publicized its abiding

* The forgery actually dates from the mid-eighth century. It was declared false by imperial scholars of the Ottonian Renaissance around A.D. *1000*, but was widely accepted before and afterward.

anticlericalism in ribaldry and mordant humor.

If the humanists were abrasively anti-clerical, they were not irreligious; quite the contrary: since one of their dearest pretensions was to instruct society (including the Church) in true morality. Nowhere does the long retreat of the Church's influence show more clearly than here. In a vacuum of moral leadership the humanists became the formulators and the guardians of standards of right; even their attacks on the clergy were possessed with conviction as to what ought to be.

It was in this evangelical spirit of restoring purity that some of the finest scholarly work was done in bibical studies. Erasmus lavished years of labor on his Greek New Testament in an attempt to present a text that was scrupulously accurate and in the original language. Erasmus' particular interests owed something to the encouragement of humanists such as John Colet (1466–1519) and Thomas More (1478–1535) whom he met in England. Colet inspired men by his gentle personality. More inspired them by his ability and, to this day, by his *Utopia* which is still read by idealists and critics of societies' evils. Erasmus, because of his unsurpassed style, his wit, and his knowledge, became the most renowned scholar of his generation. His *Paraphrases* were recommended to English churches; his Greek New Testament became a source for later vernacular translations of the Bible. He was, for a time, the moral leader of Europe. Educated in the Netherlands by the Brethren of the Common Life—a mystic pietist order—his teaching avoided their mysticism (for he was a rationalist) and emphasized piety. He called for a return to apostolic simplicity, for forbearance and mutual understanding, and for lives to be lived by a Christ-like ethic. By criticizing the failings of the Church, he inadvertently fed the fires of religious dissension and, in the heat of the Reformation, he found his former influence turning to ashes and all

that he had worked for melting away. Just before the conflagration, however, he congratulated Leo X (1531–1521) on what he had done to restore piety and erudition in the Church. The humanist was instructing and encouraging the pope!

As far as erudition was concerned, this was not always necessary. Aeneas Silvius Piccolomini was a scholar in his own right before he became Pius II (1458–1464). He was typical of Renaissance popes who patronized art and learning freely and who spent more energy consolidating their power than in improving the spiritual state of the Church.

Five popes before Pius II had employed Poggio Bracciolini (1380–1459), a super-sleuth in discovering ancient manuscripts and, through men like Poggio, thousands of Greek and Roman manuscripts were preserved from destruction by men or from decay by way of time. Boccaccio once wept when he saw the state of the manuscripts in the Benedictine monastery of Monte Casino. We owe an incalculable debt to the humanists for their feverish hunting since, in their reverence for the past, they guaranteed that its treasures could survive into our own time. (Of course we owe an even greater debt to the monks who had been copying these manuscripts for the past thousand years).

Roman manuscripts fared somewhat better than Greek, partly because Greece was distant and partly because classical Latin was more easily recovered than Greek. In the middle of the 14th century, both Petrarch and Boccaccio undertook to study Greek but from poor teachers. Not until the Byzantine scholar, Chrysolaurus, was inveigled to Florence in 1394 to teach Greek to anyone who would learn did a full knowledge reach the West. Then the Renaissance was able to enter the second temple of antiquity and to pay Greece its deserved homage. The fresh renderings of the Bible, already mentioned, utilized these new, more sophisticated, linguistic skills. At this point the Renaissance made its crucial contribution to the Reformation: for Luther repeatedly stressed that his grasp of the principle of "justification by faith" was prompted, aided, and sustained by linguistic insight.

Facility with Greek, combined with salvaged manuscripts from the East, meant the recovery of scriptural accuracy, poetry, drama, history, science, and geometry—Leonardo knew Euclid by heart—and of philosophy crowned by Plato and Aristotle. Both Plato and Aristotle had long been available in Europe; Aristotle by way of direct translations, but Plato by way of Neoplatonists and Augustine. Now Plato and Aristotle could be read in their original Greek. Padua became the chief of a number of universities with a heavy Aristotelian leaning, and Cosimo de Medici founded a Platonic academy in Florence in 1439. It nurtured devotees, like Ficino (1433–1499), who affirmed that Plato and Christianity were really compatible, and Giovanni Pico, Count of Mirandola (1463–1494), who was the most eclectic humanist of all.

Giovanni Pico, like Ficino, was a Neoplatonist and a devout Christian who, in his celebrated "Oration on the Dignity of Man," ignored the cooperation of Christ and the sacraments in the process of moral improvement. Man was a creation of infinite variety and capacity. He could abase himself to the level of a brute or raise himself to the level of an angel, with the special help of philosophy. As Alberti, the architect, philosopher, and scientist observed, "Man can make whatever he will of himself."

Doctrines of this sort glorified individual human freedom and abandoned spiritual discipline. By asserting them, the more radical humanists were reviving a pagan philosophy of ethics that had been largely dormant since the Greeks. Man alone, and not God and grace, was the source of moral energy. In this aspect humanism stood in sharpest contrast to the Reformation. Luther was to have his most violent quar-

"The Madonna of the Chancellor Rolin", by Jan van Eyck. (Cliché des Musees Nationaux)

rel with Erasmus on the subject, though Erasmus was thoroughly moderate. Giovannia Pico was an admirer of St. Thomas Aquinas, but his more radical followers were categorically rejecting the medieval past. Although St. Thomas said that grace had need of nature and reason, he firmly believed that grace was indispensable to the process of moral endeavor. The new Aristotelians, the Neoplatonists (absorbed by the phenomena of nature as a reflection of truth), Machiavelli, and the secular historians, were all unshackling the spirit of man from metaphysical trappings.

Since their time, science and technology, statecraft and politics, have become increasingly divorced from religion and ethics. Their separation from morality may well be the Renaissance's darkest legacy.

Art and Architecture

During the fourteenth and fifteenth centuries Italian Renaissance artists developed new forms of expression that contrasted sharply with the late-Gothic art of the North. Until the sixteenth century northern architects continued to build in the Gothic style, creating churches and secular buildings that were much more opulently dec-

"Le beau dieu", west portal of Amiens Cathedral. (Marburg/Art Reference Bureau)

was all but photographic. Their "Gothic realism" was kindred in spirit to the detailed representationalism of the Gothic sculptors and stone carvers. It also echoed the nominalism of late-medieval philosophers such as William of Ockham, with their emphasis on particular things rather than universal categories—on individual men rather than mankind.

The new styles of Renaissance Italy were inspired by Greco-Roman classicism and, in particular, by the classical canon of realism subordinated to a unifying idea. This was to be the style of the future; by 1500 it was streaming northward, with the general flow of Renaissance thought, to bring a new vision to transalpine artists. Classicism came naturally to Italy, where the memory of imperial Rome still lingered, and where Roman monuments and

Michelangelo, "David".   (Alinari/Art Reference Bureau)

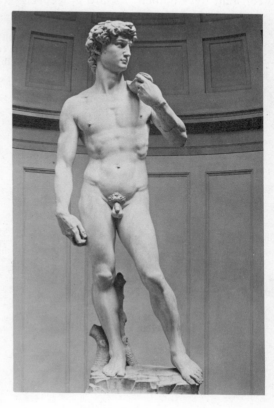

orated than those of the thirteenth century, yet structurally much the same. The "flamboyant Gothic" style emerged in late-medieval France, while English churches were evolving from the "decorated Gothic" of the fourteenth century to the "perpendicular Gothic" of the fifteenth and sixteenth, with its lacelike fan vaulting, its sculptural profusion, and its sweeping vertical lines. Northern sculptors, meanwhile, were going beyond the serene, idealized naturalism of the thirteenth century into a greater emphasis on emotionalism and individual likenesses. Painting north of the Alps reached its height in the mirrorlike realism of the Flemish school. Painters such as Jan van Eyck (*d.* 1440), pioneering in the use of oil paints, excelled in reproducing the natural world with a devotion to detail that sculpture abounded. Thus, during the fourteenth century, Renaissance artists rejected the predominantly French culture of the High Middle Ages for the styles of ancient Rome. Abandoning the Gothic spire and pointed arch, architects created buildings with majestic domes and round arches and gracefully balanced classical facades. In sculpture, likewise, the calm spiritual nobility of stone saints gave way to a classical emphasis on the shape and sinews of the human body.

Painting: Expressiveness and Perspective

Renaissance painters, with few actual classical models to follow, pioneered in techniques of perspective and imposed a classical unity and emotional expressiveness on their lifelike figures and landscapes. The result was a most remarkable outpouring of artistic genius and, in the generations between 1300 and 1500, a constant development toward a deeper ex-pressiveness and a more accurate naturalism. The painters of the early Renaissance struggled heroically, if often lucklessly, to master perspective. The vast chasm between fourteenth- and fifteenth-century ability to portray depth on a flat surface can be shown by a commonplace illustration from two editions of the same book a century apart. In the later illustration the feminine beauties are depicted in the north-European style of Jan van Eyck rather than in the manly and sometimes Amazonian Italian concept of womanhood. Perhaps there was a regional variation in physique. Cupid has changed from a crowned angel into a lecherous courtier, the attendants are wholly disrobed, and there is greater facility in the drawing of figures and the water surface. But, most obvious and most important, the flat medieval background has become a deep, distant landscape. Space-denying art had given way to space-affirming art. And as the illustration also makes clear, advances in perspective

Two versions of Venus with the Sea Goose from one of Ovid's works: the earlier one (left, about 1380) shows the flat medieval background, the later one (right, about 1480) shows the movement to deep landscape.   (Bibliotheque Nationale, The Royal Library, Copenhagen)

Lorenzo Ghiberti, "Story of Abraham".   (Alinari/ Art Reference Bureau)

technique were occurring in Northern Europe no less than in Italy. The Flemish school was less fascinated wtih muscled torsos than the school of Renaissance Italy but was no less realistic (not everyone is blessed with visible muscles).

But it was in late-fourteenth-century Italy that perspective was finally conquered, not by a painter but by the sculptor Ghiberti (1378–1455) in his bronze panel of the *Story of Abraham* for the doors of the Florentine Baptistry. Ghiberti's depiction of the young Isaac is a work of breathtaking beauty, closely modeled on a classical torso that he had in his possession. Depth was achieved by overlapping the figures in the foreground and placing them over a rock formation behind them. To complete the effect, the shoulders of both

Leonardo da Vinci, "Adoration of the Magi".   (Alinari/Art Reference Bureau)

Leonardo da Vinci, "Mona Lisa".   (Alinari/Art Reference Bureau)

Raphael, "The Dispute".   (The Vatican Museum)

Isaac and his father Abraham slant into the panel itself.

The High Renaissance

In the course of the fifteenth century Renaissance painters mastered perspective with sufficient success that it became second nature to the artists of the High Renaissance (the generation around 1500). The supreme figures of this period—Leonardo da Vinci (1452–1519), Raphael (1483–1520), and Michelangelo (1475–1564) applied the new perspective techniques effortlessly in the creation of deeply moving artistic interpretations of man and his natural and spiritual environments. The vanishing point of Leonardo's *Adoration of the Magi* leads to infinity. Uniform space had become the common property of artists and would continue to typify European art until the twentieth century. There is deep pathos, too, in Leonardo's *Adoration*, and a blur-

Raphael, "Portrait of Pope Leo X with His Nephews".   (Alinari/Art Reference Bureau)

ring of forms whose shapes are merely suggested in the shadows. This clever manipulation of light and shade is called chiaroscuro—and there is no sculptural or architectural equivalent to it. In Leonardo's *Mona Lisa* there are two distinct horizons, to heighten the mystery of the face. All this shows that by the High Renaissance the artist's use of dimensions had become highly self-conscious, complex, and articulate.

Whereas in the *Adoration*, Leonardo used triangles to give unity to his groupings, Raphael, in *The Dispute*, used different geometric constructions, noticeably the semicircle after the semidomes common in Renaissance architecture. In this work Raphael placed the wafer (representing Christ's body) precisely on the vanishing point. So everything converged there. By

Michelangelo, "The Creation of Adam", Sistine Chapel.   (Alinari/Art Reference Bureau)

this device Raphael could subtly announce his faith in the Catholic doctrine of transubstantiation. To him, there was no dispute, and his art was a testimony to his orthodox theology. Vasari called Raphael a "mortal god." Yet he was not all pure spirit and undiluted light. His portraits were supremely realistic, and he was quick to take advantage of the new possibilities of the printing press by selling prints of his own paintings for profit.

The Renaissance ideal of the many-sided artist was fulfilled by Raphael (who not only painted but was also an architect, sculptor, and designer of tapestries, engravings, and small ceramic pieces), and more com-

Michelangelo, "Captive Slave", Galleria Antica e Moderna, Florence.   (Alinari/Art Reference Bureau)

pletely still by Leonardo da Vinci (painter, sculptor, architect, musician, scientist, engineer, and natural philosopher). But the ideal achieved its fullest expression in Michelangelo—whose architecture, sculpture, and painting equally embody a spirit of monumental grandeur. In stone, in fresco, and on canvas his figures are heroes and demigods. Adam in *The Creation of Adam*, on the ceiling of the Sistine Chapel, is a dynamo of controlled power languidly at rest. His *Captive Slaves* writhe in their stone. The hesitant steps of earlier Renaissance artists in the direction of tactile reality and sense of movement culminate with Michelangelo, whose prestige in the Western world was rivaled only by Raphael.

Michelangelo personified the "cult of genius." All through the fifteenth century the independence and authority of the artist was coming to be increasingly recognized. Architects no longer had to supervise their buildings, but merely drafted the plans. Patrons became tolerant of artistic temperament, for as Cosimo de Medici remarked, "One must treat these people of extraordinary genius as if they were celestial spirits, and not like beasts of burden." The material rewards of excellence were immense, and a talented artist could amass a considerable fortune. The greatest became "superstars" whose art provided an avenue of rapid social advancement. Often of petty bourgeois or lower social origin, they were now accepted on terms of equality by the highest nobility. Late Renaissance grandiosity may reflect this "arrival" of the artist, and it may also display the increasing affluence and power of their upper-class patrons.

The Venetian School

The Venetians developed a special ability to dramatize an event with shafts of luminous light piercing deep shadow. Tintoretto (1518–1594) made use of the light in *The Last Supper*, presented as something

Tintoretto, "The Last Supper", Church of St. Giorgio Maggiore, Venice. (Alinari/Art Reference Bureau)

of a feast, in contrast to the usually re-strained treatments of the theme. The Ve-netians indulged in the lush and plush, as Titian's (1490–1576) *Bacchanale* shows. Here there is no movement in the bodies, no passionate frenzy: instead there is a mild revel or romp that he could build into a canvas of placid and resonant colors. The passivity—even in his most dramatic work —suggests the placidity of Venice herself. Although Venice suffered in her mainland possessions, she was free from the succes-sive foreign invasions that shook the main-land. No conqueror set foot in Venice until Napoleon Bonaparte. Isolated and serene in this island world, the Renaissance could continue in dignified repose. But elsewhere it was subject to violent disruption.

The Contribution of Renaissance Art

For two centuries, Renaissance artists and architects had grappled with a series of specific problems (perspective, expression,

form and space) and had mastered all of them brilliantly. Unlike classical art, which moved from idealism to realism, the oppo-site movement occurred. The early fifteenth century concern with space led to a some-what static and artificial style in the late

Titian, "Bacchanale".   (Museo del Prado, Madrid)

fifteenth century. Then the simplicity, harmony, and monumentality of the early Michelangelo gave way to disintegration, seen in Leonardo's interest in flux and change; an ultra realism, that hardened into "mannerism"—the sculpturelike, distorted art of Michelangelo's middle period. Similarly, architecture traced regressive steps from Gothic style back to antiquity. But the idealism and classicism of the Renaissance were more complex and grander in conception and execution than the ancients had attempted. Renaissance art, after all, served an ampler and less simple society. The journey back had not brought back the past, but had hastened the dawning of new styles.

The Invasion of Italy

When King Charles VIII of France invaded Italy in 1494, the age of the Italian city-republics was doomed. In the years that followed, north European powers fought to extend their influence into Italy, and the devastations and victories of the invading armies subdued the elated tone of the Italian Renaissance. The cynicism of Machiavelli marks the change of mood. Leonardo da Vinci's sketches of battles and floods are alive with turbulence. Michelangelo's *Last Judgment* throbs with violence, despair and disarray. Classical harmony was dissolving.

Yet vitality continued. The waters of the Renaissance mingled with those of the Reformation in the North. The best of Italian literature and music was yet to come. Italy was yet to give Galileo to science. Her commerce would be overshadowed, but its decline was not absolute, only relative. Epochs blend into one another; it is the historians who separate them.

Leonardo da Vinci, "The Deluge".   (Royal Library, Windsor Castle. Reproduced by gracious permission of Her Majesty Queen Elizabeth II)

Suggested Readings

The asterisk indicates a paperback edition.

Margaret Aston, *The Fifteenth Century* (*New York: Harcourt, Brace, Jovanovich, 1968).

B. Berenson, *Italian Painters of the Renaissance* (*New York: Meridian Books, 1957).

Jacob Burckhardt, *The Civilization of the Renaissance in Italy* (*Many editions).

Joseph Calmette, *The Golden Age of Burgundy* (New York: Norton, 1963).

Robert Ergang, *The Renaissance* (Princeton, N.J.: Van Nostrand, 1967).

John Fennell, *The Emergence of Moscow: 1304–1359* (Berkeley: University of California Press, 1968).

Wallace K. Ferguson, *Europe in Transition: 1300–1520* (Boston: Houghton Mifflin, 1962).

Myron P. Gilmore, *The World of Humanism: 1453–1519* (*New York: Harper and Row, 1962).

Denys Hay, *The Italian Renaissance in its Historical Background* (Cambridge, Engl.: Cambridge University Press, 1961).

J. H. Hexter, *Reappraisals in History* (*New York: Harper and Row, 1961).

George Holmes, *The Later Middle Ages: 1272–1485*. (*New York: Norton History of England, 1966).

Johan Huizinga, *The Waning of the Middle Ages* (*Garden City, N.Y.: Doubleday Anchor, 1954).

E. F. Jacob, *Essays in the Conciliar Epoch* (Manchester, England, 1953).

P. W. Lewis, *Later Medieval France: The Polity* (New York: St. Martin's Press, 1968).

J. H. Mariejol, *The Spain of Ferdinand and Isabella* (New Brunswick, N.J.: Rutgers University Press, 1961).

Lauro Martines, *The Social World of the Florentine Humanists: 1390–1460* (London: Routledge and Kegan Paul, 1963).

Michelangelo, "The Last Judgment", Sistine Chapel. (Anderson/Art Reference Bureau)

G. Mollat, *The Popes at Avignon: 1305–1378* (*New York: Harper and Row, 1965).

T. Morrison, ed., *The Portable Chaucer* (*New York: Viking, 1949).

Edouard Perroy, *The Hundred Years War*, trans. by W. B. Wells (*New York: Capricorn Books, 1965).

Henri Pirenne, *Early Democracies in the Low Countries* (*New York: Harper and Row, 1963).

Raymond de Roover, *The Rise and Fall of the Medici Bank* (*New York: Norton, 1963).

Brian Tierney, *Foundations of the Conciliar Theory* (Cambridge, Engl.: Cambridge University Press, 1955).

G. Vernadsky, *The Mongols and Russia* (New Haven, Conn.: Yale University Press, 1953).

Part 6 The Age of the Reformation

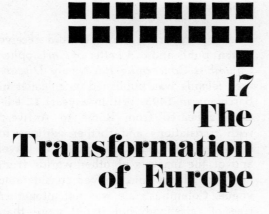

17
The Transformation of Europe

Early in the sixteenth century three young monarchs acceded to the major thrones of Western Europe; Henry VIII, the Tudor king of England (1509–1547); Francis I, the Valois king of France (1515–1547); and the Hapsburg Charles V, king of Spain (1517–1556) and Holy Roman Emperor. Their reigns began with high hopes. Europe was recovering from the depression and disorientation of the Late Middle Ages, and the prospects of the great kingdoms had never been more promising. England, France, and Spain, after generations of civil disorder, had achieved stable, centralized governments and were on the road to nationhood. The papacy was failing and, with it, the medieval dream of an international community of Catholic Christendom. The future lay with the rising nation kingdoms and, so it seemed, with the three young kings.

As the sixteenth century opened, the ideas of Renaissance humanism were influencing an international body of scholars. And all across Europe commerce was thriving once again. By 1500 European frontiers were open once more; European ships had reached America and India, and cargoes direct from the Orient were arriving in Portugal. And late-medieval inventions were changing the ways men lived—inventions such as the three-masted caravel, gunpowder, and the printing press.

Printing

A discussion of printing, as if it were an entirely novel process, refers strictly to the invention of movable metal type. Between 1440 and 1450, John Gutenberg perfected the idea in Mainz and entered a partnership. Of course, as with most inventions, the ingredients were available: there was paper; artists' oil paint could be easily modified for a suitable ink; imprints were used in the textile trade, and even separate letter stamps were used in foundries to identify metal wares. Books already were being printed by the use of wooden blocks; and block books continued to compete with type-formed books for a period. Indeed, for work that required no revisions, block prints were better. Movable type vastly increased the range and flexibility of production, and cheapened its cost, and woodcuts continued to be set in type for illustrations.

Within two decades, printers had carried their skills from Mainz to every corner of Europe, and by the end of the fifteenth century they were flooding the continent with a torrent of books. Venice alone had a hundred printing offices by 1500.

What did they publish? The Italians welcomed editions of the classics, while the Germans' output was more heavily religious. Overall, religious topics accounted for more than half of the works published before 1500. The Church Fathers, St. Thomas and other scholastic works, edifying religious tracts, editions of canon law and, above all, the Bible were most sought after. The Vulgate (Latin) Bible went through 133 editions in the fifteenth century, and it entered numerous vernacular printings in German, French, and Italian. There were fewer publications in Bohemian, Spanish, and Dutch, and none in English until the next century. Thomas à Kempis' The Imitation of Christ proved a best seller.

If anything, public taste was old fashioned. In science, books of alchemy and witchcraft and recipes for miraculous herbal cures vied with Galen in medicine and Ptolemy in astronomy. Numerous medieval commentaries on Aristotle appeared alongside Pliny's Natural History and similar encyclopedic works from antiquity.

To their credit, presses in the early decades managed to issue a vast backlog of writing, dating back to Aesop's Fables and beyond. Contemporary work formed a slender proportion of the whole, and the fact that few authors were published in their own time suggests that the reading public was as busy, or busier, devouring the past as keeping up with the present.

Exploration

One contemporary, however, did receive instant publication. A Letter of Christopher Columbus Concerning the Newly Discovered Islands was published as a leaflet in Barcelona in 1493. Within a year, 12 editions appeared from Rome to Antwerp with translations and further editions to follow. Already, enthralling tales of travel and of the marvels of other worlds from men like Marco Polo enjoyed considerable vogue. Columbus' tale was not altogether free of falsehood, but it did more than cater to a taste prepared in advance. His journey established that Europe would extend its influence over the globe, would embroil the world in its continental struggles, and would dispense its technology, religion, and values to the nethermost regions. At one bound, Columbus had reopened the frontiers of Europe.

Columbus was a Genoese who had sailed in the Portuguese service and had mastered every advance then current in Mediterranean navigation—the compass, the astrolabe, the latest charts, and the stern-post rudder. Fired with a desire to do what others had guessed at, he nursed and touted the idea of sailing into the unknown for years before he finally gained support from Spain. His contract guaranteed him 10 percent of the returns from his discoveries.

After 10 weeks at sea, in October 1492, he landed in the Bahamas and was convinced that he had discovered islands just off the coast of Cathay. On his return he enjoyed a brief summer of glory; he was feted by the populace and the government named him Admiral of the Ocean and Viceroy of the Islands.

But for all his vision, Columbus' dreams turned to dust; he had traveled only halfway to his goal. All his later voyages (1494–1504) bore out this bitter truth. The islands yielded little gold, and a colony that he had planted in Haiti (Hispaniola) gave so much trouble that his reputation as an administrator was destroyed. He was sent back from his third voyage in fetters, to be released at home, but to be stripped of his titles. His contract was broken, so he spent his last days near poverty. He hoped that his rights would be renewed and, dreaming beyond the grave, disposed of vast sums in his will.

Even the continents whose Isthmus he discovered were named after another explorer, Amerigo Vespucci, who sailed in 1497 and 1499. Amerigo claimed Brazil for Portugal, and Cabot, a Venetian, explored Nova Scotia for England. By 1497 it was beyond doubt that new continents had been discovered. Although Columbus came close to seeing the ocean that separated him from China, it was not until 1513 that Balboa gazed upon it from a peak near the gulf of Darien.

To this date Spain's spectacular explorations had brought her scant reward, whereas little Portugal, whose feats were less impressive, was already reaping the harvest of overseas trade.

Portugal's methods contrasted sharply with those of Spain. Columbus had ventured a breath-taking leap of imagination while the Portuguese sailors traversed the

Wood engraving from Columbus' letter of 1493. While this is not the Santa Maria, it is a typical explorer's vessel. As the engraving suggests, these ships were not large; the Santa Maria was 117 feet long and the two caravels which accompanied her on the voyage were only 50 feet long.   (New York Public Library)

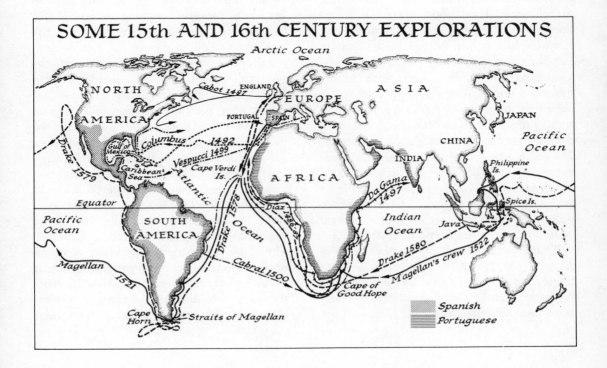

SOME 15th AND 16th CENTURY EXPLORATIONS

known over and over again before venturing any further. The courageous sailing into the sunset was not for them; they hugged the coast, feeling their way hesitantly and empirically.

Despite persistent encouragement from the third son of the king, Prince Henry the Navigator, the Portuguese sailors were, for a decade, too fearful to venture farther south than Cape Bojador (Northwest Africa); and, although Henry set up a school of navigation and equipped it with the latest charts and instruments, by the time of his death (1460) his protegés had not passed Sierra Leone—a mere 1000 miles —in 50 years. At least the lure of trade had begun to encourage others. In 1488, Diaz rounded the Cape of Good Hope because of the prospect it gave for reaching India. At this point, if the crown had been less preoccupied with finding the coastal route to the East, Columbus might have been kept in Portuguese employ, and Portugal might have owned the world. As it was, the reward waited until 1497 when the Portuguese explorer Vasco da Gama reached India.

Not without difficulty the Portuguese elbowed the Arab traders from their sphere of influence. Then they threw out a far-flung line of trading posts from Calicut, through Malacca to Macao, near Canton, in China itself. By 1520, the Genoese and Venetians, whose ties were with Arabs, had been undercut, and the price of spices began to drop in spite of a general inflation. From this time the Mediterranean declined as the centerboard of commerce, and did not revive until the Suez Canal was cut in 1869. With the spice market saturated, slaves proved to be a more reliable staple but, since this was a trade whose bulk did not pass through Lisbon, Portugal never became a great commercial center.

Neither did Spain. Sizeable treasure arrived after 1502; it rose steadily after Cortes began his conquest of Montezuma's Aztec empire in Mexico in 1519. That same year Magellan left Seville, crossed the South Atlantic and sailed around the tip of South America into the Pacific. Magellan died in the Philippines, but one of his three ships reached home three years later—the first ship ever to circumnavigate the world.

Trade and Commerce

Spain had little industry and lacked the wares to export in return for the goods that the new world showered on her. Cadiz, the principal port, was in a poor geographical position to feed the distant European hinterlands, and the city was under severe restrictions from the Crown, who decreed who could trade there and on what terms. Thus, financiers operated through agents in Cadiz and established their headquarters in the freer atmosphere of Antwerp in the Netherlands.

Antwerp had long been famous for its fairs and its freedom. It had splendid access to the sea and to the interior, and deliberately cultivated its open and unrestricted market. Indeed, for the benefit of traders, in 1537 the city built the Bourse which became the model for those Exchanges at Amsterdam and London which would later succeed her in eminence. In the early sixteenth century, Antwerp was the hub of European commerce and the most cosmopolitan city in the world.

European commerce quickened on the gold and silver that began to reach Spain from Mexico and, after Spain's conquest of the Incas in the 1530s, on more silver from Peru. As fast as the precious metals arrived in Spain, Charles V spent them to supply his armies and to meet his creditors' high interest rates. Through the bankers, the wealth of the New World filtered down to the lowest levels, fostering inflation as it went. Prices rose, credit became more abundant, and interest rates slowly fell. The Low Countries gradually replaced northern Italy as the commercial leader of Europe, but Italy still flourished. And, though less trade plied the route to Venice, Germany did not become a backwater overnight. Indeed, with the increased supply of bullion, German capitalists came into their own—Welsens, Haugs, Hochstetters, Imhofs and, greatest of them all, the Fuggers. The Fuggers never shifted their headquarters from the south German city of Augsburg, though they drew their biggest profits from their Antwerp branch.

Reformation Germany, like all Europe, was beset by rising prices and also by an increase in the number of rich bourgeoisie who were blamed for the spiral. Agricultural classes, from knights to peasants, found that the returns from their produce lagged behind the inflated prices of urban goods, and some ill-feeling was inevitable.

The dramatic upsurge of the sixteenth century had begun when gold dust began to reach Europe from Portuguese trading stations along the African coast and in the Congo basin. Slaves, ivory, ostrich plumes, parrots, and sugar filled their caravels, yet the exotic trade can be grossly exaggerated.

What mattered was the larger flow of staples: the exchange of the three main foodstuffs—cereals, fish, and wine—for industrial tools and textiles. Textiles were specialized. Italy still excelled in fine silks and satins, France and the Low Countries in linen, tapestries, and carpets, and England in wool and woolen cloth. Spain depended too heavily on raw wool production. The Baltic countries traded lumber and salted fish, Venice boasted delicate glassware, France and the Rhineland fine wines. Amsterdam led in shipbuilding. Eastern Europe and Sicily were the granaries that supplied the cereal-deficient areas of the Netherlands, northern Italy, Spain, and Portugal. All in all, Europe, on the eve of the Reformation, was more prosperous than it had ever been before.

Population Growth

It was rapidly becoming more densely populated than ever before. Demographic histories testify that the sixteenth century saw a recovery of population from well below pre-plague levels to well above them. The change from death surpluses to birth surpluses seems to have happened around the middle of the fifteenth century. Couples married younger and families grew larger. By the early sixteenth century, populations were still below pre-plague figures, but in the remainder of the century a population revolution of staggering proportions was underway. In one of the best documented principalities of Germany the increase in population between 1500 and 1604 was 84 percent. Other areas appear to have had even greater increases. Detailed studies of parish registers in England (started in 1528) suggest a similar drastic trend. French figures are the same. All over Europe, in fact, a long upward wave had begun, which was not to subside until the middle of the seventeenth century. It would rise again in the eighteenth century. Why the baby boom should have started nobody quite knows, nor is it known why it stopped suddenly two centuries later.

Population growth expands markets, it increases mobility — "surplus" children would move to other villages or towns. On the other hand, population growth makes the distress of bad harvests, famines, other disturbances, and deliberate depopulations more acute. That is, population growth encourages commercial growth but renders social problems more urgent and pressing. Maintenance of tillage, control of the poor, punishment of vagabonds, and the regulation of trading, manufacturing and wages become a matter of grave concern to governments. By the same token, social problems become a matter of unavoidable concern for reformers.

Population growth also seems to have had an adverse effect on rates of literacy. It was not the cathedral schools nor the new secular foundations that carried the burden of mass education. Numerically, their influence was slight. In the countryside, and in the villages, it was the parish schoolmaster who passed on literacy to the children. Reading and writing were in the main for boys. Daughters were largely ignored. As a group it appears that tradesmen made the most headway. Except in London it seems that the less densely populated areas in the North and South of England remained at high levels of literacy, and the more densely populated Midlands and East Anglia fell by comparison. Of course, it is hard in a "conjugal" family unit (husband and wife only, without grandparents) for the burden of teaching to fall on the father. Throughout our period the percentage of "multigenerational" family units was low. This is a characteristic of the West—families set up separate economic units. In the East, married couples and their children normally lived with one set of parents or the other. It is an important social difference between East and West, but precisely where the line should be drawn between Eastern and Western Europe is not quite clear. Nor, indeed, is it clear what inferences can safely be drawn from the pioneer work presently underway on literacy. The evidence is too flimsy to bear much weight. But perhaps an area of lowering literacy would be inclined to welcome Protestantism: it was a religion of the Word, with more oral instruction from the pulpits than Catholicism offered. And Protestantism was also an educational force since, in the main Protestant branches, children were intensively instructed in religious doctrine. With Protestantism using the press and the pulpit, it is probably fair to assume that Europe's swiftly-expanding population was becoming better informed on matters of general knowledge than previously.

Divided Europe

If Europeans were more knowledgeable, Europe (fortunately for the reformers) was also more deeply divided than previously. The Reformation would have been nipped in the bud had it not been for the power struggle between two Catholic dynasties—the Valois Kings of France and the Hapsburg Holy Roman emperors. The emperor, Charles V, earnestly desired to crush the Reformers, but King Francis I placed his political ambitions so far above religious principle that he encouraged the Protestant cantons of Switzerland and the Lutheran princes in order to embarrass the emperor. He even allied himself with the infidel Turks.

By accident of inheritance, Charles V's lands encircled France and threatened to dominate the whole of the continent. He inherited the Hapsburg lands of southeastern Germany, the territories of Burgundy (between Germany and France), and the Kingdom of Spain with its oversized empire and its jurisdiction over Sicily and Naples. And in 1519 he was elected Holy Roman emperor. It was far too much for one man to handle, and Charles chose to sacrifice the greatness of Spain for the will-o'-the-wisp prestige of the Empire. His own sense of justice defeated him, for Francis I was a cunning, faithless opponent. Charles won all the victories, and after each one Francis would submit to the emperor's modest demands, only to flout them at the first opportunity. After his sally to take the Imperial fief of Milan, for instance, Francis was captured in 1525. He agreed to waive his claim and pledged his good faith on the Gospels and before a wayside shrine. But, as soon as he reached France, he cried "Now I am King, I am King once more." He continued to press his claim for Milan on his own behalf and on behalf of his son (later Henry II) until mutual war-weariness brought the protracted and fitful war to a halt in the Treaty of Câteau Cambrésis in 1559.

Meanwhile Charles had defeated the Lutheran princes in 1547, but his other concerns prevented him from consolidating his victory. The Protestant cause revived with sufficient energy to force Charles to commit the settlement of religious matters into the hands of an Imperial Diet. Predictably, the Diet's solution, called the Peace of Augsburg (1555) was an anti-imperial peace which gave each territorial prince the absolute right to decree the religion of his own state. So the Reformation survived with the power of the princes enormously strengthened. And Emperor Charles V, who wanted for nothing but imperial and religious unity, was forced to play midwife to intensified German particularism and religious division.

18
The Protestant Reformation

The Reformation, like the Renaissance, was born in the fold of little states. Indeed, without them, it could not have survived, nor could it have survived without the rivalry of Spain and France. Like the humanists, the reformers were opposed to the cloister and were thoroughly committed to life in the world. The culture roughly described as humanist, and the Reformation, arose as papal vitality ebbed. Both were movements of emanicipation, drawing their inspiration and their legitimacy from a distant past. In their recasting of values, and their attempt to shape new views of man, the humanists and reformers were akin, but their visions of life and of human capacity and their sources of authority were quite different.

The reformers were guided by early Christian authority rather than pagan classics. They were less Greek and Roman than Hebrew. While the humanists satirized the abuses of the Church, the reformers denounced them; the one group tolerated the papacy and concentrated its scorn on superstitions and on the medieval religious orders; the other was alienated by the practice and pretension of the Renaissance papacy. It was not simply that Renaissance popes had been derelict in their duty to cure souls, or that they were politically minded and materialistic, and often guilty of gross nepotism and flagrant immorality. What mattered was the abuse of the spiritual office of the pope. And the abuse rested on claims that became the focus of the intellectual and theological grievances of the reformers. By and large the humanists had assumed that they knew the way to salvation and devoted themselves to enriching the possibilities of life, while the reformers were seeking new avenues to assurance.

Social Origins

Behind this quest lay a deep soul-sickness or, perhaps, sensitivity that had continued in Northern Europe alongside the Renais-

Michael Wolgemut, "Death Dance".
(Germanisches Nationalmuseum, Nurnberg)

flanks his righteous Christian knight on his way to a "city on a hill" with a figure of death holding an hourglass, and a monstrous devil—half wolf, half pig. Luther

Jan and/or Hubert van Eyck, "The Last Judgment".   (The Metropolitan Museum of Art, Fletcher Fund, 1933)

sance and, despite the new prosperity, persisted into the sixteenth century. It existed in the country rather than in the gay and elegant court and it shook the middle and lower orders more than the aristocracy.

A sense of doom had lingered long after the Black Death of the mid-fourteenth century. Even during the plague the reaction in the North had been more hysterical and ghoulish than in the South. Dancing frenzies and flagellations were less frequent in Italy. And one is tempted to attribute this to climate. Throughout the fifteenth century the North was preoccupied with death, judgment, and hell fire, and an abiding pessimism about man's fate runs through its prose and poetry. A peculiarly macabre dance fashion cropped up, performed by men with skeletons. The dance was intended to remind watchers of their mortality and their equality before the relentless swathe of time. Woodcuts popularized the steps and stages of it. Also, a spate of the early printed pamphlets dealt with the art of dying. In art, morbid undertones took on a bizarre realism. Van Eyck's *The Last Judgment* portrayed the subterranean horror to which the evil were to be committed. Bosch's strange sermons in paint are inhabited by wild, nightmarish creatures. Even Dürer, the German realist,

Hieronymus Bosch, detail from "The Garden of Delights". (Museo del Prado, Madrid)

believed deeply in the reality and power of Satan and his demons.

As somber as the Northern climate may be, it was also the proximity to death and the frequency of it that kept morbid pessimism alive. In France and Burgundy, for instance, the desolation of the Hundred Years War was followed by decimations between rival factions, not to mention recurrences of the Black Death plague. So, from the time of the plague, through wars, famines, and civil wars, there had been no respite from the threat of death and no guarantee against the onset of disaster.

Martin Luther's Progress to the Reformation

A high level of death-consciousness was fertile soil for the Reformation and offers insight into Luther's unusually persistent concern about salvation. For it was the terror of death that sent him into an Augustinian monastery. Born the son of a miner and foundry owner, at Eisleben in Saxony (1483), he did so well in school that his father urged him to become a jurist. He studied arts at the University of Erfurt for four years until, in 1505, a flash of lightning struck him to the ground in a thunderstorm. Without consulting his father he abandoned his intention to go on to law for the robe and cowl. A psychologist, interested in history, has called this Luther's "identity crisis." Then he began to seek a new "life-style." These phrases are ways of describing the mystery of conversion.

In the monastery the earlier terror of death became a fearfulness and trembling before God. And his inner torment was not eased by the fact that his father disapproved of his course. Had he done wrong? He felt inadequate to meet the demands of the Mosaic code, let alone Christ's new commandment. The law condemned him. He was a worm in the dust; how could he stand before the Omnipotent Judge? He underwent vigorous austerities to make himself holier, and could not find assurance. An errand to Rome shook him

Albrecht Durer, "The Knight, Death and the Devil". (The Metropolitan Museum of Art, Harris Brisbane Dick Fund, 1943)

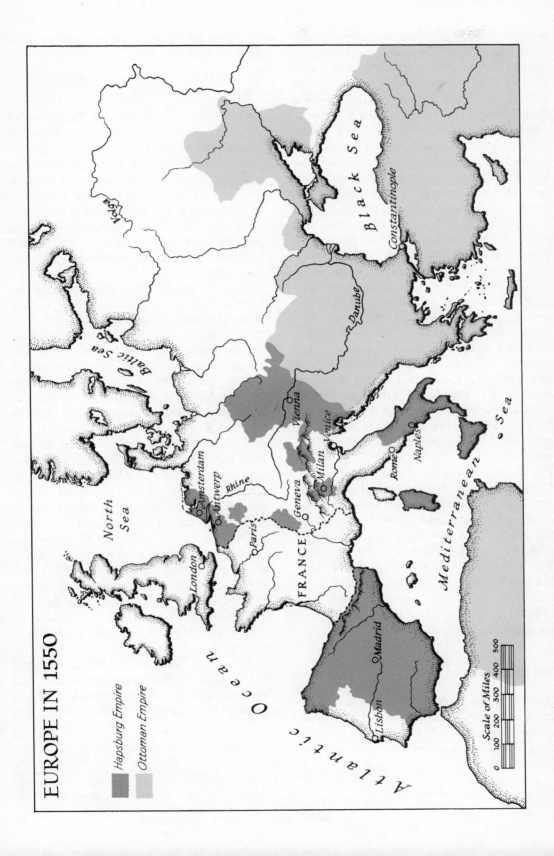

EUROPE IN 1550

Hapsburg Empire
Ottoman Empire

Volga

Black Sea

Constantinople

Danube

Baltic Sea

Vienna

Venice

Milan

Amsterdam

Antwerp

Rhine

Geneva

Rome

Naples

Paris

North Sea

London

FRANCE

Mediterranean Sea

Madrid

Lisbon

Atlantic Ocean

Scale of Miles
0 100 200 300 400 500

further. He did not notice the glories of the Renaissance or the reminders of antiquity; instead, he saw the worldliness and levity of the clergy, both high and low. He climbed the *Scala Sancta*, 28 stairs, with a Pater Noster* and a kiss on each in order to release a soul from purgatory, and at the top he found his faith in the indulgence clouded by doubt. His doubt redoubled on his return. Confession of particular sins seemed inadequate for man's plight. The whole man needed release from total inner corruption. Piece by piece and doubt by doubt, Luther came to view the all-pervasiveness of sin as the only solution that could satisfy his wounded conscience. Since man was too deeply sunk in sin to do anything for his own salvation, he had to be saved, or justified, by faith alone.

Meanwhile he was lecturing on Scriptures and was feeling his way toward a new principle of hermeneutics, a new method of expounding the Bible. Like the medieval friars, he abandoned the allegorical approaches to the texts. But unlike the friars, who preached on particular biblical episodes, Luther concentrated on the inner meaning and underlying unity of Scripture. His attention was fixed on the agony of Christ, forsaken because of the sins of man that He had taken upon Himself. Man could accept his utter worthlessness and yet take joy in the faith that was made possible through Christ's sacrifice. God was a merciful and righteous father, and not a fierce, irrascible judge. The Reformation, one could say, occurred because a brilliant professor was doing his job—preparing thoughtful, original lectures.

The Reformation

Luther's thoughts tumbled out of the classroom into the marketplace in 1517 when plenary indulgences* were being hawked by a Dominican, Tetzel, near Wittenburg.

For one fourth of a florin, buyers were assured that

As soon as the coin the coffer rings
The soul from purgatory springs.

Faithful to academic custom, Luther nailed 95 propositions (or theses) in Latin on the door of the castle church as an open invitation to a debate on their merits. They began with a popular attack on the venality of Rome, passed through the doubts as to the pope's right to remit punishment inflicted by God, and finished by asserting that nothing but contrition could remit spiritual guilt and nothing else was necessary.

Luther's doubts about the extent of the pope's power to indulge were, indeed, legitimate, for the question had never been definitively settled. Beyond that, however, he had implied an unorthodox way to salvation, and had begun the Reformation.

The newly-invented printing press quickly turned his traditional appeal for a debate into an appeal to the people. The 95 theses were translated into German and widely publicized. And as the dispute over indulgences waxed, Luther grew progressively bolder and his criticisms of the Church became more and more fundamental. Finally—after he had been excommunicated—Luther declared that he could not recognize the authority of popes and councils because they had often contradicted each other. He staked his faith and, indeed, his life on Scripture and reason. "Here I stand," he is said to have declared at the Diet of Worms (1521), "I cannot do otherwise." His Latin works, published at this time, sold out rapidly.

For a year, Frederick the Wise of Saxony hid Luther in his strongest castle, but meanwhile under the direction of Luther's close friend, Philipp Melanchthon, the

---

* "Our Father." The Lord's prayer.

* An indulgence is a spiritual gift granted by the Church, through which the period of a soul's suffering in purgatory is shortened by some specific number of days or years. A plenary (full) indulgence frees the soul from purgatory altogether.

Reformation in Wittenberg was proceeding. Luther directed it with letters while he translated the New Testament into rich German. Revisions of this work, and a German translation of the Old Testament, followed later.

In 1520 Luther had published three treatises defining his position and calling for action. In the *Address to the Christian Nobility of the German Nation* he appealed to the German ruling classes to throw off the yoke of Rome. He maintained that each believer is his own priest—a doctrine that could yield embarrassing results. Luther meant that any layman could attain forgiveness independent of a priest. The priesthood was only one of many vocations. With this stroke, he broke the power of the Church over secular authorities—the power to give or withhold the means of salvation—and encouraged civil authorities to reform an erring church. In *On the Babylonian Captivity of the Church* he attacked the sacramental system, denied four of the traditional sacraments, and kept only Baptism, the Eucharist and, in a revised sense, Penance. Confession was possible between laymen. Marriage was a civil affair to which the Church could give its blessing. Ordination and confirmation were rites of the church but were not sacraments. Extreme unction was unscriptural and, therefore, was wholy renounced. As for the Eucharist, he wanted both the bread and the wine distributed to the laity (rather than the bread alone, which had been Catholic custom since the twelfth century). Moreover, he denied that the Eucharist was a reenactment of the sacrifice of the Cross, and deviated from the Catholic doctrine of transubstantiation. Finally, his *Liberty of A Christian Man* set out the doctrine of justification by faith, making faith primary, and a free gift of God, and good works of no heavenly merit but simply the fruit of faith. God, in His mercy, gratuitously declared men just and sinless, men who were, in fact, riven with sin. God would, like a merciful judge, declare the guilty criminal to be not guilty because someone else had made reparation for him. Then the unworthy man could feel free from the terror of God's justice, free from the duress of judgment and death, and live in the joy of an eternal salvation given for no reason of his doing but because Christ's righteousness had been imputed to his credit. Liberty was conceived as a spiritual rather than a political attribute—a liberty, or power, to act righteously—yet, here again, Luther's words were extended to ends that he did not intend. These early writings laid the groundwork for the later additions and subtractions of Reformed theology.

Anabaptism and the Peasants' Revolt

The priesthood of all believers was never meant to make every man his own prophet. In several areas (Strassburg, Augsburg, Zurich, and Moravia), separate movements of Christian radicalism developed, some passive, some active. Under the inspiration of radical Lutherans who had turned apocalyptic, the latter sort spread their mystic millenarianism through Germany and the Low Countries, and quoted Luther for support. Unlike Luther, these wanted to bring society, not just faith, under the law of the gospel. Some were even prepared to use force to bring the whole society to purity. Naturally, they attracted the lower classes in town and country. Theirs was a Utopian movement and also a vent for class bitterness. Others were less millenarian, stressing the need to separate the church from worldly society, and emphasizing pacifism and the love-ethic. Luther fulminated against both branches as fiercely as the Catholics, but neither burnings, drownings, nor massacres seemed to halt their spread. Amsterdam caught the enthusiasm around 1530; and in 1534 prophets of the revolutionary wing penetrated the city of Munster to establish the Kingdom of God on earth. The city had just rebelled against its prince-bishop and was in terror of subjection. During a twelve-month siege the Anabaptists instituted a communistic state. Since supplies were running low, this was practical as well as Utopian. Similarly, as the supply of men was depleted by skirmishes, polygamy was instituted for the protection of the womenfolk as well as for personal and unorthodox ethical reasons. To the respectable, this New Jerusalem was an enormity to be crushed and scattered without hint of mercy. Only in this century were the cages containing the bones of the leaders—John of Leyden and Burgomaster Knipperdalling —removed from a steeple where they had swung in derisive display for centuries.

Munster's inglorious defeat cut the heart out of the aggressive branch of Anabaptism, but its pacifist, pietistic aspect continued to conquer the hearts of the downtrodden and dispossessed.

Luther was even more violent in his denunciation of the peasants who demanded "liberty" in social terms on the basis of scriptural authority. The German peasants were in an ambivalent position in the sixteenth century. Rising prices were in their favor, but the gap between prices for agricultural produce and industrial equipment was growing instead of decreasing. Not that peasants needed many tools. But their returns were not as large or fast as the city merchant's returns, and the growing disparity was irksome. More trying than this, though, were the downward pressures foisted on them by the Knights and magnates. The Knights as a class were threatened with decline because their rents and services, being relatively fixed, fell behind climbing prices. They were eager to reimpose maximum obligations on a peasantry that was eager to escape them. The Peasants War (1525) was one of a series of agrarian disturbances protesting the injustice and oppression of these landlords. Coming as it did in the early stages of the Reformation, and encouraged as it was in some areas by convinced Anabaptists, it threatened to drown Luther's work in a torrent of civil strife. At first

Luther was non-committal; he recognized that many of the peasants' grievances were genuine, but as the peasants indulged in indiscriminate pillaging he realized the danger to his own cause and turned against them with extraordinary venom. Princes, he urged, could better merit heaven by smiting, slaying and stabbing rebellious subjects than by prayer.

It was said that over 100,000 peasants were killed in battle or executed afterward, and crippling fines were laid upon those who escaped with their lives. From this time the peasantry ceased to count in German politics; princes and magnates had vindicated their power once and for all. Where the revolt had been most vigorous, in Bavaria and Austria, the savage reprisals alienated the peasantry from Luther and the decline of Lutheranism in southern Germany dates from the crushing defeat of the Revolt rather than from the Counterreformation.

Luther's Ethics

Luther was a consummate theological politician. His ultimate concerns were inner, yet he had to take political stands to protect the Reformation he desired. Although not excusing them, political needs go far to explain his dubious moral stands on this and other issues. Above all he was fearful for the future, and his siding with the princes was a frank recognition that it was only in their support that the Reformation had any chance of success. Social revolution, chaos, Anabaptism, and even Judaism were threats to the cause, and he was swift to denounce them. His anti-Semitism was religiously rather than racially determined, but here, as in other matters, he failed to rid himself of the current prejudices of his place and time.

Happily, the dictates of political realism coincided with the ethical consequences of his doctrines. Man was such that he needed the civil sword to contain him in order and tranquility and to bind him in a tolerable state of social cohesion. His liberty was a purely spiritual freedom from the duress of death. It was an inner grace that enabled man to fulfill the law because he had been made righteous by the free gift of God. So Luther preached absolute and unconditional obedience. He refused to condone even passive resistance to the secular arm except by princes. He did nothing to alter the habit of the authoritarian conscience. Indeed, he regarded wicked rulers as God-sent scourges. Lutheranism exchanged obedience to the pope for abject obedience to the state.

Luther's economic ethics were equally conservative, and in this he expressed the resentments of his petty bourgeois background. He did not visualize money as a productive thing in itself and therefore forbade all usury. This was to be more medieval than the schoolmen. Like St. Thomas, he believed that each person had his proper place in society and should keep it, and he used the word "calling" to suggest that God wants a Christian to be dedicated to his vocation.

If this was old-fashioned, his appeal to German nationalism was radical and modern, foreshadowing the virulent German-consciousness of the nineteenth and twentieth centuries. The Imperial Knights had early rallied to his standard, prepared to do battle for the emancipation of Germany from the Roman yoke. Although this was one of Luther's themes, his hopes were for peaceful reformation. But his vigorous German style and his outcries against the exploitation of Germany by foreigners were calculated to raise feelings of outraged patriotism.

Luther and Humanism

It was Luther's periodic fury and what seemed to be his reckless rending of the unity of Christendom that alienated the majority of humanists from him. Some, like Melanchthon, were persuaded, but most found his convictions hard to stomach because they were held so passionately. The humanists' temper was more urbane.

A vast temperamental gulf separated them from the "true believer."

Yet the root of the differences lay in their views of the nature of man and of human destiny. It was no less than the difference between the Renaissance and the Reformation. Erasmus went to the heart of the problem in a tract *On the Freedom of the Will* (1524). Initially he had sympathized with Luther. Had not Erasmus also attacked the barren formalism and legalism of the Church, its manifest corruptions, its archaic superstitions, like the veneration of relics? He had also disapproved of the abuse of indulgences, and may be regarded as a forerunner of the Reformation. Nevertheless Erasmus accepted the authority of the Church. He wanted to reform it morally from within, and to trim off its dead wood. But he was not pressed by disparate doubts to reach out for a new way to salvation. Morals were his concern as salvation was Luther's. Their debate over free will must be taken in a spiritual sense: the free will was not the mundane choosing of this or that during the day. The issue was whether a man could help himself toward salvation by his own voluntary acts. Erasmus thought so, without denying the cooperation of grace in bringing about good works. Luther thought not. Granted that a heathen could be upright and decent, but no man, no matter how pure, was worthy of justification because every human deed was tainted by selfishness and pride. God alone, Luther taught, had the freedom to justify whomever He chose. The humanists believed that man could, to some extent, make his own destiny, while Luther believed that all man could do was throw himself on the love and mercy of God. The difference was insoluble.

Protestantism in Germany and Scandinavia

In an age when such differences mattered more than life, it was inevitable that the Church should encourage the emperor to root out the Reformation with fire and the sword. Many were burned and executed and, to his dying day, Luther expected to be arrested at any time for trial as a heretic. When he died (1546) he was full of forebodings about the future.

He need not have worried. Although there was precious little idealism in the princes, they had much to gain from the Reformation. They could seize Church property for themselves, and they could add the domination of the Church to their power over the state, and more than double their influence. These advantages caused several electors and princes to declare for Luther and to impose a local Reformation settlement from above. Territorial churches, subject to the prince, replaced the universal church. When the Holy Roman emperor, Charles V, attempted to force the princes to abandon their caesaropapist claims in 1529 they protested, and *Protestant* became the name of all Luther's partisans. In 1531 the dissident princes formed a League of Schmalkald for their mutual defense. And so long as Charles V was occupied in fighting the king of France and the Turkish Sultan, the League held the field. In 1547, during a peace with France, Charles defeated the Protestant forces. Yet he could not prevent them from recovering their strength again because of the obstreperous Valois kings. France and the Turks saved the Reformation in Germany. Finally the Peace of Augsburg (1555) established the principle of princes' choice, and secured Protestantism its future.

By this time, Lutheranism had spread far beyond the German states. Nowhere was the Lutheran Church more of a political creation than in Sweden. Without declaring himself, Gustavus Vasa (1496-1560) found Lutheranism a useful ally in his leadership of the struggle for Swedish independence against Denmark. After his victory and election to the crown in 1523, Gustavus filled both church and state offices with staunch Lutherans who dutifully preached obedience. He brought church lands under his control in 1527, and then declared himself a Lutheran (1530). From this time his domination of the church was absolute. Henry VIII of England was to take a page from his book.

In Denmark and Norway Lutheranism flourished with the tacit consent of the King. It spread more from below than above, and by 1536—with the establishment of King Christian on the Danish throne after a civil war with the Catholics—the Lutheran victory was complete. Church ordinances drawn up in the following year have governed the Danish church to the present day. While the Danes did not take Lutheranism undiluted, it was inevitable that their reform movement should assume a Lutheran form in preference to any other. Denmark's lines of communication were direct with Germany and circuitous to the other reform centers. The distance from Rome, as much as the mutual interests of crowns and peoples, accounts for the stability of the Lutheran settlement in Scandinavia.

The English Reformation

English divines hailed Luther as the Father of the Reformation, and so he was, but it is possible to exaggerate his achievement. At the time of his disparate bouts with doubt and despair, there were many who were seeking fresh faith in the scriptures. The Swiss reformer, Zwingli, claimed to have announced the principles of "Scriptures only" and "Justification" before Luther in 1517. The work of humanist biblical scholars such as Erasmus was pointing in the same direction.

The Reformation was more than one man's conviction; it was a groundswell of religious disaffection. When parishioners were not being offered satisfying spiritual nourishment, the Bible provided it. And this is why the town of Wittenberg did not become the only (or even the leading) center of the Reformation.

Still, Luther had considerable effect on the English Reformation. The first English translation of the New Testament (1526) was done by William Tyndale, an English Lutheran in exile. It was hawked about England by Lollards, who had suffered severe persecution after Wycliffe's death but had never been completely stamped out. Later, the King's chief minister of the Reformation, Thomas Cromwell, authorized another and complete English translation of the Bible by another English Lutheran, Miles Coverdale (1535). The Boleyn family, whose pretty daughter caught Henry VIII's eye, represented the Lutheran faction at court, and Anne Boleyn's chaplain, Thomas Cranmer, became the Archbishop of Canterbury who finally pronounced Henry's divorce from his first wife. Cranmer's father-in-law was a leading German reformer. In spite of the language barrier, important connections with Lutheranism had been made long before the Reformation occurred in England. The merchants of the Hanseatic League freely imported Luther's work, and his doctrines were discussed by academics at Cambridge and by laymen in London. But, when all is said and done, the English Reformation was the King's and not Luther's business.

Indeed, the King was opposed to Lutheranism. Pope Leo X granted him and his successors the title "Defender of the Faith" for a sturdy defense of the sacraments that Henry had written against Luther in 1521. Luther's reply, which referred to "Henry, King of England, by the disgrace of God," did nothing to mollify him. One reason for Thomas Cromwell's sudden fall (1540) was that he tried to enmesh Henry in a Lutheran alliance. Toward the end of his reign, Henry recognized that doctrine was bound to change but, until then, he kept the Church in England well within the folds of orthodoxy—with the exception that he transferred the sovereignty of the Pope to himself.

The Divorce

Thus Henry VIII was unmoved by doctrinal considerations; unmoved, too, by the mounting tide of anticlericalism and complaint against the Church. Yet he played on popular resentment and on patriotic sentiment for his own personal and dynastic ends. It is not entirely fair to view Henry's divorce from Catherine of Aragon as a cold and heartless act; the welfare of his kingdom was involved. His wife had had nothing but a procession of miscarriages and stillbirths after the birth of Princess Mary. And the consequences of a female succession could prove disastrous, for treason was never far below the surface. The Wars of the Roses were a living memory, and treason had twice inflamed rebellion in Henry VII's time. By 1525 Henry VIII despaired of a boy from Catherine and began to scour the canon law, the Fathers, and papal decrees for grounds for a divorce. He did have some grounds in law and scripture, because his wife had first been his brother's wife, though that marriage had not been consummated. Moreover, there was hope in that the pope had granted a divorce to his sister and his brother-in-law for less grounds than he could show.

At this time, or soon after, Henry became infatuated with coquettish Anne Boleyn who had recently returned from the French court. She inflamed his passion by refusing to submit to him. Unsympathetic historians do have some reason for portraying the English Reformation as the illegitimate offspring of a monumental lust. We may wonder why Henry could not have slaked his desire without divorce and remarriage, like other monarchs. Either Anne was made of stern stuff, or if she wasn't, the dynastic considerations were preeminent. Through his thoughts and studies Henry had also convinced himself that he was living in sin with Catherine, and all three factors combined to make the divorce the overwhelming single object of his policy.

Regardless of his own judgment of the case, the pope was in no position to grant a divorce at the time Henry was pressing for it. Catherine was the aunt of Emperor Charles V, and Charles' forces were, at that moment, the masters of Italy. They were then, in fact, occupying Rome itself. How could the defeated pope shame the family of the victor? By 1529 it was clear in England that the papacy could never yield to the importunities of the frantic English emissaries. For satisfying one man's familial pride the pope lost the allegiance of a nation.

The Solution

Thomas Cromwell offered Henry the obvious way out of the impasse—the subjection of the Church to the crown. For eight years (1532–1540) Cromwell was the King's alter ego, entrusted with the remaking of the Church of England, and with the remaking of the state accordingly. Cromwell's vision far overreached the King's obsession with divorce and, unlike most politicians, he realized his vision in practice. He established England as a realm with indivisible sovereignty, and the sovereignty he established was not that of the crown alone, but of the crown in Parliament. After Cromwell, the Reformation could never be unmade by the King alone, since any change needed the consent of Lords and Commons assembled. Ultimately, the polity, doctrine, and liturgy of the Church fell under the control of Parliament. This solution (neither Lutheran nor Calvinist) has lasted with little interruption ever since.

It was not achieved in a day. First the clergy were intimidated into submission; then the king, with Parliamentary backing, claimed the right to nominate bishops —a right the British crown still wields. Above all, appeals to Rome were forbidden. The divorce question could now be "legally" settled in England by the Convocations and pronounced by Archbishop Cranmer (May, 1533). He did so with alacrity because Anne Boleyn was pregnant

and gave birth to Princess Elizabeth four months later.

Having achieved a revolution in church and state, Cromwell guaranteed its permanence by dissolving the monasteries. The profits of their sale went to the crown, where they were squandered; the land went to the nobility and gentry. In a sense, the dissolutions were a gigantic bribe. And, though doctrine would change and change again, Parliament would never vote to return church land to the church. Thus, one permanent effect of the sales was to impoverish the Establishment forever; and indirectly the crown was impoverished, for instead of conserving its fixed assets, Henry preferred quick sales for immediate gain. Finally the speculative boom in land entwined the interests of landed gentry and urban bourgeois in a peculiarly intimate way to enhance the solidarity of the members of the House of Commons. The future was theirs but, for the moment, the King's power was omnipresent.

As for Anne, she did not live up to her expectations. She could not bear a son and was executed for her failure. Jane Seymour, the next Queen, managed to bring Prince Edward into the world but died immediately afterward. There followed three more marriages whose squalid tales need not be told.

Edwardian Reformation

Just before Henry died, "full of years and sin," he purged his Council of Catholics and left the Duke of Somerset as Protector in charge of the child King Edward VI (1547–1553). Affairs of state became anarchical. Somerset started well-meaning reforms but lacked the acumen to succeed with them, and he alienated the privileged classes by proceeding against enclosers of land and depopulators of villages. As a result of his political blundering, Somerset was overthrown and, after a time, executed for treason. But his fall did not halt the forward movement of the Reformation.

Meanwhile, Archbishop Cranmer had added a doctrinal reformation to the political reformation. He did it in two stages, by measured advance. First, a moderate prayer book (1549) caused some outcry in the West for where Cornishmen spoke neither English nor Latin, Latin was the more familiar tongue. Their rebellion, also economically motivated, was swiftly crushed. A second prayer book of 1552 and 42 Articles of Faith of 1553 were unequivocally Protestant; and these were essentially reinstated in Elizabeth's time. There were slight modifications in the prayer book and the 42 Articles were distilled to 39. In Edward's reign, however, they had little chance for acceptance because the precious little prince died in 1553.

If England's doctrinal Reformation had occurred alongside its political one, it doubtless would have been less radical than it was. Since Luther's time a host of reformers had arisen, and most of them stood to the left of the originator. Cranmer drew his theology not only from Luther but from earlier critics of the Church, including Wycliffe, and from Calvin, Zwingli, and other continental reformers. Anglican doctrine, then, was thoroughly Protestant, and yet the episcopal governing structure of the Church remained unchanged. This was the *via media,* or middle way, to which Elizabeth returned in 1558.

Reaction: The Reign of Queen Mary Tudor (1553–1558)

Mary overturned it all. She was accepted after Edward's death because she was a Tudor rather than for her Roman Catholicism. Her obsession was to save the state from sin. As long as no attempt was made to restore church lands, Parliament could be rendered pliable. The doctrinal changes were unscrambled; then there began a fierce persecution of Protestants that made Mary abominable to English memory. Not only were hundreds burned in baleful fires at Smithfield near London but Mary prostrated English interests to the interests of her Spanish husband, Phillip II. England was taxed to support the Hapsburg's fight against France—a war in which she had little interest; and England's seamen were forbidden to venture across the Atlantic to disturb the Spanish monopoly in the new world. The affront to national feeling was as harmful to Mary's memory as her intolerance. She died a pathetic woman, loving a husband who did not love her, and hoping to have a child that she could not bear.

During her reign, hundreds of Edwardian Protestants fled abroad. Most of the exiles clung to the second Edwardian prayer book, but those who reached Geneva came away with a sterner theology and a sterner view of church order than they had arrived with.

Elizabethan Settlement

Unfortunately for the Genevans, the exiles from Zurich, Frankfurt, and Strassburg reached England before they did. They immediately struck up an alliance with Queen Elizabeth (1558–1603), reinstated the last Edwardian settlement, and outmaneuvered the Catholics. That staunch alliance between church and state has lasted to this century. The Geneva exiles, soon to be called Puritans, were too late to alter the *fait accompli* and spent the next three generations trying to amend it.

One historian called Puritanism the true English Reformation. That is unfair to Anglicanism, but certainly Puritanism brought a new earnestness and energy to the English temper, and its achievements were immense. Puritans led the fight to curb the prerogatives of the crown and to enlarge the power of the Commons. In the seventeenth century, Puritans carried liberty and bigotry to New England, and conquered a wilderness. At home they fought their own King and condemned him to a scaffold block. And when their force was spent, and church and crown had been restored, the fame of Puritanism's leaders like Oliver Cromwell lived on, and the works of its poets and preachers, of Milton, Bunyan, and Fox, achieved an earthly immortality that is but a shadow of the unspeakable joy they hoped to have in heaven.

Calvin and Calvinism

Calvin was the source of Puritan vitality, and it is curious that he, the most unbendingly religious of the major reformers, should have had the most secular background. Most leading reformers were priests made over. Calvin was a humanist versed in law. Of course, as a brilliant youngster and son of a Picard lawyer, he had been destined for the Church, but his father later preferred him to take humane and legal studies in Paris, Orleans, and Bourges, which he dutifully did. Everywhere Luther was to be encountered. The head of Calvin's College in Paris was a violent opponent of the new theology, whereas Calvin's Greek teacher at Bourges was an avid Lutheran. When Calvin was back in Paris studying Greek and Hebrew, possibly in 1533, he experienced a sudden conversion: the humanist became a reformer.

Late in the year he was driven from Paris and into hiding by the capricious persecutions that were then occurring. He wrote the first and shortest version of his masterpiece, the *Institutes of the Christian Religion*, while he was at Basle in 1535. When it was published, in 1536, he was taking refuge in Ferrara, but could not stay long. He settled his estate at Noyon and set off for Strassburg via Geneva, where history was lying in wait for him.

Geneva was destined to outshine all other reformed Swiss cantons, but at this stage it had just emerged from a nerve-wracking struggle for independence against the duke of Savoy and its own bishop.

With the help of Protestant Bern, it had secured its independence, and had declared itself in the Protestant camp by suspending the Mass. A dedicated Protestant named William Farel—who had been instrumental in reforming Bern—was laboring hard to induce Geneva to declare against Catholicism, sensing his own limitations and Calvin's inner strength, Farel begged him to stay and help the work. Calvin was reluctant, so Farel predicted that the wrath of God would fall upon him, whereupon Calvin trembled and accepted.

Geneva's precarious independence and the fact that the Reformation had already succeeded in other parts of Switzerland made his task easier. And even before Calvin had arrived, a strict moral regimen had been instituted by the executive or Little Council and approved by the Common Council, made up of all heads of families in the city. This was early in 1536.

Zurich, like the free Imperial City of Strassburg, had embraced reform as early as 1523. Bern followed in 1528 and Basle in 1529. The more populous Swiss cantons soon declared for reform while the larger number remained Catholic. By 1531 the equilibrium was fairly stable.

That year, by the death of Zwingli in an affray against a Catholic force, the Swiss cantons lost their spiritual leader and Zurich lost its preeminent influence. Calvin in Geneva presently wrested leadership from Bern by sheer force of personality.

He brought Geneva a mind utterly untroubled by self-doubt, a frightening presence and a genius for discipline and organization. All along, the success of his Reformation depended on the support of the Councils of Geneva—the Common Council of citizens, the Little Council of 25, the Council of 60, and the Council of 200. The austerity of his regime and his refusal to accept the dictates of the Councils as to the manner in which he should administer sacraments led to his expulsion in 1538. For three years he stayed at Strassburg, learning from the celebrated reformer, Martin Bucer, while Geneva fell prey to factions.

Imminent chaos forced the Councils to recall him, and the city's weakness put him in a powerful position; even so, he did not win all the independence of action he desired. By watching and waiting, he so molded the executive Councils that they became more Calvinistic than he. Then Geneva became something like the theocracy he wanted. It was an impressive political achievement, since Calvin never held a civil office.

Church Organization

Discipline was thoroughgoing and his organization complete. Each city ward had an upright man to oversee its morals and report faults to the clergy. Pastors, teachers, elders, and deacons shared overlapping functions in the church; the pastor was to administer sacraments and preach; the teachers were to instruct the young in true doctrine; elders (nominated by the Little Council) were to have coeval power with pastors in the running and discipline of the church. Finally, deacons dispensed charitable funds to the sick and needy. Elders and pastors together made up the highest court and policy-making body called the Consistory. Since Calvin's day, this system has been modified. In Scotland, the local church known as the Kirk elected its own elders—the meeting of elders and clergy in a small area was called a Presbytery, for the province it was a Synod, and the supreme gathering was a General Assembly. What distinguished this system from a hierarchy of bishops and priests, or superintendents and pastors, was that the laity, through representatives, participated fully in the administration and policy making of the Church. This was the peculiar genius of Calvin's system. The opportunity for laity to participate made the Calvinist church form (now not limited to Presbyterians) attractive to the respectable and religiously earnest in the Low Countries, Britain, and the New World.

In Geneva this type of organization guaranteed the Church a fair measure of integrity, because it was the substantial citizens who were chosen for elderships, and also it gave the Church direct representation (through these same elders) on the executive councils of the city.

If this interlocking system had not been in force, Calvin may well have been expelled again, for he faced continual opposition from those who ruffled at the over-severe moral discipline of the Consistory—Calvin called these opponents Libertines—and from visiting or resident heretics who were as frequently executed as banished. The Consistory declared them heretics, and the Council decided the punishments.

By 1555 Geneva was in practice, though not in theory, a theocracy. And some liked it that way. John Knox, who reformed Scotland after imbibing Geneva's bracing spirit, found the city "the most perfect school of Christ that ever was since the days of the apostles." Yet after Calvin's death, in 1566, and after Theodore Beza stepped into his shoes, it was said that Genevans did for him for love what they had done for Calvin out of fear and respect.

Theology and Ethics

Appropriately so, for Calvin's theology was one of fear and respect, rather than love. He followed Luther in his view of man, and even exaggerated the totality of man's perversion after the Fall. Whereas Luther had resolved man's hopeless predicament by faith in the love and mercy of God displayed in Christ, Calvin concentrated his attention on the glory and justice of God. Whether man belonged to the saved or not, his purpose was to worship God and glorify Him forever. Most theologians who believed that God foreknew and forechose those whom he wanted to elect did not like to specify precisely what would happen to the nonelect. Calvin, however, displaying the lawyer's tendency to announce clear and unambiguous categories, propounded a doctrine known as double predestination: a few were chosen for heaven, the rest must surely be damned. And Calvin thought it vindicated God's justice that this should be so. His arbitrariness—or rather the arbitrariness he attributed to God—seemed abhorrent to some, and when he was baited on this point he was led into emphasizing the doctrine rather more than he intended. In fact, it was not one of his major doctrines at all and simply an inference from them. Like Luther, he upheld justification by faith, though he could not accept Luther's somewhat mystical view of the Eucharist. Like Luther, and like Zwingli, or Wycliffe or Hus, he was a thoroughgoing scripturalist.

An intense scripturalism and a moral rigorousness marked the Calvinist off from others. Life was a sermon, to be lived for the edification of society, and every precept for living was assumed to be available in scripture. This was a life that could never relax, that was acutely duty conscious, with no heart, little emotion, and no eye for beauty except in the stark. The fellowship of the Church, in communion with living saints, was the only compensation for the loss of soft or romantic longings.

Discipline equipped Calvinism to be the fighting arm of the Reformation. Its belief in the Word (interpreted by Calvin) was as absolute as the Catholic's belief in church authority. The distinctive organization of Calvinism, partly oligarchic and partly representative, part clerical, part lay, made it proof against the rational unity of a monarchical church. Bible study was as absorbing to Calvinists as rosary saying was to Catholics, and congregational communion and free prayer were the Calvinists' catharsis for the feeling of sin; as satisfying, apparently, as Penance and Mass were for the Catholic. Calvinism made fewer conversions back to Catholicism than any other reform movement.

To describe it as "worldly asceticism" is to forget that the great Catholic religious movement of the sixteenth century, the Jesuit order, was at least as ascetic and equally committed to the world. Otherworldliness was, now, hardly possible. The faith had to be fought for, and monasticism had long since broken down as an ideal under the charges of the humanists before the Reformers attacked it. Calvinists, though strict, enjoyed some pleasures in moderation. They drank wine and cultivated music. Calvinism was neither a new form of monasticism nor a sanctimonious form of worldliness; it was the single-minded pursuit of moral integrity for the greater glory of God.

But God's glory was shown in politics and economics as well as in the Church. Church experience conditioned the Calvinist to participate—or to want to participate—in affairs of state and commerce or in the education of the young in right religion. More often than not the Calvinist's business enterprises (following the Church pattern) were communal, joint-stock ventures. And Calvin's attitude toward business was ambivalent: what benefited the community was encouraged; what did not was curbed. Calvin's ethics in every sphere were demanding but were practical and flexible enough to meet every challenge and contingency of life.

Scotland

Calvinism seeped into France and into Hungary; it conquered Scotland through the fiery ministrations of John Knox. After an adventurous career, Knox became a disciple of Calvin, and returned to Scotland after a stay in Geneva to build an alliance with the nobility against Mary, Queen of Scots. As it happened, Mary, after 1559, became Queen of France when her husband became Francis II. She was an absentee queen, and a French one. Knox played upon Scottish nationalism, on anti-French sentiment, and most effectively on

Mary's frivolity. He called her "Jezebel."

Even so, without England's aid the outcome would have been dubious. Elizabeth's intervention in Scotland was a decisive stroke of foreign policy. Having settled her realm into comfortable Protestantism, she realized that a Protestant neighbor would be less troublesome than a Catholic. So English troops and an English fleet were sent north for no other purpose than to help the Scots drive the French out. The English were withdrawn immediately, and within the year (1560) the Reformation was hastily accomplished.

The Scots Confession of Faith was close to the Anglican articles of faith, and their first Book of Discipline allowed for superintendents (bishops or superior clergy) along with a Presbyterian system. At the initial stage the Scots and Anglican church were not so far apart, though the provision for superintendents was soon dropped.

Mary returned to Scotland after her husband's death and found that there was nothing she could do. So she devoted her life to torrid love affairs and to a vain pursuit of the English succession. The Scots deposed her in 1567 because she was scandalous and a Catholic, and they crowned James, who was her abandoned child and a Protestant. She took refuge in England where, in spite of herself, she became the focus of plots against Elizabeth that cost her her life.

Pockets of Catholics remained in Scotland's Highlands, which is not surprising —and pockets remain there, even now, of Presbyterians who live as strictly as Genevans must have done under Calvin.

Calvinism and Capitalism

There is a theory that Protestantism, and especially Calvinism, gave a great boost to the rise of capitalism. To a large extent the argument hinges on what, precisely, is meant by capitalism. If it is individualism that is considered, then Calvinism was less individualistic than congregational and regimented. If it is the rationalizing of business organizations, then Calvinism is not especially rational, and perhaps less so than a hierarchical system such as Catholicism. Calvinist ethics are considered to be conducive to money making, but thrift, sobriety, and industry seldom, in themselves, result in large fortunes. Scotland is the glaring example. Capitalism relies on a variety of ingredients in a variety of combinations for a variety of enterprises. Prodigality is often as rewarding as miserliness; adventurousness is as rewarding as care; and a lax morality is no less appropriate than moral restraint. A capacity for hard work and a devotion to the pursuit of wealth can flourish in any confession. Far more important for success than religion is accessibility to rich resources and the wealthy markets. While connections can fruitfully be drawn between religion and the social context, the Reformation was not the simple reflex of an economic movement, nor was capitalism its illegitimate child. The Reformation was a spiritual chapter in man's endless search for self-illumination.

CHRONOLOGY OF THE REFORMATION

1509–1547:	Reign of Henry VIII of England
1515–1556:	Reign of the Hapsburg Charles V, king of Spain and (1519 ff.) Holy Roman emperor
1517–1547:	Reign of Francis I of France
1517:	Luther posts 95 Theses at Wittenburg
1520:	Luther publishes Three Reformation Treatises
1521:	Luther appears at Diet of Worms
1525:	German Peasants War
1532–1534:	Henry VIII breaks with Rome; creates independent church
1536–1566:	Calvin dominates Geneva
1547–1553:	Reign of Edward VI of England; Protestantism advances

1553–1558:   Reign of Mary Tudor: English
              Catholic revival
1555:   Peace of Augsburg settles
              religious disputes in Germany
1558–1603:   Reign of Elizabeth I: moderate
              protestant settlement

1559:   Treaty of Câteau-Cambrésis
              ends Hapsburg-Valois wars
1559–1560:   John Knox wins Scotland for
              Calvinism

19
The Catholic Reformation and the Counterreformation

Times occur in history when mortal dangers are clearly perceived but nothing is done to avoid or minimize them. The Reformation was such a time for the Roman Catholic Church and one cannot but wonder why no shift was made to meet the heresy spreading like wildfire across the North. Past experience had not fitted the Renaissance papacy to meet the challenge. Its concerns were local. Rome badly needed beautification and Italian politics were all-absorbing; the civil arm could hunt down the heretics.

Such confidence was misplaced, for while the emperor was a devoted Catholic, in the last resort he would rather close and bar the doors of Milan to the French than disperse the Lutherans. Politics, to the politician, came first; the semblance of power was holier than holy faith.

Confidence in the powers that be was also misplaced because any political counterthrust to the Reformation needed to be girded with righteousness. Troops alone could never conquer; they needed the reinforcement of a thorough reexamination of doctrine and church administration. This need was deeply felt by some pious Catholics, if not by the popes.

Catholic Reform

Even before Luther had attacked the sale of indulgences, a mystical and moral revival was beginning to develop in the South. Savonarola of Florence is a striking example. He came as a notable Dominican preacher to the cathedral of Florence in 1491 and quickly established himself as a visionary, a prophet of death and destruction, and also a dedicated defender of the liberties of the citizens against the Medici. After the defeat of Pietro de Medici by the king of France in 1494, and the subsequent French withdrawal from the city, Savonarola became the lawgiver and virtual dictator of Florence. His doctrines, his unbending rigidity and strictness, and his bold denunciations of Rome's and the

Pope's corruptions brought down a bull of excommunication upon his head. Yet he continued to organize the youth and to encourage the citizenry in various religious austerities and celebrations. On one occasion, in 1497, under the influence of his intense charisma, the townspeople disgorged their "vanities"—dice, trinkets, ornaments, cosmetics, false hair, and pornographic books—for public burning. This carnival was repeated just before Savonarola's fall in 1498. Although the Medici faction desired and the pope contrived his destruction, it was the fickle mob who stormed his convent and carried him off from the church to an intimidated and hostile signory. Fearfully tortured, subjected to a mockery of a trial by commissioners who had been ordered by the pope to sentence him to death, "even were he a second John the Baptist," he was ceremonially degraded then hung on a cross between two disciples. Crosses and bodies were then burned to the delight of the crowd. Tired of purity and moral earnestness the populace had found that Savonarola too, like a vanity, was expendable. To this day, flowers are strewn each year on the spot where he died.

But Florentine piety under Savonarola was only a brief flurry. His movement did not rekindle the zeal of the Dominican order, nor, indeed, make any lasting impact outside the city. More lasting and more effective was the forming of a non-monastic Catholic group called the Oratory of Divine Love (founded 1497). It included laymen as well as priests, and from its numbers in Rome came a clutch of outstanding cardinals. The Oratory spread spontaneously throughout the length and breadth of Italy, taking hold amongst the cultured, and weaning them away from cynicism. Paul III, himself a nepotist, had the vision to ask members of this group to prepare for him a report of the state of the Church in 1538. The report did not mince words; it lashed the papacy by naming every vice and scandal, even to the prosti-

tutes who milled about St. Peter's attended by clerics—presumably not for the care of their souls. Protestants made great sport of it.

One outgrowth of the Oratory was a new order that lived under a rule though not in a monastery. In 1524 the Pope sanctioned the Order of Theatines who were dedicated to maintaining high standards among ordinary clergy. Another new group—the Capuchins—tried to recapture the pure idealism and evangelistic fervor of St. Francis of Assisi. By 1619 they numbered 1500 houses.

These and lesser orders were responses to the Renaissance and not counters to the Reformation. Similarly, the rise of mysticism in Spain was an indigenous development owing nothing to the growth of Protestantism elsewhere. Many of the more enthusiastic mystics, alight and afire with their dreams, fell under the suspicion of the Inquisition. The most famous of them was St. Theresa of Avila (1515–1582), a shrewd organizer whose deep religious experiences were so affecting that they made her ill. She founded a number of monasteries and nunneries in obedience to her visions, and her young disciple, St. John of the Cross (1542–1591), reformed others. His poetry expressed the quintessence of the mystic spirit in lofty cadence and sublime imagery. These saints belong to the long tradition of those who have heightened the spirituality of the Church, and owe little or nothing of their drive to the pressure of Protestantism.

Counter-Reform: Loyola and the Jesuits

The Counterreformation developed during the mystic revival in Spain and was led by Ignatius Loyola, a soldier before he was a mystic. His chances of a life-long military career were ruined by a bullet wound in the hip, and as he recuperated, his enforced idleness and his new-found reading matter—lives of the Saints and of Christ—redirected his mind and talents toward the service of the Church. He spiritualized his earlier experience as a knight; the Virgin became his lady; and he envisioned the Christian progress as a continuing military campaign. His Christianity was medieval and chivalric.

But first he became a hermit (1522) and saw a vision that confirmed his faith. He began to write the *Spiritual Exercises* at this time, though they were not published until 1548. A source of inspiration to which Jesuits return again and again to this day, Loyola's *Exercises* begin with a contemplation of man's sinfulness, move to consideration of Christ's struggle against evil, then to the Passion, and finally, to the joy of the believer joining God. To participate in the *Exercises* is an agonizing, compelling, cleansing, and spiritually renewing experience.

After a pilgrimage to Jerusalem, Loyola decided that he needed education to increase his influence; first he attended grammar school with young boys, then went on to the University of Toledo. After a time his enthusiasm earned him the suspicion of the Inquisition and he thought it prudent to continue his studies in Paris. By strange coincidence he arrived at the college that Calvin had attended just months after Calvin's departure. Already he had five Spanish disciples and now he attracted four Frenchmen to him. Returning to Spain for theology, the band decided on a pilgrimage to Jerusalem, but war and politics preventing them, they met in Rome to beg for papal approval for a new order. They won it in 1540.

The Society of Jesus (or Jesuit order) was organized on quasi-military lines. Its ranks, in ascending order, were novices, Scholastics, and the Professed of the Four Vows, who elected the General of the Order for life. To the usual vows of chastity, poverty, and obedience, Loyola added a fourth vow of absolute obedience to the pope. By the Bull of 1540 Jesuits were charged to hear confession, to teach, and to preach. Thus was formed a clerical body more disciplined than the Calvinists, more

flexible, and more highly centralized. Like the Calvinists, the Jesuits did not shun the world, but embraced it in order to lead it to higher truth and sanctity.

What success did they have? At first their education was restricted to their own novices and scholastics, but they soon offered schooling to the laity, and it was so effective that it became their enemy's chief ground against them. Their preaching raised standards in pulpits throughout the Church, and their catechisms instructed millions of youngsters.

The reclamation of Poland from Protestantism was their signal achievement. They had three advantages over the divided and leaderless Protestants. Their leader, St. Peter Canisius, was in every way remarkable. He had the ear and the heart of the king. And the Jesuits' educational system was better than its rival's. Although Poland's backward social structure may not have been conducive to the growth of Calvinism, Lutheranism might have succeeded with royal support. But it was unthinkable that King Ferdinand of Poland, Charles V's brother and later emperor, would turn his back on his family's traditional policies—the twin goals of regaining souls for the Church and land for the Hapsburgs.

Finally Jesuit missions, led by St. Francis Xavier, revitalized the Church's missionary endeavor. Jesuits were not the only missionaries, of course. Carmelites pushed into Persia, and Franciscans into California, but at this early stage the Jesuits stood in the vanguard. Xavier died in Japan. Others penetrated into India, China, and Peru. By the time of Loyola's death in 1556, there were 1500 members of the Society and they had studded the globe with enclaves of missionaries.

Council of Trent (1545–1563)

Yet the church's spiritual and evangelical revival would have lacked force without theological and administrative reform. Although the need was obvious enough, the obstacles in the way of calling a reforming council were immense. Not only were clergy of laxer habits opposed to it, but even purer souls, members of the Oratory of Divine Love, felt that reform should come from below and from the heart, rather than be legislated from above. Political dissension was the prime obstacle: a council was called in 1536 but the war between France and Spain kept it from meeting until 1545. By then it was too late to nip Protestantism in the bud.

Secular political rivalries were compounded by ecclesiastical politics. Since the attempted conciliar revolution of the fifteenth century the popes' dread of councils had not abated. So the council was ordered in such a fashion that papal power would not be lessened. The votes in the councils of the fifteenth century had been by national delegation; but at Trent the abbots and theologians were excluded from power. The vote was given to bishops and heads of orders, and their majority was to be binding. Needless to say, there were many more Italian than non-Italian bishops and the Italians could be counted on to maintain papal supremacy.

The choice of Trent, too, was a political compromise between France and the Empire. Also it was sufficiently close to Italy to attract a full turnout of Italian bishops. Even so, the pope would have liked the council to deliberate closer to home, and he took advantage of an outbreak of plague in Trent to suggest removing it to Bologna —in papal territory. Charles V, however, ordered his bishops to remain in Trent and the first session of the council ended in deadlock. A new pope allowed the calling of another session early in 1547, and a third session in 1562 and 1563 was called by a pope wholeheartedly dedicated to reform. Pius IV (1559–1565) had been a member of the Oratory of Divine Love. But he was not above politics. He hated the Spanish in general and Charles V in particular, and was not prepared to con-

cede to the far-reaching reforms advocated by the Spanish bishops. Among other things, they would have liked the authority of councils declared superior to that of popes.

Bitter controversies and intrigue permeated every session. The political outcome, however, was assured by the predominance of the Italians—of the 255 prelates who signed the official Acts of the Council, 189 were Italians. Thus any revolutionary conciliar stirrings were beaten before they had begun. The immediate result of the council was a tremendous boost to papal prestige. Ultimately the outcome of Trent was the dogma of Papal Infallibility, defined in 1870.

Theologically speaking, the council ended all possibility of union with Protestants and it closed the door to much of the rich theological speculation of centuries past. While it may be true that the council drew on the best of its tradition, drawing heavily on St. Thomas Aquinas, it is also true that the breadth and flexibility of medieval Catholicism were summarily abandoned. The Church became narrower theologically as it grew more authoritarian politically. This, perhaps, is in the nature of powerful institutions beset by powerful challengers.

Index and Inquisition

Against the wildfire of Protestant reform, the Catholic Church instituted the *Index* and expanded the scope of the Inquisition. The *Index* (1558) was a list of books prohibited in whole or in part to the ordinary Roman Catholic. At first, all of Erasmus' works were among those condemned, but later this indiscriminate sentence was modified. It is a tribute to the power of the printed word that books should seem such dangerous emissaries of heresy that they merited repression. Both the *Index* and the office of Inquisitor were abolished by Vatican II in 1966.

Long an instrument of medieval Spanish

rulers, the Inquisition was reconstituted in Italy as the Roman Inquisition in 1542. That it was pathologically afraid of heresy, that it was sinister and occasionally cruel, that its procedures were unfair, and that it was drastically effective, none deny. It literally burned out the small pockets of Protestantism in Spain and in Italy. No one except the pope was free from suspicion: the Archbishop of Toledo was swallowed up for a 17-year trial and forced to abjure certain errors. Even St. Ignatius Loyola and St. Theresa of Avila fell under suspicion. The Inquisition proved more powerful in Spain than in Italy because it had firmer support from above, from the king, and perhaps from below as well. In Italy it long continued to function, arresting Galileo in the seventeenth century and the great lover, Casanova, in the eighteenth century but, by then, its main work had been accomplished.

Harsh as it may seem, the Inquisition was the Roman Catholic equivalent to the purges of their lands by Lutheran princes, and to the unbending discipline of Geneva's Consistory and Little Council. When heresy was considered damnable, death at the stake, or by drowning or strangling seemed a kindness. Fire, sword, water, rope, torture, and terror were not too drastic to root out the virus of sin. From this point of view the Inquisitors were being cruel to incorrigible sinners, only to be kind to the Catholic majority. In cases of hallucination, witchcraft, and sexual perversion they showed a good deal of restraint and common sense.

Trent and Doctrine

If the *Index* and the Inquisition were alien to the spirit of the Renaissance, the theological settlements of the Council of Trent, in part at least, enshrined the Renaissance philosophy of man. On the questions of justification by faith and predestination the council emphasized the freedom of man and his potential for moral endeavor. He could prepare himself for faith and cooperate with it, even though he was insufficient, without grace, for salvation. Man lived neither in absolute freedom nor in total bondage. Thus the council managed to preserve human integrity and responsibility as well as the might and mystery of divine grace.

The council was equally unconciliatory to Protestantism in other matters. Whereas Protestants revered tradition only insofar as it conformed with scriptures, the council distinguished scripture and tradition and placed both on an equal footing as sources of authority. Transubstantiation was judged to be the only permissible doctrine of the Eucharist: no quarter was given to Protestant views. The seven sacraments were reaffirmed, indulgences were declared effective and a proper adjunct to the pope's power. Although Protestants ever so stoutly denied it, Trent threw the weight of its authority in favor of the existence of purgatory, and claimed that intercession and the sacrifice of the Mass helped those souls detained there. Finally, in the Tridentine* Profession of Faith of 1546, to this day recited by all bishops and beneficed clergy and imposed on all converts, there was a vow of obedience to the Roman pontiff.

The dogmas of Trent reflect the wisdom that the sixteenth century Roman Church found most acceptable in its past—wisdom sharpened by the witness of what seemed to be the errors of the Protestants. Catholics are bound to accept what this council defined—to reject any Tridentine dogma is heresy. So thorough and exhaustive was its doctrinal analysis that even the recently promulgated dogmas of the Virgin Mary's Immaculate Conception (1854) and of the bodily Assumption of the Virgin into heaven (1954) were foreshadowed in a decree of Trent that exempted Mary from the otherwise universal taint of original sin. Trent, then, was a consolidation and

* The word "Tridentine" is derived from "Trent."

codification of Roman faith, expressing the conscience of the upper hierarchy of that time and remaining a touchstone and repository of Roman Catholic truth down to the present age.

Administrative Reform

For all its troubles and tribulations, Trent's achievements were stupendous. Exhaustive administrative reforms accompanied its doctrinal utterances: assaults were made on absentee churchmen and the holding of a plurality of benefices and against lax, corrupt, immoral, or unchaste clergy. The pope was implored to choose cardinals worthy of their dignity, and all religious orders were subjected to a regulatory code. Seminaries were proposed for the education of priests, so that the Renaissance humanists' favorite butt, the unlearned priest, could be pushed into the past. Princes were commanded not to interfere with church affairs and property, while laymen were ordered to attend Mass regularly. In short, the whole fabric of the Church was refurbished, no corner and no quarter went uncleansed, no level and no rank escaped fervent prescription and exhortation.

Happily for the Church, the duty of implementing the decrees of Trent fell to the austere Pope Pius V (1566–1572), the first pope in half a millennium whom the Church considered worthy of canonization. An uncompromising man, he punished disobedience with severity. He was as strict on himself as with others, visiting barefooted like a pilgrim in his diocese, praying and fasting at length. Also he reformed the curia, had the police rid the streets of prostitutes, and cleared the papal palaces of moveable pagan nudities, to the infinite benefit of the Capitoline Museum. He looked and behaved a little like Calvin.

Under Pius V a new Catechism, Breviary (daily service book), Missal (mass book), and translations of St. Thomas' *Summa* were published. These new works contributed greatly to the unification and clarification of doctrine. The Missal replaced the four permissible modes of celebration and remains virtually unchanged today, though a new mass is now being used in some areas, which is novel in form—in vernacular, for instance—and, implicitly, in theology.

Under the divisive stresses of Protestantism and nationalism it is quite possible that Catholicism might have disintegrated without Pius V and the Council of Trent: the Inquisition would have had less clearly defined principles to act upon and the impetus to reform might have been lost in a thousand individual directions. With Trent behind it, Catholicism took heart. Its hopes for reuniting Christendom began to flow again; a fervent crusading spirit began to grip Church leaders and Catholic monarchs alike. Yet their hopes and dreams were dreamed too late. One result of the definition of dogma—no matter how valuable it was for the Roman Church—was that Protestantism could never come to terms with it on the basis of the Tridentine settlement. The gulf had become unbridgeable, yet the Church ardently believed that it could fly the gap, occupy the Protestants' domains, and transform their spirits. Both sides, in fact, suffered under the delusion that they could overturn the social, political, and spiritual circumstances that had given rise to the deep division. Rivers of blood would flow before the impossibility of these misapprehensions would be accepted. Ironically, the Council of Trent completed its monumental labors in 1563, the same year that England issued its Protestant 39 Articles of Faith. The coincidence testifies that just as the Roman Church had finally and effectively prepared itself for battle against apostasy the Protestant camp was stronger than ever.

The Cultural Aftermath of the Reformation

There is some reason to suspect that the decisions of various European peoples to remain Catholics, or to become Lutherans,

Anglicans, Calvinists, or Anabaptists had distinct political and economic implications. Wherever Protestant ideas could circulate, Calvinism appealed to educated commoners but not, by and large, to nobles —although there were exceptions. Lutheranism found strong aristocratic support and royal backing in Scandinavia and Germany, for Lutheranism appealed to those who favored reform yet detested social disruption. Anabaptism, with its millennarian dreams of a heaven on earth, could stir the dispossessed to revolutionary fervor as no other movement could.

Wherever it spread, Calvinism undermined royal pretensions while Lutheranism and Catholicism both bolstered princely power. Calvinists erected an ecclesiastical structure in which power was shared between clergy and representatives of the congregation. Here was imbedded a revolutionary principle in church affairs; a representative system instead of a monarchy. And, in turn, the Church in which members of the congregation could participate so fully became a school of experience that conditioned members to clamor for a voice in affairs of state. Republicanism in the Church, and in the state, demanded that sovereignty be shared; and republicanism made headway wherever sizeable groups of Calvinists existed.

This is not to imply that Calvinists were democrats. Extremer sects who split from the Calvinists often carried the participative and congregational principles to more radical conclusions in both church and state. In contrast to these groups, Calvinists maintained a narrow oligarchy. But, in the context of the sixteenth century, Calvinism was much feared by conservatives for its radicalism.

Calvin had allowed the right of resistance to constituted authorities only to "inferior magistrates" and a new-found Moses, but these strict limits covered a variety of cases: they could apply to Knox (Moses) and the Scottish lairds and nobles, or to members of the English House of Commons or the French Estates-General. Radical political treaties on sovereignty drew their rationale from scriptures—a covenant existed between governors and governed, and when it was violated by rulers failing to protect their people or failing to observe the "fundamental laws and liberties" of the land, then rulers could and ought to be disobeyed. If Caesar's and God's wills ever clashed a Christian's first duty was to God. Covenant thinking was an early form of the contract theories which became so popular in the seventeenth and eighteenth centuries. New images clothed old reasonings: the vague fundamental laws and liberties of the sixteenth and early seventeenth centuries became the inalienable rights of later times. Occasionally a Catholic theorist justified the right of rebellion by arguing that a prince became a tyrant when he threatened his subjects' immortal souls, in which case it was no sin to remove him. Theories upholding the divine legitimation of kings were countered by ideas of the ultimate sovereignty of "the people." As a group in the English House of Commons put it, in 1604, "The voice of the people, in things of their knowledge, is said to be as the voice of God." Absolute moral obligations faced other compelling imperatives, and divine rights were set against divine rights. Modern soul-searching about abuses of power and the propriety of civil disobedience has its origin in these religio-political debates.

That a peculiar church form encouraged Calvinists to seek a share in sovereignty does not mean that Calvinists were also advocates of toleration. The discipline of their church was as rigorous as that of the state; the intolerance of the congregation was as constraining as the intolerance of secular authority. Intolerance was never the preserve of any one system; it flourished in monarchy, in oligarchy, and it has been known to flourish in democracy.

Rather than tolerance, Calvinism moulded a distinctive character type, with a degree of conscience unknown in other religions. Catholicism provided a conscience-stricken person with the outlet of frequent expiations through penance and sacrament; Lutheranism encouraged the sinner to throw himself on the mercy of Christ to feel the ecstatic inner joy that comes with sublime assurance. Calvinism offered no such rituals for purification; it assumed that guilt was ever present. Mass or Eucharist could never wipe the slate of conscience clean, and conscience sat like the old man of the sea on one's shoulders forever. Calvinists made a fetish of conscience. Yet often the Calvinist was self-righteous and morally callous; his conscience was self-centered rather than socially concerned. This was a conscience with severe drawbacks as well as with merits, a special conscience; but insofar as Calvinists carried it into every sphere of their daily lives as a matter of cosmic duty they illustrate a far wider theme in the history of the later sixteenth century.

El Greco, "The Burial of the Count of Orgaz", Church of St. Tome, Toledo. (Anderson/Art Reference Bureau)

The Art of the Reformation Era

The medieval dichotomy between the sacred and the profane was being replaced by a pervasive and free mingling of theological dogma with all aspects of life. A cosmic seriousness suffuses the art of the later Renaissance: Raphael's *Disputa* was a theological polemic; Dürer sketched vivid sermons on paper; Michelangelo painted a vast religious epic, replete with Biblical allegories, on the ceiling of the Sistine Chapel. In Spain, the work of El Greco captured the militant spirit of the Jesuits and also embodied the ecstasy of the mystics. El Greco's (1541–1614) hues were dark blacks, greys, and pallid lighter shades; his figures were elongated, their faces wearing a pious and prayerful aspect. *The Burial of the Count of Orgaz* exactly fits the dimension of the wall above the count's tomb and this setting lends an intimate, tactile quality to the spiritual apotheosis painted there. The distinctions

between the earthly and the unearthly were being blurred. Hence, the seventeenth century would inherit two contrary tendencies: one, to remake the earth in conformity with notions of heaven; the other, to review beliefs of heavenly things in the light of earthly knowledge.

World and Spirit in Sixteenth Century Literature

This interweaving of worldly and spiritual themes is exemplified by Lope de Vega, possibly Spain's greatest and certainly its most prolific author. He wrote drama, religious and historical epics, as well as pastoral poetry and comedies. Comedy itself became a vehicle for savage and probing social comment. Cervantes' *Don Quixote* can be read as a spiritual physiognomy of Spanish life. Quixote and Sancho Panza represent the polar contrasts within Spain herself, of romance, of chivalry, and of idealism, and also of coarseness, baseness, and rampant cynicism. The Spain of the past is held against the Spain of the present, the foolish and noble against the mundane and crass.

A world was passing, and authors tried bravely to revive it. In Italy, indeed in all Europe, following the pessimism of Machiavelli, Guicciardi, Luther and Calvin, a resplendent literature of chivalry and heroism captured public taste. The courage and the high endeavor of this kind of writing were actually lost possibilities for the Italy of the late sixteenth century. Returning to epic style for their form, authors were creating a feeling of nostalgia. Ludovico Ariosto (1474–1533) cast back to the days of Charlemagne for a drama of infidelity and its retribution by the Christian Roland against the heathen Saracens in *Orlando Furioso*, or Roland Enraged. The Christian-versus-heathen motif was taken up by Torquato Tasso in *Gerusalemme Liberata*, or Jerusalem Freed, which chronicled that first Crusade when Christians captured Jerusalem. Here, for a moment, the grandeur and nobility of the past were revived to strut in stylized postures of good and evil.

Right triumphed over evil, but peace and victory did not always prevail. In Guarini's (1538–1612) *Il Pastor Fido*, or The Faithful Shepherd, there is a tone of pessimism and a strain of tragedy in a love comedy. Simplicity and guilelessness were being mixed with darker forces. The "majestical" heavens could be called "a foul and pestilent congregation of vapours," and man, so "noble in reason" and "infinite in faculty," could be seen as "quintessence of dust" (Shakespeare, *Hamlet*, Act II sc. 2). The Frenchman, Montaigne (1533–1592), author of the celebrated *Essays*, passed through a phase of profound skepticism. Unlike Erasmus, whose questionings were shallower, he was driven to probe and test the fundamental tenets of his religious faith. Perhaps nothing better illustrates the mood of doubt infusing Renaissance opti-

mism than Claudio Montiverdi's opera *Orpheo* (1607)—the first extant opera performed in musical history. In glowing phrases, reminiscent of Pico's *Oration on the Dignity of Man*, a chorus vaunts man's powers just before Orpheus fails and Eurydice succumbs to her second death. The opera proceeds with Orpheus' piteous lamentations, lamentations for a world of lost delights.

The Revival of Tragedy: Marlowe and Shakespeare

For the first time in centuries in the history of the West there was an audience receptive to and ready to be moved by tragedy. The exuberance of the past seemed to be hollow, and a sense of doubt and decay seemed to represent the bitter realities of life much more closely than the heady optimism of the Renaissance humanists. Indeed, the word Faustian that we use to describe the Renaissance's overweening ambition and its superhuman hopes comes from a tragedy, *Dr. Faustus*, by Christopher Marlowe (1564–1593). Faustus cheerfully sold his soul to the devil for unlimited power, pleasure and knowledge. He was not afraid to do so, for he thought hell was a fable, a mere old wives' tale. Ultimately the skeptical and worldly-wise doctor learns the dreadful truth and descends into the cavern of hell. The knowledge that he sought was necromancy, improper knowledge, and after he gained it he used it merely to impress his colleagues and do parlor tricks for potentates. One wonders whether Marlowe was subtly castigating the new knowledge of the Renaissance and the uses to which it was put in his day.

Nowhere were irony and tragedy more forcefully exploited than in England. Even more than Marlowe, William Shakespeare (1564–1616) was the master of the sardonic twist. In *The Merchant of Venice*, for example, Shylock, the Jewish usurer, representing the old law (Jews had long since been banished from England), demands that the letter of the law be levied on his defaulting debtor, who had pledged, as security for his debt, a pound of his own flesh. Portia, the debtor's counselor and lover, pleads for the new law, the Law of the Gospel, but her pleas fall on deaf ears. Shylock refuses to relent, only to be trapped by the rigidity of the law which he himself advocates: he may have his pound of flesh, but not a drop of blood, else his life is forfeit. Thus the debtor's life is saved; and Shylock is charged with intent to murder, stripped of his fortune, and advised to become a Christian.

Shakespeare raised tragedy to consummate perfection. As in classical tragedies, his dramas were worked out against a back drop of cosmic and natural order. Wrongs have been committed against the order of nature and retribution inexorably follows. In *Hamlet* there are murder, adultery, and the consuming passion of revenge. In *Macbeth* the crimes are vaulting ambitions and murder most foul; in *King Lear* the discord is a father's unnatural spurning of a loving daughter; in *Romeo and Juliet* there is civil disorder and a sudden passion; in *Othello* jealousy and a devilish tempter. Terror, pity, passion, and compassion lead to their inevitable climax in death and violent destruction. Within this *métier*, Shakespeare worked with an unrivaled flair for drama: his theatre is enthralling, though one may not believe in witches or ghosts. As Dr. Johnson once observed, there are no heroes in his plays, only men. His characters touch universal chords of experience, they are unbound by time and place, and he clothed his perceptive human insights in the richest language and verse, especially in brilliant free verse. But it is the sense of the cosmos that interests us here, for it must have been shared by his audience.

The cosmos was, above all, a place of settled hierarchical order and harmony. So it had been for centuries. This was the cosmos which the painters of the 1400s had sought to mirror. By the sixteenth century the reality of flux and change had begun to disturb the harmonies of art and to appear more frequently in vernacular literature. Disturb the cosmos, Shakespeare thought, and ruin would surely follow. In *Troilus and Cressida* Ulysses muses,

The heavens themselves, the planets, and this centre
Observe degree, priority, and place,
Insisture, course, proportion, season, form,
Office, and custom, and in all line of order. . . .
Take but degree away, untune that string,
And hark what discord follows . . .

This serried universe observed change within its prescribed motions. The cycle of seasons, the ebb and flow of the tide, the periods of the moon, the ceaseless changes of day into night, these were of a piece with the repetitive nature of things. Thus the last cantos of Spenser's (1552?–1599) *Fairie Queen*, called the "Cantos of Mutabilitie," make mutability an integral part of orderly creation.

The cosmos of the sixteenth century—the great chain of harmonious being—seems archaic to us now, just as our conceptions will seem silly to future generations. Few of us now believe that stars influence our destinies, or that planetary motions affect our health, though we still use astrological symbols in medicine, for male (δ) and female (φ), for example,— a relic of the old connection. A fire and brimstone Hell, white-winged angels, and a personified Satan do not wring assent from many in the twentieth century. But in the sixteenth century, as in the Middle Ages, these symbols and allegories represented what were felt to be facts of the human condition. Symbol became fact. Although the symbols of the past have been largely rejected, our moral condition seems no better if perhaps no worse for it.

The abiding sense of doubt that we find in writers like Marlowe and Montaigne, the sense of tragedy, the belief that perhaps in the high endeavor of the Renaissance there lay profound futility, the unease, the self-doubt and critical self-transcendence, the stoicism in the face of final things, all these qualities twist and mar the picture of an optimistic Renaissance. While the common assumptions about the cosmos link the Renaissance most closely to the past, the literature of the late sixteenth century exposes an understanding of change and a capacity to doubt that seem relatively new. Change was not always welcomed; there was a good deal of nostalgia. Change was often equated with decay; there was a sense of loss and longing for a world that was passing, and anxiety about what was to come.

CHRONOLOGY OF THE CATHOLIC REFORMATION

1494–1498:	Savonarola dominates Florence
1515–1582:	St. Theresa of Avila
1540:	Loyola wins papal approval for the Jesuit order
1542:	Establishment of the Roman Inquisition
1545–1563:	Council of Trent
1558:	Establishment of the *Index* of prohibited books
1566–1572:	Pontificate of St. Pius V

Suggested Readings

The asterisk indicates a paperback edition.

Roland Bainton, *Here I Stand: A Life of Martin Luther* (*Nashville: Abingdon Press, 1950).

Karl Brandi, *The Emperor Charles V* (London: Jonathan Cape, 1954).

Quirinus Breen, *John Calvin: A Study in French Humanism* (2nd ed. Hamden, Conn.: Archon Books, 1968).

Edward M. Burns, *The Counter-Reformation* (*New York: Van Nostrand Reinhold, 1964).

Owen Chadwick, *The Reformation* (*Baltimore, Md.: Penguin Books, 1964).

A. G. Dickens, *The Counter Reformation* (*London: Thames & Hudson, 1968).

Geoffrey R. Elton, *Reformation Europe: 1517–1559* (*New York: Meridian Books, 1964).

H. Outram Evenett, *The Spirit of the Counter-Reformation* (Cambridge: Cambridge University Press, 1968).

H. A. E. van Gelder, *The Two Reformations of the 16th Century* (The Hague: Martinus Nijhoff, 1961).

Harold J. Grimm, *The Reformation Era: 1500–1650* (2nd ed. New York: Macmillan, 1965).

Hans J. Hillerbrand, ed., *The Reformation: A Narrative History Related by Contemporary Observers and Participants* (New York: Harper & Row, 1964).

Hajo Holborn, *A History of Modern Germany. Vol. 1, The Reformation* (New York: Alfred A. Knopf, 1959).

Philip Hughes, *A Popular History of the Reformation* (Garden City, N.Y.: Doubleday, 1960).

Hubert Jedin, *A History of the Council of Trent* (2 vols., St. Louis: B. Herder, 1957–61).

John T. McNeil, *The History and Character of Calvinism* (*New York: Oxford University Press, 1957).

Jasper Ridley, *Thomas Cranmer* (*New York: Harper & Row, 1963).

Gordon Rupp, *Luther's Progress to the Diet of Worms* (*New York: Harper & Row, 1964).

R. H. Tawney, *Religion and the Rise of Capitalism* (*New York: New American Library, 1950).

H. R. Trevor-Roper, *Religion, the Reformation, and Social Change* (New York: Harper & Row, 1968).

Max Weber, *The Protestant Ethic and the Spirit of Capitalism* (*New York: Scribner, 1958).

George Hunston Williams, *The Radical Reformation* (Philadelphia: The Westminster Press, 1962).

Part 7 Europe in Crisis: From Reformation to Enlightenment

20
State Churches and Religious Wars: 1560-1648

By 1560, one result of the Reformation seemed certain: Protestantism was going to survive, in spite of the Homeric efforts of the Catholic reformers. But other issues still sought solutions. European monarchs and statesmen knew they faced the limitless catastrophe of civil war. Religious passions had reached the dangerous temperature reserved today for race, and prevailing political doctrine and popular opinion denied that two religions could inhabit one state. Bankruptcy and exhaustion had led to a truce among the warring princes of Germany in 1555 (the Peace of Augsburg) and had brought the Valois and Hapsburg monarchies to temporary peace in 1559 (the Treaty of Câteau-Cambrésis), but no one thought it would last. Religious minorities were too threatened and threatening. Nor were monarchs secure in control over their own state church. Both pastors and cardinals continued to argue for the superiority of religious over secular concerns and to demand that the Church be liberated from state control.

Europe in 1560 was precariously balanced between the ecstasy of religious renewal and the travail of incorporating the new religious settlements into a stable political, institutional, social and intellectual framework. The old, universal Christian Church was gone. The new denominations were still volatile and unstable. New currents of thought disturbed ancient and comfortable verities. European monarchies, having survived reform itself, now faced the greater task of accommodating religion to the state.

Religious War

Sixteenth-century monarchs strove desperately to establish and protect their state churches, for the consequence of failure was civil war. But the heightened religious passions of the Reformation were not always amenable to royal direction. Many people preferred martyrdom to compromise. Monarchs frequently stung outraged zealots among their subjects to acts of revolt. In France and the Low Countries, and later in Bohemia and England, governments and peoples moved to this sinister form of confrontation. These conflicts in no way involved religious toleration, although the minority sect usually made some vague mention of that most untraditional virtue. Instead religious warfare meant an armed attempt by dissident Christians to set up a state church, to which everyone must belong, different in doctrine and liturgy and organization from that which the king had in mind. Such enterprises normally failed, and the king, after some serious difficulties, put his own state church in power. In an age when Church and state were inseparable, religious war only postponed the inevitable and prolonged the agony.

After 1560, major religious revolts were invariably the work of Calvinists. Lutherans, Anglicans and Roman Catholics settled into patterns of the alliance of throne and altar with fairly good grace. Calvin's doctrine of the independence of the Church from the state, and the fact that Calvinists were almost always a decided religious minority demanded that Calvinists reject the concept of a state church. Instead, they slowly elaborated a theory of the right of a Christian (Calvinist) to revolt against a Godless tyrant. Moreover, the tight organization of the Calvinist congregation, bound together by common beliefs and policed in morals and doctrine by elected deacons and elders, made it an ideal revolutionary cell. This tight community life, combined with the exalted feeling of being God's small band of elect, drew communicants to Calvinism. As the Calvinist minority grew in France, the Low Countries, England, or Bohemia, and as religious persecution grew with it, the more zealous Calvinists moved inexorably toward revolt.

The French Wars of Religion (1562–1598)

In France, the wars of religion began with the confluence of several trends and events. Calvinism had grown so rapidly in the 1550s, particularly among the bourgeoisie and nobility, that Catholics were seriously alarmed, and demanded that the king persecute the heretics. But the king could not. The crown had gone bankrupt in 1557, and the years thereafter were ones of decline. France lost the war with Spain, King Henry II was impaled on a lance in a tourney in 1559, and his sons and successors were not only children, but stupid, sickly, ignorant and weak. Royal authority, therefore, became the prize in a deadly struggle between the wily and corrupt queen mother, Catherine de Medici, and the three greatest families of France, the Catholic Guise, the largely Protestant Bourbon, and the religiously mixed Montmorency. Under these conditions, royal aid in the work of persecution could only be sporadic and ineffectual. Both Catholics and Calvinists, therefore, settled in to do the job themselves.

In spite of the frantic attempts by the crown to keep the peace, religious war began by private massacre in 1562. A group of Catholics at Vassy murdered about 30 Protestants. This act provoked counter atrocities by Protestants. Slowly, a war of pillage and butchery spread over France. The resulting religious mayhem and massacre, which disturbed the government as much as it soothed inflamed religious passions, held great political significance. War ended the drift toward Protestantism—indeed, reversed it. Slowly, families reassessed the implications of belonging to the religious minority, and returned to the old faith. War also added treason against the king to the crimes of the heretic, and gave French Calvinism a suspicious, occasionally pathological republican flavor. Moreover, the crown swung back to loyal

Francois Dubois "St. Bartholomew's Day", oil painting in the Musee Cantonnal des Beaux-Arts of Lausanne.

Catholicism, and began to search for ways to end the war by destroying the Protestants.

Having abandoned hope for a diplomatic solution to religious war, Catherine de Medici threw herself into the hands of the ultra-Catholic Guise family, which was desperate to return to power. Opportunity came with the marriage of the Huguenot Henry of Navarre to the king's sister, Margaret. Many Huguenots were in Paris attending the wedding and, on October 23, 1572, St. Bartholomew's day, they were massacred. Of the Protestant leaders, only Henry of Navarre and his cousin, the Prince of Conde, survived. About 6000 others were butchered.

The massacre of St. Bartholomew's day did not end the wars or eliminate Protestantism. The Huguenots closed ranks, with the ministers and urban bourgeoisie assuming the leadership. Moreover, not all French Catholics were enchanted by Catherine's program of slaughter. Many were outraged,

and many others viewed Catherine's policy as leading to the partition of France or domination by Spain. Moderate Catholics who placed peace and their country ahead of religious passions took the name *politiques*, and rallied to the banner of Henry of Navarre. By 1575, the *politiques* and Huguenots controlled all France south of the Loire River, and had established their own government in defiance of the queen mother, who was now forced to grant limited toleration to Protestants. The policy of Catholic repression had failed.

Limited toleration of Protestants, desultory civil war, and widespread disobedience to the crown characterized French politics in the decade after 1575. This abruptly changed in 1584, on the death of the Catholic prince who had been next in line for the throne (currently occupied by Catherine de Medici's incompetent son, Henry III). The crown prince's death left the Protestant Henry of Navarre as Henry III's heir, and Catholics faced the prospect of being ruled by a heretic. It was too much. The Duke of Guise formed a Holy League, financed by Spain and tied to the Spanish monarch's hopes of gaining the French crown for himself. Enjoying strong papal support, the Holy League soon grew into a major political force. It maintained an army, intimidated the king and Catherine de Medici, collected taxes, and conducted its own foreign and domestic policy. In 1585, Henry III was forced to revoke all edicts of toleration for Protestants, and in 1588, the League took over Paris, forcing the king into exile. Henry III struck back and had Guise murdered. Infuriated, the League partisans called for the assassination of the tyrant, and, in August, 1589, Henry was stabbed by a Dominican friar. The new king, Henry of Navarre, was a Protestant.

Henry IV (1589-1610) was a welcome change from his incompetent, and sometimes degenerate, predecessors. He was strong and healthy, hunted and fought well, and enjoyed a degree of mental health that would astound a psychologist. He was amiable and generous and could hold his liquor. He chased women, and caught them. Henry's shrewdness and good sense came through his most famous sentence:

. . . I hope to make France so prosperous that every peasant will have a chicken in his pot on Sunday.

He meant that, and everybody knew it.

Possessed of sound military talents and great political skills, Henry IV began to claim his country. He was the legitimate king, and Catholic nobles and towns slowly came over to his side. Frenchmen were ready for peace and the *politique* position. In 1593, Henry IV converted to Catholicism, remarking that "Paris is worth a mass." He entered his capital, and began a systematic reduction of the remaining League fortresses. By 1598, it was all but over. The Spanish were driven out, the provinces pacified, and Henry issued the Edict of Nantes, an attempt to bring the

religious wars to a political solution. In the Edict, Henry granted liberty of conscience to all Protestants, and liberty of worship to Protestants in selected towns. As a guarantee of their limited religious liberty, Huguenots were given the right to garrison about 400 towns, mostly in southern France, and Huguenot judges were placed on the major royal courts.

The Edict of Nantes ended the war. It acknowledged the basic Catholic victory by restricting the practice of Calvinism, banning it from Paris, and insuring a Catholic monarch. French Catholics, recently touched by the fervor of the Counterreformation, were more intent than ever on converting the Huguenots. For the Huguenots, Nantes was merely an armed truce. Faced with a reviving Catholicism and a Catholic monarchy, they could hope for no more than simple survival. They knew that Catholics, the overwhelming majority of France, would tolerate Calvinism no better after the Edict than before it. Thus the real guarantee of the Edict of Nantes and religious peace was Henry IV himself. A strong king, intent on increasing royal powers, Henry refused to allow religious divisions to be the occasion for war. But Henry was murdered in 1610, and his successors departed from his pragmatic and secular policy. Thus within a generation of the Edict, royal persecution of Huguenots had begun again. It did not end until after the middle of the eighteenth century.

Spain and the Netherlands

During the last half of the sixteenth century Catholicism's most ardent royal champion was King Philip II (1556-1598), who fell heir to all of Charles V's Spanish dominions—from the Netherlands to the Americas. In 1580 he inherited Portugal and her empire, joining them to the crown of Spain. For Philip, religion and national motives were one. He saw no distinction between the good of the Church and the interest of the Spanish state. He was a

THE LOW COUNTRIES IN THE EARLY MODERN PERIOD

- - - - - - - *Boundaries of the Spanish Netherlands in 1560*

The Netherlands in 1609

French conquests of Louis XIV

The Spanish Netherlands in 1609

ENGLAND

North Sea

HOLLAND

○ *Amsterdam*

○ *Utrecht*

The Brill

Rhine

GERMANY

○ *Antwerp*

○ *Bruges*
Ghent

FLANDERS

Brussels
○

BRABANT

BISHOPRIC OF LIÈGE

× *Oudenarde*

× *Waterloo*

Ramillies ×

Lille ○

Fleurus ×

Malplaquet ×

BISHOPRIC

LUXEMBOURG

FRANCE

Paris

Scale of Miles

0   25   50   75   100

devoutly religious man whose prayers and fasting were legendary. His palace, unlike that of any other contemporary ruler, was partly a monastery so that it might give glory to God as well as grandeur to the crown.

Yet Philip II would suffer no slur upon his majesty, and his relations with the popes were not always amiable. He disapproved of the Jesuits on his own territory because their loyalty to the pope seemed to compromise their loyalty to him. Through the Spanish Inquisition and through his ecclesiastical appointments he exerted a control of the Church fully as powerful as that of Henry VIII.

Unlike Henry, Philip was austere and less effective. He was the arch bureaucrat who pored day and night over his papers. His solemn marginal comments appear beside the significant and trivial alike, and, in truth, he was not able to distinguish the one from the other. His days were burdened with religious exercises and political busywork so that he lost his distance and his perspective on larger affairs.

Bureaucrat that he was, he began a drastic centralization of power in the Netherlands and rode roughshod over the customary privileges of the provincial nobility. Theirs had formerly been the right to advise the Regent, but henceforth only a Council of three was to do so, and both Regent and Council were to be closely supervised from Spain. Although economical and rational in theory, this pruning of power was politically disastrous.

Philip also tampered with taxes and banking. In 1569 he instructed his viceroy in the Netherlands to collect a new sales tax, the Tenth Penny, fashioned on the Castilian model. In a region where commerce, not agriculture, supported people, the Tenth Penny would have been a dreadful blow. The towns and nobility of the Low Countries resisted its establishment and persuaded the viceroy to postpone it for two years. But they could not talk him

out of it altogether. Netherlands saw Philip II consistently sacrificing their own interests to those of Spain.

And to compound the offense, Philip II proposed a thoroughgoing reform of the Church which, by reorganizing dioceses and recalling all ecclesiastical nominations to the Spanish crown, would rob the nobility of the powers and preferments that they had come to look upon as adjuncts to their rank. In many ways a splendid reform, when coupled with the political centralization it doubled the fears of the Netherlandish nobility for their privileges. Furthermore, the proposal to reform the Church discomfited the laxer clergy and united the Protestants—formerly divided—who feared that reform would cut much of the ground from under their feet.

Protestantism became a rallying point of Netherlandish dissent. It was one source of opposition that touched all classes down to the various Anabaptist and sectarian enthusiasms of the urban proletariat. But Protestants were a minority in every province—at least at the onset. What mattered initially was the particularistic claims of the nobility, wanting their privileges guaranteed in full. The story of the revolt is one of the broadening of a narrow selfish aristocratic protest into a national movement of liberation, spearheaded by militant Calvinism.

The first spasm of revolution occurred in the late summer of 1566. Calvinist cloth workers and petty bourgeoisie, goaded by their pastors, their zeal, their hatred of the Spanish, and their social grievances, sacked Catholic churches, destroying the statuary, communion plate, breaking up the altars and murdering the priests. The furious destruction ended only when the symbols of the old faith lay in ruins. The Calvinist fury began at Poperinghe on August 14, spreading northward to the great cities of Antwerp, Ghent, Amsterdam and Utrecht. A month later it was over. The mob simply went home to their jobs, their rage exhausted. Terrified, the government had done nothing.

Philip II was shocked and outraged. He sent the Duke of Alva as viceroy to Brussels with 20,000 Spanish veterans and instructions to crush heresy and revolution. Alva was a hard man, who combined aristocratic arrogance with a taste for blood. He moved at once to smash dissent. His Council of Blood dealt with the great nobility who had become Protestant or were lukewarm toward the government. The army marched against the towns and the Inquisition followed. Municipal privileges were destroyed, heretics were rounded up; and the new tax of the Tenth Penny was imposed. The Low Countries were at last being governed like Castile.

At first, Alva carried all before him. He struck with such force that no single town or noble could resist. But it was a transient triumph. Alva intimidated, but he did not convert. Opposition soon transcended Calvinism and became patriotism. As such, it was irresistible. When a group of Dutch Calvinist sailors captured the island town of The Brill in 1572, open revolt spread rapidly. Flushing fell next, and the Spanish garrison evacuated Middleburg, capital of the province of Zeeland. By 1574, the provinces of Holland and Zeeland were in the hands of Calvinist rebels, and the Spanish were in retreat everywhere. The Spanish sack of Antwerp and Ghent simply added to Dutch anger. By 1576, revolt was so general that all the provinces of the Low Countries signed the Pacification of Ghent, in which they pledged unity to drive out the Spaniards. Religious differences were submerged in an attempt at nationhood.

In this crisis, Philip II sent his best general to the Low Countries. He was Alexander of Parma, an Italian duke descended from popes, shrewd and subtle, as clever in dissimulation as he was decisive in war, far abler and more realistic than Philip himself, and—incredible in a politician—he was a man of dignity and courage. As soon as he arrived in Brussels in 1578, Parma played on the differences between the largely Catholic and Flemish provinces of the south and the more Protestant Dutch provinces north of the Rhine River. By promising the southern provinces their political liberties, he was able to restore obedience to the king of Spain.

The Protestant north was not appeased by promises. In 1581, they declared independence from Spain and made William of Orange, the leading Protestant noble of the Netherlands, *Stadholder*—a sort of king. The war settled into conflict between Dutch and Fleming, between Catholic and Calvinist.

Parma had an excellent army, and he pushed campaigns for the conquest of the north. He enjoyed a certain success, recapturing Antwerp and confining the rebellion largely to Holland and Zeeland. This was good work, but it could not end the war. Parma could never capture the major Dutch cities, Amsterdam, Hoorn, Rotterdam, Utrecht, Leyden, which were protected by rivers and the Dutch navy. The Dutch held absolute naval supremacy in the rivers and along the coast and, increasingly, in the ocean as well. Thus the Dutch held out, in spite of losing battles, in spite of losing territory. Time was a Dutch ally; they had merely to wait out the Parma cyclone, and then win the war against his unworthy successors.

The decisive factor in the eventual Dutch victory was the war at sea. The conflict that thrice bankrupted Spain (1575, 1595, 1608) built the framework of Dutch wealth. The Dutch shut off Flemish commerce, and appropriated Flemish markets for themselves. Amsterdam replaced Antwerp as the *market* and banking center of northern Europe. The Dutch invaded Spanish markets in the new world, took over the slave trade, and gained a near monopoly in spices. They turned to commerce raiding and drove Spanish merchantmen from the seas. In the sixteenth century, war was an expensive business that ruined the greatest kings, but the Dutch grew rich from it, a phenomenon hitherto unheard of. When the Spanish accepted a 10-year truce in 1609 they were thoroughly beaten.

Spain and England

At the height of the Netherlands revolt Queen Elizabeth had sent troops to aid the Dutch rebels. The English soldiers did poorly, but their appearance in the Low Countries was enough to stir the wrath of Philip II. He determined (1585) to conquer England, to win her for Spain, and to wean her from Protestant heresy.

That Elizabeth had managed to avoid a war thus far by diplomacy alone was something of a feat; that she interfered in the Netherlands seemed foolhardy. It was a blatant act of war, and England's only defense was the Channel. Her population was even smaller than that of the Netherlands, and the English government's annual income was a pittance compared to the

Queen Elizabeth I (Brown Brothers)

revenues that Spain drew, not from taxes, but from imported treasure alone.

The Enterprise of England, as Philip called it, was something of a crusade. It received the cautious blessing of the pope—Elizabeth was a heretic and the Bull of Excommunication had been issued against her in 1570—yet the pope rightly suspected that not only souls for the Church but the crowns of England and Scotland were the prize.

England's plans were flexible and pragmatic, while Spain's were ponderous. Philip planned to dispatch a mighty Armada with a huge invading force aboard, and never veered one degree from this strategy. Elizabeth was inclined to wage a Channel battle; her sea dogs, Sir William Hawkins and Sir Francis Drake, who had learned their skills in illicit trading and piracy along the Caribbean, were all for waging a global war, both in the Channel and across the Atlantic, attacking the colonies and cutting off Spain's treasure supply. In fact, English strategy was a hodgepodge of notions tailored none too well to the opportunities. Elizabeth always hoped that English expeditions would return with a profit as well as a victory, and given her straightened circumstances one can hardly blame her.

Philip began to assemble his fleet in Cadiz, only to be set back a year by a daring raid by Sir Francis Drake (1587), who called it singeing the King of Spain's beard. That daredevil sailed into the harbor, sank 30 ships, destroyed naval supplies, and temporarily dislocated Philip's prestige and his credit. Temporarily only, for within a year the armada sailed; 130 ships, bound for the Netherlands for more soldiers and supplies from Parma before delivering its blow to England. Meanwhile, death had carried off Spain's finest admiral and there was no experienced man to replace him.

In size the fleets were fairly evenly matched, and they were equally ill-provided for. But in sailability and firepower the English were superior. Sir William

Hawkins had reorganized the English Navy, concentrating his building on fast, maneuverable ships with long-range guns so that English fighting ships could sail rings around the stately Spanish galleons. Hawkins hoped to win by seamanship and accurate gunnery, while the Spanish tactics were to come alongside and board with soldiers. Spanish seaman were merely sea-scouts for the troops, and their ships were huge rafts on which what was essentially a hand-to-hand land engagement was to be fought.

The Armada left Corunna to sail northward in a cresent-moon, line-abreast formation that stretched seven miles across the sea. When they were sighted off the southern coast of England, the main English fleet was bottled up in Plymouth harbor by a contrary wind. At this point, if instructions had permitted, the Spanish might have entered and destroyed the English in the confines of the harbor. But inflexible orders prevented such a diversion. Also the Spanish had no idea that the main fleet was in there. So the English rowed and towed their ships to open sea and began a running battle up the Channel lasting for nine days.

Spanish defense was remarkable, for though the fleet sustained damage, at no time was its tight formation broken. The disaster came only when the formation was broken open after it had put into port at Calais. For after the Spanish anchored behind the sands, the English sent in fire ships during the night, causing panic and forcing the Spanish to cut their cables and drift out into the sea. In the morning they were seen to be scattered and the English were able to use their advantages to devastating effect. In several hours' bombardment the Armada was crippled. Even so, the Spanish admiral managed to restore the fleet to order and move northward. His valiant efforts were nullified by the wind, for a storm completed what the English had begun, driving the Spanish up the Channel followed by English ships whose

ammunition was long since exhausted. Doubling through the islands north of Scotland, the Armada ran into the Atlantic gales that flung tens of ships and thousands of soldiers upon the rocky isles and inhospitable shores of Scotland and Ireland. Sixty-seven vessels returned. Ten thousand soldiers had drowned or otherwise perished. England struck a medal bearing the motto "Afflavit Deus, et dissipati sunt"—God blew and they were scattered—but, in fact, the defeat had occurred off Calais before the squall had struck. English prowess became the stuff of legend.

Although it was a fearful defeat, the threat from Spain remained ever-present. England's offensive degenerated into a series of publicly supported privateering ventures, while Spain was rebuilding the Armada. England was to enjoy only one other resounding success, when Sir Walter Raleigh led English seamen into Cadiz in 1596—as Drake had done before. In a brilliant engagement they captured and sacked the city. And the loot covered the cost of the venture. In swift retaliation, Philip loosed a new Armada from Lisbon, 90 ships strong. No sooner had it reached Cape Finisterre (1598), en route to Ireland (in all probability), than a gale wrecked half the vessels on the shore, and the remainder beat back to Lisbon where the seasick soldiers deserted as fast as they could. England's later ventures were equally fruitless and ill-managed. Although Spain made a last attempt to turn the tables, sending troops to aid an Irish rebellion, in imitation of Elizabeth's support in the Netherlands, the war grew cold. Philip died in 1598, dreaming of a third Armada. A desultory truce reigned, the fiery spirits were becalmed, and peace was finally signed in 1604, the year after Elizabeth's death.

Philip and Elizabeth were striking contrasts, the man a fond father, the woman at times a waspish spinster. The King was imperturbable, phlegmatic, and melancholy; while the Queen was both imperious and petty, pretty and gay. Elizabeth never aimed higher than the possible and worked to her ends with every trick and skill and every charm she could muster. Philip piled grand design on grand design and squandered his patrimony in the process. While she was often dilatory, he was immovable in his resolves; she left bureaucratic details to her faithful councillors; Philip carried the whole burden on himself. Like so many Europeans since and before him, he was haunted by the vision of a united Europe, united in faith and obedience, but he could never realize the dream for all his prodigious, if pedestrian, industry.

Both loved their countries dearly, presiding over golden ages of art, literature, music, and adventurous endeavor. The age of Elizabeth was also the age of supremely gifted poets and dramatists—Christopher Marlowe, Francis Bacon, William Shakespeare; Philip II's Spain harbored famed writers such as Cervantes and Lope de Vega —and the artist El Greco. Elizabeth served her kingdom with charm and regality, Philip with prayer and devotion. As it turned out, Elizabeth's pragmatism triumphed over Philip's vision of a world without the Reformation. It was bound to be so because his vision was impossible.

The Thirty-Years War (1618–1648)

The Spanish Hapsburgs were not alone affected by religious dissent and political rebellion. Their Austrian cousins also suffered from these twin plagues. In Austria, Protestantism affected most of the crownlands, and was a particular problem in Bohemia, where Calvinism grafted itself on the native Hussite heterodoxy. The Austrian emperors in the sixteenth century were unable to mount efficient and continuous programs against their Protestant subjects; the Turks were too close, the royal income was too small, and provincial privileges were too substantial. Thus the Austrian monarchs slid into a sort of quasi-toleration. They didn't like it, and various

popes berated them for it, but it was the best they could do.

This policy began to change when Ferdinand of Styria became emperor in 1619. He was a strict Catholic, and a strong believer in royal absolutism. As soon as he entered upon his inheritance, Ferdinand had both these beliefs challenged. The Protestant nobility and gentry of Bohemia, anxious about the safety of their religion and privileges, revolted against the monarch. In 1618, they expelled the imperial officials from Prague and elected the Protestant Frederick, the Elector Palatine, as king of Bohemia. Aided by the Catholic League of German princes, Ferdinand invaded Bohemia and defeated the Protestant forces at White Mountain in 1620. He threw Frederick out, executed the leading rebels, destroyed provincial privileges, and began the elimination of Bohemian Protestantism. It was the opening round in the Thirty Years War.

If the war had remained confined to Bohemia, restricted to hanging nobles who fought for provincial liberty or the butchery of Protestant peasants, the Bohemian episode might have remained a footnote in the annals of political rebellion and religious crimes. But Ferdinand pursued his enemy into Germany and involved both Catholic and Protestant states in an expanded conflict. Ferdinand's victory over Frederick, and the consequent extension of Catholic power brought Christian IV of Denmark in as the Protestant champion. The Catholic League, supported by the revamped imperial army under Albert of Wallenstein, routed Christian, and drove him out of the war. Christian's collapse was followed by the Catholic conquest of most of northern Germany.

The symbol of Catholic victory was the imperial Edict of Restitution of 1629, which declared that all ecclesiastical property secularized since 1552 must be returned to the Church and that toleration would extend only to Lutherans, not to Calvinists. This settlement threatened to so upset the precarious religious balance in Germany that many believed Protestantism would not survive. It also reversed 300 years of German constitutional development, in which the princes had been getting stronger and the emperor weaker.

Such developments were intolerable to two of the empire's powerful neighbors. France, a state rapidly gaining in internal coherence, could not allow Germany to be dominated by her ancient Hapsburg enemies. And Lutheran Sweden, ruled by the warrior king Gustavus Adolphus, was unwilling to see either a united Germany or a Catholic one. Catholic France, unready to intervene herself, was prepared to give Gustavus Adolphus financial and diplomatic support for a Protestant crusade so long as it was also anti-Hapsburg. With the entry of Sweden in 1630, the Thirty Years War turned from a religious conflict into one in which political motives counted for as much as religious ones.

Gustavus Adolphus was a superior general. He defeated the troops of the Catholic League and the emperor at Breitenfeld (1631) and Lutzen (1632), where he was killed. But the Swedish forces were too small to drive their enemies out of the war or conquer northern Germany. For their part, the imperial forces, particularly after the assassination of Wallenstein in 1634, were generally unable to win the battles, but they could not be crushed. Even the entrance of the French into the war in 1635 did not break the power of the Hapsburgs. Although the Hapsburg emperors never regained the position of political and religious dominance they enjoyed in 1629, their progress in centralizing the Austrian crownlands and in eliminating Protestantism in Austria, Bohemia and southern Germany was permanent. In northern Germany the Protestants survived, and the Edict of Restitution was never enforced. As for the German princes, they emerged from the conflict with their powers intact. Thus, the religious and political situation in 1648, when the Treaties of Westphalia ended the Thirty Years War, was the same as it had been in 1625, before the disasterous Danish intervenion.

Although the last 23 years of the war had brought no changes in the ultimate form of the peace settlement, the various states had continued fighting. Monarchs and ministers were reluctant to admit that their war aims could not be won. The religious passions inflamed in 1618 died hard and slowly. The political ambitions that swallowed them up were abandoned with even greater reluctance. The peoples of Germany paid for this. As the war spread over central Europe, brutality and destruction grew with it. Unable to win victory in battle, armies tried pillage. Sacked in 1631, Magdeburg was completely destroyed, and 24,000 of its 30,000 inhabitants were killed. Perhaps a fifth of all Germans died of slaughter, disease or starvation. Trade and agriculture collapsed. Whole villages were abandoned by their peasants. When peace finally came at Westphalia in 1648, it came from exhaustion, and from the realization that Germany could not be conquered and religious uniformity could not be attained. Indeed, the Treaties of Westphalia were an explicit recognition that the religious wars were over.

Anglicans and Puritans

In England, as well as in the Holy Roman Empire, a religious compromise that had seemed well established at the time of Elizabeth's death in 1603 broke down in the course of the seventeenth century. The efforts of the Calvinist Puritans to modify the Elizabethan establishment in minor ways met with blank disapproval from James I (1603–1625) and his Anglican hierarchy. The Puritan demands for simpler liturgy, and for preaching clergy in every parish, were read as insidious attacks on the bishops and, ultimately, on the royal supremacy. The Anglicans were undergoing a liturgical revival with greater emphasis on ceremony and a greater drive toward uniformity. In practice, the efforts of those at the top had only spasmodic application in the localities. But in the 1630s under Archbishop Laud there was mounting pressure against the Puritans and increasing governmental hostility to all Puritan points of view. Church and state had been fused together since the Reformation; and the idea that any attack on the established church was a veiled attack on the status and power of the monarchy had become a fixed principle with both Archbishop Laud, and James I's successor, Charles I (1625–1649). Authors of books critical of the hierarchy were fined and jailed; Puritans were reprimanded and threatened: some had their ears cut off. James I had earlier warned "No bishop, no King," and his son, Charles, staked the prestige and the life of the government on adherence to this advice and all that it implied.

In 1637, Charles and Laud began the final acts of religious folly that led to a civil war and their separate executions. The episcopal system and an Anglican liturgy were imposed on Scotland without consulting the Scottish Parliament or the Presbyterian General Assembly. Charles and Laud wanted to unseat the Scottish Reformation! Attempts to use the new Prayer Book in Edinburgh caused a riot, then a national outcry, and then a war. Charles lacked the money to fight those Scots who had solemnly sworn to defend their church and state to the death; and his financial desperation drove him to call Parliament in England, something he had not done for 11 years.

When Parliament met in 1640, it focused all the religious and political discontents of the nation in one body in one place. Many Puritans were elected to this Parliament who had a bitter distrust of Charles and his advisers, and who had wide views of the prerogatives of the Commons. First issues were political, and all the constitutional and legal props were ripped out from under the edifice of Charles' previous personal rule. Then, shortly afterward, Parliament authorized the meeting of a Great Assembly of Divines at Westminster to advise on what form of religion it should prescribe. Instead of the earlier close identification of Church and state, Parliament was asserting the Calvinist notion of some separation of identity and of function between the Church and the state. As it turned out, having agreed in the destruction of the episcopal church system, the Puritan divines were not all united in knowing what should replace it. Should it be a Presbyterian system, or a system with final religious authority vested in individual congregations? Should there be religious toleration? Should the Church or the state decide who was and who was not to be excluded from the sacraments? It was on such questions as these that the Puritan front gradually disintegrated. For a time, though, the negative work succeeded: Charles was beheaded and a Puritan Commonwealth replaced the Anglican monarchy. James I's prophecy, "No bishop, no King," was fulfilled.

Conclusions

For more than a century and a half, Europeans fought unremitting and savage struggles over religion. Out of this vast and gloomy conflict emerged a compromise, differing from the religious configurations of 1565 only in detail. The haulings and tuggings, the mayhems and massacres over the course of an entire century had led to only fractional Catholic advantages. The principal sects of 1560, Anglicans, Calvinists, Lutherans, Roman Catholics, remained a century later. Although the Catholics had made gains in Bohemia, southern Germany, Hungary and Poland, they had failed by miles to achieve their announced aim of returning Europe to a single faith. Coercion had not worked.

After 1660, the passion to burn or convert ebbed rapidly in most Europeans of all classes, at least among the laity. There was a steady decline of belief in the notion that a single faith was necessary for political stability. Loyalty to religion became secondary to loyalty to a king or state. In many Europeans the idea took hold that religion was a private matter, not a public one. Others simply cared less about it than their parents had. Ministers, seeing the useless wreckage caused by confessional strife, advised their monarchs against it. A few free spirits even began to suspect that the differences between the various christian sects were minor, that no sect was susceptible to rational proof of superiority over another, that it was all personal preference, and that religious persecution was a low and unchristian act. In 1660, this view was still quite rare, but its day was coming. Put simply, the compulsion to persecute was dying, and the efforts at persecution were seen to be exhausting and unsatisfactory. And these realities signal the end of an era of religious conflict.

CHRONOLOGY OF THE WARS OF RELIGION

1555:   Peace of Augsburg in Germany
1556:   Accession of Philip II of Spain
1557:   Great international fiscal and banking crisis

1558:   Accession of Queen Elizabeth I of England
1559:   Peace of Cateau-Cambrésis
1562:   Beginning of the Wars of Religion in France
1566:   Beginning of the Dutch revolt against Spain
1588:   Defeat of the Spanish Armada
1589:   Accession of Henry IV of France
1598:   Death of Philip II of Spain
         Edict of Nantes in France
1603:   Death of Elizabeth I and accession of James I of England
1609:   Truce between Spain and the Netherlands, recognizing the Dutch victory
1610:   Assassination of Henry IV of France
1618:   Beginning of the Thirty Years War
1630:   Entry of Gustavus Adolphus of Sweden into the Thirty Years War
1640:   Beginning of the English Civil War
1648:   Treaties of Westphalia, ending the Thirty Years War
1649:   Execution of Charles I of England

21

Europe Overseas: The Growth of Empire

On April 2, 1595, a modest fleet of four small vessels sailed from Holland toward a far place. The captains had no maps, and relied for their route on hearsay, gossip and speculation. They were to sail around Africa to the Indies and capture the Portuguese spice trade. They hoped to make a fortune and strike a blow at the Spanish who ruled Portugal and were at war with the Netherlands. Conscience and inclination rode together, a happy circumstance all too rare in human affairs.

The trip was a major turning point in European colonial history. The Dutch, once embarked on colonial adventure, created an immense empire of colonies and commerce. The Portuguese and Spanish, once they had slipped into decline, lost much of their empire and the profits from all of it. This Dutch voyage was also symbolic of changing patterns of European power and prosperity, which were shifting from the Mediterranean to the Atlantic. In the seventeenth century, the Dutch, French and English would dominate Europe, as the Spanish had during the Reformation.

The Dutch bid for commercial and colonial power reflected a desire common to many European states of the sixteenth and seventeenth centuries. For it was widely understood that colonial empires meant stupendous wealth. The river of silver that ran from Peru to Spain had impressed Reformation statesmen as much as the writing of theologians and the cries of preachers. No one had doubted that Spanish political predominance rested on America, or that the brief, bright glory of Portugal came from colonial trade. When contemporary statesmen analyzed Iberian decadence, they saw imperial defeat at the hands of the Dutch. When they meditated on Dutch power and prosperity, so maddening in a time of general distress, they saw the accoutrements of imperialism: colonies, joint stock companies, and fleets. When they advised their kings on the ways to wealth and power, they stressed the need to emulate the Dutch. "What we

A. van Salm, "Fluit", oil painting in the National Maritime Museum, Greenwich.

want is more of the trade that the Dutch have," said the duke of Albemarle before the Dutch war of 1664. No one argued with that. It expressed the general view.

The Portuguese Empire

Portugal was the first European colonial power. After the voyage of Vasco da Gama to India in 1497, the Portuguese swiftly conquered an empire that stretched from Mozambique to Macao, and included forts and trading stations in India, Ceylon and Indonesia. At home King Manoel the Fortunate (1495–1521) presided over a great boom, as Lisbon became the western entrepot for spices. A spacious prosperity and an exciting sense of power and optimism had rewarded imperial enterprise.

Although vast in extent, and potentially rich, the Portuguese Empire had serious structural and economic deficiencies. Naval superiority in the Indian Ocean was maintained only because Portugal's enemies were so badly divided that they could never combine against her. Portuguese merchants never exploited the full trade possibilities in the Far East. Even at their height, between the 1520s and the 1540s, the Portuguese seldom carried more than 15 percent of the spices. The rest went by Arab ships to Egypt. Nor did the Portuguese exploit the far more valuable trade in silks and tea, or calicoes and cottons, that remained in the hands of Asians and Arabs. The Portuguese simply did not have the ships to carry much beyond spices, which brought the highest profits. A further problem was the Portuguese propensity to loot. The Portuguese never understood that loot and trade were incompatible, and they pirated Arab ships and seized the goods of Asian merchants as standard practice.

Economic difficulties were compounded by administrative ones. The Portuguese empire was not composed of colonies, but forts and trading stations. Most of them sheltered only a few dozen Portuguese, and at Goa, seat of the viceroy, there were not more than a few thousand. These scattered stations remained alien outposts among the Arabs, Indians or Indonesians, and the officials in them, unsupervised on the spot, were equally beyond reproof from home. Portuguese officials carried corruption and graft to new levels of ingenuity and greed. They stole from the king, received bribes from merchants, cheated on taxes, and stole from the natives. "In India there is no justice," wrote the High Judge of Goa, "either in your Viceroy or in those who are to mete it out. The one subject is 'the gathering of money by any means.' There is no Moor who will trust a Portuguese. Help us, Señor, for we are sinking."*

After the middle of the century, these disabilities combined to drag the Portuguese from profit to loss. After 1560 only one of three ships returned from the two-year voyage to the East. The reestablishment of the Venetian spice trade after 1550 cut into Portuguese profits at a time of general inflation and rising costs. The Portuguese also grew weary and conservative after the middle of the century. There was more profit in administration and graft, and the Portuguese had neither the money nor the will to set their imperial affairs in order. They did not develop the silk, tea or calico trade, or invest to expand the sugar or slave trades, or to maintain the navy. These difficulties were compounded by the accession of Philip II of Spain to the Portuguese throne in 1580. Tied to the fortunes of Spain, Portugal became a silent victim of Spanish decline. The Portuguese Empire had been started by Prince Henry the Navigator, one of the genuinely origi-

nal men of early modern Europe, who amply fulfilled the predictions of his astrologer," . . . to engage in great and noble conquests, and above all . . . to attempt the discovery of things which were hidden from other men."* Now the Portuguese Empire was falling into ruins; it lay open to European conquest.

The Spanish Empire

Viewed from the perspective of 1560, the Spanish Empire was the wonder of the western world. Spain and her colonies were at the height of expansive vigor and prosperity. Beginning with the discoveries of Columbus, the Spanish had spread rapidly over the Caribbean and into Mexico and South America. Unlike Portugal, Spain established colonies rather than mere trading stations. Spaniards cleared plantations, and, using slaves, began to grow sugar, indigo and tobacco. Small towns grew up, as sites for churches, government, markets and soldiers. Boom towns near the mines, which produced the most desirable colonial product, silver, became the largest settlements in the new world. San Luis Potosí in Peru grew to nearly 150,000 and attained a wild and gaudy lawlessness that was the envy and scandal of the colony. Thus the Spanish Empire attracted large numbers of settlers, more than 150,000 from Castile in the sixteenth century alone. But the great majority of the immigrants were black slaves, and thus reluctant participants in the Castilian effort to reproduce abroad the society left behind in Europe.

The administration of the Spanish Empire, both at home and abroad, closely reflected the aristocratic domination of Castilian society and the crown's fixed policies of increasing royal power and showing great solicitude for the Church and faith. Definite institutional patterns were emerging as early as the first decades of

---

* Letter of the Judge and Aldermen of Goa to the King, November 25, 1552, in George Massleman, *The Cradle of Colonialism*, 221.

* Gomes Eannes de Azurara, quoted in Parry, *The Establishment of the European Hegemony*.

Anonymous 16th C primitive painting of the silver mines at San Luis Potosi, Bolivia. (The Hispanic Society of America)

the sixteenth century. In 1503, the crown established at Seville the *Casa de la Contratación*, a combination board of trade, mint, customs house and joint stock company, which was given a monopoly over colonial trade. And a central administrative body, the Council of the Indies took its place in the highest levels of the royal bureaucracy. A stable form of government also evolved rapidly in the colonies. In 1511, the *Audiencia*, a tribunal of judges, was formed to provide a court for the colonists and a counterweight to the royal governor. The *Audiencia*, however, proved to be an inadequate instrument of royal authority, so the crown sent viceroys with virtually sovereign powers to Mexico in 1535 and to Peru in 1542. The viceroy system worked, and the colonial empire was gradually but steadily brought under tight royal control. By 1560, both in Spain and overseas, the institutions of imperial

government were firmly established and working effectively.

Political absolutism was matched by firm royal control over the Church. The *patronato real* (royal patronage) made the colonial Church a department of state. Thus, the government rapidly replaced the earliest missions with bishoprics and parishes. These were followed by the Inquisition, established in Mexico in 1569 and in Peru two years later. Missions, of course, were not abandoned. They moved to the frontiers of colonization, where they performed the double role of converting the Indians and of extending the area of effective Spanish control.

A final function of the Colonial Church was to spread Hispanic culture and submerge that of the Indians. Although the missionaries and colonists were too few to eradicate Indian civilizations, they did apply a patina of Castilian mores over the

Indian customs. Acculturation was carried out by means of language and art, as well as religion and law, and the result was a huge caste of workers, peons and slaves who were loyal to Spain. Thus the Spanish achieved both their civil and their ecclesiastical goals: to guard the power of the king and the Glory of God.

In ecomonic and commercial affairs the Spanish were not so uniformly successful, despite the river of silver that made the Spanish Empire the envy of the European world. In America, the colonial economy rested on the twin supports of plantations and mining, both providing goods that Europe could not do without. In spite of this immense advantage, the Spanish colonies did not grow as they should have. Fundamental administrative errors led to serious economic mismanagement. Spanish officials thought the purpose of colonies was to bring profit to the king and the merchants at home. Thus, they prohibited colonial manufacturing. Colonial merchants were sacrificed to those of Spain; the *Casa de la Contratación* priced Spanish exports at outrageous levels and paid less than market price for colonial products. This scheme to bilk the colonials could increase domestic profits only so long as trade flowed through official channels, the colonies were dependent on European manufactures, and Europe demanded colonial products. Only the last continued indefinitely. By 1585 the Spanish were unable to provide European manufactures in sufficient quantity or quality, or to provide enough slaves, or to curb smuggling, or to prevent colonial manufacturing, or to maintain their pricing policy. Spanish trade policies collapsed in the face of modest foreign competition and the inadequacies of the Castilian economy.

Serious as the trade losses were, the Spanish crown was far more concerned over the flow of treasure. In the 1590s, the influx of colonial silver reached its zenith, with the royal share coming to more than two million ducats a year and private imports, both legal and illegal, probably eight times that. After 1605, however, the mines at San Luis Potosí began to play out, and specie shipments dropped alarmingly. By 1615 they were less than half the 1595 total. This catastrophe cut to the core of Spanish politics, for power in Europe rested, to a large extent, on shipments of silver.

In spite of these problems, Spain was in no danger of losing her empire altogether. There were too many Spaniards overseas, and they were too well armed with cannon and Hispanic-Catholic culture to be conquered by heretics from the north. Despite the decline of Spanish wealth and power, the colonial Church continued to Christianize Indians and blacks. Hispanic culture was stamped permanently on most of the new world. The creole gentry and the high colonial officials lived a spacious, noble life in pursuit of the aristocratic and Catholic ideals inherited from home. And to many Spaniards of the seventeenth century, these ideals seemed more important, and far more lasting, then the flow of Peruvian silver.

The Dutch Empire

Trade was the opening wedge of colonial competition and the Dutch were prepared to sustain and extend overseas commerce at a time when virtually all the rest of Europe was suffering from a severe and prolonged depression. In the early seventeenth century, the Netherlands became the focal point of European trade and finance. The Dutch navy dominated the oceans, and Admiral Tromp tied a broom to the mast of his flagship symbolic of his determination to sweep the seas clean of foreign shipping. Finally, the Dutch state was dominated by merchant oligarchies from the major towns, who believed the proper end of government was trade and profit, not war or glory.

In the first half of the seventeenth century, the Dutch turned these advantages into a great colonial and commercial empire. Their first ventures were in the Far East, where they seized virtually all of the Portuguese Empire. The Dutch government moved quickly to organize the eastern trade, and Jan de Oldenbaranveldt, the Grand Pensionary of Holland and real ruler of the country, brought the merchants and towns together in 1602 into the Dutch East India Company.

The purpose of the East India Company was profit, not colonies. The company operated less as an arm of the state than as the agent of the shareholders. In the East, spices had been the queen of trade, but silks, tea, calicoes, jade and ginger were also profitable, and the Dutch exploited them, too. Thus the Dutch copied the Portuguese patterns of imperialism and improved upon them.

This policy paid immediate and immense dividends. So large were the shipments that the Company's spices, stored in huge warehouses, gave a pungent odor to an entire quarter of Amsterdam. In its first years the Company paid annual dividends of 20 percent and, although the profits fell after 1650, they were still substantial. Moreover, the imports of the Company stimulated Amsterdam industry. Amsterdam merchants contracted with the Company for raw silk, to be woven at home, and the same was done with calicoes. Eastern woods were made into furniture, and drugs and dyes were processed from roots and herbs imported by the Company. As they looked at their empire, from Capetown to the Moluccas, the 17 directors had reason to be content with their work and vision.

The Dutch West India Company was far less successful. It was founded in 1626, with the dual purpose of trade and war on the Catholic Spanish and Portuguese. War was expensive, even for the Dutch, and costs got out of hand. The Company lost huge sums trying to conquer Brazil from the Portuguese, and it lost New Amsterdam to the British. On a couple of occasions the Company had to be reorganized, so uncertain had its solvency become. Even so, the West India Company had its moments. In 1628, Piet Heyn captured an entire Spanish treasure fleet worth 11 million ducats. The Company declared a dividend. It also made a steady profit from sugar, and sugar refining became a leading Amsterdam industry. There were over 50 factories in the city by the middle of the century, and the port handled about 10 million pounds of sugar a year. Nonetheless, the Company lost money, Dutch possessions in the New World remained meager, and the anti-Catholic crusade was a distinct failure. For Amsterdam merchants the lessons were clear: avoid war, avoid fanaticism, and keep the costs of imperialism low.

In spite of enormous initial success, the momentum of Dutch colonial expansion could not be maintained after 1660. The Dutch had grabbed their empire largely from the Portuguese and had done so when France and England were preoccupied with economic depression, foreign wars and domestic revolutions. Such opportune times could not last forever, and their passing exposed serious weaknesses in the Dutch method of colonial administration. The Dutch had established trading stations, not colonies, to cut costs and increase profits. They discouraged emigration, and the outposts remained tiny and scattered. Moreover, the directors at home tried to rule the colonies from their desks in Amsterdam and allowed too little initiative and discretion to their servants on the spot. This meant a narrow concentration on the known profits of traditional trade and a marked reluctance to try something new. Such scrutiny of detail restricted commerce and harmed the colonies. A broader and more generous view might have paid better in the end.

Beyond this, Dutch imperialism suffered from the decline of The Netherlands itself. The country was too small to compete successfully in both colonial and European politics, particularly against France and

England. French and English economic recovery after 1660 meant that Dutch trade failed to grow as it had previously, and war meant resources had to be diverted from trade and empire to defense at home. The Dutch lost Brazil and New York, suffered the French invasion of 1672, and fought almost constantly from 1689 until 1713. The English and French raised tariffs and placed all sorts of ingenious restrictions on Dutch trade. In these circumstances Dutch commercial supremacy faded and profits declined. Merchants shifted their capital from trade to investment banking, which was safer and paid better. By the end of the century the Dutch were a great power by courtesy only, and the age of expansion was over.

The French Empire

During the sixteenth century, the French were too busy with their domestic religious wars to pay much attention to the world overseas. But, when Henry IV cut confessional strife back to routine hatred, the French government was able to consider claiming its share of the non-European world. In 1603, the French explorer Samuel de Champlain landed on the Canadian coast and sailed up the St. Lawrence River, looking for gold and the northwest passage. He found neither, but the French settled in Canada anyway. French missionaries, explorers and fur traders pushed up the river to the Great Lakes and into the heart of the American wilderness. La Salle followed the Mississippi River south, and reached the Gulf of Mexico in 1682. Realizing that this vast forest empire was vulnerable to the English, the French government tried to tighten its hold on the Great Lakes and the Mississippi valley. Forts and missions were established at Chicago and Detroit, and colonies were planted in Illinois and Louisiana. These struggling and starving outposts were to guard the flanks of empire.

French colonialism followed patterns already established by previous European conquerors. In the West Indies, the French established sugar plantations on the Spanish model and were extremely successful. By the eighteenth century, French sugar, which was both good and cheap, dominated the European market. The French established slave stations in west Africa in imitation of the Dutch and Portuguese, and French commercial outposts in India followed the Portuguese pattern of commercial exploitation without colonization. Frenchmen searched for gold, or were set to cultivating a cash crop in great demand at home.

This colonial domain was governed and exploited along definite principles articulated by clerics and officials who remained safely at home. French colonies were designed to benefit the mother country, both politically and commercially. Colonies were the result of government action, and royal control was extremely tight. Large commerical companies, on the order of the Dutch East India Company, were continually being organized to exploit the colonies and to move colonial trade in the proper channels. And serious efforts were also undertaken to spread the Catholic faith. Hundreds of missionaries, mostly Jesuits, were sent to the new world where they worked, often with courage and compassion, to Christianize the Indians. But, in general, the principles of tight control and profit to Mother France inhibited colonial growth and prosperity, to France's own disadvantage. French colonial officials, like their Spanish, Portuguese, and Dutch counterparts, bound their colonies in a web of inflexible rules and regulations; colonial initiative fell victim to the letter of the law. ". . . The letter killeth, but the spirit giveth life," as St. Paul has reminded us. French officials, observing the general ruin of their plans and hopes, forgot this maxim and blamed the failures of colonialism on British and Dutch competition. There was some truth in that, but not much. The basic malfunction of French colonialism occurred in France itself. The French restricted emigration to the colonies, for both political and religious reasons,* and so the colonies never supported themselves. Canada and Louisiana were too big and empty to be exploited by a few fur traders. Furthermore, the French failed to grant sufficient self-government to the colonials. When it took six months to receive a letter, all decisions could not be made in Paris. Nor should they have been. Colonials deserved more from Paris than a constant stream of officials, letters, directives, orders, and reminders of their duty.

They also deserved more than expensive goods, irregular shipments from home, and low prices for their own products. But the colonial economy took second place to the short-range profits of merchants and commercial companies at home. French royal officials had a touching faith in the ability of commercial companies to bear the costs of colonization in return for trade monopolies. Soon or late the companies always went broke, and they damaged the colony by discouraging investment and by rigging prices. Beyond this, the crown consistently refused to commit sufficient resources to the navy and merchant marine.

French imperial ventures were not without success, particularly in the slave trade and the sugar islands of the West Indies, but they never justified the hopes and cash invested in them.

The British Empire

British imperial expansion did not begin until the seventeenth century, largely because Queen Elizabeth I was too cautious and impecunious to seek a direct confrontation with Spain. By 1600, however, victory over the Spanish Armada, prosperity, and the optimism of the Elizabethan era had pushed the British to the brink of colonial

establishments. The new colonies were still not government ventures. A residual diplomatic and financial caution remained. Private companies, such as the British East India Company (1602), the Virginia Company of London (1606) or the Massachusetts Bay Company (1629) carried the financial burdens of commerce and colonization in return for trade privileges and governmental powers. On occasion, the king granted a charter to a single proprietor, such as Lord Calvert (1632), who received extensive powers in exchange for planting a colony in Maryland as a haven for oppressed Roman Catholics. Thus the king could give or deny support to the companies or proprietors in their quarrels and petitions, as finances and diplomacy required. British colonization, like that of the Dutch, was the result of private enterprise.

This policy changed very slowly after the restoration of Charles II in 1660. The crown still made grants to companies and proprietors. In 1663, the Carolinas were given to eight proprietors, and a year later, New Jersey was divided between Lord Berkeley and Sir George Carteret. New Amsterdam was granted to the Duke of York on the condition he capture it from the Dutch, which he did (and renamed it, immodestly, New York). William Penn received Pennsylvania in 1681, and the Hudson Bay Company was founded in 1670 to exploit the furs of northern Canada. Even so, the crown steadily increased royal control over the colonies. Navigation Acts were passed to force colonial trade into strictly British channels and to increase the profit from the colonies. In 1675 the Lords of Trade were established to supervise colonial affairs, and were replaced in 1696 by the more efficient Board of Trade, which included customs and vice-admiralty jurisdictions. Finally, by the end of the seventeenth century, the Royal Navy had established a more or less permanent Caribbean squadron. Growing royal jurisdiction, however, was still for imperial

---

* The Huguenots, who had strong motives to emigrate, were denied admission to the French colonies.

purposes only, and was rarely exercised in the internal affairs of the various colonies.

Mercantilists and ministers regarded colonies in the West Indies, Africa, India, and the American South as the heart of the empire, largely because of the tropical and oriental products they sent home. Nonetheless, in spite of mercantilist prejudices, the economic and political importance of colonies north of the Chesapeake Bay grew steadily after 1700. Of the northern colonies, Pennsylvania exemplified the patterns of growth, prosperity and freedom that were ultimately to wreck the old empire. Established as a haven for persecuted Quakers, Pennsylvania also extended toleration to other religious minorities. Mennonites, Moravian Brethren, Swendenborgians and others from the persecuted churches of the continent joined the Quakers in the colony. Equally welcome were the Calvinist dissenters from England, Roman Catholics and Jews. Nationalities other than English migrated to Pennsylvania. In the years after 1730 Scots-Irish settled broad tracts of land in the Susquehanna valley, while Germans went to Bethlehem, Germantown and Lancaster County, still known as Pennsylvania Dutch (Deutsch) country. This unlimited migration reinforced the necessity for toleration, and enabled the province to boast a quarter of a million inhabitants by the American Revolution.

Pennsylvaina's prosperity equalled the growth in population. Philadelphia became one of the largest cities in the British empire, enjoying an extensive commerce in grain, lumber and livestock with the West Indies, whose sugar and molasses and dye woods were then sent to England and northern Europe. It was a prosperous pre-industrial commerce, although it did not fit into the theoretical patterns established by mercantilists. The Pennsylvania economy was too close an approximation of England itself and was regarded in London as a potential competitor. Dark suspicions were entertained in London concerning the origin of the sugar, dyewood and molasses that Pennsylvania ships brought to England. Did these products come from Jamaica and Honduras, as they were supposed to, or had they been bought from the French and Spanish in violation of the Navigation Acts? Too often it was the latter, the Board of Trade thought, and there was a tightening up of the customs service, designed to correct these regrettable lapses in commercial activities.

Pennsylvania government generally followed the lines established in the English Bill of Rights of 1689. Religious toleration was enlarged, and Quakers, English nonconformists and German sectarians were allowed to vote and hold office. Electorial districts were far more equitably drawn than in England (although Philadelphia and the nearby counties were favored), and the franchise was substantially more extensive. Finally, the lower house of the Pennsylvania assembly was considerably more powerful than the House of Commons in England. It did not have to contend with a resident king, the pervasive influence of the Lords, an established church or a royal bureaucracy. Both Council and governor had less real authority than the Assembly, for both taxes and authorization for expenditure had to be initiated in the lower house. Popular control over government was immensely greater than in England, a crucial distinction between colony and mother country.

The British were the most successful of the early modern imperial states, however that term was measured. Although the British empire did not produce the mountains of silver that had financed the political and religious domination of sixteenth-century Spain, it showed even greater profits through trade, argiculture and industry. Nor were British colonies political and military liabilities, like those of France and the Netherlands. Finally, the British were just as successful as the Spanish in planting their culture abroad. By the eighteen century the British empire was the wonder and envy of all Europe.

The European Colonial Experience

Although the colonial experience of the European states varied, there were several unifying factors that cut across political lines. The most significant, certainly, was the technological superiority that Europeans enjoyed over nonwestern peoples, which steadily increased until European empires were invulnerable to native revolt, though not to the uprisings of ungrateful colonials. European treatment of nonwestern peoples was another constant of colonial expansion; it was horrible in the fifteenth century and never rallied from its barbaric precedents. Finally, colonials, in spite of the best efforts of their governments at home, generally enjoyed more freedom and a higher standard of living than their fellow subjects who stayed in Europe.

Europe's receptivity to nonwestern customs, in an age of intense religious convictions, was naturally quite limited, and the Europeans' first impulse was to loot. Nonwestern peoples were to be exploited, and slavery, or at least due subordination, was the natives' proper estate. Atrocities were quite common. Vasco da Gamma cut off the ears, noses and hands of about 800 Muslims, and suggested that the ruler of Calicut make curry out of them. Arabs, Indians and Indonesians regarded Europeans as dirty and degraded gangsters, whose word meant nothing and whose conduct was pathological.

Asians fared well compared to American Indians. Even in Canada, where the French needed the Indians to supply furs and Jesuit missionaries tried their best to understand and protect them, contact with Europeans debauched the Indian and extinguished his tribal life. Brandy and furs did it.

. . . the fur traders make them [Indians] quite drunk on purpose, in order to deprive these poor barbarians of their reason, so that the traders can deceive them more easily and obtain almost for nothing their furs . . . Lewdness, adulteries, incests and several crimes which decency keeps me from mentioning are the usual disorders through the trade in brandy, of which some traders make use to abuse the Indian women who yield themselves readily in their drunkenness to all kinds of indecency.

Chrestien Le Clercq,
Nouvelle Relation de la Gaspesie
(Toronto, 1910), pp. 254-255

This tale of woodland wickedness was reported too often to be utterly inaccurate, and what we know of the morality of commerce confirms it.

The Spanish, like the French, endeavored to find some use for the native Americans, and the use they found was slavery. The Indians were rounded up and entrusted to the care of a Spaniard, who was to work them, feed them, and see that they became Christians. But the Indians of the Caribbean basin did not adjust well to slavery, and they retaliated by dying. The Spanish had no intention of doing the labor themselves and replaced the departed Indians with black slaves imported from Africa. These stood up better under the regimen and soon became the basic labor source for Caribbean plantations.

Treatment of the black slaves who replaced the Indians was none too gentle. Brutality began with the slave trade. Blacks were stuffed head to toe into the dirty and airless holds of the ships. It was common for one third to die on the voyage over, as the slavers gave them little food and water and paid no attention to sanitation. Indeed, one of the reasons the British and Dutch did so well in the slave trade was their efficient brutality. The Portuguese, even the Spanish, were too soft to compete.

A further characteristic of Europeans abroad was a greater wealth and freedom than their relations at home enjoyed. In part, this was the result of an abundance of land which contained fewer seigneurial or ecclesiastical encumbrances. Farms in America were bigger and taxes less. In part, also, wealth came from the large assortment of cash crops from the colonies which commanded premium prices at home. Sugar, tobacco and indigo were the most profitable, but lumber, pitch, furs and grains also contributed to colonial affluence. Colonials also enjoyed a relative shortage of nobles, a class noted for its ability to consume and its reluctance to work. The framework of seigneurial privilege might be transported to the new world, but nobles enjoyed fewer privileges abroad than at home. Thus colonials lived in a society where wealth determined class structure and social mobility was greater.

Finally, colonies tended to enjoy more self-government than was common in Europe. Direction from home, although theoretically substantial, was, in fact, quite sporadic, and governmental decisions could often be responsive to local needs and pressures. Moreover, colonial officials tended to come more and more from the local aristocracies and, by the eighteenth century, this practice was permanent. City governments, *audiencias,* superior councils, colonial legislatures, all came to dominate imported officials and to represent colonial interests against the king. There was some complaint about this trend from ministers at home, but nothing was done. Colonies were politically autonomous long before they became officially independent.

The Theory of Mercantilism

European colonial expansion attracted the careful attention of merchants, pamphlet propagandists, promoters both lay and clerical, and government lawyers and bureaucrats. They all advanced numerous explanations and justifications for their own particular scheme or swindle. Priests, political theorists and other practitioners of politics in the abstract sought intellectual justification for the things their kings

did. Kings, themselves anxious to appear in an appropriate and constitutional guise, issued elaborate rationales for their imperial policies. The habits of theology had spread to statecraft, as officials sought to explain and organize the arts and mysteries of imperialism.

These collections of thoughts, ideas, impressions, prejudices, mistakes, axioms and epigrams were called mercantilism. They did not form a coherent system of economics and politics, but were a mixture of notions both true and false, many of which were mutually contradictory. But the mercantilist literature was believed anyway, in part because most of it seemed reasonable, in part because no real alternatives appeared, but mainly because mercantilists were devoted royalists, who stressed the need for royal centralization of political and economic power. Kings responded to this support against their towns, estates and nobles by subsidizing mercantilist pamphlets, organizing mercantilist companies, passing mercantilist laws, and giving solemn credence to mercantilist canons and doctrines.

The origins of European mercantilism are to be found in the economic policies of the medieval city. Royal officials, trained in law, theology, or war, were unprepared to enact the complicated commercial regulations thought necessary for proper exploitation of the new empires. Their search for precedents and guidance led directly to the laws and practices of towns. Urban governments and guilds were constantly preoccupied with the prosperity of their citizens and passed all manner of rules to insure it. Trade in the town was confined to citzens, as were crafts, such as carpentry or shoemaking. Tariffs, quotas, currency restrictions and money-changing regulations were all designed to aid the home market and manufacturers. Prices were controlled, quality and quantity of manufactured goods were regulated, export products were encouraged, and trade secrets were jealously guarded. By the seventeenth century, urban regulation had been subordinated to royal power, but the same spirit of competition and exclusion had been adopted by the King's ministers. The road to prosperity and power was to be the same for kings as for merchants.

The doctrines of mercantilism, distilled from urban precedent, imperial experience, and persuasive pamphlets, were actually quite simple, and bore a remarkable resemblance to the propaganda that flows from American Chambers of Commerce. Foremost among them was the notion that growth was good, and more growth was better. This applied to population, money, trade, industry, colonies, navies, and merchant fleets. Mercantilists were ardent expansionists. Although the term Gross National Product had not been devised, mercantilists were on cozy terms with the concept, and they claimed that their prescriptions would produce sustained and inevitable economic growth. Mercantilists also placed great faith in the new science of statistics, which first emerged in the last years of the sixteenth century. Exact figures were hard to come by, but mercantilists were untiring in their efforts to obtain them and discover new areas of human endeavor that were applicable to quantitative measurement. Furthermore, mercantilists tended to see the world as an arena for constant economic warfare. The prosperity of one state would be at the expense of another, as Sir Francis Bacon commented: ". . . the increase of any Estate must be upon the Foreigner . . . (for whatsoever is somewhere gotten is somewhere else lost . . .)." Wildly inaccurate during the boom years of the sixteenth century, this comment was a shrewd observation in the depression years after 1600. Thus, a major object of statecraft was to beggar one's neighbor, to seize his trade, to ruin his industries, and to conquer his colonies. The decline of the Netherlands meant the decline of Spain; the rise of Britain meant the decline of the Netherlands. Finally, mercantilists believed in a substantial amount

of government regulation to achieve the aims aforesaid. Government programs and laws would foster industry, manipulate and control overseas commerce, produce a favorable balance of trade, and strengthen royal authority. These good things would not occur on their own. The king must make them happen.

The most obvious monument of mercantilist ideals was the immense number of laws and regulations concerning trade and industry. Mercantilist trade regulations were first issued by the Portuguese in the fifteenth century in an attempt to centralize African commerce in Lisbon, thus assuring that the king would get his cut. The Spanish adopted this system with the *Casa de la Contratación* (1503). The *Casa* had a legal monopoly on American commerce, and its functions were three: to make certain that the king received his fifth of the silver, to provide maximum profit for Spanish merchants sending goods abroad, and to exclude foreigners from Spanish colonial commerce. In this last the *Casa* failed completely, for by the end of the sixteenth century foreign goods accounted for more than half of the legal trade with Spanish America, and all of the smuggling.

By the seventeenth century, Europeans had invented a new scheme for exploiting colonial trade. This was the joint-stock company, such as the various East India companies, the Hudson Bay Company, or the numerous French companies that failed to develop Canada. The commercial companies had certain advantages. They could provide a larger capital investment than individual merchants and market for colonial products; they confined trade to approved routes and enhanced royal control. In spite of this, however, the companies usually failed. The capital they raised was never enough to carry the immense and continuing expenses of colonialization and defense. Profits from colonial trade were simply devoured by military and administrative expenses. Moreover, the colonials were stubbornly unwilling to labor cease-lessly for the merchants and directors back home. In general, the companies were too small and poor to accomplish what the king himself could not. But these sad facts made little impression on contemporaries. New companies were chartered all the time. The French, in particular, had a touching and simple faith in commercial companies, which was never rewarded.

Navigation Acts

Mercantilists also called for laws to regu-late trade. These rules were collectively called Navigation Acts, and all countries had them. Despite certain differences in detail, the Navigation Acts included the following principles: (i) the development of a merchant marine by excluding insofar as possible, foreign sailors and ships (usu-ally Dutch) from colonial and internal trade; (ii) the establishment of a national monopoly on colonial trade; (iii) the estab-lishment of a colonial monopoly of the home market; with (iv) the colonies pay-ing for the system by customs dues. If these principles were followed, mercantil-ists were convinced, the road was open to increased wealth, trade, and power.

The most clearly articulated system of Navigation Acts was that of the British. It took its classic form after the collapse of Oliver Cromwell's Puritan Common-wealth and the restoration of Charles II. In 1660, a Navigation Act stated that all Eng-lish colonial trade must be in English ships with English masters and crews. Moreover, certain English colonial products could go only to England and nowhere else. These "enumerated commodities" were few at first. In 1660 they included sugar, tobacco, cotton, indigo, ginger, speckle-wood and dyewoods. The list was later enlarged. In 1673, coconuts and cacao were added; in 1704, rice, molasses, and rum; in 1705, naval stores; and in 1721, copper and furs. In 1663, an Act for the Encouragement of

Trade introduced a new aspect to the mer-cantilist system. All European products destined for the colonies must be unloaded in England and then shipped overseas. Thus England became the "Staple," or en-trepot for all European goods sent to the colonies. English merchants and the cus-toms revenue were bound to prosper under such an arrangement, and foreigners were bound to suffer. From the mercantilist viewpoint, the arrangement could not be better.

Although thousands of amendments, in-terpretations and legal opinions were added to the Navigation Acts, the Staple Enumeration and national shipping re-mained the basic principles of trade regu-lation. The problem was enforcement. Charles II established commissions to supervise British trade and colonial affairs as soon as he returned from exile. Their mission was to stem "the immoderate de-sire" of continental states ". . . to engross the whole traffic of the universe."* But the commissions did not work very well, nor did the Lords of Trade who followed them in 1675. This inefficiency could not be allowed to continue, and the Navigation Act of 1696 reorganized the administration of colonial trade. Customs and vice-ad-miralty officials in the colonies were given stronger backing by being allowed forcible entry to seize goods traded in defiance of the law, and a Board of Trade was estab-lished in London to direct the entire sys-tem. The new law did not eliminate trade outside the legal patterns, but increasing British prosperity made strict enforcement unnecessary, and none was attempted until the Sugar Act of 1764.

Mercantilism at Home

The second basic element of mercantilism was government encouragement of do-

* Lord Clarendon, quoted in C. M. Andrews, *The Colonial Period in American History*, IV, 54.

mestic industries. Every state passed laws and concocted hundreds of schemes both sensible and outlandish to support industry. Bounties and rewards were promised to enterprising merchants and, now and then, were actually paid. Privileges were granted new manufacturers and tariffs were raised against foreign competition. The modern patent system arose from mercantilist solicitude for industry and invention. Government support, although frequently unintelligent, was certainly genuine.

The scope of royal regulation was clearest in France, where a strong bureaucratic government was animated by classic mercantilist principles. In 1601, as soon as he had pacified the country, Henry IV set up a Commission of Commerce, which held hundreds of meetings and considered all sorts of schemes. Its most ambitious project was to increase the French silk industry. The Commission invested large sums in a scheme to plant 400,000 mulberry trees, supply silkworm eggs, and print a pamphlet telling peasants how to care for both. The Great Mulberry Mirage ran into immediate difficulties—financial, human, and botanical. Even so, silk production in Southern France grew several times over its previous level, so the king's money was not totally wasted.

Under Jean-Baptiste Colbert, finance and colonial minister under Louis XIV from 1661 to 1683, efforts to stimulate industry were redoubled. Colbert was fairly successful in dealing with tariffs. In 1664 he suppressed many internal duties, making central France the largest free trade area in Western Europe. Colbert produced the first single external tariff for the entire realm. He also subsidized canal construction. The largest and most successful of these projects was the Canal du Languedoc, which joined the Atlantic to the Mediterranean. There were also failures. Colbert was never able to abolish many river, bridge and road tolls, nor to extend free

trade to all France. He could not get a uniform system of weights and measures. These reforms awaited the French Revolution of 1789.

Colbert's most persistent efforts were toward the stimulation of French manufacturing. He had an aristocratic bias and thought luxury products for the nobility were more profitable than cheaper goods for common people. Thus he concentrated his efforts on quality as much as on quantity and was rarely concerned about high productivity. Colbert was particularly interested in French silk, lace, furs, glass, china, rugs, and tapestries. He gave numerous privileges to the glass industry, including tax exemptions. His efforts built up French glassworks, and cut deeply into a traditional Venetian industry. The crown also established the Gobelins tapestry works, which received enormous subsidies, lost vast sums of money, and produced magnificent works of art. In silk and lace, Colbert extended privileges previously granted.

All of this regulation required a large bureaucracy and continuous administrative attention, as it does today. Colbert sent out thousands of orders, exhortations, opinions, criticisms and complaints to merchants, artisans and officials. He understood merchants well, commenting that they ". . . always consult only their own individual interests, without examining what would be for the public good and the advantage of commerce in general."[*] The crown must lead the way and, if necessary, compel.

Along with advice went inspectors to see that French manufacturing attained the level of quality Colbert thought essential. The inspectors and bureaucrats were a plague on the land, then as now. Industrialists had to buy them off to keep them from enforcing rigid and stupid regula-

[*] Cole, *Colbert and a Century of French Mercantilism*, 2 vols., I, 334.

tions. On rare occasions, graft did not work, and Colbert's rules were enforced. Goods that did not meet specifications were destroyed, at enormous cost in time, work, materials and markets, as merchants could not produce what their customers demanded. The officials and inspectors were sent out with a noble and impossible purpose: to persuade businessmen to see a general good beyond their ledgers. Overall, Colbert's policies probably stimulated French prosperity more than they harmed it. But his goal of a productive, efficient national economy, highly centralized and thoroughly regulated, remained a dream and nothing more. For ultimately, Colbert's mercantilism was a crusade against human nature.

The Decline of the Old Colonial System

During the Old Regime (i.e., prior to the French Revolution) colonial enterprise bore a close relationship to power and prosperity at home. Many of the products most wanted in Europe originated overseas, and such goods—sugar, silk, tobacco, spices and indigo—brought high profits to both king and merchant. The value of these goods was so great that the colonies were able to trade with Europe for manufactured products on a fairly equal basis. Colony and mother country maintained a symbiotic relationship, each able to supply the other's needs. Under these conditions, a state without colonies or colonial trade was substantially poorer than her neighbors. Such economic advantages were not always translated into military power, as the rise of Prussia was to show. But British commercial and colonial supremacy in the last century of the Old Regime was quite clearly a major factor in her military and economic preeminence, and contemporaries grasped that equation with their accustomed ease.

By the third quarter of the eighteenth century, however, Europeans were not as convinced as their fathers had been of the value of colonial enterprise. Support for imperial adventure waned everywhere. In part, this disillusionment reflected the total British victory in the Great War for Empire (1739–1763), which placed all colonial powers in the unfortunate position of seeing the profits of empire go to the British while the expenses remained at home. In part, also, the disenchantment with far places coincided with a growing rambunctiousness among colonials, who demanded more autonomy and revolted to get it. It also reflected a continuous decline in the price of colonial products and a reduction in the profits of growing them. The costs of empire—economic, military and intellectual—were becoming greater than the profits, even for the British. Thus European imperial expansion, begun with such huge hopes for gain and glory, having played such a great part in the affairs of kings and commoners, faded out in losses, rebellion, disillusionment and disinterest. It would not resume until the late nineteenth century.

22
Hard Times: The Great Depression 1590-1660

The Coming of the Depression

Like all kings, Henry II of France (1547–1559) was desperately short of money. He had all the usual expenses, along with a demanding mistress, Diane de Poitiers, for whom he was building the stupendous chateau at Chenonceaux. To pay his bills, Henry resorted to borrowing and, when ordinary loans failed, he consolidated his debts in 1555 into a huge fund, called the Big Deal. The Big Deal tapped the money market of Lyon, and it paid 16 percent a year. People rushed to invest. The king's debts increased marvelously. There seemed to be no end to the river of cash—until September, 1557, when Philip II, king of Spain and the richest monarch in Christendom, bankrupted. Confidence collapsed, but Henry II, with regal bravado, announced he would never default on the Big Deal, as his debts were a sacred royal trust. Although not entirely convincing, that bald lie did keep the king afloat for another season, until December, when Henry, too, suspended payment on his debts.

The great fiscal crisis of 1557 affected all of Europe, and was the first major break in nearly a century of continuous economic growth. Depression did not come at once. After a kind of shudder, the European economy continued its upward movement. People forgot that kings could go bankrupt. New speculations began, kings drifted back to the money markets, trade expanded, silver flowed into Europe from the new world and everything seemed all right again. But, prosperity rested on too narrow a foundation. Primitive technology, inefficient agriculture, a vicious price inflation, and the waste of war and persecution, all inhibited European economic growth. There were new crises, like the one in 1557, and new shocks even more severe and destructive. By the end of the century the golden years were over, and Europe was headed into the most profound and prolonged depression since the Black Death.

The Instability of the European Economy

During the sixteenth century, when money was easy and trade was good, prosperity seemed permanent and hard times banished forever. Alas, they were not. The European economy suffered from serious structural shortcomings that made a new depression almost inevitable. These included considerable waste and mal-investment of scarce resources in nearly continuous wars and religious persecutions. Constant inflation and a progressive credit collapse after 1574 were also fundamental economic problems and were reminiscent of an earlier economic collapse during the crisis of the fourteenth century.

The most basic structural deficiency was an agricultural system that kept most Europeans working on the land in an endless war against poverty, famine and malnutrition. This situation existed all over the globe and always had. Indeed, ever since the High Middle Ages, Western European agriculture had led the world in productivity, and serfdom was a thing of the past. But although European agrarian productivity far exceeded that of ancient Rome or contemporary Islam, it was primitive by modern standards and inadequate to support the grand enterprises of the rising European states. Harvest yields of six bushels of grain for each bushel of seed were exceptional; three or four were far more common. Livestock were scrawny (by Texas standards), and many were slaughtered in the fall because winter feed was inadequate. One third to one half of the land lay fallow each year as primitive systems of crop rotation tried to compensate for the lack of the legumes and fertilizer that farmers use today. Likewise, agricultural implements were simple and inefficient, and poor storage methods ruined part of the modest harvest that was collected. Prosperity did stimulate some clearing of waste, and opened the western market to Baltic grain, but there had been little increase in agricultural efficiency or improvement in agricultural technology since the High Middle Ages.

Industry and commerce in the sixteenth century seemed to show a much brighter prospect, at least on the surface. Here there was genuine growth: more ships, more cargoes, more mines, more looms, and more foundries and shops. There was even some technological improvement, particularly in metallurgy and shipbuilding. But the industrial and commercial expansion was still rather small, and rested on too narrow a market. There was no general increase in the depth of the market. Luxury goods, and many ordinary products as well, remained well beyond the reach of most people.

In addition to a relatively primitive agricultural and industrial technology, there was the steep and general inflation that lasted the entire sixteenth century. The causes of the price inflation are clear enough to modern historians and economists, but they escaped contemporaries almost completely. During the period from 1475 to 1620, Europeans found two new sources of coined wealth—mines in Bohemia and specie from America. They added about one billion ducats to the economy, an incredible sum for a society in which a family could live comfortably on 25 ducats a year. There was, however, no corresponding increase in industrial production, commerce, or productivity. The modest growth in these areas simply fell far short of the steady and spectacular increase in cash.

Therefore, prices rose. They moved up slowly at first, in the last decades of the fifteenth century but, by 1520, the price rise was steeper and more rapid. Inflation was most severe in the Iberian peninsula, where the prices of everyday goods rose 400 percent between 1500 and 1640. Elsewhere the rise was more moderate, averaging between 150 and 300 percent. Wages rose, too, but not as fast and not as much. And the wage lag produced a steady erosion in the real wages of workers, in spite of formal increases wrung from reluctant masters. In all of Europe, the lower classes suffered a general decline in their living standard. In England, the drop in buying power between 1475 and 1640 was about two thirds, and there were similar losses everywhere.

Income erosion affected persons more exalted than workers and journeymen. Princes, nobles and bishops suffered the same affliction. The cost of magnificence, status, war, government and politics went up alarmingly, just when overseas trade had made new and expensive products available. Country nobles who had converted their manorial dues into money payments suffered the most, and many were forced to sell out. Kings borrowed money and issued paper, bishops hunted for plural benefices to exploit, and the secular aristocracy bought government offices that allowed them to benefit from rising royal incomes. It was hardly accidental that everywhere in the sixteenth century there was a general and inexorable rise in the number and variety of royal officials. The aristocracy were more successful in their search for additional money to spend than were workers, which is only what we might expect.

The related phenomena of rising prices and increasing amounts of money had a dual impact on the finances of kings. In formal terms, their incomes rose to unheard of heights, and they appeared rich. But the money bought so much less, particularly expensive items such as armies and navies, that many monarchs were actually poorer than ever. Kings scrabbled desperately for money. "I believe that lack of funds will ruin the state . . .," wrote Jean-Baptiste Colbert to Cardinal Mazarin in 1652, a year of severe depression, and that complaint echoed the continuous wails of bankrupt monarchs a century earlier during a time of prosperity. Kings were as needy as ever, in spite of the relative abundance of cash. To cover expenses they increased taxes as much as they could or dared and, when this was not enough, they borrowed.

Fiscal Disasters

Early in the sixteenth century royal borrowing was relatively modest. The interest was usually paid and the privileges given creditors were worth the risk, even if no one pretended that the principal could ever be repaid in cash. But by the 1550s, under the pressures of war, inflation and religious reform, this all changed. Royal borrowing increased rapidly, and kings issued paper to cover their debts. By 1557, monarchs had acquired an immense debt, far heavier than they could manage. Philip II had borrowed over 5 million *ducats* in Antwerp, largely from great German bankers like the Fuggers or the Welsers. In Castile his debts reached beyond 40 million ducats. Henry II of France had skimmed 12 million *livres* just from the merchants and bankers of Lyon, along with a great deal elsewhere, and his resources were far smaller than Philip's. The merchants and bankers who had lent these princely sums found their own resources strained. The crash came in the fall of 1557. First Philip II and then Henry II slid into bankruptcy. They stopped payment on their debts and issued paper to cover the default.

The financial crisis had severe repercussions. The Fuggers and Welsers were badly hit, and the latter, at least, never really recovered. Smaller German bankers who depended on the giants were forced into semiliquidation. Many banking houses in Lyon went out of business, and those that did not cut their investments in trade and industry. Commerce between Seville and America was sharply depressed and did not recover for five years. The city of Antwerp was compromised, and borrowing on its bourse never again reached the precrisis levels.

Bad as it was, though, the crisis passed. Silver shipments from America held up, losses were absorbed, trade picked up again, especially in the Mediterranean, and royal expenses grew as smartly as they ever had. Prosperity returned, even in France which was slipping into civil war. *Faits rouler les bons temps* (let the good times roll) say the Cajuns, and European monarchs fell in with this spirit by borrowing a lot more money. They borrowed too much. By 1572, Philip II was again in trouble and was pressing his bankers for even more to tide him over the immediate emergency. There was only so much the creditors could give, and in September 1575, the Hapsburg monarch went under again. This time he ruined a large number of Spanish bankers and began a general run on Italian banks that lasted until 1584. In the wake of Philip's default, 24 Italian banks closed, with a net loss of more than four million ducats. There was the usual depression in American trade, and the international trade fair at Medina del Campo closed down, only opening three years later when Spanish private and royal credit was somewhat restored.

The Spanish catastrophe had its repercussions in France, now firmly mired in the religious slaughter of St. Bartholomew's day. The Lyon money market suffered a sharp slump in 1574, and never really recovered. Although general failure was avoided, individual banks continued to collapse regularly. The fairs at Besançon, in Franche-Comté, did even worse. They folded altogether in 1579.

In spite of everything—the losses, the uncertain future, the continuing wars, the increasing costs of trade and manufacturing—Philip II was able to borrow more money. But his credit rested on a thin foundation. American silver and Genoese bankers were all that supported him. That was not enough, even though taxes were increased and the revenue from America reached its highest level. In 1596, the Spanish crown again suspended payment on its debts.

This time, the ill effects of royal financial failure were permanent. The trade fair at Medina del Campo closed for good, and the commerce in woolens that used to support it went to the French, English and Dutch. The number of ships trading with America fell by two thirds after 1596 and never recovered. Among Philip's creditors, only the Genoese survived, and they went under in the Spanish bankruptcy of 1608. The financial and credit center of Europe moved from the Mediterranean to Amsterdam. Spanish industry was as depressed as trade, and Italian manufacturing also felt the credit squeeze. After 1596, the entire western Mediterranean basin moved swifty into a severe and prolonged depression.

Repeated royal bankruptcies had a disastrous impact on the activities of merchant-bankers, and on the amounts of cash and credit available for investment in commercial and industrial ventures. Kings used their greater political powers to sop up the large capital accumulations that might otherwise have gone into commercial and industrial investment. Bankers and merchants, therefore, became a species of tax collector, functioning as private agencies to funnel investment capital to the king. Eventually, the king's needs outran the bankers' ability to supply fresh funds. Whenever that happened the king bankrupted and left the merchants to absorb the loss. Over the course of the half century following 1557, kings simply devoured their merchants and bankers.

For most of the sixteenth century, the adverse factors in the European economy were not strong enough to throw the balance from general prosperity to depression. Commercial growth, increases in industrial production, new sources of food, and a somewhat expanded agriculture all combined to sustain general economic growth everywhere until the 1580s, and in northern Europe until 1620. Eventually, however, the accumulated burdens of technological limitations, inflation and extensive credit disorders polished prosperity off.

Depression in Southern Europe

When prosperity cracked and faded, it did so first and most severely in the Mediterranean basin, long the richest area of Europe. As early as the 1580s, there were definite signs of decline and by 1600 the real depression had come. The economic crisis in the Mediterranean basin was composed of several elements, all transcending national and imperial boundaries. Plague, famine, regressive tax policies, capital flight, declining trade and industry, price inflation and technological backwardness affected Turkey and Italy as well as Spain. These general conditions were joined by a host of local, individual catastrophes, many of which had been surmounted during the prosperity of the previous century but now added to the general woe. These misfortunes included the expulsion of the Moriscos from Valencia, growing piracy in the Adriatic Sea, the decline of the silk industry at Messina, and the end of the trade fairs at Medina del Campo. The Mediterranean depression, therefore, was a mosaic of disasters, some general, some particular, and all combined so that only a few places escaped the general ruin.

Inflation, capital flight and currency manipulations were common in southern Europe after 1600, and followed the patterns set in the previous century. The Turkish silver asper, traditionally stable, scarce and sound, enjoyed a high value until the end of the sixteenth century. Then, as Spanish silver moved east to pay for Oriental goods, the asper became more abundant, and suffered a severe loss of purchasing power. After 1580, the asper fell dramatically, and the Ottoman government accelerated the process by debasing the coin. By 1620, the asper was no longer acceptable for international payments, and the Ottoman government was forced to mint the silver para as its replacement. Within a few years it, too, was debased.

In Spain, there was a similar story of currency manipulation. Debasement began in earnest under Philip III (1598–1621), when the crown tampered with the value of the copper coinage, and only ended in 1680 with a general currency revaluation that was a severe jolt to what remained of Spanish economic life.

Along with currency manipulations and royal bankruptcies went a substantial capital flight from the Mediterranean states. In part, this was a transfer of funds to northern Europe, particularly to the still prosperous Dutch Republic. In part, also, capital flight meant a sharp increase in investment in office, land, church and titles of nobility. These forms of investment were not unprofitable; by 1600 they offered a higher return in Spain or Italy than did trade. Moreover, noble rank and official position were the essential elements of social status, a crucially important value in an aristocratic and hierarchical society. But such investments while reasonable and attractive, only deepened the depression in trade and industry.

Financial problems in southern Europe were accompanied by a depression in the real economy. Agriculture, trade and industry failed to keep pace with northern competition. Spanish wool production declined steadily after 1580, the victim of high costs and soil erosion on grazing lands. By 1600, the Mediterranean basin had become a consistent importer of foodstuffs. Commerce also dropped off. By 1600, most of the goods sent to America by legal channels of trade were Dutch. In Venice, long the major entrepot of eastern trade, goods entering the customs house dropped decade by decade after 1600, and the rich spice trade was lost forever. Spanish and Italian shipping, even in the Mediterranean, cost more than the Dutch, was technologi-

El Greco, "View of Toledo". (The Metropolitan Museum of Art. Bequest of Mrs. H. O. Havemeyer, 1929. The H. O. Havemeyer Collection.)

cally backward, and suffered from insufficient investment capital.

Southern European industry also declined. Italian woolen manufacturing, the industrial staple of the peninsula since 1100, dropped continuously during the seventeenth century, particularly in established industrial centers such as Milan. Part of the loss was to the Dutch, and part was the result of industrial decentralization, as shops moved from the larger cities to small provincial centers. The significance of such a trend was unmistakable. Instead of producing for an international market, Italian manufacturers were making cloth for local consumption.

If the decline in industrial production was relatively moderate in Italy, in Spain it was catastrophic. Spanish textiles, iron, and leather products virtually vanished from the market, and Spain became an importer of manufactured goods as well as food. Spanish mercantilists proposed various remedies for this industrial depression, but none worked. Indeed, so disorganized had Spain become that few remedies were even tried.

Moreover, Spain was unable to keep abreast of technological advances that were stimulating the economies of the North. During the seventeenth century, Dutch shipbuilding and textile manufacturing increasingly employed new and sophisticated techniques unknown in Spain. The Spanish were also outstripped by the English and Swedish in the manufacture of guns. And Dutch civil engineers used techniques in drainage and water control that the Spanish had never heard of.

A further factor in technological backwardness was the attitude of southern European urban craft guilds, which assumed an increasingly defensive position after 1590. Possessing considerable local power, and anxious to preserve their members' livings in a time of depression, Spanish and Italian guilds fought any changes in technique on the grounds that they would force craftsmen out of work. Featherbedding became a way of life, as guilds restricted industrial technology and forced the production of goods that few wanted at a price even fewer would pay.

The cultural and social factors in the depression were vividly illustrated in the expulsion of the Moriscos from Spain. Ordered to convert from Islam to Christianity by Ferdinand and Isabella in 1502, the Moriscos had complied, but with reluctance, and were suspected by everyone of secretly retaining the old faith. High taxes and religious persecution drove the Moriscos of Castile to revolt from 1569 to 1571, which only confirmed the prevailing suspicions. Between 1609 and 1611, about 300,000 Moriscos were driven out, about 85 percent from Aragon and Valencia. In these two provinces they formed the bulk of the peasantry and petty artisans, and their departure produced an immediate and devastating economic collapse that aggravated the already depressed conditions.

Political revolution compounded economic and social problems. In Spain, the gap between Castilian resources and ambitions grew so alarmingly that the government tried to increase taxation in Catalonia and Portugal. Both provinces revolted in 1640, with Portugal eventually winning independence in 1668. Three other revolts shook the Hapsburg imperium—in Palermo in 1647, in Naples a year later, and in Messina in 1671 to 1674. Similar conditions caused all three: general economic stagnation, unemployment, high bread prices and the taunting memory of better times.

The final blow to the Mediterranean economy came from nature. Soil erosion and overgrazing in Spain and southern Italy restricted sheep pasturage and the output of wool, and had begun to encroach on the arable land as well. From 1599 to 1601, an outbreak of plague and a series of bad harvests struck Spain, causing widespread mortality and hastening the process of urban depopulation. In 1630 and again in 1657, Italy and Spain suffered from outbreaks of the plague. As a result, the larger industrial towns—Milan, Burgos, and Medina del Campo—showed sharp population losses, which were not made up until the next century.

In the Mediterranean basin, the depression was so severe and prolonged, and had so many adverse effects on all levels of government, that it may be called a general crisis of state and society, reminiscent of the disasters of the fourteenth century. Previously powerful Mediterranean states suffered a reversal in every aspect of public life, and their peoples lost the sense of openness and confidence and the impulse toward expansion so evident during the Renaissance and Reformation.

Depression in Germany and France

The depression in northern and central Europe began a generation later than in the South. Economic collapse coincided with the outbreak of war in 1618 to 1620: in Germany between the Hapburg emperors and their Bohemian Protestant subjects to open the Thirty Years' War; in the Low Countries between Spain and The Netherlands at the end of the Ten Years Truce of 1609, and in France between the King and the Huguenots. Universal war was more than the northern European economy could stand. The sharpest statistical indication of depression was the dramatic break in sound tolls, duties charged by Denmark on ships entering and leaving the Baltic seas. These taxes dropped by two thirds in the years after 1620, and only slowly recovered afterward.

The great depression in France began in the ordinary way, with a collapse of royal credit and a break in international trade. In 1619, King Louis XIII (1610–1643) declared bankruptcy, having spent all the money saved in the peaceful reign of Henry IV. War, both civil and foreign, worsened the fiscal problems. This combination threw the fragile French economy into a sustained depression that was marked by numerous peasants' revolts against seigneurial and royal authority. As in southern Europe, economic difficulties were reflected in political and social turbulence. The slump reached its nadir in the 1650s with stagnant trade, depressed agricultural prices, regressive royal taxation and an apparently endless war with Spain (which dragged on from 1635 until 1659).

A certain recovery came after 1660. France entered a decade of peace, and the mercantilist minister, Jean-Baptiste Colbert, struggled to create prosperity.* Colbert's efforts had some success, and French trade and industry showed genuine growth after 1660.

But after Colbert's death (1683), his royal master, Louis XIV, reduced the crown's aid to industry and concentrated once again on war and religious persecution. The war years, from 1685 to 1715, were a time of profound depression. The textile industry of Languedoc faded badly because of the renewed persecution of Huguenots, and overseas trade was nearly shut off by the British and Dutch navies. Royal finances fell into incredible disorder, and the few private lenders charged usurious rates. What money there was went into hiding or the purchase of nobility or royal office. Once again, poverty and persecution were accompanied by uprisings; the revolt of the Camisards in 1703 was so serious that the government was forced to negotiate

with the rebels. In spite of abundant royal folly, however, this second depression was not all the fault of the government. From 1691 to 1694 and again from 1709 to 1710 there were tremendous famines. The last was the worst natural disaster in the nation's history, and a million people perished from starvation, exposure and disease.

As a result of these catastrophes, French recovery from the seventeenth-century depression was delayed until 1720. Nonetheless, eighteenth-century France enjoyed a sustained prosperity, marked by a large population rise, sharp increases in trade, and a general growth in agricultural output. But in spite of its prosperity, France did not experience an industrial revolution on the British model until the nineteenth century. French manufacturing, although it expanded, did not undergo any substantial technological change. Thus French economic history diverged sharply from the British in the century after 1675 and was also quite different from patterns in the Mediterranean basin and central Europe, where recovery was slower yet and far less pervasive.

Prosperity in England

Not every European state experienced a general economic collapse in the first half of the seventeenth century. England and Holland did not experience a genuine economic retreat: less trade, demographic decline, fewer manufactured goods and a reduction in agricultural productivity. Instead, they benefited from a shift of trade and industry from the Mediterranean basin northward. The British and Dutch cornered the market on banking and credit, overseas trade, and basic industries at a time when most states were becoming progressively poorer. Although the total amount of European wealth was smaller in 1640 than it had been a half century earlier, it was much more highly concentrated and confined to a remarkable degree to the northwestern corner of Europe.

* See above, page 283.

J. Berck Heyde, "Old Exchange, Amsterdam", oil painting in the Rijksmuseum in Amsterdam.

Although the British did not enjoy the enormous prosperity of the Dutch, England escaped the awful economic carnage that occurred in Spain, Germany and Turkey. Continuous war in the early seventeenth century maintained the demand for British cannon and textiles, and English shipping had a small, although profitable share of the trade in sugar, slaves, tobacco and fish. English coal and iron production grew after 1600. Agricultural productivity did also, in part because of the continuing enclosures of the land and the draining of fens and marshes. Nonetheless, this modest prosperity had some soft spots, which showed up most clearly where the English were competing directly with the Dutch. The British carrying trade remained markedly inferior to the Dutch, who even captured a large share of the English, coastal trade. In the Far East, the Dutch expelled the English from the Spice Islands in 1620,

forcing them back on the less profitable Indian trade. It was the same with manufacturing. The Cockayne project (1614–1622), an attempt to prohibit export of undyed wool to the Netherlands, and thus encourage domestic dyeing, was a disastrous failure and damaged the British textile industry.

Reflecting on their economic position, seventeenth-century English merchants saw numerous opportunities and loudly lamented that the Dutch were everywhere ahead of them. Dutch ". . . riches and multitude of shipping is the envy of the present . . . and yet the means whereby they have advanced themselves are . . . in great measure imitable . . . by us of the Kingdom of England," wrote the Restoration merchant Josiah Child. Along with envy and imitation went increasing hostility. Oliver Cromwell warned that the Dutch wished to drive British Baltic trade from the seas and implied that war would be needed to stop them. The trade was worth it, and the wars were fought.

Boom in Holland

Dutch prosperity in the midst of universal distress was genuine and marvelous, and contemporaries sought explanations for it in every area from divine intervention to criminal conspiracy. Actually, the reasons were both simpler and more complex. Holland's success resulted partly from fortunate economic and political circumstances, and partly from the industry and audacity of the Dutch themselves.

The Dutch alone possessed a government that gave first place to trade and profit, and opposed war and religious conformity. "Above all things, war, and chiefly by sea, is most prejudicial and peace very beneficial for Holland," wrote the Dutch merchant and politician, Peter de La Court, and he spoke the simple truth. Even for the Dutch, wars against the decaying Spanish monarchy ate up the profits of peace, despite isolated triumphs such as Piet Heyn's capture of an entire treasure-laden Spanish fleet. After the middle of the century, war with France and England would be even less rewarding, and the Dutch government consequently made great efforts to preserve peace.

In the seventeenth century, the booming Dutch economy rested on three pillars: a diverse and technologically sophisticated industry, the universal domination of the carrying trade, and the control of European banking, credit and insurance. Dutch industry was the most varied and profitable in Europe and grew spectacularly on the ruins of industry elsewhere. Leyden became the center of the light and cheap "New Draperies," which were rapidly replacing the "Old Draperies" of Flanders and Italy. Amsterdam became the center of sugar refining and brewing, and the Dutch dominated printing, papermaking and the book trade well into the eighteenth century.

Glass, pottery, tiles and silk were all prosperous Dutch industries, migrating there from Italy and France. Dutch manufactures were largely finishing trades, where the profits were larger, the required skills greater, and the technology more sophisticated.

The most important Dutch industry, of course, was shipbuilding, which was a major concern of most of the towns along the Zuider Zee. The great shipyards at Zaandam near Amsterdam turned Baltic timbers into dozens of ships a year. These were mostly vessels of a new type, called *fluit*, invented at Hoorn about 1597 by Jan Linschoten. The *fluit* was the most advanced ship of the age, an immense improvement over conventional galleons, for it was easier to handle and carried far more cargo with one third the crew. The technological superiority of Dutch shipping amply reinforced their overwhelming numbers. In the early seventeenth century the Dutch owned between one half and two thirds of all European ships. They sent more than 1000 ships a year to the North Sea fishing fleet, another 1500 or 2000 into the Baltic, another 2000 or so to Spain and the Mediterranean, as well as hundreds to Africa, the Far East and America. The Dutch controlled every trade that was. They were the only European nation allowed to trade with Japan and, in 1619, a Dutch ship arrived at the new colony of Virginia with its first load of slaves.

Dutch superiority also extended to banking, credit, marine insurance and business methods generally. Amsterdam became the banking capital of Europe after the collapse of Antwerp and the failures of Italian and Spanish banking houses. The Bank of Amsterdam, founded in 1609, and the Loan Bank, founded in 1614, attracted liquid funds from everywhere. The Exchange Bank quickly became the strongest financial institution in Europe, surviving the panic during the French invasion of 1672, and increasing its capital in the long years of war that closed the seventeenth century.

Amsterdam likewise possessed a bourse that was both a commodity exchange and a stock market. Marine insurance was also available in the Netherlands, at better rates and from more reliable underwriters than anywhere else. The Dutch had rationalized business methods beyond anything developed outside of the now decayed Italian city states.

The vigor of the expanding Dutch economy was also evident in the export of capital, business expertise, and engineering skills. Dutch engineers were employed to drain marshes all over Europe, in Poland, Tuscany, Rome, France, Germany and England. Only Spain escaped the Dutchman's improving hand. Holland also played the dominant role in developing the economies of the Baltic kingdoms. Louis de Geer and Elias Trip, Amsterdam merchants, exploited the resources of Sweden, using Dutch capital and technology and business skills. They mined iron and copper, built sawmills, warehouses and retail stores, marketed Swedish products and dominated Swedish public finances after 1618. At the same time, the Marselis and Irgens families were managing a similar empire in Denmark.

The most dramatic example of Dutch economic dominance, however, was the incredible Tulip Mania of 1634 to 1636. Imported from Turkey, tulips slowly became an aristocratic status symbol and increased sharply in value. Naturally, the Dutch controlled trade in this important commodity, and they organized a market to sell rare bulbs. Tulips so captured the aristocratic imagination that their price rose phenomenally, and the rarest specimens were selling for thousands of gold guilden each. In 1636, a single bulb went for

two lasts of wheat
four lasts of rye
four fat oxen
eight fat pigs
twelve fat sheep

two barrels of wine
four barrels of beer
two barrels of butter
1,000 pounds of cheese
one bed
one suit of clothes
one silver drinking cup

The crash came in November 1636, and many lost heavily, especially those caught with bulbs. But the general prosperity continued, and no one was discouraged by the tulip catastrophe from investing in Dutch banks, trade or industry. Not until the sharpening of English competition after 1660 and the French war of 1672 did the Dutch lose their economic preeminence. And even then, there was no absolute decline in trade or banking; rather the English, and later the French, grew so fast that the Dutch were simply left behind.

The Transformation of the European Economy

The seventeenth-century depression marked the boundary between the medieval and modern configurations of European society and economy. Before 1600, the Mediterranean basin was the richest area of Europe, and had been since the end of the High Middle Ages. Wealth had been accompanied by technological superiority and a greater knowledge of science. In the sixteenth century, everyone bought Italian cannon and studied at Italian universities. Southern Europe also possessed the social and political attributes of wealth. Mediterranean society was more urban, more literate, more industrialized and more polished. Governments were better organized, and several states—Venice, Turkey, Aragon, Castile and Portugal—came equipped with empires. By comparison, northern Europeans were crude and their society was backward; sophisticated Renaissance Italians had called them barbarians.

In the late sixteenth century this all began to change. English and Dutch towns grew rapidly while those in Italy and

Spain declined. Scientific and technological knowledge steadily expanded in the North, and Cambridge replaced Padua as the most important university in Europe. Trade routes had shifted from the Mediterranean to the Atlantic, to the great benefit of northern Europeans. English, Dutch, and French manufacturing eclipsed that of the Italians and Spanish, particularly in the basic industries of textiles and metallurgy. Banking and credit institutions flourished in Holland, but no longer in the South. Religious toleration crept into northern Europe, and intellectual freedom accompanied it. Northern governments gradually became more efficient and energetic than those of the Mediterranean basin. By the middle of the seventeenth century, Englishmen were speaking sadly of the past glories of Italy and were condemning the sloth, poverty and backwardness of Spain.

The great depression hit sooner in the Mediterranean basin, hit harder, was much more pervasive and remained far longer. Recovery in the Mediterranean area was not well under way until 1750, and even then remained slow and uneven. In some areas of the economy, such as the American trade, the Mediterranean spice trade, or the Italian woolen industry, the losses were never made up.

In the North the general picture was quite different. There the economic retreat, though genuine and severe, was temporary. The old economy was restored. Losses in trade, industry, population, and agricultural output were made up after 1660. Northern and central Europe were richer and more industralized, and their traditional sources of wealth were on a firmer footing in 1730 than they had been a century earlier. Thus Europe emerged from the depression with an ecomonic map that persisted into the twentieth century—an industrialized and wealthy North and a backward, agricultural and impoverished South.

23
The World Reconsidered: The Development of Modern Science

Men once believed that the seas were full of monsters ready to devour sailors who ventured too far from land. Mermaids would sing to sailors and entice them to their doom. Many thought that the southern seas were boiling and would destroy ships. The land was populated with strange animals, such as unicorns and the basilisk, a winged serpent, whose very glance killed men. The earth itself stood in the center of the universe, and everything on it was composed of four basic elements, air, earth, fire and water. In 1600, many uneducated people still believed that the earth was flat, and almost none could be found to deny that it was God's will that kept the stars in the heavens.

Some of these myths were mere fairy tales, and others were based on logic and learning. Some were believed by common folk, and others were taught in universities, as psychiatry is today. But these differences were only superficial. What mattered were attitudes and habits of thought. For centuries, as soon as Europeans had cast off one myth they substituted another, no less false or fanciful. Before the advent of modern science, with its experimental and mathematical methodology, there was no test for truth about the physical universe other than revelation (which was not chiefly concerned with physical reality) and pure logic. These were as likely to give a coherent wrong answer about nature as a right one. Patient scientific endeavor changed that and, in the process, enabled western man to develop the technology of modernity.

The development of modern science was a distinct although gradual break with the intellectual past; it also divided European civilization from the rest of the world. It changed the way men thought and set them searching for verified facts as the way to solve problems. Philosophy became sharply divided from science. The scientific revolution was one of the transcendent factors of Western Civilization. It outweighs "everything since the rise of Christianity and reduces the Renaissance and Reformation to the rank of mere episodes."*

Precondition of the Scientific Revolution

The astronomer and physicist Galileo Galilei (1564–1642) did not work in isolation. He taught at the University of Padua and later gathered around him a group of assistants and students. At his death they did not all disperse or abandon scientific studies. Two of them, Viviani (1622-1703) and Evangelista Torricelli (1608-1647), remained in Florence and, in 1657, established the *Accademia del Cimento*, the first formal scientific society in Europe. The purpose of the *Accademia* was to stimulate scientific research, publish the results and bring scientists together to discuss their projects. This seemed like such a good idea that the English copied it in 1662 when Charles II granted a charter to the Royal Society. In France, too, an academy was established, developing from informal meetings of scientists and mathematicians and receiving recognition and support from Louis XIV in 1666. Such societies filled the role played in medieval Europe by universities, now in deep decline.

Academies were not the only factor bringing scientists together in the seventeenth century. There was also the coincidence of birth and nationality, which was reflected in centers of research. Scientists gathered in four areas in the seventeenth century, not far from the birthplaces of most of them. These were Holland, where there was no formal academy, southern England, Paris, and northern Italy, particularly the major towns of Florence, Padua and Bologna. Three of these clusters were in northwestern Europe and there was constant and general contact among them. Thus the French mathematician-philoso-

pher René Descartes (1596-1650) worked in Holland, claiming there was more freedom there, while the Dutch physicist Christian Huygens (1629-1695) spent much of his time in Paris.

The Academies and the clusters of scientists illustrated two of the basic social factors responsible for the development of modern science: convergence (groups of scientists who compared their work) and impetus (the building of one scientific discovery on another). These two factors were obviously interrelated; both impetus and convergence were clearly apparent in the functioning of the scientific centers in northern Italy and northwestern Europe. Scientists born outside these general areas traveled toward them. Gottfried Leibnitz (1646-1716) came from Germany to Paris, the anatomist Andreas Vesalius (1514-1564) came from Belgium to Padua, and the astronomer Nicolaus Copernicus (1473-1546) came from Poland to study at Padua, Bologna and Rome. Such personal and professional contact was essential in an age of poor communications, imperfect scientific vocabularies, inexact mathematical notation, widely varying skills in instrumentation and the constant threat of religious persecution. No one, working alone, could break through the ancient and medieval theories of nature. The body of new scientific information only grew with communication—with impetus and convergence.

These factors first occurred at the universities of Oxford and Paris in the fourteenth century. They existed to a degree in fifteenth and sixteenth-century Italy. But with a few exceptions, the humanists and artists of the Renaissance were interested in the beauty and grace of antiquity rather than in scientific experiments. Moreover, by the 1580s Italian science, letters and philosophy were beginning to suffer the conformist pressures of the Counterreformation. Galileo was arrested by the Inquisition in 1633 for having supported Copernicus' views and

* Herbert Butterfield, *The Origins of Modern Science*, p. 7.

J. Goyton, "Louis XIV and Colbert at the Academy of Sciences" engraving frontispiece to Memoires pour servir a l'histoire naturelle des animaux (Paris, 1671).

spent the rest of his life under house arrest. The papacy persuaded the Republic of Venice to censor the University of Padua, and the *Accademia del Cimento* in Florence closed down in 1667 when its Medici patron became a cardinal. With the collapse of the *Accademia*, one of its members, Antonio Oliva, was arrested by the Inquisition and killed himself to escape torture for heresy.

In northwestern Europe conditions were different. The scientific traditions of Oxford and Paris dated back to the Middle Ages. Moreover, the established churches in England and Holland were relatively weak and had too limp a hold on political power or the people's affections to impose scientific, or even theological, orthodoxy. In both states there was a modest toleration; religious persecution, although it existed, was sporadic and ineffectual. Furthermore, technological improvements were more numerous in the North, and the instrumentation for experiments was correspondingly better. Finally, governments were, at least marginally interested in science be-

cause it was good for business. Improvements in draining technique and navigation were essential to Dutch prosperity, and the government gave some encouragement to men with technical and scientific expertise. In northern Europe, convergence and impetus tended to mean an increase in the number of scientists and technicians, a greater range of subjects studied, an increase in the number of books published and a general expansion in the amount of scientific knowledge. And, at least in England, these factors contributed ultimately to the coming of industrialization.

Ancient and Medieval Cosmology

During the Renaissance, western man thought of his world in much the same way that his ancestors had for centuries. Christian philosophies of nature, built on Greek and Roman foundations, were generally accepted as true. The traditional natural concepts and ideas were logical, coherent, reasonable and in accord with what could be seen and verified by observation. They had the additional merit of being relatively consistent with most of the mathematics inherited from antiquity. Finally, they seemed to glorify God and His handiwork. There seemed no reason to abandon them.

The most elaborate of the inherited concepts of nature involved the heavens. Celestial bodies appeared to be revolving around the earth, and what was observed was incorporated into an elaborate theory of astronomy. The earth itself stood still at the center of the universe and was infinitely heavy and solid. Everything else moved in allotted curved paths through the sky around the earth. This earth-centered (geocentric) theory had been inherited from Claudius Ptolemy, a Greek scientist of the second century A.D., who had synthesized the work of several of his predecessors. Ptolemy's work had survived into the Middle Ages through Islamic intermediaries, and was absorbed by Christian scholars of the twelfth and thirteenth centuries. It accounted for most of the phenomena that could be observed with the unaided eye and had a satisfactory, indeed, excellent level of predictability. What deviations there were could be corrected by minor adjustments to the system. By and large, geocentric astronomy worked well.

Allied to Ptolemaic astronomy was a system of physics that had been developed by Aristotle. It, too, was reasonable, coherent and explained the observed data. Aristotelian philosophers argued that no object moved without a mover; when the mover ceased his pressure, the object returned to its natural state—rest. Certainly, an apple on a table did not move on its own. Neither did the earth, which was so large, so solid, and so heavy that nothing could move it. The Prime Mover, who had set the heavens in motion, had given things the impulse to move toward the center of the universe which, of course, was the earth. Heavy things, like iron, naturally fell faster than light things, such as feathers, as anyone could see. It all seemed to make sense.

Although subsequently proved wrong, these notions were far from unscientific. They rested firmly on observed reality and were supported by a rigorous system of logical analysis. Symbols or myth, the bulwarks of medieval and Renaissance art and sculpture, were absent from Aristotelian or Ptolemaic science, which were based on natural rather than supernatural phenomena. Much of this exactness derived from medieval scientists, such as Jean Buridan, Roger Bacon, Nicolas D'Oresme and Robert Grosseteste, who based their philosophy on the careful observation of nature. To this must be added the intellectual precision of medieval theologians, particularly the Scholastics. Thus the scientific revolution did not occur out of nothing but grew logically and directly from the traditions and habits of medieval thought.

None of the medieval scientific notions survived the assault made on them in the seventeenth century by higher mathema-tics, disciplined investigation, numerous experiments, new scientific instruments and the insights of genius. As the traditional axioms were discarded, they became not merely false but ridiculous. No educated man could believe in them, and many wondered how their ancestors, so wise in other things, could have been taken in by such transparent nonsense. But Ptolemaic astronomy and Aristotelian physics were not transparent and, for a society with a primitive technology and modest mathematics, they were not nonsense. The sun seemed to circle the earth, not just once a year but every day. Common sense and long experience combined to assure everyone that nothing moved without a mover; when the oxen stopped pulling the plow, the plow stopped also. Ancient and medieval scientific notions about the natural world may have been wrong, but they conformed to experience and observation to an exceptional degree, and they still do.

In the late Middle Ages, however, the validity of ancient and medieval science began to be questioned. New investigation showed areas where ancient masters such as Aristotle and Ptolemy had not achieved the last word. The erosion of old scientific doctrines was fairly slow in the centuries after 1300; even after 1500 it was hampered by the tumult of the Reformation, the opposition of both Catholic and Protestant churches, the lack of a widely accepted scientific method, and insufficient mathematics. But the old science, in spite of its prestige and orthodoxy, was slowly being transformed.

Copernicus

The first fundamental advance from inherited scientific doctrine occurred with the publication of *The Revolution of Heavenly Bodies* (1543) by Nicolas Copernicus, a cathedral canon who was trained not only in science and mathematics but in medicine and canon law as well. He even dabbled in painting. A devoted churchman, Copernicus dedicated his work to Pope Paul III but did not publish it until on his death-bed, fearing the ridicule and hostility that must come from espousing a radically new doctrine in a time of religious troubles. Despite his delay in announcing his views, Copernicus had held them for a long time. In 1500 he had been teaching mathematics in Rome, and had come into contact with the theory of the ancient Hellenistic scientist, Aristarchus of Samos, who held that the earth rotated on its axis and revolved about the sun. Aristarchus' theory lacked the precise and detailed formulation of Ptolemaic astronomy, and it had not won wide acceptance in antiquity. But it intrigued Copernicus. Using his mathematical knowledge, he uncovered a number of errors and inconsistencies in the Ptolemaic theory, and he swung to Aristarchus' heliocentric notion despite all appearances to the contrary. Most important, he expanded Aristarchus idea into an exact, systematic theory—a geometrical model that accounted for the observed motions of the sun and planets just as precisely as Ptolemy's system did, and much more simply.

Copernicus did not free himself completely from past preconceptions. He did not make the astronomical observations necessary to confirm his heliocentric theory. Instead, he argued from mathematics, logic and old observations, just as Ptolemy himself had done. Furthermore, Copernicus argued that the earth moved in a circular orbit around the sun, because the circle was the most perfect geometric form and anything less would be contrary to the perfection of the divine order. He was much influenced by the Neoplatonic preference for the sun at the center of things; and his theory was open to grave objection on this and other grounds. It was rejected by philosophers, most scientists, and men of religion from the pope to Martin Luther.

Nonetheless, Copernicus had made a serious dent in Ptolemaic astronomy, which was now shown to need constant, numerous and significant readjustments. Other mathematicians and philosophers examined these discrepancies, but without new observations and data no one could prove the truth of either theory. As the experiments were made, however, they went beyond merely providing additional data to solve a cosmological argument. Experimentation widened the scope of discussion immensely, offering the distressing possibility that both theories might be wrong. Much more, the experiments in astronomy initiated a change in the methodology of science. Logic and reason, the tools that medieval scientist-philosophers had used to comprehend the physical universe, were proving inadequate; for theories both logical and reasonable were shown to be untrue. Logic was seen to require the guidance of experimentation, of precise and continuous measurement and observation. After Copernicus, astronomy became heavily experimental, as scientists concentrated on accumulating reams of data and making computations from them. Copernicus had been a mathematician-philosopher who had happened to be more or less right. But his mathematics and logical deductions might as easily have led to the opposite conclusion, as for most men they did. The method of experimental verification moved the heliocentric issue from the arena as philosophical debate into the observatory.

Tycho Brahe and Johan Kepler

The accumulation of data began with the work of the Danish astronomer-astrologer Tycho Brahe (1546-1601), who designed and constructed the most advanced astronomical instruments of his time. With these instruments (which did not yet include the telescope), he was able to pinpoint the locations of planets and chart their motions against the background of the stars. Brahe made mountains of measurements, and they tended to discredit both the Copernican and Ptolemaic views. Brahe advanced

Anonymous engraving of "The Octagon Room in the Royal Observatory in Greenwich". (Science Museum, London)

a theory of his own, a compromise between the two systems, in which the planets moved around the sun, while the sun itself circled the earth.

If Brahe's theory fell through at the first push, his measurements were invaluable. His sometime assistant, Johan Kepler (1571-1630) showed what could be done with them, using the new mathematics of logarithms recently perfected by John Napier. Kepler worked for years over Brahe's data, to which he added his own. He calculated the orbit of Mars according to the systems of Ptolemy, Copernicus, and Brahe, and the descrepancies between the results led him to formulate two laws: (1) planets do not move in circular orbits but in elipses, with the sun in one focus; (2) planets do not move at uniform speed, but at varying speeds, so that a line joining the planet's center to the sun would sweep out an equal area in an equal time. Thus Kepler had broken the "spell of circu-

larity" and had smashed the myth of a simple harmony in the cosmos, without discarding the idea that the complex harmonies of the universe could yet be reduced to simple laws. His two laws were published in 1609. A decade later he published a third and much more technical law: that the times needed by the planets to complete their orbits were proportional, when squared, to their cubed distance from the sun. This was difficult to understand, and it still is. It is a benchmark in the journey of science from something that could be comprehended by all educated men to a group of disciplines that only specialists can grasp, and then only in part.

Kepler himself was as much a mystic as a scientist. His discoveries arose ultimately from his search for the underlying harmonies that lay behind physical reality and from his desire to express those harmonies in numerical relations. These relations represented, for him, the true nature of things. Thus Kepler's inquiries were metaphysical in scope rather than strictly scientific. His discoveries appear alongside and are imbedded in discussions on the nature of the Trinity and the Source of Celestial Harmony. Kepler believed, along with the Neoplatonic philosophers and artists, that archetypal ideas existed in God's mind from eternity, and that God reproduced these ideas both in the universe and in the human mind. Kepler's search for observable laws in nature was a search for just such a portion of God's mind as He wished to reveal to man; the visible universe was a sign of a greater, intangible Reality. In the minds of Copernicus and Kepler alike, science was not yet the secular and functional business that we imagine it is today.

While Kepler was struggling toward his three laws of planetary motion. Galileo Galilei was also observing the heavens. And, unlike Kepler, Galileo used a telescope. The first telescope had been built just recently by a Dutch lensmaker; Galileo built one of his own and, turning it on the planet Jupiter, he discovered four of its moons. Turning it elsewhere he saw individual stars in the Milky Way and discovered the rings of Saturn and the phases of Venus. Seeing the planet Venus as a crescent convinced him of the Copernican theory, and he said so. He presented his views in an explosive book, *Dialogue on the Two Principal Systems of the Universe* (1632), which discredited the Ptolemaic theory and outraged the seventeenth-century Italian Establishment. The Inquisition had stated in 1616 that "the view that the Earth is not in the center of the universe . . . is philosophically false." Galileo was brought to trial and forced to recant. He also had to give up astronomy.

Newton's Law of Gravitation

Galileo and Kepler had destroyed the Ptolemaic theory and had proved the validity of the Copernican system—with

its Keplerian amendment. But the basic laws that governed the universe still eluded precise and mathematical definition, in spite of the vast amount of data that had been acquired. Sir Isaac Newton (1642-1727) fitted it all together. In 1687 he published (in Latin) his *Principia Mathematica*, after considerable prodding from his colleagues. Newton stated that gravity varied according to distance and to mass, which was the amount of matter an object contained. The amount of gravitational force exerted between two bodies was directly proportional to the product of their masses, and was inversely proportional to the square of the distance between their centers. Newton also described inertia, the force that kept bodies moving continuously on the same line. Thus the solar system was the balance between inertia and gravity and, by extension, this principle applied to star systems as well.

Newton's work not only contained new and startling scientific insights, which completed the work of Kepler and Galileo; it also presented laws of such grandeur and general validity that his synthesis passed into philosophy. In simple and general terms, although not in technical detail, the heavens were comprehensible again, Philosophers came to compare the stars and planets to a giant and stable clock, running in absolute and placid obedience to Newton's laws. God was no longer needed, at least, He was no longer continually on call. He was viewed as the primeval engineer who had put the system together in the beginning and had given it motion. Now he was retired. Newton himself would have disagreed sharply; for like Copernicus and Kepler, Newton was a deeply religious man. He spent more time on biblical chronology than on science.

The Revolution in Physics

During the seventeenth century, work in the physical sciences included more than astronomy. There were numerous experiments in light, mechanics, heat, sound, magnetism and gases and liquids, far more, indeed, than in astronomy itself. The progress made in physics was even more significant than in astronomy, but physics and mechanics attracted far less attention. There were several reasons for this. Aristotelian physics had never become a basic part of religious speculation and, hence, the new physicists did not attract the interest of the Inquisition. Nor had medieval physics been very complete; most of the experiments and theories of seventeenth-century scientists dealt with phenomena previously unknown or unexplained. Medieval philosophers had themselves disagreed sharply about various components of Aristotle's work, and various alternative theories were already in the public domain. Finally, the work of physicists rapidly became heavily technical and very hard to understand, so few could follow or cared to debate the implication of the new, experimentally verified theories.

As important as the insights of scientists was the development of adequate instruments, without which there could be no experiments. So closely were theory and instrumentation connected that the experiment frequently revolved around the equipment, and success in one meant success in both. Nowhere was this relationship sharper than in experiments with air pressure and vacuums, which destroyed the old axiom that nature abhorred a vacuum. A German nobleman, Otto von Guericke (1602–1686), conceived the experiment but could not perform it until he had built a vacuum pump and two perfectly round metal hemispheres. Having constructed his equipment, von Guericke performed a spectacular experiment before the Imperial Diet at Ratisbon in 1654. He bolted the copper hemispheres together, pumped much of the air out, then unbolted them and hitched a team of horses to each hemisphere. The horses did their best, stimulated by the whip, but they could not pull the hemispheres apart, proving the im-

mense power of air pressure and the fact that air has weight and volume. The same relationship between instruments and experiments could be seen elsewhere, with astronomy and the telescope, with the clock and studies of motion.

Galileo was the real founder of modern physics, and his achievements in that field were even more substantial than in astronomy. He was interested in several things: the motion of a pendulum, laws concerning falling bodies, the paths of projectiles, theories about sound, and the weight of air. Galileo's work was both mathematical and experimental, although the most famous experiment of all, dropping unequal weights from the Leaning Tower of Pisa to see them hit the ground together, never took place. Experiments to discover the laws of falling bodies were performed on an inclined plane, not from a leaning tower. After considerable effort, part of which was devoted to using a pendulum to measure elapsed time, Galileo discovered that objects fell at a uniform, accelerating velocity, which he expressed mathematically. From this, Galileo calculated the arc of a projectile, such as a cannon ball, to be a parabola. This research became the basis of the science of dynamics. He presented most of it in his last book, *Dialogue on Two New Sciences*, published in Holland in 1638 after his ordeal with the Inquisition, and after he had become blind.

Scientists throughout the century kept busy following Galileo's leads. His assistant, Evangelista Torricelli, invented the barometer and provided irresistible proof of Galileo's contention that air had mass and weight. The English physicist Robert Boyle (1627-1691) elaborated on the experiments of Torricelli and formulated Boyle's law, which stated that air can be compressed by pressure, and when the pressure is removed, it returns to its former dimensions. Boyle also conducted experiments that supported and improved on Galileo's theories about sound. And the Dutch scientist Christian Huygens followed Galileo's theories about pendulums and invented a pendulum clock—by far the most accurate timepiece in Europe.

The area in which scientists went farthest beyond Galileo was optics. Although Galileo had worked with both microscopes and telescopes, he had not really investigated the properties of light, other than to try to determine its velocity—which was far too great for him to measure. Kepler was concerned with light and arrived at a basic law of photometry: that light intensity varies as the square of the distance from the source. He found this formula in a truly inspiring manner. He more or less guessed it, for his experimental proof was primitive and inadequate. Nonetheless, he was right.

Kepler's work, both its success and its limitations, led directly to the optical research of Sir Issac Newton. Newton became interested in optics because of the chromatic aberration (color distortion) around the edges of the lens of his refracing telescope. Newton experimented with prisms, and arrived at some enlightening results. Isolating the various colors produced by the prism, he found that they emerged at different angles and thus discovered that the laws of refraction applied to each color separately. White light was made up of all the various colors of the spectrum, and the colors of things resulted from various colors being refracted in different degrees. Newton published these experiments and conclusions from time to time, and included them all in *Opticks* (1704). He also gave up trying to correct the lenses of refracting telescopes and built a reflecting telescope instead.

In spite of vast and astounding progress, during this period, physics and mechanics produced a few general laws that brought a sense of order to man's view of his world. The feats of astronomy were not duplicated. Terrestrial mechanics never assumed the guise of certainty that caressed astronomers. No one thought of this world as a giant clock. Moreover,

physics had become so technical, so dependent on precise instrumentation and higher mathematics, so contrary to common sense, that most people never thought of it at all, but consigned it to the experts. In the seventeenth and eighteenth centuries there were few popular handbooks on physics like Voltaire's little work, popularizing Newton's astronomy: *Newtonianism for the Ladies*.

Advances in Mathematics

The stupendous progress in astronomy and physics rested on equally large changes in mathematics, which made it possible to explain and to compute motion, mass and gravity. In 1400, Europeans were still assimilating algebra and geometry inherited from the Greeks and Arabs. This was relatively simple mathematics, and its notation was primitive and variable. In spite of this, however, mathematics was the most advanced science Renaissance Europeans knew, and the most highly esteemed.

Mathematics was a traditional discipline, of course, taught in medieval universities and occasionally incorporated into theological speculations, although not into doctrine. Under these conditions, progress in mathematics followed traditional lines. Algebra, geometry and notation were the first areas of improvement. The initial leap was the invention of logarithms by John Napier (1550-1617), a Scottish nobleman. Napier's two books included his tables of logarithms and rules for their use. Logarithms made the extraction of roots a simple matter of division and enabled Kepler to calculate his three laws of planetary motion. So useful were Napier's logarithms that mathematicians began compiling logarithm tables for ever larger numbers; a Dutch book of 1628 covered all numbers up to 100,000, enough to take care of most ordinary needs.

Although work in geometry had been continuous since the Renaissance, the French philosopher-mathematician René

Descartes made some serious and original contributions. In his book, *Geometry* (1637), Descartes presented, in a rather sketchy fashion, the principles of analytical geometry. This was reinforced by a more complete exposition of analytical geometry by Pierre Fermat (1601-1665), a leader in the Paris group of scientists that evolved into the French Academy of Sciences. At the same time Blaise Pascal (1623-1662), a young French prodigy in mathematics and theology, produced a book on conic geometry at the age of sixteen. Pascal corresponded with Fermat on the problem, and produced some tentative theories. His work fulfilled a widely felt social need.

The most complicated mathematics of the period was the work of Isaac Newton and Gottfried Leibnitz. This was the elaboration of the principles of integral and differential calculus, complicated and difficult stuff as every student knows. Newton believed that mathematical quantities resulted from motion, thus: "lines are described . . . by the continued motion of points." This added a new dimension to geometry. Always reluctant to publish, Newton held his work back, and some of it was not printed until his death. Thus Leibnitz, working in the same direction, came up with similar theories, somewhat after Newton but before Newton's work was known. Although basically the same, Leibnitz' papers contained a clear, precise, and superior notation, which has since been retained.

These new discoveries in mathematics were far beyond the capacity of most people to understand, and they surpassed the capacities of many philosophers as well. In medieval Europe, mathematics had been the ally of philosophy and the guide to logic. Now, it was becoming part of science. This change in the use of mathematics did much to increase the separation of science from philosophy in western culture. Recently logicians have attempted to revive the medieval alliance between mathematics and philosophy but thus far they have won few converts.

Medicine

Controversies about the heavens had far less impact on the daily life of most Europeans than more homely discoveries in biology and medicine. These raised almost no fuss at all but were important just the same. Official medicine during the Renaissance was no worse—perhaps better—than the medicine of previous eras and of other cultures. But by modern standards it was atrocious; and worse yet were the ministrations of witches and other non-Euclidean quacks, with their remedies of bat wings and pulverized lice. In 1550, faith healing was still the high road to recovery. The discoveries of anatomists, surgeons and biologists began to change this situation, providing the basis for medical cures and vastly increasing man's knowledge of life around and within him.

Eighteenth-century Londoners sang a ditty about one of their most famous physicians, a certain John Lettsom. It was not encouraging.

When any sick to me apply
I physicks, bleeds and sweats 'em
If, after that, they choose to die,
Why, verily, I Lettsom.

In spite of the pessimism that permeates such passages, and such practices as fire-axe amputation, medicine had made considerable progress by the eighteenth century. Gains in medical practice occurred primarily in three areas—in improved instruments and treatment, in new medications, and in the increasingly detailed study of particular diseases. But these changes did not come easy. As a rule, both doctors and patients were against them.

Improved medical instruments changed diagnosis radically, introducing quantitative data into the tricky business of deciding what ailed the patient. The thermometer was a good example. Probably invented by Galileo, it was first used extensively in clinical practice by his friend, Sanctorius Sanctorius (1561–1636). Previously, a doctor could only tell for sure if a patient had a fever when he approached delirium. It was the same with the pulse. Prior to the pulsimeter, again introduced by Sanctorius, doctors had no idea what a normal pulse was, and were reduced to saying that a patient with no pulse at all was quite sick. These two instruments alone added immensely to the exact statements that could be made about various diseases.

Doctors also improved their treatment, which they badly needed to do. The great French surgeon Ambroise Paré (1510–1590) commented that the "operations of Chirurgery are learn't by the eye and by the touch," and his years as a military surgeon demonstrated the wisdom of that view. In his first campaign in Italy in 1537, Paré immensely improved the method for treating gunshot wounds. It was customary to pour boiling oil in the wounds, but Paré, running out of oil, used a poultice instead. The following morning Paré's patients were recovering and were not feverish, while many of the others were in great pain with infected wounds. Paré also began treating burns with soda and salt, and invented the tourniquet for use during amputation. Perhaps Paré's greatest insight, which he shared with the English physician Thomas Sydenham (1624-1689), was that many of the old medications and treatments were harmful to the patient and ought to be abandoned. The doctor would do well if he did not damage his patient more than the disease did, and most people would get well faster if doctors did less for them. They followed the maxim of the ancient Greek physician, Hippocrates: "Do no harm." Both Paré and Sydenham frequently prescribed rest and a good diet, and both were regarded as the greatest physicians of their age.

Doctors also improved their ability to recognize varieties of disease, clearly an important matter. Effective medicine rests "upon getting as genuine and natural a description, or history, of all diseases as can be procured," wrote Thomas Sydenham, stating a view widely held by everyone. Beginning with a poem on syphilis in 1530 by Girolamo Fracastoro (1478-1553), there appeared a steady stream of books on particular illnesses. Some were excellent, most were less than that, but they all had the merit of being based on observation of the facts—more or less. Gradually, physicians came to distinguish between diseases, even ones they could not cure.

Although medical knowledge grew enormously in the century and a half following Luther, it remained disorganized, scattered in hundreds of separate books and pamphlets in various languages written over 15 decades. Much of the new knowledge was not taught in the medical schools. More important still, there was no theoretical base for medicine. Sydenham flirted with the germ theory of disease, but he was far from specific and no one followed the hint. Nor was there much attempt to explain mental illness except by resorting to the pernicious intervention of devils. Medicine remained an almost completely empirical profession, and treatment involved mainly trial and error, particularly error.

A final barrier to improving medical knowledge and care was the easy way people entered the profession. Medical schools were not much good, but they gave better training than that received by a barber's apprentice, who practiced a crude therapy indeed. The sixteenth-century charter of the Royal College of Physicians stated that "a great multitude of ignorant persons . . . as smiths, weavers, and women boldly and accustomably took upon them great cures, to the high displeasure of God . . . and the grievous hurt, damage and destruction of many of the King's leige people." During the eighteenth century they still did. But the damage was not quite so great, and the slow increase in biological knowledge meant that medicine would get better yet.

The study of biology in the years after 1550 lay primarily in three areas: anatomy and physiology, the description and classification of plants and animals (taxonomy), and investigations with the microscope. The progress in anatomy was particularly dramatic and involved a sharp break with inherited doctrine. During the Renaissance, Europeans still accepted the notions found in the writings of the ancient Greek physician, Galen—the biologists' Aristotle. Galen taught that the four elements—heat, cold, wetness and dryness (fire, air, water, earth)—found their counterpart in the body, in the form of humours: blood, phlegm, and black and yellow bile. Health was the proper balance of these substances, illness the opposite. Blood was thought to be formed in the liver, and various parts of the body produced incorporeal "vital spirits," also necessary to health. This elaborate and quite reasonable theory was sharply attacked in the sixteenth century. Andreas Vesalius, a professor at the medical school at Padua, published a monumental study, *On the Structure of the Human Body* in 1543—the very year that Copernicus' *Revolution of Heavenly Bodies* was published. Hence, revolution in anatomy began the same year as the one in astronomy. Vesalius took his doctrine from nature, from numerous and careful dissections, and his book contained elaborate and accurate plates. Vesalius' work was a masterpiece, and also a revolution.

Vesalius' method of study by dissections continued at Padua after his death. The English physician William Harvey (1578-1657) studied at Padua, absorbed the methods used there, and described the circulation of the blood in his great treatise, *On the Movement of the Heart and the Blood.* Harvey showed that arteries carried blood from the heart to the rest of the body, and veins carried it back. He did not

understand the capillary system, which was only described in 1660 by Marcello Malpighi (1628-1694). Nonetheless, Harvey's work superseded the physiology of Galen, and opened new avenues of medical treatment.

Botany and Zoology

Along with their increasing knowledge of the human body, scientists deepened their understanding of plants and animals. Botany grew out of the aristocratic practice of maintaining gardens of rare and useful plants, more as a status symbol than anything else. The curators of these gardens wished to classify their plants and, finding no satisfactory system at hand, made up their own. These early botanists, Clusius (1525-1609), Lobelius (1538-1616), and Kasper Bauhin (1560-1624) made many mistakes in their classifications, but they worked directly from the plants, and were right more often than they were wrong. Zoology, however, was not so far advanced, since it lacked aristocratic patronage and depended solely on scientific curiosity. Nonetheless, some work was done. The English biologist John Ray (1628–1705), who wrote a book on plants, published a classification of animals as well, dividing them into species and families and recognizing that fossils were the remains of extinct forms.

Botany and zoology involved large species, which everyone could see, whether or not he knew what they were. The microscope opened a new world that no one had known about before. Crude microscopes existed around 1610, and both Galileo and Harvey used them, although sparingly. The first extensive microscopic investigations were made by Marcello Malpighi and Jan Swammerdam (1637-1682). Malpighi examined silkworms and chicken embryos, and first explained how lungs worked. Swammerdam's research with microorganisms led him to reject the hallowed and ancient notion of spontaneous generation.

The premier microscope investigator of his age was the Dutch civil servant Anton van Leeuwenhoek (1632-1723), who was entirely self-taught and who constructed his instruments himself. He looked through the microscope because he enjoyed it, and his research was vast and disorganized. As a result of immense, random viewing, Leeuwenhoek discovered both bacteria and protozoa and could tell them apart. He did not attempt to fit his diverse observations into any coherent theory. Leeuwenhoek was no philosopher and, basically, he did not care how his discoveries affected current doctrine. He left that to others.

By the early years of the eighteenth century, Europeans probably knew as much biology as astronomy, mathematics or physics. But the biological knowledge was not organized into any theoretical framework, and scientists were unaware of the implications of what they did know. Not until Linneaus was there any attempt to integrate Leeuwenhoek's discoveries into a consistent theory of taxonomy. Little effort was made to incorporate biological knowledge into public sanitation or medicine. Indeed, scientists were sometimes hostile to the implication of their own work. John Ray's insights on fossils and extinct species were incompatible with both biblical and popular notions about the Creation and the age of the world. For biology, the struggle between science and orthodoxy was just beginning.

The Divorce of Science from Philosophy and Religion

"We were entirely mistaken . . .," wrote Blaise Pascal in 1656 in his *Provincial Letters*. "It was only yesterday that I was undeceived. Until that time I had labored under the impression that the disputes in the Sorbonne were vastly important, and deeply affected the interests of religion." Pascal intended to ridicule his Jesuit opponents and, in a light and agreeable manner, make a serious case for his own religious doctrine. The great mathematician and philosopher believed that the interests of religion were peculiary important, the central question for all mankind. Once, everyone had thought that. Now, religion was losing its overriding importance in the minds of many Europeans. The insights of science were replacing those of revelation, and Pascal's mathematics seemed to some of his contemporaries more important than his theology. The new science was not, of course, incompatible with a religious view of life, but it was fatal to theological speculations that attempted to explain the functioning of the natural world in supernatural terms.

Although the great doctrinal struggles were ending, religious systems and religious speculation continued. Knowledge of the natural world was still imperfectly separated from belief and faith, and all learning, of whatever origin, was regarded as a unity, a whole. Men still aspired to combine all knowledge into a single, coherent system of thought. The division of learning into science and humanities had only begun. It is one of the supreme tragedies of European intellectual history that this unity of thought did not survive the extraordinary expansion of science after 1600. Knowledge was increasingly divided into compartments, each with different methods of inquiry, separate areas of study, and large and complicated bodies of data. There was simply too much to know, and people who knew different things drifted apart into different fields of study. Questions that scientists asked had become separated from those about which philosophers might speculate.

The most serious problem faced by theologians and philosophers was the collapse of credibility in large speculative systems. Traditionally charged with explaining everything in a precise and logical manner consistent with revelation, theologians had advanced theories now and again since antiquity. But in the seventeenth century their most fundamental questions—the purpose of human life, man's relationship to God—were beginning to be regarded as unanswerable, and some of the best minds had turned to the problems of science: narrower problems than those of the theologian, yet more susceptible to rational and experimental verification. With the growth of science, moreover, speculative thinkers of all sorts suffered a substantial loss of intellectual territory. The advance of experimental science completed the work of the fourteenth-century nominalist William of Ockham and his school—severing the natural world from the world of methaphysics.

People still asked questions that science would never be able to answer—questions about the meaning and purpose of the world. But some philosophers were now rejecting such questions out of hand, turning from the realm of purpose and meaning to the natural realm of cause and effect, experiment and observation. Francis Bacon (1561–1626), Lord Chancellor of England until he was convicted of taking a bribe, harbored a monumental and unreasonable contempt for theology. Bacon stated that ". . . this kind of degenerate learning did chiefly reign amoung the Scholastics, who, having . . . small variety of reading . . . and knowing little history, either of nature or time, did, out of no great quantity of matter . . . spin out unto us these laborous webs of learning . . ." (*Advancement of Learning*, Book I). Traditional theories about the universe, so Bacon believed, were worthless; and no new theory ought to be accepted unless it corresponded rigorously to empirically and experimentally verified data. Observation and experiment, that was what was needed but, instead, philosophers just chopped logic. Their grand speculations might be stitched together with meticulous precision, but they were not grounded in experiment and never could be. Therefore, they were based on false premises.

Bacon's theories had serious drawbacks when examined in detail. His idea of inductive, scientific reasoning was awkward and clumsy and, in his antagonism to theory, he equated any attempt at synthesis with nonsense. Bacon's own scientific speculations were undistinguished, they resembled the philosophy he detested far more than the experiment he admired. But his notions took root and were the basis for the foundation of the Royal Society in 1662.

Bacon's insistence that philosophy should be based on experiment was matched by René Descartes' demand that it follow mathematics. Brought up in a humanist tradition, Descartes suffered an adult conversion to mathematics, much as Luther had embraced justification by faith. Descartes came suddenly to believe that the universe could be expressed in mathematical, symbolic terms, and he set out to do it. The methods of mathematicians were the best because they were the most exact and began with the simplest notions and axioms, proceeding only then to the more complex. Thus Descartes did the same thing. He reduced everything to one single statement, which he took to be unqualifiedly true: "I think; therefore I am." From this small start, Descartes built an entire vision of the universe by rigorous application of deductive logic based on mathematical models. His universe was sharply divided into two halves: a spiritual world that included God and the minds and spirits of men; and a mechanical world that included the bodies of men and the world of matter. Thus the cosmos of Descartes involved a sharp, irreconcilable division between mind and body; and philosophers of subsequent generations set themselves to the task of joining mind and body together again.

The Cartesian system, because of its mathematical rigor and simplicity, proved to be incompatible with observed reality about both man and experimental science. Descartes' deductive method of logical analysis excluded exceptions and complexity, and that assumption of radical simplicity was its downfall. The "fabric of nature" simply did not conform to the precise and total simplicity Descartes had imagined. His notions were attacked by philosophers and theologians, but their most evident failure was in the school of experiment.

A third philosopher whose work was greatly influenced by scientific methods and discoveries was the English physician John Locke (1632–1704) who spent most of his life in politics. These absorbing pursuits did not obliterate his interest in philosophy: in his *Essay Concerning Human Understanding* (1690) Locke denied the existence of innate ideas, those inborn in the mind. Instead, man obtained all he knew from sense perceptions. Thoughts, ideas, impressions, reflections, all began with seeing, hearing, touching, and so on —with physical and intelletcual contact with the environment. Experience was the book of knowledge. The mind then organized experience into general patterns and theories, and reflected on and refined them as new experiences and new knowledge indicated. Locke's views thus reflected the empirical and experimental traditions of Bacon, rather than the tight, simplistic logic of Descartes. Indeed, Locke depended only marginally on logic. Instead, he undertook the first serious attempt to explain how we know what we know in terms of exclusively natural and material phenomena, in terms of what was observed to occur.

In Newton's time, the sharp boundary that we now draw between philosophy and science did not yet exist. Men worked in both fields and were not embarrassed to use different methods in different areas of thought. Thus Pascal was both a mystic and a mathematician and was best known for his religious thought. The mathematician Leibnitz believed in something called monads, with God as the Great Monad, and worked all his life to find a formula to reconcile Catholics and Protestants. Descartes was both a Catholic and a Platonist and believed in the reality of ideals; the physicist Robert Boyle tried to find a place for God in the science he knew; while Johann Kepler was an astrologer and a number mystic. These pursuits were not viewed as personal aberrations—as lapses from scientific rigor. On the contrary, they were highly respectable and were well received. A man of learning was traditionally expected to have general interests, and to be well versed in philosophy and theology. Seventeenth-century scientists were too close to this tradition to be exempt from it, or to ignore it themselves. Few were willing to accept the consequences of their work: that science and philosophy increasingly occupied separate domains and dealt with separate topics. Perhaps some of them glimpsed the danger involved in divorcing science from the humanities—a danger that today has become a tragic reality.

The Growth of Knowledge and the Decline of Understanding

In 1733, Voltaire wrote a small book, *Letters Concerning the English Nation*, and included seven chapters on science, so justly celebrated in the nation of Newton. He exaggerated in one of them to say that "nobody before Chancellor Bacon had understood experimental philosophy," a statement not completely true, but not so far off that in Bacon's time experiment was either common or frequent. Writing in a later chapter, Voltaire commented that "hardly any read Newton . . . for it takes considerable knowledge to understand him."

In this offhand way, Voltaire, who did not miss much, illuminated two of the basic facts about science, both in his own time and in ours. Since Brahe and Vesalius, science had become increasingly experimental, and also overwhelmingly technical. Enthroning experiment as the fundamental method of testing hypotheses and guesses is the very nature of science. Logical consistency was not discarded, of course, but it was no longer the ultimate test of truth. That depended on the facts, which scientists arranged into a growing body of knowledge that became increasingly difficult to understand. Once every educated man had known the rudiments of scientific knowledge, and some of the fine points as well. But the discoveries and insights of the seventeenth century put an end to that. By 1700, some of the bare scientific laws might be generally comprehensible, but the data and computations that supported them were not.

Thus, as scientific experiments became more numerous and sophisticated, there occurred a strange paradox. The natural world became more ordered and comprehensible—at least, it appeared to be governed by predictable natural laws that could be understood, rather than by divine mystery that could not. But very few could understand the laws, and the premises of theory were denied in fact. Western man knew more, yet was less able to explain what he knew. The dedicated efforts of scientists have meant that we all have much more accurate ideas about the nature of things, but we understand very little of it. Perhaps this is true for the scientists themselves. I have always thought so.

Selected Readings

Joel Hurstfield, ed., *The Reformation Crisis* (New York: Harper, 1965).

Richard S. Dunn, *The Age of Religious Wars: 1559–1689* (New York: Norton, 1970).

J. H. Elliott, *Europe Divided: 1559–1598* (New York: Harper, 1968).

Sir John Neale, *The Age of Catherine de Medici* (New York: Harper, 1962).

Charles Wilson, *The Dutch Republic* (New York: McGraw-Hill, 1968).

Pieter Geyl, *The Revolt of the Netherlands: 1555–1609*, (London: Benn and Barnes and Noble, 1966).

C. V. Wedgwood, *Richelieu and the French Monarchy*, (New York: Collier, 1962).

C. V. Wedgwood, *The Thirty Years War* (London: Penguin, 1957).

Garrett Mattingly, *The Armada* (New York: Houghton-Mifflin, 1959).

C. M. Andrews, *The Colonial Period in American History*, 4 vols. (New Haven: Yale University Press, 1966).

Charles Gibson, *Spain in America* (New York: Harper, 1968).

J. H. Parry, *The Establishment of the European Hegemony* (New York: Harper, 1966).

George Masselman, *The Cradle of Colonialism* (New Haven: Yale University Press, 1963).

Trevor Aston, ed., *Crisis in Europe: 1560–1600* (Garden City: Doubleday, 1967).

Violet Barbour, *Capitalism in Amsterdam*, (Ann Arbor: University of Michigan Press 1966).

J. H. Elliott, *The Revolt of the Catalans* (Cambridge: Cambridge University Press, 1963).

A. R. Hall, *The Scientific Revolution: 1500–1800* (Boston: Beacon, 1954).

T. R. Pledge, *Science Since 1500* (New York: Harper, 1959).

A. Wolf, *A History of Science, Technology and Philosophy in the Sixteenth and Seventeenth Centuries*, 2 vols. (New York: Harper, 1959).

J. Bronowski and B. Mazlish, *The Western Intellectual Tradition from Leonardo to Hegel* (New York: Harper, 1962).

Part 8
Enlightenment, Revolution, Industrialization

24
State Building and State-Craft: 1648-1789

Theories of Royal Absolutism

In 1589, the Italian political theorist Giovanni Botero published an influential book, *On the Reason of State*. Princes read it with excitement and approval, for Botero advanced the theory that the interests of the state took clear precedence over the medieval privileges of towns, nobles, church or provinces. Botero envisioned a rationalized monarchy freed from inherited restraints both sacred and secular. The revitalized monarchies would be governed only by their needs and goals, and would be responsible to no one.

Botero's book brought to the surface of debate ideas that had been stewing and simmering for a long time. Belief in the virtues of the older constitutional monarchies of the Renaissance and the later Middle Ages had been in decline before Botero's public condemnation. The late medieval states had been constructed on theories of the divisibility of public power between the king, the magnates and the lesser orders. The king was supposed to rule within a complex web of mutually contracted feudal obligations, not trespassing on the privileges of his subjects. Thus the "state" was but one element in a network of government that included all the nobles, towns and churches in the realm.

This system had not worked too well for a long time. During the Reformation, princes had been unable to keep the peace against the religious zeal of their subjects. Monarchs had not dispensed justice or protected their subjects' rights and liberties. Continuing disasters in public affairs demanded changes in the way people thought about their government.

Botero's ideas about the supremacy of state power over subjects were given a religious articulation appropriate for a Counterreformation audience, and emerged as divine right absolutism.* It was a simple doctrine, claiming only that all power be-

* The idea runs back through Machiavelli to the propagandists of Philip IV of France (1285–1314) and beyond. Glimmerings of it can be found in the medieval notions of the Holy Roman emperors as God's agents by divine appointment.

longed rightfully to the king because he received it from God. This assertion was buttressed by numerous scriptural, historical and theological authorities, which added a rich pattern of variations to the main theme. During the seventeenth century, with its need for stable government and the general belief that religion was a necessary part of secular legitimacy, divine right absolutism was both satisfying and convincing.

Although divine right absolutism was the majority doctrine, it did not stand alone. In England and Holland parliamentary institutions had long been developing, although seventeenth-century monarchs made tremendous efforts to abort them. Along with the parliaments went political doctrines to support their pretensions to power. Here, the medieval ideas of contract and consent did not die, and to these were added a miscellany of theories about the rights of man, the constitution of a commonwealth and other antiabsolutist ideas. In spite of their unfashionable insistence on the limits of royal authority, however, ideas of parliamentary power were convincing enough in two states to justify revolutions against the king.

There was a third political possibility in the aftermath of the religious wars. This was the path of feudal decentralization, a continuation of patterns of government that had taken hold in medieval Germany and Eastern Europe, and had already failed. In Poland, Spain and the Ottoman Empire, theories of divine right absolutism failed to persuade powerful feudal and provincial magnates to surrender real power to the crown. In Poland, ideals of feudal liberties held sway and, in Turkey, tribal and religious notions of unlimited royal power were never organized into a coherent doctrine of state authority that applied to all the peoples of the empire. In an age when even the strongest governments depended heavily on the consent of the governed, failures in political theory were reflected in the decline of the state.

Military Organization: The French Army

The rise of absolute monarchies was indistinguishable from the growth of royal armies. With reliable armies, kings could defeat their own subjects, a major consideration in an era of religious wars and aristocratic conspiracies. Thus monarchs put the bulk of their resources into the military —five sixths of the royal income in the case of Spain—and made the condition of the army the primary concern of the state.

During the old regime, the king's troops might be his own subjects, or they might be mercenaries. In general, mercenaries were more reliable and in the years before 1660 when armies were relatively small, mercenaries were used exclusively. Even after armies had become too large to be recruited entirely from abroad, most monarchs continued to use mercenaries as specialists while relying on native peasantry and convicts for cannon fodder. Naval captains, navigators, artillery and engineer officers, drill masters and generals were frequently foreigners. In Russia they invariably were.

The king's struggle to build a loyal army was successful first in France, where Henry IV combined his own forces with those of the duke of Lesidiguières into a fairly large and efficient army. To support this army, Henry placed his closest friend and adviser, the Duke of Sully, in charge of the royal arsenal and instructed him to acquire and maintain weapons. Sully was an able man who did his job well and, in 1610, when Henry IV was assassinated, royal power dominated France.

At Henry's death, the government fell into the hands of his widow, Marie de Medici, a fat, suspicious and stupid woman, who dismissed Sully and let the royal army fall apart. Royal power went down with it and, by 1618, the French crown was again fighting its subjects and not doing too well. Not until after 1630 was a new chief minister, Cardinal Richelieu, able to rebuild a loyal army, mostly from mercenaries. His success was demonstrated dramatically during the revolution of the Fronde (1648-1652), an unsuccessful assault on the growing power and coherence of the state. France's leading general, the Prince of Condé, defected to the Spanish, but his army refused to go with him. A century earlier it almost certainly would have.

Under Louis XIV (1643-1715) who was immensely interested in military affairs, the French army became an efficient instrument of royal policy. Louis' war minister, Louvois, worked for three decades to recruit, organize, equip and train the royal army. He established a table of ranks and issued a promotion policy that was actually used in the few cases where family influence was not decisive. He insisted on uniforms, and housed many of the troops in barracks where they could be watched instead of having them billeted in private homes. He ordered noble officers to live with their regiments, and his discipline was so severe that some actually did. He organized a supply service, established military hospitals and stocked military maps. He wrote drill regulations and insisted that the troops march until they learned how to do it right. There were frequent audits and inspections designed to make certain that the regiments were up to strength and that the officers were not stealing the ration money. Permanent garrisons were established at frontier fortresses and, where forts did not exist, Marshal Vauban, the chief of engineers, had them built.

These were massive reforms, but remnants of the old system remained. Louvois was unable to end the practice of buying commissions. Colonels still raised their own regiments and captains their own companies, and there was a great deal of fraud in the process. The troops continued to be recruited by jail delivery and kidnapping. Military punishments remained barbarous, seldom stopping before actual murder, but the atmosphere of fear could not prevent a desertion rate that ran more than one third. Even so, France possessed the finest army in seventeenth-century Europe—not only the biggest but also the best equipped and organized. Only in command was it frequently deficient.

What the French did the Prussians did also, and did better, though on a smaller scale. Like Louvois in France, Frederick-William the "Great Elector" of Prussia (1640–1688) also built an effective and loyal army. He eliminated mercenaries almost entirely, and recruited both his officers and soldiers from Prussia. As in France they were housed, fed, equipped and commanded by the king. As in France, too they were used to curb domestic revolt as well as in foreign conquest. But the Great Elector went a step farther than Louis XIV. He made the Prussian army the basic, unifying institution for the entire state.

Administrative Organization: The French Bureaucracy

Armies did not exist alone, of course, since the state had to be governed, not occupied. Absolute monarchs developed massive civil bureaucracies to cope with the arts and intricacies of taxation, justice, police and general regulation appropriate to the public good and royal glory. Again, France led the way. Here, the bureaucracy was the largest, the most expensive, the most pervasive, the most powerful and, occasionally, the most efficient in Christendom. It was also the most envied, and its better features were copied in the other bureaucratic monarchies.

The central figure in the French civil bureaucracy was the provincial intendant, who ruled a province in the king's name. Appointed by the crown and responsible to it, the intendant possessed wide powers of police, justice and taxation. He could evoke cases from the regular courts and judge them himself, or arbitrarily arrest almost anyone in his jurisdiction. He appointed the direct tax burden in his district and supervised the collection. He built roads, established hospitals and workhouses, fed the destitute, encouraged farmers and checked the local authority of nobles and towns. Toward the end of the seventeenth century he acquired subordinates, subdelegates, who enforced his orders in the remote and wretched towns he himself seldom visited. In the past, officials that powerful had often escaped from royal control. Now they did not and were thus the vital link between royal orders and provincial obedience.

Above the intendants were the ministers, appointed by the king and in intimate contact with him. During the course of the seventeenth century, the ministers had come to exercise definite functions; one was in charge of finances, another controlled foreign affairs, a third ran the army, and so on. Each minister had his own bureaucracy to deal with the increasing loads of paper as the king extended his purview into more and more areas of the nation's life. Louis XIV watched his ministers closely, and checked on their activities, since he had no intention of allowing them to usurp the king's authority for themselves. His successors were not so careful.

In an age of general illiteracy, and one that still retained a respect for pomp and symbol and ceremony, kings had to display themselves as absolute monarchs as well as give orders to ministers. Visual propaganda was far more important than the written word. In this endeavor, Louis XIV excelled. His palace of Versailles was a huge and splendid stage, the biggest, most expensive, most sumptuous royal palace Europeans had ever seen or heard of. In it, Louis was treated like a sort of god. Everything depended on the "Sun King." A complicated etiquette emphasized his grandeur. His menial servants were dukes and princes. He was flattered and imitated, to such an extent that when he had an anal fistula removed several courtiers had the same dangerous surgery performed on them. Surely, such a powerful monarch was God's viceregent on earth. Every

sacred and secular symbol known at the time shouted that he was.

Weaknesses in the French Royal Administration

But the glittering facade of Versailles masked failures as well as shouting success. The ranks of officials and clerks concealed two serious failures in French administration, both of which contributed to the coming of the French Revolution, two generations later. No French monarch or minister ever solved for long the problem of insufficient finances, nor were they free from the opposition of royal officials who owned their offices. These evils were recognized by everyone, and there were numerous programs to reform them. All failed. Over the years things just got worse.

French finances were a complicated mess. Taxation was regressive, falling most heavily on the peasants who were least able to pay. The privileged nobility and bourgeoisie escaped most levies and evaded others. The social costs of such taxation were enormous, and the revenues were inadequate. Equally serious was the failure of the crown to account for its income. There was no budget, no central treasury and no uniform system of accounts or payments. No one knew how much the king made, only that it was never enough. Nor did anyone know what the king had spent or borrowed, only that it was too much. It was not a good system, and nothing was done about it.

A second administrative problem was venality, ownership of office by the men who held them. Whole groups of offices fell under this curse, particularly the judiciary. Venality had grown from two roots; the king's need to reward his servants, and his equally pressing need to extract money from those who could pay. By the end of the sixteenth century venality had become an irrevocable custom, and royal legislation thereafter only concerned extending it to other offices and extracting more money from the purchasers. As a result, the government lost control of a large number of its officials and found itself inventing new positions, such as intendants, to carry out orders that venal officials refused to obey. This whole problem was made more galling by the fact that the orders venal officials evaded were generally those that concentrated power in the king's hands and aided the process of state-building.

There were also failures in policy. The power of the state was often used simply to exalt the glory of the king or the interests of the dynasty, while the interests of the nation were forgotten. Prosperity, except in tax revenues, was not high on Louis' scale of values. Nor did the Sun King use his authority to attack social, legal and political privilege. Manorialism remained, venality of office was extended, the courts became increasingly expensive and corrupt, the privileges of guilds, towns and provinces were confirmed and nothing was done to systematize the French legal system. The increased power of the state was used to reinforce privilege and, in general, the nobility and gentry were richer and more secure after Louis XIV than before him. Finally, the Sun King engaged in a squalid persecution of his Protestant subjects, which failed to make France Catholic and damaged the economy. Thus absolutism in France presents a paradoxical picture. Royal power and glory were mixed with substantial remnants of independent local authority. The government was strengthened and enlarged, only to be overthrown a century later because of the privilege, bigotry and lack of political liberty that it sustained—and because of the problems of royal finances that it failed to solve.

The Administration of Czarist Russia

In Russia, also, the crown succeeded in imposing the authority of the government on a reluctant people. Until Peter the Great (1689–1725), Russia had no army or government in the western sense, relying instead on feudal levies, the Church, the gentry and the weakness of her neighbors. Peter began to change all that, swiftly and brutally. He had been brought up in some contact with western ways and was eager to learn more. In paritcular, he was anxious to absorb the military techniques that westerners in Moscow described for him. In 1698, he made a tour of Western Europe, visiting arsenals, shipyards, shops, and working as a carpenter himself. The trip was cut short by a revolt of the Streltzy, a feudal guard whose leaders could see well enough where Peter's western ideas were leading. The revolt was crushed by Peter's German mercenaries. Peter rushed home, took a pitiless revenge on the Streltzy, and began a rapid and hodge podge westernization of all around him.

Driven by the pressures of the Great Northern War against Sweden (1701–1721),* Peter the Great tried to do everything at once. He organized, trained and equipped a new army and, when that was destroyed by the Swedes at Narva in 1700, did it all again. To support this army, Peter and his advisers, invented hundreds of new taxes. Taxes were placed on vodka, water, beards, births, marriages, graves, coffins, anything likely to produce a profit. These revenues were collected by a bewildering welter of agencies and bureaus. Only after 1712, when Peter imported over 150 foreign administrators, was any order brought out of the bureaucratic chaos. Even then, they only made a start. To enforce obedience to his new government, Peter established the first Russian secret police, a social and political institution that has become a permanent feature in Russian life.

Peter the Great reformed provincial and local government as well. Between 1705 and 1711 he established provincial districts, each ruled by a governor responsible

* Below, page 337.

to the czar. Municipal government was taken away from the old military governors and given to the urban bourgeoisie, because of the "waywardness and excessive stealing of our military governors." Equally important, however, was the hope that bourgeois management of the cities would add to the czar's taxes.

All this, radical though it was, had a smaller impact on Russian life than the social revolution that Peter the Great forced through. He ordered nobles to trim their beards, to wear European clothes, to use tobacco and to send their sons to European schools. He personally clipped some beards himself. These measures were neither silly nor superficial, nor without effect, for they drove a wedge between the Europeanized court aristocracy and the rest of Russian society, a division that lasted until the Russian Communist Revolution of 1917.

Peter changed the status of both the nobility and peasantry. The latter were locked more tightly into serfdom, owing labor to their lords and sons to the army. The nobility were forced to do state service. As there were not enough lords for all the new slots in the army, bureaucracy and diplomatc service, Peter the Great created thousands of new nobles. The nobility in Russia were less an independent caste than in Western Europe; in Russia, nobility was a status dependent on the good graces of the czar. Such an arrangement was a formidable weapon in the royal drive for control of the state.

Although Peter's reforms accomplished their immediate objectives—military victory and the beginnings of "westernization" they were chaotic, incomplete and, in some cases, impermanent. State service for the nobility had to be abandoned, as the crown could not demand this from the class on which it depended for support. The Russian army was still mainly a mob, in spite of the veneer of western officers who commanded it. The administrative system Peter left his successors needed

constant revision. But the main battle was won. Russia was on the way to being a bureaucratic and absolutist state on the western model, a process that is continuing today.

Administrative Centralization in Austria and Prussia

The process of political centralization that transformed Russia and France also occurred elsewhere, notably in Austria and Prussia. Here, too, a more modern army was accompanied by a growing bureaucracy. State-building encountered less resistance in Prussia than in Austria. Austrian nobles were richer and more powerful than their Prussian colleagues, and the Austrian government was diverted from the task of centralization by the constant threat from Turkey. Within a century of the accession of Frederick-William the Great Elector, in 1640, the Prussian civil service was the most efficient in Europe, while Austrian administrative reform was concentrated after 1750. The result was the same in both states, however. The dramatic increase in military strength and internal political coherence meant great power status. For kings, this was a worthy goal. The subjects, of course, were not consulted.

The Parliamentary States: Holland

"I will govern according to the common weal, but not according to the common will," replied James I to his House of Commons in 1621. He spoke for kings everywhere. In the seventeenth century, monarchs viewed parliaments as stumbling blocks on the path toward political centralization. In most countries, royal armies and bureaucracies destroyed the power and often the existence of representative institutions. In England and Holland, the kings failed. Here, parliaments survived because of victory in civil war and revolution.

Politics in England and Holland, therefore, followed different patterns from those elsewhere. The political battles were fought, as it were, on two fronts. There was the inexorable increase in the power of the central government, common to all the great powers. But there was also a struggle for control of that power, fought between kings and the representative institutions that defeated them. Contemporaries, astounded at the deviation from absolutism, concentrated their attention on the latter. Yet, it was the increase of power at the center that began the struggles between crown and parliament, for centralization enormously enlarged the rewards of victory.

In the Netherlands, the institutions and patterns of government were an inheritance from the wars with Spain. At the center of the state were the *Stadhouder* and the States General. The *Stadhouder* was a prince from the House of Orange, who held the supreme military command and some of the powers, although not the title, of king. The powers of the *Stadhouder* naturally expanded in war and dropped off in peace. Opposing the *Stadhouder* were the representatives of the seven provinces, the States General. Descendant of a medieval parliament, the States General was particularly sensitive to the wishes of the nobility and urban patriciate. The deputies viewed the preservation of provincial liberties and privileges as their major function, and carried over into their relations with the *Stadhouder* their distrust of Philip II of Spain. Below the States General came the towns and States Provincial. They had borne the brunt of the war and now expected the rewards of victory. They had fought to preserve local autonomy and were sharply hostile to any steady siphoning of local powers to the center. Finally, towering above all the cities and provinces and, occasionally above the state itself, was Amsterdam, the economic and psychological center of the nation. Amsterdam so dominated the Netherlands that nothing could succeed without her support. Amsterdam's rulers took the lead in opposing the *Stadhouder* and, paradoxically, because they were so powerful nationally, in reducing provincial and municipal autonomy. Thus they established and owned the United East India Company while they forced reluctant smaller towns to accept the company's monopoly of East Indian trade, but kept its revenue and colonies out of the *Stadhouder's* reach.

In the years after the truce with Spain in 1609, the endemic conflict between the *Stadhouder* and Amsterdam became acute. The issues were both religious and political. Amsterdam, led by its advocate, Jan de Oldenbarneveldt, supported a liberalized Calvinism and states rights while the *Stadhouder* Maurice, adhered to a rigid predestination in religion and royal power in politics. In 1618, Oldenbarneveldt led the province of Holland to the brink of secession. Maurice invaded Holland, executed Oldenbarneveldt and established a considerable measure of royal control. He was assisted in this program by the outbreak of the Thirty Years' War (1618), and by the renewal of war with Spain in 1619.

Maurice's brother, Frederick-Henry (1625-1647), continued the politics of royal absolutism. He prosecuted the war against Spain, gained control over foreign policy and created a magnificent court. When William II succeeded his father, he continued to increase royal authority. He moved against the Estates of Holland and the city of Amsterdam, but died in 1650 before he could complete his plans. As his son, William III, was born posthumously, there was a vacancy in the stadholderate. Led by Jan De Witt, the Grand Pensionary of Holland, the estates party, with the firm backing of Amsterdam, seized control of the government and virtually eliminated the *Stadhouder*. This lasted until 1672, when the French invaded the Netherlands and came very close to conquering it. In the military emergency the nation turned to the *Stadhouder*,

William III, and political power shifted rapidly from the States General to the prince. William sustained himself through domestic political manipulation and an alliance with England. The English connection was strengthened by marriage to Mary, daughter of the English monarch James II and, after the Glorious Revolution, William and Mary became the joint rulers of England.

After William III's death in 1702, power flowed back to the States General, and it was not until 1747 that the Netherlands had a new *Stadhouder*, William IV. Although the powers of the *Stadhouder* increased after the middle of the eighteenth century, the old traditions of states rights, provincial privilege and municipal autonomy did not collapse. They were revived during the Dutch Revolution of 1780 to 1787, were responsible for the welcome given the revolutionary armies of France in 1795 and formed the basis for the liberal Dutch institution of 1815. The Dutch *Stadhouders* never succeeded in conquering their country.

England: The Early Stuart Kings

When Elizabeth died in 1603, mourned by her subjects, she was succeeded by the King of Scotland, James VI (1603–1625), a Stuart, who became James I of England (1603–25). His accession joined the crowns, but not the parliaments of the two countries. He was a sorry contrast to the regal queen, ill-favored physically and something of a debauchee. He gave England over to the haphazard and erratic politics of favorites. Immensely learned, he was also pedantic, and was called the wisest fool in Christendom. His most attractive quality was his wit, which was considerable. His greatest problem was the "eating canker of want." With growing inflation, the sheer cost of government had risen: a cost that was compounded by his own extravagance.

Attempts to raise royal revenues by jacking up customs rates and other levies were fiercely resented. The bawdy life of the court offended the Puritans. The rising tide of ceremonialism in James' church hierarchy they denounced as "popery," and they objected strongly to the arrangement of a marriage between the English crown prince and a French Catholic princess.

James' view of his own divine right to rule was also offensive to Englishmen who revered the "balanced" constitutional arrangement of parliamentary government. James' view of his royal prerogatives seemed to jeopardize the sovereignty of Parliament, which was "the ancient and undoubted birthright and inheritance of the subjects of England" as the Commons complained in 1625.

James' son Charles I (1625–1649), with his more dogged and more thorough approach to government, aggravated the fears of many parliamentarians by continuing his father's policies. In 1628 the Lords and Commons induced him to sign a celebrated Petition of Rights, which should have established Parliament beyond all question as an integral part of the government of the realm. But thereafter he turned his back on the substance of what parliamentarians assumed he had agreed to, and summarily dispensed with Parliament for 11 years. During this time the government devised several ingenious ways of raising revenues without Parliamentary consent by reviving old, half-forgotten feudal rights of the crown. Despite widespread opposition, it looked as though, for once, the crown would balance its budget. But at the same time aggressively Anglican policies of the chief Archbishop, Laud, drew Charles into a war with the Scots; and without the funds to carry it on, the king was forced to call Parliament.

Parliament met in 1640 in an ugly mood. Fearing the despotic implications and tendencies of the past decade, it attacked Charles' ministers and dismantled, statute by statute, the whole apparatus of personal rule that Charles had built up. Under pressure Charles accepted Parliament's attacks on his powers. Many, distrusting his intentions, wanted to set more and more limitations on his authority. Finally, when Charles' control of the militia was questioned, he refused to accede. A round of political skirmishing broke into real fighting after June, 1642. The eastern shires and London supported Parliament, and Puritans supported Parliament. The gentry were divided; while the aristocracy for the most part remained with the King. It was only after the parliamentary army was reorganized and remodeled under Cromwell's influence that Parliament clearly gained the upper hand in the struggle. In 1644 at Marston Moor and in 1645 at Naseby, Cromwell defeated the King with an army fired and disciplined by some of his own Puritan spirit. After Naseby the royalists gave up and Charles surrendered. But he struck an agreement with his former enemies, the Scots, who allied themselves with him as a result of his promise to support Presbyterianism in their land. Cromwell went north to defeat them; then to Ireland to crush Charles' allies there. It was in Ireland that his reputation was forever sullied by two massacres during siege operations.

In 1649, a radical minority of Parliament with army backing had the King executed for crimes against the fundamental laws and liberties of his subjects. Kings had been deposed and assassinated before, but never had they been, in effect, "legally" charged with treason against their own peoples! It was a weighty precedent.

The Era of Cromwell and the Stuart Restoration

The aftermath of the monarchy was a series of attempts to find a satisfactory constitutional and religious settlement under which the majority of the nation could live peacably. Ultimate power lay

with the army, and with Cromwell. From being an obscure country gentleman Cromwell was caught up by the civil war and propelled to greatness. After the experiments of a republic and of a "Parliament of Saints" had failed, Cromwell assumed the title "Protector"—he would not take the title King. But in the face of failure with his own parliaments he resorted more and more to military counsel and militia rule. His one fixed principle was religious toleration. All else was ephemeral; even constitutions he said, quoting St. Paul, were "but dross and dung in comparison of Christ." But the bulk of the nation was not yet ready for toleration. After his death the dissident elements in the old parliamentary side and in the army fell apart; and one of Cromwell's generals—General Monk—was called to restore order. Finding the situation hopelessly anarchical, General Monk decided to restore the monarchy. Charles II had learned something from his father's fate, and he never wanted to go into exile again, consequently, he moved circumspectly with his parliaments. As witty as James I, he was intelligent without pedantry, and his roisterings and affairs with women were more acceptable than James' affection for his favorites. Indeed, they seemed to be welcome to a nation grown tired of Puritan restraints. His most famous mistress, Nell Gwynne, the actress, quite captured the public's fancy. Of all England's rulers, the Merry Monarch was the most popular and the most accessible.

In politics and religion, Charles tried to follow a moderate line. He supported religious toleration, although opposition from the Restoration Parliament (1661–1679) prevented him from accomplishing it. Parliament insisted on several repressive and intolerant laws, known as the Clarendon Code, and Charles reluctantly went along with them. He also supported the expansion of trade and colonies, and here he had parliamentary support.

The general success of the Restoration,

however, could not overcome one large deficit. It was the problem of succession. Charles II's brother, James, duke of York, was next in line, and he was a stiff-necked absolutist and a Roman Catholic. In Protestant parliamentary England, accustomed to the agreeable and slightly debauched Charles II, these were not good qualities. Charles himself recognized the problem and once commented that the future of the Stuart house depended on whether he or James died first. Charles did, on February 6, 1685, and James became England's first Catholic monarch since Mary Tudor.

The Glorious Revolution and its Aftermath

James quickly fulfilled his subjects' worst fears. He paid little attention to Parliament and began to fill official positions with Catholics. Most Englishmen were not prepared to accept Catholics in government and resisted James' efforts at religious toleration as a blind for the establishment of a Catholic regime. In 1687, James had a son, thus insuring that his policies would be continued into the indefinite future. This was more than the Anglican Church, many of the peers and the merchants could stand. An invitation was issued to William of Orange, *Stadhouder* of the Netherlands, to come to England and rescue Protestantism and Parliament. William came in November 1688, and James II, utterly bereft of support, fled to France. There was a bit of rioting in London, but no major disorders. The Glorious Revolution was a general and peaceful success.

Parliament met in January 1689, offered the crown jointly to William and his wife Mary and passed the Declaration of Rights. The Declaration stated that the monarch could not make or suspend laws without Parliament's consent, nor could he tax or maintain a standing army unless Parliament agreed. Parliamentary elections were to be free, the king's judges could not set excessive bail, nor dispense with juries, nor confiscate the people's arms. In the

Declaration of Rights, Parliament went beyond its own prerogatives, important though these were, and added several general civil liberties as well. It was a crucial document, which became the basic statement of British government principles and was copied later in the American Bill of Rights.

The reigns of William and Mary (1689–1702) and Anne (1702–1714) were dominated by war with Louis XIV, not domestic politics. At home the general drift of power toward Parliament continued, and both monarchs were careful to make certain that their ministers and policies had the confidence of the Lords and Commons. Abroad, the war went well, at least most of the time and when peace came in 1713, the Treaty of Utrecht established England as the foremost power in Europe.

England in the Eighteenth Century

Anne died on August 1, 1714, the victim of obesity, a general decline and lots of liquor. She left neither children nor close relatives. In this new succession crisis, the leading contenders were James II's son and the Protestant Elector of Hanover, George. George won out, and the party that had opposed him, known as the Tories, began to intrigue with the exiled Stuart prince. They attempted to raise Scotland against George I, and the pretender, "James III," actually landed. Government troops put the revolt down easily. The leading Tories were arrested, and the government, now secure, fell into the hands of their opponents, the Whigs.

English government in the eighteenth century was the product of two great political facts, the Glorious Revolution and the disinterest of George I (1714–1727) and George II (1727–1760) in domestic politics. The Glorious Revolution had established the powers of Parliment, and the king could neither govern against its wishes nor sustain ministers who had no friends there. This arrangement assured Parliament a coordinate share in government, but it did not reduce legitimate royal power or make the king the servant of his subjects, nor was it designed to. Royal disinterest in politics, however, led to the domination of government by the ministry and Parliament. Thus power slowly-drifted away from the crown to the ministers and Parliament, and public opinion drifted toward regarding this reduced royal role as legitimate.

All royal power did not vanish, of course. It was still possible for George III (1760–1820) to manipulate elections and bribe members of Parliament with offices, pensions and favors. But, generally speaking, executive authority and policymaking powers in eighteenth-century England passed from the king to the prime minister and the cabinet. The cabinet ministers guided bills through Parliament and, increasingly, also wrote them. They ran the government bureaus, although usually not very well. They awarded favors and peerages, commissions and commands in the armed forces and did their best to keep a majority in Parliament. No one was better at this complicated and endless game than Robert Walpole, prime minister from 1721 to 1742.

In Parliament itself, the ministers followed well-established customs of political management. The members tended to fall into two large groups, the Court party, or the King's Friends, and the Country party, or those who were not his friends. Within these broad divisions, the members attached themselves into loose factions or blocs, held together by family connections or personal interests. These interests and connections were usually led by a peer, who was frequently a minister. By controlling several electoral districts, the peer could manage the election of his relatives and friends, and then could direct their votes and speeches in Parliament. He could reward his followers with pensions and places, and coerce them with threats of defeat at the polls. Most of the factions

were small, from three to a dozen men, but they were the cellular units of a parliamentary majority.

None of this delicate web of custom, interest and connection could have worked unless both Houses were composed of men who came from the same social class. Most of the members of Commons were related to peers, and many were younger sons. Those not related to the peerage by blood were wealthy merchants or country gentry, who also belonged to the social aristocracy. Both Commons and Lords agreed on the rules and nuances of the political game and had the same expectations and hopes from it. They were able to maneuver deftly within complicated political customs, dealing with issues far more by personal negotiation and informal understandings than by debate and resolutions. In a very real way, therefore, the elections were unimportant. Whoever was returned would be an aristocrat or a gentleman, accustomed to the system.

The election procedures reinforced aristocratic control and the complex arrangements of interest and connection. Each shire sent two members to Commons, as did selected boroughs, precisely as they had since the fourteenth century. Electoral districts had last been assigned in the sixteenth century, and time had changed some of them. A few boroughs had no population at all, and were called pocket boroughs, as the owner had its seats in his pocket. The most famous pocket borough was Old Sarum, the Pitt family seat. Less decayed boroughs had fallen to a handful of voters, a dozen or twenty, few enough so that the local magnate could control each of the voters personally. These were called rotten boroughs, after the methods used in elections, and there were several dozen of them by the mid-eighteenth century.

Pocket and rotten boroughs did not exhaust the list of electoral anomalies. Each borough set its own electoral standards. Sometimes owners of certain properties could vote, elsewhere all the freeman of the city had the franchise. In total, there were not more than 250,000 voters in all of England, and fewer than 10,000 of these could control the House of Commons.

In such a system, political parties and political issues meant relatively little. Issues were seldom discussed in Parliament. Party affiliation, whether Whig or Tory, meant much less than family connections and interests. Nonetheless, the system had its advantages. The quality of the members, although not very high, was still better than that of the hacks and poltroons who so often infest American legislatures. Furthermore, the system was successful, and people enjoyed a degree of freedom unmatched in Europe. Morever, England was able to defeat her foreign enemies from Louis XIV to Napoleon (George Washington was the single exception). Critics found it hard to argue with success.

The Disintegrating States: The Holy Roman Empire and Poland

When the philosopher Samuel Pufendorf described the decaying feudal anarchy and incoherence of the Holy Roman Empire, he found that the traditional Aristotelian categories of monarchy, aristocracy and democracy did not describe it. Nor did it seem to have any element of sovereignty, since its head, the emperor, did not rule its members; the princes defied him at will. In the end, Pufendorf called the empire a monster, an organism alien to the laws of nature and nation. Such a judgment on the disintegrating empire would have been impossible as late as 1630 but, by the middle of the seventeenth century, with the changes in political theory and administrative practice, Pufendorf's conclusion was not merely appropriate, it was mild.

Pufendorf's judgment applied to states other than the empire, and Poland was one. During the seventeenth century Poland became the classic example of feudal

anarchy in which the nobles counted for everything and the king nothing. Poland was a monarchy in name only. Kingship was elective, and the nobles who voted for the king took care to elect someone as weak and innocuous as possible. They almost invariably succeeded. Polish kings were generally undistinguished, and they had very little independent power to support their royal rank. By the eighteenth century the monarchy had become a bad and bankrupt joke. It was held by figures such as Stanislas Poniatowski (1764–1795), a discarded lover of Catherine the Great of Russia and made king as a consolation; or August the Strong (1697–1733), whose exploits were mainly sexual (he was reputed to have fathered 365 bastard children). "Power [is] one of the things most necessary to the grandeur of kings and the success of their government," Cardinal Richelieu commented, and the Kings of Poland lacked it altogether.

The weakness of Polish kings lay in the absence of any royal army or bureaucracy. For government, Poland relied on the moral authority of her kings and Diet, along with the vouutary consent of the governed. No coercion was possible, and in the more remote provinces it was difficult for the king even to learn whether he had been obeyed or not. For defense there was only the feudal levy. In an age of more sophisticated military technology and increasing use of highly trained military professionals, the Polish feudal levy was a fiasco. Whereas Poland's chief rivals—Prussia, Austria and Russia—had modernized their governments and armies on the Western European model, Poland herself failed to do so, and her failure eventually brought disaster to her.

Politics in the Old Regime reflected social patterns, and the "aristocratic republic" of Poland possessed an archaic social structure even for the seventeenth century. In Poland, the dominant class was the landed nobility, who numbered about 12 percent of the population, far more than anywhere else. Polish nobles were a diverse lot, ranging from the Potocki clan who owned estates the size of Connecticut to thousands of landless gentry, who owned nothing but their honor. The poor gentry became retainers for the rich, enabling the magnates to have private armies and to become virtually independent of the crown. Beneath the lords were the peasants, so far beneath that Rousseau's description of them as "less than nothing" exaggerted their status. They were serfs, owned body and soul by their lords who regarded them as animals and treated them accordingly. The urban bourgeoisie were better off than the servile peasants, having personal freedom and a modest income, but their political power was insignificant. Except for Warsaw and Cracow, the towns were small miserable places where the inhabitants were as likely to speak German as Polish. Alienated from the peasants whom they did not know and from the nobility who despised them, the bourgeoisie lived in a narrow and constricted world, without power, influence or wealth.

In such a society, only the nobility could wield any real power. The nobility was organized into the Diet, a sort of legislature that had the right to elect the king and pass on all legislation. Each noble could vote, and unanimity was required to pass a law. A single veto, and the bill or treaty failed. The Diet was thus able to frustrate any attempt to strengthen the crown far more easily than it could develop any coherent policy of its own. Moreover, politics within the Diet reflected the power of the great nobles, who were virtually sovereign themselves. Families such as the Potocki and Braniki had their own foreign and domestic policy; the Potocki, for example, were pro-French and wished to to retain the aristocratic constitution that Poland had. Such magnates could also call foreign powers into Poland, and Russian intervention frequently followed calls from Polish nobles. The result of these political arrangements was evident by the end of the seventeenth century. Poland had become a classic power vaccum, and her disposition was one of the main elements of the Eastern Question in eighteenth century diplomacy.

The Ottoman Empire

The other eastern state that failed to consolidate its administration or modernize its army was the Ottoman Empire. In the two centuries after the onset of the great depression, the empire declined markedly, although it did not disintegrate to the extent that Poland did. From the viewpoint of Christian Europe, Turkish decadence was a startling and welcome reversal from her previous strength and vigor which, in two centuries, had extended Ottoman control across the eastern Mediterranean, the Black Sea, and Hungary and the Balkans. After the fall of Constantinople in 1453, Europeans had shuddered at the Turkish menace and had concocted dozens of schemes and crusades to throw the Turks back. Nothing had worked. The Ottoman hordes crushed the Hungarians at Mohacs in 1526, besieged Vienna in 1529 and threatened to push into Poland and Bohemia. Although the gates of Vienna marked the farthest Turkish advance into central Europe, no one felt secure. Even during the Reformation, Protestant princes occasionally contributed troops and arms to Catholic Hapsburg emperors for the constant wars against the Turks. Now, in the years after 1600, the Turks seemed stricken by a mysterious langor, and the monarchs of eastern Christendom were immensely relieved.

Turkey's weaknesses were many—political, administrative, cultural, social—but chief among them was a growing economic decline. The trade routes around Africa diminished commerce through Egypt, and the eastern Mediterranean slowly ceased to be the source of spices, silks and other oriental products. The decline of Turkish trade was compounded by a severe monetary inflation. The expenses of government soared as the Ottoman rulers expanded their bureaucracy and tried to convert the feudal and slave hordes into a modern, professional army. Taxes were increased, and the feudal lords, who were abandoning their role as soldiers, demanded increased dues from their peasants. As a result, brigandage increased alarmingly, and so did graft and extortion. The military and administrative magnates who had once plundered the infidel now began to plunder the empire itself, and no one could do anything about it.

The Decline of Spain

A third great power sinking into irreversible decay in the seventeenth century was Spain, once the greatest and proudest power in the western world. Like the Turks, the Spanish had enjoyed immoderate power, prosperity and glory in the sixtenth century, and then had come upon hard times. Unlike the Ottoman Turks, the Spanish collapse was swift and complete, with no period of seeming recovery, no ephemeral successes. So total and absolute was the Spanish catastrophe that observers between 1600 and 1700 were moved to awe and sought explanations in the realm of religion and demonology as well as politics, diplomacy and trade. A seventeenth-century Spanish lawyer, after recounting the more mundane ills of his land, added a plaintive comment on divine disfavor:

It seems as if one hand wished to reduce these kingdoms to a republic of bewitched beings, living outside the natural order of things. . . .*

But there were explanations for the Spanish decline beyond those of collective sins and expiation. They were partially economic. The savage depression in the

Hapsburg states during the seventeenth century was a big factor in military defeat abroad and revolutions at home. Politically, Spanish commitments had exceeded her powers even in the sixteenth century, and by 1620, the gap was so wide that defeat could only be delayed. Efforts to prolong Spain's position as a great power simply made the final disaster worse by adding revolts to the other problems of government.

In the Old Regime Spain was composed of three Iberian kingdoms: Castile, Aragon and, after 1580, Portugal. Each was governed separately under its own laws. Only in Castile was the royal authority clearly dominant over the towns, Church and Cortes (parliament). Here, the king did about as he wished, and he taxed cruelly. In Aragon and Portugal, royal power was far less extensive. Portugal retained its own administrative structure and was ruled by Portuguese officials. In Aragon, parliaments retained great powers, and the king could not override them easily. In the Aragonese province of Catalonia, he could not override the parliament at all.

The most important thing in Your Majesty's Monarchy is for you to become King of Spain; by that I mean, Sire, that Your Majesty should not be content with being King of Portugal, of Valencia and Count of Barcelona, but should secretly plan and work to reduce these Kingdoms of which Spain is composed to the style and laws of Castile, without any difference.*

This was good advice, and Olivares as chief minister from 1621 to 1643 did his best to carry it out. But he failed. The economic disasters forced him into a series of improvisations both domestic and diplomatic, none of which had much hope of long-term success. When the resources of Castile ran out, Olivares tried to tax the other states of the Hapsburg Spanish

* Gonzales de Cellorigo, quoted in J. Elliott, "The Decline of Spain," in T. Aston, *Europe in Crisis: 1560–1600*, p. 193.

* Memoir of Count-Duke Olivares to Philip IV, 1624.

crown, and the consequence was revolt. On Corpus Christi Day, 1640, the laborers of Barcelona rose in riot and sparked a revolt in Catalonia against the royal government at Madrid. Later in the same year, a Portuguese national revolt broke out under the leadership of the duke of Bragança. In 1647, the area of rebellion widened, with the revolt of Masaniello in Naples against atrocious misgovernment, high taxes, high bread prices and unemployment. Such events made peace essential. But although the treaties of Westphalia in 1648 ended the Thirty Years War in Germany, the war between France and Spain dragged on for another 11 years, to the increasing disadvantage of the Spanish. Although the Spanish Hapsburgs were able to restore this authority in Naples and slowly recapture most of Catalonia, Portugal was lost forever.

Peace with France in 1659, (the "Peace of the Pyrenees") did not bring recovery to Spain. She was economically prostrate, and Castilian government had degenerated into a morass of corruption and inefficiency. The new king, Charles II (1665-1700), could not give the leadership the state needed. He was retarded and sickly, and his jaw was so large and heavy that he could not close his mouth. He drooled constantly, and could not control his bowels. He suffered from an astonishing variety of respiratory ailments and was constantly expected to die—but, in fact, he lived on and on. The so-called government fell into the hands of the queen mother, who ran an indolent and corrupt regime, notable only for its vicious palace intrigue. In 1680 Castile reached its nadir. A currency revaluation destroyed what remained of trade and industry and again bankrupted the crown. Royal government was nearly lifeless. It even stopped promising better times, and presented a facade of quiet futility. Attempts at reform and recovery awaited the new Bourbon dynasty, who entered their paltry inheritance in 1700. And the Spanish Bourbons, though not without grave faults, were an improvement. Shorn of its power, Spain made a modest recovery in the last century of the Old Regime.

The circumstances of decline varied widely in the Spanish, Polish and Ottoman monarchies. Spain had a developed bureaucracy and a powerful royal army, but fell prey to the seventeenth-century depression and unattainable religious and imperial goals. Formerly a semimodern state, Spain deteriorated into poverty and red tape. Poland was just the opposite. An expanding market for grain made the magnates rich but did nothing for a monarchy that possessed no army or administration. And the Ottoman Empire became an army without a state, a tribe without a country as Christians and Arabs took over nearly all the functions of government. The results, however, were the same in all three: defeat abroad and political disintegration at home.

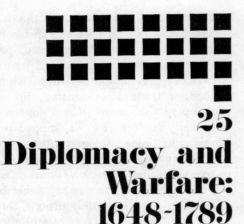

25
Diplomacy and Warfare: 1648-1789

Warfare in the Old Regime

"A great country can have no such thing as a little war," said the Duke of Wellington in 1815, after a particularly big one. In the Old Regime, the European Great Powers managed to live up to Wellington's standards as, for the most part, they have since. But during the Old Regime, wars, although big and long enough, were seldom conclusive. Total military victory was impossible. Armies were too small, they moved too slowly, and the territories they had to conquer were too large to hold. Commanders found it difficult to administer conquered provinces. Moreover, the technology and tactics of defense were superior to those of offense. Each walled city had to be besieged, and that often took months. Each fortified village had to be reduced. Even castles still blocked an enemy's advance. Furthermore, an opposing army might be defeated in battle, but was seldom destroyed. It retreated into a walled town, and recovered. Beyond that, armies fought by the season, campaigning in the summer when food was plentiful and retiring into winter quarters when it was not. Finally, a preindustrial technology limited offensive military effectiveness. Unpaved and ill-kept roads meant that an army moving three miles a day was marching rapidly. Guns were undependable, giving the advantage to fortifications. Armies were ill equipped to achieve victory.

Military strategy and tactics conformed to the limitations mentioned above. Generals maneuvered for position, hoping to force their opponents to retreat, leaving fortified towns without hope of reinforcement. Whole campaigns were designed to reduce a single town or to secure a single district. Battles were fought only when necessary. Pillage was as important a tactical weapon as battle or siege; after all, the troops must eat and enjoy. Generals measured victory in relative terms; if they ended a campaign in a better position than they began it they were all satisfied. Only the greatest commanders transcended these limited concepts of war. Eugene of Savoy, the duke of Marlborough, or Mauriec de Saxe sought to destroy the enemy. But total victory eluded even them. In spite of battles won, technological limitations held them back. They were like speedboats trapped in the mud.

Balance of Power Diplomacy

Such strategy, of course, made diplomacy more important than fighting. Since war was not fought to victory, it had to be fought to negotiations. Battles or sieges won were diplomatic poker chips to be used at the peace table. Diplomats traded these advantages, attempting to gain by skill in their profession what soldiers lost through incompetence in theirs.

This type of diplomacy, which dealt in limited liability, was christened "balance of power" by the English diplomat, Sir William Temple. This meant that no state could be allowed to gain a general hegemony in Europe. Should a country become too powerful, the others would combine against it, thus keeping its gains within acceptable bounds and preserving the existing state system based on national sovereignty. Temple presented this as an observation on the way things worked, but balance of power soon became a canon of diplomacy, a reason constantly invoked by diplomats to justify their actions.

A second fundamental factor in the Old Regime state system was the existence of two district spheres of diplomacy. One was western, comprising Spain, France, England, the Netherlands, and Austria. In this arrangement, the small Italian and German states, as well as Portugal, were viewed as provinces to be conquered or as spheres of influence. Territorial aggrandizement in the West, therefore, often came at the expense of these small states. Only Spain, the weakest of the western countries, had to part with her provinces.

Territory was not the only object of western warfare. Wars were fought on both land and sea, in Europe and abroad, for trade and colonies. Treaties reflected these diverse interests. They included tariff schedules and colonial adjustments, as well as provisions for European provinces and royal marriages.

In Eastern Europe the diplomatic web included the Ottoman Empire, Poland, Russia, Sweden and Prussia. Here, diplomacy was simpler. Eastern European states were generally behind their western neighbors in political centralization, so questions of colonies and trade were unimportant. Eastern powers fought only for land, for huge provinces with uncertain boundaries, few towns, little wealth and less government. In spite of this, the military and diplomatic struggles in Eastern Europe possessed both purpose and coherence. The wars resolved themselves into one basic theme. The central issue was the disposition of three empires that had become too weak to sustain themselves: Sweden, Poland and Turkey—an issue that eventually became known as "The Eastern Question."

Until 1740, these two spheres of war and diplomacy were generally separate. Wars were fought simultaneously, and the Austrians, who had vital interests in both halves of Europe, were frequently engaged in the East and West at the same time. But aside from this, what happened in the West seldom affected Eastern Europe, and the reverse was also true. Indeed, the Austrians, who had a habit of losing wars in the West, were usually winners in the East. In 1740 this pattern broke down, and most of the Great Powers were drawn into a single interconnected conflict, the War of the Austrian Succession (1740-1748). And it took a dynastic crisis in the one great power that belonged to both diplomatic spheres to bring all Europe into the same war. The last years of the Old Regime (1740–1789) saw a single European balance of power, thus insuring that every state

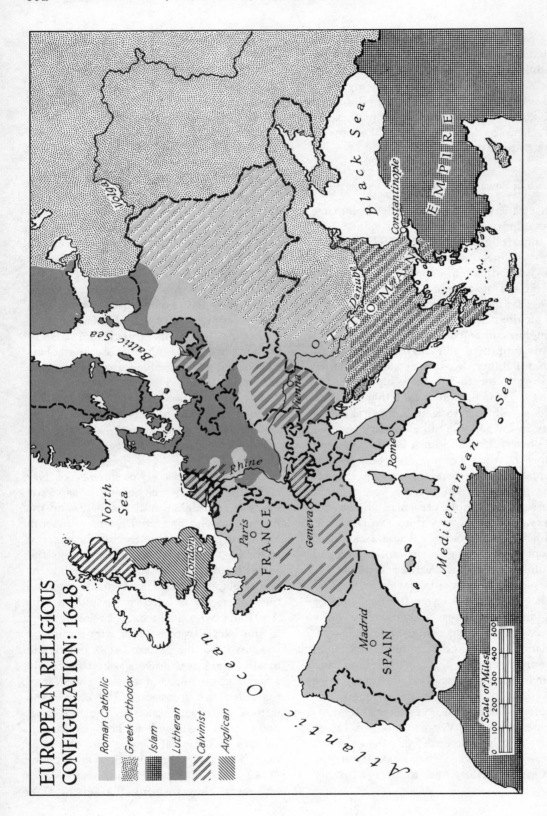

EUROPEAN RELIGIOUS
CONFIGURATION: 1648

Roman Catholic
Greek Orthodox
Islam
Lutheran
Calvinist
Anglican

North
Sea

Baltic Sea

Volga

Black Sea

Constantinople

OTTOMAN   EMPIRE

Danube

Vienna

Rhine

Paris

FRANCE

Geneva

London

Rome

Mediterranean   Sea

Madrid

SPAIN

Atlantic   Ocean

Scale of Miles
0   100   200   300   400   500

Jacques Callot, "The Battle" from Miseries and Misfortunes of War, a book of gravures. (The Metropolitan Museum of Art, Rogers Fund, 1922)

would eventually become involved in the wars of the French Revolution.

The Early Wars of Louis XIV

In Western Europe after the Treaties of Westphalia (1648), the basic issue of international affairs was the French attempt to establish political hegemony over her neighbors. France had emerged from the Thirty Years' War with territorial gains in Alsace, and she was also the best organized state in Europe. French gains at Westphalia were reinforced by victory over Spain in a long and desultory war that ended in 1659 with the Peace of the Pyrenees. France added territory in Belgium as well as the Spanish province of Roussillon. By 1661, when Louis XIV assumed personal power, France was uniquely prepared for sustained expansion on a large scale.

Louis, of course, took advantage of the situation as soon as he could. After careful diplomatic preparation, he launched a massive invasion of the Spanish provinces in the Low Countries (Belgium), and grabbed them all. Such rapid and overwhelming success frightened the Dutch, who organized a coalition against France. Louis chose to negotiate rather than to continue fight-

ing and, in 1668, the War of Devolution ended with France giving up much of Belgium. But the Sun King was still compensated for his troubles. He kept a strip of territory in southern Flanders, including the fortress city of Lille.

This was nice, but it was not enough. Louis had settled for considerably less than he wanted, and nobody likes to do that. Outraged at the Dutch success in reducing the scope of his victory, the Sun King organized a coalition against the Netherlands. In 1672 he was ready, he invaded, and was only prevented from occupying the entire country when the Dutch opened their dikes. The war then settled down into campaigns of maneuver and diplomacy. The coalition against the Dutch contradicted the principles of balance of power, and crumbled away within two years. By 1675, France was fighting against Spain and Austria as well as the Netherlands. And by 1678, everyone had had enough. The Spanish, as usual, paid the price of peace. In the Treaty of Nijmwegen, Spain ceded the province of Franche-Comté and some more Flemish towns to France. Everyone else got nothing.

After Nijmwegen, Louis XIV changed his tactics a bit, but not his aims. Instead

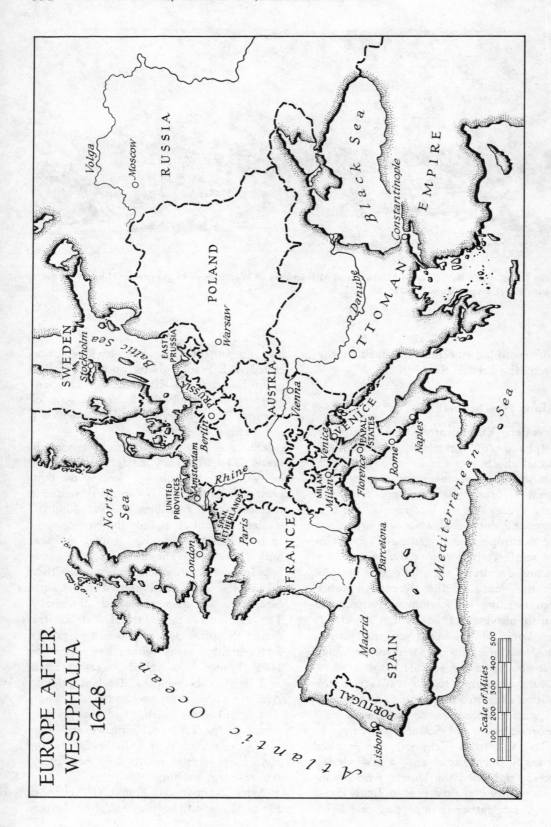

EUROPE AFTER
WESTPHALIA
1648

RUSSIA

Volga

Moscow

SWEDEN

Stockholm

Baltic Sea

EAST
PRUSSIA

PRUSSIA

Berlin

POLAND

Warsaw

Danube

Black Sea

Constantinople

OTTOMAN EMPIRE

North
Sea

UNITED
PROVINCES

Amsterdam

Rhine

AUSTRIA

Vienna

VENICE

Venice

MILAN

Milan

PAPAL
STATES

Florence

Rome

Naples

Mediterranean Sea

London

SPAN.
NETHERLANDS

Paris

FRANCE

Barcelona

Madrid

SPAIN

PORTUGAL

Lisbon

Atlantic Ocean

Scale of Miles

0   100 200 300 400 500

of declaring war on his neighbors and invading them, he haled them into French courts and invaded them. He established "Chambers of Reunion," which were to decide the true boundaries of the cities, provinces and territories recently ceded to France. Since medieval boundaries were notoriously vague, it was possible to claim that France was owed far more land than she had received. Louis' courts solemnly claimed everything they could, and the French army occupied it, including Lorraine, Luxembourg, Strasbourg and a good deal of the Rhenish Palatinate. There were protests, of course (there always are), but for a decade after 1678 there was no serious armed resistance. For France, "Reunion" was even better than war.

The War of the League of Augsburg

The Chambers of Reunion, together with French victories in the last several wars, convinced most western diplomats that only a powerful coalition could stop the Sun King. Therefore, England and the Netherlands submerged their colonial rivalry, and were joined by Spain and Austria in another effort to defeat France. In the War of the League of Augsburg (1688-1698) the allies did fairly well, fighting the French to a stalemate. In the Treaty of Ryswick (1698), Louis XIV was forced to make some important concessions. He recognized William III, the Dutch *Stadhouder*, as king of England, thus accepting the results of the Glorious Revolution. He disgorged most of his Reunions, including Luxembourg and Lorraine.

Exhaustion was certainly a factor in the Treaty of Ryswick. France had suffered famine, depression and disguised royal bankruptcy, and the allies were also feeling the pinch. But there was another factor, perhaps more important: the partition of the Spanish empire. At long last, it looked as if the drooling Charles of Spain was finally going to die. He had no heirs, of course, and the disposition of his empire was the subject of an intense diplomatic auction. The two leading contenders, France and Austria, agreed to a Bavarian candidate, who outraged everyone by dying even before Charles II. Seeing no alternative to Austrian control of Spain, the French managed to get it for themselves. In 1700, Louis XIV's grandson became Philip V of Spain—the first of the Spanish Bourbons.

The War of the Spanish Succession

England, Austria and the Netherlands could not acccept this spectacular expansion of Bourbon power. By 1701 they were again at war with France. In the War of the Spanish Succession (1701-1713), France fought in a defensive posture. Even so, in 1704 the war turned against the French. At Blenheim, the duke of Marlborough obliterated a French army and drove them out of Germany.* Two years later, Marlborough broke through French defensive lines in Belgium at Ramillies and pushed the French back to the frontier. At the same time, Eugene of Savoy pushed the French out of Italy, and Philip V's troops barely escaped destruction in Spain. But the worst was still ahead. In 1708, Marlborough and Eugene destroyed a French army at Oudenarde and invaded France itself. The next year France was struck by the worst famine in her history, which killed over a million people.

Somehow, the French fought on. The bankrupt king managed to raise one more army by recruiting starving peasant youths who could find bread nowhere else. The French built another defense line across northern France, which the allies attacked

---

* The nineteenth-century poet Robert Southey celebrated the battle of Blenheim in these words:

" 'It was the English,' Kaspar cried, 'who put the French to rout;
But what they fought each other for I could not well make out;
But everybody said,' quoth he,
'That 'twas a famous victory.' "

at Malplaquet. There were more than 40,000 casualties in the battle, including the French commander, Marshal Villars, but the French held and denied Marlborough his chance to march on Paris. When peace came, therefore, it was, like the others, a compromise. Philip V held on to Spain; the French surrendered a few colonial possessions to the victorious British, and it was stipulated that the Bourbon crowns of France and Spain could never be united. The Treaties of Utrecht (1713), however, masked rather than revealed the diplomatic reality. The French were badly beaten, and it would be a century before they made one last effort to dominate Europe—in the wars of the Revolution and Napoleon.

War and Diplomacy in Europe: The Turkish Decline

In Eastern Europe, during these years, the main concern in diplomatic affairs was the Turkish menace, the most pressing aspect of the Eastern Question. The Turks controlled, more or less, a vast amount of Eastern Europe. It was a powerful empire, even though Turkish control over much of it was loose and sporadic. Most of the Eastern powers felt threatened by the Turks, and were frequently at war with them. Things had been this way since the fourteenth century when the Turks had first gained a foothold in Europe.

In the middle years of the seventeenth century, this accustomed diplomatic pattern continued. Venice was at war with the Ottoman Empire. It began in 1645, and gradually settled down into an Homeric seige of Candia, in Crete. Although the Venetians won some important naval victories, they were unable to hold Candia, which the Turks finally took in 1669. The peace treaty in 1670 ceded the island of Crete to the Ottoman empire.

Austria also fought the Turks, continu-ously in border skirmishes, more seriously in a short war from 1661 to 1664. The Austrian general, Montecuccoli, won a major victory at St. Gotthard, but the Truce of Vasvar in 1664 merely reaffirmed the existing boundaries. Poland tried her hand at war with the Turks in 1672 and was promptly defeated. In the Treaty of Zuravna in 1676, the Turks gained most of Podolia, a large province with unknown boundaries and no central administration. Only the Russians did well against the Turks. In a short war from 1677 to 1681, Turkey lost her nominal suzerainty over the southern Ukraine to Russia.

In these desultory wars, the Ottoman Empire rarely faced more than one Christian power at a time, and fought on one front only. Although the power of Turkey was declining, it was sufficient to deal with such modest threats. Moreover, Turkey's enemies only nibbled around the outer edges of empire and never threatened the center. Even if the Turks lost, as at St. Gotthard, it was not too serious. The basic power balance remained.

In 1681, the traditional diplomatic patterns were changed. A new Turkish vizir, Kara Mustapha, decided to invade Austria, and he provoked a general Christian alliance against him. Austria was joined by the papacy, Venice, Poland, and ultimately Russia in the Holy League, whose avowed aims were to liberate "oppressed" Christians, conquer territory and end the Turkish menace.

The Turks struck first. Urged on by the French, Kara Mustapha launched a slow and ponderous march up the Danube to Vienna. It took two years to get there but in 1683, the Turks laid siege to Vienna. Although ably defended by Rüdiger von Stahremburg, the city might have fallen had it not been relieved by a Polish army under King Jan III Sobieski.

The siege of Vienna of 1683, like the earlier siege of 1529, was the high point of the Ottoman efforts. As the Turks retreated down the Danube, the Austrians followed. in 1686 the Austrians took Budapest, the capital of Hungary, and in 1687 the defeated the Turks at Mohacs and drove them south into Serbia. At the same time, the Venetians invaded Greece and conquered the Peloponnesian peninsula. They even captured Athens, although in the process an ammunition dump in the Parthenon exploded and severely damaged that ancient and celebrated building.

In 1695, the Russians joined the alliance against Turkey. They besieged Azov and after a year took it. The Austrians were also active. In 1697, Prince Eugene of Savoy cornered a Turkish army at Zenta in southern Hungary and destroyed it. Such an overwhelming defeat persuaded the Turks to seek peace. In 1699, the treaties were signed at Karlowitz. They reflected the magnitude of the Christian victory. Austria gained Hungary, Transylvania, Croatia and part of Serbia, while the Russians retained Azov, the Venetians kept the Peloponnesus and most of the Dalmatian coast and Poland got Podolia. Karlowitz marked the end of the Ottoman Empire as the most powerful eastern state, a role now assumed by Austria and soon to be shared with Russia.

The Great Northern War

No sooner had war ended in the south than it broke out in the Baltic. Here, the issue was the disposition of the Swedish empire. In 1697, a young boy of fifteen became Charles XII of Sweden. His neighbors, Russia, Poland and Denmark, thought it might be a good time to partition an empire that Sweden could no longer hold. In 1700 they attacked, and began the Great Northern War.

No one could know it, of course, but Charles XII was a natural military genius. In six months he had driven the astounded

Danes out of the war and turned on Russia. At Narva, in November 1700, Charles attacked 40,000 Russians with only 8000 of his own troops. The Russians were not expecting him; it was snowing and already dark when Charles attacked. People did not fight in such wretched weather. But Charles did, and he utterly routed the Russians. He then turned on the Poles, and drove them out of the war in 1706.

Having dealt with Poland and Denmark, Charles turned back to Russia. But Peter the Great had used the respite to reorganize his army, and in June 1709, Peter defeated the Swedes at Poltava. In effect, this victory won the war for Russia, although desultory fighting and serious pillaging continued until 1721. Charles XII could never again regain the strategic initiative. The allies had been right. Sweden was too poor and small to defend her extensive Baltic empire. In the treaties of Nystadt (1721), Russia got the entire Baltic coast from Finland to Prussia and took her place as a legitimate Great Power.

The Polish Question

The Great Northern War demonstrated with dreadful clarity that Poland had become a power vacuum, a part of the Eastern Question. During the eighteenth century, her neighbors intervened in Polish affairs with increasing force. As early as 1715, Russia actively supported the Polish nobles against their king and, by the 1730s, the Polish king had to be chosen abroad. In 1766, the grant of religious toleration to Protestants and Greek Orthodox Catholics brought Poland to civil war. Her great power neighbors moved to protect their interests in Poland, and Austria and Russia came to the verge of war. Not wishing a general conflict, Frederick the Great of Prussia proposed a partition of Poland. In August, 1722, Russia, Austria and Prussia each grabbed a slice of Poland.

This worked so well that it was repeated in 1793 with a second partition, only this time Austria was left out. In 1795, a third partition, with all three great powers participating, finished Poland off. Everyone, except the Poles, seemed pleased by this neat solution to a difficult aspect of the Eastern Question. In 1668, the retiring king, Jan Kasmir, had predicted exactly that result. Rarely has a prophecy been so accurate.

The Power Shift in Eastern Europe

In the years between Westphalia and the French Revolution, there had been a complete reversal of the diplomatic and military relationships in Eastern Europe. In 1648, Poland, Sweden and Turkey had controlled, in a rather disorganized fashion, huge empires in Eastern Europe. Russia was still an Asiatic state, Austria was glad to hold her defensive lines against the Turks, while Prussia was still a minor German principality. During the following century and a half, all that changed. Three new great powers, Austria, Russia and Prussia, came to dominate Eastern Europe, largely through modernizing their armies and creating an effective civil service. They conquered many provinces from their fading rivals, and wiped one out altogether. In the process, Russia, Austria and Prussia discovered that they could gain more by cooperation than war. Russia and Austria established a cooperationist diplomacy as early as the 1720s, and Prussia joined them after 1763. The partitions of Poland signaled the change. Diplomacy replaced war as the preferred method of dealing with the Eastern Question.

The Wars of the Eighteenth Century

After the War of the Spanish Succession and the Great Northern War, the great powers were exhausted. By 1715, they had been fighting almost continuously for a generation. It was time for peace. But peace only adjourned the quarrels; it did not end them. Prussia was not satisfied with its small gains from the Great Northern War. Austria and Russia hoped for more from Turkey. The Franco-British colonial and trade rivalry grew steadily worse. The British thought themselves strong enough to grab a large piece of the Spanish Empire. In the eighteenth century, as today, peace was frequently a temporary expedient, a last resort when ministers could think of nothing else.

War came at last—in 1739 in the colonies and in 1740 in Europe, after an appropriate and recuperative interval of peace. The new hostilities were a conjunction of two separate conflicts, the continuing colonial quarrels between France, England, and Spain, and the efforts of Prussia to become a great power. The war was immense, like that of the Spanish Succession and the crusade against the Turks put together. The English were reaching for colonial and economic domination, and the Prussians were trying to annex a rich and extensive Austrian province. Stakes like that brought everybody in and merged the two previously separate diplomatic spheres into one, as nations sought allies wherever they could.

The mid-century war was fought in two installments with an eight-year respite between them. The first, the War of the Austrian Succession (1740-1748), was a kind of preliminary. The second, the Seven Years' War (1756–1763), saw the British and Prussians finally victorious. In between the two, there was some juggling of alliances. The French, who had been allies of Prussia in the War of the Austrian Succession, switched over and became allies of Austria for the second round. A "diplomatic revolution" contemporaries called it, as France and Austria had been enemies steadily for a quarter of a millenium. But it was not really a revolution, for the essential struggle remained the same. Austria was still fighting Prussia, France was still fighting Great Britain. The issues in the

Seven Years' War were the same as those in the Austrian Succession.

The Wars of the Austrian Succession

The war in Europe, between Austria and Prussia, began with an Austrian succession crisis. Charles VI had no sons, and so he prepared to leave his empire to his daughter, Maria Theresa. To insure her succession, he had her rights acknowledged by the provinces of the realm and the major foreign powers. When Charles died in 1740, Maria Theresa assumed the throne of Austria. The new king of Prussia, Frederick the Great, sensing an opportune moment to grab a piece of Maria Theresa's inheritance, invaded and conquered Silesia. He also provoked a general European war. The French were drawn in as Prussian allies, and the British joined Austria, thus binding their colonial rivalry to the war in central Europe.

In the colonies, the Great War for Empire had begun in 1739, after two decades of nagging disagreements between England and Spain. The English had received limited trading rights in the Spanish Empire in the treaties of Utrecht (1713) and, in the endless search for profits, English merchants had consistently gone beyond the letter of the law. The Spanish had retaliated by licensing coast guards to prevent illegal English trade. The coast guards were paid out of the profits from captured ships, so they captured as many as they could, regardless of what kind of trade the merchants pursued. There were protests, court cases, diplomatic representations, reparations claimed, and increasing hostility between England and Spain. In 1738, Captain Jenkins, testifying before a parliamentary committee, announced an unusual and horrible atrocity. He said the Spanish had cut off his ear. It was too much: in 1739, England declared war on Spain. This so called "War of Jenkin's Ear" expanded swiftly into the larger conflict involving Anglo-French colonial rivalries and the Austro-Prussian struggle.

When war began, the English expected to drive the Spanish out of Latin America in a short and glorious campaign. It did not happen. The English were unprepared for war, and the Spanish, however feebly, fought back. Not until 1745 were the British really ready. Thereafter, they did well. They swept French and Spanish shipping from the seas and took Nova Scotia from the French. Only defeats in Belgium prevented the British from completing their triumph.

By 1748, both sides were ready for peace. The French were nearly bankrupt and in danger of losing their American colonies. The British cabinet was composed of nervous and petty men, who feared that the war debt would mean higher land taxes. Frederick the Great of Prussia, firmly in possession of Silesia, had wanted peace for six years. Maria Theresa of Austria reluctantly concluded that her armies and treasury were too battered to go on. The Treaties of Aix-la-Chapelle (1748), therefore, were a kind of truce. Except for Silesia, which remained Prussian, conquests were restored. The great powers concentrated on getting ready for the next round.

Part of the preparation was the search for allies. Austria, in particular, was dissatisfied with her friends. The British paid nice subsidies, but they concentrated their efforts in the colonies and their army was truly pitiful. The Austrian search for new allies ended in 1756, when Russia and France agreed to help her win Silesia back. Prussia and Great Britain, diplomatically isolated and outmaneuvered, formed their own alliance in self-defense.

The Seven Years' War

Frederick the Great could see that his position in 1756 was precarious, and his enemies, at least on paper, were far stronger than he. So he struck suddenly in August, 1756, conquering Saxony and invading Bohemia before the allies were ready. Although Frederick failed to drive the Aus-

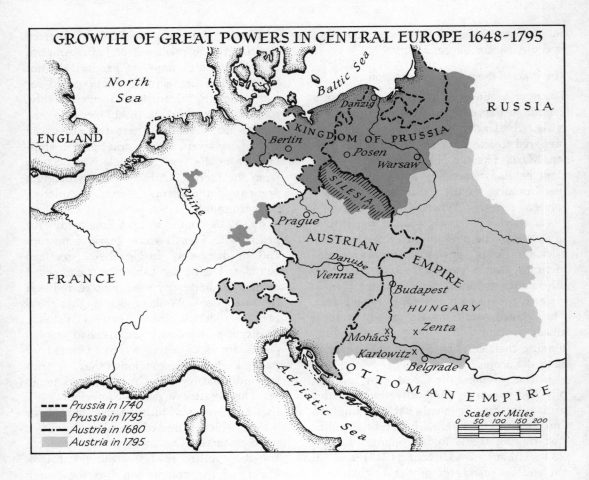

GROWTH OF GREAT POWERS IN CENTRAL EUROPE 1648-1795

North Sea

Baltic Sea

Danzig

RUSSIA

ENGLAND

KINGDOM OF PRUSSIA

Berlin

Posen

Warsaw

SILESIA

Rhine

Prague

AUSTRIAN EMPIRE

FRANCE

Danube

Vienna

Budapest

HUNGARY

Zenta

Mohács X

X

Karlowitz X

Belgrade

OTTOMAN EMPIRE

Adriatic Sea

- - - - Prussia in 1740
▨ Prussia in 1795
—·—·— Austria in 1680
▨ Austria in 1795

Scale of Miles
0   50   100   150   200

trians out of the war with the first blow, he did maintain the upper hand for the first two years of fighting. He destroyed the French at Rossbach (1757) and forced them back over the Rhine. He held Saxony and part of Bohemia and drove the Russians back in disorder at Zorndorff (1758). But by 1759, the allies' superior strength began to tell. The Russians captured Berlin, and the Austrians occupied most of Saxony and Silesia. Only the death of the Czarina Elizabeth in 1762 saved Frederick from certain defeat. Her successor, Peter III, was a great admirer of Frederick and pulled out of the war. The French, being beaten down by Great Britain, could give no help, and Austria was too weak to win alone. In 1763, the Treaty of Hubertusburg ended the fighting on the basis of mutual restor-

ation of conquests. Seven years of savage war had changed nothing. Prussia still held Silesia, and was, irrevocably a great power.

Overseas, no one had observed the fragile interval of peace that obtained in Europe between the two wars. The Great War for Empire continued without interruption. In India, the British and French continued fighting through the medium of native allies. In North America, Indian raids were nearly continous along the borders of the northern English colonies. In 1753 the French occupied the Ohio valley. They fortified Niagara, and built posts on Lake Champlain. General Braddock attempted to drive the French from Fort Duquesne (Pittsburgh) in 1755, and lost his whole army. The formal declaration of war a year later changed nothing.

This time, the British fought the war with immense vigor. The little men cleared out of the way, and a great man took their place. In 1757, William Pitt became the British war leader. He was a man of incredible energy who knew just what he wanted—victory. His intensity had frightened his petty colleagues, who kept him out of power as long as possible. In 1757 it was no longer possible. This war could not be fought like the last.

Pitt demanded offensive action in all quarters. He ordered his admirals in the Caribbean to capture the French sugar islands of Guadeloupe and Martinique, which they did without much difficulty. In India, Robert Clive defeated the French and their allies at Plassy in 1757 and secured British domination of the subcontinent. Pitt sent armies to North America to conquer New France. He also sent the right generals. Wolfe and Amherst redeemed years of timidity and bungling by capturing Quebec (1759) and Montreal (1760); and Canada became British. In 4 years of war Pitt did what his predecessors had failed to do in 40. He had triumphed everywhere.

The key to British success in the Great War for Empire was the Royal Navy. Naval superiority, firmly established by the victories at Lagos and Quiberon Bay in 1759, enabled the British to maintain communications and supply, while isolating the French in little outposts that merely waited their turn to be reduced. French shipping disappeared and French trade collapsed. In the sugar islands the French faced defeat by starvation before the British invasions. Montcalm, the defender of Canada, was a skilful general, but he had a small army and no means of communication with home. His only real hope was to hold out until the British got tired and settled for a compromise peace. Naval supremacy gave the British a basic strategic domination that could surmount tactical defeats, the inevitable stealing by bureaucrats and flag officers, and the timidity of military timeservers. A leader like Pitt, of course, put an end to all that, and the Royal Navy promptly won the war.

In trying to translate military victory into peace, the British faced an embarrassing and unforeseen problem. They had won too much and had overthrown the imperial balance of power. Something had to be given back. In the Peace of Paris (1763), the British returned the sugar islands to the French and Havana to the Spanish, recognized French fishing rights off Newfoundland, and refrained from expanding their trading privileges in New Spain. But the British kept India, Canada, Florida and the Ohio valley. There must be some reward for victory.

The treaties of Hubertusburg and Paris in 1763 established the power relationships in Europe for more than a century, until the Franco-Prussian War in 1870. British empire overseas was balanced by four great powers on the continent, none of which could dominate Europe. The result of massive war had been to confirm the supremacy of diplomacy over fighting, to make total victory even less likely. The wars also served to raise the concept of balance of power to the level of sacred dogma, as the partitions of Poland, the alliance against Britain during the American Revolution, and the course of the wars of the French Revolution would show. Old Regime wars, then, merely changed the names of the great powers; Spain and Poland, for example, succumbed from external defeat and internal rot while Prussia and Russia took their places. But the state system continued unaltered. In an age of relative social, technological and political stability, it could hardly be otherwise.

The Growth of State Sovereignty

The French prime minister, Cardinal Richelieu, understood what government meant. He outlined a simple and ambitious program to his king, Louis XIII.

I promised Your Majesty to employ all my industry and all the authority which it should please you to give me to ruin the Huguenot party, to abase the pride of the nobles, to bring all your subjects back to their duty, and to restore your reputation among foreign nations to the place it ought to be.

Allowing for local variations, this is exactly what happened during the seventeenth and eighteenth centuries. The state became greater than its people. Where the nobility, the Church and the towns had previously been stronger than the king (or king in parliament), the reverse was now true. Thus the state began to claim larger and larger portions of the people's resources, energies and loyalty. The state taxed, drew people into government service, and supported doctrines of patriotism and nationalism.

The state also grew bigger. It absorbed independent enclaves within its boundaries, for instance, federal principalities and ecclesiastical territories. It also extended those boundaries considerably. States fought almost constant war to annex new provinces: the Austrians conquered Hungary from the Turks; the Prussians conquered Silesia from the Austrians; the French tried to conquer Belgium. Ministates, like Venice or the Netherlands, no matter how rich or well organized they were, slipped behind in the race for power.

These were not inconsequential trends. They resulted in the transformation of war from a private to a public pastime. They meant that government had become more important than religion, or even class. The growth of the power of the state is the most important political process of modern history. And it is not over.

CHRONOLOGY OF THE OLD REGIME

1640–1688:	Reign of the Great Elector of Prussia
1660:	Restoration of the monarchy in England
1672–1678:	War between France and Holland
1681–1699:	Great Christian Crusade of Austria, Poland, Venice, Papacy and Russia against the Ottoman Empire
1683:	Seige of Vienna
1688–1689:	Glorious Revolution in England
1697:	Battle of Zenta
1699:	Treaty of Karlowitz, ending war between Austria and Turkey
1701–1713:	War of the Spanish Succession
1701–1721:	Great Northern War
1715:	Death of Louis XIV of France and accession of Louis XV
1740:	Accession of Maria Therese of Austria
	Accession of Frederick the Great of Prussia
	Beginning of the War of the Austrian Succession
1748:	Treaty of Aix-la-Chapelle, ending War of the Austrian Succession
1756–1763:	Seven Years' War
1760:	Accession of George III of England
1772:	First Partition of Poland
1775–1783:	American "Revolution"
1780–1790:	Joseph II Emperor of Austria
1786:	Death of Frederick the Great
1787–1789:	Beginnings of the French Revolution
1793:	Second Partition of Poland
1795:	Third and final Partition of Poland, which now disappeared

26
The Age
of Enlightenment

"The more things change, the more they stay the same," runs the French proverb and, generally, it is true. But not this time; the Enlightenment, while it bore a resemblance to thoughts past, marked a sharp and surprising departure from the way men had once thought. The Enlightenment was the intellectual divide between a medieval and modern climate of opinion, between a religious and secular view of the world. It contained elements of both visions, but novel ideas predominated. The break with the past, while not total, was loud and enthusiastic, and was accompanied by scorn for ideas that everyone had once believed.

So rapid a change in the prevailing opinions magnified disagreement. Sides were sharply drawn between those who attacked Christianity and those who defended it, between those supporting existing social arrangements and others who condemned them. The Enlightenment was a time of controversy and noise, of shouting and insults, of hordes of petty propagandists, of popularization rather than creation. The climate of opinion was more significant than the notions of particular philosophers. In the midst of universal ferment, only the high culture, art, music, drama, architecture, with its continued dependence on aristocratic patronage, remained the same. Elsewhere the tone of eighteenth-century thought and debate was set by critics, dealers in new notions, prophets of a new Utopia and those who shocked and alarmed.

The New Intellectual Climate

In December 1680, Halley's Comet passed over Europe in its usual manner and aroused discussion everywhere. It revived the old superstition that comets were the portent of political catastrophes, natural calamities and the death of princes. Men freely predicated the worst, from the end of the world to less general but still startling disasters. Such pronouncements were received solemnly and with real concern. They were the traditional reaction to comets. Nothing appeared to have changed.

This time, however, there were different opinions on the subject. Edmund Halley (1656-1742), the British astronomer, viewed the comet as a natural phenomenon and published a sober treatise calculating its orbit and predicting future appearances of this wayward star. In France, the Huguenot pastor Pierre Bayle (1647–1706) wrote a powerful book, *Divers Thoughts on the Comet* . . . , which assailed the superstitution about comets, denounced supersition in general, and belabored the miracles of the Christian faith. From this beginning, the infection spread to everything. Within a decade of the comet, both Bayle and John Locke had written imposing pleas for religious toleration. Locke proposed a new knowledge theory in his *Essay Concerning Human Understanding* (1690), and defended liberal politics in his *Two Treatises on Civil Government* (1690 also). Sir Isaac Newton published his *Principia Mathematica*, completing the journey of astronomy from being part of the Faith to a secular science. In only a decade, the intellectual landscape of Europe changed with a speed and abruptness previously unknown.

Established ideas had been challenged before, of course, both singly and in battalions, but this time the notions of the heretics received almost instant applause. The ideas of Newton, Locke and Bayle became the new orthodoxy as soon as people heard them. Traditional notions, such as approval of religious persecution, or the efficacy of superstition and magic, or the divine right of kings, or the earth as the center of the universe, each hallowed by long usage and universal acceptance, suddenly lost all standing among men of letters and were mentioned with scorn and derision. The speed with which the climate of opinion shifted from the old to the new was as startling as the ideas that now came into fashion.

The fact is, of course, that religious toleration, scepticism toward superstition, ideas of limited monarchy, anticlericalism, a scientific view of the heavens had all been seething and stewing underground before they commanded wide and astounding acceptance. People had been preaching religious toleration since 1560, to a very small audience. There were anticlericals even in the height of the Reformation, and they were by no means unknown in the Middle Ages, but now they expanded from a platoon into an army. Galileo had thought along the same lines as Newton but had been far less successful in convincing others. Superstition had been denounced before Bayle discovered it. The Great Remonstrance (1621) and the Petition of Right (1628) elaborated the rights of Englishmen and the powers of Parliament, but the King ignored them. Nonetheless, circulation of subversive ideas continued. And by the eighteenth century their time had come. The notions that no one had previously believed now became the new orthodoxy and dominated the new climate of opinion.

Although Locke, Bayle and Newton disagreed with their predecessors about the answers to questions of political theory, religion and science, they were still agonizing and arguing over the same problems. The proper relationship between kings and their subjects had interested Thomas Aquinas as well as John Locke, and both sought to define the duties of monarchy. Both the Scholastics and Enlightenment philosophers placed great emphasis on the doctrine of natural law, and they differed only in detail on what it meant. Theologians and philosophers each searched ardently for the absolute—absolute truth, absolute values, absolute virtue, absolute proofs. Locke and Bayle were as concerned about human virtue as any Jesuit. Newton and Leibniz thought that understanding God was a crucial human endeavor. And, finally, the philosophers used logic and reason precisely as did their theologian opponents; they bent and shaped it to prove what they already knew to be true. Nonetheless, Enlightenment thought contained an unspoken presupposition: that old problems might be solved in a new way, with new answers. Old bottles were to be refilled with a new brew.

Progress and Perfectibility

"Born to lament, to labor and to die . . . ," wrote the poet Matthew Prior about the human condition. Theologians dwelt often on this theme, and elaborated on the ambiguous nature of man—created in God's image yet inclined toward sin, standing midway between angels and beasts in the hierarchy of creation, and drawn in both directions. But many Enlightenment philosophers took issue with the priests and theologians, arguing that man was basically good and had been corrupted only by society. They asserted the cheerful doctrine that Nature was kind and beneficent, that both man and society might progress indefinitely. Alexander Pope incorporated such views in his epic poem *Essay on Man* (1733), declaring optimistically:

All discord, harmony not understood
All partial evil, universal Good
And, spite of Pride, in erring Reason's spite,
One truth is clear, whatever is is right.

Yet so soothing a notion, which dominated the early Enlightenment, collapsed overnight. In 1755, an earthquake and tidal wave destroyed Lisbon. The kind and bountiful Nature of song and theory had just reached out and obliterated a great Christian city. Why? In an effort to explain the catastrophe, Voltaire (1694-1778), the leading spirit of the Enlightenment looked again at the philosophy of Optimism, and the problems of evil, sin and unmerited disaster. In a long poem, "The Disaster of Lisbon," Voltaire expressed his disillusionment with Optimism, and argued that evil and disaster had been accounted for no better by Enlightenment philosophers

Hyacinthe Rigaud, "Louis XIV", oil painting in the Louvre. (Alinari/Art Reference Bureau)

than by theologians; indeed, the new philosophers had denied them altogether. Voltaire followed this poem with his most celebrated work of fiction, *Candide*, a short satirical novel that described a series of unparalleled disasters which befell the hero and his companions, most of which were undeserved and could hardly have occurred in the best of all possible worlds. Voltaire's concluding advice was reminiscent of Job —let us stay home and cultivate our own gardens.

For a while, it appeared as if Voltaire and the Lisbon earthquake had obliterated all notions of optimism, progress, and moral improvement. But optimism is a seductive notion, and it reappeared toward the end of the century under a new name. Now called the doctrine of progress, it found a home in the philosophy of the Marquis de Condorcet (1743–1794), a pathologically cheerful aristocrat who finished his book while hiding from the police. Condorcet argued that the regular operation of natural laws applied to human affairs as well, and he perceived a progression of ages in human history, each marked by greater virtue and enlightenment. The French Revolution was the last age, and the principles of peace, virtue and justice were about to triumph. The tyrants and priests could no longer prevent it. Under the circumstances, Condorcet's arguments were not altogether convincing. He was imprisoned by the revolutionary government and died in prison while awaiting the guillotine.

Education and Ethics

If Condorcet's hymn of faith in human perfectibility failed to win converts, it was not merely because of the Revolution. In the two decades before 1789 the Enlightenment climate of opinion had begun to change, away from dependence on the harsh rigor of science and reason toward the more human terrain of emotions. Virtue and justice were still the goals, but the immutable and impersonal laws of science might not lead there. Virtue must come from within. It must be inculcated through education, said the Swiss philosopher Jean-Jacques Rousseau (1712–1778) in *Émile*. A natural education, far from the corruption and artificiality of society, would produce a truly moral man. The novelist Bernardin de Saint-Pierre carried this theme forward in his romantic books, notably *Paul et Virginie*. In this early soap opera, two children were abandoned on an East India isle and grew up living with nature rather than society. They were profoundly virtuous, the product of a beneficent nature and their own innate goodness. This touching tale mirrored the new mythology precisely. People were tired of logic. Feelings were more important.

These various inquiries into the human condition were prompted by a general search for a new system of ethics and morality. Moral strictures had traditionally come from God, but religious morality was distasteful to this secular age with its emphasis on science and man. One of these, or both, must be the foundation of moral virtue, and the moral laws might be as absolute and unshakable as when they were derived from God. No one took this view more seriously than Benjamin Franklin, a rising young man from Philadelphia. In his *Autobiography*, Franklin described his plan to reach moral perfection. He listed 13 salient virtues, and emphasized each one until he mastered it. Alas, it did not work. "I soon found I had undertaken a task of more difficulty than I had imagined," Franklin wrote, "While my care was employ'd in guarding against one fault, I was often surprised by another." His contemporaries, lacking his sturdy realism, kept searching for the origins of virtue in all the disciplines they knew. They, too, failed. The religious explanations of virtue and morality remained intact.

Enlightenment Science

The age that venerated virtue held the same opinions about reason and science. They were the essential tools to unlock the secrets of man and nature. There would be no more arguments about the soul, or angels, or heaven, or the nature of God himself; such things were the domain of belief, and reason could shed no light at all. Instead, reasoned inquiry would be limited to areas where there was evidence, to secular or scientific problems, which could be solved. Philosophers no longer regarded reason as a substantive thing, as Plato or Aquinas had, around which a whole speculative system might be built. It was to be a tool, subordinate to facts that must be gathered and arranged according to the scientific method. Research and experimentation, the patient observation of man and nature, and a careful reasoning from this sure foundation would lead to the fundamental truth about everything far more quickly and certainly than the vague and grandiose notions of theologians. Or, at least, that is what many eighteenth-century intellectuals believed.

And yet, in spite of the prestige given to scientists and their marvelous method, the Enlightenment did not see a general continuation of the great discoveries of the previous century. What occurred, instead was a mass of detailed experimental work. The researches of the Bernouilli family were typical. Three generations of Bernouillis worked on higher mathematics, popularizing calculus, working out problems in analytical trigonometry, infinite series and mechanics. This was important work, certainly, but it was along lines already well established. The same was true of the Swedish biologist, Karl Linneaus (1707–1778), who made a general classification of plants and animals. Linneaus incorporated much previous work into his *Systema Naturae* (1735), which went through repeated editions and enlargements. Linneaus based his classifications on external appearance, as Aristotle had, rather than on internal structure. A further error in Linneaus' work was the idea that species remained constant, thus eliminating any concept of evolution. In spite of this, however, the Linnean categories survived, and became the basis for modern taxonomy.

Only in chemistry did eighteenth-century scientists move well beyond the theoretical framework they had inherited. In 1775, an English Unitarian minister, Joseph Priestley, published experiments proving he had isolated and identified oxygen. Four years later, the Dutch scientist Jan Ingenhousz proved that plants exhaled oxygen. Then in 1781 the French chemists, Claude Berthollet and Antoine Lavoisier established oxygen, hydrogen and carbon as the basic elements of organic substances. In 1789, Antoine Lavoisier theorized that oxygen was the vital element in both combustion and breathing, and his book, *Elementary Treatise of Chemistry*, made basic contributions to both organic and inorganic chemistry. Chemistry had hardly existed when the Enlightenment began; now it was a science exact enough to rival physics.

Although the French Revolution disrupted or destroyed most lines of Enlightenment thought, scientific investigation was hardly affected. A couple of scientists were beheaded during the revolution, but their numbers continued to increase, and their successes gave an increasingly scientific cast to western thought. Patient measurement, constant experiment, endless investigation and questioning, these attributes of science do not succumb to mere political upheaval or war.

The Cult of Reason

For Enlightenment philosophers, reason was as important as science in the long campaign for human betterment. The use made of reason in the eighteenth century was in critical analysis of society, law, religion, of everything previously thought immutable and ordained by God. For example, reason became the flail of miracles. "A miracle is the violation of mathematical, divine, immutable, eternal laws . . . ," Voltaire argued in his *Philosophical Dictionary* (1764), "a contradiction in terms: a law cannot at the same time be immutable and violated." Those things alleged to be miracles never happened or, if they did, there was quite a simple explanation that had escaped contemporaries or was omitted by pious chroniclers. It was the function of reason to point this out, not to rationalize and defend "miraculous" events, as was the habit of theologians.

The same mode of critical thought applied to secular customs, many of which were unreasonable and indefensible. In the *Persian Letters* (1721), Baron de Montesquieu (1689–1755), wrote a trenchant satire on contemporary French government and society. The magistrate is made to say that he sold his law library to buy a judicial office, and does not regret the sale, for a judge does not need to know any law at all. The French mistake honor for virtue, and fight duels over nothing. They mistake virginity for virtue, and care more for their bride's purity than for her character or personality. They make marital sex a legal duty, and sue each other in court for nonperformance or malfeasance. They sell public offices to fools, and complain when government is inefficient and tyrannical. They practice legal torture, even though judges know torture produces far more lies than truth. Can reason sustain such customs?

Used as a tool of criticism, reason had its limitations, and might lead to unreasonable ends. It could be pushed to radical scepticism and complete doubt. Pierre Bayle, the first of the Enlightenment philosophers explored this cul-de-sac with his demand that each doctrinal and philosophical assertion be based on facts and hard evidence. All too often, there was no evidence, at least none that could be trusted or checked; frequently, the evidence on one side of an issue was as good as that on the other. The process of destroying myth, of establishing truth, of finding virtue, Bayle discovered, was endless and impossible.

The trouble with radical doubt, of course, was that it demolished everything, including the doubter's capacity to distinguish between what was probably true and what was probably false. This was useless and self-destructive, and the exiled Huguenot pastor Elie Benoist proved it in his *Collection of Historical, Philosophical and Theological Remarks . . .* (1712). How do you know, asked Benoist, that Pierre Bayle is really the author of the famous *Historical and Critical Dictionary* (1697)? Bayle can amass evidence, of course, in the form of sworn witnesses and solemn depositions, but these may well be lies, the witnesses perjured or perhaps mistaken.

Such things have happened before, given the nature of man. There was no absolute proof of Bayle's authorship, Benoist concluded, only partial and approximate proof. What applied to this case applied to them all. We must take things, in part, on faith. We can only ask that the evidence be as sound as possible. To demand more is useless.

Benoist's temperate treatise failed to cool philosopher's dreary ardor for absolute certainty. Nothing could do that. But, it did point to one of the main themes of Enlightenment rationalism; that ideas and knowledge should be useful. The cult of useful knowledge reached its apex in the *Encyclopedia*, a stupendous collection of 21 folio volumes with 13 volumes of plates (1751–1780). It was edited by Denis Diderot and Jean le Rond d'Alembert, both widely known philosophers and publicists who subscribed to the rational, secular and scientific bent of their age. The articles of the *Encyclopedia* were quite uneven. Those dealing with topics such as mechanics, agricultural technology, handicrafts and architecture were excellent. Perhaps these were humbler things than philosophical truth, but the happiness of countless human beings depended on them.

The Attack on Christianity

"Every sect, of whatever opinion it may be, is a rallying point for doubt and error . . .," wrote Voltaire in his *Philosophical Dictionary*, and he expressed a general Enlightenment opinion. Beginning with Bayle, Enlightenment philosophers had mounted a general assault on both the Christian Church and Christian Faith, pronouncing them major impediments to progress and virtue. The philosophers' immediate demand was for religious toleration. Bayle and Locke began the campaign. In *A Letter Concerning Toleration* (1689), John Locke argued that religion was a private matter, an affair of the heart between a man and his God. It was no business of the king. Moreover, given the weakness of human thought, religious differences were inevitable, and one opinion had as good a chance as another to be the truth. Heresy might send one to hell—theologians could argue that—but it should not send a man to the hulks or gallows. Pierre Bayle said much the same thing under far more trying circumstances. A victim of Louis XIV's persecution of the Huguenots, Bayle produced a bitter tirade against intolerance. He described persecution as an offense against both God and man, as a sin as well as a crime.

The demand for toleration broadened rapidly into a general assault on the Church. Critics repeated the old charges that the clergy were corrupt and lived spaciously off the pennies of the poor. They had abandoned apostolic poverty, and received when they should have given. Now, it was said that the church itself was a fraud and a crime, apart from the casual sins of any individual clerics. Bayle, in his *Historical and Critical Dictionary*, discussed church history and argued that the massacres, atrocities and inquisitions were caused by the clergy who urged their flocks on to these monstrous crimes. Pietro Giannone took up the same theme in his *Civil History of the Kingdom of Naples* (1723). He concentrated on the efforts of bishops and abbots to seize temporal power, to establish a theocracy. The Church was the main barrier to human progress, therefore, as well as being an affront to reason and decency. It was unworthy of a Christian people.

The growing popularity of these ideas was sharply tested in Toulouse in 1762. A Huguenot merchant, Jean Calas, was executed after being convicted on the trumped-up charge that he murdered his son to prevent his conversion to Catholicism. The evidence was flimsy; it was fairly obvious that the son, who was seriously depressed, had committed suicide. The whole case was so clearly the product of religious fanaticism that the Calas Affair became a general scandal. Voltaire himself denounced the persecution, and demanded rehabilitation of Calas and the release of his imprisoned family. Continued outcry embarrassed officials in Toulouse and, ultimately, the Calas family emerged from jail and the conviction was reversed. Thus the philosophers' ideas on toleration were beginning to affect popular opinion and the behavior of courts; the ardor of the sixteenth-century religious wars was in full retreat.

While most Enlightenment commentary on religion dealt with persecutions and the general silliness or improbability of various dogmas, there was also an attempt to find an acceptable substitute for Christianity. Voltaire, for instance, turned to Deism. "I was absorbed in the contemplation of nature . . . ," he wrote in the *Philosophical Dictionary*, "A man must be blind not to be impressed by this Spectacle, he must be stupid not to recognize its author, he must be mad not to adore Him." There certainly is a God, whom we ought to worship, but beyond that we know little about Him. Such a view comforted men who had lost their faith in revelation, miracles and dogma, but still wished to worship. In place of the Judeo-Christian God of Hosts they were given Voltaire's God of Reason.

The general assault on Christianity left an indelible mark on western culture. Ridiculed and doubted, the Christian faith moved steadily away from the center of intellectual life toward its periphery. Christianity had once informed and sustained the entire culture; it remained still the religion of the masses but was losing its credit among the most advanced thinkers of the age. Enlightenment criticism of religion was a major step in the secularization of western thought. From having been interpreters of the general culture, the theologians of eighteenth-century France and England came to echo the Psalmist:

Engraving, "The English Parliament". (The Trustees of the British Museum)

"How shall we sing the Lord's song in a strange land?"

Political Theory

In political theory, as in everything else, the Enlightenment involved a sharp shift from the orthodoxy of the seventeenth century. It began with John Locke, whose *Two Treatises on Civil Government* were written to refute divine right absolutism and support the notions of limited government and political liberty that triumphed in the English Glorious Revolution (1688–1689). Locke presented the myth that government began when men abandoned a primordial "state of nature," and delegated authority to a prince or a parliament for private convenience and the general good. Thus following the lawyers of ancient Rome, philosophers of the Middle Ages,

and Reformation Calvinists, Locke asserted that ultimate sovereignty resided in the people. Such views entailed two consequences. The people, who were the ultimate rulers anyway, could retrieve their lent power from the king if he should abuse it, and there were certain natural rights, defined as life, liberty and property, which the government could not abridge. People were not placed on earth for the glory of the king.

Locke openly admitted his intellectual debt to the sixteenth-century theologian Richard Hooker ("The Judicious Hooker," Locke called him), whose theories of natural law, popular sovereignty, and social contract were themselves inspired by the political thought of St. Thomas Aquinas. But Locke gave these ideas a secular cast of which Aquinas and Hooker would not have approved.

These old ideas in new clothing intrigued the eighteenth century, and they became standard Enlightenment doctrine. They formed the basis of the political theories of Jean-Jacques Rousseau. In his *Social Contract* (1762), Rousseau began with the large assertion that "Man is born free; he is everywhere in chains . . ." The state of nature had been glorious, while the present governments were all tyrannical and unjust, having usurped man's natural rights and freedoms. The only free government would be one responsive to the "general will," a vague phenomenon that was like a consensus reached in a Quaker meeting. In such a system, Rousseau claimed, government would be legitimate and men would be virtuous. That double promise was too much for contemporaries to resist. Rousseau's doctrines were repeated endlessly by revolutionaries who seldom had any idea what they meant.

The proper form of government could also be ascertained by examining the law. The monumental effort of this genre was the immense and labored volume by Montesquieu, *The Spirit of the Laws* (1748). Montesquieu tried to derive the natural laws of political development, to determine which climate, which peoples, which institutions inclined normally to despotism and which to liberty. No one doubted that these formulas existed. The laws of Nature were universal, and Montesquieu's ponderous prose convinced everyone he had found them. One observation seemed particularly pertinent. Montesquieu observed that the liberties of England were the result of a division and separation of powers between the legislative, executive and judicial branches of government. This notion, incorrect regarding England, became exceedingly popular, and was incorporated into the constitutions of France and America.

The natural laws of government could also be understood by observing the imperfect world of the Old Regime. The laws actually in effect were peculiarly unenlightened, which everyone agreed was the result of centuries of obscurantist and clerical rule. The natural liberty and equality of man, his inheritance from the state of nature, could hardly be found anywhere. All of this was clearly pointed out by a Milanese aristocrat, the marquis Cesare de Beccaria (1738-1794). A morose and unprepossessing gentleman, Beccaria nonetheless wrote a significant book, *On Crimes and Punishments* (1764). Beccaria's experiences with visiting and managing Milanese prisons convinced him that the ferocious punishments then common failed to deter crimes. Judicial torture was barbarous and seldom succeeded in convincing criminals to tell the truth. The aim of punishment should be the rehabilitation of the criminal, thus protecting society. Criminal law should be reordered on a rational basis, to serve society and adhere to the natural rights of man.

In order for a punishment not to be, in every instance, an act of violence of one or of many against a private citizen, it must be essentially public, prompt, necessary, the least possible in the given circumstances, proportionate to the crime, dictated by the laws.

Beccaria closed his book with that maxim, which instantly became a part of Enlightenment political philosophy.

The proper aim of government could be found in an appeal to history as well as arguments from law and philosophy. David Hume traced the development of British constitutional liberty in his *History of England,* (1754–1761). He wished to know how the English enjoyed liberty while other peoples were ruled by despots unfettered by law. The answers were to be found in the peculiar history of England, particularly in the constitutional struggles of the seventeenth century. Equally instructive was the story of enlightenment lost. In *The Decline and Fall of the Roman Empire* (1776-1788), Edward Gibbon chronicled the catastrophic collapse of the greatest civilization man had ever known. The villain was Christianity, with its intolerance, its emphasis on salvation rather than citizenship, its obscurantist hostility to all that was best about classical culture. Acquaintance with this dismal tale might warn us of present dangers, and help preserve what liberties we have.

These doctrines of natural rights and political liberty did not remain the exclusive possession of philosophers and their public. As the century wore on, political struggles increasingly were articulated in terms of natural rights and Enlightenment philosophy. The demand for parliamentary reform rocked England in the 1780s, between the Peace of Paris and the French Revolution. The inalienable rights of man were written into the American constitution and Declaration of Independence. Dutch and Belgian revolutionaries quoted liberally from contemporary political philosophy, and the Poles cast their struggle for natural reform in terms of natural rights. In the course of a century John Locke's views on political liberty, legal equality and the rights of man had been transformed from philosophical speculation into revolutionary slogans brought into battle.

Atheism

The Enlightenment, which attacked orthodox opinion in every quarter, had orthodoxies of its own that were vigorously defended, and its own heresies, all attacked roundly. The most obnoxious heresies, the ones most consistently denounced, were atheism, the evils of private property, and the hideous neo-Calvinist possibilty that social progress rested not on virtue but on man's incurably perverse nature. These doctrines were assaulted by both polemic and philosophical treatise. Ultimately, however, Enlightenment philosophers failed to produce a definitive defense of property, or rebuttals against atheism or the social

utility of evil, and so fell back on repeated assertions that such thoughts were repugnant to decent men. Yet these heresies showed a sturdy capacity to survive in a hostile climate of opinion.

"Theology is only ignorance of natural causes reduced to a system . . . a long tissue of chimeras and contractions . . .," wrote the atheist Baron Holbach in 1772. Voltaire and his friends could not argue with that; they had said as much and more themselves. But they were horrified at the conclusions Holbach drew from his statements. Holbach went far beyond the conventional Deism of the Enlightenment. He denied the existence of God.

Atheism attracted public attention only toward the middle of the century. In 1748, Julien Offray de La Mettrie published a small book called *Man: A Machine*, in which he denied the existence of the soul and argued that man was only a physiological mechanism. This notion made a great uproar, and La Mettrie had to leave the country. His ideas survived, however, amply supported by Baron Holbach, who maintained a salon where atheists and anticlericals gathered to insult God. Holbach himself contributed to the ferment with a long and mediocre book, *System of Nature* (1770), republished and condensed in 1772 as *Common Sense*. Holbach said nothing new about atheism, which is a simple religion, but he did keep the faith alive and provide a center for respectable blasphemy.

There were atheists in the streets as well as the parlors. A printer named Boulanger published dozens of atheist and antireligious tracts, running them off in his shop as fast as the hacks could turn them out. For a while Boulanger did very well in his enterprise. His pamphlets were denounced by the authorities, they seemed daring and clever, they possessed radical chic. Eventually, however, the public became bored with polemics denouncing monks and throwing mud at God. Enthusiasm for atheism waned.

The basic objection most Enlightenment

philosophers had to atheism was not its scepticism, nor its hostility to church and clergy, but its adverse impact on society. Almost everyone except the atheists believed that the common man needed a belief in God to remain virtuous and obedient to social superiors and moral laws. Without religious faith, most men would give in at once to their numerous evil desires, and sin without stint or limit until it hospitalized or killed them. This was an unsavory prospect, and the good of all demanded that everyone believe God lived. "If God did not exist, it would be necessary to invent him," Voltaire wrote, and, as usual, he struck the proper note. So sharp a philosopher as David Hume agreed, and his devastatingly skeptical *Dialogues on Natural Religion* lay unpublished in his desk until after his death.

Attacks on the Doctrines of Human Virtue and Private Property

Almost as disreputable as atheism, perhaps even worse, were the alarming ideas of Bernard Mandeville (1670–1733), a Dutch physician living in exile in London. Mandeville attacked head-on a favorite Enlightenment notion: that private virtues added up to public benefits and ought to be encouraged for the general good. In 1705 Mandeville published the *Fable of the Bees,* a short poem to which he added long appendixes and explanations. The message was clear and simple.

Millions endeavouring to supply
Each other's Lust and Vanity . . .
As Sharpers, Parasites, Pimps, Players
Pick-Pockets, Coiners, Quacks,
South-Sayers . . .
Fraud, Luxury and Pride must live
While we the Benefits receive . . .
So Vice is beneficial found.

The Enlightenment optimists found such notions obscene. A society trying to find a firm secular base for virtue did not relish being told that private vices led to public good. And it was no good trying to shout the monster down. He was a tough debater and stoutly defended his criminal thesis. Not everyone was convinced by Mandeville that man's rottenness had social value, but his ideas were never quite dismissed. There were enough realists and cynics to keep them afloat.

Equally abominable in theory, although expressing a more abstract and distant danger, were ideas of communism. In an age of criticism, when everything was questioned, there were even critics of private property. In 1775, Morelly published *Nature's Code,* in which he outlined the laws and precepts for a communist society. Morelly argued that original sin was fatally increased by the personal possession of property, the abolition of which would ". . . cut off at the root the vices and all the evils of society." Although they sympathized with the goals, most philosophers were not taken in by the simple delusion that poverty made men virtuous. In fact, few philosophers took communism seriously. They may have harbored illusions about man giving up his vices, but they knew he would never surrender his property.

All of these heresies offended the conscience of the age. Yet, they emerged clearly enough from the general tendencies of Enlightenment thought, from religious skepticism, from the passionate search for virtue. The heretics simply carried Enlightenment premises to their logical conclusions. But most of the eighteenth-century philosophers fought ardently to defend their new, secular orthodoxy against the new heresies.

The Legacy of the Enlightenment

These were optimistic men, the Enlightenment philosophers, who felt the joy and challenge of standing at the edge of a new and better world. They wrote and argued with the untroubled gusto of men who thought their labors would help make a more perfect society. When the occasion demanded it, they even sanctioned revolt with the same clear conscience, appealing their case from vicious kings or recalcitrant nobles to the good opinion of mankind and the gratitude of posterity. They were confident of the result.

The revolutions that they worked best, of course, were those of the mind. Enlightenment philosophers eroded the moral foundations of Old Regime society, government and religion. They had appealed beyond tradition to reason, and destroyed much of the sense of legitimacy that once supported the existing order. Conditions and ideas once regarded as normal became an affront to God and reason. The old ways, the old verities became incredible and unworthy of belief.

In all of this, the Enlightenment philosophers were enormously convincing. Their ideas triumphed. The democratic ideals and the pervasive secularism of modern culture, the adoration of science and the cult of utility, the habits of criticism and the facile assumption that every problem has a solution, all have been inherited from the Enlightenment. We may no longer give these notions unreserved belief, but we have not discarded them either. They still inform and guide our thought.

27
The Eighteenth Century: The Crisis of the Old Order

Discontent with the Old Regime

The last century of the Old Regime was a time of contradictions, when European society showed contrasting aspects of health and sickness. The eighteenth-century was one of sustained economic growth and prosperity. A slowly improving agricultural technology made famine less threatening. Industrialization had begun to increase the supply of goods and lower their price. There were fewer wars and they were less destructive. Europeans were generally governed better than they ever had been.

Yet signs of decay were everywhere. After 1765 there was a series of revolutions throughout the western world, largely the result of popular discontent with political and social conditions that seemed unjust yet were, in reality, clearly improving. Their improvement, however, was gradual and uneven, and it lagged behind the rise in expectations. The problem was most acute in France, the richest state on the continent. Here the government declined into irresolution and incompetence—the despair of minister and observer alike. An equally clear indication of trouble was the Enlightenment climate of opinion, which was highly critical of judicial torture, arbitrary arrest, legal inequalities and social privileges, all common practices in Old Regime Europe.

By the middle of the century, the political and social structure of the Old Regime was losing its moral authority. The consensus that the existing way of doing things was right and valuable was fast slipping away. Traditional privileges and institutions, previously unquestioned, came increasingly to be criticized as unjust and unnecessary. Respect for ancient forms of rank evaporated. Efforts to defend privilege, or divine right monarchy, or legal inequality met only ridicule and scorn. Instead, reformers viewed the condition of contemporary France as unenlightened, unjust, and altogether monstrous—and they preached the doctrine of progress. Few of them saw their attack on the moral legitimacy of existing social and political institutions as an overt call for revolution. But the criticisms hit home. The complaints convinced. The Old Regime was falling apart.

Enlightened Despotism

Criticism of social inequality and political injustice was not limited to Enlightenment philosophers. Every monarch or minister sensed that the usefulness and legitimacy of his government no longer commanded total respect. Kings ceased to talk of divine right and stopped insisting that their subjects owed unquestioning obedience in all circumstances. They talked, instead, of efficiency and justice, of making the crown the focal point of reform. "I am the first servant of the state," said Frederick the Great of Prussia, and when he was thanked by a group of townsmen for replacing their burned out homes, he replied, "You had no need to thank me. It was my duty. That is what I am here for." Absolutism was abandoned as a political justification, replaced by Enlightenment ideals of religious toleration, legal equality, administrative efficiency and social justice. This new doctrine, called enlightened despotism, also involved a generous increase in royal power and royal revenues. Reform is never cheap.

The Enlightened Despots and Anticlericalism

In spite of the differing circumstances in various European states, there were certain trends of reform common everywhere. The most popular, and the most clearly aligned with Enlightenment thought, was a general assault on the power, wealth and privileges of the Church. The Spanish monarchy concluded a concordat with the papacy in 1754 that made the Spanish church practically independent from Rome. A similar agreement in 1741 had placed the Neapolitan church under state control.

The campaign to reduce Church independence and power was most vigorous and thorough in Austria. Emperor Joseph II (1780–1790) was an Enlightenment rationalist, and he regarded the Church as an obscurantist relic of the past. He granted toleration to Protestants, established state schools, closed about 800 monasteries and seized great tracts of church land. An effort at personal diplomacy by Pius VI, who visited Vienna in 1782, had no effect on the emperor's anticlericalism. Destruction of church privileges continued until his death in 1790.

Monasteries and church wealth were not the only targets of reforming monarchs. The Jesuits were also an object of suspicion, largely because of their reputation as secret political agents of Rome. In Portugal, some Jesuits were implicated in the Conspiracy of Tavoras (1758) to overthrow the prime minister Pombal, and Pombal expelled the Society from Portuguese domains. This was followed by the expulsion of the Jesuits from France in 1764, and from Spain three years later. Intense diplomatic pressure on Rome finally forced the dissolution of the Society of Jesus in 1773. Whether the temporary suppression of the Jesuits was a triumph of Enlightenment or not, it was certainly a victory for the bureaucratic state.

The Enlightenment of Law and Administration

Enlightened despots also tried their hand at reforming and codifying the law. Frederick the Great pushed this plan for most of his reign, and a consolidated Prussian law code emerged in 1794, after his death but as a result of his efforts. In Naples, the minister of justice Bernardo Tanucci worked on a law code, trying to mitigate barbarous punishments and to reduce the traditional legal inequalities between social classes. An important part of his work, therefore, was the reduction of the numerous privileges of the nobility, and Tanucci was only partially successful

William Hogarth, scene from "The Marriage Contract". (National Gallery)

before he fell from power in 1776. In general, however, codifying the immense tangle of civil law, feudal law, common law and royal statute, and harmonizing them with the most advanced Enlightenment principles, was too great a task for Old Regime monarchies. They talked more about legal reform than they practiced it.

Allied to reform of the law was royal administration. Here, enlightened despots were directly enlarging their own authority, so they put their hearts into it. Nowhere was the government more thoroughly reorganized than in Austria. After the peace at Aix-la-Chapelle in 1748, Maria Theresa and her advisers completely overhauled the central administration, clarifying the functions of various bureaus and ending overlapping jurisdictions. The primary aim was to increase military efficiency and financial accountability in preparation for another go at Frederick the Great. This was followed in the 1750s and 1760s by greatly increasing the power of the district officials in the provinces and by instructing them to take the peasant's side against the nobles. These reforms initially applied only to Austria and Bohemia, and attempts by Joseph II after 1780 to extend them to

Belgium, Lombardy and Hungary led to widespread revolt.

The Iberian states, long dormant and depressed, also experienced the winds of eighteenth-century reform. In Spain, Charles III created a new council of state to coordinate all the activities of the central administration. He abolished many of the inefficient councils that had existed since the early sixteenth century and that were incapable of doing the work. Charles III also tightened up the activities of the provincial intendants and reinvigorated the Spanish colonial system. In Portugal, the prime minister, Pombal, tightened royal control over an administration that had become practically an independent entity within the state. He suppressed many useless offices and reduced the nobles' power over peasants and local government. Here, also, enlightened despotism meant an assault on the privileges of the nobility.

Enlightened Economic Policy

A final area of enlightened reform was economic and fiscal policy. Government action to stimulate the economy was approved by mercantilists and philosophers,

Frederick the Great of Prussia. (Culver)

and enlightened despots saw it as a royal duty. Frederick the Great subsidized the textile industry in Silesia and induced more than 300,000 colonists to take vacant lands in Prussia. He established a royal land bank to provide capital for farmers. In Austria, Maria Theresa and Joseph II were ardent mercantilists. They gave as much protection and support to industry as they could afford and they established land banks to improve agriculture. In both Prussia and Austria, the tremendous prosperity of the eighteenth century assured at least a modicum of success.

Taxation also engaged royal attention, naturally. Both Joseph II and his brother Leopold of Tuscany greatly reduced their inherited debts, and they took pains to prevent royal borrowing from devouring all the liquid capital of the realm. Frederick the Great did even better; not only did he end deficit financing but even accumulated a yearly surplus. Tax structures were also reformed. Leopold of Tuscany abolished tax farming, on the double grounds that it squeezed the people without enriching the king. Even in Spain and

Naples, backwaters though they were, the powers of the tax farmers were greatly reduced. Enlightened despots began to view taxes as part of an integrated royal economic policy, not merely as the art of plucking the goose with a minimum of popular complaints.

The Limitations of Enlightened Despotism

Although monarchs and ministers claimed to have made enormous changes, all for the better, this was an exaggeration. By and large, the reforms were superficial, involving the appearance of things far more than their realities. Left untouched was all the vast, interlocking array of social and economic privileges enjoyed everywhere by the nobility, urban patricians and the clergy of the established church. The legal immunities of the nobility to lawsuit, arrest and imprisonment were only marginally lessened. Reforms in the tax system rarely meant that the clergy, nobility or upper bourgeoisie paid much more than they had before, and their opportunities for evasion remained extensive. Primogeniture* remained, and land reform, where attempted, failed. Careers were not opened to talent, but remained a function of birth and connection, both by law and custom. Privilege was simply eroded a bit around the edges, largely because it had become a hindrance and a nuisance to the increasing centralization of royal power. People talked endlessly about equality, but it remained just talk.

Moreover, even in those areas where progress toward legal equality was made, the law was frequently negated by custom. Royal officials could hardly be blind to rank in an hierarchical society, and they could not ignore the real power that noble status gave. Many royal officials were themselves nobles (all the important ones were and the rest hoped to be), and they

* The law that lands and authority pass intact from aristocratic father to eldest son.

were quite hesitant to call their friends and relatives to account. Custom everywhere supported legal privileges and was often more respected than the law itself. As late as the 1890s, a French peasant replied to a question about his politics by saying that he was the subject of the viscount. Before the Revolution this attitude was universal. Men followed their patrons, their lords, their betters, and the attempts of reformers to alter these patterns of custom invariably failed. Social, legal and economic privilege continued as before.

So did un-privilege. Those social and legal groups that were most burdened by the privileges of others continued in that condition. Manorial and seigneurial courts, where the lord was judge and prosecutor as well as a participant in suits, were retained everywhere and insured that even the land-owing peasant would remain the subject of his lord. Seigneurial taxes were also retained, continuing as a type of permanent lien on the peasant's land. The urban laborers were totally without rights, protection or privilege, and city fathers viewed them uneasily as criminals, bums and fomentors of riots.

Moreover, Old Regime governments made little progress in civil liberties. Arbitrary arrest continued, censorship of books and the press was universal, and the public hangman was kept busy burning subversive literature, particularly that produced by Enlightenment philosophers. Resistance to authority was a major crime, and those so foolish as to insult royal officials were fortunate to suffer merely exile and property confiscation. Torture was still used for both interrogation and punishment, and prisons held numerous persons accused of nothing at all. Trials themselves were conducted on the assumption that the accused was guilty; why else would the authorities have him in custody and under torture? Self-incrimination was normal. Unprivileged persons were often arrested on the grounds that they were guilty of some crime for which they had not yet been

punished, or that they were about to commit a crime and society profited from their timely arrest. Only a small minority thought that a citizen had natural rights which his government must not impair, and even fewer thought these ideals applied to the peasant and urban worker.

Finally there was little increase in political participation to include new, less privileged groups. The constituted bodies, such as guilds, self-perpetuating municipal and provincial councils, and local estates, all resisted enlightened reforms. These corporations opposed any extension of local or provincial power and were generally successful in doing so. This pattern seldom varied. It characterized the politics of the English Parliament, the Parlement of Paris, the Diets of Hungary and Poland, the municipal governments of the Dutch cities and Milan and the feudal nobility everywhere. Those with corporate political power kept it, in spite of enlightened despots' efforts to win control over the peasants from their lords or to extend urban political participation beyond the circle of hereditary oligarchs. Traditionalism and social hierarchy were deeply rooted in eighteenth-century Europe, as they had been in all previous civilizations everywhere. Now, for the first time in human history, they were under serious and general attack. But they were not easily uprooted. For the time being, the privileges of the nobility and bourgeoisie survived.

The American Revolution

Not all of the reforms achieved or attempted by enlightened despots pleased everybody. There were people who demanded more legal equality, more administrative efficiency, more humanity and justice in the working of courts, more political participation and power. There were also many who wanted less of these things, who only wanted the king to mind his own business and leave them alone. There were also those less interested in social and political reform, but who cared passionately about the new idea of nation and wanted their king to care as well. All of these people were left dissatisfied by the cautious reforms of enlightened despotism. In an era of reform, liberals and nationalists still felt their time might come, soon. When it did not, they soured on their governments. The conservative, constituted bodies feared the loss of their privileges and, therefore, sponsored increasingly militant resistance to their king. The result was a spate of revolutions, supported by some who wanted more reform and by others who wanted less. These revolutions covered the entire western world from Poland to America. By 1770, change was coming from below as well as from above.

The first of the revolutions was a civil war between two aristocracies, two groups of legally constituted institutions, one in Europe and the other in America. The 13 English colonies of North America had grown marvelously in the eighteenth century, in size, population, wealth, experience in self-government and consciousness of their rights. These trends did not make a sufficient impression on British political leaders who, in 1763 (after the Peace of Paris), tried to tighten the political and economic bonds of empire at the time when the external threat from France had vanished. These new policies were to be paid for in part by the colonials in America —who had been far more lightly taxed than the English at home.

Such notions, embodied in the Sugar Act (1764) and the Stamp Act (1765), were extremely galling to the colonial gentry, who protested that their rights as Englishmen were being violated. By 1765, Americans had come to view the British constitution differently from the British, who saw Parliament as the supreme imperial authority, able to tax and rule in the colonies as well as at home. Colonials disagreed, claiming that Parliament had no legislative authority over them. Governor Bernard of Massachusetts Bay put the issue succinctly in 1765:

In Britain, the American governments are considered as Corporations empowered to make by-laws, existing only during the pleasure of Parliament. . . . In America, they claim . . . to be perfect States, not otherwise dependent on Great Britain than by having the same King.

Repeated political confrontations led to war in the spring of 1775. Early in the war the strategic equation became clear. The British, with their naval superiority, had no difficulty in capturing the major Atlantic seaports, but expeditions into the interior ended disastrously, as at Saratoga in 1777. The colonials won the decisive battle at Yorktown (1781)—with the aid of French troops and a French blockading fleet. After Yorktown, the British, who were getting tired of the war, began to cast around for a way out, and agreed to independence for the United States in 1783. Having won the war, the colonial aristocracy now struggled to win the peace; and, with the creation of an effective constitution in 1787, they did that as well.

At the time, the American Revolution seemed quite revolutionary indeed—far more so than it would appear after 1789. The Americans, after all, fought for the same principles of liberty, increased political participation, and an end to privilege that animated later revolutionaries in Europe. Moreover, a large number of Loyalists emigrated from revolutionary America, and their property was confiscated outright. There was also a certain turnover in local ruling cliques, as conservatives, less enthusiastically hostile to the king, were replaced by more radical and reliable gentlemen. Finally, there were a few legal changes in a democratic direction.

In spite of this, however, the American Revolution, from the perspective of 1789, did not seem very radical and, by the 1790s, respectable authorities were claiming there had never been a revolution. There was no wholesale destruction of social classes, political institutions, legal systems or traditions. America in 1790 seemed pretty much like America in 1775. There were three overriding reasons for this. First, America was democratic already by contemporary standards. Voting and landowning were quite widespread. Religious toleration was genuine and respected. There was no feudal aristocracy and, with minor exceptions, there were no seigneurial and manorial encumbrances on the land. In America there was much less to revolt about.

Moreover, conservative or Tory opinion in America was weak, badly articulated, and poorly presented. There was no Tory declaration of obedience, no Tory appeal to great constitutional principles. The Tories confined their case to obedience to George III, and this was not at all inspiring. The notions of the revolutionaries were more widely supported in America than elsewhere. Ideas of religious toleration, wide political participation, legal equality, and end to privilege were common currency over here, but not in Europe. The American Revolution had less to overcome in ideological terms and was comparatively modest in its own pronouncements and politics.

Finally, the American political institutions, legally constituted and functioning, sided with the revolution. Americans claimed they were fighting in defense of legality, not against it. This simple fact robbed the revolution of the character of a popular uprising. It also produced a political paradox. In London, the Americans were revolting against the legally established authority of Parliament. In America, the Tories were the rebels, defying their legally constituted local authorities.

In spite of its conservatism, the American Revolution had a considerable impact on Europeans. Several European officers had gone to the new world to fight for the Americans, and had come home as heroes to tell everyone about the glories of liberty, equality and victory over the tyrant. Printed propaganda was equally powerful. The "Declaration of Independence" made a great impression abroad and seemed to promise a new government, free from injustice, oppression, and noxious privilege. Finally, the unexpected American victory seemed nearly providential, proof of the virtues of freedom and an inspiration to enlightened Europeans. It made America seem the ideal land, the inspiration of mankind, the best hope of everyone. The reality was far less, of course, but the myth became part of the moral condemnation of the Old Regime, part of the collapse of approval in existing institutions.

The Abortive Revolution in the Netherlands

The American Revolution also affected European politics. France and Spain went to war against Great Britain in America's behalf (and to settle old scores with the British), and most of Europe was sympathetic to the American cause. The Dutch Republic was caught in the middle of all this. Traditionally neutral, fearful of British seapower, but mindful of trade advantages in America, the Dutch government slipped into war with the British in 1780. From the beginning the war went badly for Holland. The Dutch fleet was unready, and Dutch merchants lost about 80 million gold guilders in shipping to the British. At the peace table, the British demanded new privileges from the East India Company, and got them.

Bad as the British were, many Dutch thought the attitude of their own government was even worse. The *stadhouder*, William V, an irresolute booby, remained tied to the British and refused to take any real measures of national defense. William supported in this policy by his court, many of the great nobles, and the Dutch Reformed Church, all traditional supporters of the house of Orange in its struggles with the towns.

The *Stadhouder's* policies aroused considerable opposition. The rulers of the major Dutch cities, known as regents, added this new grievance to their traditional opposition to royal power. The regents, in general, wanted to eliminate royal influence in the towns and to bring the government back to a closer understanding of the needs of trade. In these times of universal criticism, however, the regents were joined by a group new to politics, the urban middle class. They found their leader in a provincial nobleman with the beguiling name, Jan van der Capellan tot der Pol.

This new liberal faction did more than merely issue manifestos. They organized into an armed militia, known as the Free Corps. In December, 1784, the Free Corps held a national meeting at Utrecht and demanded political changes that went far beyond anything the regents had in mind. The Free Corps wanted a genuine democratization of Dutch political life. They wanted a wide increase in political participation, which was aimed at the regents as much as at the *Stadhouder*. At Utrecht, the local Free Corps elected 24 of their number to supervise the city council. A year later, they dissolved the old council of regents, choosing a new one in a general election. The actions of the Free Corps at Utrecht was the program of the liberals everywhere.

Such assaults on the sovereignty of the regent oligarchy split the opposition to the *Stadhouder* down the middle. The regents had only wanted a diminution of William V's power so that they could rule instead, while the Free Corps were opposed to both and wanted a liberal regime. By 1786 the regents began to seek an alliance with the *Stadhouder* as privileged elements drew closer together. They could only survive if the Free Corps were defeated, so the

Stadhouder and the regents began to negotiate with Prussia and Great Britain. When the Free Corps and the Dutch army fired on each other in 1787, foreign intervention was assured. The British spread some cash around and the Prussians invaded, restoring the *Stadhouder* to his powers, chastising the regents and dispersing the liberals. But the restoration solved nothing. Although the revolution failed, the *Stadhouder*, in his turn, failed also. He made no reforms in his government. He stood apart from his people, popped up with foreign guns and money. By 1789, kings could no longer get away with that.

Revolution and Repression in Poland

The revolution in the Netherlands had a curious parallel in Poland, a land that differed from it in almost every way. As in Holland, the power of the king was a basic issue. Both revolutions took the better part of a decade to unfold, and both were crushed by foreign intervention. Both involved national as well as political and religious issues.

The differences, however, were even greater. The Netherlands was the richest, most urban, most commercial, most middle-class state in Europe, and Poland was the least. The Polish "aristocratic republic" that had failed to keep pace with its neighbors in the seventeenth century continued without change in the eighteenth. The elected monarch continued to agree to the "liberties" of the nobles, and remained at their mercy. The "liberum veto" in the Diet continued to paralyze legislation as before; the taxes remained nominal, the bureaucracy and army were virtually nonexistent. The great magnates conducted their own foreign policy and, by the eighteenth century, foreign intervention had become customary in a state that lacked internal coherence.

Such conditions were becoming increasingly intolerable to many Poles, and reform sentiment, advocating changes in the constitution and a restoration of Polish glory, grew steadily during the eighteenth century. Enlightenment ideas added to the ferment. The University of Cracow became a center of nationalism, and the appearance of newspapers in the 1760s intensified demands for reform.

The chance came in 1788, when the Russians were preoccupied with a war in Turkey, the Prussians with the Netherlands, and the Austrians with revolts and threats of revolt. The Polish king, Stanislas Poniatowski, a liberal reformer, called the four years Diet to discuss constitutional reform. Discuss was about all the delegates did. Not until April 1791, did they pass the Statute of Cities, which gave the urban bourgeoisie national political rights and control over their own municipal governments. On May 3, 1791, a constitution was adopted, making the crown elective in the House of Saxony, abolishing the "liberum veto," and strengthened the king's power.

The process had taken too long, however. Inspiring as national and liberal reform was to the Poles, it frightened and irritated their principal neighbors. Russia, Prussia and Austria did not want a rejuvenated Poland in their midst. Moreover, the eastern monarchs, seeing the explosion in France, were wary of revolutions, especially those close to home. Catherine the Great of Russia organized Polish nobles who were opposed to reform into the Confederation of Targowica in 1792 and, using them as an excuse, she invaded Poland. Prussia followed and, in January, 1793, the two great powers partitioned Poland for a second time. Enraged, the Polish liberals, led by Thaddeus Kosciuszko, rose in revolt to defend their nation and constitution. Russia and Prussia invaded again, won again, and with Austria, partitioned Poland again. The third partition, in 1795, wiped Poland out. It also ended liberal reform in Eastern Europe until after the middle of the nineteenth century.

Revolt in the Austrian Empire: Belgium

Between Poland and the Netherlands, both in geography and social patterns, lay the immense Austrian Empire, a series of widely diverse and nearly autonomous provinces that were being ruled with increasing efficiency by the Hapsburg emperors. Persistently liberal, humanitarian, and interested in increasing their own authority, Maria Theresa and her son, Joseph II, tried ceaselessly to ameliorate the conditions of the peasants and to reduce the authority of the nobles. There were limits to what an enlightened despot could do by administrative pressure, however, and the career of Joseph II proved this. By 1787, the Austrian Empire was wracked by revolution or, rather, by an aristocratic counterrevolution launched by the nobility of Hungary, Transylvania, Milan and Belgium against Joseph's reforms. Austria was the first great power to be torn apart by the conflict between new ideas and the old social realities.

The liberties, privileges, immunities and rights of Belgium had been defined in 1355 by the Duke of Brabant in a document called the "Joyeus Entry." It guaranteed the authority of the provincial estates, along with the powers of several specific groups within them. The first estate was represented by the abbots of the great monasteries, the second estate by a few wealthy nobles, and the third estate by delegates from the guilds of the major towns. The society governed by these small privileged groups was basically stagnant and quiescent, the results of the great depression after the Dutch war. Dutch victory in 1609 had closed the Scheldt River to Belgian commerce, which declined to depression levels and stayed there. The numerous towns were accustomed to unemployment rates of 25 percent, while the industry that remained produced mainly for local consumption. The Church owned about half of the land, most of it concentrated in the hands of a few large abbeys.

The nobility dominated the countryside, while the guilds controlled the towns. Thousands of officials staffed the numerous medieval courts, boards, councils and assemblies that really governed the province. The Austrian presence was limited to the viceroy, a few troops, and the lowest possible taxes, and this arrangement suited the Belgians precisely. Everything was the way it should be.

Joseph II was too energetic, too committed to reform to accept this, and the initial Belgian revolution came from the emperor himself. He decreed toleration for Protestants, suppressed a few monasteries and reduced the rigid trade and craft monopolies of the guilds. In 1787 he went much further, reorganizing the complex network of seigneurial, municipal and district courts. Many were abolished, judicial and administrative responsibilities were separated, and a new system of uniform appeal courts was established for the whole country.

This imperial interference provoked an immense outcry from all who benefited from the existing constituted bodies, and that was everyone in Belgium who had any political voice at all. By 1789, outrage had become revolution. A new Belgian secret society, "For Altar and Hearth," succeeded in driving the Austrians out. This victory promptly split the revolutionaries into two groups. The conservatives, with their power in the Church and the provincial Estates, wanted to retain the existing order; they fought Joseph II only because he was changing things. The liberals supported much of Joseph's program. They wished to widen the limits of political participation and to allow the urban middle classes a share of power.

These two views were irreconcilable and, in March 1790, the conservative party won. Liberals were rounded up and thousands fled to France. There was a general persecution, which ended only with the return of the Austrian troops in December 1790. But the Austrians could not bring them-

selves to support the liberals. Reluctantly and hesitantly, they sided with the conservatives who controlled the Estates. For the time being, counterrevolution had won.

Revolt in the Austrian Empire: Hungary and Transylvania

Belguim was not the only province provoked into revolt by the reforms of Joseph II. They had the same impact on Hungary. Here, Joseph's reforms had two aims: to increase royal authority, and to limit the power of the lords over their peasants. In the political sphere, Joseph tried to bypass the Hungarian Diet and county assemblies, handing over their traditional powers to civil servants appointed in Vienna. This was bad enough, but there was worse. In 1789, Joseph II issued a decree that proposed to tax all land, whether noble or peasant, at the same rate, to eliminate peasants' forced labor for their lord, and to secure the peasantry in their tenures as landowners. The nobility could not permit that, and they prepared to resist Joseph's decree. The peasants prepared to enforce it. Class war broke out in many parts of Hungary and Transylvania as peasants began to butcher their lords. Class hatreds were aggravated by ethnic ones; in Transylvania Vlach peasants were particularly brutal to Magyar nobles and generally left Germans alone.

Faced with a major social war, the Hungarian nobility in the Diet and county assemblies were unable to press their demands for political independence from the Hapsburg empire. They compromised with Joseph's successor, Leopold II. Leopold agreed to surrender the bulk of Joseph's reforms, though not all, and to return local government and the peasantry to the Hungarian nobility. In return, the Hungarians forgot about independence. Thus the Belgian experience was repeated. Aristocratic counterrevolution had defeated an enlightened despot. Reform by the crown, no matter how enlightened or badly needed, could move only so far without the support of public opinion. In the Austrian Empire, apart from the nobility and privileged, there was no such thing as public opinion; thus, any reform that seriously compromised existing status or privileges was bound to fail. The reforms that Joseph proposed awaited something stronger than his decrees. They waited for revolution.

Cracks in the British System: The Association Movement

"The constitution of England is without doubt the most perfect form of government that was ever devised by human wisdom," wrote a British literary critic in 1775. Almost everyone agreed with him. Smug self-congratulation was the common opinion, and few were bashful about expressing it. British liberty was also admired abroad. Voltaire and Montesquieu had written approvingly of English politics. Even enemies, such as Benjamin Franklin and John Adams, thought well of the British system and wished to have its virtues retained in the new world. In the minds of most, the English were caressed and soothed by the best government ever seen or heard of.

With governments, however, even the best is not very good and, after 1763, the admirable British system began to show disconcerting signs of imperfection. A large chorus of Babbitts arose to deny this, but facts are facts and the evidence was there. One sign of disarray was the Association movement (1778–1780) which demanded increased parliamentary independence from the king and reform of electoral procedures. Under the heading of independence from royal control went the abolition of numerous lucrative and useless pensions and offices that the king had used to bribe Lords and Commons to see things his way. The other plank was for change in electoral procedures, eliminating some of the inequities of pocket and rotten boroughs. This was the more radical demand, since it involved real political changes rather than lightly retouching the surface.

The Association Movement called for a mass meeting—a "General Association" of representatives from all the nation to reform the Parliament by means of the sovereignty of the people. The Movement also urged universal male suffrage, an advanced notion even for the radical Americans. Such ideas, naturally enough, frightened the conservative and substantial people, and these were even more alarmed at the Gordon riots which convulsed London in June, 1780. The reform movement split in two and lost momentum. No General Association ever met. No electoral reform passed. There was no sovereignty of the people or universal male suffrage.

William Pitt the Younger: Efforts at Electoral Reform

Although the Association Movement failed, there were still many who thought that electoral reform was a good idea. These included William Pitt the younger, who had just entered Parliament through the family pocket borough of Old Sarum. In 1782, he brought in a reform bill, which was only narrowly defeated. He tried again in 1783 and lost, and supported another member's bill unsuccessfully in 1784. In 1785, as chief minister, Pitt tried once again. It was a moderate bill. Pitt proposed to abolish only 32 depopulated boroughs, transferring the seats to larger towns and the shires, and to extend the suffrage slightly. His bill was very similar to the Reform Bill finally passed in 1832.

Although Pitt was head of the ministry, his bill was in trouble from the start. There was no large faction in Parliament committed to reform. The king was against it. The ministry was divided. Support from the merchants in the large towns was unenthusiastic. Finally, electoral reform already had a tainted aroma—the legacy of the Associations, and radical rhetoric. Pitt could not overcome all this, and his bill failed by a very comfortable margin of 248 to 174. That was it. If Pitt could not carry electoral reform, no one could. The issue remained on the margin of British politics until after the Napoleonic wars.

Prerevolutionary France: The Pressures for Reform

"Nobody dreamed of a revolution, although it was rapidly effecting itself in public opinion," wrote the Comte de Ségur, son of the last war minister of the old regime. ". . . Every class of the old social order, undermined without expecting it, still preserved . . . its antiquated distinctions and all signs of power. The deepest foundations of the old social edifice were entirely undermined, although the surface showed no symptoms that could indicate approaching ruin. We felt no . . . anxiety for the future, and gaily trod a land bedecked with flowers which concealed a precipice from our sight." Ségur's astonishment was shared by many, who were stunned at the swift passage of events in 1789 from murmurs of reform to riots and revolution. Such surprise was unwarranted. Ségur himself remarked that the words liberty and equality were heard everywhere. The King's ministers themselves grumbled about the existing system, for they realized more than anyone that the government was inefficient, clumsy, expensive, unjust, burdensome and profoundly irritating. Periodically, the ministers would suggest a large block of reforms of the type being promoted by enlightened despots elsewhere, and would publish their condemnation of current practice and their hopes for the improvement in an edict, to be posted everywhere and read from the pulpit in church. The word went out. The government was working badly; those in power knew it and they were going to change it.

But the proposed reforms, although often announced, never seemed to take place. Something always interfered. Some aspect of privilege always prevented the crown from reforming the administration or social structure. Louis XV (1715–1774) was a weak and irresolute king, far more interested in women than government, and yielding to privilege was the easiest thing for him to do. Although the pressure for reform was greater in France than anywhere else, few changes took place. The forces of privilege and conservatism were immensely powerful.

Prerevolutionary France: The Structure of Privilege

Privilege, in Old Regime France, had variable meanings. It was partly honorific, partly economic, partly social, partly political and partly a form of license entitling the fortunate to enjoy immunity from the law. Many Frenchmen had varying degrees of all these types of privilege, with the wealthy nobility having the most. But privilege was not solely an attribute of nobility. Even a cursory glance at the social structure of the Old Regime explodes that myth. The carpenter or mason who belonged to a guild had a substantial grant of economic privilege, since his guild excluded others from his trade and guaranteed him a living. A rich peasant who was a receiver of seigneurial dues enjoyed his lord's privileges. A poor parish priest was privileged by his occupation. In Old Regime France, not only did the nobility and clergy enjoy privilege, the entire urban middle class did also. Perhaps a quarter of the nation was privileged to some degree, and the great majority of these persons were not nobles. Indeed, privilege was primarily a bourgeois phenomenon, enjoyed by craftsmen in their guilds, merchants in chambers of commerce and municipal governments, royal officials in their positions and titles. Most merchants and officials, in fact, possessed greater privileges than the country gentry,

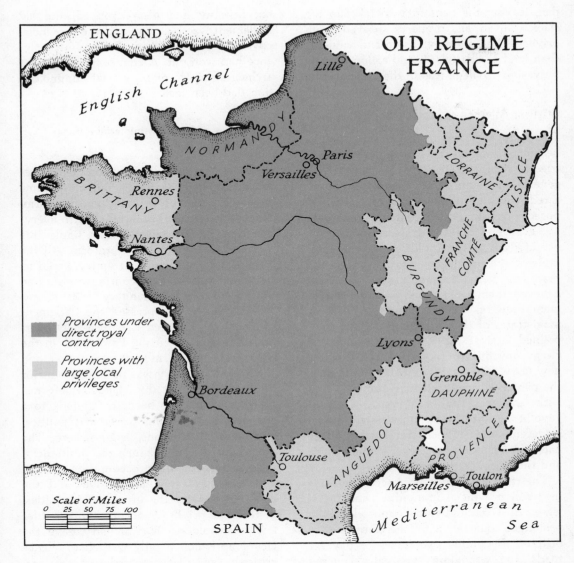

particularly in terms of political power, legal immunities, and opportunities to make a living.

Many forms of privilege had become so entrenched that they were considered property, like land or furniture. Included among them were the seigneurial taxes and rights of justice that lords had over their manors and villages. In much of France, these ancient dues and privileges accounted for the bulk of the lord's income, exceeding what he got from the land itself. Royal offices were also a form of privilege, since they were owned and could be bought, sold or willed like any other property. There were regular quotations of the price of high offices, and people even bought blocks of them at discount and later sold them at retail. Most administrative and judicial offices were venal, and their owners, besides the salaries, enjoyed immunities to many forms of lawsuit and certain rights of graft. High judicial office, such as a judgeship in a Parliament, conferred noble status on its owner. Finally, royal office greatly reduced one's tax burden, leaving the peasantry to take up the slack. All in all, property derived from privilege was more extensive and valuable than land or chattels, in indication of how pervasive privilege was in the Old Regime.

Privilege Attacked and Defended

The political power or organized privilege became starkly clear when the government tried to reduce it. In 1749, the comptroller-general of finances, Machault, proposed a redistribution of the tax burden. He imposed a new tax, the Twentieth, to be paid by everyone with no exceptions. This would destroy the traditional tax exemptions of the privileged, which were so old that the nobility and urban patriciate believed them to be a natural and fundamental law of France. Outraged, the noble magistrates of the Parlement of Paris complained against the Twentieth, while the clergy, meeting in 1750, declared that the new tax was heresy. Everywhere in France, the privileged were reluctant to pay. Faced with an awful public uproar, Machault gave in, and the Twentieth was withdrawn in December 1751. Social and legal privilege had won a major victory over simple justice and the needs of the treasury.

The crown had no more success in dealing with provincial immunities and privileges. In 1753, it became embroiled in a prolonged quarrel with the Province of Brittany. Beginning over taxes to pay for roads, the wrangling eventually covered virtually every aspect of provincial autonomy and involved both the Parlement of Brittany and the provincial estates. By 1765, Louis XV lost patience with Breton hostility to commands from Paris. The Parlement of Brittany was dissolved, and a new supreme provincial court, more attentive to royal wishes, was put in its place. Defenders of provincial privilege were arrested. This brought the Parlement of Paris in as a defender of its sister tribunal in Brittany, and the war now extended to two fronts. By 1770, plans to tax Brittany had been dropped, the old Parlement was restored, and the provincial governor had resigned. Breton intransigence had won out. A chance to reform the archaic structure of provincial administration had been lost.

The Failure of French Ministerial Reforms: Maupeou and Turgot

Following the pitiful conclusion of the Breton fiasco—in fact, arising out of it—came a new experiment in Enlightened reform. Since Machault, it had been clear to everyone that the Parlements were implacable and effective opponents of reform. All the ministers agreed that the country would be better off if these vocal courts were snuffed out. Accordingly, in January, 1771, Chancellor Maupeou suppressed the Parlement of Paris. He replaced it with a new court and then started on the Parlements in the provinces. By November it was all over, and the French judiciary was no longer a major political force. But the Maupeou reforms, which should have been the prelude to a systematic revamping of French political and social institutions, led nowhere. The chancellor did not disturb the multiplicity of legal systems, the procedural delays, the endless costs of litigation. Nor did the ministers modify the gross tax inequities, or the legal privileges of merchants, nobles and officeholders. The ministry gave the clear impression it only wanted to silence criticism, and was prepared to accept any injustice if no one complained.

But people did complain, and the silence of the new courts was added to their litany. When Louis XVI came to the throne in 1774, his ministers, in an effort to win popularity for the new king, decided to restore the old Parlements. The magistrates soon demonstrated that three years of exile had not changed their opinions, and they were denouncing the reforms of a new enlightened minister, A. R. J. Turgot. In 1774, Turgot freed the grain trade from its numerous traditional restrictions in an effort to increase the size of the harvest. Two years later he ended the royal *corvée*, a compulsory road service that fell exclusively on the peasants, and abolished urban craft guilds. The Parlement of Paris complained, and was aided in its efforts by a large bread riot in May 1776. This combination drove Turgot from office and his reform measures were immediately repealed.

The Financial Crisis and the Calonne Reforms

After Turgot's dismissal, the drive for reform slackened. New ministers, contemplating the fate of so many predecessors, were more cautious. But the problems continued. All of the old tax inequities stood. All forms of legal and social privilege remained. The ranks of the privileged stood ready to defend their property and status should the ministry be so foolish as to launch further reforms. But, to the ministers, royal finances were the most serious problem. By 1787, the annual deficit had grown to one fifth of the king's income, while interest on the accumulated debt consumed 60 percent of the royal revenues. In 1787, Louis' chief minister, the marquis de Calonne, communicated these dismal figures to the dull and astonished king. The crown was bankrupt. Large reforms were needed, not just because enlightened ministers thought they were a good idea, but to save the state.

Calonne's program, in effect, was a recapitulation of the reforms of his predecessors. He wished to abolish internal customs barriers, free the grain trade, abolish the peasant *corvée* and establish a uniform land tax with no exemptions. Calonne's program was designed to do many things later carried out in the Revolution. It was a large step toward administrative uniformity. It meant the end of privileged tax exemptions, and it eased the burdens of the peasantry. It would create the largest free trade area in Europe. Most important, of course, it would avert bankruptcy, and

Calonne would be universally recognized as an enlightened benefactor of the people.

Calonne knew that the Parlement of Paris, which had already rejected all these ideas, was unlikely to accept them now. So he persuaded the bewildered Louis XVI to call an Assembly of Notables. The Assembly contained the most privileged men in France: 7 princes of the blood royal, 14 prelates, 37 magistrates from the Parlements, 36 of the richest nobles and other assorted magnates The Notables were surprisingly agreeable. In general, they were willing to accept everything in Calonne's reform programme but the land tax, which was its heart. The Notables solemnly claimed that the land tax was a wicked measure, contrary to ancient privilege, destructive of good social order, and so forth. No sort of pressure could make them approve so bad a bill.

Calonne, of course, could not survive this defeat, and he was replaced by his most ardent and incompetent enemy, Lomenie de Brienne, one of the Notables. Brienne found it easier to get rid of Calonne than to solve the problems of state. He was forced to adopt Calonne's program, and began to feed the edicts into the Parlement of Paris for approval and registration. The magistrates reacted as the Notables had. They accepted everything but the land tax. Desperate, Brienne tried force. In August 1787, he banished the Parlement to Troyes, but public outcry and the need for money forced him to recall it a month later.

France Slides Toward Revolution

Brienne was not content with his catastrophe. He compounded it. In May 1788, he turned on the Parlement of Paris as the author of all his troubles. He proposed a judicial reform even more thorough than Maupeou's had been. He established new courts and made justice both cheaper and more certain. But it was too late for these half-measures or, indeed, for any royal reforms. French saw Brienne's policies as an assault on their liberties. A great outcry arose, and it was not confined to discussion, petitions and pamphlets. On June 7, 1788, there was a serious riot in Grenoble, and this was followed by disorders in Brittany, Béarn, Provence and Franche-Comté. The king called the troops out but, often as not, they refused to fire on the citizens. As if that were not enough, Paris bankers refused the bankrupt government any more loans, and the clergy followed their example. In August 1788, Louis XVI gave in. He dismissed Brienne, suspended the judicial reforms, and announced that an Estates General would meet in May 1789— for the first time in 175 years.

This was the last political decision made by the monarchy of the Old Regime. Since 1749, the French monarchy had made consistent efforts to reform both government and society. It had tried to improve royal administration, redistribute the tax burden and eliminate some of the grosser forms of privilege. These plans had all failed, and in the effort to carry them out the monarchy had collapsed. The crown had resigned in favor of the people. Louis XVI would await the representatives of France. The changes these representatives would make would not be so very different from those proposed by royal ministers from Machault to Brienne, or those attempted by Joseph II in his Hapsburg domains. But they were accomplished by war and terror, by a revolution that spread new doctrines across all of Europe. The people were entering the political stage and, in 1788, the astute could hear the movement described by Anatole France:
Wooden shoes going up the
stairs of history pass the
velvet slippers coming down.

28
Industrialization

Between 1789 and 1814 a series of shattering revolutionary experiences plunged France from monarchy to republic to Napoleonic empire, transforming Europe in the process. But before turning to these tumultuous events, we must explore another revolution that was unfolding during these same years in England—with far less fanfare yet with even deeper significance for the future of mankind.

The Impact of Industrialization

When a mechanic named John Kay invented the flying shuttle, which made the weaving process more efficient, his neighbors denounced him and drove him into exile in France. His invention would put weavers out of work, they said. Only the rich merchants would benefit, as was usual when things changed. It was better to keep to the old ways. At least the poor would find work. But the old ways were slipping from men's grasp. Kay's invention was just a straw in the hurricane. The irrevocable and continuous process of industrialization had begun.

Industrialization is not an event, like a battle or the passage of a law—something that occurs once and not again. It is a continuous process, endless as far as we can tell, of applying increasingly sophisticated technology to the production, distribution and use of goods, services and ideas. While natural resources such as coal or oil, are limited, technology appears to be limitless; industrialization has become a process of continuing innovation in certain basic areas, such as the transportation of goods, the dissemination of ideas, or the techniques of manufacturing. The railroad, for example, was an improvement over the stagecoach, which was better than the oxcart, which was itself better than a backpack. Thus a single industry had experienced substantial technological change over the centuries, and after 1750 this process became much more rapid.

The implications of industrialization are incalculable. In the place of a stable social system there has come mobility. Continuous and rapid economic growth has replaced a static economy. Affluence has become more common than poverty. Governments have used the new technology to increase their power over the citizen; they were far more successful at this dismal business in the century after Napoleon than in the millennium before him. Science and technology slowly replaced religion as the informing principle of Western culture. Instead of continuity and stability, westerners have had to accustom themselves to endless change. The process has made us rich, and given us comfort and power beyond anything our ancestors dreamed of. I wish I could say it has made us happy.

The Causes of Industrialization

Industrialization had diverse origins, like all major historical trends. Some were cultural, others political and social, still others rooted in the economic history of the sixteenth and seventeenth centuries. But only in England did these historical trends lead toward industrialization. Elsewhere, in Prussia or Austria for example, even the most devoted support given agriculture and manufacturing by mercantilist ministers did not provide the impetus necessary to move from a traditional economy to an industrial one.

The economic origins of English industrialization go back into the great depression of the seventeenth century. Although the English had suffered from depression and civil war, recovery after 1660 had been extraordinarily rapid. As the Dutch economy leveled off, the English forged ahead. The English also profited from the French depression of 1683 to 1725, and from the extremely slow recovery in central Europe and the Mediterranean basin. As a result, the English economy began to diverge rather sharply from its continental neighbors.

A basic difference came in the rate of capital accumulation. After the Civil War, the English began to acquire capital at a rate similar to that of the Dutch in the years before 1650. By 1700, the English were fitted out with their own national debt, the Bank of England, and marine insurance companies, all in imitation of Amsterdam. But, whereas the Dutch fiscal institutions had ceased to grow very much after 1660, the English ones expanded with only small interruptions throughout the entire century and a half from Cromwell to Napoleon. Thus the English possessed a vast source of capital, which they invested in canals, roads, industry, trade and technology. The costs of industrialization were immense, on a scale larger than any Old Regime commercial or colonial venture. Only the English had that sort of capital.

A major factor in English capital accumulation was the increasing concentration of overseas trade in English hands during the eighteenth century. Although English merchants faced rugged competition from the French and Dutch in such things as the slave, spice and sugar trades, they increasingly dominated commerce in manufactured goods. They could not keep up with the demand. Increasing markets first forced English manufacturers to hire more workers, still using the traditional methods of production. That did not suffice. By the middle of the eighteenth century, therefore, there were solid economic reasons for Englishmen to search for new ways of making things—for a new and more efficient technology.

Economic origins and causes of industrialization were probably less important than cultural ones. Market pressures, after all, existed everywhere in Western Europe, but only in England did they lead to technological change. Perhaps the most important cultural factor in England was the habit of tinkering with machines and techniques. This went back into the sixteenth century, and was supported by the government. The first royal patent for smelting iron with coal dates from the reign of Elizabeth I. Dozens of subsequent patents were granted in the seventeenth century for the same process; alas, none of them worked. But inventors kept at it, and one of them, Abraham Darby, eventually succeeded. It was the same with steam engines. The first two practical models were both invented by Englishmen, Thomas Savery (1698) and Thomas Newcomen (1706). Gadgets to improve spinning and weaving were offered to the public—at a price, of course—long before the crucial innovations of the eighteenth century.

These habits of tinkering interested men far above the usual social level of mechanics and, in the stratified society of the Old Regime, aristocratic patronage was essential for success. Noble owners of estates interested themselves in "improvements," which included new types of farm machinery. The first canal was financed by a duke, and James Watt's steam engine attracted the capital and business acumen of a successful manufacturer of buttons. Even American scientists and inventors found friends and encouragement among the English aristocracy.

Added to this were the habits of business and investment acquired in centuries of foreign commerce. Trade had attained social acceptance as a legitimate and worthy occupation. Englishmen of all classes invested their savings in commerce, and there were neither laws nor customs to prevent the aristocracy from engaging in trade. In this, England differed from all continental countries except the Netherlands. Not only did the nobility and gentry invest in commerce; many others did as well. The number of smaller investors was also in contrast to the continent, where the government was the principal source of risk capital. In Austria, for example, the largest industrial and agricultural investor was the emperor, Franz-Stefan. His activities were not the result of conviction, how-

ever. His wife, Maria Theresa, would not allow him any role in government, so he invested to give himself something to do.

A final factor in the development of industry in England was the government. As with all Old Regime governments, the English adhered to the tenets of mercantilism and encouraged industry and commerce with state aid. Direct government investment in England fell far behind France, Prussia, Austria or Russia, but the English put great emphasis on the navy which, in the long run, was probably the most useful thing the crown could have done. Beyond this the English government was particularly sensitive to commercial interests, which were expressed in the House of Commons and in merchant's petitions. These latter were responsible for most of the Navigation Acts. Finally, the government supported trade and industry by winning its wars, something that the French neglected to do. To the English passed the fruits of victory, and they were substantial. No government is perfect, however, or even very good; and Britain promptly squandered her advantages in the debacle of the American Revolution. Even so, the English recovered rapidly and, when they next fought the French, managed, after much difficulty, to crush Napoleon.

The factors mentioned above were all vital parts of the origins of industralization, but it is more crucial yet that they all occurred together. There had been previous periods of large capital accumulation and a remarkable concentration of trade, as in thirteenth-century Venice, Milan, Florence or Flanders, but these had not led to the cluster of technological innovations that mark industrialization. Colbert had mobilized the resources of seventeenth-century French states in the cause of trade and industry, but the technology had remained almost static. Hellenistic Alexandria had been the site of considerable capital accumulation and sustained research into science, mechanics and mathematics, all without industrialization. Only in eighteenth-century England technological change and industrialization were slow and sporadic; they were not fully established until the 1780s.

The Rise in English Population

The industrial revolution was more than factories and machines. Mechanization of industry was accompanied by four other social movements, each an integral part of industrialization. There was a sharp population rise in the eighteeenth century, along with a sustained and remarkable expansion of English trade. England also experienced a complex agricultural revolution and a general reconstruction of her transportation system. These four areas of change were indivisible from the mechanization of industry and the rise in production. They were as important as invention to the progress of industrialization.

English population at the beginning of the eighteenth century hovered near six million. It did not begin to climb until the decade of the 1740s, when the rate of increase grew from less than one percent a decade to more than 3 percent. By the 1780s, the English population was growing at 11 percent a decade, and after 1814 it grew more than 16 percent a decade. This was a phenomenal increase, only partly explained by the general absence of epidemics, a long run of good harvests, and an increase in agricultural output. Industrialization also played a part. The new machines provided additional jobs, additional goods, and a generally rising Gross National Product. For much of the population, it also meant a rising standard of living and, for almost everyone, increased opportunities.

The population rise also affected the process of industrialization. It provided a constant pool of labor and meant that labor was cheap, a major consideration for the inadequately capitalized factories of the early industrial revolution. A growing population also added to the number of consumers, thus widening the market at the precise time when manufacturers were producing more goods than ever before. People were as basic a resource of industrialization as coal or iron or cotton, and were as ruthlessly exploited.

The English Agrarian Revolution

Along with the spectacular growth in population came a slow but genuine revolution in the methods and output of English agriculture. Agricultural change had several facets. It involved the introduction of new crops and new machinery. Farmers slowly discarded the ancient methods of crop rotation. They began to plant artificial meadows and to experiment with improved stock breeds. There was also large-scale enclosure of the land—both the wastes and commons, and the medieval strips of arable. Each of these contributed to a general result, a continuous rise in agricultural productivity, which meant more food.

The introduction of new farm implements spanned the century, beginning with Jethro Tull's seed drill, developed about 1700. The seed drill enabled the farmer to plant his seed in straight rows, far enough apart to allow continuous cultivation between them. The weeds were kept under control, the expenditure of seed was reduced, and the yield was increased. In the 1730s the Rotherham steel plow was invented. The Rotherham plow allowed the farmer to use two horses in place of the eight-ox-two-man team inherited from the Middle Ages. To the plow and seed drill were added threshing machines, first produced in the 1780s. These were only the first steps on a continuous road of change in agricultural technology, but they broke the old medieval patterns of farming.

The English also developed new crops during the eighteenth century. The most famous was probably the turnip, tirelessly extolled by an amiable eccentric, Turnip Townshend. More important, though, were the legumes and grasses that made up artificial meadows and replenished the soil, thus permitting the farmer to cultivate all his land all the time. Along with new meadows came experiments in cattle breeding, now that the land could support them. The new crops did not supplant traditional ones, such as wheat, rye, barley or oats, but were added to them, enabling the English to use more land and to use it more efficiently.

In spite of their manifest advantages, all of these new crops and equipment made slow progress against the ingrained conservatism of the countryside, the lack of capital that plagued most farmers, poor transportation and the medieval patterns of land ownership and use. Indeed, many of the new tools and techniques, which could be quite expensive, brought real profits only on large farms that produced for the market rather than at subsistence. Since the population rise after 1750 guaranteed good profits from large farms using the improved methods, many lords and squires consolidated their holdings, a process known as enclosure.

Enclosures of both arable and common lands had been known since Tudor times, and quite a rash of them had occurred during the prosperous years of the Restoration. The scattered strips of arable had been consolidated into units, with each farmer getting approximately his original acreage. Frequently, the waste, pastures and commons of the village had also been enclosed and divided proportionately. Such an event made the lord's fortune, since he could now farm for the market, and it was catastrophic for the cottager, who needed his rights on the common and waste to survive.

In the eighteenth century, rural magnates used Acts of Parliament to force enclosures on their reluctant tenants and villagers. In the years after 1750, when agricultural prices rose consistently, there was an increasing volume of Parliamentary enclosures. Between 1760 and 1814, there were about 1800 individual Enclosure Acts and, in 1801, Parliament passed a General Enclosure Act that made the process much easier. Between the peace of Paris (1763) and Napoleon's Fall (1814), one and one-half million acres were enclosed—a considerable chunk of the English countryside.

Enclosures, primarily benefiting the large farmers, made the transition to new agricultural methods almost inevitable. Profits alone would insure that, but pride was also involved. It was a time when George III, in his fleeting moments of sanity, took to calling himself "Farmer George" and maintained a model farm and breeding station. Great landlords did likewise, and provided their estates with the latest crops and equipment. Agricultural societies encouraged this trend. Year by year, English agriculture slowly shifted away from medieval patterns toward modern, heavily capitalized, farms.

The Reconstruction of the Transportation System

Agricultural modernization would have taken even longer than it did if the English had not also improved internal transportation. English roads in the early eighteenth century were said to be the worst in Europe, trails of mud or dust according to the weather. After 1750, however, there was a sustained effort to improve them. Unlike France, where such activities were undertaken by the government, English road building was largely the result of private enterprise. Turnpike companies were formed, received a charter from Parliament to improve a section of public road, and charged tolls for its use. Between 1750 and 1810, Parliament passed from 40 to 60 Turnpike Acts a year, and most of the major English roads were affected.

Some improvements were marginal, merely fixing the worst ruts at the least expense and charging the highest tolls possible. Other roads were completely remade. The engineers used methods copied from the Romans, putting down layers of rock and gravel that settled into a hard surface. Such expensive repairs were in the minority, but they were concentrated on the main roads. Travel times between London and the main provincial cities were cut by about one third and the number of stage coaches went up astronomically. By 1820 there were about 1500 coaches leaving London each day over the improved roads. Costs of land transport went down also, but not so far as to compete with waterborne traffic. That development would await the railroads.

Although the improvement in roads aided industrialization, the major element of the transportation revolution was canals. Commerce by water was far cheaper and faster than by land, and the canals tied England together into a single market and allowed exploitation of resources previously unusable. Like turnpikes, canals were built with private capital, except that a far greater amount was required. The first canal was financed by the duke of Bridgewater, and it cost him over a quarter of a million pounds. It was to carry coal from the duke's mines at Worsley to Manchester. The canal was designed by James Brindley, an almost illiterate engineer, who made all of his calculations in his head, using the powers of memory and concentration. Unable to explain to the duke his canal plans, Brindley carved a model in soap. Work began in 1759 and was completed two years later. It was a gigantic achievement, containing a tunnel at Worsley and a huge viaduct over the Irwell River at Barton.

The Worsley Canal was a stupendous success. It cut the price of coal at Manchester by one half, made pots of money for the duke, and established Brindley as a great man. The people who lived in the district were also caught up in the project. They painted the canal boats bright colors, and held annual competitions for the most beautiful coal boat. On Good Friday, families would picnic at Barton, in the shadow of the viaduct. People spoke of Brindley and the duke of Bridgewater in Biblical accents, as great and wondrous men who had brought fame and prosperity to their district. Today the canal is no longer in use, but it is still kept up as a public monument to times and glories past.

The canal at Worsley also set off a wave of canal building elsewhere in England. Brindley himself designed the Grand Trunk Canal, which connected the Irish and North Seas, though he did not live to see its completion in 1777. By 1814 the country was tied together by almost 4000 miles of internal waterways, which connected all the major ports, mines and industrial cities.

Canals were the highways of the early industrial revolution, for they made it possible to move bulk items such as wood, stone, grain, coal and iron to any spot in the country. Land transportation was still too slow and expensive, nor could the roads accommodate the huge amounts of coal and iron the new factories needed. The canals thus overcame the localism of the thousands of petty markets and economies. Industrialization could not have occurred without them.

The Growth in Foreign Trade

The final dramatic change that accompanied industrialization was in trade. During the eighteenth century, British overseas trade grew dramatically, particularly after 1780. With the wars of the French Revolution, the British acquired virtually a monopoly of international trade. The numbers of ships increased along with trade volume, and by the 1790s every major port was starting an extensive program of dock construction. The seventeenth-century mercantilist, Thomas Mun, had declared that England's treasure was by "forraign trade" and, by the end of the eighteenth century, this seemed truer than ever.

The boom in foreign trade after 1780 was more than simply a commercial bonanza, however. It was also connected with the processes of industrialization. Overseas trade created a continuing, growing, demand for British manufactures, as well as the habit of buying them. The English domestic market, although the deepest in the world, was still too small to absorb all of the products of industrialization. Foreign commerce took up the slack. It also gave the English access to needed raw materials that would not grow or were not found at home. Cotton from India and the southern United States was a prime import, as was high-grade Swedish iron ore. Beyond that, the English imported dozens of items for resale abroad, mostly to Europe. These included rice, tobacco and sugar. Moreover commerce produced a large capital surplus, much of which found its way into industrial investment, rather than back into trade. Canal-building was financed largely from the profits of commerce. Finally, trade was a major factor in building a business ethic and supporting institutions such as banks, insurance companies, and a stock market. Because of trade, London was the financial capital of the world, and the habits of investment built up in trade were transferred to the expansion of industry.

The Impact of Technological Innovations

The process of industrialization itself, taken in isolation from associated social and agricultural movements, can best be described as a clump of technological innovations, some processes and some inventions, which changed the way things were made, and changed them sharply and rapidly. Time is important. Both printing and radio radically altered communications, but they did it half a millennium apart, and no one considers these two inventions as part of a single "industrial revolution," a single shift from a primitive economy to an industrial one. "Clustering" or "convergence" of technological innovation was a basic factor in the dramatic and irrevocable eco-

nomic shift that occurred in England toward the end of the eighteenth century. It was the short time span in which they occurred, as much as the nature of the innovations themselves, that had such a revolutionary effect on English industry.

These clusters of innovations occurred in two distinct industries: iron manufacture, and textiles. These occupied a strategic location in the English economy. Textiles, particularly woolens, had been a basic English export since the early twelfth century, and iron products had joined them in the sixteenth century. Both products enjoyed international as well as home markets, and both were plagued by insufficient production and inadequate quality. Technological change in these industries, therefore, had a disproportional impact on the English economy, far greater than if the changes had taken place in the manufacture of paper, or even shipbuilding.

Innovations in Textile Manufacturing

Textile manufacture in 1750 followed traditional lines, similar to production patterns on the continent and those of medieval Europe. The domestic, or putting-out, system was common, wherein the worker owned or rented his machinery and worked in his house. Manufacturing was thus scattered about in the villages, with the peasant supplementing his agricultural income with industrial labor. The supplies of wool, flax or cotton were brought to the village by a merchant-industrialist, who paid by the piece to have it made into thread and then cloth, and picked it up when the work was done. Much of the labor was concentrated in rural areas in order to escape guild regulations which, on the continent at least, were extremely strict.

There were several social advantages to to the domestic system. It spread the work around. If no one got rich, almost everyone could eat. It also kept the peasant in his village, where life was familiar and comprehensive, where he enjoyed the dignity of working the soil and, perhaps, owning a scrap of land. Domestic manufacturing required only a modest capital outlay. No factory need be built, the merchant paid only for the raw materials, and the workers, more often than not, could afford their own looms and spinning wheels. Finally, it fit into the hierarchical structures of Old Regime society, preserving the traditional relationships between peasant and gentry, worker and master, townsman and countrymen. It was a comfortable system, and most people spoke well of it.

There were disadvantages also, and these became more acute as the eighteenth century wore on. In the first place, the quality of work done by yeoman weavers and spinners was at best, bad. Quantity was inadequate also; the market snapped up all cloth made, no matter how shoddy. Agricultural work interfered with manufacturing, and supplies of cloth were periodically interrupted. The disadvantages were mainly economic and technological and were resented chiefly by the merchants, while the benefits were essentially social, and were conferred, as it turned out, mainly on the poor. Under these conditions, it is obvious that there would be a massive effort to improve the way cloth was made.

Within the traditional textile industry, there existed a basic imbalance which no juggling of supplies or organization of labor could solve. This was the gap between spinning and weaving. Using hand looms and wheels, weavers could do more work than the spinners. It took four, sometimes six women working at their spinning wheels to supply thread for a single weaver. This imbalance was aggravated in 1733, when a mechanic named John Kay invented the flying shuttle, which could be attached easily to existing looms. The flying shuttle did two things: it enabled the weaver to dispense with his assistant, and it made him more than twice as efficient as before. Now, he could absorb the work of

a dozen women at their spinning wheels. For these very reasons, the flying shuttle was attacked as being destructive of good social order, and it therefore spread very slowly; it was not at all common until the 1770s. But it did spread, and it did make a spinning machine absolutely necessary. It was either that, or the English would have to import a great many women.

Spinning Machines

Efforts to invent a spinning machine had begun in earnest as early as the 1720s, but not until the 1760s was the problem solved —by two inventors, working independently. In 1765, James Hargreaves, a weaver and carpenter, invented the spinning jenny, which he named after his daughter. It was a simple machine, rather like a spinning wheel set on its side. A moveable wooden frame contained a number of spindles, allowing the operator to twist the thread and draw it at the same time. The jenny was more efficient than the spinning wheel, and it produced finer quality thread as well. Finally, it was designed to be used at home, thus fitting into the framework of the domestic system.

The other inventor was Richard Arkwright—a ". . . bag-cheeked, pot-bellied . . . much-inventing barber," Thomas Carlyle called him. In 1768, Arkwright invented the water frame, patented it at once, and began to produce a coarse tough thread by means of water power. The water frame was simply a huge, vertical jenny, but it produced thread strong enough to be the warp as well as the weft of cotton cloth, which neither the jenny nor the spinning wheel could do.

Both the jenny and the water frame were immediately successful. Ten years after Hargreaves' death in 1778, there were said to be more than 20,000 of his jennys in England, and the smallest of these had six or eight spindles. The water frame, producing its strong thread, was also indispensable, so much so that others took it up, in defiance of Arkwright's patent. They fought him in Parliament and in court, ultimately winning a legal decision in 1785. But Arkwright was not defeated. He may have had an unprepossessing appearance, but he was also a man of exceptional business skill, and his establishments were the best managed and most profitable in all England. His original mill, established in 1771 had, within a decade, grown to several thousand spindles and employed 300 workers. He himself worked constantly to improve his mills, to extend his education, and to increase his fortune. He was knighted by George III, became high sheriff of Derby, and died in 1792 leaving an incredible fortune of half a million pounds (about 250 million dollars in modern purchasing power) and a legend for industry, astuteness, and achievement.

Arkwright's invention was significant beyond the immediate increase in thread. His was the first machine that did not fit into a cottage, that did not come to the worker but demanded instead that the worker come to it. The water frame meant factories. At one stroke, the worker lost ownership of the machines and control over his own working conditions and hours of labor. All these passed to the owner of the mill. The textile worker was transformed from an independent petty producer into a hired hand, with all the loss in autonomy and status that that implies. On the other side, the entrepreneur was obliged to lay out immensely greater amounts of capital. He had to build the factory, construct the machines and maintain them, purchase huge quantities of raw materials, pay wages in cash, and be able to ride through periods of slack demand when his expenses outran his income. The owner also had to know how to manage his business, a talent that Arkwright possessed but that many others did not. In return, however, there was the chance of getting rich.

Thus the worker and the owner, who had once been partners of a sort, who had once belonged to contiguous social classes, who had once shared risks and the capital outlay, now became opponents. The factory worker saw his interests as opposed to the owner's. The worker wanted higher wages and shorter hours, and the owner usually did not want him to have them. Owners wanted newer and more efficient machines, while the men who ran them feared being thrown out on the street. These changing attitudes spread only slowly as the implications of the factory system became clearer. But with the spread of factories, the new social attitudes came to overshadow older conflicts between lord and peasant, or lay and cleric, or town and countryside.

The next spinning machine, the "mule" of Samuel Crompton, was a combination of the jenny and the water frame. Developed between 1774 and 1779, Crompton's mule produced thread both fine and strong, and thus improved on older machines. Within a decade, the mule had been hooked to both water and steam power, while the number of spindles per machine had been increased from a few to a few thousand. By 1800, the mule was the basic spinning machine, and it remained such. It completed the technological evolution of cotton spinning, and the transformation of that industry from domestic production to the factory.

The Mechanization of Weaving

These new machines radically increased the supply of thread, and its quality as well, and thus reversed the traditional imbalance between spinning and weaving. Now, it was the weavers who could not keep up. By 1790, skilled weavers were being paid in pounds instead of pence. William Radcliffe, a contemporary entrepreneur, wrote that, about 1800, ". . . there was not a village within thirty miles of Manchester . . .

in which some of us were not putting out cotton . . . in short, we employed every person in cotton weaving who could be induced to learn the trade." That could only mean a weaving machine. And one was invented, by Edmund Cartwright, the youngest son of a country gentleman. In 1785, Cartwright produced a very crude machine, which had a distressing tendency to break down. He kept at it, though, and two years later had made a much better model. By 1789, he had hooked it to a steam engine. The first factory, at Manchester, was burned to the ground by hostile weavers, and Cartwright lost everything. But the logic of the machine was irresistible and, in 1800, the Scottish industrialist, John Monteith, established a power-loom mill, which was the prototype for the hundreds that followed. By 1815, both spinning and weaving were mechanized, with complicated machines being hooked to steam engines, housed in factories, and owned by great capitalists. And it had all happened, for the most part within 40 years.

The Cotton Gin

Industrialization of both spinning and weaving again shifted the pressure point in the manufacture of cotton. It was now raw material, the cotton itself that was in short supply. Neither India nor America, nor both together, could keep up with the insatiable new machines. A Yankee gunsmith, visiting the Georgia plantation of General Nathaniel Greene, solved the problem. In 1793, Eli Whitney invented the cotton gin, which replaced the slow and laborious separation of cotton fiber from the stalk. Whitney's machine had immediate and powerful results. It increased the supply of raw cotton to the point where it could not all be used, and it gave the American slave system a new lease on life. The English were certainly pleased with the first, although Americans have had some difficulty in adjusting to the latter.

Economic Consequences of the New Textile Industry

Some of the results of this industrial transformation we have already mentioned: factories, new social classes and relationships, and changing social attitudes. There were other results, equally significant. One, already hinted at, was the sharp increase in the quality of cloth. There is a myth today that handmade goods are better than those made by machine. Usually, the reverse is true. The machines were more consistent than man, made fewer mistakes, and eliminated the coarse and fragile patches that characterized handmade products. The quantity produced went up, of course; that was the main reason for the new machines. And it kept going up, with no end in sight. No matter how much the factories produced, the market absorbed it. Growth seemed endless and fantastic to men accustomed to the static economy and inelastic demand of preindustrial days. Finally, most wondrous of all, the price of cloth dropped. Prices for cotton cloth were slipping steadily before 1814, and afterward they fell by three fourths again. Mass production meant lower costs, lower prices, a greater market, better goods, sustained economic growth, and all of these things, so astounding to contemporaries, were as much a part of the "industrial revolution" as the technology itself.

Innovations in Iron Manufacturing

Cotton was not the only industry that experienced radical technological change during the eighteenth century. Ironmongering did also, and its technological and economic development, while less spectacular, was probably the more important. For the development of metallurgy made it possible for other industries to move beyond the stage of simple wooden machines powered by hand.

Englishmen had long recognized the importance of the combined industries of mining and the manufacture of iron products. From cannon to horseshoes, the iron industry was essential to the nation's power and prosperity. It was also sick and had been for some time. There was plenty of domestic iron ore, but it was of inferior quality. So the English imported, largely from Sweden or Russia. Between 1710 and 1720, the ore imports were between 15,000 and 22,000 tons a year, and by 1765 this figure had risen to more than 55,000 tons. These two facts meant that the production of pig and bar iron was small, and on a small scale. During the first half of the eighteenth century there were never many more than 60 blast furnaces, some producing less than 150 tons of pig iron a year. The iron was expensive, and the operation suffered from the distinct disadvantage of requiring a great deal of capital investment for a small return.

An additional problem was the general technological backwardness of iron mining. The mines were little more than dog holes, a few yards deep. Mining was mainly scraping the ore from the surface. One furnace in Surrey even used slag from Roman foundries, rather than ore from new mines.

The metal finishing industries reflected these sad conditions. They, too, were organized into small shops, on the domestic system. Most craftsmen worked in their own homes with their own tools. Guild regulations still survived, particularly in the north, with the "Holy Fellowship and Company of Cutlers and Makers of Knives within the Lordship of Hallamshire in the County of York" (founded in 1624). The Holy Fellowship was dedicated to the noble goals of finding work for the masters, keeping others out, and freezing the technology of metal working at its current unsatisfactory level.

Beyond all of this, the worst problem was fuel for smelting the ore. Charcoal was used, and it presented serious problems. It was in short supply and extremely expensive. And since it was also hard to

ship, the ore diggings had to be near forests, not where the best ore might be. Thus, the forges drifted across England, hunting for oak trees, and leaving slaughtered forests behind them. As wood was the basic material for wagons, ships, machines, and buildings, such timber butchery had evil economic consequences. Forests were also necessary for the survival of small farmers, who used them for poaching, grazing their pigs, firewood, and construction materials. Finally, when the forests ran out, the iron industry would die. By the eighteenth century, that day was not far off.

The answer to this problem was at hand, and everybody knew what it was. Coal must replace charcoal as the fuel for smelting ore. Since the sixteenth century, men had been trying to find a way to use coal for refining iron. All attempts sank on the same reef. English coal had a high sulfur content, which the burning coal released and which the molten iron absorbed. Sulfur in the iron made it extremely brittle, and pig iron refined with coal was useless. Not until the eighteenth century was this problem solved, and then only slowly. A Quaker ironmaster, Abraham Darby of Coalbrookdale, conducted numerous experiments, smelting iron with cooked coal, or coke. It was all trial and error; the chemistry behind the process was completely unknown. Between 1709 and 1713, Darby got excellent results, smelting a good pig iron with coke and cutting his costs by about two thirds. He died in 1717, however, before he could perfect the process, and the experiments were not taken up again until 1730 when his son, also Abraham Darby, took over the furnace. The second Darby extended the range of his tinkering. He improved and enlarged the bellows, thus making the fire hotter, and he began adding limestone to the molten ore to add to the purity of the pig iron. By the 1760s, the whole process—coke, lime and bellows—was a distinct economic and technological success and had greatly increased English production of pig, or cast iron.

This was all to the good, but it did not solve the iron industry's problems completely. The bottleneck moved from fuel to the refining process itself. Pig iron could be produced in large quantities, but it still remained too full of impurities, too brittle for every use. A further refining step was needed. The pig iron must be heated and hammered, again and again and again, into wrought or bar iron. This cost time and money, and some pig was so impure, so contaminated with carbon, that heating and hammering would not work. Thus the English, even after they had increased their production of pig iron, were still importing bar iron from Russia and Sweden. This in itself was bad enough, but a sharp rise in the price of Baltic iron after 1770 made things even worse.

In 1783, two men found the answer simultaneously. One, Peter Onions, was an obscure Welsh ironworker, but the other, Henry Cort, had influential friends and could publicize his process. Cort took out a patent in 1784 for his invention, called puddling and rolling. The pig iron was first refined again over a coke fire, which drove some of the carbon off. It was then put into a furnace with clinkers containing iron oxides that combined chemically with the carbon given off by the molten pig iron. The whole mess was stirred, called puddling, then hammered, and finally rolled into a long metal strip. The process both purified the iron and rolled it into a usable sheet. It solved at one blow all the major existing technological problems in the iron industry.

Although Cort's process was an immediate and spectacular success, many of the biggest ironmasters remained unconvinced. James Watt, inventor of the steam engine, was outraged at their blindness and stupidity, and wrote, "Cort is treated shamefully by the business people, who are ignorant asses, one and all." Only up to a point, however; for when Cort lost his

patent in the bankruptcy of his backer, they all converted to puddling and rolling at once, now that it was free.

The final invention that transformed metallurgy was the steam engine, which found two primary uses. It powered bellows far larger than man or horse could move, and it thus made possible larger furnaces and more efficient smelting. Steam engines were also used in the mines. The need for both coal and iron ore could not now be satisfied with strip mines, dog holes, and the like. But deep mines flooded and could not be used in the rainy season, which in England is always. James Watt's steam engine, finished in 1775, enabled miners to pump water out of the mines faster than God put it in. The English could now mine at any depth and, consequently, the production of coal and iron ore increased so swiftly that they were exporting both by the wars of the French Revolution.

The Impact of the New Iron Industry

The results of these inventions and changes were momentous, as contemporaries could clearly see. As with textiles, the quality of the product, both pig and bar iron, improved dramatically, and the price fell as well. England ceased importing and began to export iron, not merely ordinary iron,

James Watt's first steam engine now in the Science Museum, London. (The Bettmann Archive)

but metal of such high quality that it competed favorably with the Swedish. Again, as in textiles, the new innovations meant a concentration of the industry into factories and signaled the doom of domestic metal workers. Iron had always required large amounts of capital, and now it demanded even more. But it began to pay better. Some ironmasters became almost feudal lords of an industrial empire. John Wilkinson fit this mold. He was progressive about technology and was one of the first to use the new Watt steam engine. He owned coal and iron mines and built blast furnaces all over England. In 1777 he established the Indret iron works near Nantes, in France, which were the most advanced and efficient in that country. He made his own coins, which showed his face and the majestic inscription, "Wilkinson Iron Master." He ran all of this with a high and hard hand, even driving his brother out of the firm, but his abilities were great and his decisions usually correct. He led the world in finding new uses for his product, including an iron bridge, iron canal boats and iron pipes. Equally large and important, although in another field, were the Carron iron works, established in 1760 by John Roebuck. He, too, used the most advanced technology and produced goods famous throughout the world. They were guns, so efficient and deadly that "carronade" became a European synonym for cannon fire.

A final consequence of the improvement in ironwork was its enormous impact on all other industries. Before puddling and rolling, every industry used wooden machines; iron ones were too expensive and fragile. Now, that was no longer true. Metal machines replaced wooden ones in the textile industry rapidly after 1800, since they alone could tolerate the power output of steam engines, and now they cost less. The machine tool industry also dated from puddling and rolling. In 1797, Henry Maudslay invented the screw-cutting lathe, the basic tool and die machine.

It was an invention that awaited high quality and low cost metal. Thus innovations in metallurgy affected the entire economy as the technological transformation of the textile industry had not. The changes in ironworking were basic to the entire process of industrialization.

Industrialization and the Human Condition

The industrial revolution, with its accompanying process of uprooting multitudes of rural peoples and jamming them into grim factory towns, is apt to leave a bitter taste in our mouths, and with good reason. The brutal living and working conditions in the new industrial cities has produced a moral tradition condemning the industrial revolution, or more specifically, technology, for creating slavelike conditions and smoky skies.

But the moral tradition has always omitted considering factors that are equally moral. For one thing, the principal commodities whose production was revolutionized by technology were chiefly commodities of general consumption, most notably food and textiles. Imperfect as the distribution system may have been, and miserable and unjust though the conditions of labor were, industrialization offered for the first time the possibility of a production level sufficient to raise the living standards of masses of ordinary people from subsistence-starvation to security and decency. It would require another 150 years for this possibility to approach realization, but without the industrial revolution it could never have occurred.

The anti-industrial moral tradition too easily implies that the evils of material existence first arrived with industrialization. But those who have known rural poverty stripped of its bucolic facade, or who know something of the realities of life in regions untainted by technology, know human life for what it has been for most men throughout history: appalling disease, poverty, and early death. Whatever the abuses or misuses of technology from the eighteenth century to our own day, the possibility for a better material existence for mankind has depended on the proper application of modern scientific knowledge to the process of production.

TECHNOLOGICAL CHANGE IN THE EARLY INDUSTRIAL REVOLUTION

Mining and Metallurgy

1702–1712:   Development of the Newcomen atmospheric pump

1709–1730:   Development of coke by Abraham Darby

1759–1761:   James Brindley builds the Worsley Canal to take coal to the sea. First of the great English canals.

1775:   James Watt invents the steam engine

1784:   Henry Cort invents puddling and rolling process

1802–1803:   Richard Trevithick invents the high pressure steam engine

Textiles

1733:   John Kay invents the flying shuttle

1765–1770:   James Hargreaves, spinning jenny

1769:   Richard Arkwright, water frame

1775:   James Watt, steam engine

1784:   Samuel Crompton, Crompton's mule

1785–1787:   Edmund Cartwright, power loom

1800:   John Monteith, steam-driven factory of power looms

29
Europe in Revolution: 1789-1814

The Optimism of 1789: The Enlightenment Triumphant

Long live the fortunate moment,
When everything is born again,
The Kingdom is regenerated,
Alleluia.

The stanza of a popular song expressed the feelings of most Frenchmen in the spring of 1789. The European revolution had come to France, and democracy, gained in America, would soon grace and illuminate the French. The evils of politics, society and character that had plagued men were now going to vanish. As another popular ballad announced, the Estates General would eradicate pride, jealously and drunkenness, fill the treasury and the markets, and reconcile all men to the new golden age. Virtue would replace vice, civic spirit would overcome diffidence and apathy, liberty and equality would reign forever. The renewal of the world was here.

An ambitious program, composed of generous hopes and limitless promise, it also concealed another side to the public mood in the spring of 1789. There was impatience for reform and a deepening hostility to privilege, the result of years of Enlightenment political theory and the failure of the government to undertake any real change. Anticipation and impatience, the eagerness to embrace the New Jerusalem, all met at the first meeting of the Estates General. When Louis XVI was late, an indignant deputy protested, "A single individual should not keep a whole nation waiting."

The Estates General of 1789

Although the King and his ministers were resigned to consulting the nation, they were not agreed on the form the Estates General should take. Most thought in terms of the last meeting, in 1614, with three estates of about equal size, voting separately. Jacques Necker, the prime minister, had heard enough popular songs to realize that this was impossible, and he obtained a concession. The Third Estate, which included everyone not a noble or a priest, would elect 600 deputies, equal to the First Estate (clergy) and the Second Estate (nobility) combined. But they were still supposed to vote separately—as Estates, not as individuals. The crown had gone as far as it wanted in meeting public opinion.

The elections to the Estates General confirmed the hopes or fears of those who wanted large social changes. In the First Estate, almost half the deputies were peasant parish priests, who were hostile to the privileges of their noble bishops. Even in the Second Estate, about 50 liberal nobles were elected amidst a crowd of poor and reactionary country gentlemen. The third Estate was totally dominated by bourgeois lawyers, merchants or officials, who had been molded in the Enlightenment and wanted major changes.

Election was only half the process. The deputies brought *cahiers*, or statements of their constituents' grievances. These lists were as important as the deputies themselves, for they were supposed to be the basis of reform legislation. The *cahiers* generally reflected a liberal, reformist position. Most of them demanded a constitution for France, freedom of the press, equality before the law, and reforms in the royal administration. The *cahiers* of the Third Estate also insisted on abolishing the fiscal privileges of the clergy and nobility. Nobles and clerics were less enthusiastic about this last reform.

Along with elections and drafting *cahiers*, Frenchmen engaged in a lively pamphlet campaign during the winter and spring of 1788 to 1789. Royal censorship broke down, and a torrent of pamphlets, poems and songs amused and aroused the public. Most denounced privilege and flayed nobles and bishops. The most trenchant was published by a cleric, Abbé Sieyes. *What Is The Third Estate?*, Sieyes

asked, and he replied that it was presently nothing.

What does it demand?/To become something . . .

The Third Estate, which was virtually all of the nation, wanted fiscal and legal equality, a constitution, an end to obnoxious privilege, and a share of the political power in France. The urban bourgeoisie could agree with that, and Sieyes' program found its way into many *cahiers*.

From Estates-General to National Assembly

In the spring and summer of 1789, as the Estates General met to set France right, there occurred four separate and distinct revolutions, each the product of different groups and classes, each concerned with different problems. At Versailles, the lawyers and deputies to the Estates General were creating a National Assembly and were beginning work on a constitution. In the streets of Paris, mobs formed in July and took the Bastille. In the countryside, peasants revolted against their seigneurial lords and taxes. And in hundreds of provincial towns, bourgeois revolutionaries took over municipal governments and forced royal officials into retirement. Together, these events formed the first of several waves of revolt that swept France during the Revolution.

In the Estates General, the immediate issue was quite clear. How would the deputies vote, by order or as individuals? The Second Estate organized itself, and announced that vote by order was fundamental to monarchical government. The Third Estate refused to organize itself or transact business; instead, it invited the two privileged orders to join with it in a National Assembly. The First Estate, split between peasant priests and noble bishops, temporized, and finally, on June 19, decided (by one vote) to join with the Third. The next day, when the National Assembly tried to assemble, they found the hall shut. Greatly indignant, and suspecting the king of siding with the nobility, the deputies met in an indoor tennis court and swore that they would never disband until they had given France a constitution. The Tennis Court Oath symbolized the deputies' demand for reform, and attempts by the king to override it failed. On July 27, Louis gave in and accepted the National Assembly.

The Declaration of the Rights of Man

Having won the procedural question, the liberal deputies turned to what they thought was their main task: to give France a constitution. A constitutional committee was organized, and debate began on what sort of constitution it should be. Every politician had a speech to make, and many had quite a few, and debate dragged on in an endless chain of pompous orations. Nonetheless, the deputies actually made progress; on August 26, they adopted a fundamental document, "The Declaration of the Rights of Man and the Citizen." A short and general document, the Declaration set forth the natural rights of man— rights that were not to be curtailed by the state. These included freedom of religion, habeas corpus, abolition of torture, guarantees of due process of law, and careers open to talent, not merely birth. The Declaration combined an affirmation of natural rights derived from Enlightenment philosophy with a prohibition against some of the most grating features of Old Regime government.

The Storming of the Bastille and its Aftermath

While the deputies spoke at leisure about dignity and imperishable principles, the people of Paris faced a more basic problem. Starvation stalked the city; bread prices had been at famine levels for a year. Uncertainty accompanying the collapse of the old monarchy had held up grain shipments to the capital, as farmers, fearing they would not be paid and hoping for even higher prices, kept their grain back. In June, rumors of royal troops marching on Paris added to the anxiety and fear. On July 12 Paris exploded. Mobs pillaged markets and shops in search of bread and wine and sacked public buildings looking for guns. The municipal customs barriers were burned and the city government was overthrown. Many of the troops joined the people and, on July 14, a neighborhood mob took the ancient royal fortress, the Bastille, destroying the symbol of royal power in Paris as it had previously ended the reality.

Although the mob violence was satisfying, and brought sharp changes in municipal government and police, capture of the Bastille had not meant more bread. Prices remained high and stocks stayed low. People were still starving. On October 5, a crowd of hungry and angry women marched through a cold, steady rain the 20 miles to Versailles to present their grievances to the king and National Assembly. The next day, the women insisted that the king and Assembly move to Paris. Unprepared to resist, both Louis and the deputies agreed. At the time, the move to Paris seemed an insignificant concession to calm a frightened and turbulent city. It turned out to be far more than that. After October, the course of the Revolution was tied to the moods and politics of Paris, while the wishes of the rest of France fell into the background. After October, it was more the Paris Revolution than the French Revolution.

Revolution in the Provinces

When the news from Paris reached the provincial cities, it provoked an immediate reaction. In hundreds of cities, the old municipal and provincial bureaucracies simply collapsed, to be replaced by self-constituted Committees of bourgeois, who took over local administration and formed national guards for police and defense. Sometimes violence accompanied the change. At Tours and Bar-le-Duc men were murdered. Most often, however, the change was peaceful, even quiet. The centralized state French kings had been building for seven centuries dissolved in one month.

The fourth revolution was in the country, a national uprising of peasants against enclosures, the manorial system and royal taxes. Having been asked to state their grievances in the *cahiers*, the peasants assumed that the king meant to end them. Isolated instances of rural unrest and violence had occurred throughout the spring of 1789. Peasants refused to pay manorial dues and attacked chateaux. Provincial authorities fought back; at Mâcon, 33 peasants were hanged. After Bastille, however, the uprisings became too general and the government too disorganized to save the detested manorial privileges. Between July 18 and August 6, the Great Fear, six separate and independent peasant revolts, churned up the French provinces. Roused by the cry, "The brigands are coming!," peasants armed and, when no brigands appeared, they directed their attention to manorial dues and land enclosures. Local authorities were helpless, and the only response from Versailles was an evening session on August 4 when privileges already lost were formally renounced. The manorial institutions of France, which originated during the time of the fall of Rome, were destroyed. Of all of the revolutions of 1789, the peasant revolution succeeded most completely.

Revolution, Church, and Monarchy

During the cold and rainy winter of 1790, the pace of revolutionary change slowed appreciably. Instead of action there was sharp debate, both in the country and Assembly, on what was to be done. The basic issues had changed after 1789. Manorial dues, class privilege, the old government, these were all gone beyond recall. Now, men clashed over the place of the Roman Catholic Church in the new France, the role of the king, or the increasing threat of war. None of these questions was easily solved, and the process of confronting them led the French into further renewed revolutions, counterrevolution, wars, and the Terror.

The most serious problem faced during the years 1790 to 1792 was religion. Everyone agreed that the Roman Catholic Church must abandon its privileged position in the state, and most agreed there should be freedom of religion. In July 1790, the Assembly passed the Civil Constitution of the Clergy, which was to be the new institutional framework of the French Church. The Civil Constitution required priests and bishops to be elected by their people. The number of dioceses was reduced from 135 to 83, corresponding to the departments, which were the newly framed administrative units of provincial government. Finally, bishops were forbidden to recognize the administrative supremacy of Rome. The ties to Rome would be doctrinal and sentimental, nothing else. The Civil Constitution of the Clergy was the culmination of efforts by French kings to establish a state church, which dated at least from the fifteenth century. The revolutionary deputies completed the policies of the old monarchy.

In Rome, of course, this all went down badly. Relations with the papacy worsened when the Assembly imposed an oath of obedience on the French clergy. Half the priests and all but seven bishops refused to uphold the Civil Constitution of the Clergy. Strengthened by this French resistance, the pope condemned the Civil Constitution in March 1791. This swung the king against the Revolution. Louis was a man of deep though simple faith. Now he sought relief from his religious and political woes through flight from France.

In July he tried to escape to Germany, but he was captured before he could cross the French border and was returned to Paris. Having exposed his treason, he was no longer really king but an object of suspicion and contempt. The growing conflict over religion had dragged the crown in as well as the Church. And opposition to the Civil Constitution of the Clergy was soon to become the focus of counterrevolution.

The Economic Policies of the National Assembly

The National Assembly also followed the policies of the Old Regime in dealing with government bankruptcy, which had been the immediate cause of the Revolution. The deputies first confiscated Church lands, a favorite royal remedy from Charles Martel to Henry VIII. When this failed to fill the treasury, the Assembly issued paper money, called *assignats*, which differed only in name from the various notes and bills of the Old Regime. As the new government could not collect its taxes, the deficit grew, and the Assembly, following hoary precedent, debased the money by issuing *assignats* at will. The resulting inflation had the serious political repercussion of helping keep bread prices high.

The Constitution of 1791 and the Legislative Assembly

In spite of the burdens of running a disorganized country on a daily basis, the National Assembly made slow but steady progress on a constitution and finished it in September 1791. It was a poor document. The deputies of the National Assembly disqualified themselves from running for office; hence, the new Legislative Assembly would consist of entirely new men. Only the bourgeoisie got the vote, and as a result the new legislature lacked a broad political base. With the restricted franchise, religious division, distrust of the

king and an inexperienced legislature, the new government was going to have to fight for simple survival.

The Legislative Assembly met on October 1, 1791, and from the start it failed to direct events. The chamber was badly divided into factions and was unable to cooperate with the king. Bickering replaced debate. Bread prices continued to rise, reflecting both political uncertainty and inflated money. Religious hostilities grew, as the government drove "refractory" clergy, who had not sworn to support the Civil Constitution, from their parishes. There was a steady dribble of emigration, as men foresaw trouble and took themselves and their cash to safety. Everyone knew the king was intriguing with foreign powers. In April 1792, France drifted into war with Austria and Prussia, and the war went badly. The army was disorganized, officers fled to the enemy, frontier fortresses surrendered at once, and the allies slowly occupied much of eastern France. The Legislative Assembly seemed helpless, paralyzed by problems it could not solve. The French people, increasingly restless and frightened, demanded that the government do something. In Paris the public mood swung erratically to the left, while the provinces became more conservative—an ominous split that mirrored the ancient hostility between capital and country. In the provinces men wanted peace, the old priests, and to be left alone to run their own affairs. In Paris citizens talked of plots and traitors, wanted a defense of the Revolution and nation, cheaper bread, and an end to the suspect and ineffectual monarchy. In the summer of 1792 Paris became more turbulent and moved rapidly toward a new spasm of revolution.

The Fall of the Monarchy and the National Convention

On August 9 and 10, 1792, the anger and fears of Parisians exploded into revolt. A well organized mob occupied the city hall

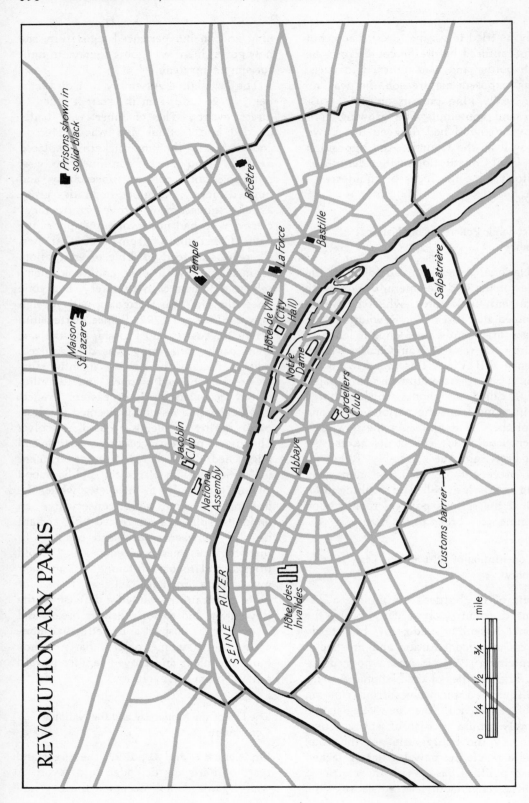

REVOLUTIONARY PARIS

Prisons shown in solid black

Bicêtre

Temple

La Force

Bastille

Salpêtrière

Maison St. Lazare

Hôtel de Ville (City Hall)

Notre Dame

Cordeliers Club

Jacobin Club

National Assembly

Abbaye

Customs barrier

Hôtel des Invalides

SEINE RIVER

0   ¼   ½   ¾   1 mile

and dispersed the municipal government. A new and more radical government, the Commune, was formed from delegates from the Paris sections (electoral wards) and dominated by a rising revolutionary personality, Georges Danton. The next day the mob invaded the royal palace and made the king a prisoner. The Legislative Assembly bowed to these events and called a National Convention to draw up a constitution for a new, republican France. The monarchy was ended.

The August Days did nothing to solve the problems the old government had failed to face. People were still hungry, and a foreign army was still marching on Paris and threatening dire revenge on revolutionaries. As the days passed, and nothing was done, Paris tempers and fears began to rise again. Now it was rumored that the multitude of nobles and churchmen who had been imprisoned were planning an immense jail break, which would be the signal for a slaughter of patriots. On September 2 armed mobs formed. They proceeded to the prisons and began a methodical execution of prisoners. For five days the massacres went on. More than 1200 prisoners were slaughtered, half of those held in Paris jails. Then, for the moment, Paris seemed calmer, but the savage butchery had signaled a new era of revolution, a time of Terror.

When the National Convention met on September 20, 1792, the deputies were confronted at once with the problem of the king. The Paris Commune and the radical deputies insisted that Louis be executed, while moderates from the provinces sought frantically for a way out. A search of Louis' private papers proved his treason beyond doubt and, for that, revolutionary justice demanded death. On January 21, 1793, Louis XVI was guillotined. The king's execution had great symbolic importance, making reconciliation with conservatives almost impossible. But its immediate political impact was slight, for Louis had long ceased to play any real role in the government.

In the months after the Convention met, several factions struggled for control of the chamber and the Paris Commune. The most moderate group was called the Girondins, because several of its leaders came from the department of the Gironde (Bordeaux). This was a loose faction, composed of provincial deputies with no support in Paris at all. The Girondins had only the loosest political program and no party discipline. In spite of a majority in the Convention, therefore, they were unable to turn this advantage into control over Paris or the national government. A second faction, with strength in Paris and the provinces, was known as Jacobins, named for the former Jacobin convent where their political club met. The Jacobins, led by Maxmillian Robespierre, were the more radical deputies of the Convention. Although a minority in the chamber, the Jacobins enjoyed superior party discipline and leadership. They had allies in Paris and also directed a network of local Jacobin clubs in many provincial cities. These were considerable elements of strength, and gave the Jacobins decisive advantages in dealing with their enemies. A third group, confined to Paris and without real influence in the Convention, was comprised of the radical, urban leadership of the Paris sections and city government. This faction, too, had a political club, the Cordeliers, which controlled the poorer section of Paris and commanded an armed and semidisciplined mob. The Paris radicals were hardly a unified group. Those in the Commune were constantly menaced by more extreme politicians from the sections and the streets. Even so, the armed force of their mob made them a serious political power.

In the months after the September prison massacres, politicians of the rival factions struggled to control the state and to meet the problems of war and revolution. In this contest the Girondins steadily lost ground to the Jacobins. While they held their majority in the Convention, the Girondins were blamed for military defeat in Belgium and Germany. They were denounced as traitors and monarchists and food hoarders. Thus the power of the Jacobins grew steadily as the mistakes and misfortunes of their enemies accumulated.

In the city, a similar political evolution occurred. High bread prices and fears of a counterrevolutionary plot undermined the moral authority of the Commune. Radical orators from the sections took advantage of this. A foolish attempt by the Girondins to arrest some of the leading radical Paris politicians sparked a new revolt. On May 31, 1793, the city government was overthrown, to be replaced by the Revolutionary Commune, a collection of Paris politicians somewhat louder and more radical than their predecessors. Two days later, on June 2, the Convention bowed to Parisian demands for a purge of 29 Girondin deputies. Once again, an organized Paris mob had overthrown both the municipal and national government.

The Reign of Terror

Although workers and shopkeepers from the poorer sections of Paris had made the *coup* of May-June 1793, the real victors were the Jacobin politicians in the Convention. Having defeated their Girondin enemies, even if by proxy, the Jacobins created a strong and successful revolutionary government over the course of the next year. The instrument they used was terror. Imitating the Paris example, the Jacobins, by their policy of mass executions, made terror into a system of government. Terror became an acceptable substitute for strong local administration, and took the place of the departed royal bureaucracy. It filled the army with recruits, encouraged officers to do their duty, and persuaded peasants to release their grain to the market at an acceptable price. Terror punished counterrevolutionary and food

hoarder alike. It was used as an instrument of daily administration as well as revolutionary security.

Terror had a number of advantages over traditional means of government. It freed the government from dependence on reports and red tape and allowed it to make rapid and flexible decisions, appropriate for the emergency conditions. The law's delay meant nothing now. A sense of urgency was reinforced by the guillotine. The government was brutal, but it was also efficient.

Although terror was the mainspring of government, the Jacobins also built institutions to carry out their policies. At the center, the Convention abdicated most of its executive power to the Committee of Public Safety. The Committee consisted of 12 able men, dominated politically by Robespierre. Within the Committee, the men worked in quasiministerial fashion. Lazare Carnot, a former regular army captain, directed the creation of the revolutionary armies, and earned the title, "Organizer of Victory." Bertrand Barere, the most astute parliamentary politician in the Convention, managed the chamber. Jean-Bon Saint-Andre, a former Protestant pastor, became a sort of minister of the navy. Together, their energy and efficiency dominated French government as no ministry had since Chancellor Maupeou in the 1770s.

The Committee of Public Safety's orders were carried out largely by three groups—the army, the network of local Jacobin clubs, and deputies of the Convention sent on missions to the provinces or the front. Of the three, the deputies on mission were the most important. Sent out on the Committee's orders, their task was to recruit men for the army, collect grain for Paris, purge unreliable local officials, execute subversives, and monitor the activities of the army. "I found this department religious, royalist, Girondin, public spirit killed, a small group of patriots molested, scarcely daring to call themselves Jacobins," wrote

A Scene in the Reign of Terror. (Culver)

Taillefer, the deputy on mission to the department of Cahors. "I de-Christianized, republicanized, Jacobinized, regenerated it . . .," he added. It was just what the Committee expected him to do.

Many of the deputies were not too particular about the means they used to do these things. At Nantes, Carrier drowned over 1200 prisoners, sinking them in the Loire River in large rafts. At Lyons, after the Jacobin army captured the city from the Girondins, Fouche shot about 2000 "counterrevolutionaries." Milder men often began their work with arrests and an execution or two, to set the proper tone of seriousness for their mission. Occasionally, the deputies and local Jacobins could not cope with the opposition and had to call in the army. In these instances, of course, the slaughter was appreciably increased.

In spite of the provincial revolts, the Jacobin Committee paid particular attention to Paris, an attitude of great political wisdom. To deal with the countless subversives everyone believed infested the city, the Committee relied on the Revolutionary Tribunal. Trial procedure was simple. The accused was permitted no de-

fense. Hoarding grain and counterrevolutionary activities were the usual crimes. Between the execution of Louis XVI in January 1793, and that of Robespierre in August 1794, the Revolutionary Tribunal condemned 2672 persons to the guillotine, imprisoned some and even acquitted 857. The Tribunal was assisted in this patriotic work by watch committees in the 48 Paris sections, securely under the control of loyal Jacobins. The Committee also watched the Paris municipal government and gradually purged it of enemies, replacing them with Jacobins. On the whole, Jacobin rule in Paris worked effectively, paralleling the growing Jacobin control of the countryside.

The basic problem faced by the Committee was the war. On the frontiers the spring of 1793 had brought serious defeats. On April 5, the Girondin commander in Belgium, Dumouriez, deserted to the Austrians, who then drove the disorganized French back across the border. In July two key fortresses surrendered, and it appeared that the Austrians were about to march on Paris. In Lorraine and Italy, French troops were also in retreat or on the defensive.

Carnot and his associates reversed that and turned defeat into victory. By autumn, Carnot's new armies were ready. The French defeated the Austrians on the Belgian frontier and began another invasion of Belgium that culminated in the victory at Fleurus in July 1794 and opened the Low Countries to French conquest.

The civil war also went well for the Jacobins. In April 1793, a royalist-clerical revolt had begun in the Vendée in western France, and it was soon serious enough to require regiments from the frontiers. Furthermore, in July 1793, a federalist revolt, tied to the expulsion of the Girondin deputies from the Convention, broke out in many of the large cities of southern France, including Bordeaux, Lyons, Marseilles and Toulon. Again, the regular army was needed. The Jacobins pushed the campaigns against counterrevolution with energy and brutality. In December, at Savenay, the army caught up with the Vendéans, and defeated them. In the south, the major cities were recaptured. It was all accompanied by reprisals and butchery. Suspects were executed without trial and prisoners were shot. The Jacobin deputies on mission showed what revolutionary justice really meant.

The instrument of victory was a new army, organized and equipped by the Jacobin Committee. Lazare Carnot directed this effort, and his general orders were simple, far different from the cautious strategy of the Old Regime. Seek battle. he commanded,

. . . keep the troops in constant readiness . . . use the bayonet on every possible occasion, and follow up the enemy without pause until he is completely destroyed.

Carnot's recruiting methods were also revolutionary. He was not content with convicts and bums but drafted sturdy peasant youths for his regiments. Command no longer went automatically to incompetent nobles. Carnot sought ability. Unlucky and defeated generals were cashiered and guillotined. Others took their places, including Napoleon Bonaparte and eight of his marshals. Carnot's 14 armies, animated by nationalism and revolutionary fervor (to say nothing of the guillotine), were victorious everywhere. In a year they repressed revolt and conquered the Rhine frontier. It was an immense achievement, the real beginning of national armies and modern war. It also made the other European powers exceptionally nervous.

Victory in war would be meaningless if the Revolution were overthrown internally by its enemies. The Jacobins, who had come to power by conspiracy, were extremely sensitive to plots and rumors of plots. Everyone must be loyal to the Revolution. There was no room for dissent. The emergency demanded total vigilance. Nobles, priests, food hoarders, slackers and defeatists were all subversives. As the gray and rainy winter of 1793–1794 closed in on Paris, with political tension high and bread prices higher, these sentiments were translated into executions and purges.

The first to perish were the Girondins. Already compromised in the federalist revolts, the Girondins were also implicated in a suspected though imaginary counter-revolutionary plot. Haled before the Revolutionary Tribunal, they were guillotined on October 31, 1793. The Paris radicals came next. Their demands for total price controls were opposed by Robespierre. Arrested without warning, the radicals were executed en masse in March 1794. Immediately, Robespierre turned on a dissident Jacobin faction. Georges Danton and his friends were arrested on charges of corruption and hostility to the Committee of Public Safety. They were unquestionably guilty on both counts and were guillotined on April 5.

Extermination of the factions, however, did not end the Terror. Instead, it became worse. The executioners never lacked work. The Republic of Terror now added a new dimension to its public philosophy. Madame la Guillotine would do more than enforce political conformity. In their season of triumph, the Jacobins would establish the "Republic of Virtue." Virtue, in the Jacobin state, was given a civic cast. It meant a willingness to fight for the revolutionary government and ideals, to care for them and sacrifice for them. Idleness was prohibited, and hoarding of food became a crime as black as royalism. *Civisme* was a badge of honor and loyalty, while *incivisme* merited death and often received it. The New Jerusalem was at last at hand. A final effort, and the corrupt would be cast down, while the virtuous, once downtrodden, the stone the builder had despised, would inherit the Kingdom.

Long live the fortunate moment
When everything is born again.

Psychologically, the French Revolution had come full circle.

The Republic of Virtue enforced conformity more savagely than Calvin's Geneva, Nero's Rome or the Inquisition. But for the faithful, for the true believers in the Jacobin vision, the Republic of Virtue was awesome and inspiring. They applauded such laws as the edict of November 10, 1793, which prohibited the worship of the Christian God. Good Jacobins supported discarding the traditional Christian calendar in October 1793, and advocated replacing it with a patriotic and revolutionary one. Certainly, Jacobins approved of the law of 22 Prairial, II (June 9, 1794), which made it possible to execute corrupt deputies to the Convention and greatly extended the range of *incivique* crimes. But to others, to priests and nobles, to federalists and skeptics, the Jacobin paradise was a vision of hell. For Jacobins who had quarreled with Robespierre, the law of 22 Prairial was a death warrant. So, a plot was hatched by dissident Jacobins to end the Terror. Some, like Billaud-Varennes, were on the Committee of Public Safety; others, like Fouché were deputies in the Convention. On the ninth of Thermidor, II (July 27, 1794), Robes-

Robespierre guillotines the Executioner. (Bullox/ Art Reference Bureau)

pierre and a dozen supporters were arrested. The next day they were executed. Robespierre had been shocked at being taken in a *coup* and had protested violently. But execution at the hands of fellow conspirators is a common end for revolutionaries, and an appropriate one.

The Thermadorian Reaction

Politically, the *coup* of the 9th of Thermidor was the turning point of the Revolution. In the years since 1788, the Revolution had been supported by fewer and fewer people as the groups in power drifted farther away from the generous ideals of 1789. At the same time, the political factions became better and better organized, and enjoyed the total support of their adherents. The execution of Robespierre checked this trend. It was, in effect, the triumph of general opinion over political organization, and it was the first time during the Revolution that this had happened.

Robespierre's death also ended the Terror. Practical men, who were untouched by the Jacobin vision, thought the Terror was no longer needed. Once, it had been necessary for survival. Terror had fed Paris, overthrown the factions, defeated enemies both foreign and domestic, and held France together. But those days were over. It was time to stop. Men doubted the promises of the Republic of Virtue, doubted that the Jacobins could lead France to perfect liberty, equality, fraternity and justice. They believed that the continuation of the Terror was horrible and inhuman and, what was worse, pointless. Did the Jacobins want the horror to continue forever? Nobody wished that. Frenchmen were tired of heroism and sacrifice, tired of the faith and fear that accompanied the Jacobin heaven. In a debate in the Convention, a Jacobin called for justice only for patriots. France wanted justice for everyone.

The Government of the Directory: 1795–1799

With the war going well and the Terror ended, the Convention turned to its ostensible task and drew up a constitution for France. The Constitution of 1795 (year III) was extraordinarily complex, designed to keep the people at bay and to prevent the government from governing. Executive power was given to five directors, and the government that they headed came to be known as the Directory. The Legislature was bicameral, a Council of Elders of 250 and a lower house called the Five Hundred. Each chamber had one third of its members elected annually by a restricted electorate that excluded workers and the poorer peasants. It was a middle class constitution, designed to uphold bourgeois values, virtues, property and power.

The Directory never really established itself, however. It was plagued by *coups;* the habits of conspiracy and faction died hard. In 1796, a proto-Socialist named Gracchus Babeuf led his Conspiracy of Equals against the regime. Its aim was to abolish private property. The government suppressed this mini-rebellion with ease and executed Babeuf, who was later canonized by Marxists as an early prophet of socialism. The second *coup* came from the Directors themselves. On September 4, 1797 (18 Fructidor, V), three republican Directors exiled their two conservative colleagues, including Carnot, and purged Conservatives from the legislative Councils. A third *coup*, in 1798, followed this pattern. The Directors annulled the elections, which they had lost, and appointed their cohorts to the legislature. It all went smoothly enough, but the third resort to extralegal means in as many years revealed the political bankruptcy of the regime.

The Directory also failed to solve the social problems inherited from the Jacobins. The most insidious was the inflation of the *assignats,* which had fallen to less than a penny on the dollar. Consequently, bread prices remained artificially high. Efforts to deflate the *assignats* and assign them a fixed value only brought about a depression in 1798–1799. Nor was the Directory able to do anything about the religious divisions in France. The regime neither renounced the de-Christianization of the Jacobins nor settled its differences with Rome. Instead, the government intermittently persecuted both priests and Jacobins. These loathsome practices helped discredit the Directory in the eyes of decent and moderate Frenchmen, as indeed they should have.

The most serious problem, however, was the rampant and cynical corruption. All the politicians could be bought, though this is not unusual, and business with the government was normally conducted by bribery and influence-peddling. The degraded psychology of the *nouveau-riche* businessman pervaded the regime. People assumed that everyone had his price and politics was simply the art of finding it. These attitudes extended to women. It was an era of courtesans, not the least talented of whom was Josephine Bonaparte. Fashionable ball gowns consisted of gauze draped tastefully over a nude body. Parties given by the Director, Paul Barras, were elegant orgies, which everyone enjoyed attending. For a brief period, this open and public corruption was exciting, sophisticated and fashionable. After a few years, however, it disgusted the middle class Frenchmen who were the regime's main support. It was a moral revulsion that finally doomed the Directory.

Yet the Directory was not without its successes. Its legislation laid the basis for Napoleonic administrative reforms, and anticipated Napoleonic edicts in law, education and finance. Most important, the Directory won the foreign war. In 1796, a young general, Napoleon Bonaparte, was appointed to command the French army in Italy, an advancement he owed to the political and sexual intrigues of his wife Josephine. Napoleon promptly attacked the Austrians, defeated them, and drove them out of Italy in a series of brilliant campaigns. In October 1797, he wrung spectacular concessions from the Austrians in the Treaty of Campio Formio. Austria recognized the French conquest of Belgium and the new French client states in Italy. Even the Sun King had not won such a victory.

But military success and the beginnings of institutional consolidation were not enough to save the Directory. It had never inspired much loyalty, or commanded much fear. Its politicians and generals thought in terms of overthrowing the regime. The last *coup* came on November 9, 1799 (18 Brumaire, VIII), when the most successful general, Napoleon, aided by the Directors themselves, captured the machinery of state. There was no resistance. France was apathetic. Most citizens simply wanted an end to adventure and revolution. With the advent of Napoleon, France came full cycle, from an incompetent monarchy to an effective one, from a floundering king to an enlightened despot who meant to end revolution at home while extending it abroad.

Napoleon as Enlightened Despot

The new regime, the fifth since 1789, bore a surface resemblance to those it followed. There was a written constitution that contained the usual provisions for a legislature, legal equality, modest political liberty and a plural executive. The constitution created three Consuls, with only the first Consul, Napoleon, having any real power. There were four legislatures, with their functions strictly divided. The legislative body voted on bills, but could not debate them. The Tribunate debated bills, but did not vote. The Senate decided on the constitutionality of bills, while the Council of State drafted legislation, but neither debated nor voted on it. The electoral laws were as carefully manipulated. All adult males voted, thus keeping faith with the Jacobin tradition. But they voted only for the commune list, who then chose one tenth of their number as the department list, who chose one-tenth of their number as the national list. From these came the members of the legislature. The whole system was designed to concentrate all real power in the hands of the First Consul. It was eyewash for dictatorship. But it was not unpopular. A plebiscite in 1800 ratified the constitution by a vote of 3,011,107 to 1657 a comfortable margin.

The man who devised the constitution was born into a petty and turbulent Corsican family, with loads of brothers, sisters, debts and feuds. Napoleon was an unmanageable boy, so his family packed him off to military school, a solution that has since occurred to many American families, although not with such spectacular results. In due time, the troublesome and moody Corsican got his commission. He was even

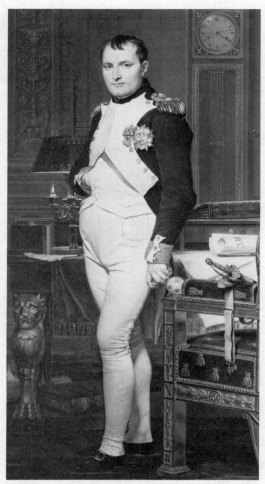

"Napoleon in His Study", oil painting by Jacques Louis David. (National Gallery of Art, Washington, D.C. Samuel H. Kress Collection)

promoted to captain, in spite of an abrupt and abrasive personality and numerous absences without leave. He was destined for unhappy obscurity, until the Revolution. By sheer luck, he was at the siege of Toulon when the artillery commander was wounded. Posted to his slot, Napoleon set up his guns and took the town. This display of military aptitude, plus some opportunistic Jacobin oratory, persuaded Carnot to make him a general. When the Jacobins went down, Napoleon went with them, but Josephine restored him to grace and

obtained for him the command of the army of Italy. It was considered a poor post, with little chance for glory. Director Paul Barras gave it to Napoleon as much in pity and contempt as anything else, just to satisfy Josephine, get the importunate young man out of town, and bury him in a minor but honorable position. For the elegant and cynical Barras, the appointment to Italian command was a form of dismissal; for Napoleon, as he surveyed his ragged and complacent troops, it was the beginning of everything.

Once in power, Napoleon turned immediately to domestic reform. He swept away some of the debris of the revolution, and included elements from both the old regime and the five revolutionary regimes that preceded him. He had two basic aims, an efficient government, and one that would inspire loyalty. Anything less, and Napoleon would lose power as others had before him.

Peace with Rome was probably Napoleon's most popular achievement. He indicated his intentions his first month in power by returning churches to the priests for worship. He reestablished Sunday. He began negotiations with the pope, and reached an agreement in 1801. The Concordat incorporated many of the characteristics of the Old Regime, Gallican Church. The government (Napoleon) appointed the bishops, who took an oath of loyalty to the state. The government also controlled the seminaries, and paid the salaries of priests and bishops. The Church acquiesced in the loss of its lands, and gained the right to accept gifts and bequests.

In spite of some complaint from anti-clericals, the Concordat was generally popular. It reassured Frenchmen that they could keep their church lands, and it ended the squalid religious persecution. Grateful for that, the Church constantly praised Napoleon and his government, and even included some of this praise in the catechism. The Concordat was also popular with Napoleon, which is what counted. He believed a state supported by the Church would be seen as legitimate, and this sense of permanence was what he wanted most.

Having settled with the Church, Napoleon turned to the civil administration. Building on the work of the Directory, he created a civil service that surpassed both the Jacobins and the Old Regime in administrative centralization. In fiscal policy, Napoleon reverted to the system of the Old Regime. He partially repudiated the *assignats*, in imitation of countless royal swindles. He reinstated the Old Regime land tax and excise taxes, though without tax farming and aristocratic exemptions. He founded the Bank of France and established a firm budget and accounting system, all of which had eluded the Bourbon kings. As a result of these reforms, Napoleon received about 400 million francs a year, approximately the amount Louis XVI had had coming in, but he did it with the most efficient and honest tax system the French had ever known.

Finally, Napoleon completed the codification of French law, a project begun during the Revolution. He pushed this project hard and, in 1804, the Civil Code was approved. Two years later came the Code of Civil Procedure, in 1807 the Commercial Code, then a Code of Criminal Procedure and finally a Penal Code. As with his other domestic legislation, the law codes contained both revolutionary and Old Regime legislation, as well as Naopleon's own ideas. It was also in the tradition of Old Regime enlightened despotism, of which Napoleon was the heir. Continuity in politics is as instructive as change.

Napoleon at War

Domestic reforms, which never occupied more than a fraction of Napoleon's attention, were designed to keep him in power. That power was to be used for war. Basically, Napoleon was a soldier, and he thought war was the only profession worthy of his talents. Once his *coup* was

complete, and domestic reform begun, Napoleon went to the front. His presence made a decided difference. The French offensive of 1800 was extremely successful. Napoleon defeated the Austrians at Marengo, and drove them from Italy for the second time. Routed in Italy, the Austrians suffered a further defeat in Germany and were obliged to sue for peace. At Lunéville, in 1801, Austria agreed to abandon Italy and the left bank of the Rhine to France. With Austria out of the war, Great Britain lost her last continental ally and began to think of peace. After long negotiations, France and Britain ended a decade of war with the Peace of Amiens in 1802.

This was the most critical moment of Napoleon's career. He had defeated his enemies and had concluded peace. He had established a firm regime at home. At Amiens and Lunéville, he had reached the limits of conquest that the European state system, based on the balance of power, could concede and accept. "A conqueror, like a cannon ball, must go on," wrote the Duke of Wellington of Napoleon. After Amiens, Napoleon chose to become a conqueror, pursuing the visionary goal of European domination. His sense of realism abandoned him. He moved into the realm of dream.

This decision was symbolized for all to see by Napoleon's coronation as Emperor of the French on December 2, 1804. It was a stupendous ceremony, with the pope himself attending. Afterward, Napoleon I created a brilliant court. He made kings and princes of his family and friends, and established an elaborate etiquette to emphasize his grandeur. It was a creditable imitation of the Sun King, less grandiose perhaps, but certainly an effective statement of Napoleon's intention to be the embodiment of France and the arbiter of Europe.

Napoleon's expansion resumed less than a year after the Treaty of Amiens was signed. In 1803 he undertook the reorganization of the ramshackle Holy Roman Empire. Most of the ecclesiastical states and imperial cities were destroyed, along with the smaller imperial dignities. Although not immediately affected, the British saw clearly enough where this blatant aggression must lead, and they declared war on France in May 1803. In 1805, they were joined by Russia and Austria in a third coalition against the French Emperor.

The allies won their only battle at sea, but it was a permanent strategic victory. On November 25, 1805, Lord Nelson destroyed a Franco-Spanish fleet at Trafalgar. French hopes of defeating the British went down with the navy. Napoleon would never invade England.

On land, Napoleon, who was at the height of his powers, did much better. On December 2, 1805, the first anniversary of his coronation, Napoleon annihilated a combined Austro-Russian army at Austerlitz. This disaster drove the Austrians out of the war and the Russians out of Germany. Again, Napoleon reorganized the smaller German states, this time into the

Lord Nelson. (Culver)

Confederation of the Rhine, a bloc of satellite kingdoms. Almost as an afterthought, he abolished that important medieval relic, the Holy Roman Empire.

At this point, when it was too late, Prussia joined the allies. In October, 1806, in the twin battles of Jena and Auerstadt, Napoleon crushed the Prussian army. Moving fast, the French Emperor took Berlin and marched east against Russia. At Friedland, in 1807, Napoleon completed his triumph by soundly beating the Russians. That was it. Only the British could go on. Russia and Prussia asked for peace.

The peace negotiations were conducted at Tilsit, in Prussia, with Napoleon, Czar Alexander I and Frederick-William III of Prussia acting as their own negotiators. Napoleon proved less apt in diplomacy than in war. His terms, although not unrealistic in view of the magnitude of his victories, made any permanent peace impossible. Russia was treated rather leniently and actually gained some territory. But she was forced to recognize Napoleon's German settlement, as well as the Grand Duchy of Warsaw, a Napoleonic client state on her borders. Prussia paid the price of peace. She lost most of her Polish lands to the Grand Duchy of Warsaw, and all of her provinces east of the Elbe River. Prussia was forbidden to keep an army of more than 40,000 men and was condemned to pay a huge indemnity and admit French occupation troops to her fortresses. The Treaties of Tilsit dropped Prussia from the ranks of the great powers. These treaties also involved Napoleon in Polish affairs, which Russia had traditionally regarded as vital to her national interests.

Peace at Tilsit left only the British still in the war. Invasion of England was impossible, so Napoleon tried to defeat the British by cutting off their trade. In 1806 and 1807, he issued the Berlin and Milan Decrees, which closed continental ports to British goods and ships. By these means, Napoleon hoped, Britain would be driven

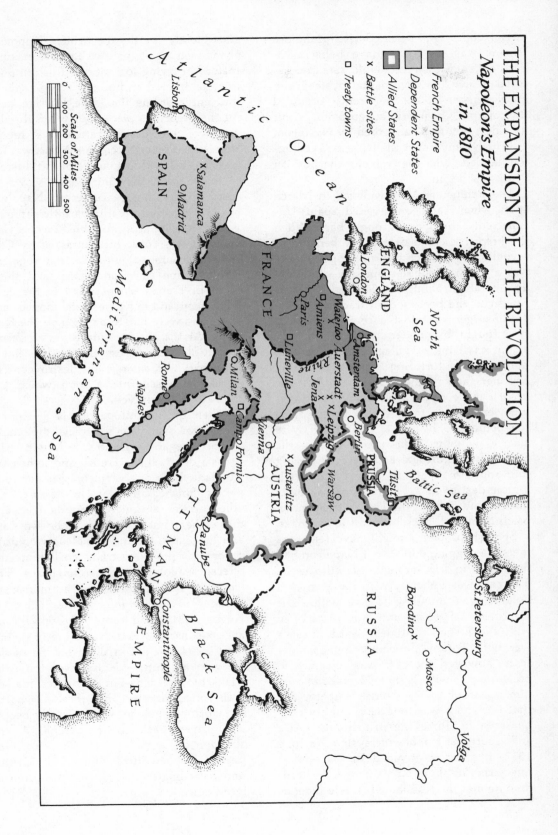

THE EXPANSION OF THE REVOLUTION

Napoleon's Empire in 1810

French Empire
Dependent States
Allied States
× Battle sites
□ Treaty towns

Atlantic Ocean

Scale of Miles
0 100 200 300 400 500

Lisbon

SPAIN

×Salamanca
○Madrid

Mediterranean

Rome○

Naples○

Sea

FRANCE

×Waterloo
Paris○ ×Amiens
□Lunéville
○Milan
□Campo Formio

Rhine

Amsterdam○

London○

ENGLAND

North Sea

Auerstadt× ×Leipzig
Jena×
○Berlin

PRUSSIA

Tilsit

Baltic Sea

St.Petersburg○

Vienna○

AUSTRIA

×Austerlitz

Warsaw○

Danube

OTTOMAN

EMPIRE

Constantinople

Black Sea

RUSSIA

Borodino×

○Mosco

Volga

to bankruptcy and peace. Such a grandiose scheme was bound to have holes in it. Portugal, a British economic satellite, refused to join the Continental System and, in November 1807, the French occupied the country. Great Britain could not permit its oldest ally to be absorbed by Napoleon. A British army under the Duke of Wellington landed, and the war in the Iberian Peninsula began.

The Peninsular War widened in March 1808, when Napoleon invaded Spain. Unexpectedly, the Spanish fought back. When the French tried to extend the benefits of revolutionary church reform to Spain, there was a massive popular uprising—the Vendee revolt on a huge scale. The war was fought in the best modern tradition, peasant insurgents against a regular army. It was fought by modern methods, mainly against civilians, by pillage and murder and burning, by torturing priests, shooting prisoners and raping women. Initially the French made gains against the insurgents but were unable to drive the British from the peninsula. By 1811, the British were clearly winning. They had driven the French from Portugal and were advancing into southern Spain. In July 1812, Wellington destroyed a French army at Salamanca, and obliged the French to abandon Madrid and fall back toward the Pyrenees.

Spanish problems might have remained merely a nagging difficulty if Napoleon had not begun to drift into enmity with Russia. The czar was unhappy with the French in Poland, was unwilling to live within the Continental System, and was dissatisfied with the French attitude toward Russia's war with Turkey. Remembering past defeats, however, the czar was reluctant to break openly with France. Napoleon saved him the trouble. The French emperor felt that one more war, one last, mighty conquest would force the British into peace and secure the Napoleonic system. In June 1812, the French invaded Russia with a huge army of about 600,000 men. At Borodino he met the Russians. It was a hideous

and bloody battle, in which Napoleon abandoned all of his own tactical maxims. Instead of trying to flank the Russian position, he ordered an infantry charge against the center of the line. The Russian guns cut the French to pieces but when the day was over the Russians retreated. A month later, the French occupied Moscow. The Russians refused to concede defeat. Instead of negotiating, they burned Moscow. Instead of dictating peace terms, Napoleon began a ghastly retreat toward the frontier. As his starving army stumbled toward Germany, it was constantly harassed by Cossacks and pursued by the Russian regulars. Winter came early and hard, and thousands of Frenchmen perished in the cold. Equipment and guns were abandoned, and stragglers were left to be shot by the Russians. At the icy Beresina River the army fought its way across the bridge, but a large part was cut off and destroyed. The retreat collapsed into a rout, which less than 100,000 survived.

When the magnitude of his defeat became clear, Napoleon's artificial diplomatic alliances began to crumble. In March 1813, Prussia deserted the French and joined the Russians. Even so, Napoleon was not completely finished. In May, he defeated the allied armies at Lutzen and Bautzen and drove them out of Saxony. The Russians and Prussians, fearing Napoleon would recover, accepted Austrian mediation and offered Napoleon a generous peace. The emperor refused. It was a monstrous blunder. Austria joined the allies in August, 1813, and turned the power balance against the French for the first time since 1794. Napoleon did what he could. He won an initial victory over the Austrians at Dresden, but the allies massed their forces anyway. In a three-day battle at Leipzig, Napoleon was decisively beaten and driven back to the Rhine. As he abandoned Germany, Napoleon received unwelcome news from Spain. The British under Wellington had crossed the Pyrenees into France.

Although Napoleon was on the run, the allied generals were still wary of him. On November 8, they offered peace again, conceding France the Rhine frontier. Napoleon again refused. The war continued with an allied invasion of France. In his defensive campaign, Napoleon fought as well as he ever had. In February 1814, he defeated various detachments of the allied armies in six rapid battles, driving them back in some disorder. Again, he was offered peace, this time with the frontiers of 1792. Again, Napoleon refused. Twenty years of continuous fighting and negotiation had badly eroded his grasp of strategic and diplomatic reality. He was badly outnumbered; he might win tactical victories but not the war. Each of the allied offers had been generous, as everyone but Napoleon could see.

After Napoleon's last refusal, the allies pushed on to Paris. They entered the city on March 13, 1814, twenty-two years after the first Austro-Prussian invasion had set out for Paris to end the revolution and restore a Bourbon to his throne. Although the Bourbon Restoration had been delayed, it was not forgotten. Louis XVIII, old, fat, safe and complacent, was placed on the French throne, and Napoleon was packed off to the island of Elba. Except for the brief epilogue of the Hundred Days, which began with Napoleon's return from Elba in 1815 and ended in the catastrophe at Waterloo, the Napoleonic era was over.

The Revolutionary Legacy

The heavens themselves, the planets and this centre
Observe degree, priority and place
Insisture, course, proportion, season, form,
Office, and custom, in all line of order . . .
Take but degree away, untune that string,
And, hark, what discord follows.

When William Shakespeare wrote *Troilus and Cressida* he described social values that were widely accepted yet already beginning to erode. By the end of the eighteenth century their erosion was all but complete. Order, hierarchy, privilege and rank, these essential attributes of Old Regime society and government, were badly mangled by the Revolution and wars. Nobles, clerics and kings could be pardoned for seeing the Revolution as satanic and the Napoleonic wars as a crusade against them.

Certainly, the Revolution had been more successful than Enlightened Despots in clearing out the remaining centers of Old Regime private political power. Aristocratic, ecclesiastical and municipal privilege had generally withstood the best efforts of Old Regime reform. The old constituted bodies, whether guilds, Parlements, manors or churches, had not done so well, however, after 1789. Such privileges had been destroyed or damaged in much of Europe. The government now faced most of its citizens without noble or privileged intermediaries. A basic result of the Revolution was the immense and permanent growth in the power of the state.

Equally important were the changes in the way men thought. In the long interval of war and revolution, society had become more equalitarian, more individualistic, more secular. Liberalism was a popular ideology even in 1815, and the traditional social conflicts between the privileged and the commoner were by no means over. Notions of legal equality and careers open to talent dissolved allegiance to traditional concepts of social hierarchy and status. Even worse was the new secular religion—nationalism. The French had rallied to defend their nation in 1793 and then drove all Europe to do the same 20 years later. The relatively decorous contests between dynasties were being replaced by savage struggles between peoples. Without wishing it, the Revolution and Napoleon had created a Europe of nations.

The revolutionary era, therefore, witnessed the triumph of the two basic political forces of modernity: the state and the people. Not everybody, certainly not the former masters of society, was pleased with this, or with the prospect of more of it. "No one who has not lived before 1789 knows how sweet life can be," commented the French foreign minister Prince Talleyrand, and he expressed the spirit of 1814. It was the voice of the past.

CHRONOLOGY OF THE FRENCH REVOLUTION

1789:	Estates General meets
	Bastille Day riots in Paris
	Dissolution of royal government in the provinces
	Great Fear
	Declaration of the Rights of Man
	Revolution in Belgium
1790:	Civil Constitution of the Clergy
	Revolution in Poland
1792:	War between France, Austria, Prussia
	Establishment of the Republic
	Beginning of the Reign of Terror
1793:	War with England, Holland and Spain
	Reign of Terror
1794:	Death of Robespierre and the end of the Reign of Terror
1795:	Establishment of the Directory
1796–1797:	Napoleon Bonaparte's Italian campaign
1797:	Treaty of Campio Formio
1798:	Russia declares war on France
1799:	Napoleon seizes power in France
1801:	Treaty of Luneville
	Concordat with the Papacy
1802:	Treaty of Amiens
1804:	Napoleon becomes Emperor
1805:	Battle of Trafalgar
	Battle of Austerlitz
1806:	Napoleon abolishes the Holy Roman Empire
1806:	Battles of Jena and Auerstadt
1807:	Treaties of Tilsit
1808:	French invasion of Spain and the beginning of the Peninsular War
1812:	French invasion of Russia
1813:	Final allied coalition against Napoleon
	Battle of Leipzig
1814:	Abdication of Napoleon
	Congress of Vienna
1815:	Napoleon's One Hundred Days
	Congress of Vienna makes peace for Europe for a century

SUGGESTED READINGS

Pierre Bayle, *Historical and Critical Dictionary: Selections*, ed. R. Popkin, (New York: Bobbs Merrill, 1965).

John Locke, *A Letter Concerning Toleration*, (New York: Bobbs Merrill, 1955).

John Locke, *The Second Treatise of Government*, (New York: Bobbs Merrill).

John Locke, *Essay Concerning Human Understanding*, 2 vols. (New York: Harper).

Voltaire, *Philosophical Letters*, (New York: Bobbs Merrill, 1961).

Cesare de Beccaria, *On Crimes and Punishments*, (New York: Bobbs Merrill, 1963).

Frank Manuel, ed., *The Enlightenment* (Englewood Cliffs, N.J.: Prentice-Hall, 1965).

Charles Hendel, *Jean-Jacques Rousseau: Moralist*, (New York: Bobbs Merrill, 1962).

Paul Hazard, *The European Mind*, (New York: Meridian, 1963).

Paul Hazard, *European Thought in the Eighteenth Century*, New York: Meridian, 1963).

Ernst Cassirer, *The Philosophy of the Enlightenment*, (Boston: Beacon, 1955).

Carl Becker, *The Heavenly City of the Eighteenth Century Philosophers*, (New Haven: Yale University Press, 1969).

The Duke of Saint-Simon, *Versailles, the Court and Louis XIV*, L. Norton, ed. (New York: Harper, 1966).

C. A. McCartney, ed., *The Hapsburg and Hohenzollern Dynasties in the Seventeenth and Eighteenth Centuries* (New York: Harper, 1970).

H. B. Hill, *The Political Testament of Cardinal Richelieu* (Madison: University of Wisconson Press, 1961).

Carl Friedrich, *The Age of the Baroque: 1610–1660* (New York: Harper, 1962).

Friedrich Nussbaum, *The Triumph of Science and Reason: 1660–1685* (New York: Harper, 1962).

John B. Wolf, *The Emergence of the Great Powers: 1685–1715* (New York: Harper, 1962).

Penfield Roberts, *The Quest for Security: 1715–1740* (New York: Harper, 1963).

Walter Dorn, *Competition for Empire: 1740–1763* (New York: Harper, 1965).

Leonard Krieger, *Kings and Philosophers: 1689–1789* (New York: Norton, 1970).

Franklin Ford, *Robe and Sword* (New York: Harper, 1965).

R. Rosenberg, *Bureaucracy, Aristocracy and Autocracy* (Cambridge, Mass.: Harvard University Press, 1958).

Thomas Paine, *Common Sense* and *The Crisis* (Garden City, N.Y.: Doubleday, no date).

R. and E. Forster, eds., *European Society in the Eighteenth Century* (New York: Harper, 1969).

Karl Roider, *Maria Thresa* (Englewood Cliffs, N.J.: Prentice-Hall, 1972).

John Gagliardo, *Enlightened Despotism* (New York: Crowell, 1967).

Albert Goodwin, ed., *The European Nobility in the Eighteenth Century* (New York: Harper, 1967).

L. H. Gipson, *The Coming of the Revolution: 1763–1775* (New York: Harper, 1962).

R. R. Palmer, *The Age of the Democratic Revolution*, Vol. I and II (Princeton, N.J.: Princeton University Press, 1959).

Edmund Burke, *Reflexions on the Revolution in France* (New York: Bobbs Merrill, 1955).

Albert Goodwin, *The French Revolution* (New York: Harper, 1962).

J. M. Thompson, *The French Revolution* (New York: Oxford University Press, 1966).

Albert Mathiez, *The French Revolution* (New York: Grosset and Dunlap, 1964).

Alexis de Tocqueville, *The Old Regime and the French Revolution* (Garden City, N.Y.: Doubleday, 1955).

Crane Brinton, *Decade of Revolution* (New York: Harper, 1963).

Georges Lefebvre, *The French Revolution*, 2 vols. (New York: Columbia University Press, 1962).

Georges Lefebvre, *The Coming of the French Revolution* (New York: Random House).

R. R. Palmer, *Twelve Who Ruled* (Princeton, N.J.: Princeton University Press, 1941).

George Rude, *The Crowd in the French Revolution* (Oxford: Oxford University Press, 1959).

Charles Tilly, *The Vendee* (Cambridge, Mass.: Harvard University Press, 1964).

Alfred Cobban, *The Social Interpretation of the French Revolution* (Cambridge: Cambridge University Press, 1964).

Paul Mantoux, *The Industrial Revolution in the Eighteenth Century: The Beginnings of the Modern Factory System in England* (New York: Harper, 1961).

Phyllis Deane, *The First Industrial Revolution* (Cambridge: Cambridge University Press, 1969).

M. Dorothy George, *London Life in the Eighteenth Century* (New York: Harper, 1964).

Part 9 The Nineteenth Century: 1814-1914

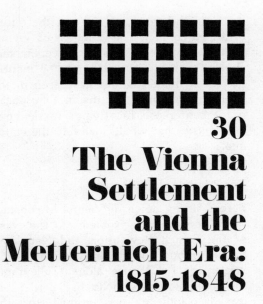

30
The Vienna Settlement and the Metternich Era: 1815-1848

The Conflicting Claims of Cosmopolitanism and Nationalism

The era of the French Revolution and Napoleon gave birth to modern European nationalism in association with liberalism—the impulse to free the common people from the traditional domination of king and nobility. The combination of nationalism and liberalism had immense appeal in the decades following Napoleon's fall. It is all too easy to miss, in these same decades, the strong residue of cosmopolitanism —of a larger sense of European community. The politics of the nineteenth century can be seen, in part, as a prolonged struggle between the idea of nationalism and the ancient cosmopolitan tradition.

If we have come to think of Europe as a hodgepodge of nation-states, we may overlook those roots common to all European nations which for many centuries gave Europeans a sense of community (despite local differences), and which Europeans have been endeavoring to recover in recent decades. During the medieval era, the dim memory of a powerful Christian empire— the myth of Rome or Byzantium—inspired the creators of Christendom. And the universalism of that Roman and Christian heritage continued to argue against parochialism despite the steady advance of localism and secularization that, together, chipped away at the foundations of the universalist or cosmopolitan dream.

Even the French Revolution, although the breeder of nationalism, also came to promote a new universalism—one based not on traditional notions of Christian empire or papal monarchy but on revolutionary republican axioms legislated and evangelized by one ecstatic nationality. The very energy of the French nation, in fact, defeated the new cosmopolitanism by revealing to its rivals the enormous power an emancipated nation could engender. The ultimate defeat of France by a Europe in coalition set the stage for a lengthy conflict between the principles of cosmopolitanism and nationalism.

The Congress of Vienna: 1814-1815

Many months before the advancing Allies reached Paris in the spring of 1814, they had been formulating their war aims in a series of treaties which were chiefly necessary to hold the wartime alliance together. For the uncomfortable truth of the matter was that the four great powers (Britain, Russia, Prussia, and Austria) had little in common beyond their mutual mistrust of Napoleonic France. Their coalition-warfare against the French had too often been coalition in name only, with their private ambitions and rivalaries always working behind the facade of their alliance. Napoleon's very brilliance in the defense of France that spring repeatedly opened the possibility that one or more of the Allies would abandon the campaign and sign a separate peace with the French, providing the opportunity for a French recovery. British diplomacy, backed up by generous subsidies, succeeded in keeping the alliance in the field until the French royalists, led by the realistic Talleyrand, were able to negotiate the restoration of the Bourbon monarchy as a basis for peace. This uneasy experience meant that when it came to constructing the actual peace settlement, the Allied representatives came to the peace table encumbered with prior (and sometimes conflicting) commitments; and that the threat of a French revival loomed large if Allied solidarity should evaporate with the end of the fighting.

This accounts for why the peace conference, known to us as the Congress of Vienna, was so lengthy and tortuous, and why the British in particular extended the line of their wartime diplomacy into the peace settlement. In recent times we have come to expect that in the aftermath of great and devastating warfare, all diplomatic energies will be aimed at providing new international institutions designed to maintain the peace and prevent the return of armed conflict. The Congress of Vienna (1814–1815), even if its peacekeeping machinery was far less elaborate or institutionalized than what we have seen in the twentieth century, was the first European peace conference to attempt to define a *mechanism* that would maintain the status quo.

The Principle of Legitimacy

Before sitting down in Vienna to consider the European-wide problems in the wake of the French Revolution and Napoleon, the victorious powers first worked out a settlement for France alone. Talleyrand, the foreign minister who had earlier betrayed Napoleon, had argued for the restoration of the Bourbons in the person of Louis XVIII (1814–1824) on the grounds of his *legitimate* right to the throne. That is, the Bourbons had the hereditary right to the crown, which they had been denied by the now-defeated revolution. Tallyrand's argument not only prevailed, as the victorious statesmen all represented legitimate monarchies, but the principle he advocated came to be a convenient principle of authority when those same statesmen turned to European questions.

It was understood, however, that Louis XVIII would not be allowed to have the absolute power available to the monarchy before 1789. He must grant the French a constitution limiting his powers, as it was recognized that a nation that had gone through the liberalizing period of the revolution would never consent to a return to absolutism. To make the king further acceptable to the French, the Allies blessed him with a peace settlement (the First Treaty of Paris, May 30, 1814) that returned the French to their prewar boundaries, exacted neither indemnity nor territory, and spared them an army of occupation. Such were the first measures taken by the peacemakers in their hope to stifle further revolutionary zeal in the defeated

J. B. Isabey's "Congress of Vienna", November 1814. (Giraudon)

nation, thereby checking the militarism that the revolutionary zeal had earlier produced.

In the autumn of 1814, the representatives of many states gathered in Vienna to discuss the disposition of the great empire that had been won and lost by the French. But the major decisions were made by the chief delegates of the four victorious powers: Chancellor Metternich for Austria, Czar Alexander I for Russia, Viscount Castlereagh for Britain, and Prince von Hardenberg for Prussia; as well as by the wily Talleyrand for France, who exerted critical pressure when disagreements developed among the great powers. He had already advocated legitimacy as the guiding principle in making political and territorial decisions. One alternative would have been to admit the right of each nationality to determine its future. Excepting Britain, where the sovereignty was regarded as vested in the crown *and* in Parliament, the victorious powers regarded sovereignty as the property of the crown

alone, and there could be no admission that the people—the nation—shared the sovereignty. The latter notion, in fact, had been held by the revolutionaries in the 1790s, and the peacemakers of 1814 did not mean to embrace revolutionary idealism. Legitimacy it had to be.

Applying the principle, however, proved to be something else. Not only did "legitimate" claims rather generously overlap, but prior commitments necessarily made to ensure wartime cooperation did not always coincide with "legitimate" rights. Moreover, Britain, which had no territorial claims on the continent, preferred to see territory redistributed in a manner that would maintain a balance of power on the continent. Since French miltary power had not been destroyed in 1814, there remained four military powers on the continent. The British reasoned that on most critical issues these powers would line up two against two, and such a balance would discourage war by making its outcome uncertain. Or, the British could support the weaker pair to restore the balance. In any case, maintaining the balance of power was held to be the key to maintaining the peace.

Conflicting ambitions and goals at the Congress of Vienna finally came to a head in the Polish question—whether to repartition Poland exactly as she had been partitioned in the eighteenth century. The Russians, backed by Prussia, demanded a greater share of Poland than they had previously possessed; but even though the other powers would have been equally compensated elsewhere, this particular transaction would have had the effect of upsetting the balance of power by making Russia the paramount power in Europe. Austria and Britain resisted the demand and finally sought Talleyrand's support to break the deadlock, thus bringing France into the deliberations of the great powers. If war should be resumed, it meant that France would have two major allies.

Napoleon's Return: 1815

This bickering in Vienna, meanwhile, was not lost on Napoleon in exile. Being Emperor of Elba had lost its allure; the Bourbon regime had fallen behind in paying his promised pension; and he knew that many of the French were resentful of this government that had come "in the baggage of the Allies." All seemed to point to a successful return. His landing at Cannes on March 1, 1815, however, shocked the gentlemen in Vienna into quick resolve to mend their differences and deal with the real enemy; whereas Louis XVIII, seeing Napoleon rally many French troops as he moved on Paris, began a discreet retirement northward to await Allied help. Napoleon soon discovered, however, that the most responsible elements of the French population did not favor a renewal of the wars against Europe, which led him to pose as the defender of revolutionary ideals to attract support from the urban masses. He did not wait for the Allies to concentrate against him, but took the offensive northward where he would

meet only British and Prussian contingents. Despite initial successes that raised his confidence, he was checked and beaten decisively at Waterloo on June 18. Though he escaped from the battlefield, he abdicated the throne four days later and went to the coast to put himself in British hands, hoping by this voluntary submission to be allowed to live in Britain. Instead, he was caged on the remote island of St. Helena, where he died of cancer in 1821.

The Completion of the Vienna Settlement

His adventure, meanwhile, prompted the Allies to complete the Treaty of Vienna (June 9, 1815), with the Russians obtaining the heart of Poland, and Prussia and Austria obtaining booty elsewhere. The shuffling of frontiers altered the map of Europe dramatically and without much regard for the sentiments of the various nationalities. While the territorial changes can best be understood from a map, it is useful to point out that Prussia, for instance, in annexing the northern half of Saxony, the city of Danzig, and Rhenish territory, was annexing German-speaking people. Whereas Austria, in annexing Lombardy, Venetia, Illyria, Dalmatia, the Tyrol, and the city of Salzburg, gained largely Italians and Slavs, making the Austrian Empire conspicuously cosmopolitan as Prussia became increasingly Germanic. Austria did abandon the Southern Netherlands, which had been an imperial headache during the eighteenth century, so that the two Netherlands could be combined into the Kingdom of the Netherlands to make a more formidable buffer along the northern French frontier.

The Vienna peacemakers necessarily had to eliminate Napoleon's Confederation of the Rhine, but to replace it they could agree neither on the restoration of the Holy Roman Empire nor on the creation of a united German state—a dangerous concession to the principle of national self-determination. The ultimate compromise

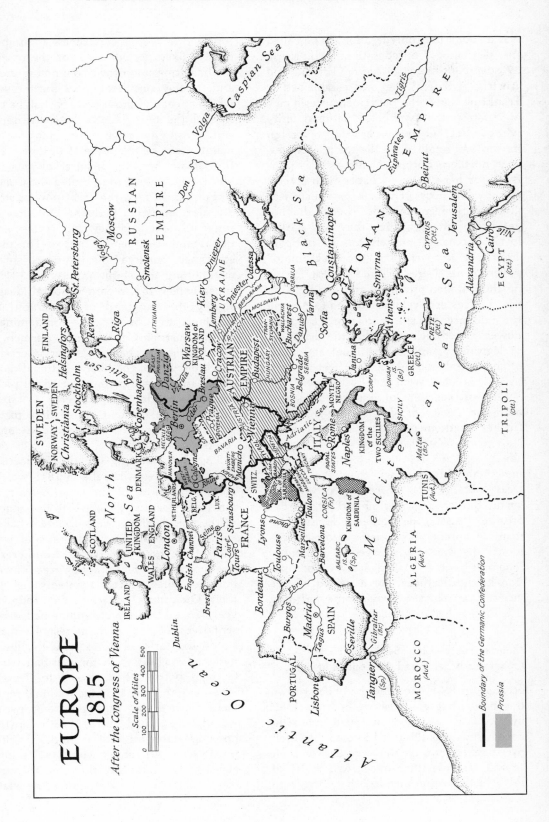

was a substitute confederation, to be called the Germanic Confederation, comprising 39 sovereign states including Prussia and Austria. A federal Diet was established at Frankfurt under the permanent presidency of Austria: the symbol of national unity without its substance, as the sovereign power was retained by the member states.

In northern Europe, Denmark was punished for her wartime alliance with Napoleon by the loss of Norway, which was given to Sweden. But the Swedes did not get back Finland, which they had earlier lost to Russia. In southern Europe, in Spain and Italy in particular, the "legitimate" governments were restored except in the northern Italian provinces annexed by Austria. The restored regimes looked to Austria for guidance, for she more than any other power came to be regarded as the champion of legitimacy; and the national ambitions of many Italians, which had been excited by the French, went totally ignored.

One further item of business remained after the Treaty of Vienna was signed: a further settlement with France after Napoleon's Hundred Days. The Second Treaty of Paris (November 20, 1815) was understandably harsher than the earlier treaty. France was forced to cede some small, but strategically important, border areas to Prussia, the Netherlands, the Germanic Confederation, and Sardinia-Piedmont; she was now charged a substantial indemnity for an Allied army of occupation in the northeast for a period of five years. Even so, she avoided the partition that Prussia had proposed.

Maintaining the Vinns Settlement: The Quadruple Alliance and the Concert of Europe

Because, in 1815, the Allies had been shown the peril that could emerge from their bickering, they signed the Quadruple Alliance, which was designed to maintain their peace settlement, on the very day of their second treaty with France. Article VI of the Alliance recommended that "the high

contracting parties . . . renew their meetings at fixed periods . . . for the purpose of consulting upon their common interests, and for the consideration of the measures which at each of those periods shall be considered the most salutary for the repose and prosperity of nations, and for the maintenance of the peace of Europe." Lord Castlereagh was the inspirer of this proposal, which came to be called the Concert of Europe. In fact, the great powers never did meet at "fixed periods," but they did convene periodically when issues arose threatening the general peace. For many statesmen, "maintaining the peace" meant maintaining the status quo as of 1815, a conservatism that regarded liberal ideas as simply the vanguard of revolution. Accordingly, the Concert was soon dominated by the Austrian Chancellor Metternich, for no other power had a greater interest in checking the rise of liberal-national movements than cosmopolitan Austria. In Metternich's hands the Concert of Europe became an instrument of reaction, just as did the Germanic Confederation under Austria's presidency.

The first meeting of the Concert of Europe at Aix-la-Chapelle in 1818 was the most harmonious of the congresses in the nineteenth century. Called at the request of the French, the powers declared that the French indemnity was paid up and withdrew their occupying forces from France. She now joined the family of great powers, but the Allied powers pointedly renewed their Quadruple Alliance. The following year, 1819, Metternich summoned representatives of the nine largest Germanic states to Carlsbad to deal with liberal-nationalist agitation in the German world. German patriots had looked to Prussian leadership, hoping that the national movement, born during the Napoleonic period, would be crowned in 1815 with constitutional government. But Frederick William III (1797–1840), under Metternich's influence, had abandoned this liberal movement in favor of maintaining the status quo. Out of Carlsbad came proposals for repressive decrees outlawing liberal societies, introducing anti-liberal censorship of the press, and putting universities under police surveillance. These proposals were promptly ratified by the Germanic Diet at Frankfurt.

1820–1823: Crisis in Spain and Naples

The liberal-nationalist sentiments unleashed by the French Revolution, however, were not to be denied. In Spain, the restored Bourbon Ferdinand VII (1814–1833) was preparing his armed forces for the recovery of the Latin American colonies, which had been lost during the Napoleonic occupation of Spain. A revolt led by army officers on the first day of 1820 against the King's vicious and capricious governance made the King a virtual prisoner of the army. He had no choice but to restore the Bonapartist Constitution of 1812. This example encouraged liberals in the Neapolitan army during the summer of 1820 to rise against the despotic Bourbon Ferdinand I (1759–1825), who hastily granted the kingdom of Naples a constitution; and before the summer was over, Portuguese liberals overthrew the regency which had been established in 1807 after the flight of the royal family to Brazil to escape the French.

This led to a crisis in the international establishment, for Austria, Russia, and Prussia, all autocracies, meant to stifle revolution everywhere as inimical to international peace and the Treaty of Vienna. On the other hand, Britain and France, both constitutional monarchies, regarded such intervention into the internal affairs of any nation as a misuse of the international machinery to keep the peace. The upshot, early in 1821, was that Austria acted on behalf of the three despotic powers alone to restore Ferdinand I of Naples to his full powers, following which there was a furious repression in Naples. And the Austrians aided the government of Sardinia-Piedmont in crushing the Italian liberal movement in that country.

Before anything could be done about the Spanish situation, the powers were faced by a Greek national rising in 1821, against the Ottoman Turks. The Greeks, because of their ancient contributions to Western Civilization, were sentimental favorites in Europe; but two issues combined to prevent any immediate European assistance to their cause. The British feared that any weakening of Turkey would simply be the opportunity for Russian expansion in that corner of Europe, with the result of unsettling the balance of power. While Metternich argued that the powers must not support revolution anywhere. Thus, the great powers at the Congress of Verona in 1822, turned their attention to Spain.

None of the powers had any stomach for a Russian offer to send an army to Spain on behalf of the Concert, but only the British opposed a French offer to restore Ferdinand VII. Louis XVIII's government might argue that their assistance would surround such a restoration with as liberal an atmosphere and perhaps preserve the cause of constitutional government; but the British balked at any encouragement of French militarism. Moreover the British had developed important trade relations with an independent Latin America. They had no fear that Spain alone could ever recover her authority there, but if the Franco-Spanish Bourbon monarchies were able to revive their eighteenth-century cooperation, it might be another story.

Britain thus separated from the Concert when France was given the mandate to restore Ferdinand VII and warned the French that the British fleet would block the way of Latin America. British hopes that the United States would join in the warning were disappointed, though their proposal did lead our government to issue unilaterally the Monroe Doctrine. In the meantime, the French defeated the Spanish rebels in 1823, but promised the British that they had no intention of intervening elsewhere.

The restored Ferdinand VII embarrassed the French by failing to honor his pledge to pardon all revolutionaries, and engaged in a savage extermination of liberals.

The Greek Revolution

Except in Greece, the liberal-national cause seemed cushed by these events, but European enthusiasm for the Greek cause (known as Philhellenism) survived the official indifference of the great powers. As the balance in the struggle began to swing against the Greeks by 1824, the literate classes agitated for intervention. The Greek nationalists, at first led by Alexander Ypsilanti, although inspired by the ideas of the French Revolution, expected Russian aid against the Turks. Not only were the Turks and Russians old enemies, but the Greeks and the Russians were coreligionists with a common desire to see the Muslims driven from Constantinople, their holy city. When Metternich prevailed upon Czar Alexander I (1801–1825) to maintain neutrality, the Greek national cause seemed doomed. The Greek uprising in 1822 had caught the Turks off guard, but in 1824 the Sultan was prepared to invade Greece with new forces from the northeast and had engaged his vassal, Mehemet Ali, the Pasha of Egypt (1811–1848) for a seaborne invasion of the Peloponnesus.

The accession of Czar Nicholas I (1825–1855), a Russian expansionist, brought the question of intervention to a boil, just at a moment when public opinion in both Russia and the West was sufficiently inflamed to permit the Russians to strike at the Turks under the guise of helping the Greeks. It was a difficult moment for the Western governments, forced by public clamor to do something for the Greeks, yet wanting to keep the Turks strong as a barrier to Russian expansion—the old balance of power problem. Initially, three powers (Britain, Russia, and France) tried to force a negotiated settlement that would give the Greeks autonomy under Turkish suzerainty; but the Turks resisted compromise in view of their continuing military success. To underscore their proposal, the three powers then formed an Allied naval squadron which was sent into Greek waters (1827), and these ships inadvertently were engaged by the Egyptian fleet in Navarino harbor, which put an end to the Egyptian fleet. Knowing that the Western governments were embarrassed by this incident, the Sultan still refused to sign an armistice. Nicholas I, taking advantage of pro-Greek sentiments in the West, soon declared war unilaterally upon the Turks (1828). Britain and France, not wanting Russia to go it alone, then forced the Egyptians to evacuate Greece by threatening military intervention. The Greek cause was finally saved.

The Turks made peace with Russia at Adrianople in 1829, paying a war indemnity and recognizing Greek independence. But the ultimate settlement for Greece, ridden with internal factions, was necessarily worked out by the powers in London. Greek national pride was injured first when the powers chose not a Greek but a Bavarian for the Greek throne, Otto I (1832–1862), and again when the new national frontiers omitted much territory regarded traditionally as Greek by the Greeks: Epirus, Thessaly, and Crete, all of which remained Turkish. Thus, the Greeks had their independence, but cosmopolitan considerations dictated the peace. And a Europe that had officially declared liberal-national movements taboo, had been brought to recognize their possible respectability.

The Revolution of 1830: France

The Concert of Europe faced a new wave of revolutions in 1830; its firm resolve to squelch revolutions had been badly dented by the events of the previous decade. Conservatives were not surprised, however, when this new wave began in France, which they considered to be the source of most dangerous ideas. Louis XVIII, after 1814, had made an honest attempt to give his people moderate, constitutional government. He faced in Parliament, however, a strong Left wing made up of ex-revolutionaries and ex-Bonapartists, and a strong Right wing made up of ultra-royalists who were absolutist in spirit. The two extremes would often coalesce to make middle-of-the-road government difficult, yet the King felt it necessary to keep the center in power at any price. If either extreme came to power, it could jeopardize the arrangement of 1815 and invite Allied intervention. For a time the stratagem of juggling the electoral laws before parliamentary elections worked to ensure the vitcory of moderate candidates, but by 1820 it was understood that this dubious practice could not work indefinitely. The governemnt must seek a more permanent alliance with either Left or Right. The very fact that the heir to the throne was the leader of the Ultra faction suggested the practicality of a drift to the Right.

Despite a warning from Metternich that the "established order" in France was the key to the general European peace, Louis XVIII's government introduced reactionary measures in 1821, notably the renewal of censorship and arbitrary arrest, and altered the electoral laws to ensure an Ultra victory that year. The reaction expectedly deepened when the chief Ultra succeeded to the throne as Charles X (1824-1830), with the new king giving clear evidence that he meant to restore a pre-1789 absolutist and Catholic regime. The Constitution of 1814 itself, in other words, was at stake; and moderate royalists began to speak of the necessity of a French version of England's "Glorious Revolution." In July, 1830, the hostility between the crown and parliament had reached such a point that the king determined to rule by decree and without parliamentary sanction. When he dared to issue four repressive ordinances, which amounted to a *coup d'état*, republicans and liberal royalists aroused Paris

against the king. Alarmed too late, the king withdrew the ordinances, then fled from Paris and finally to England. The French Bourbons had fallen for the second and last time.

The constitutional monarchists, rather than the republicans, then got hold of the situation, promoting the candidacy of the Duke of Orleans for the throne. With republican concurrence, he became Louis-Philippe I (1830-1848), King of the French "by the grace of God and the will of the people"—a title which admitted the end of divine right. He promised to uphold the Constitution of 1814, a gesture to reassure Metternich as well as the French; and he took as the national flag the revolutionary tricolor rather than the white banner of the fallen Bourbon. The electorate was immediately broadened by reducing both the voting age and the property qualification for the vote. If not a democracy, the regime announced itself as liberal.

The Concert of Europe was irritated at having to accept the existence of a revolutionary regime; but it made no sense to back Charles X, given his intentions, and refuse to recognize a regime dedicated to upholding the 1815 settlement. What is more, the success of the July Revolution in Paris distracted the attention of the other great powers by reviving revolutionary activity elsewhere.

The Revolution of 1830: Belgium

In August of 1830 Belgian nationalists rose against their Dutch king, William I (1815-1844) The union of the Dutch and Belgian peoples, contrived by the Congress of Vienna, had been unhappy from the start; the majority Belgians claimed that they were being governed as a dispised minority, subject to economic and anti-Catholic discrimination. Faced with rebellion, William I offered the Belgians autonomy within the kingdom, but they would have no more of him. Instead, they prepared a constitution for an independent liberal monarchy, and rumor had it that the new French king would be asked to supply one of his sons for the Belgian throne. Meanwhile, the Dutch appealed to the great powers to maintain the settlement of 1815.

Louis-Philippe, however, knew perfectly well that the great powers would regard a close Franco-Belgian tie as the beginning of a French resurgence. Knowing that the British in particular were sensitive to a great power moving into the Lowlands, he hastened to reach an understanding with them. The three despotic powers were inclined to intervene on behalf of the Dutch, but the British and French agreed to back Belgian independence. The Concert, therefore, gathered in London to discuss the crisis, and there agreed to recognize Belgian independence. When the Belgians finally selected Leopold of Saxe-Coburg (1831–1865) as their first king, the great powers ratified the choice. The international settlement for the Belgians was known as the Twenty-Four Articles, the sixth article of which recognized Belgium to be "independent and perpetually neutral" under the guarantee of the powers.

Revolutions Elsewhere in 1830–1831: Germany, Italy, and Poland

With the Greeks newly freed and revolutions succeeding in France and Belgium, it might appear that the machinery forged to maintain the 1815 settlement had broken down. What the events of 1830 revealed, in fact, was that reactionary government could not be sustained in western Europe: Britain and France, although they were traditional enemies, were being forced together by the liberality of their political institutions. Whereas to the east of them, reactionary regimes could still cooperate to throttle liberal movements. The story of 1830 is full of liberal-nationalist revolutions that were vigorously contained. Uprisings in Hanover, Saxony, Hesse-Cassel, and Brunswick, for instance, forced the respective princes to grant con-

stitutional government. But Metternich, with the backing of Prussia, got the Germanic Diet to vote the Six Acts (1832), leading to the restoration of the absolute authority these German princes had yielded.

Italian secret societies, having failed to achieve national independence in 1820–1821, were inspired to try again by the success in Paris and the foundation of the July Monarchy. Their insurrections began in Parma and Modena, and spread into the Papal States. Metternich, aware of support from Prussia and Russia, repeated his performance of ten years before, and Austrian arms crushed the uprisings. This second failure led the most notable of the Italian nationalists, Mazzini, to believe that Italian unity would never be achieved through the plotting of local secret societies and sporadic uprisings. Fleeing to Marseilles in 1831, he founded the Young Italy movement, designed to organize nationalist agitation on a national rather than a local basis to give unity to what he called the *Risorgimento*—the national regeneration.

The Poles experienced a similar unpleasantness in 1830. Since 1815 the heart of Poland had been within the Russian Empire, and the Czar, as King of Poland, had tried to reconcile the Poles to the arrangement by granting Poland a large measure of autonomy: a constitution, a parliament, and an army. Polish patriots remained dissatisfied with anything short of independence. What is more, they claimed not only territories still held by Austria and Prussia, but provinces to the east taken from Poland in the eighteenth century which were clearly Russian in population. In short, both the nationalist and the "legitimist" claims by the Poles conflicted with those of her three powerful neighbors. When the Poles broke into revolt against Russian rule late in 1830, they recognized the need for outside help and naively expected it from the government of Louis-Philippe. None came, and the poorly organized movement collapsed before a large Russian army.

With this failure went the autonomy, and Poland became simply another Russian province subject to a Russification program. Consequently, the Polish refugees who fled (principally to Paris) devoted themselves to keeping Polish culture alive.

The Eastern Question

The Empire of the Ottoman Turks was extraordinarily cosmopolitan. Not only did it include many nationalities, but they were both Asian and European, Muslim and Christian. That Empire had been decaying since the seventeenth century, and various schemes had consequently been advanced for partitioning it in a way that would maintain the balance of power in the east. Yet the Turks lived on into the nineteenth century, with their territory only nibbled away as by the Greeks in their successful revolt. As Russia had been a major benefactor of Turkish weakness in the previous century, European statesmen in the nineteenth century feared that Russia sought to fill the Turkish vacuum unilaterally as a step toward achieving hegemony on the European continent. The Concert must not merely contain France—but any one power suspected of seeking hegemony.

In the aftermath of the Greek Revolution, the Egyptians inadvertently played into Russian hands. Mehemet Ali had come to the Turk's aid in that conflict at the Sultan's promise of territorial compensation after victory over the Greeks. But the failure of Egyptian arms meant that Mehemet Ali received nothing, and in 1832 the ambitious Pasha occupied Turkish Syria and began an invasion of Anatolia itself. The Sulan Mahmoud II (1808–1839), unable to halt the Egyptian advance, appealed to Britain for support but received none because the British were caught in a domestic political crisis. The desperate Sultan then turned to Russia for help, which was only too eagerly given. The Egyptians discreetly retired from Anatolia as the Turks and Russians concluded a mutual assistance treaty (1833); and western Europe was shocked to realize that Russia had taken a major step toward domination of the eastern Mediterranean.

France responded by encouraging Mehemet Ali in his dream of complete national independence from Turkey and in his hope to build a great Arabo-Egyptian Empire. Turkey, aware of Egyptian ambitions, slowly prepared to counter them, and in 1839 sent an armed force to Syria to expel the Egyptians. The mission miscarried, producing a major European crisis, for it was feared that either Russia or France would exploit the situation. Britain insisted on an international regulation of Turko-Egyptian affairs, and Russia agreed to cooperate, recognizing the opportunity to increase tension between the western liberal powers. The upshot was that the two powers forced Mehemet Ali out of Syria, and the Russians neglected to renew their treaty with Turkey when it came due. The settlement, a diplomatic defeat for the French, gave the Turks a lease on life.

CHRONOLOGY: 1814–1848

1814–1815:	The Congress of Vienna
1815:	Battle of Waterloo
1815–1848:	The Metternich Era
1818:	Congress of Aix-la-Chapelle
1819:	Carlsbad Conference
1820–1823:	Revolutions in Spain and Naples
1822–1829:	The Greek Revolution
1830–1831:	Revolutions in France, the Netherlands, Germany, Italy, and Poland
1830–1848:	Reign of Louis-Philippe in France
1848–1849:	Revolutions in France, Italy, the Austrian Empire, and Germany

31
The Replacement of the Vienna Settlement: 1848-1871

1848: Year of Revolution and End of the Metternich Era

While the many revolutions in 1848 varied in detail according to nationality, to study them together is to see how many liberal, national, and radical ideas—the heritage of the French and the Industrial Revolutions —came to a head that year. Each group of revolutionaries, whatever the nationality and whether liberal or radical, struggled to found regimes reflecting the ideals of the turn of the century, the very ideals that the statesmen of the Metternich era had tried to eradicate. As these revolutionaries, in general, failed to establish durable regimes, their failures did great damage to the prestige of their ideals. Thus, although the revolutionaries did manage to upset many established regimes in 1848, including that of Metternich himself, the failure to plant successful liberal regimes in their place opened the way for an entirely new species of political leadership. Looking back, 1848 seems not simply to have been a political watershed, heralding an era of tougher, more realistic government, but also a cultural watershed—of which more later.

The Revolution of 1848: France

As in 1830, the wave of revolutions in 1848 began in France. The period of the July Monarchy, which fell between these two dates, saw the beginning of the French industrial revolution; which happened to coincide with a government that was officially liberal, indeed, revolutionary in origin. The liberal of that day, however, as his creed grew out of the eighteenth-century attempt to check royal absolutism, was largely concerned to protect the individual from the tyranny of the state. Let nature rather than the state regulate the system, and freedom would be the result: "*Laissez faire la nature.*" The July Monarchy, in short, was too committed to laissez-faire to permit legislative measures to improve the social and economic conditions born of industrialization or urbanization. Not that France became industrialized by 1848—far from it. But what industrial workers there were, along with the artisans in small establishments, soon became alienated from a state that neither set minimum wages nor made any attempt to abolish miserable living and working conditions in the new industrial towns. Understandably, such workers soon felt betrayed by liberalism and began to toy with the various socialist and radical schemes that, in this very period, offered new formulas for the democratization of society. The government responded with repression and censorship, thus gradually losing its claim to be liberal.

Other segments of French society, too, were hostile to the regime: The Legitimists (followers of the House of Bourbon) regarded Louis-Philippe as a usurper; the clergy objected to the government's official anticlericalism; and French nationalists were angered because the government had failed to exploit the Belgian opportunity in 1830 or to back Mehemet Ali successfully in 1840. After that date, a familiar pattern of government reemerged. Guizot, the king's chief policymaker, answered criticism by manipulating elections to Parliament, buying votes in Parliament, and sharply limiting the electorate through increasing the property qualifications for the vote. Such a regime was doomed in a country that had experienced the liberalization of the French Revolution. When this combined with a severe economic depression in 1846-1847, demands for reform proved to be beyond the moral competence of a government based on corruption. Rioting in Paris, led by republican politicians, brought down the monarchy; the king went into exile, and the revolutionaries proclaimed a provisional Second Republic (February, 1848).

This provincial regime was a coalition of liberal and socialist republicans led by Lamartine and Louis Blanc, respectively, meaning that the two groups could agree upon little more than the republican form of government, though they had in common the old Jacobin faith that political democratization would lead to social reforms. When national elections were held in April for a new Assembly, the more moderate or conservative candidates won overwhelmingly against the known radicals, and we know today that many candidates who called themselves republican under the circumstances were in fact recent monarchists with no particular devotion to a republic. By June of 1848, the radicals knew that their dreams of a socialist republic were doomed, and the Parisian mob became convinced that it was again the victim of betrayal by the propertied classes, that the revolution itself had again been betrayed. An insurrection lasting four terrible days in June was crushed by the army, leaving over 5000 dead, after which the Assembly completed work on a constitution for the Second Republic.

In contrast to 1789, this revolution in 1848 never succeeded in establishing a radical regime in France—the reaction set in almost immediately. Moreover, the Left became permanently hostile to political association with moderate liberals. The constitution of 1848, it is true, was a liberal document, providing for universal suffrage and for checks on executive power. But when new elections were held under this constitution, the electorate revealed itself to be solidly antiradical and more concerned for order than for liberty. In the presidential election, Prince Louis-Napoleon Bonaparte, nephew of Napoleon I, swamped the moderate and radical republican candidates nearly three to one. Part of his appeal lay in his name, especially attractive after the June Days, when a man of order seemed required. In the parliamentary elections, avowed monarchists won two-thirds of the seats. Though the republic would live on until 1852, it had been given a mortal blow at its birth.

Italy: The Problem of Achieving National Unity

The Italian national movement, after the failures in 1831, produced three major formulas for achieving national unity. Of the three, that of Mazzini, philosophical child of the eighteenth century and the French Revolution, had the particular characteristic of being at once nationalistic and cosmopolitan. He thought that all nationalities ought to be free and self-governing, that each nationality had unique qualities which could contribute to the enrichment of civilization only when that nationality achieved liberty. As for form of government, Mazzini argued for the French-style anticlerical republic (to be achieved through revolution) as the best guarantee of individual liberty once national independence had been won. From exile, Mazzini endeavored to coordinate various national movements with his own Young Italy movement, giving the revolutionary movement the aspect of an international conspiracy in the eyes of established monarchical regimes.

Mazzini's hope for a united and anticlerical Italy with its capital at Rome was unacceptable to those Italian nationalists who remained devoted to Catholicism and to the integrity of the Papacy. The so-called Roman Question included arguments not simply about the proper extent of the Pope's spiritual authority within the various secular states, but about his temporal power within the Papal States. Since that temporal power, dating from the eighth century, had been justified as a device to guarantee the spiritual independence of the Papacy, many Catholics feared that to surrender Papal territory to an Italian state would ultimately be to subject Church to State. The experience of the Church during the French Revolution, in other words, seemed to leave the Church no alternative but to be antirevolutionary and antinationalist.

A Piedmontese priest named Gioberti, however, proposed in 1843 a compromise that would give the substance of unity without despoiling the Papacy: a confederation of independent Italian states with the Pope as president of the confederation. That same year, the third formula was proposed by Count Balbo favoring the ruling house of Sardinia-Piedmont. That is, he wanted the house of Savoy to take the lead in Italy, first by banishing Austrian influence from Italy, then by turning Sardinia-Piedmont into a progressive, liberal, constitutional monarchy, to become the nucleus of a united (and monarchical) Italy.

The Gioberti scheme seemed to have the inside track when Pius IX (1846–1878) took the Papal throne and gave early evidence of liberal governance in the Papal States. Many Italian patriots became convinced that he would break his predecessor's association with the Metternich system to become an Italian nationalist. Before the end of 1847, the Pope, to his discomfort, found himself a hero of the Italian revolutionaries; for, as the head of a cosmopolitan institution, Pius IX could hardly afford to become recognized as the champion of one nationality against another—especially when the two nationalities concerned were both Roman Catholic. Nevertheless, popular enthusiasm for the Pope forced King Charles Albert of Sardinia-Piedmont (1831–1849) to grant liberal reforms at home in his bid for national popularity.

Early in 1848, however, the focal point suddenly shifted southward, where a purely local uprising in Sicily spread to the Neapolitan mainland. Ferdinand II (1830–1859) at once asked for Austrian aid to maintain the status quo, but as Pius IX refused to permit Austrian troops to cross Papal territory to get to Naples,

Ferdinand was obliged to grant a liberal constitution to his people. In short order, Piux IX, Charles Albert, and the Duke of Tuscany followed suit. Then, with the astonishing news of a liberal uprising in Vienna and the consequent resignation of Metternich, the Milanese rose against Austrian rule in Lombardy, and the Venetians proclaimed their independence as a republic. Charles Albert of Sardina-Piedmont, seeing in this his dynasty's great opportunity to take the lead in Italy, announced himself as the champion of the Milanese and declared war on Austria.

This bright beginning for the Italian national cause soon turned sour, beginning with the Pope's refusal to allow his troops to join in an offensive against Austria (though he appealed to the Austrians to withdraw from Italy). In July of 1848, the Austrians overwhelmed Charles Albert, recovered control of Lombardy, and forced an armistice upon the Piedmontese. Meanwhile, Ferdinand II had recovered his own position in Naples by hiring Swiss mercenaries. Through it all, patriotic anger heightened against Pius IX, increasingly seen as the key to the disasters, until the Pope felt obliged to flee to neighboring Naples for protection. Early in 1849, the Mazzinian republicans sought to take advantage of the vacuum in Rome and Charles Albert's defeat by establishing the Roman Republic; but this venture, too, was doomed, and it was a sister republic that brought the Mazzinians down.

The Second French Republic, of course, was republican in name only by 1849. It was a Catholic country with a president whose name and personal ambitions made him an enemy of the 1815 settlement and especially of that country most identified with the maintenance of that settlement—Austria. As the Austrians were recovering from their own revolutionary turmoil, it was assumed they would soon intervene to restore the Pope. Thus the French decision to go to the Pope's aid really reflected

more hostility to Austria than to the Roman Republic, which fell to French arms by midsummer of 1849. Shortly after, the Austrians besieged Venice and destroyed the Venetian Republic—the last of the revolutionary regimes.

Liberal and National Uprisings in the Austrian Empire

The Hapsburg Empire, the very citadel of cosmopolitanism, was itself severely shaken by liberal and national uprisings in 1848. Nationalist sentiments had been on the rise among the various minorities that comprised the Empire in the aftermath of the French Revolution; and even before the news of Louis-Philippe's fall triggered demonstrations and speeches in both Veinna and Budapest, the Hungarian liberal Deák had drafted a plan providing for Hungarian autonomy within the empire. When the trouble began in 1848, Emperor Ferdinand I (1835–1848) accepted Metternich's resignation, accepted Deák's plan as a constitution for Hungary, and promised the Austrians a constitution of his own manufacture. Rioting continued in Vienna, however, as most Austrian liberals wanted a hand in the drafting of a constitution; and the constitutional movement spread to Prague, with the Czechs insisting on a separate constitution for Bohemia.

Indeed, the Hapsburg Empire seemed to be falling apart at the seams. Other Slavic minorities now aspired to autonomy, and the Czech nationalists launched a pan-Slav movement that proclaimed the solidarity of all Slavic peoples against their German oppressors. When the Croats and Slovenes demanded autonomy from Hungary (which was rejected), the government in Vienna perceived the opportunity to turn the various minorities against each other and thus to recover Austrian hegemony within the empire. This strategy worked well in Bohemia, where the Austrians exploited quarrels between Germans and Czechs to crush the Czech revolutionary movement. It backfired when the Austrians sought to humble the Hungarians by egging on the Croats. Led by Kossuth, the Hungarian liberals now rejected their newly won autonomy in favor of complete independence, and they invaded Austria to win their point.

Metternich's fall, meanwhile, had particularly shocked Nicholas I of Russia, who felt he must assume the role of policeman of Europe now that Metternich had abandoned it. If the Hungarians were to succeed in making good their claim to independence, their example might inspire the Poles. The new Austrian government, faced with invasion, appealed to Nicholas for help, which he readily granted. Russian forces invaded Hungary from the east in 1849, and the Austrians moved in from the west, smashing the independence movement. After more than a year of of turmoil, the Hapsburg domains were reunited by force; the currents of nationalism were at least temporarily confined.

Liberalism and Nationalism in Germany

In the German world, the news from Paris in 1848 excited liberal-nationalists into believing that the moment had at last arrived to achieve representative government within a united Germany. The revolutionary movement caught fire, forcing many German rulers to promise liberal reforms. Frederick William IV (1840-1861) of Prussia feared he might have to place himself at the head of this nationalist zeal if he were to maintain his throne. Yet, he had no taste for liberal government and feared retaliation from Austria and Russia if he abandoned them apparently to lead a revolution. At Frankfurt, in the meantime, a self-appointed committee of liberals supervised national elections on a democratic basis, and in May of 1848 the Frankfurt National Assembly convened, suspending the Diet of the Germanic Confederation. In Prussia, meanwhile, the

King permitted a constituent assembly to begin preparation of a constitution.

It was all for naught. When news reached Berlin that the new regime in Vienna had successfully dispersed revolutionaries there, Frederick William IV dissolved his own constituent assembly. He then rejected an offer of the throne of a united Germany from the revolutionaries in Frankfurt, making a shambles of their constitutional project. Wanting a united Germany, but on his own terms, Frederick William then toyed with a plan that would have created a Prussian-dominated central European confederation. Neither Austria nor Russia would tolerate this half victory for German nationalism, forcing the Prussian King to cast aside his project in 1850.

The Ascendency of Napoleon III in Europe: 1851–1870

After the failure of the liberal-nationalists to achieve their political goals through revolution in 1848, Europe entered a period of reaction similar to that after 1815. More or less autocratic governments justified themselves as the guardians of "order" after the upheavals. Nationalist aspirations, on the other hand, did not fade away; and in the period between 1851 and 1871, a new breed of tough-minded, skillful politicians emerged to advance the claims of nationality. They challenged not merely the liberals' cosmopolitan or European conception of nationalism as a movement that would release unique energies for the benefit of all. The newer view saw nationalities as units of hostility, with each nation-state obliged to strengthen itself for the inevitable competition with other nation-states. By 1871, the liberal-nationalists had been overwhelmed in both the political arena and on the battlefield by the conservative-nationalists, and Europe started her dreadful slide toward total hostility and total war.

The most representative figure of this transitional period was Prince Louis-

Napoleon Bonaparte, the man elected to be president of the Second French Republic in 1848, later Napoleon III (1852–1870). As heir to both the "princples of '89," as he himself put it, and the Napoleonic tradition, he sympathized with all subject nationalities and believed it to be his destiny, once he had achieved power, to work for their emancipation. In the liberal-nationalist tradition, therefore, he represented the view that to liberate subject nationalities would be to remove a major source of conflict and war in Europe. Despite this idealism of an earlier generation, he was also a shrewd, calculating politician, who believed that the national movement could benefit France. He was ready to obtain through diplomacy and war, like the men of his own generation, what the liberals had failed to accomplish in 1848. This uncomfortable mixture of qualities not only baffled his contemporaries, but contributed to the ultimate triumph of other leaders devoted more singularity than he to politics based solely on the realities of power— *Realpolitik.*

The rise of a new Bonaparte to power was understandably disquieting to the European establishment, based, as it had been since 1815, on containing French militarism. On the other hand, the earlier days of great-power intervention to eradicate regimes thought to be inconsistent with the 1815 settlement were long past, and it would have been folly to have attempted to unseat the elect of such an overwhelming majority of the French. His restoration of the Papacy in 1849, however anti-Austrian its real aim may have been, could be seen as the work of a good conservative maintaining the status quo. And when he cunningly outmaneuvered his opponents at home to make possible the supplanting of the Second Republic by the Second Empire after the *coup d'état* of 1851, the great monarchies half hid their irritation over the news by noting with satisfaction the passing of a republic. That the new emperor's despotism was sanc-

tioned by universal suffrage, a recognition of popular sovereignty, was ominous for the old order; but at least it was despotism. Thus was the Vienna settlement, with its provision against a Bonapartist restoration, peaceably defied.

The Crimean War: 1854–1855

The Eastern Question remained quiescent for a decade after the containment of Mehemet Ali in 1841, until the new French Emperor, responding to pressure from Roman Catholic opinion, approached the Turkish government on the matter of the Holy places in Palestine, most of which had fallen under the control of Greek Orthodox monks. Napoleon III, in reviving the traditional French right to protect Roman Catholic monks in the Holy Land, thus made his first move to restore French greatness in Europe; and he succeeded in retrieving some of the holy places for the Catholics through Turkish agreement (1852). As the political implications of this success far outweighed the religious, Nicholas I of Russia demanded of Turkey not merely equality with France in the Holy Land, but also the right to protect Greek Orthodox churches in Constantinople and throughout the Turkish Empire.

Even though Britain had been distressd by the appearance of a new Bonaparte in France, and though Britain had previously cooperated with Russia in containing the spread of French influence in the Eastern Mediterranean, the demands made by Nicholas I were so threatening to Ottoman integrity that the British dared not support them—which the Turks soon understood. And their worst fears about Russian intentions were soon confirmed when Nicholas sent troops into Turkey's Danubian Principalities to back up his demands. The remaining great powers now tried to resolve the crisis through diplomacy; but the Turks, increasingly confident of European support, endeavored to exploit this opportunity to give Russian expansionism a sharp slap. Sending Russia an ultimatum to evacuate the Principalities, the Turks declared war upon Russian refusal (1853).

During the Greek Revolution, the British and French had briefly experienced the odd necessity of cooperating to maintain the balance of power. Now the logic of politics forced them together again, and their alliance was popular in the West to the degree that Russia had become odious in the eyes of many western Europeans: a divine-right autocracy was, of course, anathema to liberal opinion; there was much pro-Polish sentiment, especially in France; and the Russian intervention to destroy Hungarian independence in 1849 had awakened horror in the West. Russia, on the other hand, counted on Austrian support, thanks to 1849, to counteract Franco-British pressure. In some respects, therefore, Austria played the decisive role in what became the Crimean War in 1854, even though she never became a belligerent. For the Austrians, whatever their recent debt to Russia, were hardly ready to see Russia dominate the Balkans and the Eastern Mediterranean. After Britain and France went to the aid of Turkey that year, with the public seeing the war as liberalism versus autocracy, the Austrians astonished the Russians by sending them an ultimatum to evacuate the Danubian Principalities. Already at war with three powers, the Russians felt they must comply.

Neither Britain nor France wanted an expensive war, which precluded an invasion of Russia. Their ultimate strategy was to seize the naval base at Sevastopol on the Crimean peninsula and hold it as a pawn, meanwhile applying diplomatic pressure upon Austria to force her active participation against Russia. Vienna was thus the scene of continual negotiations as the fighting developed in the Crimea. Even the Piedmontese joined the western Allies in the hope of a seat at the peace table. The limited nature of the Allied campaign was more than offset by the inefficiency of the Russians in meeting this invasion on the periphery of their Empire, but it took the Allies until the autumn of 1855 to force the Russians to evacuate Sevastopol. Even then, the Russians were reluctant to make peace, as they knew already that the Allies hoped to solve the Eastern Question by forcing the demilitarization of the Black Sea. It took a second Austrian ultimatum to make the Russians agree to make peace.

Early in 1856 the powers convened for the Congress of Paris to sign the terms which, for the most part, had been worked out in Vienna during the war. Russia and Turkey mutually accepted the neutralization of the Black Sea (a blow to Russia alone); and the Danubian Principalities, the nucleus of the future Romanian state, were put temporarily under the collective jurisdiction of the powers signatory to the Treaty of Paris. The Congress of Paris also proved to be a sounding board, thanks to Napoleon III, for various national groups seeking self-determination and for the revision of the Vienna settlement of 1815. And the general unpopularity of Austria in 1856 for her wartime neutrality—when both sides had sought her belligerency—contributed to a more general willingness to listen to national claims. Between 1857 and 1862, Romanian nationalists developed the foundations for a nation-state and, in 1866, were granted autonomy within the Ottoman Empire.

The Unification of Italy

The chief spokesman at the Congress of Paris for Italian nationalism was the prime minister of Sardinia-Piedmont, Count Cavour, who represented in particular the Balbo formula for Italian unity: that Sardinia-Piedmont and her ruling dynasty should become the nucleus of an Italian monarchy. Above all else, Cavour was a political realist and he knew, after 1858, that Italy would not be forged by the Italians alone. Recognizing Napoleon III's sympathy and ready to sacrifice Sardinia's two French-speaking territories—Nice and Savoy—to gain the rest of Italy, Cavour bargained privately with the French Emperor. Both men knew that Austria would have to be expelled forcibly from Lombardy and Venetia; while Napoleon III, whose troops had garrisoned Rome after the Pope's restoration in 1849, felt at least temporarily constrained by the need to support Papal independence. Consequently, he favored the Gioberti formula for Italian unity; the formation of a confederation of independent Italian states.

In 1859, Cavour provoked Austria into an attack upon Sardinia-Piedmont, making it easier for Napoleon III to come to the side of Sardinia. After two military victories by the French over the Austrians, however, Napoleon's luck in Italy began to run out. Prussia suddenly mobilized on the French frontier and volunteered to come to the aid of Austria, clearly a bid to seize the leadership of the German world from the Austrians. Since neither Austria nor France welcomed Prussian intervention, they hastened into armistice and arranged terms far short of what Napoleon had originally promised Cavour. Austria ceded only Lombardy to France (which gave the province to Sardinia), but retained Venetia. Napoleon's hopes for an Italian confederation were soon dashed, partly because of the Pope's continuing refusal to become its president, and partly because Cavour's agents, some of them Mazzinian, stirred up Italian opinion in favor of a unitary state. Following nationalist uprisings (1859 and 1860) in Tuscany, Parma, Modena, and Romagna (part of the Papal States), plebiscites were held in those territories, and the inhabitants voted overwhelmingly to be annexed by Sardinia-Piedmont (1860). Plebiscites were also held in Nice and Savoy, where the vote was to join France.

Meanwhile, in the south, a flamboyant revolutionary named Garibaldi successfully invaded the territories of the Neapolitan Bourbons. Fearing that he might move next against Rome, where he had commanded briefly in 1849, the Sardinians quickly sent a force to occupy Naples to avoid an embarrassing clash with French arms. Pius IX tried to prevent the Sardinians from crossing Papal territory to reach Naples, but lost his tiny army in the process. The result was that two more bits of Papal property, Umbria and the Marches, as well as Naples, were given the option of voting to join Sardinia. Consequently, by the end of 1860 only Venetia and Rome itself remained outside the realm. Early in 1861, Sardinia renamed herself the Kingdom of Italy. Napoleon III, in short, had done much for Italy, if not exactly in the manner he had anticipated. In the process, French Catholic opinion had been offended and the Pope was outraged—hardly grateful for the French troops who still protected him.

The Waning of French Prestige

Napoleon III was thus instrumental in producing a modern Italy and a Romania, in the process of which he apparently returned France to the continental paramountcy lost in 1815. But his luck with other nationalities turned sour in 1860s, paving the way for the rise of the modern Germany. Some of the reverses were due to French miscalculations, and others to foreign misreading of French intentions abroad.

An example of the former was the French intervention in Mexico, beginning in 1861. No doubt the Mexican Republic invited trouble by suspending payments on debts to European investors, but the real motives for Napoleon III's conquest of Mexico were those of a visionary. He had long been interested in the construction of a Central American canal as the focal point for Latin American economic development, a cosmopolitan scheme worthy of a Napoleon. When he became convinced that the Mexican Republic was depriving the majority of Mexicans of their preferred Catholic monarchy, he intervened on behalf of Mexican monarchists, enabling them to install the Austrian Archduke Maximilian as Emperor in 1864. When the truth dawned in Paris that Napoleon III had been misled about the state of popular opinion in Mexico, a French evacuation was inevitable and it came toward the end of 1866 when alarming developments in the German world made it necessary to bring the troops home.

A costly and apparently senseless expedition such as this only increased European mistrust of French ambitions. And a foreign policy that sought European-wide benefits, rather than benefits for France alone, was an anachronism in a day of the new nationalism and, thus, easily misperceived. The British, in particular, still haunted by the image of the first Napoleon across the Channel, concluded that his successor ought to be isolated. When in 1863, the Poles rose a second time against Russian domination, the great powers were given an opportunity to behave toward a revolution as they had in the 1820s and to contain the supposed militarism of the French as they had in that era.

The Polish revolt of 1863 was a highly complicated movement, as the revolutionaries were deeply divided into factions. In the aftermath of the Crimean War, which had revealed gross inefficiencies in Russian government, Alexander II (1855-1881) had begun major social and administrative reforms within his empire, which eliminated many of the abuses and hardships endured by the Poles after their rebellion in 1831. Though the Czar hoped to reconcile the Poles to integration with the Russians, the relaxation in fact aroused hopes for independence. As earlier, Polish patriots dreamt of reestablishing their pre-partition boundaries of 1772, meaning territory that was not strictly Polish in population, and that by 1863 was claimed by Prussia and Austria as well as by Russia. Polish demands, in other words, soon exceeded what Alexander II either would or could concede.

When fighting broke out, the hopelessness of the Polish cause was underscored by a Prussian offer to give Russia any aid that might be necessary to quell the revolt. Polish appeals to France for aid put Napoleon III in a quandary: On the one hand, the Polish cause was popular in the West and consistent with well-known Napoleonic principles. On the other hand, he had striven to be conciliatory to Russia ever since the Crimean War, his aim being the reconciliation of all the Crimean opponents as the basis for a durable peace. He tried to save both causes by avoiding unilateral action in Poland, calling upon the great powers to do something for Poland in concert. The three eastern powers, with their common interest in the subjection of the Poles, were unenthusiastic, and Britain found in the crisis the opportunity to promote French isolation. Consequently, Polish independence went down the drain, and Napoleon III's attempt to reconstruct a new European authority suffered a fatal defeat. The future belonged to those whose ambitions were parochial rather than cosmopolitan.

The Unification of Germany

The gradual isolation of France provided a favorable climate for the aggrandizement of Prussia under its Hohenzollern king, William I (1858–1888), just as the Franco-Sardinian success against Austria encouraged Prussia to play a Sardinian role in the German world. Vigorous attempts to reform and enlarge the Prussian military establishment were for a time stalled in the Landtag (legislature) by the Liberal majority, which wanted control of the budget and saw the army as the bulwark of the autocracy. Indeed, when the monarchy had granted constitutional and representative government during the crisis of 1848, the royal intention had been to preserve royal authority behind the mere facade of representative government; and the crown took a dim view of this liberal attempt to check royal power. In 1862, after several years of parliamentary squabbling, William I appointed as his minister-president a tough conservative known for his hatred of parliamentry institutions: Otto von Bismarck.

Bismarck was not so much a German nationalist as he was a Prussian patriot, but his policies soon won him the support of nationalist opinion and ultimately the acclaim of many liberals. This despite the fact that he ordered the collection of taxes without parliamentary consent and thus destroyed the liberals' position. His quick successes in foreign affairs were the key to his popular support; and German nationalists, in abandoning their earlier alliance with liberalism, effectively promoted the Prussification of Germany in the name of unification. Both Napoleon III and Bismarck were consummate politicians, but unlike Napoleon III, Bismarck was not harnessed to a set of political ideals. His genius lay, therefore, not in promoting a preconceived program, but in exploiting international crises for the benefit of the Hohenzollern dynasty of Prussia.

Since the eighteenth century, the rise of Prussia in the German world had been at the expense of Austrian power, and certainly in the nineteenth century Austria had used her power to bind the Prussian government to antinationalist policies. Thus the wedding of Prussia to German nationalism in the 1860s was seen as a great peril in Vienna. As an empire whose vulnerability had been exposed in 1848 and again in 1859, the Austrians would have done well to cede Venetia to Italy after 1863 in exchange for a firm understanding with Italy and France, freeing Austria to face the north. Napoleon III, in fact, proposed a characteristically elaborate scheme by which the Austrians would annex Turkey's Danubian Principalities (then preparing for autonomy) as compensation for the loss of Venetia; and Italy would pay the Turks an indemnity for the

ceded Principalities (which they seemed likely to lose ultimately anyway) as the price for Venetia.

As the Austrians rejected any such transaction, they became the victim of an Italo-Prussian alliance (1866) which had the blessing of Napoleon III. For he not only was anxious to see Italy obtain the Venetia he had been unable to deliver in 1859, but he was logically sympathetic to German as well as Italian nationalism and had long expected that Prussia must one day be enlarged into a Germany. What is more, Bismarck hinted at territorial compensation along the Rhine, presumably those areas lost by France in 1815, in exchange for French neutrality. It remained for Bismarck to provoke a war with Austria, which he accomplished by suddenly proposing that the Germanic Confederation be abandoned in favor of a new federal system which would eliminate Austria. Most of the small states in the Germanic Confederation sided with Austria to avoid being swallowed up by Prussia and the Austrians, fearful of French intervention, at once ceded Venetia to France to guarantee French neutrality.

The shortness of the ensuing Seven Weeks War (1866) astonished European military opinion, which had expected a lengthy, indecisive conflict. Even though the Italians were defeated by Austria, the Prussians won a great victory for the Alliance by routing the Austrians at Sadowa. Bismarck at once offered the Austrians an easy peace, based on the exclusion of Austria from further participation in the German world, and the Germanic Confederation was scrapped. In its place he formed the North German Confederation under Prussian presidency, to include the states north of the Main River. Napoleon III, of course, handed Venetia to the Italians but when the French approached Bismarck for the expected bits of territory that would have wiped out the vestiges of the 1815 settlement, they had their first experience with his deviousness. During 1866 and 1867, he methodically scuttled the very projects for territorial adjustment which he himself initiated. In retrospect it is easy to see that, having pushed Austria from the German scene, Bismarck used the occasion to enrage French opinion as the basis for future conflict. That conflict, when it came in 1870, was a major tragedy that ought to have been avoided, since Napoleon III had long since accepted the legitimacy of Prussian aggrandizement in Germany. Instead, Bismarck believed that Prussian aggrandizement required a national war against a common enemy as the context for unification, and the French defeat in 1870 did much to destroy what remained of a sense of a European community.

This is not to say that Bismarck plotted the Hohenzollern candidacy for the Spanish crown, which proved to be the incident leading to the Franco-Prussian War. Instead, when a Hohenzollern prince seemed to be the Spanish choice to fill the throne that had been vacant since 1868, Bismarck secretly abetted the cause, certain that the French in general would see this Hohenzollern "encirclement" as intolerable. The House of Hohenzollern itself was far from anxious to become the cause for another war, and Bismarck very nearly saw his plans go awry as the Hohenzollern candidacy was withdrawn in the face of French pressure. The French, however, too anxious to avenge their humiliations of the recent past, pressed the Prussians to promise that there would never be a renewal of the candidacy in such a way as to force them to admit they had been guilty of wrongdoing in the first place. William I rightly rejected the demand, and Bismarck altered the report of the king's last interview with the French ambassador to make it appear that the French had made insulting demands on the king, and that the king had dismissed the ambassador in an insulting

manner—which had not been the case. The French fell into the trap, and, in declaring war, appeared to be the aggressors.

To general surprise, the army which had won in the Crimea, in Mexico, and in Italy did poorly from the start, notably outgeneraled by the Prussians under Moltke. After the capture of Napoleon III and a portion of the army at Sedan, the Parisians overthrew the Second Empire and established a Government of National Defense which was republican in form. Energetic attempts to mobilize the entire nation for defense in the manner of the 1790s stood some chance of success had it not been for the untimely surrender of a second French army at Metz. Paris itself endured a dreadful siege during the winter of 1870–1871, until the responsible elements in the provisional government knew they must seek an armistice. For a time, they had hoped for European intervention to prevent Prussia from becoming too overwhelming on the continent. The other powers, however, could not be roused to act in concert. Britain rejoiced to see Napoleon III in captivity; the Russians announced that they would remilitarize the Black Sea; and when the Italians were certain of the French defeat, they seized the city of Rome as their national capital.

As for Prussia, she crowned her victory by swallowing up all of Germany. The other German states no longer dared to defend their sovereignty, and the King of Bavaria was induced to invite the King of Prussia to take the imperial title. Early in 1871, the German Empire was proclaimed at Prussian military headquarters, the Palace of Versailles. Peace terms were then given to the French: the loss of Alsace and Lorraine, an indemnity of five billion francs (which was believed to be beyond the power of the French to pay), and an army of occupation in the northeast until that indemnity could be paid. The intent of such terms was obvious, and the treaty marked the beginning of a new era of harshness and bitterness in international relations.

CHRONOLOGY: 1848–1871

1848–1849:	Revolutions in France, Italy, the Austrian Empire, and Germany
1851–1870:	Ascendency of Napoleon III
1854–1855:	Crimean War
1856:	Congress of Paris
1859–1870:	Unification of Italy
1863:	Revolution in Poland
1864–1871:	Unification of Germany
1866:	Seven Weeks War (Prussia versus Austria)
1870–1871:	Franco-Prussian War

32
The Road
to Total War:
1871-1914

The Fundamental Factors in Bismarck's Diplomacy

Having been the architect of Prussian aggrandizement, Bismarck became the first chancellor of the German Empire; and having achieved his aims he emerged after 1871 as the devoted champion of the European status quo. His diplomacy had to cope with three major factors that would remain constant right down to 1914: First was the need to keep defeated France isolated, for her unanticipated financial recovery by 1873 raised the specter of a war revenge if she could find an ally against her larger neighbor. The foundation of the Third Republic in 1870, however, seemed to suggest France's indefinite isolation amidst the monarchies of Europe. Since Britain had been following an isolationist policy herself after the Crimean War, Bismarck felt that an understanding with the Russian and Hapsburg Empires would suffice to contain France.

Second, the Hapsburg Empire had been much altered by the reverses beginning in 1859. After their defeat in 1866, the Austrians felt obliged to make concessions to Hungarian nationalism, and in 1867 the Austria Empire was formally converted into the Dual Monarchy of Austria-Hungary. Bringing the Hungarians into foreign policymaking amounted to a diplomatic revolution. They were able to deflect Hapsburg energies from the traditional involvement in German and Italian affairs, forcing the monarchy to devote its attention to the Slavic minorities within the Empire, a stance which in time came to be a policy of hostility to Slavic peoples. The new orientation may have facilitated Bismarck's desire for reconciliation with the Hapsburgs, but it jeopardized his plan to develop close ties between Germany, Austria-Hungary, and Russia. Not only did the Russians remember with bitterness what they called Austria's "betrayal" during the Crimean War, but the Hungarians nurtured a passionate hatred of Russia for suppressing their national movement in 1849.

One can see the extent of Bismarck's diplomatic task when one adds to this picture the traditional rivalry of these two eastern empires to replace the declining Turkish Empire in the southeast. Toward that goal, the Russians increasingly picked up the banner of pan-Slavism, first flown by the Czechs in 1848, as the device to increase Russian influence among the peoples of southeastern Europe. The Dual Monarchy tried for a time to counter this by opposing Slavic nationalism and favoring maintaining the status quo in the Turkish Empire.

Finally, the third factor in the diplomatic picture was the rise of little Serbia under the leadership of Prince Michael Obrenović (1860–1868), an ardent Serbian nationalist. During his brief reign, he reached an understanding with the Prince of Montenegro and with the Bulgarian Revolutionary Committee (within the Turkish Empire) for an eventual union with Serbia, clear evidence of Serbian expansionism in the Balkans. This Slavic nationalism was as distressing to the Hungarians as it was to the Turks.

These three factors—Bismarck's desire to keep France diplomatically isolated, Austria-Hungary's rivalry with Russia in the Balkans, and the upsurge of Balkan nationalism—governed European diplomacy in the decade after the Franco-Prussian War. And all three were closely related. In brief, (1) Bismarck's goal of forestalling French revenge by depriving France of potential allies impelled him toward allying Germany with Austria-Hungary and Russia, but (2) these two powers were becoming more and more at odds with one another over their rival interests in the Balkans, and (3) the Balkans themselves were growing increasingly unstable with the continued disintegration of the Turkish Empire and the rise of nationalism among the Serbians and other Balkan peoples. Thus, Bismarck's efforts to woo Austria-Hungary and Russia became increasingly difficult as time passed.

The Three Emperors' League

In the immediate aftermath of the Franco-Prussian War, Bismarck's policy of isolating France achieved its first success when, in 1873, he brought the three eastern empires—Germany, Austria-Hungary, and Russia—into the Three Emperors' League (*Dreikaiserbund*). This arrangement, not a formal alliance, simply provided for mutual consultation in case the peace should be threatened. The fragility of this arrangement was soon revealed in 1875 and 1876 when insurrections in the Turkish provinces of Bosnia and Bulgaria provided opportunities both for Slavic nationalists and for international intervention into Turkish affairs. In the summer of 1876, the little Slavic states of Serbia and Montenegro invoked the pan-Slavic ideal and declared war against Turkey, entrusting the command of their armies to a Russian general well-known for his pan-Slavic views. Though the representatives of the *Dreikaiserbund* tried to regulate the crisis by agreeing not to allow the formation of a large Balkan state, the quick defeat of the Serbs by the Turks put Serbian independence in jeopardy and offered Russia a fine opportunity for intervention.

To meet this general Balkan crisis, the great powers convened in Constantinople. The Turks, however, confident of British backing in resisting Russian pressure, rejected the international attempts to meddle in Ottoman affairs—all while negotiating a status quo-antebellum peace with Serbia. In secret, meanwhile, Russia and Austria worked out an agreement, which revealed that neither power was seriously concerned for the welfare of Serbia. Both reaffirmed that the formation of a large Balkan state would be blocked, and agreed that Russia might unilaterally declare war on Turkey for refusing to improve the administration of her Christian subjects. After the expected Russian victory, she would annex Bessarabian territory along the Danubian frontier, while the Austrians would be free

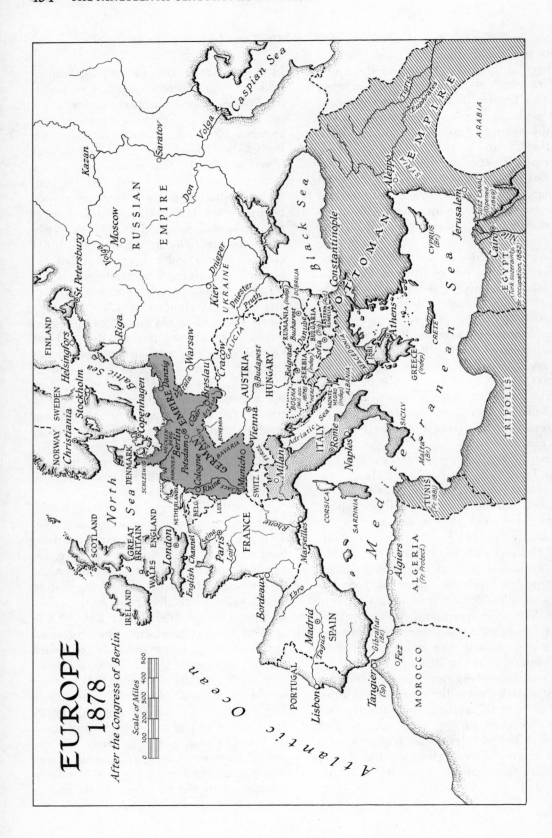

EUROPE
1878

After the Congress of Berlin

Scale of Miles

0   100   200   300   400   500

to occupy Turkish Bosnia and Herzegovina at any time. Accordingly, Russia declared war on the Turks in 1877 and was promptly joined by Romania, who hoped to transform her autonomy within Turkey into complete independence.

The Congress of Berlin: 1878

Once the Turks were overwhelmed and agreed to Russian peace terms (1878), Bismarck learned how difficult it was to keep Austria and Russia on good terms. The Russians had dictated peace terms to Turkey that were entirely inconsistent with the prior understanding with Austria. They provided for the creation of a large, independent Bulgaria (which Russia hoped to dominate), and for an autonomous Bosnia and Herzegovina. To avoid a possible war between Austria and Russia, Bismarck invited the great powers to resume their Balkan deliberations in Berlin.

This Congress of Berlin (1878) forced the Russians to invalidate their previous peace terms and to accept the Treaty of Berlin, which greatly whittled down Bulgaria and left her merely autonomous within the Turkish Empire. Romania, however, did win her complete independence. As for Bosnia and Herzegovina, the treaty put a brake on the Austrians, too, by permitting them a *temporary* occupation of the two provinces if order there should need to be restored. The events of 1878, in sum, revealed that both Russia and Austria had expansionist ambitions in the Balkans: Russia by trying to create a large Bulgaria, Austria-Hungary by her increasing interest in Bosnia-Herzegovina.

The Dual and Triple Alliances: 1879 and 1882: French Isolation Continues

The events of 1878 also revealed the ineffectuality of the *Dreikaiserbund*, and as the angered Russians hinted that they might seek an alliance with France, Bismarck felt he must draw closer to Austria-Hungary.

He found the Austro-Hungarians willing to sign an alliance with Germany, providing it was directed against Russia alone. Thus the Alliance of 1879 pledged the two countries to assist each other in case of an attack by Russia; but they were under no obligation in case of an attack from another country (France or Italy, for instance) unless that country was aided by Russia. This agreement was the first of the arrangements that would become effective in 1914.

Both partners in the alliance, meanwhile, had been aware of potential trouble from France and Italy: the former was anxious to recover territories lost in 1871, the latter was claiming the Trentino (the Italian-speaking part of the province of Tyrol). Consequently, both Germany and Austria urged France and Italy, respectively, to seek their territorial goals in North Africa rather than in Europe; and for reasons we must consider in greater detail elsewhere, both powers settled upon Tunisia as their proper area of expansion. The French suddenly occupied Tunis in 1881, to the dismay of the Italians, and established a protectorate. Bismarck, though personally disdainful of Italy, preferred under the circumstances to accept Italy as an ally. Otherwise, the frantic Italians might feel themselves forced to reach an understanding with France for the partition of North Africa, in which case France would cease to be isolated. The upshot was that Germany and Austria formed the Triple Alliance with Italy (1882), the terms of which were specifically anti-French rather than anti-Russian.

Bismarck had not, in fact, abandoned his hope of reestablishing the *Dreikaiserbund*, and had cajoled the Russians into renewing the ties ruptured at the Congress of Berlin. Toward that end the three emperors agreed in 1881 to consult on matters relating to the Eastern Question. And to rebuild this accord, Bismarck, who had presided at the Congress of Berlin as a self-styled "honest broker," now secretly agreed to the undermining of the Berlin settlement. Austria withdrew her objection to a large Bulgaria and received in exchange the right to annex Bosnia and Herzegovina at any time.

The years after the Congress of Berlin were increasingly worrisome for the small Balkan states, caught as they were in the crossfire of Russian and Austro-Hungarian ambitions. Moreover, each Balkan state had its own expansionist dreams, the revival of some ancient or medieval greatness before the arrival of the Turks; and without exception each national ambition was incompatible with that of every neighboring nationality. Add to this hints from some Italian nationalists that Italy might well lay claim to territories within the Roman Empire, and one had in the Balkans the ultimate madness that the new nationalism could create. Under the circumstances, these small states sought the protection or sponsorship of a great power; but in becoming clients, they risked becoming mere pawns of the great powers. The domestic politics of these small states, therefore, reflected these gross ambitions and elaborate fears, which gave to Balkan politics the atmosphere of comic opera based upon nightmares.

The potentiality for disaster in this mixture of great-power and small-power rivalries was illustrated in 1885. Bulgaria, hoping to convert her autonomy into complete independence, had taken advantage of Russian sponsorship to prepare to seize Eastern Rumelia (a Bulgar-speaking territory in Turkey immediately south of Bulgaria, which she had been denied in 1878), meanwhile quietly mobilizing Bulgarian national opinion to resist becoming a Russian puppet. When the Bulgarians suddenly moved into Eastern Rumelia in 1885, the jealous and anxious Serbs declared war on Bulgaria. Austria, for the moment regarding Serbia as her client, failed to intervene until the Serbians were quickly defeated by Bulgaria. Then, without informing her

Dreikaiserbund partners of her intention to intervene, Austria forced an end to the conflict and prevented the unification of Bulgaria. Had not the Russians already been irritated by their inability to manipulate Bulgaria, a general war could have developed that year, for Russia was infuriated by Austrian high-handedness.

The *Dreikaiserbund* failed to survive this second major clash of Austrian and Russian interests, and in 1887 Bismarck endeavored to keep his foreign policy intact by seeking a treaty with Russia that would be compatible with his treaty with Austria. This meant that he could not guarantee German neutrality in case of an Austro-Russian war. The result was the three-year Reinsurance Treaty, more a testament of good will than a document guaranteeing mutual aid. Germany's real alliances, indeed, were those with Austria and Italy.

The Accession of Kaiser William II (1888–1918) and the Franco-Russian Alliance of 1894

Bismarck's system, if already in difficulty, did not long survive the accession of a new emperor in 1888. Much influenced by the military and political views of the German General Staff, William II believed that an Austro-Russian war for domination of the Balkans and the Straits was unavoidable. As the national interests of Germany were more reconcilable with those of Austria than with those of Russia, the German General Staff favored an Austro-German "preventive war" against Russia while she was relatively weak. Bismarck had opposed that view, arguing that such a war would be the opportunity for France to try to recover Alsace-Lorraine. But Bismarck's long-term policy had been to maintain the European status quo, whereas William II was nurturing ideas of German expansionism. Clearly, the two divergent views could not long remain in the same house, and when, in 1890, Bismarck offered his resignation, the emperor accepted it. An immediate result was a German failure to renew the Reinsurance Treaty, apparent proof that Germany was abandoning Bismarck's policy of being friendly simultaneously with Russia and Austria.

In retrospect, German foreign policy between 1890 and 1914 seems to have been as erratic as the restless, ambitious Hohenzollern emperor himself. Its first result was to drive the Russians into an alliance with France, no matter how repugnant such a marriage was for the autocratic Czar Alexander III (1881-1896). Though it was known in Europe that the two powers were seeking an agreement, the actual terms of the military convention signed in 1894 were kept secret (Russia wished to avoid irritating Germany). Completely defensive in nature, the alliance was to remain in force only as long as the Triple Alliance existed. Even so, it marked the end of French isolation.

Aware of the negotiations, William II tried to tie Britain to the Triple Alliance. The British, arguing that their cabinet system of government precluded binding future governments with long-term obligations, would enter no alliance system. The Germans believed the British argument was intended to deceive them, and it made them suspicious of British intentions. William II consequently had second thoughts about his rejection of Russia, and his uneasiness was underscored when the questionable effectiveness of Italy as an ally was revealed to all by a monumental defeat inflicted on the Italians when they tried to establish a protectorate over Ethiopia in 1896.

In the 1890s, therefore, a new German policy gradually evolved which was based not upon securing the isolation of France, but upon securing the isolation of Great Britain. The effect would have been to merge the Triple Alliance with the Franco-Russian Alliance, to destroy the balance of power on the continent, to give Germany practical hegemony on the continent, and

to leave Britain alone facing a situation uncomfortably reminiscent of the Napoleonic Empire. William II found the key to this new orientation in East Asia, where Britain had commercial interests and where Russia had become the competitor of Japan—both powers were endeavoring to expand at the expense of the declining Chinese Empire. The encouragement of Russian expansion in the Manchurian-Korean region was a German bid for Russian friendship, and it had the added advantage of turning Russian energies away from the Balkans and a possible clash with Austria. The strategy seemed the more workable since it coincided with Anglo-French squabbling in North Africa.

This rivalry had begun to fester in 1875, when the British government, taking advantage of the Egyptian ruler's indebtedness, purchased his shares in the Suez Canal Company, and became the majority stockholder in what had been a French enterprise. In the ensuing years, the French saw their traditional influence in Egypt replaced by that of Britain, with the British gradually drawn southward up the Nile valley to defend Egypt's claim on the Sudan and to protect the water supply for the canal region. In the 1890s, French nationalists counter-attacked with a scheme designed to give France control of the headwaters of the Nile; and the two Western powers seemed near war in 1898 when the French established a small base at Fashoda in the Sudan.

By then, however, the British were too alarmed by German policies and tactics to allow relations with French to degenerate into war. In 1896, for example, on the twenty-fifth anniversary of the German Empire, William II proclaimed an aggressive "pan-German" program:

The German Empire has become a world empire. Everywhere at the most distant points on the globe dwell thousands of our fellow countrymen. German merchandise, German science,

German energy sail the oceans. The value of our sea trade amounts to thousands of millions. It is your duty to aid me in creating firm links between this greater Germany and our fatherland.

Already possessing a formidable army, the Germans announced in 1897 the development of a large navy to implement the new global policy. The British read the challenge correctly and knew that their security depended upon naval supremacy. A belated attempt to reach an understanding with Berlin was rebuffed, as the Germans were increasingly confident in the ultimate success of their continental system. This gave the British no option but to seek a reconciliation with France. Thus was born the series of commitments that would serve to block William II's world policy.

Britain Renounces Her Isolation, 1899–1907

In backing away from her long-term isolation, Britain entered into a number of agreements with foreign powers, but never concluded an alliance in Europe such as all the continental powers had arranged by 1900. Her international position, therefore, remained ambiguous, especially in German eyes: she was suspected of having made, by 1914 firm European military commitments in secret, which in fact she never did. In 1899, she reached an African settlement with France, by which the French agreed to evacuate the Nile watershed; west of this the British gave the French a free hand. The Anglo-French settlement immediately alarmed Italy as a possible barrier to her still frustrated African ambitions, leading her to undertake secret talks with the French. In 1900 they mutually recognized Italy's "interest" in Tripoli and France's in Morocco, actually a first step in undermining Italy's loyalty to the Triple Alliance.

Britain's second move was an attempt to restrict Russia's German-backed penetra-

tion of East Asia by signing a five-year alliance with Japan in 1902. The two island empires recognized Japan's economic interests in Korea, but guaranteed the independence of both Korea and China. This treaty had the effect of making Russia promise to evacuate Manchuria, but her failure to live up to the promise gave the Japanese pretext for war. Early in 1904, the Japanese launched a surprise attack, which gained them early advantages from which the Russians never recovered. What is more, the Russian government met these disasters so ineptly as to provoke a political crisis at home and to provide opportunity for a radical uprising against the autocracy in 1905. The political crisis forced the Russians to make peace at the very moment when their forces in East Asia were finally reaching strength to make a Japanese defeat probable. The pro-Japanese American president, Theodore Roosevelt, mediated the conflict, and the Japanese were left with a foothold in Korea and the southern half of Sakhalin. Like the Crimean War, the Russo-Japanese War revealed the inefficiency of the Russian autocracy and forced both military and political reforms upon Czar Nicholas II (1896-1917). But the outcome of the war also obscured Russia's true military strength, just as the Japanese victory excited Asian and African nationalists.

Meanwhile, the French developed their African settlement with Italy by securing Italy's promise to remain neutral in case the French found themselves "directly provoked" to declare war. This gave the Italians the latitude to decide who would be the "real" aggressor in a future Franco-German conflict and, thus, the opportunity to shirk the obligation to aid Germany. No power could any longer predict how Italy would behave in a crisis, and she was mistrusted after 1902. The French also hoped to develop their African settlement with Britain, and toward that end Anglo-French diplomats systematically reviewed and compromised a backlog of disputes that had divided the two nations. Their efforts were summed up in the *Entente Cordiale* of 1904, which removed the major grievances and made close cooperation henceforth possible. William II's hope of uniting the continent against Britain was slowly being checked.

By the turn of the twentieth century, Europe as a cosmopolitan entity had almost disappeared. Even those proposals that seemed to embody an international idealism were too often expressions of mere national interest. The First Hague Conference (1899), for instance, came following a proposal of Nicholas II that the powers ought to seek agreement on the limitation of arms. No power felt it was politic to ignore the proposal. Yet Russia's motive, when she was conducting an aggressive policy in East Asia and falling behind Germany's military expenditures, was widely (and rightly) suspect. With Russian sincerity questionable at The Hague, the Germans vetoed a Russian suggestion that all armies be kept at current levels for five years. The British then proposed that the powers establish a permanent court for compulsory international arbitration, which the French warmly supported. Such a court was established at The Hague, but the Germans rejected the idea of compulsory arbitration and put themselves in a bad light. In the aftermath, the French and Russians tightened their alliance by prolonging their military convention indefinitely. Moreover, as part of the search for their *Entente Cordiale*, the Anglo-French agreed to refer all their future disputes to the International Court.

The strengthening of the ties between Britain and France, and between France and Russia, made the French logically eager to see Britain and Russia be reconciled after a century of hostility. The destruction of Russian naval power in the war with Japan did a good deal to relieve traditional British worry over Russian expansionism, while the post-1905 reforms in Russia brought to power men more sympathetic to the British than to the German form of government. Consequently, Anglo-Russian diplomats reviewed and compromised the entire gamut of Anglo-Russian frictions, especially those along the inner frontiers of Asia. And in 1907, they signed an entente—an understanding—rather than an alliance. The last of the prewar alignments had been achieved.

The Descent into War, 1908–1914

Beginning in 1908, Europe experienced a series of crises in the very regions that had long been the focal points of international tension; but the great powers now responded to such crises in the light of the recent British commitments (some real and some imagined) to her continental friends. The Austrians, for example, presumed that the British, in reaching an understanding with Russia, had abandoned their traditional support of Ottoman integrity and had agreed to aid the Russians in getting the Straits opened to Russian warships. (The Straits had been closed to all warships since the Crimean War.) For her part, Germany, learning that the French and British had been engaged in secret military and naval discussions, presumed that the Entente of 1904 masked a firm military alliance. Both these assumptions were incorrect, but the misunderstandings affected international relations.

Thus, in 1908, when a group of young Turkish nationalists dedicated to stemming the long decline of Ottoman Turkey seized power in Constantinople, the Russian and Austrian foreign ministers met at Buchlau to discuss their mutual ambitions in the Balkans, as the sudden revolution seemed to be the opportunity to annex Turkish territory. Their "Buchlau bargain" permitted Austria to annex (rather than merely occupy) Bosnia-Herzegovina, with the Russians getting Austrian support for opening the Straits to Russian warships. Evidently, the Russians assumed that such major changes could not be undertaken without obtaining the sanction of all the powers signatory to the Treaty of Berlin—and set out to secure their permission—and were thus caught short when the Austrians suddenly announced the annexation of Bosnia-Herzegovina. To their chagrin, the Russians then discovered that Britain and France would only support the opening of the Straits for *all* warships, not merely those of Russia. And nationalistic Serbia, her own eyes on Bosnia-Herzegovina, was furious at Austria's action. Germany was furious, too, for her ally had taken this major step without prior consultation. War between Austria and Serbia-Russia was a real threat when the Russians insisted that they had not approved the Austrian annexation; but that lie was so evident that the German government felt itself obliged to support Austria in the crisis, giving the unfortunate impression that Germany would support any Austrian move to maintain the Triple Alliance. The Turks put the final fires out by accepting an indemnity from Austria for the lost provinces.

A second war crisis blew up in 1911 over Morocco. A turbulent country in the nineteenth century thanks to continual uprisings and conflict among four major ethnic groups, Morocco had become as early as 1880 the subject of international intervention designed to produce order. The consequent rise of anti-foreignism in Morocco not only threatened to undermine such international efforts, but gave the French, whose interest in Morocco was evident by 1900, an opportunity for establishing the same special status for themselves in Morocco that they had won in Tunisia in 1881. The initial French move in 1905 was blocked largely by German initiative, but in 1911 anti-foreign riots in Morocco led the French to occupy Fez. Again the Germans reacted in a manner that suggested that they themselves were conniving for

naval bases on the Moroccan Atlantic coast. The British naturally backed the French in the crisis, and the issue was successfully mediated when the French gave the Germans bits of the French Congo and some adjacent territory.

With France getting a free hand in Morocco, the Italians concluded that it was high time to utilize their earlier agreements by grabbing Tripoli from the Turks, who were now the butt of everyone's nationalist ambitions. All the great powers had earlier encouraged Italian penetration of North Africa for reasons of their own, but by 1911 no great power wanted to see any further assault on the Ottoman Empire for fear it would light new fires in the Balkans. The Italians proceeded, nevertheless, but found the Turks unexpectedly well-entrenched in Tripoli. A second Italian fiasco in Africa was in the making when, in 1912, the Turks felt forced to make peace in order to confront a far greater danger in the Balkans.

After their humiliation in 1908, the Russians had been secretly urging the little Balkan states to form an alliance against further Austrian expansion. Until 1912 Balkan rivalries had precluded such cooperation; but with Turkey vulnerable during the Italian attack, Serbia and Bulgaria concluded an alliance that was ostensibly anti-Austrian (as the Russians wished), but secretly anti-Turkish (which the Russians knew). The Russians, on the other hand, expected to be able to use this alliance solely as an anti-Austrian tool. With the adherence of Greece to the alliance, however, the Russians recognized that the situation was not under their control, and they joined the other powers in warning the alliance not to disturb the peace. The warning came on the very day that Montenegro declared war on Turkey, the fight being immediately joined by Greece, Bulgaria, and Serbia.

While the Turks were easily defeated in this First Balkan War, the victors immediately squabbled over the spoils as their various national ambitions all collided. Before the year was out (1913), Greece and Serbia declared war on Bulgaria, and Turkey and Romania joined the war against Bulgaria, who was quickly defeated in the Second Balkan War. The most significant result of the two wars was the enlargement of Serbia to nearly double her former size and the subsequent whetting of her nationalistic appetite. Bulgaria was the chief, and the embittered, loser.

Turkey herself proved to be the scene of the last serious crisis before 1914. If in the nineteenth century Britain was the chief power to bolster declining Turkey, she began before the end of the century to recognize the hopelessness of preaching reform to the sultans to forestall Turkey's collapse. The waning of British interest in Turkey happened to coincide with an upswing in German interest in Turkey. At first this interest seemed little more than a German search for a place to invest capital —thanks to the phenomenal growth of German technology and industry after 1871. Though German activity in Turkish business enterprise and railroad construction exceeded that of any other power by 1900, the commercial value of this economic penetration was small. It led, however, to the Germans furnishing military missions to train the Turkish army; while the railway concessions, by tying Berlin to the Persian Gulf via Constantinople and Baghdad, were suddenly perceived in Europe (notably in Russia) as a major military advantage to the Dual Alliance powers and as a development entirely consistent with William II's world policy. Especially after 1907, the German presence seemed designed to cut Russia off from her Western friends in case of war. Thus, in 1913, when a German general was appointed by the Turks to the actual command of Turkish troops around Constantinople, the Entente powers blew up in protest. The German government admitted the legitimacy of the

opposition and worked out a compromise with the Turks, so that the officer remained in the Turkish service but not in command of troops.

The Assassination at Sarajevo, June 28, 1914

The murder of the heir to the Austro-Hungarian throne, Archduke Franz Ferdinand, by Serbian nationalists in the Bosnian capital proved to be the final straw. Even today the events surrounding that fatal incident remain somewhat mysterious. Especially after the Austrians annexed Bosnia-Herzegovina in 1908, they were seen by Serbian nationalists as the chief barrier to the creation of a large Serbia; and even though the principal Serbian nationalist organizations were unofficial, major Serbian officials joined such organizations, making it difficult to distinguish between official and unofficial Serbian actions and attitudes. As for Franz Ferdinand, although an autocrat at heart, he was widely believed to have accepted the necessity for reforming the Dual Monarchy to accommodate the minority nationalities; consequently he was as much feared by conservatives within the Empire as by ambitious nationalists in Serbia and Romania.

The announcement that the Archduke would visit routine army maneuvers in Bosnia during the summer of 1914 was made several months before the event, giving the assassins ample time to organize their attempt upon his life. Meanwhile, the Serbian government, aware of the plot but finding it impolitic to warn the Austrian government directly, sought to pass on the information through indirect channels. It remains unclear whether this method proved ineffective (thus giving the Austrians grounds to claim that they had not been properly warned), or whether the Austrians chose to ignore the warning in their search for a showdown with Serbian nationalism. The fatal shots were fired by Gavrilo Princip, a Bosnian Serb belonging to a group that advocated the unification of the southern Slavs.

The Austrians took the official line that unless they dealt promptly with Serbia, the Hapsburg dynasty, its territories, and thus the Triple Alliance would be in mortal danger. William II informed the Austrians that he would back their settlement with Serbia, thus giving the Austrians what has been called a "blank check"—perhaps anticipating that under the circumstances of the murder the Russians would not come to the aid of Serbia, and the conflict would remain local. Austria's ultimatum to Serbia was deliberately constructed to make it unacceptable to a sovereign government, and the terms were not revealed to the Germans until they had been sent off to Belgrade. In other words, the war was deliberately provoked—the Austrians declared it on July 28. Any hope that the conflict could be localized was dashed in a few days, and Europe entered the era of total war.

CHRONOLOGY: 1871–1914

1867:	Creation of the Dual Monarchy of Austria-Hungary
1870–1871:	Franco-Prussian War
1871–1890:	The Bismarck Era
1878:	Congress of Berlin
1878:	Romanian Independence
1879:	Dual Alliance (Germany and Austria-Hungary)
1882:	Triple Alliance (Germany, Austria-Hungary, and Italy)
1887:	Reinsurance Treaty (Germany and Russia)
1894:	Franco-Russian Alliance
1902:	Anglo-Japanese Alliance
1904–1905:	Russo-Japanese War
1904:	Entente Cordiale (Britain and France)
1907:	Anglo-Russian Entente
1908:	Young Turk Revolution
1912:	First Balkan War
1913:	Second Balkan War
1914:	Outbreak of World War I

33
The Gathering Centralization of Power

The Heritage of the French Revolution and Napoleon

One of the oldest traditions of the continental monarchies was their tendency to increase their power and efficiency by centralizing their authority and making their governance as uniform as possible throughout their various realms. To accomplish such a goal, monarchs had necessarily struggled against the aristocracies of Europe, whose titles reflected local powers and interests. If in those struggles over the centuries most kings gradually reduced the power of their nobles, the process of centralization was far from complete in most states by the eighteenth century—and government was still notoriously inefficient. Even the much-vaunted centralization achieved by Louis XIV before his death in 1715 left France a country without uniform or equitable tax rates, with internal tariffs detrimental to the national economy, with no national standard for weights and measures, and with a nobility so exempt from taxation as to contribute to the central government's bankruptcy before the end of the century.

As we have already seen, many eighteenth-century intellectuals, especially on the continent, responded to such imperfect government by advocating what we have come to call "enlightened" despotism —that is, government based on the same rational principles that presumably also govern the universe. Such government could only be ordained by a philosopher-king who would both understand the principles of nature and possess the authority to reform man's institutions to conform with those principles. The argument ran that such a system would not only produce a highly centralized and rational order, but liberty as well, for the equation held that inefficient government led to disorder and tyranny; whereas liberty could only derive from rational order. The whole notion depended on the assumption that nature is a state of rational order and a state of perfect freedom. Thus, the old prescription that man ought to return to a state of nature in order to find freedom was not meant to be an invitation to return to the realm of nuts and berries, but a plea to discover all natural laws and to regulate society according to them.

Many royal governments experimented with what they thought was enlightened despotism in the later eighteenth century as the newest formula for enhancing centralization. And while the French Revolution certainly did not derive from a single cause, it is very much to the point that the French monarchy failed to produce anything like enlightened despotism, led the nation into bankruptcy and constitutional paralysis, and had to be overturned before the century was out. What is more, the republican and Napoleonic heirs of the old monarchy labored successfully to perfect the centralization of government. By 1814, the revolution had transformed France into a highly centralized nation with local authority utterly subservient to Paris—the perfect political instrument for any would-be dictator—and all in the name of order and liberty.

The paradox gradually dawned on Europe as a whole. Even though most of the libertarian ideas and slogans of the French Revolution remained in the nineteenth century to inspire Europeans seeking national or individual liberty, many European liberals in fact turned to the English experience as a more practical guide to freedom. The British record by 1815 was impressive: During the long duel with France, which had begun in the time of Louis XIV and ended with the final surrender of Napoleon, British political institutions had been steadily liberalized. Royal power had been checked without destroying the monarchy; the unitary state retained its paramouncy without destroying the integrity of local government; and public confidence in the system—if occasionally strained—provided the credit the regime required to sustain the unequal contest with France. No doubt

much remained to be done if Britain were to become a heavenly city. But by European standards of that day, she stood alone and beyond as the model for the future, though she functioned through institutions out of the past. It was not lost on European liberals that this freer society had prevailed over the more autocratic one.

Nineteenth-century liberals, because their creed had been born of the long fight to contain royal absolutism, were seriously concerned to define what the state must *not* do. Though they might still thrill to the emancipatory currents undammed by the French Revolution, they were also inevitably distressed that the French Revolution had shown the way to a more effective centralization that could become a new absolutism. The liberals' desire to free nations and individuals, which they knew often required centralization, when combined with a reluctance to organize and use power, put nineteenth-century liberalism on the horns of a dilemma from which it never entirely escaped. They were often centralizers when in power, decentralizers when out of power. Just as the European liberals gradually lost direction of the various national movements because of their relative political ineffectuality, so did their reluctance to use the power of the state often make them ineffective social reformers. The particular seriousness of this impotence lay in the fact that the Industrial Revolution, already well underway in Britain, began to creep across the continent.

We know today that the Industrial Revolution did not necessarily worsen the economic conditions of life for those caught up in the transition from country to town. But whatever the momentary economic conditions of life, the long-range implication of industrialization was a higher standard of material existence for all. By raising popular expectations, industrialization contributed to the development of a revolutionary situation; not because hardships were created, but because the poor, with their eyes on immediate amelioration, were easily disenchanted. Rapid urbanization, moreover, was another form of centralization whose implications went far beyond the political or the economic. Highly self-sufficient rural folk found themselves in specialized routine factory jobs, living and working in a crowd—conditions that can affect negatively everything from morale to fertility. A sixteen-hour work day was not unusual for a factory laborer, and his wages were usually too small to support his family unless his wife and children were also employed.

The average liberal of the post-1815 period, hoping for nature rather than the state to regulate men's lives, no longer had any reason to believe that the outcome of nature's regulation would be happiness for the majority of mankind. Writing an essay on population growth in 1798, an English clergyman named Malthus had calculated that an unchecked population increases geometrically (doubling roughly every 25 years), while food production merely increases arithmetically. Workers, in particular, he believed, tend to multiply until checked by starvation and misery. He argued that nature limits our population growth through wars, poverty, and vice; and that if social reformers tried to remove those evils, the population would swiftly outstrip the food supply. This pessimism was shared by David Ricardo, another laissez-faire liberal, who believed that economic life is governed by unalterable natural laws. Among them he included the natural antagonism between the three classes: landowners, capitalists, and laborers. Believing that there is a fixed amount of goods and a fixed amount of wages to be divided among workers, (and knowing Malthus' work on population growth), Ricardo calculated that the lot of workers must inevitably decline. The supply of workers, in other words, would increase faster than the demand for them. Social reforms designed to keep them alive were actually an unkindness to them. If you paid them higher wages to keep them alive,

the capitalists' earnings, would necessarily be smaller, meaning smaller investments and fewer jobs in the future. This fixed system he aptly called *The Iron Law of Wages* (1817). The pursuit of happiness, deemed feasible by some liberals in the eighteenth century, was banished by these dismal scientists of the nineteenth.

The Liberal Regimes and the Rise of Radicalism

Doctrinaire liberalism enjoyed its heyday in Western Europe between 1830 and 1848, during which time various radical and socialist theories also found their adherents in Western Europe. In the face of a greater awareness of social problems, the fact that liberals were political, rather than social, reformers largely accounts for the rise of radicalism. In fact, following the decline of liberalism after 1848, no recovery would be possible for liberalism until liberals could find a way to accommodate their traditional concern for individual freedom with a concern for general welfare.

Radicalism in France

The first of the regimes to be officially liberal was the July Monarchy of Louis-Philippe (1830–1848). In 1831, silk workers in Lyons succeeded in negotiating better wage rates with their employers; but the government, viewing this collective activity as a violation of laissez-faire, did not regard the new wage agreement as legal. Troops were used on several occasions to maintain order, which was distressing to liberals who shrank from the idea of a government based on force; while the workers felt themselves betrayed by the state and learned that the benefits of liberalism were for the few. A similar ambiguity could be seen in the liberal Education Law of 1833. Liberals were genuinely concerned for the intellectual and moral improvement of individuals and were heirs to the French Revolutionary notion that public educational facilities must be established to make that improvement possible. The law of 1833 made all French municipalities responsible for providing primary education for boys; but, attendance was not to be compulsory to safeguard the individual's liberty. In a day when many children were employed in factories and mines, such a law gave the appearance of giving the employers' needs higher priority than the children's. On the other hand, the latest "science" sanctioned such an outlook, so that sincere humanitarian intentions were often overborne by a faith in laissez-faire.

Radicalism in Britain

In Britain, where political reform (as opposed to revolution) had often been successful in meeting abuses, both major political parties—the Whigs and the Tories—had become increasingly conservative during the long years Britain had fought the French Revolution and Napoleon. Reforms projected in the later eighteenth century had consequently been shelved.* Thus, after 1815, when the nation began to suffer from the dislocations produced by the change from a wartime to a peacetime economy, the prior failure to reform left the political system peculiarly unresponsive to the economic crisis. The parliamentary system in particular revealed two major constitutional flaws: First, constituencies had not been revised to reflect the dramatic shift in population from rural to urban areas which came with the Industrial Revolution, leaving some rural constituencies as grossly overrepresented as the new towns were underrepresented. Second, since land alone had been traditionally regarded as real property, the property qualification for the right to vote and to hold public office had the effect of disenfranchising many of those who owned the commercial or industrial property that was

* See above, pages 365–366.

becoming the economic backbone of the nation.

Though the Whigs had historically been more liberal than the Tories, both parties necessarily represented the landed interests. After 1815, a new breed of radical (or democratic) politicians emerged who saw that the new conditions of life in the nineteenth century would require the democratization of British institutions. A journalist with great credit among British workers, William Cobbett, argued that if parliamentary constituencies should be revised so that representation in the House of Commons would once again reflect the nation rather than the few, the necessary social and economic reforms would follow. Jeremy Bentham formulated a political philosophy called "utilitarianism," which advocated political democracy as the most practical political form. Wanting a system that would provide men with what they *need* and *desire*—which would bring "the greatest good for the greatest number"— Benthan also wanted to secure the greatest happiness for the greatest number. Political democracy seemed to satisfy these requirements: If each individual best knows his own interest, then it follows that the general interest can best be judged by the majority. The system reconciled individual egotism with the general welfare. Another radical, James Mill, saw popular education as a necessary concomitant of democracy and a free press as necessary to check arbitrary government.

In the 1820s, a bizarre reformist alliance appeared. The aristocratic Whigs, desperate for office after nearly a half century of Tory rule, were finally ready for the reform of Parliament even at the expense of the landed interests, making possible an alliance with the unrepresented manufacturers and with the Radicals. Their opportunity came when the Whigs won the elections of 1830. The subsequent Reform Bill of 1832 reformed the constituencies, redistributing the seats in Commons to reflect the shift in population from country to town, while the property qualifications for the vote were modernized. In fact, the bill did not greatly enlarge the electorate, since the property qualifications remained high; but the bill gave the middle class a greater participation in politics and reinforced the liberal, if not the democratic, climate.

What followed was reformist legislation by a liberal regime which, like its contemporary in France, practiced laissez-faire to the distress of those Radicals who had expected social and economic reforms. In the matter of slavery, the Whigs and Radicals did see eye to eye and cooperated to end slavery throughout the Empire in 1833. But when Parliament then took up the reform of poor relief, by then an archaic dole system by which public funds were given to parishes to make up the difference between a worker's wage and a minimum living wage, the Liberals and Radicals parted company. If the old system was both morally and economically outrageous, the new Poor Law of 1834 held no charm for workers. No relief could now be given to the able-bodied unless they resided in a poorhouse, where conditions were kept deliberately wretched to encourage a man to accept any work at any wage to stay out of them. The reform provided a large supply of laborers eager for work, while taxes for poor relief diminished. It also revealed that the liberal principle of laissez-faire could be a guarantee of inhumanity. Europe was ready for new doctrines that would reduce the exploitation of human beings.

The Rise of Socialism

Count Henri de Saint-Simon was the first well-known socialist writer of the nineteenth century. Rather than exploit each other, he argued, men should work together to exploit nature for the common good. He envisioned the future state as a giant cooperative, a highly centralized and authoritarian state, which would supervise both production and distribution of goods. As for the sharing of goods, he would have

each person receive "according to his capacity and according to his services." Toward the end of his life, Saint-Simon tried to extend the social and economic aspects of his system into a secularized morality that he called the "New Christianity," with himself the messiah for the new cult. His disciples developed his ideas into a formal religion where salvation lay in organizing the means of production so as to improve the lot of the poor as quickly as possible. The French government outlawed the cult in 1832 for advocating the abolition of private property.

Obviously, men had exploited the resources of nature long before Saint-Simon; and Christian sects had sometimes conveniently adjusted their doctrines to sanction human rapacity, especially in frontier communities. On the other hand, traditional Christianity had taught that nature, including human nature, must not be violated, just as the eighteenth-century rationalists had seen nature as our proper model rather than as our victim. The Saint-Simonian invitation to exploit nature as a moral duty was especially enticing in a day when the Industrial Revolution promised a burgeoning production, and the utilitarian ethic he substituted for a spiritual or metaphysical ethic made man's material welfare the new measure of the good and the true.

Charles Fourier was another early socialist who, like Saint-Simon, opposed an economy based on competition as likely to lead to human exploitation. Rather than antagonism, he said, let us have harmony. And he thought that harmony could best be achieved through the founding of small cooperative communities, not through a centralized administration. This idyllic communalism was rooted in the eighteenth-century faith in the inherent goodness of human nature. Where competition and antagonism were removed to make the environment sweeter, human instincts would naturally work for peace and happiness. Each person who entered such a community was to be given property to give him a stake in the community, and each person was to be free to choose his own vocation. The first of such communities was established southwest of Paris in 1832, but the movement's heyday was in the 1840s in the United States, where 16 communities were founded.

The contemporary Owenite movement was also decentralist and similar in spirit to the Fourierite movement. Robert Owen (1771-1858), a Scottish cotton mill owner, was an environmentalist who was determined to turn his typically wretched factory town into a model community with no unemployment. He raised workers' wages while reducing the work day from 17 to 10 hours; he constructed decent housing and improved factory conditions; and he required that the workers' children be in school between the ages of five and ten. He hoped this model would lead other manufacturers and the state to found similar communities, never to exceed 3000 people, but he was not emulated. His ideas, however, did contribute to the founding of many cooperative stores in Britain where workers could purchase goods at little more than cost, and to the founding of a number of Owenite communities in the United States.

During the 1830s, when the labor movement in France was being driven underground by the July Monarchy, and when British workers became increasingly dismayed by the failure of the reformed Parliament to enact social legislation, the labor movement itself became more radical. Two British artisans, William Lovett and Francis Place, drew up the "People's Charter," a petition to Parliament that asked for universal male suffrage, the removal of the property qualification for the vote, and annual elections to Parliament—terms that implied popular sovereignty and democracy. Nearly a million and a quarter signatures were attached to the petition before it was submitted to Parliament in 1839. But the Whigs and Tories, holding that sovereignty was vested jointly in the Parliament and the crown, rejected the petition. The energies of the movement were soon channeled into the drive for free trade (which would have the effect of reducing food prices for the British public). This was achieved under the leadership of Richard Cobden in 1846 after the failure of the Irish potato crop and poor harvests in England. In France, Louis Blanc published a book called *The Organization of Labor* (1839), which presented statistical evidence of the miserable conditions of employment in the industrial cities, attributing them to free enterprise. He extended the revolutionary doctrine of the Rights of Man by arguing that every man has not merely the right to live, but also the right to live by the fruits of his own labor. To provide full employment at decent wages, Blanc insisted that it was the obligation of the centralized state to provide interest-free loans to cooperatives, a device he believed would ultimately ruin private operators and pave the way for a complete socialization of capital.

Positivism

This growing awareness that industrialism was producing an entirely new complex of social problems led directly to a new field of academic study: sociology. Its father, Auguste Comte (1789-1857), ought to be specially noted as epitomizing the main currents of mid-nineteenth century thought. Originally a Saint-Simonian, Comte's studies led him to sum up mankind's thought as an evolutionary progress through three principal phases: the theological phase, a period when man's knowledge was so limited that he necessarily ascribed all phenomena to supernatural powers; the metaphysical phase, the period in which man sought to discover the causes of phenomena by observing nature and by using his reason; and finally, the *positive* phase in which man has progressed to a point where he no longer asks *why* things happen but is wisely content with the "scientific" facts which tell us *how* things happen or *what* is happening. This school of thought, known as positivism, advocated the gathering of information about man and his society so that our political, religious, and ethical systems could be given a scientific foundation. This emphasis on giving man a better life was soon transformed into a worship of mankind; and like Saint-Simonianism before it, positivism became a secularized religious cult.

Marxism

Karl Marx, the father of scientific socialism, also based his sociology on his particular views of the history of mankind; and he, too, found an evolutionary mechanism which he claimed not only explained the past but predicted the future. In his *Communist Manifesto* (1848), he introduced his fundamental premise that "the history of all hitherto existing society is the history of class struggles." This meant that he saw all historical change resulting from the conflict between the propertied and the propertyless—that the course of history had been determined by economic factors. This conflict or dialectic became known as dialectical materialism. According to his theory, the class owning the means of production inevitably becomes politically ascendant. Thus, when machines and factories became the principal means of production, the middle class replaced the feudal aristocracy. In the future, the proletariat—the operators of the machines—would replace the bourgeoisie.

In predicting the inevitable triumph of the proletariat as the outcome of the nineteenth-century conflict between the owners of capital and labor, Marx made no claim that capitalism would fail because it seemed ethically defective. Instead he predicted capitalism's collapse on the basis of an economic doctrine known as the theory of surplus value. Much influenced

Karl Marx (Radio Times Hulton Picture Library)

by Ricardo's inflexible views on wages and profits, Marx argued that capitalism would fail because the low wages paid to laborers would make it impossible for them to buy the products of their own labor. Prices would not be lowered, because this would be inconsistent with the capitalists' necessary profits. Since he believed that bourgeois governments would never act to limit bourgeois profits, the rich would get richer, the poor poorer. Much of the middle class would erode into the proletariat, which would end by seizing the state and the means of production. The immediate result would be a dictatorship of the proletariat, a totally centralized state where capitalism would be abolished in favor of a cooperative commonwealth: the first classless society in history, where workers would presumably for the first time receive full value for their labor. But since the disappearance of classes meant, according to the original premise, the disappearance of conflict in society, Marx's long-range forecast was that the dictatorship would cease to be necessary, that the state would wither away—a heavenly vision, but necessarily an earth-bound Eden.

Anarchism

Marx's French contemporary, Proudhon, also wanted the state to wither away, but he called himself an anarchist. Recognizing that when men had originally emerged from the state of nature, they had necessarily organized government to create order, Proudhon went on to argue that as men become increasingly sophisticated in society they become increasingly resentful of government authority. The rational response to this is to seek greater liberty and equality through decentralization of political authority, until such a point that authority is entirely self-imposed rather than imposed by the state. Proudhon's influence during the 1850s and 1860s in France, the most centralized of European countries, was much greater than Marx's; but Proudhon's ideas, thanks to his muddled prose, were especially open to misconstruction. He did not, for instance, advocate the abolition of private property, but merely denounced those who used their property to exploit others. And as for anarchy or self-government, he meant self-discipline, not self-indulgence, his goal being perfect justice for all.

The Aftermath of 1848

The general failure of liberals and radicals in the revolutions of 1848 left conservative governments in the saddle; these justified themselves as the guardians of "order" in the wake of the uprisings. Just as they seized control of the various national movements after 1848, so did the conservative regimes press forward with the traditional tendency to centralize power. In multinational Austria-Hungary, for example, the provincial Diets (legislatures) enjoyed by

the various national groups were now abolished, the revolts in 1848 being sufficient excuse. Local government became entirely administered from Vienna, one of the long-range goals being the Germanization of the Hapsburg Empire. In Prussia, though Frederick William IV granted his subjects a constitution of his own manufacture after the defeat of the German liberals in 1848, the constitution preserved the King's ultimate authority. Centralization was promoted by denying towns and rural districts further participation in the choice of local officials. All office holders came to be appointed by the crown.

In France, where administrative centralization had been perfected before 1815, executive power made itself once again absolute after 1848. As we have seen, popular reaction to radical violence undermined the democratic institutions of the Second French Republic. The National Assembly played into the hands of President Louis-Napoleon Bonaparte by being more reactionary than he, allowing him to pose as the heir to his uncle's alleged dual role—the guarantor of order *and* the hope of democracy—a latter-day crowned Jacobin, for the crown was his goal. And like his uncle, he staged a *coup d'état* against his parliamentary opponents (1851) to secure dictorial powers. The following year, the Second Republic was easily converted into the Second Empire, with the President becoming Emperor Napoleon III. These changes were overwhelmingly sanctioned in national plebiscites. A Caesarian democracy, in other words, a dictatorship established by popular vote.

Unlike Prussia (later Germany) and Austria-Hungary, where highly centralized, autocratic institutions remained intact until 1914, France experienced a gradual liberalization of her political institutions, but no decentralization. Beginning in 1860, when the still-popular Napoleon III enjoyed the prestige of his victories over Russia in 1856 and Austria in 1859, he began to dismantle the dictatorship. Parliament, which had lost its right to initiate or amend legislation, was periodically granted new legislative powers, labor won a limited right to organize in 1864; and four years later, the regime all but abandoned its censorial power. This led, in 1870, to a new constitution establishing the so-called Liberal Empire, a limited monarchy whose development was cut short by the untimely onset of the Franco-Prussian War. The Emperor's initiative seems to have been motivated by his realization that France (unlike Austria or Prussia), with her liberal and radical traditions dating from 1789, would not indefinitely tolerate absolutism. If his dynasty were to endure, he must move in the direction of the British model —though he hoped to be his own prime minister.

The liberal tendencies Pius IX (1846–1878) evinced on taking the Papal throne vanished after his unhappy experiences in 1848–1849. Thereafter, his reaction took several allied forms: He worked to centralize the administration of the Roman Catholic Church by increasing Papal administrative authority at the expense of the various national hierarchies (a tendency known historically as ultramontanism). His doctrinal innovations were conservative and directed toward Papal absolutism. Earlier in the nineteenth century, men who called themselves Liberal Catholics had championed ultramontanism, thinking that by strengthening Papal control, they could reverse the modern tendency of the secular states to dominate the national churches. For them, ultramontanism was a device to secure separation of church and state, a goal of all nineteenth-century liberals. Consequently, these Liberal Catholics were dismayed as they saw the ultramontanism of Pius IX lead not to greater separation, but to closer relations with illiberal governments and to doctrinal attacks on liberalism.

In 1864 he issued the Encyclical *Quanta*

Cura, to which was attached *a Syllabus of the Principal Errors of Our Time*. Its tenor was summed up in the eightieth "principal error," namely, that "the Roman Pontiff can, and ought to, reconcile himself, and come to terms with progress, liberalism and modern civilization." This Papal extremism reflected the Pope's view that modern civilization had become highly secularized; and that if religion, which he held to be the true foundation of justice and legitimacy, were finally to be excluded from society, we would enter an era of materialism and brute force. Pius IX capped his challenge to secularism by summoning a Vatican Council (1869), which he induced to proclaim the dogma of Papal Infallibility in 1870. This meant that when a pope speaks *ex cathedra** on matters of faith and morals, he is infallible. The centralization of spiritual authority, at least, seemed complete.

Meanwhile, in Russia, which had not experienced an uprising in 1848, the Crimean War exposed the shocking inefficiency of the central government. Moreover, since it had become apparent that much of this inefficiency was grounded in the archaism of the fundamental institutions of Russian life, Czar Alexander II (1855–1881) reluctantly recognized the necessity of thoroughgoing reform. Moreover, the initial reform—the long-overdue decree abolishing serfdom—dictated the nature of the subsequent reforms. It is estimated that the emancipation decree (1861) freed 40 million people, after which the state took the responsibility for providing the ex-serfs with land, compensating the original landowners. Such lands were not given outright to the peasants, but were administered by the villages where the peasants lived; and the peasants repaid the government for the land in installments over a period of 49 years. The system was

---

* That is, "from the throne"—solemnly and officially.

a financial expedient; it being easier to collect taxes and installment payments from the villages than from each peasant.

The emancipation of the serfs had profound political and legal implications: it instantly dissolved traditional feudal relationships, and Alexander II knew that he would have to provide new institutions of local government and law. He did so in 1864, first by creating local and provincial assemblies and giving them the right to levy taxes for local needs; and second, by decreeing equality before the law regardless of class. The Czar stopped short of a national assembly; Russia remained an autocracy. But his reforms did make the central government more efficient and rational; and they stimulated demands for a more thoroughgoing democratization of Russian society and government. Because there was little consensus among would-be reformers as to the methods to achieve their goals, the autocracy proved to be invulnerable until after the turn of the century, when military reverses would once again undermine Czarist prestige and, finally, destroy it altogether.

The Commune of Paris, 1871

As we have already seen, the capture of Napoleon III in the Franco-Prussian War allowed his Parisian republican opponents to seize power. But their efforts, through a Government of National Defense, to reverse the unfavorable war proved to be in vain, and early in 1871 this provisional regime signed an armistice with Bismarck. This national disaster only aggravated the internal questions that had divided the nation ever since 1789. During the final months before the armistice, the liberal Republicans in power had been continually criticized and intimidated by more radical Republicans in Paris. The latter succeeded in convincing large numbers of Parisians not only that they were invincible, but that the liberals sought an armistice simply to avoid having to inaugurate social and economic reforms. Antagonisms heightened when the national elections which followed the armistice produced a National Assembly that was overwhelmingly conservative, but with a Parisian delegation that was largely radical. The defeated nation found itself seriously divided—with Paris against the country.

The humiliation of defeat and a deep sense of betrayal were compounded when the harsh peace terms from Germany became known; and the radicals in Paris ended by defying the rest of the nation by establishing an independent government in city hall known as the Commune of Paris. While the regular government based in Versailles prepared to reduce Paris by force, the Commune struggled to define its program, a nearly hopeless task since its membership included a wide variety of radicals whose principles could not be made to coincide. Consequently, the rhetoric was far more radical than the deeds. The popular support for the regime in the city quickly fell off, but those who fought against the assaulting troops did so desperately and were massacred. In the final week, between 17,000 and 20,000 Parisians lost their lives.

Above all else, the Commune did represent the decentralist principle, whereas the ultimate victory of the central government amounted to one more example of the contemporary European drive toward the unitary state. This vicious civil war proved to be the last of the uprisings within the revolutionary tradition that had begun in 1789; and though a highly centralized republic finally emerged from that revolutionary tradition, the great majority of the French, remembering the violence, voted for a republic that was resolutely conservative. Marx's pamphlet, *The Civil War in France* (1871), saw the revolt of the Paris Commune as an attempt to establish a dictatorship of the proletariat, tailoring the facts to fit the Marxian theory of class conflict. Since both radicals and antiradicals tended to see the Commune in this

Marxian light, the misinterpretation affected French politics for several decades and served as a major contribution to Marxian mythology.

CHRONOLOGY: 1814 TO 1871

1814–1815:	Congress of Vienna
1830–1831:	Revolutions across Europe
1832:	First Reform Bill (Britain)
1839:	British Parliament rejects the "People's Charter"
1846–1878:	Pontificate of Pius IX
1848–1849:	Revolutions across Europe
1848:	Marx's *Communist Manifesto*
1861:	Emancipation of Russian Serfs
1864:	Papal Encyclical *Quanta Cura*
1867:	Second Reform Bill (Britain)
1869:	First Vatican Council
1871:	Commune of Paris

34
The Two Cultures of the Nineteenth Century

European civilization, deriving as it did from two major sources—the Greco-Roman and the Christian—had always borne within itself contrary tendencies and impulses that reflected its parentage. One has only to recall the various polarities encountered in the study of European history to illustrate the point: the spiritual and the temporal, the common law and the canon law, scholasticism and humanism, the classical and the romantic, the universal and the particular. Such tensions were challenges that contributed to the vitality of European civilization. Consequently, to find contrary tendencies within the civilization of nineteenth-century Europe is in itself hardly novel. Rather, what strikes one as new about the various nineteenth-century polarities was the deepening suspicion in that era that such tensions either could not be or ought not to be reconciled to give civilization stability and balance. One no longer rendered appropriately unto both Caesar and God. The whole was no longer the sum of its parts; instead, each part was often viewed as the whole.

The contemporary novelist-physicist C. P. Snow (1905–   ) has noted that our intellectual and practical lives have become polarized into literary and scientific groups, between which there is incomprehension, distrust, and open hostility. The roots of this dangerous schism are deep in the nineteenth century: the emergence of two divergent cultures. No single explanation suffices to account for this civilizational fragmentation, although a study of nineteenth-century history reveals that many of the ingredients contributing to the crisis were related.

We know, to begin with, that European society was becoming democratized in the nineteenth century, and that at the same time it was becoming secularized and industrialized. Also, the pace of life—or the pace of change—had begun to accelerate in a manner previously unknown to Europeans; the acceleration was due principally to the practical applications of modern science. Men were called on to adjust to novelties at a rate that often became uncongenial and seemed inhumane, and the continual need to choose between the "old way" and the "new way" introduced new tensions in every man's life and between the generations. If we can understand that the tempo of life for most Europeans in 1850 was more comparable to that of the thirteenth century than that of the twentieth, we can then get some sense of the distressing adjustments that life was beginning to require. An agonizing paradox was not lost on the intelligentsia in particular: as men were becoming freer politically, socially, and economically, the very dynamism of science, which contributed to that freedom, also contributed to the cultural crisis. The upshot was that not only would every "advance" increasingly be questioned, but that the notion of progress itself would become a matter of doubt.

The Democratization of European Society

Let us consider, for instance, the gradual democratization of European society in the nineteenth century. This movement was grounded in the revolutionary idea of the sovereignty of the people and a secularized expression of belief in the importance of every man. But it differed greatly in both form and substance from nation to nation and from region to region. Democratization tended to proceed more rapidly in Western Europe than in Central and Eastern Europe, but in no two countries was its course the same. In theory a democratic constitution was supposed to guarantee the rights of all citizens regardless of class, but in fact democratic constitutions were employed in the nineteenth century in both liberal and autocratic regimes. We have seen already how universal male suffrage was granted by the Second French Republic in 1848 as the foundation of modern, liberal government; and that the same universal male suffrage was used as the foundation of Napoleon III's autocracy in 1852, and used again by him as he liberalized the Empire after 1860.

Democratization in Germany

The new German Empire in 1871, through which Prussia really swallowed the other German states, was the oustanding example of democracy in an autocracy. The imperial constitution created the facade of a federal empire and representative government with a bicameral system. Sovereignty was vested in the upper house, the *Bundesrat*, which represented the governments of the member states. But since state delegations had to vote as a unit and their size was fixed by the constitution, the system was rigged to preserve Prussian dominance. These state delegations were appointed by the states they represented—not popularly elected. The *Reichstag*, the lower house, presumably shared the legislative duties with the *Bundesrat*, and here the delegates were elected by universal suffrage. By giving the *Bundesrat* the power, however, to dissolve the *Reichstag*, the imperial government possessed an easy means of checking the lower house and universal suffrage. The constitution did not even pretend to provide responsible government. Federal affairs were directed through the chancery, and the chancellor was appointed by the emperor and responsible to him alone. The whole apparatus enabled autocratic Prussia to give Germany a Prussian regime.

The ambiguities in this anachronistic empire were revealed by Cancellor Bismarck's attitude toward socialism. In 1875, various socialist factions fused to form the German Social Democratic party, which was dedicated to achieving social advances through the democratically elected *Reichstag*. Bismarck, suspecting that all socialists were at heart really anarchists, was horrified by their parliamentary gains; and in 1878 he pushed through an antisocialist law banning socialist and communist organizations and publications. Yet, even Bismarck realized the need for social legislation in an industrializing country, and in the 1880s he sponsored social security laws for the protection of workers—legislation that was liberal in spirit but in violation of laissez-faire: an accident insurance law (1885) which forced employers to insure their employees against accidents while on the job; a sickness insurance law (1885) which forced every employee making less than $500 a year to insure himself against sickness; and an old-age insurance law (1889) requiring employees making less than $500 a year to contribute, along with their employers, to a pension fund. Bismarck's leadership in "state socialism" inspired most western governments to adopt similar laws.

Democratization in Austria-Hungary

Democratization within the Austro-Hungarian Empire was a problem much complicated by the cosmopolitan nature of that Empire. After 1867, when the Hungarians obtained full autonomy in their half of the Empire, the Austrians and Hungarians viewed democratization differently. Whereas the Austrians tackled the problem of getting the minority nationalities to tolerate each other in their common loyalty to the Hapsburg dynasty, the Hungarians directed their energies toward keeping their minorities in check. Thus, Hungarian franchise laws reflected not democratization but attempts to Magyarize the minorities. In Austria, meanwhile, especially during the prime ministry of Count Taaffe (1879–1893), the minorities were urged to participate in elections for seats in the imperial Reichsrat; and the franchise was broadened, by a law of 1882. Since a concession to any given nationality was seen as an affront by the remaining nationalities, the Austrian government saw this greater participation in central government as the only possible alternative to granting local concessions. Similarly, the Austrians sought to play down the nationality issue by turning to social reforms in the manner of Bismarck.

The Austrian policies were from the start jeopardized by the strong appeal that nationalism had in the nineteenth century, as well as by the autocratic nature of the monarchy. While it is true that prime ministers usually gave up or lost office when unable to command a majority in the Reichsrat, in fact they were legally responsible only to the emperor. When universal male suffrage was at last granted in 1907 and seats in the Reichsrat were redistributed to national groups according to their population, the reforms had the effect of multiplying political factions along national lines. Instead of strengthening the monarchy, political parliamentary life became more chaotic.

Democratization in France

Even the democracy of the French Third Republic had its equivocal aspects. The constitution of 1875 provided for a bicameral National Assembly and for universal suffrage. But while the lower house, the Chamber of Deputies, was elected by direct vote of the people, the Senate was elected by a highly indirect and undemocratic procedure. The president was not popularly elected, but was chosen by the National Assembly for a seven-year term and his cabinet ministers were all responsible to the National Assembly. This deliberate attempt to shackle executive power revealed French awareness that their highly centralized state was a ready-made vehicle for any would-be dictator and that a dictator might just as easily be voted into office by the people as though a military coup d'état.

The turbulence of the political life of the Third Republic owed much to the fact that the democrats continually sought to eliminate the antidemocratic features from the constitution, while the antidemocrats strove in the opposite direction. Thus, every crisis and social scandal was blown up out

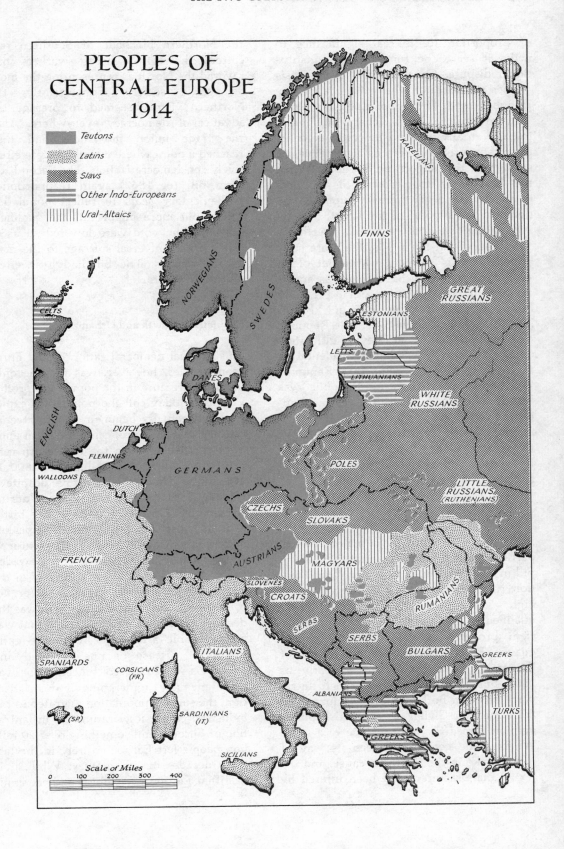

PEOPLES OF
CENTRAL EUROPE
1914

Teutons
Latins
Slavs
Other Indo-Europeans
Ural-Altaics

L A P P S

KARELIANS

NORWEGIANS

SWEDES

FINNS

GREAT
RUSSIANS

CELTS

ESTONIANS

LETTS

LITHUANIANS

WHITE
RUSSIANS

ENGLISH

DANES

DUTCH

FLEMINGS

WALLOONS

GERMANS

POLES

LITTLE
RUSSIANS
(RUTHENIANS)

CZECHS

SLOVAKS

FRENCH

AUSTRIANS

MAGYARS

SLOVENES

CROATS

RUMANIANS

SERBS

SERBS

BULGARS

GREEKS

ITALIANS

SPANIARDS

CORSICANS
(FR.)

ALBANIANS

TURKS

(SP.)

SARDINIANS
(IT.)

GREEKS

SICILIANS

Scale of Miles
0   100   200   300   400

of proportion to its real significance to make it serve the fundamental constitutional dispute. Consequently, every crisis seemed to threaten the existence of the Republic itself. The rise of a popular minister of war in the 1880s, General Boulanger, initially an ally of the democratic elements in society, was first seen as a maneuver to strengthen the democratic Republic. When the Left came to perceive his political incapacity and withdrew support, he obtained the support of the Right, thereby stimulating fear that he would overthrow the Republic. In the 1890s, the more celebrated Dreyfus Affair, growing out of an espionage case, may have begun as an attempt to obtain justice for a man probably falsely accused. But the affair quickly enlarged into a contest between the Republic and its opponents. That Dreyfus ultimately obtained justice was almost incidental in the fight to save the democratic Republic. We know today that the Republic was less threatened by such crises than it appeared to be at the time—that the great majority of the French wanted to preserve the reforms that had come from the French Revolution and would support a Republic as long as it did not become radical.

Democratization in Britain

In Britain, meanwhile, both major political parties had come to realize that the Reform Bill of 1832 had fixed a property qualification for the vote that was altogether too high. Many artisans were intellectually qualified to vote, yet did not possess sufficient property or pay sufficient rent to qualify. Proposals for a second reform of Parliament were introduced as early as 1851, but all of them fell victim to intraparty strife in both parties. The impact of the American Civil War on British public opinion forced the reform issue to a head. Whereas the gentry had seen its way of life at stake in the Southern cause, and the textile manufacturers had been injured by

the Northern blockade of Southern raw cotton, the British urban workers had favored the North as representing the more democratic society. Consequently, the Northern victory seemed to presage the advance of democracy everywhere. Also, the trade union movement had then reached a point where it could agitate effectively for democratization. The Second Reform Bill (of 1867) again reapportioned parliamentary seats to reflect population shifts; but more important, the qualifications for the vote were lowered so as to give virtual universal suffrage to the male urban workers. The bill had little effect on rural workers.

Population Growth and Urbanization

This gradual democratization of the European peoples, however, was not the only important feature in the population profile. What we today call the population explosion had actually begun in the eighteenth century, and the European population more than doubled itself in the nineteenth century—from about 187 million in 1800 to 401 million in 1900—and this despite a substantial emigration from Europe during the century. On the other hand, the birthrate in most European countries peaked and began to decline before the century's end, first in France, Norway, and Sweden before 1850, and ultimately in Italy in the 1880s. Therefore, the greatest factor accounting for the population growth was the decline in the death rate, a decline that was more notable after 1870 when the germ theory of disease became accepted and antisepsis was practiced. Since Europe was simultaneously undergoing industrialization, the surplus population migrated to the industrial cities, accelerating the urbanization of Europe; and something over 20 million people left Europe entirely in the last three decades of the century. While it is true that European technical and economic development was astounding in that period, such an emigration reveals that economic development lagged behind the population explosion.

The Prestige of Science and Technology

Science is currently unpopular among many educated people, but the opposite was true during much of modern history. For science was viewed as the key to our understanding the universe, on the basis of which we might reform human institutions; and applied science (or technology) could improve every man's standard of living. The growing enthusiasm for science and technology, often indistinguishable in the popular mind, reached its peak in the 30 years following 1870, what a distinguished historian called "a generation of materialism." By this time many in the "literary group" were highly alarmed about the future of European civilization. They saw the democratization of a rapidly increasing population as the forecast of a mass culture where creature comforts would be man's highest goal. Theirs was a vision of a new barbarism based on technology—the vulgarization of culture—a society in which individual greatness would become impossible.

Great scientific discoveries in the nineteenth century, like those in the preceding centuries, may have led to practical results but their immediate signficance was to contribute information to philosophical speculation about the nature of our universe. The climate of scientific opinion had been predominantly Newtonian in the eighteenth century, a faith that the universe is an immutable mechanism governed by unchanging laws discoverable through the proper use of human reason. But some natural scientists in that same century, by calling attention to biological evidence which suggested that species are not permanently fixed or unchanging as a result of their creation, cast doubt about the validity

of the mechanistic outlook. In 1830, Charles Lyell published his *Principles of Geology*. By showing that the earth gets its appearance from the continual action of geological processes, like erosion, volcanic action, and earthquakes, Lyell contributed evidence to those who had begun to argue for an evolutionary rather than a mechanical view of the universe.

On the other hand, Lyell's contemporary, Michael Faraday, made a celebrated report to the Royal Society in 1831 which seemed to confirm the Newtonian view. Convinced from the outset that those phenomena which he called "the forces of matter" are mutually dependent and have a common origin (in other words, that magnetism, electricity, gravitation, cohesion, heat, and light are different manifestations of the same basic power), Faraday designed his experiments to find the relation of these "forces." He was, in fact, the synthesizer of a number of contributions made by his predecessors during the 1820s in the attempt to understand electromagnetism, beginning particularly after the Danish scientist Oersted published his observation that a magnetic needle was deflected when a current of electricity flowed through it. Faraday found that a steel needle could be magnetized by subjecting it to an electric current, not only confirming the relationship of these "forces" but opening the way for practical electrical machinery, which depends on the principles of the induction of currents.

Darwinian Evolution

Theories of evolution had been in the air for a hundred years, not only in natural science, where they had been offered by Buffon and Lamarck, among others; but in philosophy, history and sociology as well, as we have seen in the cases of Comte and Marx. And Charles Darwin, in the course of his studies which led to the publication of his *Origin of Species* in 1859, knew of the evolutionary implications in Lyell's *Principles of Geology*. We ought not to say, therefore, that Darwin was the first to conceive of evolution but, instead, that he achieved a refined and novel view of evolution and successfully popularized the idea. And if the idea of evolution became acceptable after 1859, it is not merely that Darwin's views were plausible, but that many factors had paved the way for their acceptance.

In asserting that species are not permanently fixed, but are in a process of continual change, Darwin initially offered three mechanisms to explain how such differentiation and changes occur: natural selection, sexual selection, and the inheritance of acquired characteristics. He thought that the primary mechanism is natural selection, by which he meant that in the struggle for life, those individuals within a given species who possess special variations favorable to survival tend to survive and reproduce. Repeated variations and improvement through many generations result finally in a new species. It is not the least of Darwin's significance that his ideas seemed to reconcile the mechanical and evolutionary views of the universe, in that he proposed that evolution is really a mechanism. Therein lay the real grounds for intellectual dispute.

Contrary to popular notion, Darwin neither denied the existence of God nor professed to know how life was originally created. But in limiting himself to describing the mechanism that presumably governs life itself, a mechanism evidently involving neither choice nor act of individual will, he suggested that there is no purpose to life. Earlier, Lamarck (1744–1829) had explained differentiation and change through the inheritance of acquired characteristics, a deliberate response by an individual to special environmental conditions. Lamarck's view had been congenial to the romantics of the earlier nineteenth century, who not only rejected a

mechanical view of life but insisted on the ability of the individual to act and triumph in unique ways. The decline of romanticism after 1848 (of which more later) helped to provide a climate of opinion that was more congenial to Darwin's views.

Even though Darwin had emphasized natural selection, he recognized that it could only account for why a given mutation survived or failed to survive. Thus, he had reluctantly added Lamarck's assumption that acquired characteristics are inheritable to account for variation in the first place. The German zoologist Weissmann refined Darwinian theory by making a distinction between the ordinary bodily (somatic) cells and the reproductive (germ) cells. Since hereditary characteristics are transferred by the germ cells alone, it meant that acquired characteristics, being variations in somatic cells, could not be inherited. His findings left Darwinism a theory that explained the survival of variations, but not the reasons for variation.

Another major contribution to inheritance theory was made by the Augustinian monk Gregor Mendel. By carefully controlling plant fertilization, Mendel found that he could breed for certain characteristics, and that these characteristics would appear in subsequent generations in proportions that he could predict mathematically. He reasoned that this could only happen if the germ cells of each parent contained conflicting or opposite characteristics, one being dominant and the other recessive. In the union of male and female germ cells, the dominant characteristics will appear more frequently than the recessive, and always in a set mathematical proportion. Mendelian genetics could, therefore, account for the systematic perpetuation of variation in species, but it shed no more light on the purpose or meaning of evolution than Darwin had. Mendel's contribution, though published in 1870, was not discovered and publicized until 1900.

Because of the title of Darwin's 1859 book—*The Origin of Species*—it was too easily inferred that his subject was the origin of life rather than the variation and survival of species; and the misunderstanding fed the well-known controversy between the Darwinians and the religious fundamentalists. Many materialists and antireligionists of that period also misunderstood Darwin's findings, believing erroneously that he had given them a mechanical solution to the origin of life which, in particular, refuted the Bible. Scientific opinion in the mid-nineteenth century was predominantly materialistic in outlook and was prepared to accept mechanistic theories about life, including the notion that life is generated spontaneously and does not require some act of creation.

Pasteur, whose prejudices were formed by his continuing Christian faith, rejected the very idea of spontaneous generation. The experiments he began in 1860, which led to the process we call pasteurization, were based on his assumption that if one could first destroy the microbes in putrescible liquids and then isolate such liquids from microbes in the air, the liquid would remain pure indefinitely, because there would not be any spontaneous generation in the liquid. Similarly, in 1865, Pasteur was able to solve the silkworm epidemic in France only because he was prepared to treat the disease as an infectious matter rather than as a phenomenon of spontaneous generation. Having thus demonstrated the validity of the germ theory of disease, Pasteur worked for the next several decades to produce vaccines to give immunity to both animal and human diseases by learning how to attenuate the virulence of disease germs, so that a benign infection of a given disease could be used to provide immunity from that disease. Pasteur's research enabled Lister to develop procedures for antiseptic surgery in hospitals, greatly reducing the septic diseases that had always made surgery so risky and had given hospitals an evil reputation.

Advances in Chemistry and Physics

For the first half of the nineteenth century, the world of chemistry had been a battleground. In 1808, John Dalton had published an atomic theory. Each element, he proposed, has its distinctive kind of atom, and the different atoms have different weights. It was then known, for example, that water is a compound of oxygen and hydrogen. Dalton assumed that a molecule of water contained one atom of each combining gas; but when he subjected these atoms to gravimetric analysis, he found that seven parts *by weight* of oxygen combined with only one part *by weight* of hydrogen to form a molecule of water. This meant to him that an atom of oxygen is seven times heavier than an atom of hydrogen. In 1811, however, Avogadro argued that the relationship of atoms should be established by volume rather than by weight, saying that equal volumes contain an equal number of atoms, whatever the gas.

Confusion reigned until 1860 when, at an international convention of chemists, Cannizzaro proposed a way to harmonize the data on atomic weights with that on the volume of gases: Atomic proportions should be established by relative weight, oxygen being assigned a weight of sixteen; but molecular proportions should be established by gas volume. A molecule of water, therefore, since it actually contains two atoms of hydrogen and one atom of oxygen, should be written H_2O, a formula that does not reflect the relative weights of the combining atoms. During the 1860s, many chemists contributed information about atomic weights to produce the periodic table—an arrangement of the elements according to their atomic weights. And in 1870, Mendeleyev capped the work with his periodic law: When arranged by atomic weights, the periodic sequence of the elements reveals a mechanically perfect progression, and the gaps in the chart simply mean undiscovered elements. It was a stunning statement for the rational perfection of the universe.

The organization of impressive bodies of facts into systems, like that of the chemists of the 1860s and of Darwin, served the prestige of science enormously. And the field of physics had a great synthesis in that period, too, with the statement of the laws of thermodynamics. The nature of heat, and particularly the motive power of heat, had been of increasing interest beginning with the use of the steam engine. Here the key contribution was James Joule's discovery that water could be warmed by agitating it with a paddle, from which he derived a formula relating the rise in water temperature to the amount of work spent on the paddle—the mechanical equivalent of heat. This led directly to Helmholtz's statement of the first law of thermodynamics in 1847, also known as the law of conservation of energy: when heat is transformed into any other kind of energy, or vice versa, the total quantity of energy remains invariable; that is to say, the quantity of heat which disappears is equivalent to the quantity of the other kind of energy produced and vice versa. The second law of thermodynamics—the law of dissipation of energy —was described by Lord Kelvin in 1851. Admitting that the total energy of the universe is constant, he added that the useful energy was being diminished by its conversion into dissipated heat. The law implied the ultimate death of the universe with the gradual cooling of the sun.

Science and Technology

The prestige of science, however, did not depend on its discoveries or their philosophical implications, but was enhanced by the increased practical use of scientific knowledge as the pace of industrialization quickened. This activity was especially brought to public attention after mid-century in an organized manner through what we would call a world's fair—the first was the London Exhibition of 1851, which was then followed by the Paris Exposition Universelle of 1855. Visitors saw the latest application of building materials, new farm machinery, and household items designed to raise the living standards of the poor. Science, philosophy, and the arts all were engaged in the pursuit of truth; but science alone produced engines, medicine, and domestic comforts.

The phrase "generation of materialism," to characterize the last 30 years of the nineteenth century, referred both to the mechanization of thought—that is, the vogue of Darwinism with its mechanical implications —and to the enormous expansion of European industry with its promise for better material living for the average man. Even though that generation had its important skeptics, it was popularly supposed that science and technology would soon solve all human dilemmas. That the proof of such an assumption lay in the appearance of the first telephone (1876), the incandescent lamp (1878), electric cars and trams (1881), the electric sewing machine (1889), and wireless telegraphy (1896) suggests the shallowness of the popular appraisal.

Scientific Advances: 1890–1915

The discoveries in science, however, continued to be impressive. In 1895, Roentgen found x rays while investigating cathode rays, and the practical application of x rays in diagnostic medicine was almost immediate. What is more, the x rays proved to be the key to other discoveries that brought physics from its Newtonian to its modern (or quantum) stage. Studying some of Roentgen's observations led Becquerel to the discovery of radioactivity a few months later; and in 1899 Marie Curie concluded that radioactive atoms are unstable atoms in the process of disintegration, thus releasing energy. In the same decade, Thomson, trying to relate electrical and atomic properties, found particles within atoms which carried negative charges of electricity. These were later called electrons, and the phenomenon revealed that atoms are composite, not simple, entities.

Soon after the turn of the century, two more revolutionary ideas further undermined traditional physics to lead us into the atomic age. Classical physics had held time to be an absolute, so that the past, present, and future were perfectly clear and unmistakable terms. Space, too, was seen as an absolute, within which all phenomena were seen in three dimensions. The system was applicable to this world alone; but in 1905, Einstein began his description of new laws of mechanics that would be absolutely applicable in all coordinate systems—not merely to earth. Since the only constant factor to be related to motion is the velocity of light, he proposed that motion is always relative to the motion and position of the observer. This made it possible for Einstein to suggest that the interval between the past and the future has a finite extension in time which depends on the distance in space between an event and its observer. In this view, space and time attain an absolute character only when they are fused (space-time) and become part of a four-dimensional continuum. Einstein's proposal was called the theory of relativity for evident reason, but was in fact a new absolutism.

Because the Newtonians had regarded the universe as a precise mechanism whose motions could be predicted with exactness, it was disturbing to discover at the end of the nineteenth century that the classical electromagnetic theory could not account for the emission and absorption of radiation. Max Planck suggested a new physical mechanism to account for the phenomenon —the quantum theory. It had been held that the energy of an oscillator depends solely on its frequency and amplitude, but Planck suggested that an oscillator may possess only discrete amounts of energy—even

though he was distressed philosophically by the idea that natural processes could be discontinuous.

The Protest Against Mechanism and Materialism: The Romantics

The literary, philosophical, and artistic protest against materialism—and particularly the protest against the popular view that technology is the road to human salvation —was rooted in what we have called the "romantic spirit." One can, in fact, trace the origins of the romantic movement back to the eighteenth century, to those who already rejected the mechanistic, rigid view of the universe characteristic of rationalism and classicism. Instead of the eternal and the universal, the romanticist emphasized the changing and the particular—a more subjective, individualized, complicated view of reality. Nature was no longer the elegantly perfect mechanism to be comprehended rationally, but a thing of beauty revealed through our senses. The set values of the classical or rational outlook were giving way to relative values, truth defined as something individually perceived. This willingness to emphasize both the particular and those things which change contributed to the European climate which fostered empiricism and made it easier to accept evolutionary theories in a variety of fields. Therefore, one must be careful to note that the romanticist was not opposed to science itself, merely to those scientific theories that viewed man and his universe as mechanisms.

The Romantic Philosophers

Perhaps the most distinctive philosopher of the romantic period was Hegel (1770-1831), because of his idea that *being* is a process of *becoming*, which epitomized the changing, or evolutionary, view of life. In this view, to exist is to change, to grow, to evolve toward a goal. Moreover, he believed that the *striving* for a goal gives life its significance and meaning, and that the goal which the human spirit seeks is freedom. He meant us to understand that freedom emerges not from passivity, but from conflict; and he used an argument, or dialectic, to illustrate how we progress toward higher truths in our striving. It is the conflict between a thesis and its necessary antithesis, which ultimately produces a synthesis—which is at once a higher statement of truth and a new thesis. The process continues endlessly, like evolution itself, meaning that the goal is never really achieved. Thus, the meaning in our lives derives not from attaining the goal, but in our awareness of the goal and our struggle to reach it.

When one has reviewed the various traits of romanticism—individual expression, subjectivity, the rejection of classical rigidity, the reliance on intuition and the senses—one must note that not all romantics shared these qualities to an equal degree. In particular, some were equivocal in their rejection of rationalism, seeking to harmonize the universal with the individual to achieve a balanced view of reality and the human condition. Goethe (1749-1832), for instance, feared that the subjectivity in romanticism could lead to self-indulgence or despair, yet he insisted in the best romantic fashion on the striving for a rich personal life, struggling for the noble goal regardless of its attainability. We are thus introduced to a tragic vision, as in his *Faust*, of man's existence: that we must struggle for fuller knowledge in the full realization that we will fall short of fulfillment. And there can be no surrender, even though we recognize our goal to be forever elusive. "This is wisdom's final word," he wrote, "Worthy alone is he of life and freedom, Who conquers them anew each day." This tragic view of human reality, characteristic of the romantic spirit, was a far cry from the enthusiasm engendered by the technological progress of the nineteenth century.

Another aspect of the rejection of ration-

alism emerged from the apparent failure of "enlightened" laws to bring peace and order in the time of the French Revolution and Napoleon. Traditions and standards may have been destroyed by the revolution, but the perfect society had not replaced them. The general disenchantment characteristic of so much of the European intelligentsia by the beginning of the nineteenth century led some of them to seek a spiritual awakening as the key to man's dilemma. Chateaubriand (1767-1848) was the outstanding example of a former rationalist who became reconciled with traditional Christianity, claiming it to be the only salvation for mankind. Mysticism and pietism enjoyed a revival, especially in the German world—intensely private religion directed toward individual rather than universal salvation. Yet, under the influence of German mysticism, Czar Alexander I proposed his Holy Alliance in 1815, which was not so much a treaty as it was a statement of principles as a basis for international cooperation. He hoped that the European monarchs would regard each other as "brothers" and their subjects as "families" in the Christian sense.

As Goethe had recognized, romanticism could reach extremes of despair, a condition he had flatly called disease. The black melancholy of Kierkegaard (1813-1855), for example, while it clearly derived from a dreadful childhood and physical deformities, left him incapable of concern for society or mankind. In that century when most intellectuals continued to reject Christianity, Kierkegaard was a believer; but he was entirely indifferent to the misery of others in his concern for his private despair. "The thing is to find a truth which is a truth for me," he wrote in 1835, "to find the idea for which I can live and die." His Christianity was intensely private and existentialist.

Schopenhauer (1788-1860) was another philosopher of despair. Like Kant in the previous century, Schopenhauer believed that the contradictions represented by theses and antitheses are generally beyond solution by human reason, and he had no patience with Hegel's confidence in inevitable progress. For Schopenhauer, the world was inherently evil, and its only reality was what we perceive through our senses. This loathesome reality was to be avoided at all cost, all the more difficult in his view as our basic drive is our will to live in this world of misery. One could only avoid this real world Schopenhauer believed, by giving oneself to contemplation, and to the contemplation of art in particular.

The Romantic Writers and Artists

On the whole it is fruitless to try to associate romantic philosophers and artists as a group with a particular political party or faction. Indeed, if one seeks generalizations about their public attitudes, one might first note that the romantics' penchant for individual perception of truth and beauty, their willingness to break with convention, inclined them to radical postures, whether on the Left or the Right. Lacking practical political experience—and often despising those who did—their views were as brilliant and humane and imaginative as they were often impractical or naive. This in itself might not distinguish them from their counterparts in other centuries. What was characteristic of artists and writers in particular in the romantic century was their refusal to come to terms with a society caught up in swift commercial and industrial expansion, seeing themselves as the sword and shield of a civilization endangered by the dragon of crass materialism. For them, mankind was not to be saved by advancing technology or by a religious revival, but somehow to be redeemed by art. Science was fine so long as it remained speculative and unapplied, and especially when it used its heaviest guns to blast at religious positions. But the redeemer's role was reserved for art. As the century deepened, the democratization of society—the rise of the masses—was seen as

another dimension of barbaric materialism, at which point artistic protest often became elitist rather than liberal.

Lord Byron (1788-1824) and Shelley (1792-1822), who scandalized their nation with advanced opinions and erratic behavior, were characteristic of the earlier romantic generations. They were rebels against all authority and convention, seeing their own homeland as the worst possible example of obtuseness and repression. Both left England for the continent after 1815. In Paris, Victor Hugo sought to have his romantic drama *Hernani* produced in 1830. Aware that neoclassicists were out to destroy the play with hisses, Hugo mustered a throng of romanticists to defend his right to have the play staged, including Balzac, Stendhal, Gautier, Berlioz, and Delacroix. This episode should remind us that neoclassicism lived on into the nineteenth century with distinguished representatives like the painter Ingres (1780-1867),

Jean-Auguste Ingres, "Mademoiselle Riviere". (Cliche des Musees Nationaux, Louvre)

Eugene Delacroix, "Oriental Lion Hunt". (Museum of Fine Arts, Boston, S. A. Denio Collection)

even though romanticism had become the dominant creed. The neoclassical calm and impersonality, as well as the superb drawing, in Ingres' canvases, was a far cry from the boldness of design, the bright colors, and the fascination with action and struggle characteristic of Géricault (1791-1824) and Delacroix (1799-1863). Berlioz was the composer who was most revolutionary in abandoning traditional symphonic form, in the liberties he took in orchestration, and in the lavishness of his individualism. His *Symphonie Fantastique*, first performed in 1830, still sounds astonishingly modern, yet came on the scene only three years after Beethoven's death.

In its rejection of universal truths and rigid form, romanticism emphasized not simply individualism, but often the individual nationality within European civilization. The subject matter of the arts was in-

creasingly historical or patriotic; and Weber (1786-1826), endeavoring to develop a German opera distinct from the Italian, drew on folklore and folk melodies. Most of Sir Walter Scott's (1771-1832) well-known novels, appearing after 1814, were set in either historical England or Scotland; just as the elder Dumas's (1803-1870) were set in historical France. Aside from appealing to the national past, such works were nonpolitical.

Yet the romantic novelist could give his work a contemporary setting—the greatest of them did—and it is much to the point that many such novels were either acid commentaries on the conventions of bourgeois society or protests against the conditions of life in the industrializing towns. Such romanticists were but a step from the literary realism that became predominant in Europe after 1848, and they exuded the pessimism common to all those who had become disenchanted with classical idealism. In 1831, Stendhal published *The Red and the Black*, the story of a young upstart who chose clerical black rather than military red in his scheme to rise in a corrupt society. His calculated love affairs and his blatant opportunism were Stendhal's way of commenting on the public and private morality of his day, a morality that Stendhal both despised and feared he shared. In *The Charterhouse of Parma* (1839), Stendhal revealed the pettiness of the reactionary regimes restored after the greatness of the Napoleonic era. The protest movement took a feminist twist in the novels of George Sand, whose heroines were restless romantics. She drew in particular upon her own emotional experiences for *Indiana* (1831) and *Lelia* (1833).

In 1842, Balzac began a detailed survey of French life through a series of novels under the overall title *The Human Comedy*, establishing the tradition of "documentary" novels that Zola would perfect later in the century. Balzac's hatred of the society of industrializing, commercial France is continually evident in his novels. He had the romanticist's contempt for the unexciting, stingy standards set by King Louis-Philippe himself, a world in which bankruptcy was the greatest of all possible tragedies. His subjects were taken from real life, though he used his imagination freely in their rendering.

Even the Russian czar admitted that Gogol's exposure of corruption and hypocrisy in high places in his play *The Government Inspector* (1836) was fair, and Gogol went on to include a sharp denunciation of serfdom in his novel *Dead Souls* (1842). Gogol's crisp characterizations remind us of his English contemporary, Charles Dickens, the most popular of early Victorian novelists. At once realistic and melodramatic, some of Dickens' works were also propagandistic. His *Oliver Twist* (1838), for example, commented on the harshness of the Poor Law of 1834 and in *Nicholas Nickleby* (1839), he revealed the need for school reform. On the whole, Dickens' novels portrayed lower-class life. For criticism of upper-class life, one may turn to Thackery's *Vanity Fair* (1847) or to his *Henry Esmond* (1852). The lithographer-journalist Daumier (1808-1879) was spiritually akin to such novelists. His subject matter, with few exceptions, was the unpleasant, the ugly, the grotesque, the inhumanity to be found on all sides, and the shallow pompousness of the middle class. One finds here no visions of beauty or progress, but contempt for that which degrades humanity—the conviction that the human comedy is really the human tragedy.

Realism

The failure of the political romantics in 1848 and the consequent emergence of the "blood and iron" politicians had its artistic counterpart in realism. In true realism, the artists not only rejected the ideal or the rational, but abandoned the personal and the individual, deliberately choosing subjects from the everyday world, striving to be impersonal in recording what they saw. And generally they saw life as brutish and mankind as weak. Realism continued, therefore, the tradition of social criticism; and the writers became zealous fact collectors to provide the raw material for their novels. This school was most notably represented by Flaubert (1821-1880) and later by Zola (1840-1902), who called himself a naturalist. What was new in their work was a conscious desire to close the widening gap between those in the literary culture and those in the sciences. Theirs was, in fact, a faith in science. Flaubert argued that the only hope for the human race was to make "science prevail." Zola went even further by trying to turn literature into a scientific enterprise, insisting on "scientific" objectivity in the portrayal of reality. Beginning in 1870, this Darwinian of the arts sketched out a series of 20 novels through which he meant to describe all aspects of life under the fallen imperial regime: *The Natural and Social History of a Family Under the Second Empire*. This great endeavor was completed in 1893, a vast canvas of social evils. But for all its documentation, the focus on the sordid and the appalling did not provide a balanced view of life under the Second Empire. What was great in Zola was his art, not his science.

The Attack on Commercialism

The main thrust of cultural opinion after 1848, however, was hostility to materialism and commercialism, the very things which science, through technology, was aiding if not intentionally abetting. This passion took the form (as it had with the earlier romanticists) of contempt for everything bourgeois. Though they identified the bourgeois with all that was gross, they meant by *bourgeois* a spirit, an attitude, rather than a class, just as Matthew Arnold (1822-1888), condemning the barbarism of mid-century life, used the term *Philistine* to describe "exuberant self-satisfaction" of those Englishmen who saw material progress as the guarantee of human happiness. Both Arnold and John Ruskin (1819-1900) warned against the development of an ethics founded on acquisitiveness. If the right to acquire should become the standard measure, Ruskin predicted that national destruction would follow.

They referred to acquisitiveness for its own sake, and to all those—regardless of class—who never subordinate self-interest to exterior claims. To be *bourgeois* was to prefer security to grandeur, to seek wealth rather than truth or beauty. Cultural vitality, therefore, was still equated to the old romantic passion for individual greatness. The poet Baudelaire (1821–1867), in despair for the future, thought that the time was soon at hand when the young man would leave home, "not in search of heroic adventures, not to deliver a beautiful prisoner from a tower, not to immortalize a

garret with his sublime thoughts: but to start a business, to grow rich, to enter into competition with his vile papa." Indeed, since the economic realities of the nineteenth century pointed to the increasing availability of the things of this world, and to their worship, the cultural protest against materialism took on the guise of a crusade against the Philistines.

The Cultural Elite

Such cultural zealots, seeing themselves as the few pitted against the masses, often regard themselves as a new aristocracy. Their elitism, however, took a variety of forms: In some, we see the search for new energy, for boldness; in others we find extreme individualism and extravagent preciousness. In the 1860s, the word "impressionism" was used to describe the work of a new school of young painters, notably Manet, Degas, Monet, and Renoir, who were opposed in theory to both neoclassicism and romanticism. They painted "what they saw," especially the outdoor world, seeking to create the visual impression of the moment, but as the human eye sees, not the camera. Hence, they blurred, often distorted canvases to suggest how we really see things at a glance. In the following decade men like Van Gogh and Gauguin, calling themselves expressionists, went beyond impressionism by insisting that the painting should reveal the artist's emotion when he is recording his impression on canvas. The result was great individuality and vivid color.

Elitism did not necessarily bring its practitioners spiritual relief. Gauguin's well-known abandonment of his family for a life of art on Tahiti may have symbolized the artist's challenge to bourgeois conventionality, but his heroic gesture ended in wretchedness. The playwright Ibsen (1828-1906), abhoring the social conventions of his native Norway, went into Italian exile; yet, haunted by his past, he set his plays in the dark, cold country of his birth, thus achieving even a grimmer view of reality. Because the majority in any society are necessarily wedded to social conventions, the libertarian Ibsen equated democracy to mediocrity and conventionality. Similarly, Flaubert, in the 1870s, toyed with the idea of leaving France as a place likely to become uninhabitable for people of taste. The Goncourt brothers predicted that man's rash ventures into science would bring mankind to its end. Having heard a famous scientist estimate in 1869 that in a hundred years our knowledge of organic law would enable us to create life in competition with God, they recorded that at such a moment, God in His white beard would descend to earth, swinging a bunch of keys, and say to mankind as the attendant at the museum says at five o'clock: "Closing time, gentlemen."

That the great Russian novelists after mid-century seem so different from their Western counterparts reflects the backwardness of Russia and a different set of problems. Dostoevski's exile was imposed by the state in 1849—four terrible years in Siberia among the Empire's most vicious criminals—for having been a member of a revolutionary society. His later novels, especially *Crime and Punishment* (1866), were admired for their psychological insights, another characteristic of realism. Hating the social evils and the autocracy of Russia, Dostoevski still had the capacity to perceive the evil in all men. Tolstoy (1828–1910), whether in his novels or in his religious essays, was consumed by moral and philosophical problems, relating them to the way people ought to live. The ancient Russian preoccupation with the mystical flowered anew in Tolstoy. Though he struggled to believe that, in this evil world, mankind's salvation lies solely in ultimate redemption and rectification, the lack of serenity in his personal life suggests that he shared the spiritual doubts of the generation of materialism. "I have been thinking about the Divinity of God for a long time," he wrote in 1877, "Don't say that we must not think about it. Not only we must, but we ought. In all ages the best people, the true people, have thought about it."

Such concerns were a far cry from those elitists whose sense of civilizational doom led them into what we might call aestheticism. Here the manifestations ranged from dandyism to a high-minded hedonism; that is, the belief that the richest life is the one spent in pursuit of pleasure through beauty. Theirs was not an art of social criticism, but, in the phrase of Walter Pater (1839–1894), the "love of art for art's sake." In this view, art should give us nothing but the highest quality to the moments as they pass. Aestheticism seems to have been a logical protest on the part of those who rejected the implications of material progress, who associated such progress with the democratization of society, and who had come to the conclusion that the rare, creative imagination of artists was being prostituted by the vulgar fact collectors of the realist school: the mechanistic bondage of the creative soul. These aesthetes, in other words, lumped the realists with the very bourgeois society the realists had condemned.

Although the aesthetes were highly individualistic by definition, they all equated beauty with art—with artificiality. The poet Baudelaire, with a poisonous hatred of nature and for the most of society, transmuted the most appalling aspects of the industrializing, urban reality about him into poetic beauty, the *Flowers of Evil* (1857). His lines may have enabled others to see beauty where it had not been seen before; but for Baudelaire, the lines amounted to a perverted glorification of all that he hated, which included his own defects. Thus, if Baudelaire was among the first to enlarge the scope of artistic subject matter to include the vulgar, he was also among the first to protest against vulgarity.

Elitism, in its variety of forms, now seems to have been the attempt to create a cultural aristocracy to replace the fading blooded aristocracy: an aristocracy of talent made possible only by the democratization of society in the nineteenth century, yet in revolt against the democratization and contemptuous of innovations that were making the lives of ordinary people increasingly bearable. The people were seen as a stupid, destructive beast, which must be contained by the authoritarian state. The earlier hope that the arts could redeem mankind through the revelation of the most fundamental truths had given way to the notion that art is superior to life. A true religion, in other words, had been corrupted into an idolatry of the arts. The precious artificiality of the idolators was well-epitomized by Stefan George, the German poet (1868–1933): "My garden requires no air and no sun."

Violence in Nineteenth-Century Thought

After the gigantic calamity that was the First World War, historians necessarily sought its causes, looking in particular through the diplomatic records to find out which power, or powers, had been most responsible for bringing on the war. This endeavor, while intellectually respectable, often concealed the fact that the European climate of opinion after 1848 had been subtly drifting toward violence. One must hastily add that, of course, violence has always been present in history. What changes historically is our attitude toward violence: That is, the degree or the pervasion of violence can be affected by a society's view of its desirability or its inevitability. The conservative order that held sway in Europe after 1815, for instance, was determined to use both diplomacy and force to maintain the general peace settlement, holding the localized use of force to be preferable to the generalized European conflict of the previous 25 years.

Throughout the century, Britain used her monopoly of sea power toward the same end: to limit rather than to eliminate violence.

After 1848, however, we become aware that the moral abhorrence of violence had weakened, and that the future belonged to those who hitched violence to progress. The benevolent, cosmopolitan nationalism of the early century brought freedom to no nationality. That required blood and iron—notably in the cases of Italy and Germany. The history of radicalism seemed to parallel that of nationalism: A benevolent utopianism gave way to a belief in violence after mid-century. This is seen not simply in the Marxian summons to revolution, but in the anarchism of Bakunin (1814–1876), who advocated the immediate destruction of the state. His ideas, his insistence that men should obey nothing but the laws of nature, might remind us of Proudhon; but Bakunin went far beyond him in demanding the *violent* destruction of existing society. Bakunin's anarchism, in fact, illustrates another form of political extremism: the rejection of contemporary morality or religion on which all social, economic, and political institutions are based: hence, the justification for their destruction. The later nineteenth century called that prescription *nihilism*.

It takes nothing away from the elegance of Darwin's work if we recognize that his theories reached an audience well prepared to think of life as a struggle for survival. Any intellectual worthy of that name had to have an opinion on evolution after 1859, and not simply to keep apace with the nonintellectuals. Darwin himself saw "grandeur" in his view of life—that from a simple beginning "endless forms most beautiful and most wonderful have been, and are being evolved." Some of the Darwinians, furthermore, saw in the principle of evolution the guarantee of progress—that progress is not an accident but a necessity. Consequently, Herbert Spencer (1820–

1903) could happily look forward to a day when evil and immortality must disappear and man must become perfect.

Racism

Racial theories and racism had been known in Europe since antiquity, and the word "racial" had long been used loosely to mean national. So that after Darwin, when it became fashionable to discuss species and, in particular, those fittest to survive, it was but a step to compare the European "races" as to their "fitness." Thus, German political and military preeminence after 1870 was said to prove that the Germanic "race" was the fittest; hence, it was a superior "race." This seemed to square with Gobineau's *Essay on the Inequality of Races,* published in 1854. An aristocrat, Gobineau and actually not meant to ascribe racial superiority to any one nation. On the contrary, he tried to prove the superiority of the French aristocracy over the masses of the French people on the grounds that the aristocracy represented pure Germanic or Frankish stock, while the people were an impure mixture of many "races." Indeed, he thought that the German masses were just as "racially" mixed as the French masses. But because he described aristocratic superiority in Frankish or Germanic terms, he was widely understood by the 1880s to have demonstrated the superiority of all Germans. Thus Richard Wagner, working to construct a national German art, could conclude that a purely Germanic art (his own) must necessarily be superior to that of other "races."

Such racial theories were more easily swallowed in that day, not merely because Darwinian biology was claimed to sanction them; but because in an era of increasing national antagonisms, patriots grasped at any facts which seemed to justify those antagonisms. To think of nationalities or races as superior of inferior was a long step away from regarding them as unique and possessing different (and valuable) qualities. Racial theories, indeed, have historically always been advanced for deliberate political goals. After 1871, especially, "racial"' prejudices were cultivated to help justify discriminatory legislation against minorities in various nation-states in the interest of centralization and national unity. National as well as religious minorities felt the lash of discrimination: "One law, one language, and one religion," as one Russian statesman put it. A feature of such nationalist programs was an upswing in anti-semitism, in response to which a Hungarian Jew, Theodor Herzl, in 1896 launched the Zionist movement: the search for a Jewish national state, preferably in Palestine.

The Death of God and the Rise of Superman

For some like Herbert Spencer, the theory of evolution may have been an optimistic guarantee of human progress, but for others the theory seemed to underscore our brutish qualities, permitting only pessimism. Nietzsche (1844–1900), Spencer's contemporary, prepared for a pessimistic outlook by Schopenhauer, saw that the distinction between man and animal had been abolished by Darwin. This was the ultimate in secularization, if one may so state it, and led Nietzsche logically to conclude that "God is dead." Moreover, he turned the tables on those who argued for inevitable progress by pointing to the immense time it takes for evolutionary changes to be effected. It made no more sense to wait passively for mankind to evolve than to believe that our animal ancestry permits us instincts for the good, the beautiful, and the true.

Our true nature, Nietzsche said, is to strive for power, to strive for greatness, so that an aristocracy of supermen shall emerge. His was a reassertion of the romantic spirit, an elitist protest against the substitution of mass culture for vital individualism, an attack on all aspects of the vulgarization of life. The violence of Nietzsche's words were later taken to mean that he was the champion of brute force, that he thought of the superman as a superior physical animal who would smash culture as a decadent and odious phenomenon. While it is true that he hated the climate of democratization in the late nineteenth century, his supreme value was culture and its creation. His superman's strength was the vitality and refinement of the truly civilized man. He had no sympathy for racism and its associated nationalism, predicting that they would destroy the German spirit, which he defined as the concern for eternal, universal questions. Since he saw the great dilemmas of mankind as unchanging, he could not avoid being contemptuous of notions of human progress; he was clearly a man of the "literary culture."

Creative Evolution and Religious Revival

In 1907, Henri Bergson published his *Creative Evolution*. He proposed, as evolutionists like Hegel and Darwin had before him, that the world is in a state of flux, that change is the fundamental truth about reality. Bergson's particular twist, however, was his statement that, beginning with the original creation of matter and mind by God, evolution has been the continuing creation of new forms in the universe. The world may be mechanical, obeying strict laws, he argued, but man's *intuition*, his consciousness, enables him to overcome such rigidities and to be free of mechanical determinisms in his search for truth and freedom. "To exist is to change, to change is to mature, to mature is to go on creating oneself endlessly." This may not give evolution a precise meaning, but it gave evolution vitality, what he called creative vitality: *élan vital*. Bergson would admit that man may be an animal—but an intelligent animal. Our intuition, in other words, is not animal instinct, but one form of human intelligence.

The immediate popularity of his ideas suggests how eager Europeans were to find explanation for life that both coped with the latest scientific discoveries and gave man a role which transcended the mere mechanical. By the beginning of the twentieth century, in fact, one sees signs of a growing awareness that, though man may have originated in the state of nature, his emergence into the state of society put him into a realm where nature's laws do not necessarily apply. Man may still have to contend with his ancestry and with the fact that he shares the planet with the other creatures of nature; but in society man has become so various, able to manifest himself in so great a variety of forms, as to raise doubts about our ability to know about *the* nature of man. If this is so, the proper study of man cannot be limited to biology. As Wilhelm Dilthey (1833–1911) believed, "What man is, only his history tells."

Such an outlook implied that we have to settle for something less than certainty, to accommodate ourselves to the mysterious. It pointed the way not merely to religion but, as in Bergson's case, to mysticism: the private, romantic search for unique knowledge. Organized religion, too, showed signs of accommodating itself to the modern world by the end of the century. Many Europeans had come to assume that the Church was losing its fight for survival in the modern world, not simply because Pius IX had announced in 1864 that he would not come to terms with modern civilization; but because the spiritual truths the Church represented lacked believers in the generation of materialism, and the peace of God was nonsense to those who saw violence as the key to progress.

During the pontificate of Leo XIII (1878–1903), however, the papacy abandoned its traditional alliances with conservative governments, repeatedly warning that the Church was not married to any form of secular government. Through a series of encyclicals, the pope showed that Christianity had constructive alternatives to the evils of materialism, and that Christianity could become progressive and scientific in spirit. If Leo XIII attacked socialism for denying men their "natural right" to possess property, he also rejected the laissez-faire view that labor should be regarded as a commodity in a free market. He denied that class warfare is the natural state of man, but added that "it is shameful and inhuman to treat men like chattels to make money by, or to look upon them merely as so much muscle or physical power." Roman Catholicism, in other words, while still professing its faith in an otherwordly salvation, served notice of its intention to fight all dogmas that held men to be mere brutes and all institutions that reduced men to brutish existence.

Freud

Whereas Dilthey studied history as the key to mankind's "nature," Sigmund Freud

Sigmund Freud (Brown Brothers)

focused on the private history of each individual. Freud is known to us as the inventor of psychoanalysis, which he defined as the "discovery of the unconscious in mental life," and which has made us more aware of the nonrational impulses that underlie human nature. He taught a new technique of observation—that we must try to see others as full individuals: both the rational and the nonrational, the conscious and the unconscious, the obvious and the mysterious. Psychoanalysis was based on the theory of repression—that is, that society necessarily represses the individual, and the individual represses himself. Thus, the individual really disowns some of his ideas and desires, forcing them into his unconscious, where the conscious will no longer be aware of them. But banishment does not render them impotent. Dreams, neurotic symptoms, and slips of the tongue reveal both the presence and the nature of our unconscious ideas and desires.

Freud concluded that we are all neurotic, for the same reason that civilization itself, as the initial represser, is the source of neuroses. His view of man, therefore, was entirely pessimistic. Though Freudian therapy was designed to force the unconscious into the consciousness so that we might understand the wellsprings of the conflicts within us, Freud saw that human life is fraught with pain, disappointment, and insuperable tasks. We may have the right to the pursuit of happiness, but we find only suffering.

Reflections on Violence

The intellectual and cultural life of Europe in those years immediately before the outbreak of general war, in sum, was immensely vigorous, if often pessimistic. But on the whole the thinkers did not anticipate the great war, perhaps because as a group they were so nonpolitical. The intellectual and artistic elitists remained essentially indifferent to international affairs in particular. If they predicted catastrophe, it was their reaction to the technological revolution and to the decline in moral values. Yet the forces of nationalism and socialism, increasingly militant in the decades before 1914, were on the verge of destroying the old order of nineteenth-century Europe.

The case of Georges Sorel (1847–1922) illustrates the point. A retired railroad engineer, he was an advocate of violence without ever suspecting the actual form of the violence that was to come. Hating the politicians of the Third Republic and seeing its democracy as the road to mediocrity and moral degeneration, he published, in 1908, his *Reflections on Violence* as a formula for national regeneration. His ideas were a curious mash of Marxian dialectical materialism, the Nietzschen will to power, and Bergsonian *élan vital*. The energy and the regeneration of the future he thought could come only from the proletariat; and he saw the labor union (or syndicate) as the logical organization to promote the proletarian revolution. The general strike, moreover, would be the ultimate weapon in class warfare. This formula came to be called syndicalism. It called not for reason, but for violence— for direct action. Sorel may not have preducted World War I, but his ideas proved to be congenial to those men who would lead the postwar dictatorial states: men who, whether Leftist or Rightist, accepted violence as *the* solution to social and international problems. As Ortega y Gasset would later write, Sorel's system amounted to the Magna Carta of barbarism.

CONSOLIDATED CHRONOLOGY FOR PART 9: THE NINETEENTH CENTURY

1814–1815:	Congress of Vienna
1815:	Battle of Waterloo
1815–1848:	Metternich Era
1822–1829:	Greek Revolution
1830:	Lyell's *Principles of Geology*
1830–1831:	Revolutions across Europe
1832:	First Reform Bill (Britain)
1846–1878:	Pontificate of Pius IX
1847:	First Law of Thermodynamics
1848–1849:	Revolutions across Europe
1851–1871:	Ascendency of Napoleon III
1851:	Second Law of Thermodynamics
1851:	London Exhibition
1854–1855:	Crimean War
1856:	Congress of Paris
1859:	Darwin's *Origin of Species*
1859–1870:	Unification of Italy
1866:	Seven Weeks War (Prussia and Austria)
1867:	Second Reform Bill (Britain)
1867:	Creation of Dual Monarchy of Austria-Hungary
1869:	First Vatican Council
1870:	Mendeleyev's Periodic Law
1870–1871:	Franco-Prussian War
1871:	Commune of Paris
1871–1890:	The Bismarck era
1878–1903:	Pontificate of Leo XIII
1878:	Congress of Berlin
1879:	Dual Alliance (Germany and Austria-Hungary)
1882:	Triple Alliance (Germany, Austria-Hungary, and Italy)
1887:	Reinsurance Treaty (Germany and Russia)
1894:	Franco-Russian Alliance
1895:	Beginning of Freud's studies on the subconscious
1895:	Roentgen discovers x rays
1900:	Quantum Theory proposed
1902:	Anglo-Japanese Alliance
1904–1905:	Russo-Japanese War
1904:	Entente Cordiale (Britain and France)
1905:	Theory of Relativity
1907:	Anglo-Russian Entente
1907:	Bergson's *Creative Evolution*
1908:	Young Turk Revolution
1912:	First Balkan War
1913:	Second Balkan War
1914–1918:	World War I

SUGGESTED READINGS

The asterisk indicates a paperback edition. Luigi Albertini, *The Origins of the War of*

1914, 3 vols. (Oxford: Oxford University Press 1952–1957).

Fredrick B. Artz, *Reaction and Revolution 1814–1832* (*New York: Harper, 1934).

Jacques Barzun, *Romanticism and the Modern Ego* (*Boston: Little, Brown, 1943).

Jacques Barzun, *Darwin, Marx, Wagner* (*New York: Doubleday Anchor, 1958).

Robert C. Binkley, *Realism and Nationalism 1852–1871* (*New York: Harper, 1935).

Georges Bonnin, *Bismarck and the Hohenzollern Candidature for the Spanish Throne* (London: Chatto and Windus, 1957).

Louis de Broglie, *The Revolution in Physics* (*New York: Noonday, 1953).

Geoffrey Bruun, *Revolution and Reaction 1848–1852, A Mid-Century Watershed* Princeton, N.J.: Anvil, 1958).

Rondo Cameron, *France and the Economic Development of Europe 1800–1914* (*Chicago: Rand McNally, 1965).

Guy Chapman, *The Dreyfus Case, A Reassessment* (New York: Reynal, 1965).

Clement V. Durell, *Readable Relativity* (*New York: Harper, 1960).

Georges Duveau, *1848: The Making of a Revolution* (*New York: Vintage, 1967).

Loren Eiseley, *Darwin's Century, Evolution and the Men Who Discovered It* (*New York: Doubleday Anchor, 1961).

Herbert Feis, *Europe, The World's Banker, 1870–1914* (New Haven, Conn.: Yale University Press, 1950).

Harvey Goldberg, *The Life of Jean Jaures* (Madison: University of Wisconsin Press, 1962).

César Graña, *Bohemian Versus Bourgeois, French Society and the French Man of Letters in the Nineteenth Century* (New York: Basic Books, 1964).

Elie Halévy, *The Growth of Philosophical Radicalism* (*Boston: Beacon, 1955).

Carlton J. H. Hayes, *A Generation of Materialism 1871–1900* (*New York: Harper, 1941).

Gertrude Himmelfarb, *Lord Action, A Study in Conscience and Politics* (*Chicago: University of Chicago Press, 1952).

Michael Howard, *The Franco-Prussian War: The German Invasion of France, 1870–71*

(*New York: Macmillan, 1961).

J. Hampden Jackson, *Clemenceau and the Third Republic* (*New York: Collier, 1962).

Barbara Jelavich, *The Hapsburg Empire in European Affairs 1814–1918* (Chicago: Rand McNally, 1969).

Roderick Kedward, *The Dreyfus Affair* (*London: Longmans, Green, 1965).

Henry A. Kissinger, *A World Restored: Metternich, Castlereagh, and the Problems of Peace* (*Boston: Houghton Mifflin, 1957).

Hans Kohn, *Pan-Slavism: Its History and Ideology* (*New York: Vintage, 1960).

William L. Langer, *Political and Social Upheaval, 1832–1852* (*New York: Harper, 1970).

Georg Lukacs, *Studies in European Realism* (*New York: Grosset & Dunlap, 1964).

Martin Malia, *Alexander Herzen and the Birth of Russian Socialism* (*New York: Grosset & Dunlap, 1961).

Frank E. Manuel, *The Prophets of Paris* (*New York: Harper, 1962).

Arthur J. May, *The Hapsburg Monarchy 1867–1914* (Cambridge, Mass.: Harvard University Press, 1951).

Allen McConnell, *Tsar Alexander I, Paternalistic Reformer* (*New York: Thomas Y. Crowell, 1970).

Charles Morazé, *The Triumph of the Middle Classes* (*New York: Doubleday Anchor, 1968).

George L. Mosse, *The Crisis of German Ideology, Intellectual Origins of the Third Reich* (*New York: Grosset & Dunlap, 1964).

George L. Mosse, *The Culture of Western Europe: The Nineteenth and the Twentieth Centuries* (Chicago: Rand McNally, 1961).

W. E. Mosse, *Alexander II and the Modernization of Russia* (New York: Macmillan, 1959).

Lewis B. Namier, *1848: The Revolution of the Intellectuals* (*New York: Doubleday Anchor, 1946).

Linda Nochlin, ed., *Realism and Tradition in Art: 1848–1900* (Englewood Cliffs, N.J.: Prentice-Hall, 1966).

Joachim Remak, *The Origins of World War I*

(*New York: Holt, Rinehart & Winston, 1967).

Norman Rich, *The Age of Nationalism and Reform, 1850–1890* (*New York: Norton, 1970).

Priscilla Robertson, *Revolutions of 1848: A Social History* (*Princeton, N.J.: Princeton University Press, 1952).

George Rudé, *The Crowd in History, 1730–1848* (*New York: John Wiley, 1964).

H. G. Schenk, *The Mind of the European Romantics* (*New York: Doubleday Anchor, 1969).

Alexander Sedgwick, *The Third French Republic 1870–1914* (*New York: Thomas Y. Crowell, 1968).

L. S. Stavrianos, *The Balkans 1815–1914* (*New York: Holt, Rinehart & Winston, 1963).

John H. Stewart, *The Restoration Era in France 1814–1830* (*Princeton, N.J.: Anvil, 1968).

Mack Walker, *Plombières: Secret Diplomacy and the Rebirth of Italy* (*Oxford: Oxford University Press, 1968).

Basil Willey, *Nineteenth-Century Studies, Coleridge to Matthew Arnold* (*Baltimore, Md.: Penguin, 1941).

Basil Willey, *Darwin and Butler, Two Versions of Evolution* (London: Chatto and Windus, 1960).

Roger L. Williams, *The World of Napoleon III.* (*New York: Free Press, 1965).

Roger L. Williams, *The Commune of Paris, 1871* (*New York: John Wiley, 1969).

Roger L. Williams, *The French Revolution of 1870–1871* (*New York: Norton, 1969).

Cecil Woodham-Smith, *The Reason Why* (*New York: Everyman, 1960).

Part 10
The
Twentieth
Century

35
World War I and its Aftermath

Who was Guilty?

Since the responsibility, or guilt, for inaugurating the era of violence has never been historically settled, it is useful to ponder the variety of causes that have been thrown into the debate. Some historians have stressed the long diplomatic prelude to the war, the series of international crises after 1871, to suggest an almost inexorable drift toward a violent showdown. Others, in contrast, by stressing that diplomacy had successfully contained those crises, pointed to the immediate events in 1914 where international diplomacy evidently collapsed. Another group has argued that what really made a general war probable was the growing climate of violence during the later nineteenth century, a kind of fatalism which assumed that reason must ultimately fail in the affairs of men, with violence to determine what should survive. To this, the response has been that there seems to have been no general expectation that a war was coming.

Other historians labored to pin the guilt on one particular nation or alliance. The peacemakers at Versailles did precisely this when they wrote into Article 231 of the Versailles Treaty:

Germany accepts the responsibility of herself and her allies for causing all the loss and damage to which the Allied and Associated Powers and their nationals have been subjected as a consequence of the war imposed upon them by the aggression of Germany and her allies.

In the historical literature after 1918, one can find learned arguments designed to demonstrate the primary guilt of all the major participants. An alternative was to consider this evidence as proof that no nation was uniquely guilty, but that the responsibility belonged to *all* the participants to a greater or lesser degree. If this is true, then Article 231 was patently unjust.

The argument for corporate guilt was ultimately buttressed by showing that no power in the crisis of 1914 wanted a *general* European war, and that the diplomatists all worked either to avoid war entirely or to localize it. The political consequences were too uncertain, the losses in life and property were likely to be too high, for any power to have wanted general war. But if one went behind the immediate crisis of 1914 and its frantic diplomacy, then German responsibility loomed larger. For after 1890, German foreign policy, apparently aiming at hegemony in Europe and in the world, was the principal factor that threatened the continental balance of power which had succeeded in localizing conflicts since 1815. It is argued that, in those 25 years before 1914, the Germans merely sought in the world what others had earlier achieved. Be that as it may, her expansionism, often poorly planned and clumsily defined, gave Germany an aggressive posture. It took a second World War, however, when German designs were more transparent, to reveal the aggressive continuity of German foreign policy in the twentieth century. In which light, Article 231, if perhaps unwise and too exclusive, was not far off its mark.

Thus, while the well-known German invasion of Belgium in 1914 (in violation of the Treaty of 1839) served to bring Britain into the war, there can be little doubt that she would have of necessity entered the war in any case. A continental victory for William II's aggressive policy in 1914 was as intolerable for British security as a similar victory for Hitler's ambitions would prove to be for the United States in 1940. Such observations must immediately be tempered: first, by recognizing that the Germans did not plot the war in 1914, which depended on the quarrel between Austria and Serbia; and second, by noting that the United States entered the war in 1941 only when attacked, and not because the general public yet understood the consequences of a German victory in Europe.

The Campaigns of 1914

By 1914, most European military strategists had been taught by the swift Prussian victories of 1866 and 1870, rather than by the lessons of the American Civil War. Instead of a war of deadlock and attrition, they saw victory quickly achieved through vigorous offensives. The improvement in communications after 1870 confirmed their faith in the technical feasibility of swift movement. Every power had its contingency plans, the most critical of which proved to be the Schlieffen Plan, named for the man who headed the German general staff from 1892 to 1905. His plan of attack (1905) assumed from the Franco-Russian alliance that the Central Powers, in case of general war, would face a two-front war. To await an attack from two sides would have been madness, especially in view of Italy's doubtful loyalty to the Triple Alliance; and given the likelihood of a slow Russian mobilization, the opportunity to avoid a two-front war lay in the swift defeat of France.

Schlieffen expected (correctly) that the best French troops would be concentrated for an invasion of Alsace-Lorraine. If, therefore, the Germans moved swiftly and in great strength through Belgium into a region less well-defended by the French, moving on Paris from the northwest, the French would have to abandon their own offensive plans and rush to the defense of Paris. The invasion of Belgium, which the Germans admitted to be a violation of international law, was a military requirement designed to force French capitulation within six weeks. Meanwhile, the Russians would have to be held in check by inferior forces in the east, giving some ground if necessary; for the Germans were not confident that the Austrians alone could contain Russia.

The critical factor was time, and that went against the Germans in 1914 from the start. The Belgians fought hard, delaying the German advance two weeks and

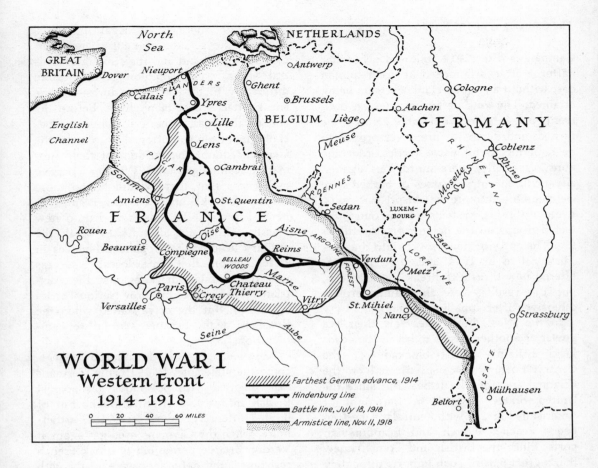

WORLD WAR I
Western Front
1914-1918

0   20   40   60 MILES

///////// Farthest German advance, 1914
∿∿∿∿∿∿ Hindenburg Line
━━━━━ Battle line, July 18, 1918
⠿⠿⠿⠿ Armistice line, Nov. 11, 1918

giving the British an opportunity to join the French. Still the Germans came on, forcing an Allied retreat eastward. So confident was General von Moltke of victory, that he detached several corps for service on the eastern front. In fact, his gigantic operation became exposed on its right flank to counterattack by French reserves; and though he saw the danger, communications with his fast-moving forces were inadequate to make adjustments in time. French counterattacks thus forced Moltke to halt his advance and to retreat into defensive positions. By the spring of 1915, a stalemate was achieved with the battle lines extending from Switzerland to the North Sea; and the Germans found themselves condemned to a two-front war.

Had the Russians been ready for war, therefore, the Central Powers would have been in serious difficulty from the very outset of the campaigns. But Russian military reforms, projected after the defeat by Japan in 1905, were not scheduled for completion until 1917. Disorganized and unready for battle, they moved prematurely into East Prussia to try to divert German pressure from the French and were beaten back. On the other hand, the Russian advance against the Austrians in 1914 was a spectacular success and came at a time when the Austrian attempt to knock Serbia out of the war had failed. Russian shortages in arms and equipment, however, forced a halt to the offensives in the late fall, and the real opportunity to eliminate Austria-Hungary from the war was lost. Thus, the eastern front became stabilized by the end of the year, much like the western front.

The Campaigns of 1915–1916

Campaigns after 1914 followed a familiar pattern: attacks launched at great human cost without any appreciable decision being attained. The long defensive lines on both fronts presented no vulnerable flanks to be turned, and defensive firepower proved to be superior to offensive tactics. Machine guns, especially, were murderous against advancing infantry, masses of barbed wire were employed to prevent surprise assaults, while elaborate systems of dugouts protected troops on the defense from artillery fire. The entry of new powers into the war, Turkey late in 1914 and Italy in 1915, offered new threats to break the deadlock, but the results were the same: broken offensives after appalling casualties.

In the West, both sides saw their sea power as another means to break the deadlock. Britain's initial blockade of the Central Powers was concentrated on the Channel and the North Sea. But since the United States insisted on the right of Americans to trade with neutrals, American goods reached Dutch and Scandinavian ports. Since the British and French knew that a great part of such imports ultimately reached Germany, they came to increasingly rigid definitions as to what constituted contraband; and late in 1914 they declared the North Sea to be a military zone. Faced with a shrinking flow of supplies, the Germans risked a naval raid against the British early in 1915. Its failure led the Germans to their last naval ace: their submarines. They declared a counterblockade of Britain and the Channel, warning that enemy ships in that war zone would be destroyed without warning—for the effectiveness of submarines depended on surprise attack. The Germans warned neutrals to stay out of that war zone, since mistakes could easily be made, especially after the British advised their merchantmen to fly either neutral flags or no flags at all in British waters as a protection against submarines.

Although there is no legal difference between the seizure of neutral merchandise as contraband and the sinking of neutral ships, world opinion reacted quite differently to the two procedures—for the sneak attacks cost many lives. Before the end of the year, American opinion, especially, had been so outraged as to make the Germans doubt the wisdom of their submarine campaign; and William II gave assurances that there would be no more surprise attacks upon passenger ships or neutral vessels. This decision led to new massive efforts on all sides to break the military deadlock with giant offensives in 1916. The one that came closest to success was the Russian drive against the Austrians, who were by now seriously demoralized. But the drive halted when the Russians again became starved for ammunition.

New weapons were introduced to overcome the stalemate. In 1915, the Germans experimented with poisonous gas against British infantry, a frightful tactic but of limited offensive value. By 1916, furthermore, when the Germans used gas again at Verdun in a desperate bid to break French resistance, the defenders were ready with gas masks. Meanwhile in Britain, Churchill had sponsored the development of a vehicle that could smash through barbed wire, protect its occupants from enemy fire, and bridge enemy trenches. The "tank" was the answer, so called because its development was hidden from the Germans with the pretense that the British Navy was constructing new water storage tanks. First used experimentally against the Germans in 1916, the 36 tanks sent into action were inadequate for any military success; but the British saw their future and ordered a thousand more.

1917: Submarine Warfare and the Entry of America

As 1917 approached, the Germans, well aware that time was not on their side, once again turned to naval tactics; for food supplies were running short, and the homefront morale was cracking. German surface ships were sent on raids in the North Sea in the hope of destroying isolated units of the British fleet without engaging the entire British navy. On one such sortie, a British advance guard was lured into action off Jutland with the main German fleet and might have been destroyed had not Britain's grand fleet suddenly appeared out of the mist. The Germans had to flee and might have been destroyed had not Jellicoe, the British admiral, been overcautious out of respect for their gunnery. (Though outnumbered, the Germans had some ship-for-ship advantage, as their navy was of more recent construction.) Though the victorious Jellicoe was supreme on the North Sea, his caution allowed the Germans to slip into the Baltic where the British dared not follow, meaning that Britain lost the opportunity to close in on the Baltic submarine bases, not to speak of the opopportunity to open a supply route to Russia.

The only remaining naval alternative for the Germans, however, was a return to unrestricted submarine warfare against almost all shipping in European waters, determined as they were to put an end to Allied purchases of munitions in the United States. The renewal led the United States to break relations with Germany, and ultimately to enter the war in April 1917. Many of the traditional reasons to account for the American intervention have since been discarded. President Wilson himself contributed to obscuring the issues at the time by seeing the conflict as a defense of international law and freedom of the seas. The fact was that Britain was in desperate straits. By April 1917, a quarter of her ships leaving home ports never returned. The traditional American suspicion of the British was nothing compared to America's abhorrence of the possible victory of the German system with its avowed policy of European domination.

The Capitulation of Russia

Despite American intervention, 1917 was a year of serious reverses for the Allies. French attempts to break the German lines with shock assaults resulted in nothing but shocking casualties. An Italian drive against the Austrians, timed to coincide with the French offensive, inched forward all summer, only to be hurled back by Austro-German units at Caporetto. After this the British and French had to keep troops in Italy to prevent a separate peace. But the most disastrous collapse of all came in Russia, whose immense efforts had come to nothing. Her economy could not sustain the demands of modern war, and British hopes to establish a supply line either through the Dardanelles or the Baltic had been frustrated. The Czarist regime, which had survived the Crimean and Japanese disasters, cracked in March 1917 with the abdication of Nicholas II.

A liberal provisional government tried to rebuild Russia's armies in the face of the advancing Germans, while the country plunged deeper into revolution. Communist agents infiltrated the army, further weakening its ability to fight. And when the Communists, pledged to peace at any price, seized control of the provisional government in November, the Russian war effort came to an end. In the general collapse, the Empire had already begun to dissolve. The Poles declared their independence in March 1917; and in November, the Ukrainians, Estonians, Finns, Bessarabians, and Latvians followed suit. The climax of the catastrophe came in the treaty of Brest-Litovsk (spring 1918) between the Central Powers and a new Russian government—now under Communist control. The Russians formally acknowledged the loss of territories to the former minorities, as well as the independence of Lithuania and Transcaucasia. Following this capitulation, the Germans occupied Finland and the Ukraine, hoping the latter would provide the food to offset the effects of the British blockade.

Despite these Allied setbacks, the Germans knew the seriousness of their own situation by the end of 1917. The British were beginning to build merchant ships faster than the Germans were destroying them; and British tanks scored a spectacular, if temporary, breakthrough near Cambrai, which seemed ominous to the Germans who had been minimizing the effectiveness of tanks. Worse, fresh troops from America would soon be crossing the Atlantic to offset the loss of Russia to the Allies. Thus the Germans gathered their forces in the west for a last great blow, substantially outnumbering the Anglo-French forces. In the crisis, the British and French achieved a combined command for the first time in the war in the person of General Foch.

1918: The Allied Victory

The German push began in March 1918, and although it reached the Marne east of Paris by May, American troops were then ready to enter the lines. Moreover, French artillery became increasingly effective in breaking up German efforts. By early August, it was clear that the back of the German offensive had been broken and that German casualties had been notably higher than those of the Allies. The initiative passed to the Allies, and in September General Foch unleashed a major counteroffensive. In the meantime, the Germans opened negotiations to seek a peace before their forces were seriously routed. The Austrians had attempted a drive against the Italians in coordination with the final German push in France. But the Austrian army was so handicapped by wholesale desertions that no success was possible. Austria agreed to an armistice on November 4.

Germany's methods and motives in seeking peace have remained controversial, for they set the stage for further international conflict. Naturally, Germany sought the softest peace possible, and she perceived that opportunity in an appeal to the well-known idealism of the American president, Woodrow Wilson. In a belated enthusiasm for democracy, William II reconstituted his government on October 4 to establish true parliamentary government; and on the same day the German and Austrian governments appealed to Wilson for an armistice based on his Fourteen Points. These had been set down at the beginning of 1918 as an outline of American foreign policy and amounted to a settlement based on the rights of *all* nationalities to self-determination. The Fourteen Points, however, had been composed before the Germans had revealed their territorial designs in the treaty of Brest-Litovsk; and they now found that Wilson demanded not simply the acceptance of the Fourteen Points, but the cessation of submarine warfare and the evacuation of all occupied territory as precedents of an armistice. Indeed, since Wilson had come to believe that the Germans did not truly adhere to his principles, he now agreed with the other Allied leaders that the German surrender must be unconditional.

Consequently, aside from the actual armistice terms, none of the Central Powers knew what the final peace terms would be. Also, William II abdicated on November 9 to make way for a republic, meaning that the defeated regime escaped the responsibility for signing the unconditional surrender. Finally, the German armistice commission was entirely civilian, though the top German generals had been the first to recommend a quick armistice. Thus did the generals seek to place the blame for defeat on others and to create the impression that the army had not been defeated—but betrayed. The armistice terms were harsh. Foch required the evacuation of Alsace-Lorraine, the Rhineland, and all occupied territories (the treaty of Brest-Litovsk became a dead letter. Not only arms, but many trucks, locomotives, and freight cars were surrendered to aid the immediate recovery of Belgium and France, whose industrial areas had been systematically razed by the retreating Germans. The terms were signed on November 11, 1918.

The Russian Revolution: The Historical Background

As in the coming of the French Revolution, we must distinguish between the revolutionary *spirit* and the revolutionary *situation* as the prelude to 1917. For one finds in nineteenth-century Russia both an intellectual protest against the premises on which the autocracy was based, and a set of circumstances which the autocracy seemed increasingly unable to manage. In contrast to the French example, however, where the *spirit* and the *situation* long remained so distinct and separate as to preclude describing them as a revolutionary movement, the coming of the Russian Revolution was a more conscious affair. Those imbued with the revolutionary spirit were also close students of actual conditions in Russia; they meant to overthrow the established order long before 1917; and the historical example of the French Revolution made it possible for them to be fully aware of what they were setting out to accomplish.

One of the notable consequences in 1917 was an acceleration of the revolutionary cycle. In 1789, most of the revolutionaries expected to reform the monarchy, to bring to an end a constitutional crisis so that financial and economic problems could be tackled. In 1917, monarchical reformers were swept aside in a few days, leaving the stage for a showdown between the Russian "Girondists" and "Jacobins." The hopelessness of reforming the monarchy had earlier been pointed up after 1905 when military disasters fed criticism of the regime. Public disorder and assassination became so serious that the government not only made an untimely peace with the Japanese, but promised the election of a national assembly—the Duma—on a broad franchise. To

the despair of liberals, however, the monarchy quickly recovered from its panic of 1905, and the Dumas between 1906 and 1916 turned out to be consultative bodies rather than truly legislative. For all practical purposes, Russia remained an autocracy.

The revolutionary movement had first developed among army officers who saw service in France between 1814 and 1818, and who were shocked to discover the superiority of western conditions of life. From this there arose a spate of secret societies dedicated to political, social, and economic reform in Russia. Their leadership came from the gentry. Some favored the establishment of a French-style democratic republic, others an English-style constitutional monarchy. They engineered uprisings on the death of Alexander I late in 1825 (the Decembrist Revolt), which were swiftly smashed. Vigorous reprisals by the new czar, Nicholas I, put new teeth in czarist absolutism and alienated the monarchy even more from the liberal gentry.

On the other hand, even well-meaning reform attempts by the imperial government produced a great deal of dissatisfaction. The emancipation of the serfs by Alexander II after the Crimean War, and the subsequent redistribution of land, angered former landowners, who felt they had been despoiled, and peasants, who believed that they ought not have to pay for lands received. (Not to speak of peasants dissatisfied with what they had received.) Peasant rioting was widespread in the 1860s, often encouraged by the new (1862) Land and Liberty Society organized by liberals and radicals. Peasants generally, however, did not trust intellectuals, many of whom concluded that there was no hope of a revolution based on the rural population. Radical opinion, therefore, increasingly favored terrorism, the traditional weapon of a tiny minority; and in 1879 the Will of the People Society was formed, openly advocating the assassination of the Czar and indifferent to his reformist tendencies—for reforms could preserve the established order and the principles on which it was based.

Furthermore, rural poverty was hardly abolished with the emancipation decree and the subsequent reforms. A small group of gentry still controlled nearly half the agricultural land, and perhaps a third of the peasantry remained landless right down to 1914. More to the point, the technical level of Russian agriculture remained so primitive that a peasant's productivity was about one third the yield harvested by a German farmer. The gentry who rented land to peasants for sharecropping often received 50 percent of the crop or other manorial forms of rent, so that a kind of serfdom existed despite emancipation.

The reign of Alexander III (1881-1894) coincided with the beginning of industrialization and its usual abuses, creating a new dimension of grievances to which the repressive czarist government was indifferent. By 1914, Russian production of coal and iron per capita was tiny compared to the western countries, and she had no machine-tool industry or chemical plants at all. Yet, what industry Russia had was modern in its high degree of concentration, which inadvertently contributed to the organization and political strength of her industrial workers. The enormous demands made by the war in 1914 on this infant industry exposed to all eyes the backwardness and underproductivity of the entire Russian economy. Leading straight to military incapacity, the situation brought the autocracy to the brink of its third debacle in a half century. As with France in 1789, so with Russia in 1917, the leadership of the old regime was inadequate in the crisis. The bankruptcy of czarist Russia was financial as well as moral, government income being a bare 10 percent of military expenditures. At a moment when the regime desperately needed to rally the nation, its vision narrowed in a jealous desire to maintain absolute authority.

With industrialization, meanwhile, had come new western-style socialist movements to compete with the native anarchist and terrorist organizations for command of the revolutionary movement. The first Russian Marxist party was formed by Plekhanov (in Swiss exile) in 1883. In 1898, Martov and Lenin dared to reorganize the party on Russian soil—the Social Democratic party or SD's—with a direct appeal to industrial workers; but they were soon forced to promote their party from exile. True to their Marxist philosophy, the SD's believed that class warfare knew no national distinctions; thus they considered themselves part of an international movement and favored international organization. A rival socialist party, founded in 1901 by Chernov as the Socialist Revolutionaries or SR's, was more narrowly Russian. The SR's viewed their cause in national terms, and worked for the improvement of the peasants' lot as had traditional Russian radicalism.

A division of opinion within the Russian SD's appeared in 1903 at their party congress in London. Lenin wanted to restrict party membership to an elite: to a few, highly disciplined professional revolutionaries who could direct the masses. Martov and Trotsky preferred a party open to all supporters as in the case of the German Social Democratic party. The difference reflected a more serious division: Lenin was uncompromising and meant to accomplish his revolutionary goals through violence; the Martov-Trotsky faction preferred to promote the eventual socialist society with parliamentary, evolutionary means. As the Lenin faction gained control of the party in 1903, it was henceforth known as the Bolsheviks (majority); the Martov-Trotsky group was known as the Mensheviks (minority). The party maintained its outer unity, but the split was never healed.

Liberals organized, too, with the Union of Liberation in 1903. Primarily seeking representative government, the liberals were often men who had taken part in local and provincial government after the reforms of 1864 and who wanted those reforms crowned with the creation of a national parliament. The Czar's hasty promise to summon such a parliament in 1905 seemed for a moment to mean victory for the liberals, just then reorganized as the Constitutional Democratic party or KD's. But the regime quickly alienated liberal support by devising a series of checks on parliamentary power and by rejecting liberal legislation designed to rally the peasantry to the government.

The Fall of the Czarist Government

The World War, which ended by revealing the utter incompetence of the autocracy, at first rallied the public to the regime. Although the reactionary ministers in power succeeded for a time in keeping the true state of affairs at the front from members of the Duma, the specter of disaster loomed large in St. Petersburg (the present Leningrad) by mid-1915. When anxious members of the Duma found themselves powerless to urge abler or more reputable officials on the regime, the suspicion developed that the autocracy actually connived at a German victory out of sympathy for the German form of government. The outbreak of revolution, however, in March of 1917, was not led by the liberal or the radical parties, but seems to have been a spontaneous outburst of public outrage at a government whose efforts had produced nothing but defeat, food shortages, and serious inflation. A wave of strikes in the capital of St. Petersburg brought great mobs into the streets, and the government found that it could not rely on its demoralized troops to keep order. Only after the government lost control of the major cities did radicals organize a workers' council (Soviet) in St. Petersburg, by which time the liberals in the Duma had already notified Nicholas II that his abdication had become necessary. He gave way without a struggle.

The Duma, anxious to prevent the more radical Soviet from assuming power, then created a provisional government under the prime ministry of Prince Lvov, a KD. This new regime, however, was handicapped from the start by the presence of the Soviet, which acted as a rival government, issuing its own orders and establishing soldiers' councils (also soviets) in all army units. It soon became clear that the Provisional Government would have to depend on the Soviet for military support. That was no problem for the moment, as the Soviet was dominated by Mensheviks and SR's, who favored promotion of the war just as the Provisional Government did. But when that regime announced, as war aims, that Russia would expect to obtain the Straits and Constantinople, the socialists in the Soviet balked. They took the line that wars are imperialistic, and that all peoples should demand that their governments conduct only defensive war and renounce annexationist policies. In any case, it seems likely that the rival regimes would have fallen out sooner or later, especially over SR plans to redistribute land.

This jockeying for control of the revolution between liberals and moderate socialists was soon complicated by the appearance of Lenin in mid-April 1917. Totally opposed to any further Russian participation in the war (on the grounds that wars are manufactured for the benefit of capitalists), he worked for Bolshevik seizure of the Soviet, after which he planned to end the war and to establish a dictatorship of the proletariat. Lenin had been permitted by the Germans to cross their territory to reach Russia in the hope that he would succeed in removing Russia from the war. It was not hard for him to convince the warweary, land-hungry masses that the time for peace and land redistribution had come, and a government dedicated to pursuing the national interest in the war faced a collapse of the home front. When the general commanding the troops in St. Petersburg tried to halt demonstrations for peace, the Soviet ordered his troops to their barracks.

This set the stage for reconstitution of the provisional government in July, with the SR Kerensky assuming the prime ministry.

The revolution, therefore, had moved a step to the Left. Yet, Kerensky appointed a well-known conservative, Kornilov, to command the armed forces in an attempt to restore discipline. The appointment put the regime in an equivocal position: while seeking harmony and unity with the Soviet, Kerensky also put his military forces in the charge of a man who regarded the Soviet as composed of pro-German traitors. Kerensky never escaped the dilemma of his dual loyalty—his responsibility to maintain the government he headed, and his attachment to fellow socialists in the Soviet who were a continual threat to his government. In the crunch, he could provide no effective leadership; and the crisis came in September when Kornilov informed Kerensky of his plan to crush the Soviet. Kerensky first wavered, then warned the Soviet of its danger. Those who wanted to save the revolution, doubting Kerensky's integrity, felt they had no alternative but to submit to Bolshevik leadership, while railway workers, under Soviet direction, managed to confuse troop movements so thoroughly that Kornilov's coup collapsed without any fighting.

The Bolsheviks in Power

Still, many of the Bolsheviks shrank from the prospect of seizing the Provisional Government, and Lenin had a difficult time convincing his party that their time had come. Kerensky took no effective means to meet the challenge he knew was coming, and in November he fled in disguise to France. In taking power, Lenin at once announced that the war would be immediately ended, and that the property rights of the nobility would be destroyed—hoping to insure his support by the mass of the population, the peasantry. He also gave notice that the revolution in Russia would be a

Lenin (Photo World/FPG)

mere prelude to the world socialist revolution. To carry out his promises, the Soviet government ordered an end to private landholding, with no compensation to former landowners. The nationalized lands were to be worked through rural soviets elected by the peasants; these soviets were to be responsible for the distribution of land for individual farming.

As for peace, an immediate armistice was followed in early 1918 by the Treaty of Brest-Litovsk. Lenin might argue that Russia had no power to resist the harsh settlement dictated by the Central Powers, but in fact he was for international socialism and relatively indifferent to the claims of Russian nationalism. In any case, a treaty that cost Russia 1,300,000 square miles of territory and over 60 million people was bound to shock patriotic opinion. Her former allies were caught in a serious bind by Russia's separate peace, which gave the Germans real opportunity for victory in the West. And Lenin compounded the agony by repudiating all debts contracted by the imperial regime, which hit the French especially hard as they had been the primary lenders to Russia.

Lenin postponed an immediate nationalization of industry in the hope of keeping it functioning. Yet, he allowed workers to form soviets for the purpose of supervising managerial personnel, a move that contributed to considerable confusion and hostility. Having always believed in the dictatorship of an elite, Lenin knew that terror would be necessary to control opposition. "Not a single question pertaining to the class struggle," he said, "has ever been settled except by violence. Violence when it is committed by the toiling and exploited masses is the kind of violence of which we approve." The All-Russian Extraordinary Commission (Cheka) was appointed to shut off opposition and illegal activities, and its chief weapon was terror. The fallen Provisional Government had promised national elections to form a constituent assembly, which Lenin recognized could become a stronghold of opposition, especially since the SR's—the traditional peasant party—might well win the elections. Lenin went ahead with the elections in 1918 only because he had control of the army by then and knew he had the power to dissolve the assembly. When the SR's indeed gained the majority in the assembly and gave signs of seizing control, Lenin disallowed further sessions. The Bolshevik dictatorship had been established.

The Postwar Settlements

The general Peace Conference opened in Paris in 1919 under the chairmanship of Clemenceau, the French Premier, whose main objective was the permanent weakening of Germany for the future security of France. In all, 32 states were represented, many having become belligerents late in the war simply to obtain a seat at the conference; and many national groups wishing to become states, aware of Woodrow Wilson's hope that the settlement would be based on the rights of *all* nationalities to self-determination, also sent representatives. Soviet Russia, having made a separate peace and by then engaged in civil war, was unrepresented, and the defeated powers were not invited. This omission precluded the possibility of the defeated sowing discord in the ranks of the victorious as Talleyrand had managed it a hundred years before. But it also lent weight to the later German claim that Germany had been unjustly treated—indeed, betrayed. Having offered to surrender on the basis of Wilsonian principles, the Germans found it easy to convince themselves that they had been swindled, forgetting that they had been defeated in the field, and that Wilson himself, after Brest-Litovsk, had insisted on unconditional surrender. Aside from the armistice terms, none of the defeated powers knew what the eventual paece terms would be.

The harsh settlement that emerged from the conference was by no means easily achieved, and not only because it was difficult to draw neat boundary lines to separate nationalities aspiring to self-government. In 1815, the peacemakers had been assisted by the fact that the principle of *legitimacy,* the basis for political and territorial settlement, was consistent with the Allied method of uprooting French militancy (that is, destroying the vestiges of the French Revolution by restoring the legitimate House of Bourbon). In 1919, because of the overlapping of national claims, the principle of nationality was much harder to apply fairly or to general satisfaction, not to speak of the national claims of the defeated powers. Moreover, the principle was soon found to be inconsistent with the attempt to guarantee that Germany would not revive as a military state. The morselization of Europe, in sum, left an immense residue of bitterness on the part of those nationalities that thought they

"The Big Four": Orlando, Lloyd-George, Clemenceau, Wilson. (Radio Times Hulton Picture Library)

had been despoiled or that were certain they had not received what was properly theirs; just as it created new states that had no particular geographic or economic viability. The stage was set for the ambitious and the revengeful.

Still, something can be said for Wilson's concern for the rights of nationalities. He had observed the nationalists' passion in the later nineteenth century and knew it to be a major source of conflict and violence. He also knew that nationalism itself had had many constructive features. One might regret that its claims, so long unrequited in the nineteenth century, had turned nationalism into a hate-filled monster. What a difference for Europe, for instance, if the Austrians had discovered early a way to make their cosmopolitan empire congenial to the component nationalities! Like Napoleon III before him, Wilson hoped in 1919 that the ambitions of the various nations could be satisfied all while preserving cosmopolitan Europe through international organizations: his League of Nations.

The Peace Provisions

The Treaty of Versailles (1919) forced Germany to return Alsace-Lorraine to France, to cede two frontier areas around Eupen and Malmédy to Belgium, to give up Posen and West Prussia to the new Poland, and to consent to plebiscites (under the auspices of the League of Nations) that would regulate what part of Schleswig must go to Denmark, what part of Upper Silesia must be given to the new Czechoslovakia, and what the future of the Saar Basin would be. German armed forces were sharply limited to numbers felt to be adequate for policing the coast and maintaining internal order. The creation of Poland (see the map) had the effect of isolating East Prussia from the rest of Germany; and within the "Polish Corridor" separating the two, the German city of Danzig was made a free city under the supervision of the League of Nations. One can see at once how the integrity of the new League of Nations was shackled at its birth to the maintenance of the peace settlement. The Covenant of the League of Nations, in fact, became the first section in the Treaty of Versailles, so that any German violation of the treaty would put her at odds with all members of the League.

The "war-guilt" clause in the treaty condemned the Germans to pay reparations for damage done to civilian property and population. The treaty required a token payment of five billion dollars, with an Allied Reparation Committee to set the final figure by May of 1921. Thus, Germany pledged to pay an unknown amount at a moment when her territorial losses reduced her ability to pay. Aside from the loss of her colonial empire (given to the League of Nations for disposal), Germany lost only one-eighth of her territory; but the eighth lost contained 65 percent of her iron ore and 45 percent of her coal. This Allied indifference to some of the economic realities of the peace settlement was repeated in the treaties that broke up the Austro-Hungarian Empire along national lines, destroying an economic unity in central Europe.

Separate treaties were signed with Austria (St. Germain-en-Laye, 1919), and with Hungary (Trianon, 1920). Austria suffered particularly, being reduced to 25 percent of her former share of the Dual Monarchy in both population and territory. Two new states comprising western and southern Slavs, respectively, Czechoslovakia and Yugoslavia, were carved out of the old Empire; despite the fact that the components groups, like the Czechs and Slovaks or the Serbs and the Croats, had never been notably congenial. Other Slavic-, Italian-, or Romanian-speaking territories were ceded to the new Poland, to Italy, and to Romania; but the German-speaking South Tyrol was given to Italy on Italian insistence that the Brenner Pass region was necessary for defensive reasons. Austria was specifically forbidden to seek a union with Germany as a solution to her territorial losses, and a restoration of the Hapsburg was denied to both Austria and Hungary. The latter retained only about 40 percent of her former population. Defeated Bulgaria had to sign the Treaty of Neuilly (1919), ceding territory to Greece and Yugoslavia, which had the effect of cutting Bulgaria off from the Aegean Sea. But the treaty agreed to by the Turkish Empire so outraged Turkish nationalist opinion that it led to the overthrow of the old monarchy and disavowal of the treaty. In any case, Turkey lost her claims on her vast empire in North Africa and the Near East, and the League of Nations inherited the task of partitioning the territory.

The Climate After Versailles

The Great War had seemed to confirm the nineteenth-century democratization of European society. Not only had the liberal states emerged victorious—with the four major autocracies crumbling—but an international agency to settle international disputes had at last been founded, which would reflect international opinion. Perhaps then, Europe now had the means to shut off the currents of corrosive nationalism and to approach her problems as a cosmopolitan community. In fact, general war would again break out 20 years later, broader in scope than in 1914. Many factors contributed to the instability of the European order after 1919 and, thus, to the failure of the peace settlement.

The war had left all manner of wounds that drastically affected the social fabric in the belligerent countries. The casualties alone were on an unprecedented scale, the major participants counting over eight million dead and more than double that figure wounded. France suffered the greatest casualties in proportion to total population; but the Russians, who would soon add millions of dead through civil war, suffered the most in sheer numbers. All the belliger-

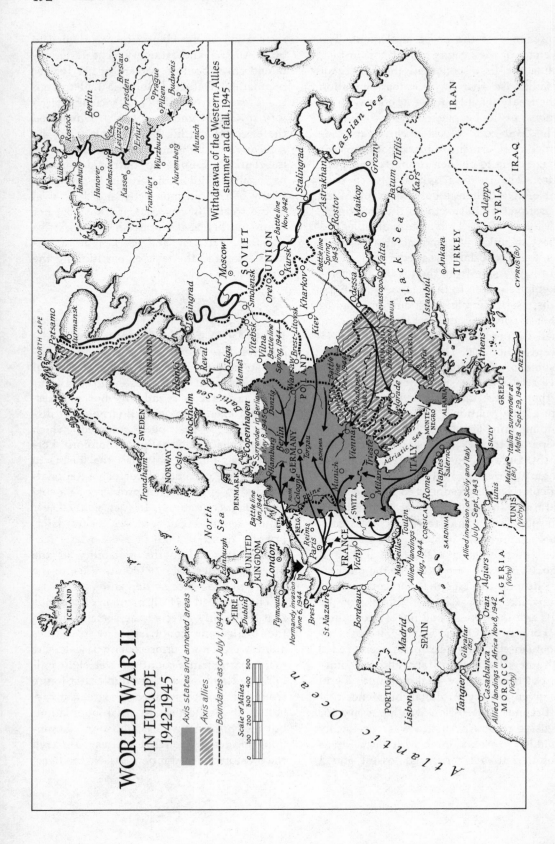

WORLD WAR II
IN EUROPE
1942–1945

Axis states and annexed areas

Axis allies

Boundaries as of July 1, 1944

Scale of Miles
0   100 200 300 400 500

Withdrawal of the Western Allies
summer and fall, 1945

ent European countries found themselves with a serious deficit of men after 1918, the discrepancy in Britain approaching the figure of 1100 women for every 1000 men. The European birth rate, already declining by 1914, dropped sharply during the war to forecast a manpower shortage for years to come. During the war, women were mobilized as never before for work on farms and in factories, leading to their greater emancipation. Britain, for instance, gave women over 30 the right to vote in 1918.

Similarly, the total mobilization of national resources, necessary for all the belligerents as the war lengthened, had a lasting effect on European economic and social thinking. Before 1914, Europe had been part of a world economy—largely an unplanned economy. Despite the rising tariff barriers that reflected the hostile nationalism of the late nineteenth century, international business relations expanded, characterized by increasing economic specialization and trade. Europe increasingly exported capital as well as manufactured goods, London being the most important source of cheap capital for worldwide investment. The wartime economic planning led to postwar demands for peacetime mobilization of the national resources, so that the benefits of industrialization could be more quickly and generally realized. Despite such demands, businessmen naturally tried to resume the prewar patterns of trade; but the impact of the Great Depression after 1929 forced European governments back to planning. Thus, it is fair to claim that 1914 was a watershed between unplanned and planned economies. The nineteenth-century liberal had dwelt on those things which governments ought not do; postwar liberalism defined new realms for government controls.

Economic planning had been foreshadowed in the late nineteenth century in both government and private business by Bismarck's "state socialism," for instance, and by the social insurance systems available in most western countries by 1914. After 1890, European businessmen showed a new tendency to plan for the future on a grand scale to increase their efficiency and competitiveness, a movement that led to the formation of giant cartels and trusts. Because of this experience, such men were called into government service during the war for economic planning in the emergency. That the impetus for peacetime planning emerged from the war years can be seen in the military metaphors used in the peacetime planning: agrarian and industrial *fronts*, production *battles*, *shock* workers, and *brigade* leaders.

The political and economic recovery of Europe after such terrible devastation called for international cooperation and planning, especially through the agency of the League of Nations. Even the victorious Allies, however, soon allowed national interests and prejudices to prevail over international requirements, a condition that gave opportunity to all those who hoped to unsettle the peace rather than to maintain it. The first sign of Allied disaffection was the failure of the United States Senate to ratify the Treaty of Versailles. Since ratification of a treaty requires a two-thirds majority, the rejection was the work of a minority (mostly Republicans). On the other hand, in the face of considerable popular enthusiasm for the League of Nations, this country returned a Republican congress in 1918 and elected a Republican president in 1920, clearly enhancing the probability that the treaty would fail. The public showed itself more eager for rapid demobilization and "normalcy" than for any other cause in the world. Sometimes seen as a sign of American immaturity in international politics, the reaction more likely reflected popular suspicion that American idealism had been trampled under foot by cynical European statesmen in the forging of the peace settlement. If the war had been more realistically approached in 1917, or even before, Americans might have been spared much of the subsequent disenchantment. As it was, those who had approached the war in 1917 as a crusade for international law and freedom of the seas ended in 1920 by refusing to participate in the League of Nations, the most idealistic aspect of the peace settlement.

The prospects for achieving Wilson's goal of "perpetual peace" were immediately dimmed. Marshal Foch had already remarked the previous year that "This is not Peace. It is an Armistice for twenty years." In fact, not only was there no real peace after 1919, but even the "armistice" was too consistently violated to be called a true armistice. Conflicts were limited in scope, some of them taking the nonmilitary form we have come to call "cold war;" but the European climate through the next 20 years was a militant one.

36
The Uneasy Peace

The League of Nations

The League was an association of sovereign states, initially designed to include the 32 nations who had broken relations with Germany during the war, plus 13 neutral nations to be invited to join. Thereafter, additional nations could be elected to membership by a two-thirds vote of the member nations. The League's work was done through a Secretariat, a Council, and an Assembly, located at Geneva in neutral Switzerland. Each member nation was on an equal footing in the Assembly, having three delegates there but only one vote. Five of the nine seats in the Council, however, were given permanently to the great powers—Britain, France, the United States, Italy, and Japan; the remaining seats were to be filled by election from the Assembly to represent the smaller states. Most decisions in both the Council and the Assembly required a unanimous vote, and a nation could resign from the League by giving two years' notice of its intention.

The postwar treaties gave the League responsibility for guiding the development of territories in the former German and Turkish empires. Such territories were mandated to more "advanced nations" by the League for the express purpose of preparing them for self-government, their progress to be reviewed annually by the League. Beyond this specific responsibility, the League was charged with reducing worldwide armaments, the mediation of disputes, and the promotion of humanitarian projects. Armed with no police power to enforce its decisions, the League depended on the willingness of member nations to honor their obligations to the international community; but the Covenant did contain a clause that obliged all members to break trade and financial relations with any nation that went to war.

Obviously, the League had been designed with an assumption of American participation, and our failure to join raised the immediate prospect that economic sanctions by League members against an aggressive power might not succeed, but would hurt in particular a trading nation like Britain if she supported such League action. American withdrawal shocked the French for a further reason: Their negotiators at Versailles had demanded, for reasons of security, the Rhine as the northeastern frontier. Opposing this annexation of German-speaking people, the Americans and British persuaded the French to abandon the claim in exchange for treaties guaranteeing French security. Yet, the American Senate refused to ratify a treaty of alliance with Britain and France in 1919 some months before our rejection of the Versailles settlement became known. The French felt betrayed by this collapse of wartime unity, which led them to assume a tougher attitude on the matter of German recovery.

The Early Alterations of the Peace Settlements: Turkey

Turkish nationalists had long suspected the European powers of conspiring to partition the declining Ottoman Empire. When the Sultan agreed to terms in 1920 with the Allies which amounted to his abandoning of all the non-Turkish territories of the old Empire, the nationalists—led by Mustapha Kemal—were prepared to overthrow the monarchy and to disavow the agreement. Consequently, it became necessary for the Allies to occupy Constantinople to save the peace treaty. The Greeks were allowed to occupy Smyrna in Turkey itself, where the population was largely Greek-speaking; and the Italians were confirmed in their possession of Rhodes and the Dodecanese Islands.

Seizing the old city of Angora (later Ankara), the nationalists announced they would establish a liberal republic and destroy the peace settlement, which led the Greeks to march on Angora. While the Greeks had British encouragement, most of the other European powers saw that the nationalists had widespread popular backing in Turkey and concluded that a new understanding with Kemal ought to be reached. In 1922, he drove the Greeks into the sea and proclaimed the overthrow of the Sultanate, following which a new peace settlement was reached at Lausanne in 1923.

Kemal had to accept the loss of the non-Turkish territories, including the Dodecanese and most of the Aegean islands; but he saved Smyrna for Turkey and recovered Adrianople and a portion of eastern Thrace at the expense of Greece. In exchange for this he agreed to the neutralization of the Straits. He also negotiated a compulsory exchange of populations with Greece in order to expel Greek residents from Turkey, where they had lived since ancient times. The League of Nations had to supervise the transfer, which uprooted nearly one million Greeks, while the Turks retrieved about 100,000 of their nationals from Greece. Tiny Greece could hardly absorb such a sudden influx of people, so that the dislocation had grievous political and economic results for Greece. Since the British and French had been on opposite sides at the beginning of the crisis, the squabble marked the beginning of their postwar antagonism which further shattered Allied unity.

Italy

Italian nationalists were another group that was dissatisfied with the peace settlement of 1919, though Italy had received the Trentino, South Tyrol, Trieste, Istria, and a few islands off Dalmatia. Given the limited value of Italian military efforts during the war, her Allies had thought these gains to be generous; but Italy had anticipated annexing the city of Fiume and the Dalmatian coast as well. Slavic Dalmatia had been awarded to the new Yugoslavia, and Italian diplomats walked out of the Paris conference when they saw their claim to Fiume rejected. Late in 1919, a small force of Italian war veterans, led by the poet D'Annunzio and wearing capes and daggers, seized Fiume for Italy. Yugoslavia refused, however, to abandon her claim to the city, and the two powers reached a negotiated settlement at Rapallo in 1920 which made Fiume an independent city-state. The compromise outraged nationalist opinion in Italy, giving Mussolini, after his rise to power, the opportunity to curry popular favor by demanding a revision of Fiume's status. The Yugoslavs gave in in 1924 and allowed Italy to annex much of the city, leaving several outlying areas of the port for Yugoslav use.

Russia

Meanwhile, Russian nationalists of various political hues were drawn together in opposition to Lenin and the Bolsheviks. The harsh terms he accepted at Brest-Litovsk (1918) were followed by an agreement to pay Germany six billion marks in reparations, leading many Russians, like their former Western Allies, to believe that Lenin was turning Russia into a German puppet state to permit Germany to turn her full military power into her last offensives of 1918. If Britain and France should fall, Germany would be in a position to annex the entire Soviet Union. Lenin found support from those in Russia who were ready for peace at any price, which gave him time to build the Red (Bolshevik) army. The threatened civil strife was no mere ideological opposition to Bolshevism, but a patriotic outburst in particular. The Bolsheviks moved the capital from St. Petersburg to Moscow as a more secure base to face the storm.

The Great Civil War (1918-1920) was really a series of struggles between the Bolsheviks and many opposition groups, together called the Whites. This White movement, however, including the whole spectrum from monarchists to Mensheviks, was never unified or coordinated, and their patriotic stance was compromised by the appearance of foreign troops—especially British, French, and American—on Russian soil, sent to prevent Russian arms from falling into German hands. Since this intervention inevitably favored the parties opposing peace with Germany, and because the West furnished supplies to the Whites, the Bolsheviks could portray the intervention as an improper interference into Russian politics. As Russian nationalists, the Whites were less than enthusiastic about the new states (Poland, Finland, Lithuania, Latvia, and Estonia) carved out of the old Russian Empire, nor were they sympathetic to demands for autonomy by the Cossacks and the Ukrainians.

This chaos of interests is best illustrated in the Ukraine, where an independence movement had been encouraged by the Central Powers early in 1918. When newly in power, the Bolsheviks overthrew a Ukrainian regime which established itself in Kiev, but they were in turn forced to abandon the province at Brest-Litovsk. With the Germans then collapsing in the West in the summer of 1918, the province was invaded by White forces, backed by a French mission that landed at Odessa. Poland, meanwhile, dissatisfied by her new boundaries, saw in this Ukrainian disorder the opportunity to rectify her dissatisfaction.

The question of a proper frontier between Russia and Poland has been one of the traditional border conflicts in European history. The peacemakers in Paris gave the Poles the Curzon Line, named after Lord Curzon, a British negotiator, as their eastern frontier, thus denying Poland her historical claim to the Ukraine, to a slice of Belorussia, and to the city of Vilna (which was given to the new state of Lithuania). In 1919, when the Bolsheviks were preparing to drive the White forces out of the Ukraine, the Whites tried to draw the Poles into an alliance against the Red regime; but being unwilling to cede to Poland territory the Whites regarded as properly Russian, no arrangement was

RUSSIAN TERRITORIAL LOSSES 1917-1921

——— Brest-Litovsk treaty line 1918

Russian territorial losses

achieved. Thus, the Poles stood aside while the Bolsheviks swept the White forces out of the Ukraine, and then opened negotiations with the Bolsheviks for a revision of the frontier, demanding the borders of 1772—those of prepartition Poland.

These negotiations failing, the Poles overran the Ukraine in 1920 and grabbed the city of Vilna. A Red counteroffensive, however, not only drove the Poles out of the Ukraine, but thrust straight at Warsaw, which the Poles managed to hold with the aid of a French military mission. After this the Reds were forced back across the frontier. A negotiated settlement in 1921 gave the Poles bits of territory beyond the Curzon Line; but the status of Vilna was only settled by a plebiscite held there in 1922—the city voted to join Poland. Lithuanian nationalist opinion was enraged by the outcome.

The Bolsheviks, meanwhile, tackled the isolated centers of White resistence in the Ukraine, in the Caucasus, and in Siberia. Japan had taken advantage of the Russian Revolution to land troops at Vladivosok late in 1917, leading the Western Allies also to send troops to Siberia, but principally to contain Japan. As elsewhere, the Allies were hostile to the Bolsheviks for making a separate peace, and an evacuation did not take place until it was clear that the Reds were winning the Civil War. The Japanese were the last to evacuate— in 1922. This foreign presence left a bitter memory in the Soviet Union.

War Debts and Reparations

The political bitterness after Versailles was soon reinforced with financial and economic conflict that greatly impeded postwar recovery in Europe. Nationalist rivalry and hostility was easily expressed in high protective tariffs, which inhibited trade. This climate hardly favored a rational resolution of the enormous tangle that the question of war debts and reparations offered Europe after Versailles. The fantastic costs of the war had driven all the belligerents into heavy taxation and borrowing. During the war years, France had doubled her tax income, and Britain had tripled hers; and both governments had been obliged to force the liquidation of overseas investments in payment for badly needed supplies. Inter-Allied borrowing had provided for the assistance of the weaker nations.

At the war's end, therefore, the three wealthiest of the victorious powers emerged as creditor nations—the United States and Britain for roughly seven billion dollars each, and France for two and a quarter billion dollars. Since the repayment of debts first required national economic recovery, most governments again had to borrow to stimulate the adjustment to peactime production. Thus, by 1922, the United States had risen to be a creditor for 10 billion dollars, France for three and a half billion dollars, while Britain had slipped to being a creditor for only four and a half billion dollars. As there was no hope of collecting the money lent to Imperial Russia, Britain and France proposed that all wartime debts be written off to the war effort and began granting concessions to their debtors, with only the postwar debts to be binding. But once again, the need for postwar Allied cooperation was shattered in Washington, where the Harding administration insisted on collection of the entire debt. Our attitude forced the European Allies to press for German payment of reparations at the very moment when the British, in particular, had begun to doubt the wisdom and the justice of assessing reparations at all.

The Reparations Commission, in the meantime, presented Germany in 1921 with a reparations bill of 33 billion dollars, to be paid in installments over 30 years: a high sum for a country that had just lost substantial resources for the production of goods, and that then had an unfavorable balance of trade. Moreover, Germany emerged from the war with notable inflation resulting from her failure to develop adequate wartime taxation to finance the war. Many Germans immediately began reinvesting their capital abroad to escape the high taxation obviously in the cards at home, a practice that crippled the effort to convert to a productive peacetime economy. The government itself contributed to the inflationary spiral by printing money to meet its expenses and through the necessary purchase of foreign currencies to meet initial reparations payment. The German mark consequently began to sink on the international market, so that before the end of 1921 the Germans had to notify the Reparations Commission that they would be unable to make the payment due in 1922 and asked for a moratorium of two and a half years.

In the face of American intransigence on the inter-Allied debt and needing immediate economic relief in the devastated areas, the Belgians and the French were opposed to a moratorium, while the British were inclined to leniency. The French, moreover, knew that the sums demanded of Germany were proportionately no heavier than what had been charged them in 1871: that even having lost the resources of Alsace-Lorraine, the French had resolutely set about paying off their indemnity and had done so ahead of schedule. Not merely had the French government faced the unpleasantness squarely, but French capital had not fled from the national responsibility. Consequently, the French in 1921 had no doubt that the Germans could pay the reparations if they had the will to do so, just as the French were indifferent to the charge that the peace terms were unjust. The example of Brest-Litovsk, moreover, left little doubt that peace terms dictated by Germany would have been even harsher than the terms of Versailles. In French opinion, the German financial maneuver in 1921 was merely the second act in the devious drama staged by the Germans in 1918 in attempting to cloud the circumstances of their military defeat.

Early in 1923, the Germans having been declared to be in default by the Reparations Commission, Franco-Belgian forces occupied the industrial Ruhr valley. The evident Allied disagreements about financial matters, however, encouraged the German government to sponsor passive resistence to the military occupation and the immediate decline in productivity spurred the inflationary spiral to ruinous heights. Allied occupation costs were greater than the reparations purchased by force, and it became clear that new reparations arrangements would have to be made.

The task fell to a new committee chaired by Charles Dawes, which granted a moratorium on payments until 1926. Annual installments were reduced to a point thought to be consistent with Germany's ability to pay—the matter of her unwillingness to pay having not yet been perceived —and the Dawes Committee recommended that foreign loans should be granted to Germany to stimulate economic recovery. In 1929, a second committee again reduced the annuities by extending the period of the debt to 1988 and arranged for further foreign financial aid. These remedies soon vanished in the world economic crisis that began in 1929, and it remains unclear today how much Germany had actually paid in reparations before the payments ceased. The suspicion is that she paid less than she received in loans, that the Allies had been led into financing German recovery and at the cost of inter-Allied confidence and cooperation.

In fact, German determination to destroy the peace settlement can also be found in her foreign policy. She signed a treaty of friendship with the Soviet Union at Rapallo in 1922, whose secret clauses provided for the illegal training of German troops in Russia; and she expected that Russo-German friendship would lead to the extinction of the new Poland and the recovery of the prewar eastern frontier. In 1923, the Germans experienced a psychological and moral collapse at the height of the economic chaos, adding fuel to their sense of outrage that had been cultivated since 1918. From this posture of innocents betrayed would spring the most dreadful barbarity yet experienced by modern Europe, a regime that would ridicule or pervert every great tradition of European civilization to the applause of the German people.

The Succession States

This name was given to the new nations that were carved out of the fallen autocratic empires. Satisfying the historical demands for self-determination, these new nations soon demonstrated that the problems generated by nationalism had not withered away with the coming of national independence. All of them suffered economically, for example, from the plethora of new frontiers—which meant barriers to trade, for ancient antagonisms were easily expressed in discriminatory tariffs. Most of them suffered internally from minority problems. Ccezhs and Slovaks, or Serbs and Croats, might all speak Slavic languages and be able to understand each other; but all had unique ethnic and historical traditions that were soon manifested in mutual hostility when two or more groups were lumped together as a nation-state. Finally, these states all suffered from a schism that was common in most European states after 1919. Those who strove to make European society more democratic were fought by those whose only wish was to destroy the postwar settlement or to recover lost territory and power.

Austria

The new Republic of Austria found itself reduced to a state where virtually half the population lived in Vienna and its suburbs. Aside from the economic significance of such an imbalance, the absence of the traditional hinterland threatened to bring to an end the traditional links between the Church and Austrian government. The rural areas, remaining strongly Roman Catholic, became the stronghold of the Christian Socialist party; while the Social Democrats, an anticlerical party, drew its strength from Vienna (and included the large Jewish community). Thus, regional and religious antagonisms aggravated the normal tension between a conservative and a liberal party. A small Nationalist party, determined to revise the 1919 settlement, followed a pan-German line and urged *Anschluss* (union) with Germany.

Such political divisions were inimical to the very notion of loyal opposition that democratic government requires. After a dozen years of party strife that frustrated the attempts of the majority Social Democrats to build a more democratic society, and after an attempt in 1931 to integrate Austria into the German economy through a customs union was blocked by the western powers as a covert attempt to seek the *Anschluss* forbidden by the 1919 peace settlement, the desperate Social Democrats felt forced to bring parliamentary government to an end. In 1933 Chancellor Dollfus inaugurated a dictatorship in the name of moderate government, to prevent a seizure of power by the conservatives, backed by a private army (the Heimwehr). But Dollfus was assassinated in 1934 during an unsuccessful attempt by the Nationalists to deliver Austria to Germany. The democratic forces maintained power, but only at the cost of democracy.

Hungary and The Balkans

Hungarian political life after 1918 was almost entirely conditioned by the frustration of nationalist ambitions. During the final weeks of the war, the Hungarians had sought to escape from the likely penalties for defeat by dissolving their union with Austria and bringing to power an aristocrat, Count Károlyi, known for his liberal views and his opposition to the war. When it became clear that his projected reforms and his expressions of concern for the subject nationalities would not save Hungary from being treated as a defeated power, he lost popularity and resigned office early in 1919. For the next five months, Hungary was a communist republic headed by Béla Kun, who proclaimed the beginning of a dictatorship of the proletariat. Though representing only a fraction of the Hungarians, he was widely tolerated in anticipation of help from Bolshevik Russia in preventing the loss of territory to Romania and the new Czechoslovakia.

Toward that end, Kun reorganized the Hungarian forces into a Red army and began an invasion of Slovakia and Transylvania. With French encouragement, the Romanians fought back, scattered the Red army, and even occupied Budapest for a time. Kun fled to Russia, abandoned by upper- and middle-class people who had favored his nationalist campaign, and power fell to the conservative aristocrats who had traditionally governed Hungary. Known communists, radicals in general, and Jews in particular were subject to a brief reign of terror; and the right to vote in the future was severely limited. In early 1920, Hungary's short experience with a republic came to an end with the reestablishment of monarchy, really a regency under Admiral Horthy, since Hungary's new neighbors threatened war in the event of a Hapsburg restoration. During the next two decades, Horthy's regime catered to the great landowners, crushing demands for social reforms, yet enjoyed considerable popularity deriving from widespread belief that he would ultimately succeed in revising the peace settlement in Hungary's favor and make possible a Hapsburg restoration. Revenge was the paramount issue.

No doubt the Hungarians were hostile to democracy as a principle espoused by the victorious powers, but democracy fared poorly elsewhere in central and eastern Europe despite initial intentions to promote it. In the new Yugoslavia, for example, the royal house was the former house of Serbia; and since nearly 50 percent of the population was Serbian, most Serbs thought of the new state as simply a greater Serbia and favored a highly centralized state that would inevitably be dominated by them. The minority Croats and Slovenes, regarding themselves culturally and economically superior to the Serbs, preferred decentralization to preserve ethnic uniqueness. When the Constitution of 1921 proved to be the embodiment of Serbian principles, the minorities opened a campaign in Parliament for autonomy that soon made a chaos of political life and culminated in 1928 with the murder of the Croatian leader on the floor of Parliament. To preserve the nation, King Alexander I then dissolved Parliament and embarked on a royal dictatorship, which had the effect of driving the opposition underground. In Yugoslavia's three Balkan neighbors—Greece, Romania, and Bulgaria —experiments with parliamentary government were equally unsuccessful; but perhaps better should not have been expected. None of them had any parliamentary tradition nor any understanding of orderly party government, and all ended with royal dictatorships in the 1930s.

Poland and Czechoslovakia

The restored Poland, too, became a disappointment for the democratizers; but here the critical factionalism that proved to be disruptive of parliamentary government was the traditional Polish cleavage between the conservative gentry and the liberal bourgeoise. Marshal Pilsudski, a national hero for his part in establishing an independent Poland and for his subsequent defense of Warsaw against the Red army in 1920, presided as Chief of State until the democratic constitution of 1922 was ready. Modeled on that of the French Republic, the constitution provided for a weak executive and a dominant parliament —a structure fatal in a country so deeply divided. As in Hungary, the gentry was able to obstruct needed agrarian reforms, and in 1926 Pilsudski put an end to parliamentary wrangling by overthrowing the constitution and becoming a dictator. Though he had flirted with socialism in his earlier years, Pilsudski disappointed both rural and urban workers who looked to him for social reform. Thereafter, Poland remained a military dictatorship, the government primarily devoted to preserving Polish independence from both Germany and Soviet Russia, who were rightly suspected of a collaboration detrimental to Poland.

Czechoslovakia proved to be the succession state where democracy functioned more successfully during the interwar period. She had various nationalities within her frontiers—Czechs, Slovaks, Germans, Hungarians, and Ruthenians (Ukrainians)—and frictions there certainly were, some of them of ancient origin. The Germans, who were really Austrians inhabiting the area of the Sudeten Mountains in particular, found it awkward to have to abandon the preferred status they had enjoyed under the Hapsburgs. The Czechs, Slovaks, and Ruthenians, if linguistically close, all had different ethnic backgrounds. Somewhat more culturally and industrially advanced, the Czechs were also inclined to anticlericalism, which did not sit well with the more agrarian, Roman Catholic Slovaks and Ruthenians.

On the other hand, Czechoslovakia had assets that overcame these liabilities. Her natural resources, her industry and agriculture, gave her a more balanced economy than her neighbors possessed; and in Thomas Masaryk, she was blessed with political leadership of the highest order. Masaryk, originally Slovak, had become an internationally famous scholar at the University of Prague, thus himself bridging the gap between Czechs and Slovaks. The new state was planned from the start on the assumption that cooperation between national groups would be fundamental to statehood, and Masaryk, as the first President, provided an inspiring example of democratic leadership in his fairness toward all groups. Not until external interests began to exploit the national divisions within Czechoslovakia did her experiment begin to crack. Meanwhile, she had demonstrated that—with good will and good leadership—a cosmopolitan state could be viable.

37
The Great Dictatorships and the Crisis of the 1930s

The Czechoslovakian leadership after 1918 was enormously assisted in its attempt to plant vigorous democratic institutions by the existence of a balanced economy that gave the promise of a progressive prosperity. In much of Europe, however, parliamentary government was undermined by economic dislocation, uncertainty, and fear, themselves the offspring of war, war debts, reparations, and discriminatory tariffs. Economic recovery generally was so slow, in no small part due to the collapse of Allied cooperation, that it soon became apparent that it had made little difference whether a country had come out on the winning or the losing side in the war. That perception itself was the cause of great bitterness. The longer the propertied classes felt the pinch, the more their faith in the democratic processes flagged. In the background was the success of the Bolsheviks in Russia, whose propaganda appealed to working people everywhere, especially in those years of hardship and dismay. As a consequence, many middle-class people came to believe that a Rightist dictatorship would be at once a guarantee of economic recovery and a barrier to communism. Much of Europe, therefore, drifted toward totalitarian regimes. Individual rights vanished, the rights of the state becoming paramount; and intellectual freedom gave way to thought-control programs administered by ministers of propaganda. Except in a few liberal bastions in western and northern Europe, the long progress of European civilization toward freedom and justice seemed stifled by totalitarian states of the Left and Right whose methods and standards were remarkably similar.

Fascist Italy

Italian bitterness was rooted, in the first place, in the frustration of national ambition. No other Allied power had entered the war with such naked territorial motives, and though Italy came out on the winning side, her contributions to the victory were a good deal less spectacular than the prizes she claimed. On the other hand, her military and economic costs had been high, making the mediocre military results a matter of national humiliation. Although the Italian negotiators gained much territory for Italy in the peace settlement, their failure to obtain every last claim led them to walk out on the conference, personifying the national hypersensitivity.

In the second place, grievous economic problems proclaimed the emptiness of the Italian victory. Agricultural productivity had declined during the war, leading to an unfavorable balance of trade; the government had borrowed heavily to prosecute the war, also printing paper money toward that end. The upshot was serious inflation, especially distressing to people who lived on fixed incomes or who had bought government bonds during the war. For purposes of wartime morale, the government had promised—once peace should come— a redistribution of land to help a peasantry whose plots were notoriously small. By 1920, with economic conditions actually deteriorating, both rural and industrial workers began seizing properties, no doubt stimulated by exaggerated rumors from Soviet Russia about the immediate benefits that would follow proletarian direct action. The police gradually restored order, and the danger of a revolution faded in 1921. Even so, the propertied classes had been frightened and, fearing the spread of Bolshevism, fell on the Fascist movement as their salvation.

Founded in 1919 by Mussolini, who had broken with the Italian Marxists, the Fascist party was not only vehemently nationalistic, but originally embodied the socialist, republican, and anticlerical views of its founder. Only when Mussolini saw that the road to power lay not in trying to gain leadership of the Marxist movement, but in appealing to the propertied classes, did he revise his principles to ap-

peal to them, to the Church, and to the monarchy. Retaining his nationalism, he emerged as an anticommunist and a champion of order. Yet, as an ex-Marxist, he knew the need for social reforms and was a master of the egalitarian rhetoric that enthralled the working classes and won their adherence. Some of the moderate politicians in Italy thought that Mussolini, therefore, could be a useful ally in promoting Italian recovery, yet were uneasy about the street gangs he was developing into paramilitary units. Their equivocation, plus Mussolini's threat to use violence, led the king to name him prime minister in 1922.

Everything in Mussolini's rise to power indicated that he would follow a militant foreign policy, attack Italian economic problems, and meet political opposition with terror. On reaching the prime ministry, he ordered that an official Fascist philosophy be constructed to provide the ideological justification for such policies. The quickly cooked result, a mixture of Sorel, the usual misinterpretations of Nietzsche, and nineteenth-century racial theories, seems to have been influenced by the work of one of Sorel's disciples, Vilfredo Pareto, especially his *Treatise of General Sociology* (1916). He accepted Marx's fundamental idea of class struggle, but rejected the idea that a victory for socialism and the proletariat would produce a classless society, concluding instead that it would produce merely a new governing elite. By elite he meant people of notable intelligence, character, skill, or capacity. And because he believed that mankind in general—the inferior people—is irrational, it must be governed by superior people, either by force or by cunning. He seems to have favored force as the better outward sign of strength; and he argued that an elite lost its mandate to govern only when it lost the willingness to use force to obtain what was rightly its own. A new elite, constantly generating among the inferiors, would then seize power. As Mussolini would recast the idea, "The Fascist State is a will to power and to government."

There followed several decades of bullying and blustering at home and abroad out of which a revived Roman Empire was presumably to emerge. Mussolini's heroics, however, always smacked of thuggery, and the suspicion remains that he always picked on the weak. In 1923, for example, the Italian member of an international commission investigating a Greco-Albanian border dispute was murdered. Mussolini assumed that the assassin had been Greek and ordered the bombardment and occupation of Corfu, demanding a large indemnity as the price for withdrawal. Greece appealed the matter to the League of Nations, where it was thought that the dispute ought to be referred to the World Court in the Hague. Whereupon the western powers, fearful of destroying Italian loyalty to the League, advised the Greeks to pay the indemnity. It was a black day for the integrity of the League. We have already noted Mussolini's quarrel with Yugoslavia over Fiume, settled in favor of Italy in 1924 because of Yugoslav weakness.

On the home front, Mussolini sought to stimulate economic productivity, first by reducing taxation through rigorous government economies—though he did raise the income tax rates. Public works were launched to provide work for the unemployed, and both strikes and lockouts were made illegal. These measures became permanent features of what Mussolini called the "corporate state." He originally took office with a coalition government, but as his paramilitary groups had become a militia paid by the state, he could more easily intimidate and purge the opposition. His old associates, the socialists and communists, were the first to feel his venom, and in 1923 he pressured Parliament into passing an electoral law giving the political party with a plurality of votes two thirds of the seats in Parliament. With 20 opposition parties to split the vote, the elections of 1924 gave the Fascists their two-thirds majority. Thereafter, the terror and censorship were more blatant, and parliamentary life was a farce. By 1928, all candidates for public office had to be approved by the Fascist party. Since all party officials were appointed rather than elected, all vestiges of democracy had been destroyed, and an "elite" held power.

Mussolini's dictatorship clearly represented the interests of the Right, yet the basic ideas for his "corporate state" came from the extreme Left—as he had—and more particularly from that part of the nineteenth-century labor movement called syndicalism. The phenomenon is hardly trivial since it contributed to the similarity of Leftist and Rightist dictatorships after 1918, led by men who accepted violence as the solution to social and international problems, and who generally began political life on the extreme Left imbued with ideas that we may loosely call "Sorelian." In the case of Fascist Italy, where independent labor and management associations were illegal, syndicates were organized within each industry to which both employers and employees belonged. All disputes had to be settled within the syndicate, and no strikes were allowed—hardly a Leftist ideal. Syndicates were also created for the professions and the trades, and the officials who directed the syndicates had to be Fascist party members. The system subjected the entire economic life of the country to the state. It eliminated much strife, and economic recovery and material progress did result. All it cost was political and personal liberty.

Germany: The Background to the Rise of the Nazis

While Germany seemed to follow Italy into fascism, the German situation after 1918, because it was more complex than the Italian, has been the subject of greater controversy. The debate has focused first on the sincerity of German support for a parliamentary republic (the Weimar Republic) and ultimately on the reasons for abandoning that republic. As late as 1928 the moderate political parties, those committed to making parliamentary government work, heavily out-polled the anticonstitutional extremist parties. Moreover, the Weimar Republic weathered several armed attacks, crushing the Left-wing Spartacists in 1919 who favored close ties with the Russian Bolsheviks, and breaking the back of the Kapp Putsch in 1920, a Right-wing attempt to restore the monarchy. On the other hand, no single moderate party ever achieved a majority that might have given parliamentary government vigorous direction, so that parliamentary government never seemed to function satisfactorily. The inherent weakness of coalition government was ominously revealed when the moderates needed Right-wing support to control the Spartacists in 1919 and Left-wing support to contain the monarchists in 1920.

Several myths were abroad in the 1920s that clearly compromised popular loyalty to the republic. The first was that Germany had surrendered in 1918 on the basis of Wilson's Fourteen Points and had then been betrayed by the victors; and the second was that the republic had betrayed Germany by accepting the terms presented at Versailles. In fact, the surrender had been unconditional beyond the actual armistice terms, and the real military collapse meant that *any* German government would have had no choice but to accept whatever terms were offered. When we see the popular drift toward Adolf Hitler's National Socialists (or Nazis) after 1928, a party whose platform rested on those myths, we must wonder whether the initial popular loyalty to the republic was genuine or an expedient.

In the matter of reparations, no German political party was convinced that Germany could pay the sum demanded, an attitude that weakened the national resolve to pay. Most Right-wingers were openly obstruc-

tionist on the issue, arguing that Germany should resist the "unjust" demands for payment. Many moderates, however, favored paying what was possible while working for a reduction in the amount due. When the western countries found themselves unable to relax their demands, the Weimar Republic sought political and economic ties with the Soviet Union in 1922 as a way of exerting pressure upon the Allies. Their agreement at Rapallo not only threatened the integrity of the new Poland, but was the first signal that Germany meant to evade the responsibilities agreed to at Versailles.

Out of the subsequent Allied occupation of the Ruhr region in 1923 came passive resistence encouraged by the government, and the loss of productivity—the final contributions to runaway inflation. Even though all the nations concerned then came to recognize that new reparations arrangements would have to be made which would provide opportunity for German economic recovery, the shock of those dreadful days of economic chaos left an immense residue of bitterness to feed the popular notion that the Germans had been repeatedly betrayed. Moderate, parliamentary government was threatened from the beginning by deep national resentments. Its instability was made manifest when the crash of the American stock market in 1929 triggered a global economic crisis that sent Germany drifting toward extremism.

The primary cause of that crash—if not the only cause—was an over-expansion of credit. Public interest in the stock market greatly increased during the 1920s, and many of the purchases by both large and small buyers were on margin. That is, the investor put up only a fraction of the purchase price for stocks, the broker advancing the rest by borrowing from banks. Perhaps as much as 90 percent of the transactions were speculatory rather than permanent investments. This speculation forced prices (and profits) to a point in 1929 where they had no real relation to wages. When the inevitable break in the market came, investors rushed to sell their holdings, merely fueling the collapse. Because the world economy was still highly integrated, the American disaster soon had international repercussions, especially critical because of the unresolved war debts and reparations.

The economic chaos that ensued not only drove European governments to permanent economic planning, as we have noted earlier, but proved fatal to the idea of a single world economy. London's traditional financial monopoly gave way to rival financial centers like New York, and the world economy was replaced by many national economies. The high protectionist duties of our Hawley-Smoot Act of 1930, consistent in spirit with our policy of debt repayment though hardly conducive to making payment possible, provoked retaliatory trade measures elsewhere. Many countries found high tariffs alone insufficient to promote their economic nationalism and imposed rigid import-export quotas. Still, unemployment figures continued to rise, reaching about three million in Great Britain by 1932 and between six and seven million in Germany.

The hardships endured by German business and labor were at once reflected in the rising strength of extremist political parties on both Right and Left. In 1930, the German chancellorship passed to Heinrich Brüning, a member of the moderate Centrist (Catholic) party whose personal conservatism and economic orthodoxy made him fear the Left more than the Right. Brüning called for new parliamentary elections, appealing to the nation to rally to the parties known to support the republic. As earlier in Italy, the moderate parties failed to join forces to face the challenge of extremism; and when the elections enabled the Communists to increase their seats from 54 to 77, and the Nazis from 12 to 107, Brüning reclared the state of emergency that entitled him to suspend constitutional rights and to govern by decree.

The Rise of Hitler and the Third Reich

This drift toward authoritarianism that culminated in the appointment of Hitler as chancellor in January 1933 featured intense jockeying for power among ultra-conservative factions and personalities. The military and the old aristocrats believed that they could regain control of national affairs in coalition with Hitler's Nazis, as social distinction divided them more than political principle; whereas the Nazis viewed such a coalition as a mere step to power. By 1932 the Nazis had become the largest of the Right-wing parties, and they had recruited a party police, the storm troopers, to bully the opposition. Even so, the decision to allow Hitler to become chancellor was a strategem of one old conservative faction to outmaneuver another. The cabinet contained only two other Nazis; the rest were true conservatives who could guard against the Rightist radicalism the Nazis represented.

Since the Nazis were not a majority party when Hitler assumed office, he called new parliamentary elections, preparing for them with a frenzied campaign against Communists. His strength only rose to 44 percent of the vote, but with the aid of the monarchical Nationalist party, he possessed the votes in parliament to have himself given dictatorial powers; and after he expelled the Communist members, his majority was absolute. The symbols of the Weimar Republic were at once replaced with the symbols of the Nazi party, including the national flag, and the state was renamed the Third Reich.* Since no one could mistake what Hitler stood for, his rise to power depended on widespread popular enthusiasm for his views (witness 44 percent of the vote) and not simply on the intrigues of Right-wing politicians whose plans went

---

* That is, the third German Empire; the first two were the Holy Roman Empire (A.D. 800–1806), and the Hohenzollern Empire that resulted from Bismarck's unification of Germany under Prussia (1871) and was destroyed by World War I.

Adolf Hitler (Radio Times Hulton Picture Library)

tional prejudices. Official propaganda not only hammered away on the old themes of betrayal at Versailles and the subsequent republican duplicity, but introduced a new party line arguing for the superiority of the German race and nation and warning against the national danger that the presence of Jews presumably constituted.

In the campaign to purify Germany, the police were given orders to shoot Communists on sight; but in introducing the official harassment of Jews, Hitler was implementing the Nazi race theory that came close to being the only "intellectual" justification the regime found. Like the racists of the late nineteenth century, the Nazis believed that race is the prime determinant in society. The party line held that pure Aryans (which meant Nordic people) are inherently superior and are biologically destined to rule over Slavs, Latins, Blacks, and Jews; and that Jews in particular contaminate a society. Hitler began by dismissing "non-Aryans" from official, military, and professional posts in 1933, a non-Aryan being defined legally to include anyone with one Jewish grandparent or Aryans who married non-Aryans. The government incited mobs to attack Jews and their property; in 1935 Jews were deprived of citizenship, and many of them were put in concentration camps. Other Germans who objected to this inhumanity, or who objected to the intellectual absurdities on which the racial policies rested, were themselves liable to confinement. The sad fact was that German culture fell into the hands of the government censors and propagandists, so that the purpose of all learning and the arts came to be the support and the glorification of the state. The educational system, too, was soon geared to train the young for nothing but service to the state and to wish for nothing but total subservience to the state. And that state was in the hands of Hitler and his party cohorts, who called themselves an elite, but whose social or intellectual credentials for such a claim were entirely invisible—men who were not

awry. Such politicians, it is true, agreed with Hitler on the goals for German foreign policy. But much of the Nazi vote had come from middle-class people whose judgment had been warped by economic distress, and from university students who saw in Hitler the opportunity to attack the entire social order and to bring about a future in which they would presumably have a greater part. Hitler's radicalism, however, had failed to attract industrial workers, who adhered to the traditional Left-wing parties.

In moving quickly to consolidate his position, Hitler recognized that his most imminent danger lay in those conservatives whom he had outmaneuvered in achieving dictatorial powers. In June of 1933, his storm troopers carried out a brutal purge of nearly a thousand Rightists to prevent a new coalition against him. Meanwhile, he established a Ministry of Propaganda and Enlightenment, acting on his belief that the masses are moved not by intelligence but by inflaming their irraso much indifferent to, as ignorant of, the morality and law that make society possible.

This totality of state control was extended to the national economy. In that era when most European governments experimented with economic planning and with limited economic controls, Nazi Germany devised extensive economic planning. The goal was to provide the means for war. Private enterprise still existed, but the state attempted to regulate production and distribution, banking, investment, and trade, not to speak of manpower. The high degree of coordination within German business and industry that had been developing for several decades before 1933 facilitated the Nazi economic policy, as the great cartels could be used as agencies to promote government designs, a fact which rallied many industrialists to the Nazi cause. Hitler also sponsored a public works program to eliminate the grievous unemployment, though by 1938 his rearmament program had created a virtual war economy that itself guaranteed full employment.

Control of foreign trade had initially been introduced in 1931 to stop the flight of capital, but in 1934 the Nazi's introduced their New Plan which was designed to reduce imports and to force the use of substitute products that could be made in Germany. Toward that end, importers had to hold balances in special marks rather than in freely convertible currency, and the government limited export commodities to items of nonstrategic value. This New Plan aimed at once at autarky—economic self-sufficiency—and at blatant trade discrimination; and it could only have succeeded in that day of international business recession. In any case, what the Germans attempted in the 1930s amounted to a reversal of the tendency toward economic specialization that had characterized the world economy in the nineteenth century. The practice of autarky was both a preparation for war and a deliberate looting of struggling foreign economies.

The Soviet Union

Whereas Italy and Germany were governed democratically for brief periods after 1918, democracy in the Soviet Union was a sham from the outset. Lenin's constitution of 1918 did provide for a national parliament, the All-Union Congress, but it met only once every two years, mainly to ratify the work of the cabinet—known as the Council of People's Commissars. Moreover, the voting system was highly complex, indirect, and discriminated against the rural population. Entire groups of people believed to be sympathetic to pre-Bolshevik regimes were simply disenfranchised. The Communist party was the only legal party, and it comprised a bare one percent of the population, an elite which in theory submitted absolutely to party discipline. At first the party had its own tribunal, the *Cheka*, which tried political opponents before executing them. But in 1922, the Cheka was abolished and its function was assumed by the OGPU, a division of the national police; the transfer illustrated the fact that the party and the state were identical.

Because Lenin's leadership of the Russian Revolution was cut short when he suffered a stroke in 1922, a struggle for power began at once—even though Lenin survived into 1924. His favored successor was his long-time associate, Trotsky, an intellectual and the man credited with building the Red Army which had triumphed in the Civil War. His chief rival, Stalin, was regarded by Lenin as a man so utterly ruthless that his leadership could jeopardize the integrity of the revolution. Yet, Stalin, then secretary-general of the party, ultimately gained the ascendancy, partly because his control of the party machinery proved to be the most powerful position in Russia, and partly because a majority of the Bolshevik leaders feared his intellectual mediocrity less than they did Trotsky's brilliance.

As their rivalry intensified during the 1920s, Stalin and Trotsky became identified with different revolutionary programs.

Trotsky, sticking closely to the Leninist line, continued to see Russia as the generator of international revolution. Stalin, seeing the failure of Marxist parties elsewhere by 1923, argued for Russian isolationism, and for building Russia into a strong socialist state capable of resisting attack from the capitalist nations if that should come. Though most of the Bolsheviks rallied to Stalin's party line, he knew that many of them had been reluctant to abandon the dream of world revolution, leading him to declare the Trotskyite position as antirevolutionary and subversive. Trotsky and his friends were expelled from the party in 1927, and Trotsky himeslf was banished from Russia two years later.

With the question of leadership settled, Stalin could turn to the economic reorganization of the country—to the construction of a totally planned economy. The first Five Year Plan (1928) was designed to transform an underdeveloped country into an industrial state without depending on either foreign or domestic private investors. Toward that end, the government decided on the collectivization of Russian agriculture as the quickest way to modernize it and to produce the agricultural surpluses necessary to free manpower for industrial labor. What is more, collectivization struck at the heart of a serious source of opposition to the regime—the wealthier peasants (or kulaks) who had resented the food rationing and price-fixing that had made agriculture relatively unremunerative. During the 1920s, the resentful kulaks had often limited their production to their own needs, refusing to deliver food to the cities.

The kulaks resisted collectivization even more vigorously, destroying farm animals and equipment, until Stalin virtually declared war on them as a class. Some two million of them, who survived a campaign of terror, ended in forced labor camps in remote areas of the Soviet Union. Not until collectivization was completed in 1931 could the state claim that private enterprise had been destroyed, with the state capturing the entire economic system. No doubt the very vastness of Russia and her economy enhanced the possibility of economic isolation, which was the counterpart of Stalin's political isolation. The government limited imports to materials vital for the developing industry, and the volume of foreign trade remained low. The standard of living also remained low as the government concentrated on heavy industry, on mechanizing agriculture, and on military preparations. Emphasis on consumer goods would have to wait. A second Five Year Plan was inaugurated in 1933, during which Russia emerged as an industrial nation.

Stalin granted a new constitution in 1936 which was heralded at home and abroad as a great advance in democracy and personal liberty. It provided for a bicameral parliament, one house to represent the many nationalities in the Soviet Union, the other house to be elected directly by the people. Not only did the continuation of one-party government reveal the reform to be mere window dressing, but it came at a moment when Stalin was engaged in a vast paroxysm of terror designed to consolidate his absolute authority. Beginning in 1935, he carried out a systematic purge of the party hierarchy, including many of the "old Bolsheviks" suspected of enjoying prestige or popularity. Some of the most prominent were induced to confess their betrayal of the revolution in trials whose evident aim was to influence world opinion. No doubt there had been criticism of Stalin's abandonment of world revolution, of his harsh treatment of the kulaks, and of his unwillingness to provide more consumer goods; just as he no doubt believed that the rearmament of Germany under the Nazis was a serious military threat to Russia and required greater unity to meet the danger. But the very savagery of Stalin's purges, which only ended in 1938, revealed a pathological distrust of those around him. It is hardly a matter of idle curiosity that the two men—Hitler and

Stalin—whose personal regimes required the death of countless millions, were both evidently victims of paranoia. We shall probably never know how many innocent millions Stalin sent to death or to labor camps, for the purges reached far beyond the party hierarchy in almost total disregard for human life.

Fascist Spain

Democracy also failed in Spain in the 1930s, but the particular brand of fascism that emerged was really a variant of ancient political traditions in Spain. Spanish national unity had been born of a late-medieval crusade led by the Christian monarchy against the Muslim Moors, the memory of which kept many Spaniards traditionally loyal to the monarchy, the army, and the Church. Yet, the brilliant successes enjoyed by these foundational institutions well into the sixteenth century were much rarer thereafter, for Spain lacked the economic resources to compete successfully with the other Atlantic states. Her response was to turn inward in defense of her traditional institutions—to reject innovations bred north of the Pyrennees. The loss of her Latin American empire not only contributed to her isolation, but dealt a serious blow to the prestige of the traditional governing triumvirate of monarchy, army and Church. In the nineteenth century, therefore, the monarchy faced increasing demands to decentralize the nation, particularly from the Basques and the Catalans; the army could no longer justify its claim on a major slice of the national budget; the Church was so conservative that it was occasionally chided by Rome; and those Spaniards wanting to stem the national decline by bringing Spain into the ranks of the progressive countries began to toy with liberal and radical ideas coming from outside, notably anarchism. Military defeat by the United States in 1898 was a humiliating blow, and when the army could not

even contain an uprising in Morocco in 1931, the antimonarchial forces were finally able to win the national elections and force the abdication of the monarch, Alphonso XIII.

Unfortunately for the new Spanish Republic, its supporters were divided into nine political parties, ranging from liberal to anarchist, making coalition government necessary. In the short history of the republic, no cabinet ever enjoyed the backing of a parliamentary majority in the hands of one party. This inherent instability was all the more threatening as only 14 of the 470 delegates elected to the Constituent Convention had had previous parliamentary experience. Grasping for the few issues on which all republicans could agree, they fell upon anticlerical and antimilitary legislation. The army was substantially reduced in size, many superfluous officers being retired on full pay; clerical control of education was sharply reduced, and the state confiscated all ecclesiastical property.

Such extreme measures served to rally the traditional factions to attempt a comeback, but in the 1930s they saw in fascism the ingredients for a Right-wing dictatorship likely to be more effective than a restored monarchy. Thus the Spanish fascist movement, calling itself the Falange, took the anticommunist line common to fascist parties elsewhere and declared itself opposed to the republic on the grounds that the republic was communist-ridden. While there can be no doubt that the communists, as one of the republican parties, did make trouble for the more moderate republicans, the poverty of the Falangist charge was revealed in the elections of 1936, when the Communists won only two and one-half percent of the parliamentary seats.

The actual attempt to overthrow the republic began as a military coup in Morocco, and rebel officers quickly seized control in portions of south, west, and northwest Spain. But the coup failed when much of the southwest, the north, and the heart of Spain remained loyal. Thus the country plunged into civil war, with the rebel government establishing itself at Burgos, and General Franco emerging as the rebel chief. Both sides appealed for foreign aid—the rebels to Germany and Italy, the republic to France and the Soviet Union. Hitler responded with transport planes (especially needed to bring troops from Morocco, since the Spanish Navy remained loyal to the government) and later with new military aircraft. Mussolini sent troops, ultimately 40,000 supported by tanks, though their performance was unimpressive.

Russian aid to the republic, through the Mediterranean, was limited by the presence of German and Italian submarines. But Soviet support compromised the noncommunist majority in the Spanish government, who were continually hampered by radical uprisings in the rear. To have refused the nominal cooperation of the radical parties would have been to write off Soviet aid. Therefore, the government would have greatly preferred its military assistance to come from the western democracies for both logistical and political reasons. Léon Blum, the socialist prime minister of France in 1936, favored giving such assistance—so great was his horror of European fascism—but that critical aid never came. The wonder is that the Spanish army, with substantial foreign aid, took three years to destroy the republic. Madrid, bitterly defended by its citizens, fell only in 1939, at a moment when the Communists were making a last bid to seize control of the republic.

Many in the civil war died anonymously. Casualties from both battles and purges probably cost over a million lives. The Franco regime, posing as a regency to prepare for a Bourbon restoration, was in fact a corporate state modeled on Mussolini's Italy. The international aspects of Franco's victory, however, revealed the true decay of western nerve when faced with the responsibility to maintain the settlement of

1919. The western policies of nonintervention in Spain were ostensibly based on a pathetic hope that they would induce the fascist powers to cut off support to Franco and on the fear that general intervention could lead to general war. On the other hand, the evil that the totalitarian states represented by the 1930s, whether Rightist or Leftist, was so transparent and so menacing to the remaining bastions of human liberty and decency, that western failure to save a moderate republic in fact reflected a moral crisis in western society.

It is no doubt true that western resolve was handicapped by the very fact that the danger appeared simultaneously from the extreme Left and Right. To some, neutrality seemed to be the moral alternative to an alignment with any totalitarian regime. Yet, a great body of western opinion had been so antagonized by the foreign and domestic policies of the Bolsheviks after 1917 that there remained a genuine reluctance to aid any regime that accepted communist support as the Spanish Republic had, which became a tendency to tolerate any regime that was avowedly anticommunist. But the failure of the western democracies to act in their own interest in Spain primarily revealed the disenchantment which they, the victors in 1918, felt about the peace that had crowned a victory won at such terrible cost.

From the outset there had been no Allied agreement as to the proper treatment of defeated Germany. The British and Americans in particular, tending to suffer from bad consciences about the harsh settlement, were susceptible to German complaints and inclined to overlook treaty violations—to the intense distress of the French. The meager fruits of victory taught an entire generation the virtues of pacifism, a public attitude that enfeebled every western government when forced to face the teeth of militant totalitarianism. This weakness, when coupled with the collapse of democratic governments on all sides, made many in the

West question the vitality and future of democracy—in the very countries that in the nineteenth century had been the hope of all peoples seeking freedom. The disillusionment reached its apex in France, where the sense of betrayal by her wartime allies was a contributing factor.

The Crisis of the 1930s: French Disunity

French economic recovery in the 1920s had been remarkable and had been accompanied by administrative and tax reforms which ought to have produced a sense of confidence and security. French uneasiness, however, was not solely rooted in the decay of the wartime alliances, but in an awareness of a declining population and in the dislocation of many people as France experienced a new thrust of industrialization. The demographic crisis reached its peak in 1935, when the number of deaths exceeded the number of births. If the loss of young men in the war was the direct cause, France had long experienced a declining birthrate, sharpening the sense of a loss in vitality.

The postwar industrialization gave France a more balanced economy than she had had in the nineteenth century, and her resulting stability made her the last major European country to be affected seriously by the stock market crash of 1929. As in the case of Germany, however, that collapse ultimately brought economic depression and unemployment, causing the industrial workers in particular to demand social legislation. The Rightist parties regarded such Left-wing demands as the probable beginning of a Bolshevik revolution, so that by 1932 a national crisis was brewing. Coalitions of Leftist parties controlled the governments at that point, but the cabinets were never stable. Each party had its own idea as to the degree of nationalization of business and industry necessary to meet the economic crisis. And the multi-party system contributed to the difficulty of getting tax increases and other anti-inflationary measures through parliament.

The result was near paralysis, a rapid succession of "caretaker" cabinets, which not only undermined public confidence in democratic procedures, but encouraged the revival of all those elements in French society that had been hostile to the republican form of government after 1870. This internal disunity contributed to a weak foreign policy when it came to facing the menace of Hitler and Mussolini, further convincing some Rightists that only a fascist-style regime in France could cope with both internal and external pressures. The so-called Popular Front, a new coalition of Leftist parties formed in 1936 under Léon Blum, did save the democratic republic from that Rightist solution; but by then France's weakness had been revealed to those who wished the destruction of the Versailles settlement.

Meanwhile, uncertain of British and American support, the French had been trying to bolster that settlement through alliances in 1934 with Czechoslovakia, Yugoslavia, and Romania, and in 1935 with the Soviet Union. But the military value of such alliances for French security was doubtful, while the tie with the Soviet Union served to heighten Rightist suspicions. As Blum discovered in 1936, no firm commitment to the cause of republican Spain was politically possible, however, necessary it may have been for French integrity and security.

Economic Depression in Britain

Disenchantment with victory overcame the British even earlier than the French, principally because Britain did not enjoy the economic recovery experienced by the French in the 1920s. At the root of the problem was Britain's traditional preeminence in industry. Whereas the French had to rebuild much of their industry after the war, the British resumed competition in the world market with an established industry that was outmoded and relatively inefficient compared to that of Germany, the United States, and Japan, latecomers to industrialization. During the dark years of sacrifice that culminated in victory, the public had come to anticipate a postwar Eden: prosperity and social reform. Instead, British export trade proved to be shockingly low in volume, and as production necessarily fell off, unemployment soared. Membership in the Labor party rose rapidly as a consequence, mainly at the expense of the old Liberals; and Labor formed its first government in 1923 under Ramsay MacDonald.

The Labor party, which had housed some pacifists during the war, also profited from a postwar wave of pacifism, as many of the disillusioned came to believe that no victory could be worth its cost. Rapid postwar disarmament reflected both this pacifism and the need for government economy. Continued depression led to a strike in the coal industry in 1926, and thanks to the ineptitude of the leaders in government, labor, and industry, the coal strike expanded into a general strike that inflamed class tensions. The middle class tended to see the general strike as Bolshevik-type direct action, and thus as revolutionary and a rejection of traditional parliamentary procedures, often losing sight of the workers' genuine grievances. After the failure of the strike, the Labor party sought to reduce hostility and enhance understanding by educating the middle class and recruiting from it.

Therefore, faced with the global economic crisis after 1929, the British parties tended to close ranks and to cooperate in defense of the British system and way of life. Unemployment remained high right down to the outbreak of World War II, but only a few extremists suggested in the 1930s that the parliamentary democracy be scrapped in favor of an authoritarian regime. Although the British preserved internal unity better than the French did, Britain's domestic scene precluded rearmament even when the designs of the fascist states became transparent. And conse-quently, Britain's foreign policy was even weaker than that of France.

The Appeasement Policy

The failure of Britain and France to counter the fascist intervention in Spain was only one of several instances in the 1930s when the western powers showed themselves ready to pay any price necessary to avoid another war. Because general war eventually came despite their good intentions to avoid it and despite their willingness to appease those determined to revise the status quo, world opinion ultimately condemned western statesmen for not putting the brakes to the likes of Hitler and Mussolini before they became so arrogant in their power and so much more difficult to defeat. The criticism misses several key points: that it was proper to seek peace; that it was not wrong to employ diplomacy to settle issues; that democratic governments cannot long act in defiance of public opinion; that when public opinion leads to disarmament (as in Britain) or to support for a military establishment essentially defensive in character (as in France) or to feigned neutrality (as in Belgium), a statesman's latitude is constrained, and he has no convincing response to those who respect only force.

One can understand the roots of popular pacifism after World War I and sympathize with its motives, while lamenting the rising barbarism which cared not for people, much less for their peace. So the day came, as it must to all civilized men, when the menace had to be destroyed if civility were to endure. The fault of the statesmen of the 1930s was their failure, as cultivated men, to recognize the essential barbarism of the movements they faced. Instead, Nazi and Fascist demands were treated simply as national or territorial claims, more or less justified, as is proper in normal foreign relations. To have perceived exactly what Hitler represented, which was hardly the national German interest, would have been to cry out in alarm for the immediate mobilization of the national resources in defense of both decency and the national interest.

The first act of aggression to be challenged weakly by the western powers in the 1930s was in fact committed by Japan in 1931. Using a minor incident in Manchuria as a pretext, the Japanese overran that Chinese province and established a puppet state called Manchukuo, accomplishing what they had failed to do at the turn of the century. China appealed to the League of Nations for assistance, but Japan ignored a League request for a negotiated settlement; and when the League formally condemned the Japanese aggression, the Japanese gave notice of intention to withdraw from the League. By 1935 Japan had pursued her invasion of North China, occupying three more provinces without any punitive response from either the League or the United States.

In 1935, Hitler made his initial challenge to the Versailles settlement by denouncing its disarmament clauses, an action that led directly to the Franco-Russian alliance, but which failed to provoke the military reaction Hitler feared. The British, in fact, seeing the Franco-Russian pact as a further example of unfairness to Germany's legitimate rights, actually encouraged German rearmament by concluding a naval agreement with Hitler that year. Though Hitler agreed to limit his navy to 35 percent of the tonnage of the British Commonwealth fleets, he clearly gained an enormous political victory.

Mussolini made his move in 1935, too, following an incident on the frontier between Ethiopia and Italian Somaliland. The Italians had had an eye on Ethiopia since the 1890s, and Mussolini boasted that he would accomplish its seizure. The League moved quickly to halt his aggression by voting to impose economic sanctions against Italy. But Britain and France, hoping to draw Mussolini into a common front against German military revival, connived to have coal and oil excluded from the commodities to be denied to Italy. No doubt Italy could have bought the oil from American producers in any case, but the western connivance in Mussolini's aggression only increased his contempt for democracy and his preference for Germany. The League's sanctions went unenforced while Ethiopia fell to Italian arms. When the League lifted the useless sanctions in 1937, Mussolini expressed his contempt by taking Italy out of the League. The collective security, presumably to be promoted by the League of Nations, was obviously nonexistent. By then, the Spanish Civil War was compounding the humiliation of the democratic states.

From then on the initiative belonged to Hitler. In 1936 he ordered the military reoccupation of the Rhineland—forbidden by the Versailles settlement—to which the western powers made no military response. To have acted to preserve the demilitarization of the Rhineland would no doubt have brought war with Germany, as Hitler's political future would have given him no choice but to fight. The crisis revealed especially the political and military vulnerability of France: A caretaker government was still in office; and the military establishment, designed solely for national defense and not for quick counterthrust, was poorly equipped for offensive warfare. The army, in fact, confessed its weakness. Many Rightists, angered by the recent alliance with the Soviet Union, openly favored strengthening Hitler as a bulwark against communism. Moreover, world opinion had gradually bought the German line that the Versailles settlement had been unjust and that Hitler was only rectifying a wrong. What the French revealed to Hitler, by not taking firm measures to safeguard their own frontiers in 1936, was the unlikelihood of their going to war on behalf of an ally.

Hitler Absorbs Austria and Czechoslovakia

The Versailles settlement had also forbidden the union (*Anschluss*) of Germany and Austria. In his own book, *Mein Kampf* (1923), Hitler revived pan-Germanism, claiming that Germans everywhere should be united into a greater Germany. He particularly desired the annexation of his native Austria. But although many Austrians had been eager for *Anschluss* after 1918 as the solution of Austrian economic problems, the idea appealed considerably less after 1933. The Christian Socialist leadership in Austria sought closer association with Mussolini, expecting that Italy would not want a strong Germany on her nothern frontier. But Mussolini's ultimate collaboration with Hitler not only isolated Austria, but commenced the slow erosion of Italy into a German satellite.

In 1938, after an unsuccessful attempt by the Austrian National Socialists (Nazis) to seize power, Hitler brought overwhelming pressure to bear on the Austrian government. Seeing no effective support from either Italy or the western powers, the Austrian government let itself be bullied out of office in favor of the local Nazis. *Anschluss* followed at once. Hitler then held a plebiscite to ask the Austrians if they approved union with Germany, and 99 percent of the population dutifully accepted the accomplished fact. Germany thus acquired over six million new citizens.

Hitler next turned on Czechoslovakia, where he had been encouraging the three million German minority, known as *Sudetens*, to enlarge on alleged discrimination by the Czechs and to demand *Anschluss* with Germany. To have tried a bald annexation as in the case of Austria would have been risky, for unlike Austria the Czechs had strong defenses and alliances with France and Russia. The Germans knew they had the military power to reduce Czechoslovakia in 1938, but not the strength to resist simultaneously an Anglo-French in-vasion from the west. Poland, on the other hand, with an eye on Czech territory in case of partition and eager to appease Hitler, let it be known that she would not allow Russian troops to cross Polish territory to aid Czechoslovakia.

Even so, Hitler thought it best to try to gain his ends by negotiation, especially after Prime Minister Chamberlain of Britain claimed that one must work out crises with Hitler in good faith to prevent war. Daladier, then prime minister of France, saw the danger Germany posed more clearly than Chamberlain, but was constrained by the French army's lack of readiness for offensive warfare and felt that France could not risk a campaign without direct British support. Given Chamberlain's insistence on a negotiated settlement, the Sudetens stepped up their demands for *Anschluss*. The agony of the Czechs was complete when both Poland and Hungary also made territorial demands, and when the Slovaks were induced to demand autonomy.

On September 29, 1938, Hitler entertained Chamberlain, Daladier, and Mussolini at a conference in Munich, deliberately omitting Russia (which might have supported the western powers.) Chamberlain, determined to save the peace, and having publicly said that "If we have to fight, it must be on larger issues than . . . a quarrel in a faraway country between people of whom we know nothing," did not even insist that the Czechs be allowed to send representatives. They were given no alternative but to surrender 25 percent of their territory and to grant Slovakian autonomy.

Chamberlain claimed that he had "won peace in our time," but when Hitler occupied the remainder of Czechoslovakia without resistance six months later, Chamberlain's faith in Hitler's integrity was shattered. Daladier already knew that the British and French had abdicated as great powers by their refusal, or inability, to exercise their responsibilities at Munich. Russia subsequently made great political capital from her exclusion from Munich, claiming that she would have honored the collective responsibility to block Hitler. In fact, the Russians made no military preparations to aid Czechoslovakia and privately notified the Germans that the Sudeten issue did not concern the Soviet Union. But at least the Russians had no illusions about Hitler's ultimate intentions and were deliberately buying time.

The Polish Crisis and the Outbreak of War

Since 1933, the Soviets and Nazis had religiously denounced each other's ideologies and declared themselves to be mortal enemies. Moreover, Hitler had made no secret of his determination, once Germany had the military strength, to acquire what he called *Lebensraum* (living space) in Eastern Europe. Even so, Stalin had long recognized the actual community of Russo-German interests: Both powers were antagonistic to the post-World War I territorial settlements, and both knew that secret German rearmament in the Weimer period had been abetted by Russian connivance. In particular, both had in the partition of Poland the grounds for eventual agreement in Eastern Europe. By 1939, Russia had the choice of either working out closer ties with the Anglo-French to check German expansion in Eastern Europe or of approaching Hitler to work out an agreement for the division of Eastern Europe between them.

The military weakness of the West hardly recommended the first option, especially after Munich; the Russians knew only too well the long term Western hostility to the Soviet system and doubted effective cooperation; and Stalin's proposal to occupy all of Eastern Europe from Finland to Turkey as the key to blocking Germany could hardly be conceded by the West. Thus, when Hitler turned his attention to Poland after the occupation of Czechoslovakia in 1938, Stalin took steps to implement his second alternative.

The Versailles settlement had given Poland territories in the west that included German-speaking people, and she had expanded to the east at the expense of the Soviet Union in the troubled years following the Russian Civil War. The treaty had also created the Free City of Danzig as an enclave, a city too German to be given to Poland. Polish nationalists nevertheless assumed that the city must eventually become theirs. Indeed, the architects of Polish foreign policy, banking on eternal Nazi-Soviet hostility, favored reaching a friendly understanding with Hitler as the basis for a greater Polish role in Eastern Europe. Consequently, they were considerably unsettled, at the end of 1938, when Hitler informed them that Danzig must become German; and in the ensuing months, they seemed slow to realize that Hitler's intentions included no room for Polish ambitions.

Meanwhile, the clear threat to Poland led the British and French governments to warn Hitler in the spring of 1939 that they would act to resist any attempt on Polish independence. To this Hitler responded by acknowledging the repeated overtures from the Soviet Union. On August 23, 1939, a German-Soviet Pact was signed. Even though most of its terms remained secret, its implications came as a bombshell, for the Pact publicly announced that in case one of its signatories were to go to war, the other would remain neutral.

While the German-Soviet Pact enabled Hitler to launch an attack on Poland, which he did in great confidence one week later, the Pact was an enormous diplomatic victory for Russia. It led to embroiling Hitler with Britain and France, who honored their pledge to Poland by declaring war on Germany, and bought the Soviet Union valuable months to prepare for the eventual collision with Hitler in Eastern Europe. It bought territory, too: The secret clauses provided for the partition of Poland, for Lithuania to become a German "sphere of influence," but for Finland, Latvia, and Estonia to come within the Russian sphere.

Evidently, Hitler presumed that his conquest of Poland, launched with no declaration of war, would be so swift that the western powers would reluctantly accept it as they had his prior annexations. By then, however, even Chamberlain had recognized that the world faced something quite different from the alleged German claims to rectify the "wrongs" of the Versailles settlement. As he put it:

We have a clear conscience, we have done all that any country could do to establish peace, but a situation in which no word given by Germany's ruler could be trusted, and no people or country could feel themselves safe, had become intolerable. . . . For it is evil things we shall be fighting against, brute force, bad faith, injustice, oppression, and persecution. But against them I am certain that right will prevail.

And so the war, which the men of peace had said was intolerable, came in September of 1939.

CHRONOLOGY OF 1914–1939

1914–1918:	World War I
1917:	Collapse of the czarist regime in Russia
1917:	American entry into World War I
1917–1920:	Russian Revolution and Civil War
1918:	Treaty of Brest-Litovsk
1918–1922:	Lenin's ascendency in the Soviet Union
1919:	Treaty of Versailles
1922–1943:	Dictatorship of Mussolini
1927–1953:	Dictatorship of Stalin
1929:	Beginning of the Great Depression
1931:	Abdication of Alphonso XIII
1933–1945:	Dictatorship of Hitler
1934:	Assassination of Chancellor Dollfus
1935:	Italian invasion of Ethiopia
1936–1939:	Spanish Civil War
1936:	German military reoccupation of the Rhineland
1938:	Union of Germany and Austria
1938:	Munich Conference
1939:	First successful atomic fission (Germany)
1939:	German-Soviet Pact
1939:	Pact of Steel (Germany and Italy)

38
World War II

The Italo-German Offensives

For all its militant bluster, the Italian government had watched the approach of war in 1939 with considerable misgiving, rightly doubtful of Italy's ability to sustain a major conflict. Yet, Mussolini's feeble appraisal over the years of where true Italian interests lay had culminated in a formal alliance with Germany early in 1939 (the "Pact of Steel") and left Italy at the mercy of German foreign policy. Even so, Italy did not immediately honor her alliance after the Anglo-French declaration of war on Germany, but adopted the "wait-and-see" tactics she followed in 1914. What she saw was encouraging. While the western allies found themselves unequipped to give Poland any direct help, the Germans turned upon the Poles the new tactics of *blitzkrieg* (lightning war). Aircraft, especially dive bombers, were used as artillery to break up enemy formations and to destroy communications; after which swiftly moving armored divisions took advange of enemy confusion to range far behind enemy lines and to develop encircling movements that cut the enemy into isolated pockets. Air attacks were used simultaneously against the civilian population to increase confusion and demoralization.

The Poles, outnumbered, outgunned, and unprepared to cope with such methods, capitulated after 27 days, and the campaign would have been even shorter had Warsaw not held out heroically when all else was lost. Russia, meanwhile, occupied the Polish and Baltic territories specified in the deal with Hitler, and approached the Finnish government with a proposal for an exchange of territory ostensibly to improve the defenses of Leningrad. Determined to do everything possible against the anticipated day of Russo-German conflict, the Russians attacked the Finns late in 1939 on Finnish rejection of the proposal. Though the Russians made a poor military showing against the valiant Finnish defense, the Finns ultimately were obliged to make the territorial concessions in 1940. Inactive on the western front, the Anglo-French had been struggling to put together an expedition to aid the Finns. Hitler used the knowledge of these futile preparations as a pretext to occupy both Denmark and Norway in early 1940, claiming that the Allies planned to use a Scandinavian route to attack his ally, Russia. This series of calamities forced Chamberlain from office, and his long-time critic, Winston Churchill, took the prime ministry.

Now powerfully based on the continent, Hitler suddenly broke the calm on the western front with an invasion of the Netherlands and Belgium on May 10, 1940. The tactics of blitzkreig were again employed to produce paralysis and demoralization, now augmented by parachutists and subversives who seized vital centers of communication. A Dutch surrender came after five days. For years, the French had spent millions on their Maginot Line, a defensive work of undeniable strength extending along the northeastern frontier from Switzerland to Belgium; but it had never been extended to the sea for fear of weakening Belgium's resolve to resist a German attack. Consequently, the Anglo-French rushed troops into Belgium to help stem the German drive, only to be confronted by the unexpected capitulation of Leopold III on May 28. His surrender had the effect of isolating the Allied forces in Belgium, and their necessary retreat was blocked by a German breakthrough at Sedan that had completely bypassed—or outflanked—the Maginot Line.

Though the French fought a successful rearguard action that enabled the bulk of the British forces, nearly 340,000 men, to escape by sea through the port of Dunkirk, the magnitude of the defeat and the outflanking of the Maginot Line convinced the French military that the defense of France had become impossible and that an armistice must be sought. At that juncture, Mussolini deemed it prudent to begin an assault against the French southeastern frontier. After an agony of indecision, the French signed an armistice on June 22 which gave Germany all of northern France and the Atlantic coastal zone. General de Gaulle, who had opposed the armistice, flew to London to organize a Free French movement, and some of the units of the French navy joined his cause. But much of the Navy remained loyal to the new French regime which established itself at Vichy in southern France under the leadership of Marshal Pétain. This regime, openly collaborationist with the victorious Germans, was no doubt supported by some who felt that defeated France had no alternative; but the regime brought to power men and factions who had long been antagonistic to the democratic Third Republic and who saw in its defeat the opportunity to construct an authoritarian (and antisemitic) state.

The fall of France left Britiain alone against the continent, almost as she had been in 1807. She had sacrificed much of her military equipment at Dunkirk in favor of rescuing her men, but she did have naval control of the Channel as a barrier to German invasion. But the Germans saw that if they destroyed the Royal Air Force, the British fleet would not dare to operate in the narrow confines of the Channel. German air attacks on Britain began in July of 1940; but the British aircraft, though outnumbered, proved to be substantially superior to the German and were assisted in seeking their targets by a new device called radar. The German air losses over Britain became so costly that plans for an invasion had to be postponed. German bombing did, of course, hamper British industrial production, and submarines inflicted heavy losses on merchant shipping. At that point in 1940, President Roosevelt, convinced that a British defeat would be catastrophic for the United States, took the lead in getting help to the British despite his country's substantial isolationism. Roosevelt traded 50 overage destroyers for

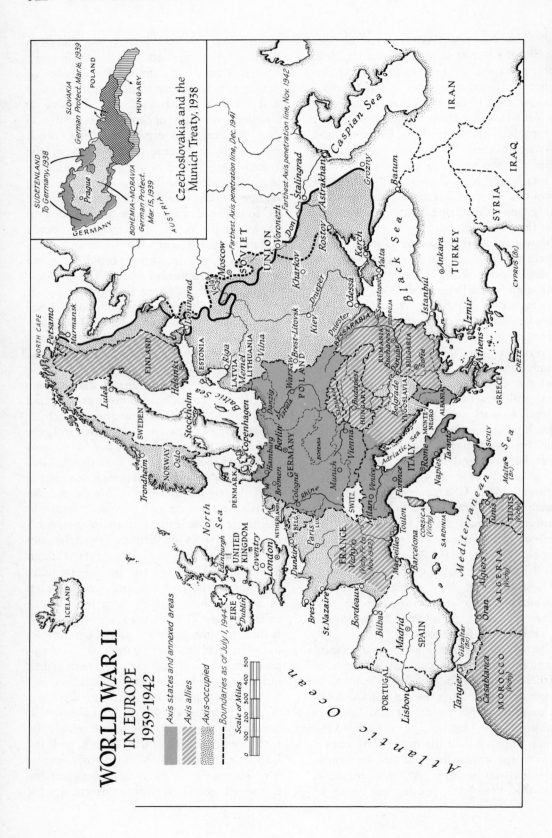

WORLD WAR II
IN EUROPE
1939-1942

Axis states and annexed areas
Axis allies
Axis-occupied
Boundaries as of July 1, 1944

Scale of Miles
0 100 200 300 400 500

Czechoslovakia and the
Munich Treaty, 1938

SUDETENLAND
To Germany, 1938
German Protect. Mar.16, 1939
SLOVAKIA
POLAND
HUNGARY
Prague
BOHEMIA-MORAVIA
German Protect.
Mar. 15, 1939
GERMANY
AUSTRIA

convoy duty to Britain for long leases on British bases in the Caribbean and Atlantic. Early in 1941, Roosevelt secured the Lend-Lease Act, which gave him authority to provide American help to any nation whose defense was vital to American security.

The Italians endeavored to contribute to knocking Britain out of the war in 1940 by taking aim at British positions in Egypt and the Near East, to be accomplished by an offensive eastward from the Italian colony of Libya and by the conquest of Greece. These campaigns were not only miserable failures, but gave the British opportunity to overrun Mussolini's East African empire and to inflict heavy damage on the Italian fleet in the Mediterranean. On the other hand, although Hitler was furious at the Italian bungling, German troops were sent to bail out the Italians in both Africa and Greece, in the process of which he forced Romania, Hungary, and Slovakia to join the war against Britain and Greece; and German troops were even sent to Italy to bolster Mussolini's regime against popular criticism. Despite the Italian fiascos, the war was really going badly for Britain.

Indeed, the threat of increasing aid to Britain from the United States, and the fact that Britain began to have the resources to begin serious bombing of Germany in 1941 did suggest that the moment had arrived for Germany to risk an all-out assault on Britain. Instead, Hitler chose to create a two-front war by invading the Soviet Union on June 22, 1941. Expecting no invasion from the Atlantic side, Hitler calculated that he could conquer Russia during the summer. Once he should have the great food-growing regions of the Soviet Union in hand he could then easily finish off the British in the Afro-Mediterranean theater. Confidence in the scheme was so great that the Germans launched it with no preparations for a winter campaign in Russia.

When the Russians retreated swiftly to avoid the outflanking tactics of blitzkreig and scorched the earth as they retired, Hitler's schedule evaporated; and the fundamental unsoundness of attacking Russia before the reduction of Britain proved to be fatal to Germany. She might inflict dreadful casualties on the Russian population but was unable to bring the Russian armies to bay. And her own forces suffered miserably in the Russian winter. Worse, supplies began reaching the Soviet Union from Britain and from the United States (under the Lend-Lease Act), most of them by way of the laborious overland route across the Middle East.

The United States Enters the War

Japanese territorial ambitions on the Asian continent had been evident for decades, and in 1936 Japan promoted close relations with Nazi Germany in recognition of common goals to be won at the expense of Russia and the West. Consequently, the Russo-German Pact of 1939 came as a shock to Japan, but the following year she joined Germany and Italy in the Tripartite Pact, evidence that Japan had been assured of an ultimate German invasion of the Soviet Union. Since the Japanese had long viewed their own plans in global terms, they logically came to regard the increasing American commitment to Britain and Russia as aimed also at Japan in the long run, not simply at Germany and Italy. Moreover, American aid to the embattled European powers meant that American industries were being retooled for military production, and the signing of the Tripartite Pact in 1940 led the Roosevelt government to request funds for a "two-ocean" navy and to adopt for the first time universal military training in peacetime. The Japanese decided to strike before American mobilization could be completed.

Six months before the Japanese surprise attack on our fleet based at Pearl Harbor (December 7, 1941), Japan extorted military control of Indo-China from the powerless Vichy French, thus obtaining an advanced base for an assault on the Philippines, Hong Kong, and Malaya, which were struck the same day as the Japanese attack on our Pacific islands. While the United States was recuperating from the initial blows, the Japanese achieved the surrender of Hong Kong, Singapore, the Dutch East Indies, and the Philippines; forced an alliance on Thailand; and occupied Burma to cut off the chief western supply route to Nationalist China. The consequent loss of prestige by the old European colonial powers contributed to the early independence of the Southeast Asian colonies in the postwar period.

The American declaration of war against Japan after the surprise attack brought Germany and Italy into the war against the United States under the terms of the Tripartite Pact, forcing the Roosevelt administration to meet the crisis with a global strategy. Given the strength of the Japanese position by 1942, Roosevelt's decision was to contain further Japanese expansion, while concentrating American energies to winning first in Europe where the enemy was overextended and already in some difficulty. The defeat of Japan would be the secondary goal. This European orientation, however logical, was controversial in this country, where many citizens had been resolutely turning their backs on Europe since 1919 and where resentment over the Japanese "sneak" attack was keen.

The strategy in the long run, of course, worked; yet, 1942 was a desperate year in Europe with Hitler dangerously close to accomplishing in Russia and the Mediterranean what he had failed to accomplish in 1941. Much of the continent was being mobilized for Nazi military requirements and forced to accept Nazi ideology as well, thus participating in what Hitler called the "final solution" to the Jewish question. From all parts of Europe Jews were shipped in cattle cars to concentration camps, where ultimately about six million of them met death after unspeakable suffering. Those

who had early recognized the essential barbarism of the Nazi movement now had their proof; and whatever the dictates of military strategy, it was proper—and overdue—that we recognized what was our primary enemy. Soviet Russia's own record in the systematic liquidation of political opponents perhaps gave her no moral claim to be a champion of humanity, but there could no longer be any doubt that Britain must be saved and France and the Low Countries liberated if civilization were to endure. Toward that end, the Soviet Union was embraced as a valiant ally, and the long western antagonism to the Bolsheviks and their dictatorship was overlooked. This necessary but uncomfortable alliance was the price we paid for our withdrawal from postwar European affairs, and the immense Russian contribution to the final defeat of Hitler gave Russia an undeniable role in the peacemaking.

German failure to win in either Russia or North Africa in 1942 passed the initiative for the first time to the Allies. Anglo-American landings in Morocco and Algeria caught the Italo-German armies from the rear, ending the stalemate in Egypt. By May of 1943, the entire North African coast was in Allied hands, Italy lay open to invasion, and the Russians were regaining much territory in the Ukraine. In Asia, meanwhile, an Allied fleet had successfully defended Australia from Japanese invasion by repulsing the invasion fleet in the Coral Sea (May 7, 1942), and a month later a Japanese fleet approaching Midway Island was driven off with heavy losses. Such victories would have been impossible had the United States waited until Pearl Harbor to increase its naval strength.

Early in 1943, Roosevelt and Churchill met at Casablanca to plan the invasion of Europe, naming General Eisenhower as the supreme commander and announcing, as their war aims, an unconditional surrender by the enemy. They wanted no room for German equivocation as after 1918. Their decision to invade Italy rather than western Europe in the summer of 1943 has remained controversial, because the Italian campaign turned out to be more costly than was anticipated and was subsequently criticized as ill-advised. The western leaders were eager to mount an offensive against the continent at the earliest possible date to divert German pressure from the Russians, as the Germans had launched a new campaign in Russia that spring. The thoroughness of German defenses along the Atlantic coast would have required greater Allied preparation than the Italian invasion seemed to require, so that the decision to strike northward from Africa provided relief for the Soviet Union months before an invasion of the Channel coast could have.

An Allied invasion of Sicily began July 10, 1943, and its success within two weeks was so obvious that the Fascist Grand Council overthrew Mussolini in favor of Marshal Badoglio, who opened secret negotiations for peace. At the beginning of September, Allied troops crossed the Straits of Messina into southern Italy, and Badoglio was granted an armistice on the basis of unconditional surrender. The Germans, however, meant to make a fight of it, taking advantage of the rugged Italian terrain. Reinforcements badly needed on the Russian front were poured into Italy, and the Germans managed to delay the capture of Rome until the following summer. They rescued Mussolini and established him as a Nazi puppet in northern Italy—the role he had unwittingly chosen even before the war by rejecting Anglo-French and Austrian overtures.

The Allied Invasion of France

The assault on the heavily defended Channel coast was finally launched on June 6, 1944. It required an overwhelming air cover, a massive fleet to provide fire against shore batteries, and enormous stockpiles of supplies in Britain in anticipation of serious initial losses. The most novel feature of the Normandy invasion was the creation of artificial ports for landing troops and supplies, done by sinking rows of ships and concrete caisons. Enemy communication lines were pounded from the air to impede strong counterattacks; but only when American armor broke through southward into Brittany, and then eastward toward the valley of the Seine, were the Allies firmly established on the continent.

In August, an American-Free French expedition from Italy and North Africa was landed on the Mediterranean coast between Nice and Marseilles to drive northward up the Rhone valley. Both Paris and Brussels were liberated before the summer's end, whereupon the Allies had to face the stubbornly held defenses of Germany itself. The German position became hopeless before the end of 1944. Russian troops had been moving westward into Estonia and Poland, and after the Ukraine was recovered, the Russians swept into the Balkans and from there northward into Hungary. Only Nazi determination to continue fighting prevented an end to the war.

The Approach of Peace

Nazi fanaticism in part rested on a sure knowledge that the regime could not survive defeat, and the government had long since perfected the instruments of terror necessary to keep the population in the war. Moreover, Nazi propaganda had convinced many Germans that a Russian victory and occupation would be worse than the most appalling costs from continued fighting. But the Nazis also hoped that the presence of the Russians advancing through eastern Europe would awaken the historical western antagonism to the Soviet regime; and German propaganda pleaded for the western powers to join Germany in an anti-Bolshevik crusade. The Nazi line was especially clever, because it sought to exploit wartime troubles between Russia and her western allies. As early as 1938, the Russians had revealed their desire to

Churchill, Roosevelt, and Stalin at Yalta, 1945. (Library of Congress)

dominate Eastern Europe, and during the war they had pointedly refused to recognize governments-in-exile (notably the Polish) and had cooperated exclusively with resistance movements led by Communists. To Allied complaints, the Russians sometimes hinted that the West connived at a Soviet defeat by failing to apply sufficient pressure on Germany. The charge was unwarranted, but was widely believed in Left-wing circles in Europe after the war. Through it all and despite the susceptibility of some Right-wing elements in the West to the Berlin propaganda line, the alliance held firm on the common assumption that Hitler and his regime must be destroyed.

With the end in sight, Churchill, Roosevelt, and Stalin met at Yalta in the Crimea in February of 1945 to discuss plans for defeated Germany. They included an ar-

rangement to divide Germany into four occupational zones (British, French, Russian, and American) with a joint control commission to be seated in Berlin, and an agreement to convene an international conference in San Francisco in April to draft a charter for a permanent international organization: the United Nations. The negotiators at Yalta also recognized the Russian right to reorganize eastern Europe, to which Churchill and Roosevelt really had no alternative unless they were prepared to drive the Russians from eastern Europe by force. And that would have been unthinkable given the popularity the Russians had gained during their desperate defense against invasion, not to speak of a war with Japan yet to be won. The historical reasons which had required the West to need, and to accept, Russia as an ally led to a peace settlement which could not

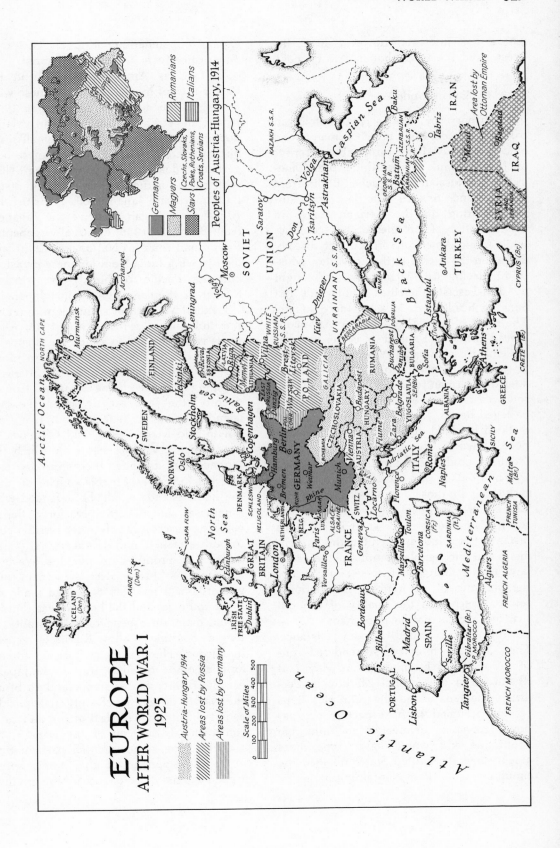

EUROPE
AFTER WORLD WAR I
1925

ignore her interests, however little the West liked the price that had to be paid.

1945: The End of World War II

By February of 1945, Anglo-American troops had crossed into Germany and quickly destroyed the formidable defenses on the left bank of the Rhine. Simultaneously, the Russians approached Berlin from the east and invaded Austria from Hungary, cutting off the German forces in northern Italy from the mother country; while Anglo-American forces inflicted heavy defeat on the enemy in the Po Valley. Mussolini, fleeing to Switzerland, was caught by anti-Fascist guerrillas, shot, and left hanging head-down in a Milanese square. The news of his death seems to have convinced Hitler that suicide was the preferable end. Russians and Western troops met at the Elbe river on April 26. Three days later the German forces in Italy capitulated, followed on April 30 by Hitler's suicide in besieged Berlin. Just before he died, Hitler dictated his final diatribe against "international Jewry." "It is untrue," he stated, "that I or anybody else in Germany wanted war in 1939. It was wanted and provoked exclusively by those international statesmen who either were of Jewish origin or worked for Jewish interests. . . . Above all," his testament concluded, "I enjoin the government and the people to uphold the racial laws to the limit and to resist mercilessly the poisoner of all nations, international Jewry." Such was the quality of thought that led a great nation into chaos.

Hitler's death ended German resistance. The German military surrendered unconditionally to Eisenhower on May 7 at Rheims, and to Marshal Zhukov in Berlin the next day, and the four victorious powers assumed their respective occupational zones as delineated at Yalta. No doubt the end would have come more quickly had the United States not had the simultaneous task of containing Japanese

expansion, something Russian critics of American efforts persistently ignored.

In fact, as American strength in the Pacific theater increased, the Japanese were forced to the defensive as early as 1943. American strategy produced an island-hopping campaign: isolated, small-scale, but murderous assaults on Japanese-held garrisons designed to provide the Allies with bases for the ultimate invasion of the Philippines and Japan itself. A British-led Allied force began to drive the Japanese from Burma in 1943, eventually reopening the ground route to Nationalist China and likely saving India from Japanese invasion; but the Pacific remained the principal theater of the campaign against Japan.

General MacArthur's campaign to retake the Philippines opened late in 1944, while plans went forward to attack the islands of Iwo Jima and Okinawa, so close to Japan that they would provide bases for intensive bombing of the home islands. Consequently, the Japanese defended the two islands with great tenacity, but Iwo Jima fell in mid March 1945, and Okinawa in June. The very bitterness with which the Japanese had defended their shrinking empire led to the inescapable conclusion that the home islands would be defended with fanaticism, and that the invasion of Japan could be successful only after terrible cost to both attackers and defenders. At Yalta, Stalin had promised to join his Western allies against Japan after a German surrender; but after May 8 he had made no move to do so, and the betting was that he would maintain a benevolent neutrality as long as possible to allow Russia to recover in Europe. The American decision to use atomic bombs to demonstrate to the Japanese the futility of resistance and to bring the war to an end as cheaply and quickly as possible became the last major, and most controversial, decision of the war.

At the time, some scientists participating in the development of the atomic bomb argued against its actual use on the grounds of its terrible destructiveness. The mere threat to use it should suffice to compel a hasty Japanese surrender. American political leaders, however, had little confidence that a mere threat would intimidate the Japanese military, especially when the details of the new weapon would be seemingly out of science fiction. Why not, then, stage an announced demonstration of the bomb's awesome power by exploding one near Japan but at an altitude that would spare the Japanese population? Here the flaw lay in American uncertainty as to whether the bomb would actually explode as advertised; a technical failure could convince the Japanese that we had been bluffing. An unannounced demonstration would have avoided that risk. But even a successful demonstration, unannounced or otherwise, might not have convinced the Japanese that we meant to use such a weapon, since the mere demonstration would have suggested our reluctance. Hence the painful decision to drop the bomb without warning on a Japanese target.

The initial bomb was dropped over Hiroshima on August 6, but it failed to provoke the expected offer to surrender—though it brought the Russians into the war against Japan out of fear of being denied a part in the East Asian peace settlement. On August 9, the second bomb was dropped on the naval base at Nagasaki; but even then the Japanese cabinet took six days to reach a decision to surrender unconditionally, perhaps the most astounding of the many evidences the Japanese gave during the war of their willingness to fight against great odds. The bombs cost approximately 130,000 fatalities and many thousands of wounded. From the immediate military point of view, therefore, since it had been feared that no Japanese surrender could be expected until an invading army had killed many times that number of Japanese, the decision to drop the bomb seemed wise.

The controversy, on the other hand, did not end with the Japanese surrender in August of 1945, but assumed new dimensions as the world awoke to the horrendous realization that mankind now possessed a weapon that could end life as we know it on this planet, either from direct bombing or from radiation poisoning that can alter genetic structure and produce incalculable mutations in future generations. In a world where colored peoples were everywhere rising to independence, the use of such a weapon against Japan, when it had not been used in Europe, was taken as proof of western disdain for the lives of nonwhites. The actual fact that the bomb was not available in time for use against Germany carried little weight in impassioned racial debate. Many nonwhites found it inconceivable that we would have used the bomb against Germans, an opinion that must be questioned in view of Allied saturation bombing of German cities and the fire-bombing of Dresden in particular.

The Japanese surrender left the United States in control of Japan and her island possessions. But the Russians, who had been at war with Japan only seven days, recovered the southern half of Sakhalin and won recognition of Outer Mongolia as their sphere of influence. It is surmised that had the western leaders at the time of Yalta known that they would soon possess an atomic weapon they would not have felt so great a need for Russian assistance and would have been able to stand firmer against Russian territoral ambitions in eastern Europe and Outer Mongolia. That probability led to later speculation that was less well-grounded—to the charge that the atomic bomb had been dropped primarily to impress and to warn the Soviet Union, not Japan. This ingenious line came to be cited in discussion about the origins of the "cold war" after 1945, but no evidence has even been uncovered to suggest that the United States had by then formulated a policy to take advantage of our nuclear monopoly and to provoke a showdown with Russia. On the other hand, neither did the United States foresee how alarming that monopoly would appear to the Soviets. Awakening their historical distrust of the capitalist West, the Russians were the more determined to retain a protective screen of satellite states. The groundwork had been laid for another uneasy peace.

But the effects of Hiroshima far transcended international politics. Beginning after the mid-nineteenth century, many Europeans within the literary culture had come to suspect that the technology born of science would lead to materialism and decadence, that the day would come when God would call a halt to man's insatiable quest for knowledge and new powers and close us down. The exhibition in 1945 of what science and technology could do seemed to such people evidence that scientific knowledge leads only to evil; or more pointedly, that evil is in knowledge and not in man. Should that notion become increasingly popular, as it steadily has since 1945, it could some day be reckoned as the most important product of the atomic bombardment of Japan. For it would be hard to generate an idea more inimical to civilization.

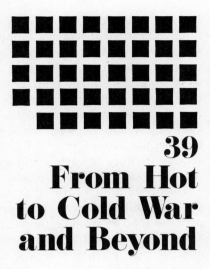

39
From Hot to Cold War and Beyond

The Idea of One World

Because World War II completed the devastation of Europe that was begun in 1914, the pivotal position of Europe in the world was gone by 1945. Gone, too, was the notion that the rest of the world was simply an extension of European ideas and power. While non-European independence and uniqueness were being championed throughout the world, the global dimensions of the recent war convinced many statesmen that most international problems could no longer be geographically confined, and that an international organization of truly global composition must emerge to guarantee the maintenance of peace. After 1918, the League of Nations had claimed to be global association. In fact, it was Europe-centered and dominated. The two great powers who came to dominate the United Nations after 1945 were never members of the League. In contrast, the United Nations, with its capital in New York, has clearly been far more global and egalitarian than its predecessor.

On the other hand, the overwhelming military resources of the United States and the Soviet Union after 1945, especially after Russia acquired her own nuclear capability in 1949, had the effect of dividing the members of the United Nations into two partisan camps, jeopardizing the organizational effectiveness in ·maintaining the peace. Just as there had been localized wars between 1919 and 1939, so have there been numerous localized wars since 1945, most notably in Korea and Vietnam. Yet, the world has so far escaped a general conflict for a period much longer than the 20 interwar years. And with the ending of the devastating war in Vietnam (1973), the prospects for World War III are fading rather than increasing. In the 1970s, Cold War hostilities are gradually giving way to active diplomatic relations, trade agreements, and an increasing sense of peaceful cooperation among the former

Cold War rivals (although tensions have increased among some former Cold War allies). The final irony may be that the terrible weapons produced by science and technology have created a balance of terror more effective in producing restraint than have the political institutions created for that purpose. Other reasons than terror have also made coexistence practical, for neither of the superpowers is nearly as dissatisfied with the status quo as major powers were on the eve of the two world wars.

Whatever may be the détente between East and West in the 1970s, the fact is that in 1945 the immediate problem of European recovery was clouded by the real possibility that the only remaining great powers in the world, the United States and the Soviet Union, might find themselves unable to maintain their wartime cooperation toward the goal of international recovery. Because Cold War did, in fact, replace the hot war after 1945, and because important sections of public opinion were wont to blame the American use of the atomic bomb as the sole cause of the Cold War, it becomes particularly important to note that the United States became heir, in the 1940s, to conflicts between the West and Russia that much antedated the postwar hostility. For all the resolve to construct a happier world, the historical and ideological antagonisms that had divided Russia from the West since 1917 were exposed anew as soon as the common enemy was prostrate.

Recall, for instance, the sharply focused grievances after 1918 when the Bolsheviks withdrew Russia from the war, and when the worried western Allies sent small contingents of troops into the Soviet Union to cooperate with Russian political groups determined to maintain military pressure on Germany. Furthermore, Russian repudiation of her World War I debts contributed markedly to the postwar finanical crisis. Although American troops were evacuated from Russian soil in 1920, we refused recognition to the Soviet Union until 1933 so great was our annoyance and suspicion; and we made no effort to cooperate with Russia in blocking militancy in Japan and Germany until 1939. By that date, the Munich agreement had suggested that the West was willing to turn Hitler's Germany against Russia, while the West had become aware that Stalin hoped to acquire territory in eastern Europe as protection against probable attack.

Twenty-four hours after that attack came in 1941, the American government announced that we would offer Russia assistance. But even that aid, augmented some months later when we became an active ally of the Soviet Union against the Axis powers, did not remove fundamental antagonisms for the war aims of Russia and the West, ostensibly the defeat of Germany, Italy, and Japan, were in fact at odds. The West, especially the United States, sought a free world under the supervision of an international agency. In contrast, the Soviet Union sought a postwar territorial settlement that would make her invulnerable to the presumed implacable antagonism of the capitalist nations. Wartime cooperation required that such disagreements be concealed, but they surfaced at once with peace in 1945— and to the dismay of those in the West who had come to idealize the Soviet Union for her dogged defense against invasion.

Thus, while the United States emerged from the war internationalist in spirit, having abandoned the isolationism of the previous decades, convinced that America must become the Good Samaritan of the entire world, the Soviet Union emerged from the war narrowly nationalistic in spirit, if still voicing the internationalism of the Marxian creed—a posture less surprising to officials who had negotiated with the Russians during the war than to those who had cheered from the sidelines. In the summer of 1944, for instance, when 44 nations had sent delegates to Bretton Woods, New Hampshire, to plan postwar economic cooperation, the Russians had merely sent an observer. Consequently, they did not sign the agreement providing for the International Bank for Reconstruction and Development or for the International Monetary Fund, instruments designed to promote economic and financial security by giving each country "the strength of all through common use of the common reservoir." In that same year, the Russians had declined an invitation for an international aviation conference in Chicago on the grounds that "fascist countries" like Switzerland would be included. We have already noted the high price paid to Stalin at Yalta in 1945 for participation in the war against Japan, which was capped several months later in San Francisco—during the organization of the United Nations—by the intransigence of the Soviet Foreign Minister, Molotov.

Although one may trace historically the explanation for Russian fears and suspicions, her behavior did not augur well for the period of postwar reconstruction. By mid-1946, opinion polls in the United States revealed a dramatic reversal in attitudes toward the Soviet Union, a quick disenchantment that helped reshape American foreign policy and, therefore, the course of Cold War. Russian domination of eastern Europe was now seen as offensive, rather than defensive in purpose, her goal being to communize all of Europe and Asia; her cooperation within the United Nations as doubtful; and worst of all, that she was likely to start a third world war within 25 years. In short, the American public came to favor a tough line to halt Soviet expansion, a line that culminated in American intervention in southeast Asia.

Political Reorganization of Europe, 1945–1948

Above all else, World II was novel in bringing its primary military damage to urban Europe. The countryside had been comparatively untouched except in areas through which armies had fought; but the air power, which flattened cities, had also destroyed communication systems and equipment. Great cities like Budapest, Rotterdam, Vienna, and Warsaw lay in ruins. Nearly every large town in England and Germany had been extensively damaged, and the French channel ports were virtually useless. Even factories that had escaped destruction had become inefficient and in need of renovation, and the European population was in a state of exhaustion and shock.

It is still too soon to know accurately the total loss of population, as several generations must pass before we can calculate the impact of war on population growth and vitality. Except on the Russian front, actual battlefield casualties were fewer than in the first war; but the civilian population was hit as never before, and large numbers of men were uprooted in Nazi-occupied countries and sent to labor camps. Add to that deliberate programs of extermination, such as the German attempt upon European Jewry that cost between five and six million lives, and one begins to sense the magnitude of the horror. The vitality of many people had been permanently sapped, since the Nazi-occupied countries had been forced to supply food to Germany to the extent that there was near-starvation throughout much of the rest of Europe.

Another matter difficult to calculate with any precision is the morale of a population. What faith in the greatness of civilization, or faith in man himself, can survive the many acts of barbarism to which Europe was witness between 1939 and 1945? The Germans and Russians in particular manipulated individuals and peoples as if they were beasts of the field. No doubt all parties in wartime are guilty of extreme actions or atrocities. What distinguished the German and Russian atrocities was their calculation. Moreover, atrocities deliberately perpetrated upon *other* nationals had already been practiced, in both spirit and technique, upon the perpetrators' *own* nationals. Brutality and indifference to humanity, in other words, was not simply spawned by war, but was a necessary extension of the political "philosophies" of the totalitarian states; all of which were governed by men ignorant of, or indifferent to, the culture and the libertarian thrust of European civilization.

Every occupied nation was looted of its goods, and retreating armies had often destroyed what they could not carry away. Even a country like Britain, never occupied by an enemy army, emerged from the war as crippled as if she had been defeated, in part because she had never fully recovered from the first war. Moreover, for nearly a century she had struggled with the problem of maintaining a large population in a tiny area, and until the twentieth century she had solved the problem by producing income through investment abroad, by carrying others' merchandise, as well as by exporting industrial goods. By 1945, although her human casualties had been grievous, her economic plight seemed even worse. Fully one quarter of her homes had been either destroyed or severely damaged; one half of her merchant marine tonnage had been sunk; much of her foreign investment had been liquidated to pay for the war; and her industrial establishment had become inefficient and noncompetitive. The war had cost her nearly one quarter of her national wealth. In sum, only the United States, which had been spared invasion and occupation, had both the material and the vitality to initiate European recovery.

Reconstruction: Soviet and Western Approaches

When it came to reconstruction, the Allies were agreed on some issues: that Germany must be demilitarized, for example, and that her industrial production ought to be curbed in favor of agriculture to reduce her military capacity and to give her a more balanced economy with a standard of living commensurate with that of her neighbors. They all agreed to be responsible for the denazification of Germany and to participate in an international court (at Nuremberg) to try the Nazi leaders, 10 of whom were executed. But they had emerged from the fighting in 1945 without clear-cut prior arrangements about national boundaries. Wartime meetings between the leading Allied statesmen had produced statements of principle and war aims, suggestive of ultimate boundaries; but the statements were usually idealistic rather than precise, and the idealism sometimes had to be modified by the actual fact of inter-Allied political differences. Roosevelt and Churchill, for instance, signed the Atlantic Charter in 1941 as a statement of principles for the postwar world: Neither Great Britain nor the United States sought territory, but rather self-determination for all peoples and free trade worldwide. The Soviet Union adhered to the Charter only with the proviso that the Baltic states and eastern Europe be excluded from its application. This Russian claim to reorganize eastern Europe was made good at the Yalta conference in 1945.

Areas liberated by Anglo-American troops were generally reorganized politically to conform to the western ideals of political democracy. In eastern Europe, where Russia had been the liberator, single-party Communist dictatorships ostensibly representing the people were organized with Russian blessing. It quickly became clear that denazification meant different things to the Russians than to the West. The Russians understood denazification as a mandate to eradicate "bourgeois capitalism" from their occupational zone in Germany, which they accomplished through the foundation of a Communist puppet regime and through the elimination of large estates and privately held industry. Conversely, the three western powers proceeded against individuals in their occupational zones in a manner consistent with western canons of justice. The inevitable slowness of such judicial procedures convinced the Russians that the West was insincere in its pledge to uproot Nazism, while the West viewed the socialization of the Soviet zone as a part of Russian colonialism in eastern Europe. Although Germany was ostensibly administered by the Allied Control Council in Berlin, it is not surprising that this administration soon broke down in a series of disagreements and crises.

Meanwhile, pursuing the western notion of democratic government, the United States and Great Britain sponsored the restoration of multiparty parliamentary democracy in western Europe and Greece. The French elected a constituent assembly in October 1945, for the purpose of writing a constitution for the Fourth Republic, and the Italians elected their constituent assembly the following June. Denazification of a sort also occurred, in that restored democratic regimes sought to bring to trial those who had collaborated with the Germans. It is now believed that many so-called collaborators, notably in France, were not so much pro-Nazi or pro-German as hostile to parliamentary democracy. Most of the formerly Nazi-occupied countries also experienced private acts of revenge against former collaborators.

Whatever injustices may have been worked in the Anglo-American attempt to restore a free society, they came to be dimmed by what occurred in the areas of Soviet influence. In the years following the war, Russia annexed 185,000 square miles along her western frontier, involving 25 million people; and she acquired control of 100 million more people in eastern Europe. The technique for acquiring control varied only in detail: Russian armies remained in occupation until coalition governments (or United Fronts) were established with local Communists devoted to Russia holding the key posts. Large private holdings were then confiscated and redistributed in the name of the people's democracies. Noncommunists were soon eliminated from the coalition regimes through intimidation or murder. Poland, Hungary, Romania, and

Bulgaria were secured by the Soviet Union in 1947. Czechoslovakia, by far the most western-oriented and democratic of the countries within the Soviet sphere, did not prove to be pliant. A *coup d'état*, by Communist-led workers, was necessary to establish a coalition government in 1948 and was followed soon after by the mysterious death of the noncommunist foreign minister, Jan Masaryk.

The Truman Doctrine

In the meantime, the western Allies had had a chance to survey the German scene and had become aware that their initial design for the German economy would have to be modified; the United States in particular soon recognized that the problem of European economic recovery would require an approach quite different from our posture of the 1920s. Since the free society envisioned in Europe could not survive without economic recovery, President Truman promised long-term assistance in the spring of 1947 in a message to Congress: "I believe that it must be the foreign policy of the United States to support free peoples who are resisting attempted subjugation by armed minorities or by outside pressure."

The Truman Doctrine came at a time when Britain had informed the United States that she could no longer afford to support the Greek government against Communist guerillas. Congress thus voted funds to provide military protection for both Greece and Turkey, an action demonstrating the degree to which American opinion had been aroused by Russian activity in eastern Europe. The Russians necessarily saw American aid to Greece and Turkey as the resumption of the capitalist conspiracy to destroy the Russian Revolution, especially since a country like Turkey was hardly one of the "free countries" we had pledged to support. She would have, it is true, free elections for the first time in 1950; but serious economic underdevelopment and widespread illiteracy have made a democratic state and society in Turkey impossible to this day.

In fact, the Truman Doctrine did not imply counterrevolution, but rather *containment* of further communist subversion of established regimes. Its economic counterpart was unveiled on June 5, 1947, by the American secretary of state, General George Marshall, and came to be known as the Marshall Plan. Under its provisions, the United States gave a total of 12.4 billion dollars worth of economic aid between 1948 and 1952 to Austria, Belgium, Denmark, France, Britain, Greece, Iceland, Italy, Luxembourg, the Netherlands, Norway, Portugal, Sweden, Switzerland, and Turkey—gifts unprecedented in the history of international relations. Czechoslovakia, originally scheduled to participate in Marshall Plan aid, was forced by the Russians to withdraw after the Communist *coup*, and no other nation within the Soviet orbit was permitted to accept American aid.

The Cold War

The American decision in 1947 to contain further Russian expansion was generally expressed as a policy to contain militant communism. The expression was doubly unfortunate in that it converted the historical issues separating Russia from the West into ideological and emotional terms, and had the effect of obscuring the similarity between Soviet foreign policy and that of imperial Russia before 1917. Given the subversion and terror practiced by the Soviets in eastern Europe, we can understand the climate in which that conversion took place: a public so recently swept up in its campaign to destroy the evils of Nazism was outraged by the brutal tactics of another totalitarian state. But obscuring issues traditionally more fundamental in the formulation of foreign policies, such as national interest or national security, hampered the subsequent development of a sophisticated American foreign policy.

The term "cold war" came to be applied

to the postwar tension between Russia and the West. Each suspected the other of imperial ambitions, and each side took what it considered to be proper defensive measures that generally appeared to be offensive in nature to the other side. The American decision to halt lend-lease aid to Russia at the end of the war was perhaps logical, but it really reflected American disapproval of Russian plans for eastern Europe and our embarrassment at having had no option but to give the Russians a free hand. Thus, the American action was seemingly unfriendly, especially in view of obvious Russian need for economic assistance and her eagerness to accept it. When the Marshall Plan was announced in 1947, American generosity was rebuffed by the Russians, who also prevented their satellites in eastern Europe from accepting American aid. Consequently, American aid went to the noncommunist countries alone, deepening the rift between East and West, a division that Churchill called the iron curtain.

The Two Germanies

In 1948, the Russians showed their teeth by cutting off all land and water communications to West Berlin, an enclave of Allied control within the Russian zone of Germany, evidently hoping to force the western powers out of the city so that it could be integrated into the Russian zone. The West responded to the blockade by supplying the city by air for nearly a year until the Russians abandoned their campaign. Meanwhile, as all attempts to reunite Germany had failed owing to Soviet opposition, the western Allies merged their zones into one economic unit; and two weeks after the lifting of the Berlin blockade, they created the Federal Republic of Germany, commonly called West Germany (1949). The Russians thereupon established the German Democratic Republic (East Germany) in what had been their zone. In 1958, the Russians renewed their pressure by announcing that they meant to turn over their Berlin obligations to the puppet East German regime, a regime unrecognized by the West; and the iron curtain became a physical fact in 1961 when the Russians and East Germans built a wall of barbed wire and concrete to prevent the flight of East Berliners into the freer society of the West.

The Korean War

The second major confrontation of the Cold War came in Korea, a country that had endured a Japanese protectorate since 1907. It was understood that a Japanese defeat would mean Korean unity and independence, but the western Allies failed to agree with the Soviet Union on the proper government for Korea. At the end of 1945, therefore, a temporary arrangement was achieved: an occupational government called the Joint Commission, whose American representatives were to command in South Korea, the Russian representatives to command in North Korea, with the thirty-eighth parallel as the dividing line. In the North, the Russians sponsored a Communist-dominated Provisional People's Committee, while in the South the Americans backed politicians favoring private property.

Because the Russians persisted in refusing to allow free elections in Korea, thus violating previous commitments, the United States finally took the matter to the United Nations in 1947. The General Assembly moved to get the elections organized, but met Russian intransigence. Consequently, elections could be held only in the South, from which emerged the Republic of South Korea in August 1948. The following month a Communist state, the People's Democratic Republic, was founded in North Korea. Both the Russians and the Americans then withdrew their troops from Korea. Almost at once, the North Koreans began to perpetrate armed clashes along the thirty-eighth parallel, and on June 24, 1950, they launched an invasion of South Korea.

The United Nations condemned the invasion and prepared to meet it with force, naming the American General Douglas MacArthur to command its army. No doubt the Russians would have vetoed the decision had they been present, but at the time they were boycotting the UN because of the continuing presence of the Chinese Nationalist ambassador. (The Chinese Communists had virtual control of the Chinese mainland by 1950). The UN military contingents came from a number of nations, heavily supported by the United States. Badly outnumbered at the outset, they were forced to retreat into a small perimeter that could be supplied from the sea; but ultimately MacArthur was able to drive his enemy northward. Not content to expel the invader from South Korea, and evidently calculating that the new Chinese Communist regime could not effectively obstruct him, MacArthur pushed on for the Yalu River, the boundary between North Korea and China. To his dismay, the Chinese sent masses of troops across the Yalu, forcing him southward. For this intervention, the UN branded Red China an aggressor. The war bogged down in dreadful stalemate until an armistice was reached in July 1953, based on the *status quo ante bellum*. Containment, in other words, was achieved, but only after three years of fighting, at a cost of $22 billion and 54,000 American lives.

Although it is too soon to reach historical judgments about events as recent as the Korean War, it may someday be reckoned that the failure to secure nothing more than a truce, after such an expenditure, was a more serious blow to the prestige of collective security than was realized at the time. But in 1953, satisfaction was taken in the apparent containment of this attempt at Communist subversion without the need to use atomic weapons and without the outbreak of a third world war.

The Growing Polarization of Power

Judging the Soviet posture in eastern Europe and in east Asia as aggressive in spirit, as a revival of the campaign for worldwide revolution, the non-communist world early began to take defensive measures. Western governments, noting that the leadership of the Communist parties in eastern Europe was loyal to Stalin, came to hold the Communist parties in the West in increasing suspicion. By 1947, cabinets in both France and Italy no longer included Communists, and the West German government banned the Communist party as unconstitutional. A series of defensive alliances were developed on a regional basis beginning with the North Atlantic Treaty (1949), originally signed by Belgium, Canada, Denmark, France, Great Britain, Iceland, Italy, Luxembourg, the Netherlands, Norway, Portugal, and the United States. Greece and Turkey joined the North Atlantic Treaty Organization (NATO) in 1951, West Germany in 1955.

Two other regional defensive pacts followed: the Middle East (or Central) Treaty Organization including Iran, Iraq, Pakistan, Turkey, Britain, and the United States; and the Southeast Asia Treaty Organization including Australia, France, New Zealand, Pakistan, the Philippines, Thailand, Britain, and the United States. Quite clearly the United States had abandoned its isolationism for worldwide commitment, determined to prevent through collective security the subversion or invasion of independent nations. Such a ring of treaties, of course, was easily viewed as an aggressive threat by the Soviet Union, a nation that had always expected a capitalist countercrusade against the communist dream of world revolution.

Thus, the Soviets moved on three fronts to consolidate Russian authority in the satellite states. First was the matter of ideological uniformity. The secret police of the eastern European countries were assisted by Russian secret police in rooting out dissent and in purging from the various Communist parties those whose Marxist interpretations differed from Stalin's. The Communist Information Bureau (Cominform), made up of representatives from all European Communist parties, became a clearinghouse for party orthodoxy and a promoter of propaganda. Mutual assistance pacts were the second method of achieving close association. Russia had such treaties with Yugoslavia, Czechoslovakia, and Poland dating from the war, but signed similar alliances with Bulgaria, Finland, Hungary, and Romania in 1948, and with Communist China in 1950. The system was given even greater unity with the signing of the Warsaw Pact in 1955, a mutual aid treaty including Russia, Albania, Bulgaria, Hungary, Poland, Romania, Czechoslovakia, and East Germany. As in the case of NATO, the Warsaw Pact provided for a single command over the multinational forces; but unlike NATO, the Warsaw Pact also created a joint committee to coordinate political life in the member countries.

The third Soviet technique, the attempt to integrate the economies of eastern Europe with that of the Soviet Union, proved to be troublesome. For economic integration appeared to be economic exploitation, despite the fact that the economic productivity of the satellites was soon on the rise. In 1948, Marshal Tito, Communist dictator of Yugoslavia, was expelled from the Cominform for resisting economic integration, and Soviet troops left the country. Evidently Moscow feared to use force in this case, knowing that Tito had much popular support and fearing that he might obtain aid from the West. While the economic integration and recovery proceeded elsewhere in eastern Europe. Stalinist trials began (1949) to purge the various Communist parties of men suspected of local loyalties similar to Tito's. By 1953, the year of Stalin's death, Communist party rule in each eastern European country had been converted into rule by a pro-Stalin boss; so that Stalin seemed to have achieved personal control, not only of the Soviet Union but of a vast integrated empire.

Reconstruction of Western Europe after 1947: Germany

In the West, it gradually became clear that the postwar goal of demilitarizing and de-industrializing Germany was incompatible, not simply with the desire to promote German recovery but with the plan to rebuild Europe itself. Despite general fear of a revitalized Germany on the part of neighbors so recently her adversaries in war, it became necessary to invent devices that would include the Germans in political and economic organizations, while guarding against a German military revival. The Russians inevitably saw the redirection of Western efforts as a covert encouragement of a German military comeback.

To begin with, the West German Federal Republic in 1949 was given the responsibility for administering what had been the Western occupational zones, with the proviso that the West Germans must accept Allied control of German industrial development. This control was guaranteed by the creation of the European Coal and Steel Community in 1951, an outgrowth of the French Schuman Plan to provide a transactional body to regulate the prices and the production of coal and steel. France, Belgium, the Netherlands, West Germany, Italy, and Luxembourg joined the community. The upshot was a sensational recovery of a nation that had been prostrate in 1945. West German industrial production doubled between 1950 and 1957. By 1962, real wages were almost double the prewar level, and unemployment had disappeared. The prosperity was the more pointed in that it occurred within a free-market economy, a tacit criticism of the rigid controls east of the "iron curtain," and a contrast with the nationalization of key industries in other western countries.

The very failure to reunite the two Germanies probably contributed to West German prosperity, as the separation of East Germany had the effect of making West Germany more heavily Roman Catholic (perhaps 44 percent of the population), enabling the Catholic, free enterprise party known as the Christian Democratic Union (CDU) to become the largest party in the first postwar election in 1949 and to gain an absolute majority by 1953. Thus, while West Germany had a legal and viable opposition party in the Socialists, the economic recovery profited from the continuity of governmental policy and American assistance.

Postwar government by Catholic parties was not confined to West Germany and has to be regarded as a moral as well as a political phenomenon. Konrad Adenauer, leader of the CDU, was chancellor of West Germany from 1949 to 1963; Alcide de Gasperi's Christian Democratic party held an absolute majority in Italy from 1948 to 1953; and the Catholic party in France (the MRP), led by Robert Schuman, was the dominant force in French politics. Such men, while committed to the separation of Church and state, had an international outlook, a cosmopolitan spirit, that was religious in origin. They worked for European integration as the practical path toward European recovery, but they also represented a revival of Christian values after the recent experience with barbarism.

The second regulatory device to guard against German militarism was NATO itself, which created a joint military organization for its member nations. Any German rearmament in the future would be subject to NATO control. The treaty required the United States to maintain troops in Europe as a member state and committed us to maintaining Western security. Eisenhower became the first supreme commander of NATO forces in 1950. The final step to integrate West Germany into the western camp was taken in 1954 when the sovereignty of the Federal Republic was formally acknowledged, and West Germany joined NATO—meaning that the occupation had ended. France became reconciled to the concomitant German rearmament only because of a renewed British pledge to keep troops stationed on the continent.

The Growth of Economic Unity

Meanwhile, the European Coal and Steel Community began to function to such mutual satisfaction that its members envisioned new dimensions of unity. At Rome in 1957 they founded the European Atomic Energy Community to make the uses of atomic energy available to all members; and they established the Common Market, an ambitious program of total economic integration aimed at the gradual elimination (over a period of 15 years) of trade barriers between members and the achievement of uniform working and social conditions. Inefficient sectors of the members' economies soon felt the pinch after the Common Market began to function in 1959, but the long-term effect on economic growth in every member nation has been spectacular.

British application for membership was blocked in 1963 by President De Gaulle of France. He considered Britain as an outpost of American interest and influence, was suspicious of Britain's ties to the British Commonwealth outside Europe, and believed that American power and investment in postwar Europe was entirely too great for the good of European integrity and morale. The relative high cost of British industrial productivity, plus the liquidation of much British capital overseas, had left the British on the brink of economic disaster, for which eventual entry into the Common Market seemed to be the only solution. De Gaulle's attitude gave Britain no opportunity of Common Market entry until his resignation from the French presidency in 1969, and it took until 1972 for Britain (and Denmark) to gain admission.

De Gaulle's Europeanism, however, did not check American financial investment in European business and industry. Even though the United States was not a member of the Common Market, American investors profited greatly from its existence, so much so that an eminent French journalist, Servan-Schreiber, argued that Europe must Americanize itself (by which he means to copy the American "art of organization") to avoid losing out entirely to American enterprise. Servan-Schreiber's goal, in other words, was to realize in Europe the close association between industry, the academic community, and the national state, already known in the United States.

Italy

Italy, although a defeated power like Germany, had never been seriously regarded as a military threat, so that her economic revival after 1945 was untrammeled by attempts to prevent a military revival. Furthermore, wartime damage to her industrial plants was considerably less than that experienced in Germany or Britain. Therefore, Italian industrial production resumed more quickly than that of any other European country, and Italian products were in great demand. Marshall Plan aid contributed to the modernization of Italian industry and to a rapid increase in the development of electric power facilities. Industrial production by 1954 was 71 percent higher than it had been before the start of the war, and urban real wages were 50 percent higher.

This apparent prosperity failed to conceal serious unresolved problems in other realms of Italian life; and even the industrial boom, by stimulating large migrations from rural to urban areas, created the distress always associated with uprooted and dislocated people. Most serious, the Christian Democrats failed to bring about agricultural and land reforms in southern Italy where poverty was worst. At the root of Italian inability to tackle obvious problems successfully was the multiparty political system that had been a feature of Italian parliamentary life since unification in the nineteenth century—except for the years under Mussolini. By 1953, the Christian Democrats had lost their absolute majority in Parliament, making coalition government necessary thereafter. The result was not simply the rapid rise and fall of cabinets, but an inability to formulate and sustain programs for domestic reform. Political paralysis stimulated the growth of extremist parties on both Left and Right, giving Italian democracy the appearance of eternal crisis.

France

French economic recovery after 1945 was confused even earlier than the Italian by political instability. Here, again, the multiparity parliamentary system provided no coherence, too often leaving the direction of government, as under the Third Republic, to the professional bureaucrats who survived the rapid changes of coalition cabinets. Most French republicans agreed that the Fourth Republic ought to be structured so as to avoid the political chaos that had plagued the Third and had delivered government to men not elected by the voters. Yet the three parties that between them received 75 percent of the vote in 1945 could not agree on the solution to the problem. The Socialists and Communists favored strengthening the legislative branch; while the Popular Republicans (MRP), initially led by General De Gaulle, favored strengthening the executive branch. De Gaulle, the provisional president, resigned his post early in 1946 when it became clear that the new constitution would give the Fourth Republic a regime very similar to the Third. Indeed, the Fourth Republic, during its brief tenure (1946-1958), featured more than 20 coalition cabinets with government largely carried on by the centralized bureaucracy and by municipal authorities. Aside from the difficulty in sustaining policies contributory to economic recovery, the system was especially costly in that the French bureaucracy had become notoriously large and self-serving after so many decades of virtual freedom from public or political control.

The temporary retirement of De Gaulle enabled the left-wing parties to take the lead early in the Fourth Republic, which meant that government approached the problems of recovery, not with the free-economy philosophy as in West Germany, but with the intention to nationalize key units of the economy. Insurance companies, the merchant marine, the airlines, and public utilities now followed the pattern of the railways, which had been nationalized earlier. A master plan for economic development and modernization, inaugurated by Jean Monnet, provided state funds and technical advice to both capital and labor. As in Italy, this modernization was assisted by the Marshall Plan.

The French scene was a complex of contradictions: government planning led to an improvement in economic conditions. Industrial production, for example, was 87 percent higher by 1956 than it had been immediately before the war. Yet, despite price controls, government loans for construction, and public works projects, wages seemed to lag noticeably behind prices. The high degree of political centralization, always a factor in contemporary France, when augmented by the nationalization of key industries, ought to have produced a sense of efficiency and order; but the contrary seemed to prevail. The factor most responsible for inflation and for slowing recovery was the high cost of government. And that derived not only from the overblown bureaucracy and the new social security system introduced by the left-wing coalitions, but by the high cost of defending and administering the French colonial empire.

Popular discontent focused in the 1950s on the Fourth Republic itself: the parliamentary system was seen as unable to provide the vigorous leadership necessary to keep pace with France's neighbors, especially Germany, and unable to reach a solution to the Algerian situation. Nationalist rebellion had produced civil war in Algeria which threatened to spread to France as the question of Algerian independence became hotter. Given the high cost of Algerian administration and the casualties incurred (5000 French and 50,000 Algerians by 1958), it made financial sense to grant independence. But the one million French residents of Algeria, backed by right-wing sentiment in France, had foiled all attempts to reach a compromise.

The impasse reached a point in June 1958, where the Fourth Republic essentially confessed its political bankruptcy. De Gaulle accepted the prime ministry on condition that he could rule by decree for six months, draft a new constitution to be submitted to popular referendum, and work out an agreement with the Algerian nationalists for their independence. Thus was born, in September 1958, the Fifth Republic under a constitution that greatly enhanced presidential power at the expense of parliament. What emerged, in fact, was representative government rather than true parliamentarianism. De Gaulle accepted the presidency in 1959, ushering in a new decade of apparent contradictions: austerity in economic programs, but a search for *grandeur* and the leadership of Europe in foreign policy.

Britain

The abandonment of empire was associated with the problem of economic recovery in Britain, too; but whereas the French began to enjoy new prosperity in the 1960s as their overseas obligations dwindled, the British reaped no such benefits. Elections were held shortly after the German surrender with Labour winning the parliamentary majority, which forced the resignation of Churchill in favor of Clement Attlee. Although Churchill grumbled about na-

tional ingratitude, the fact is that the Conservatives were belatedly paying the price for their ineffectuality in dealing with the British economic crisis in the 1930s. The Labour party was held to be more competent to come to grips with the economic dilemma of 1945.

Since the Labour party was socialist, it was understood that critical industries would be nationalized. Moreover, the Attlee government promised to build a "welfare state" which would provide security "from the cradle to the grave" for every British subject, but warned that national austerity would be required before such goals could be attained. This meant continuing the rationing of consumer goods, including food; the deliberate limitation of imports until British exports would revive; and rigid currency controls. Social legislation, meanwhile, probably helped national morale in the face of continuing austerity. The National Insurance Act (1946) provided nearly total coverage for unemployment, disability, and old age; while the National Health Service Act, carried despite the opposition of the medical profession, guaranteed free medical care for everyone.

Major economic units nationalized included the Bank of England, the transportation system, and the coal, iron, and electrical industries. Even with American financial assistance Britain's recovery was slow, and in 1949 the decision was made to devalue the currency drastically to achieve a more competitive position. Austerity was harder to bear because its economic results seemed so meager and because the cost of living remained so high. The wearied voters gave the Conservatives a chance to cope with the dilemma in 1951, but the Conservatives, although committed to free enterprise, found no alternatives to most of the nationalization undertaken by Labour. The antiquity of the British economic establishment, when compared to those of the United States, Germany, and Japan, has to this day handicapped economic recovery; and no western industrial nation is more threatened than Britain by the deepening energy crisis.

Cosmopolitanism and the New Nationalism

The United Nations Charter was signed on June 26, 1945, by the delegations of 50 countries, and future membership was left open to all "peace-loving" nations. Beyond the mission to promote friendly relations among nations, the United Nations were committed to ameliorating social and economic problems worldwide, although prevented from interference in matters judged to be the internal prerogative of a member state.

The new organization had an executive branch (the Security Council), a legislative branch (the General Assembly), and a bureaucracy (the Secretariat) for permanent administration. In the General Assembly, every nation was equal with one vote. A simple majority was sufficient for most matters, but a two-thirds majority was required in important questions such as the admission of a new member. The Security Council contained only 11 seats, 5 of which were permanently assigned to the United States, the Soviet Union, China, Britain, and France. The remaining 6 members were to be elected by the General Assembly for two-year terms. The Charter required the unanimity of the 5 permanent members on all important matters. A Secretary General presided over the Secretariat, elected by the General Assembly from a slate of candidates approved by the Security Council.

Under the Charter, the Security Council could recommend peaceful methods to settle disputes, methods like economic sanctions. But the Charter also gave the Security Council the power to recommend action by "air, sea, or land forces" to maintain the peace or to restore order, and provided for an international police force toward those ends. In fact, such a force was never organized; and the United Nations' police actions in Korea and elsewhere were carried out by forces contributed temporarily by member nations. For the first few years, such police actions as in Indonesia, Israel, and Kashmir were cause for considerable optimism. The Korean intervention, however, was only possible because of the Soviet Union's temporary absence from the Security Council, and the threat of a Soviet veto thereafter fatally weakened international resolve. As the years have passed, therefore, the political prestige of the United Nations has diminished, although its activity in social and economic matters has continued to be energetic. American initiative in abandoning the veto power of the 5 permanent members was rejected by the Russians.

The declining effectuality of political internationalism ought not be attributed alone to the use of the veto, or to the threat of a veto, by a great power. Membership in the United Nations more than doubled in the first 20 years of its existence, and a great share of the new members were countries newly formed out of the dissolution of the old colonial empires. Although their performance in the United Nations has been far more complicated than can be detailed here, the new nations, excited by their independence, naturally hostile to even hints of tutelage from the former imperial masters, too often reflected the militant nationalism that the United Nations had been formed to curb. Political life within the new countries, moreover, was frequently violent, continually confronting the United Nations with agonizing decisions as to whether international interference was required or forbidden under the Charter. Add to this the politics of the Cold War, which offered smaller countries the opportunity to play off the West against Russia, and one has catalogued a climate of hostility and opportunism hardly congenial to the spirit that founded the international association.

Colonial Independence: The British Empire

Much of the colonialism of the nineteenth century, as we have seen, had been a manifestation of European nationalism, though often an elaborate rationale was cited to justify the accumulation of an empire overseas. That rationale had long since been found faulty, two world wars had convinced most Europeans that their militant nationalism was intolerable, and the very expense of administering and protecting a far-flung realm had become insupportable by 1945. To colonial claims for independence, therefore, Europeans could only demand time to arrange the details of separation and try to protect investments as much as possible in the areas to be evacuated. The transition was rarely smooth, often embittered and violent, with the British generally handling the disengagement better than the other colonial powers or, at least, with better grace.

In 1946 the Labour government offered independence to India, a country that had never been united before British rule. In fact, religious differences made it necessary to divide India into two states (India and Pakistan) before independence could be possible. Millions of people were relocated to separate Hindus from Moslems, but bloody clashes over border disputes continued to plague the area. In 1972 a destructive civil war in East Pakistan resulted in the emergence of a third independent Indian State—the Republic of Bangladesh.

Burma, India's eastern neighbor, gained her independence from Britain in 1948; but here, too, religious and ethnic differences undermined national unity and left the new nation vulnerable to Communist insurgency. Ceylon also received independence in 1948 and was also upset by Communist insurgency. Such insurgency, in fact, so wracked Malaya that independence had to be delayed until 1963 while the British took vigorous and successful counterinsurgency action. Then the Federation of Malaysia assumed self-government. British withdrawal from Africa began in the Gold Coast, which became independent (as Ghana) in 1957. Independence followed for Sierra Leone (1961), Tanganyika (1961), Uganda (1962), and Kenya (1963).

British withdrawal from the Near East was different from that in Africa or southeast Asia. With the exception of Cyprus, the Near East had merely been a sphere of British interest and influence. The British government had become the majority stockholder in the Suez Canal Company in the nineteenth century, and the British economy and armed forces were critically dependent upon Near Eastern petroleum production. It had become important for the British, therefore, to maintain good relations with the Arab nations that became independent from Turkey after World War I. Several of the Arab states had direct British assistance in achieving their independence. Through the Balfour Declaration in 1917, however, the British had also become committed to providing a national home for Jews, the goal of the Zionist movement since the late nineteenth century. Consequently, when Britain was given a mandate over Palestine by the League of Nations, she acquired the task of reconciling the Arabs to Palestine becoming Jewish—but made little headway.

With Hitler's persecution of European Jewry beginning in earnest in 1933, Jewish immigration to Palestine increased, to Arab irritation. With the approach of international war in 1939, the British felt that they must restrict that immigration sharply; but, by then, the Arabs were sufficiently suspicious of British intentions to reveal themselves as pro-Axis during the war. In 1945, the British tried to prevent the outbreak of civil strife by forbidding any further Jewish immigration, but it continued illegally. Unable to afford the military establishment necessary to keep peace, the British withdrew in 1948, whereupon a Jewish provisional regime under David Ben-Gurion proclaimed the State of Israel. This provoked warfare between the Arabs and the Israelis, which the Jewish state survived.

In 1956, the Egyptians seized the Suez Canal Company, the profits from the nationalized canal henceforth to be used to build the Aswam Dam on the upper Nile. Britain responded by forming a secret alliance with France and Israel. The Allies suddenly attacked and swiftly defeated the Egyptians, their goal being not merely the recovery of the Suez Canal, but the establishment of a buffer region between Egypt and the Israelis. In a countermove still not clearly understood today, the United States and the Soviet Union moved within the United Nations to force a cease-fire and an evacuation of the Allied forces. There has since been warfare between Israel and the Arab states in 1968 and in 1973; and it may well be that no peace will be possible in the Near East until such a buffer region can be established and policed.

The French Colonies Gain Independence

The French emerged from World War II with diminished military prestige which encouraged nationalistic movements within their vast empire. The colonial dilemma for the French, however, was greater than for the British, because of the peculiar rationale that had governed French colonialism from the start. Britain had generally granted her colonies some measure of self-government at the outset; and even where the autonomy was little more than a legal fiction, the seeds of ultimate independence had been planted. Long before 1945, vast chunks of the British Empire had evolved into the independent dominions that chose to remain affiliated with Britain in the Commonwealth (as did some of the new nations after 1945). Consequently, when it became necessary for financial reasons to retrench after 1945, not only were the methods for abandoning empire understood, but a majority of the public were prepared in mind and sentiment for what must come.

Whatever the particular set of circumstances that governed the French conquest of territory overseas, French colonialism had always been profoundly tinged with a "civilizing mission." Colonial administration was often exploitative rather than civilizing, but the ideal came to be cherished in the mother country. The French preoccupation with universal truths (such as liberty, equality, and fraternity for all mankind), when combined with the passionate admiration of their own civilization, produced a zeal to make all men French in culture as *the* road to liberty and equality. Thus, when a variety of factors suggested the withdrawal from empire after 1945, the very idea was distasteful as a retreat from high principle. The expedients devised to hold the empire together, such as the French Union to include the entire empire, went far beyond mere concern for the economic interest of a few prominent businessmen. The problem was to find inexpensive devices to avoid abandoning "Frenchmen." Only when such devices proved to be intolerably expensive in lives and treasure, since they were ineffective in reducing militant nationalism, were the links of empire severed.

After years of fighting the nationalist movement in Indochina, the French gave up the struggle in 1954. As French withdrawal came in the aftermath of a notable defeat at Dien Bien Phu, military failure was commonly held to have been responsible, thus reinforcing the popular notion that a people convinced of the rightness of their cause, in this case the Vietnamese nationalists, could never be defeated. This notion prospered despite the recent defeat of the Germans and the Japanese, both of whom had notable convictions of rectitude and invincibility. In truth, the French decision to give up in Indochina derived less from military failure than from popular disenchantment in France itself: the dream had gone sour. Two years later (1956) both Morocco and Tunisia were granted independence.

The toughest decision, the greatest agony, was over Algeria. For not only was Algeria a legal part of metropolitan France, but more than one million of the Algerians were French colonists. On the other hand eight million Algerians were Muslims, most of whom wanted independence. Terror and counterterror produced dreadful casualties and made reconciliation increasingly remote. Matters came to a head in May 1958, when there seemed to be real danger that right-wing extremists might seize control of Algeria to prevent the establishment of a Muslim-dominated state. This threat enabled De Gaulle to obtain the dictatorial powers necessary to meet the emergency and, as we have described, to revise the constitution in favor of strong executive power. It was understood that he would grant independence to Algeria on an equitable basis.

The terms were worked out only after months of tedious negotiations with Algerian leaders and in an atmosphere of crisis. There remained the possibility that French army officers, embittered by what they called the sellout over Indochina, would either cooperate with the French-Algerians or succeed in overthrowing De Gaulle. A referendum in France on the principle of self-determination for Algeria was successful in 1961, and Algeria became independent the following year.

Meanwhile, De Gaulle's constitution for the Fifth Republic offered autonomy to all remaining colonies. This autonomy was converted into outright independence in 1962, although close cultural and economic relations between France and her former colonies survived. With the empire gone, De Gaulle set himself to remind the French of the greatness of their civilization and of their duty to offer leadership in Europe. His formidable faith was precisely suited to help restore public morale, although his insistence that Europe ought to free itself

from dependence upon American military power and financial investment seemed to some a dangerous departure from the principle of collective security.

The Vietnam War

When the French abandoned Indochina in 1954, they left three newly independent states: Laos, Cambodia, and Vietnam. Through the mediation of Britain, Russia, and the United States, a peace agreement was concluded at Geneva which provided that Vietnam be divided temporarily into a Communist North Vietnam and a non-Communist South Vietnam. North Vietnam was led by the Russian-trained Communist Ho Chi-Minh, who had long been a leader in the Vietnamese nationalist movement against the French. National elections were planned for the purpose of choosing a government for a unified Vietnamese state. Pending those elections, the country was partitioned along the seventeenth parallel in the Korean manner. The elections were not held on schedule, largely because the South feared it would lose them. And from 1958 onward the American-backed South Vietnamese regime was attacked, on an increasingly large scale, by local Communist guerillas (known as the Vietcong), vigorously aided and reinforced by North Vietnam and supported by the Russians and Chinese.

The interpretation of these events became controversial at the outset and raised difficult questions: Was Vietnamese Communism a legitimate nationalist movement with a right to govern Vietnam and tackle its social and economic problems? Or was the Vietcong another expression of systematic Communist insurgency aimed at worldwide revolution? Most Europeans, looking hopefully toward the possibility of détente between East and West, regarded the Vietnam conflict as a civil war in which the western nations should keep hands off. But the United States, still firmly committed to the Truman Doctrine, and more profoundly hostile to Communism than most European intellectuals, committed itself to supporting the non-Communist regime in South Vietnam against Communist attack. The activities of the Vietcong and North Vietnamese, so the American government believed, really masked either Russian or Chinese imperial expansion. As American assistance to South Vietnam grew into massive military commitment, European disapproval effectively weakened the NATO alliance. And since a large section of the American people increasingly adopted the European arguments as valid, the home front became divided to a point of intense bitterness.

Meanwhile the Vietnam war dragged on, seemingly without end. With wholesale domestic disaffection and no victory in sight, America was obliged in 1973 to conclude an armistice. The settlement left the South Vietnamese regime intact but far from secure. At this writing, the Vietnamese Communists seem to have resumed their military effort to bring all Vietnam under their control, and the future of the country remains in doubt. What does seem likely is that, given the national temper during the Vietnam withdrawal, the United States is abandoning its self-appointed role as Good Samaritan to the world.

Competitive Coexistence

Foreign and domestic opposition to the Vietnam War was based on the view that the traditional Cold War philosophy was obsolete—that the course of global politics need no longer be perceived as a remorseless struggle between America and the Communist world. This viewpoint had long been developing. As far back as 1953, Stalin's death had seemed to promise better relations between East and West. Nikita Khrushchev, Stalin's successor, by no means abandoned the historical goal of worldwide socialism. But Khrushchev did admit, for the first time, that war with the capitalist world was not necessarily inevi-

table. And Russia's sudden decision early in 1955 to allow peace terms to be signed with Austria came as a pleasant surprise. The open condemnation of Stalin, while perhaps a clever ploy by Khrushchev to justify his own power, nevertheless brought hope that the Soviet Union would become a freer society.

Interest at once focused on eastern Europe where, with the exception of Marshal Tito of Yugoslavia, the leaders had been personally loyal to Stalin. In Poland, the Stalinist Bierut managed to retain power, as did Ulbricht in East Germany; but in Hungary the Stalinist Matyas Rakosi lost the prime ministership to Imre Nagy. The Russians, meanwhile, sought to eradicate Stalin's hostility to Yugoslavia. In 1956 Khrushchev and Tito issued a joint statement to the effect that the variety of socialist developments contributes to the strength of socialism. This was a clear Russian admission that Yugoslavia might pursue her independent path without fear of reprisal. The message was heard elsewhere in eastern Europe where nationalists increasingly resented the subjection of local interests to Russian requirements.

Bierut of Poland had died several months before the Khrushchev-Tito announcement. Thereafter, a general relaxation, or de-Stalinization, had begun with the release of 9000 political prisoners, including Wladyslaw Gomulka who became head of the Polish Communist party. Before the end of 1956, a serious strike by workers in Poznan, while contained by force, convinced the Polish Communist party that it must seek as much autonomy as possible to speed up economic recovery and development. De-Stalinization, therefore, did not mean the end of Communism, but a decentralization of the Communist world; which is why many Europeans argued that the Soviet Union had abandoned her postwar imperialism and that the Cold War ought to be regarded as over. Indeed, the new climate may well account for why the United States, in 1956, was eager to cooperate with the Soviet Union during the Suez crisis as a means of thawing the Cold War.

The West soon learned to its discomfiture that the Russian leadership, if ready to permit a degree of decentralization in the Communist world for practical reasons, did not mean to relinquish ultimate control over the destiny of eastern Europe. This fact was first demonstrated in Hungary, where de-Stalinization had been more thoroughgoing than elsewhere. The Nagy government had been putting special emphasis on the production of consumer goods, and nearly half the peasants were allowed to leave the collective farms, some of which were disbanded. Certain disgruntled ex-Stalinists, including Rakosi, sought to recover power in Hungary by intriguing with Moscow and convinced the Russians that the Nagy regime was losing its hold on the workers and the peasants.

Although the Russians used their influence to depose Nagy and restore Rakosi, the thrust for autonomy had gone too far. The Hungarian Communist party was deeply divided, permitting non-Communist factions to encourage the anti-Moscow Communists. The establishment of the Gomulka government in Poland late in 1956 helped to ignite a rebellion in Hungary against Soviet influence. The Communist party immediately restored Nagy to power to appease the rebels, realizing that failure to quell the rebellion could lead to the overthrow of the Communist regime. In desperation, Nagy announced that Hungary would leave the Warsaw Pact as proof of Hungarian autonomy; but that decision brought on a Russian invasion, the occupation of Budapest, and Nagy's execution. The brutality of the Russian interference horrified Western opinion, but nothing was done to aid the Hungarians; Western statesmen continued to hope that the overall Russian policy was to decentralize control and to relax the Cold War.

A very similar situation gradually developed in Czechoslovakia in the 1960s. The Communist government began making concessions to popular pressure for greater autonomy and intellectual freedom until, in 1968, the Russians evidently concluded that the Czechs were drifting away from the Warsaw Pact in the direction of neutrality. Aware of the historical prowestern orientation of the Czechs, the Russians simply occupied the country with troops and crushed the movement toward greater liberty. There could no longer be much doubt that the Russians still regarded eastern Europe as their domain. Throughout the period, meanwhile, the argument had raged on both sides of the Atlantic as to how much real autonomy for Asian Communist regimes would be tolerated by either Russia or China, an argument that weighed heavily in opinion about the Vietnam War. The issue was rendered more complex by the growing hostility between the two Communist giants themselves. The Russians and Chinese massed troops along their common border and waged bitter ideological warfare against one another, dissolving the Western notion of a single Communist world.

Meanwhile, all was not serene in the West. Economic recovery had proceeded faster than in the East, but within a framework of political freedom which precluded any American crackdown in the Russian style. The American presence was strongly felt and sometimes resented, although that presence was financial and economic rather than military. Marshall Plan aid ended in 1952, but private American investment in European enterprise contributed mightily to economic growth, and European economic integration proceeded with American blessing. The implementation of the Common Market began in 1959 with a 10 percent tariff cut among the member nations, and intracommunity trade increased tremendously.

President De Gaulle, who sought to reduce American influence in Europe by keeping Britain out of the Common Market, also regarded American military protection for Europe as a decreasing need. This because of the European economic recovery, because of the alleged decline in Russian aggressiveness that would accompany de-Stalinization, and because the French themselves, at great cost, were developing their own atomic capability. Consequently, he insisted that American troop contingents serving NATO not be stationed on French soil, and he forced NATO headquarters to leave Paris for Brussels.

For all the irritations and suspicions between East and West, and despite the antagonisms within the great blocs, one can argue that Europe has progressed measurably toward coexistence since 1945. The Berlin Wall may still exist—as does much that it symbolizes, and the early optimism about the peacekeeping capability of the United Nations may have faded; but economic integration and political cooperation within Europe seem increasingly characteristic of European life. Even the threat from the nuclear weapons arsenals is lessening as a measure of the determination to coexist despite ideological differences. The Test Ban Treaty of 1963, the Non-Proliferation Treaty of 1968, and the Arms Limitation Treaty of 1972 have all contributed to an easing of the balance of terror. The détente between the United States and China, and between the United States and Russia in the aftermath of the Vietnam War in 1973, has been welcomed throughout the world.

Coexistence, henceforth, will likely refocus from the competition between East and West to the problems separating the "developed" and the "underdeveloped" countries of the world, and most immedi- ately to the ratio between global food production and the population explosion. During the first quarter of the twentieth century, the world's population increased 23 percent; during the second quarter, it increased 31 percent. The 1930 population of two billion had risen to three billion by 1960. We have reached a point where the world population increases by more than one million a week, and the greatest increases are taking place in Asia and Africa. Food production *is* up, but the population outstrips it, and the very regions where the population increases the fastest are at present the least self-sufficient in food production. Not merely world peace, but existence itself will depend on technical progress in the "underdeveloped" regions and assistance from those which are "developed."

CHRONOLOGY OF 1939–1973

1939–1945:	World War II
1939–1940:	Russo-Finnish War
1940:	Capitulation of Belgium, the Netherlands, and France
1941:	American entry into World War II
1945:	Yalta Conference
1947:	Announcement of the Marshall Plan
1949:	Beginning of the North Atlantic Treaty Organization (NATO)
1955:	Beginning of the Warsaw Pact
1957:	Establishment of the Common Market
1957:	Formation of European Atomic Energy Community
1961:	Construction of Berlin Wall
1972:	Britain enters Common Market

40

The Cultures of the Twentieth Century

Science

In the twentieth century, modern man has had to cope with much more than new knowledge unsettling to traditional belief. No understanding of the new knowledge, in fact, was even possible until he learned to accept new dimensions of vastness and minuteness, dimensions that challenged both imagination and credulity. In 1900, for instance, the distances of only about 20 stars were known with any assurance; today the distances of several thousand stars have been ascertained using improved telescopes and photography. The notion of galaxies other than our own, perhaps a hundred million of them, and the necessary use of the light-year as a measure (light travels at the rate of 186,000 miles per second), totally defeats our normal assumptions about space and distance. The most distant galaxies are, at least, 14 billion light-years away and are receding.

At the other end of the scale, until the end of the nineteenth century the atom was conceived as a hard, solid object, and as the smallest unit of physical reality. In the 1890s, however, Joseph Thomson found particles within atoms which carried negative charges of electricity, particles he called corpuscles but which came to be called electrons, and which showed that atoms are composite entities. The evidence suggested, furthermore, that electrons were identical in all atoms. Subsequently, protons were discovered: particles charged with positive electricity equal in amount to the negative charge on the electrons. It meant that each atom of a given element possessed an equal number of electrons and protons (making every atom electrically neutral). It followed then that the atoms of different chemical elements must be formed of *differently arranged groups* of electrons and protons.

In 1911, Lord Rutherford further refined atomic theory by proposing that atoms are largely empty. He saw the atom as a central nucleus with a positive electrical charge, surrounded at a distance by an outer shell of negatively charged electricity: a model that suggested a miniature solar system involving much empty space. Matter, in other words, was to be regarded as more empty than "material." A second inference was that if atoms differed chemically because of the different numbers of protons and electrons of which they are composed, then could they not be transmuted? The description of radioactivity had already shown certain elements to be in the process of disintegration. Rutherford achieved the first such transformation in 1919 by bombarding more complex elements with alpha particles to produce a simpler element—hydrogen. Further experiments showed that not only could transmuted elements be produced but even some synthetic elements could be created, such as plutonium, berkelium, and californium.

The apparent simplicity of Rutherford's atom soon underwent modification with the discovery of additional components. In 1932, Chadwick described the neutron, an uncharged particle with a mass equal to that of the proton. Then came Anderson's positron (1933), with a mass equal to that of an electron, but with a positive charge. And finally came mesons, particles of short life, variously charged or neutral. The atom, in other words, was rapidly taking on the aspects of a cosmos, just when the cosmos itself was becoming a complexity almost beyond our ability to imagine, much less comprehend. The minuteness that atomic theory requires us to accept had an analogy in the germ theory of disease. When it had been established in the nineteenth century that bacteria are the agents of disease, it became immediately possible that even more minute agents of disease existed—what we have called viruses since 1935. What viruses are, whether they are living agents or not, is not yet entirely understood.

When physicists learned in our century to measure the rate of disintegration of radioactive substances into lead or helium,

it became possible—by measuring the proportion of lead and helium in radioactive materials—to establish the age of the rocks in which such minerals occurred. This has enabled contemporary geology to confirm the great age of rocks—in the millions of years. Consequently, geological time became another measure of vastness leading to incomprehensibility. Postwar generations that were particularly motivated to demand increased personal security were not being given by science the easy or absolute answers that many people require for security. New discoveries deepened the mysteries about reality.

These new realms of vastness were the more extreme in that they were set within the narrowing of time in all other aspects of modern man's life, namely, the acceleration of the pace of change and the new speed of communications. The European of 1870 would have found the pace of life in the twelfth century more similar to his own than that of 1970. The later he lives in the twentieth century, the more pressure there is upon him to accommodate to change, a factor that hampers the development of an integrated civilization. Since 1945, moreover, he has had to face a new dimension of destructiveness that atomic theory produced. Experiments to transmute atoms by bombarding them with high-voltage devices called cyclotrons or atom smashers led in 1939 to a successful splitting of the nucleus of a uranium atom into two parts —atomic fission—by two German scientists. After this came a letter from Einstein to President Roosevelt which explained the military possibilities of atomic fission that would require a political decision of the utmost gravity. Einstein not only knew the terrible destructiveness inherent in an atomic weapon, but what it would mean if Hitler's Germany alone developed it.

Atomic explosion was not the only European concern. Already in the nineteenth century some European intellectuals worried about the population explosion in Europe itself; by 1945 the anxiety had become global. The biologist Julian Huxley, a neo-Malthusian, was the man most responsible for making the world conscious of the population problem. He was the great figure at the Conference on World Population held in Rome in 1954. Here the first international survey of the population problem was made; it was estimated that the world population of 1920 would double by the early 1980s. Such a projection implied that if food and population growth were not soon brought into balance, the world would face miseries and frustrations of unprecedented scale. More pointedly, these agonies would become the chief motives for future wars.

From Laissez-faire to Welfare

In the recent past, the social sciences in general reflect a growing recognition of the complexity of both the individual and society. This means that we are less ready than were the eighteenth and nineteenth centuries to approach man and his society with a faith in the universe as a self-regulating mechanism, with its various components discoverable through the use of human reason. Individuals are seen to behave irrationally, hence, in an unpredictable fashion; economic "laws," such as the price-regulating mechanism of supply and demand, seem less reliable than laws should be; different cultures are found to respond variously in their development of social controls; and irritating creatures called historians now insist on the uniqueness of events, making it embarrassingly difficult to generalize.

Thus, the pattern of the social sciences after World War I was similar to that of the sciences: a trend away from a rigid, mechanistic view of reality, toward a more organic or relativist view. To this perceived complexity of reality one must add the complexities wrought by improved communications and by the rapidly increasing world population, which have made universal and immediate many matters that

earlier ages could meet with the luxury of time and isolation. For all the wonders and benefits of burgeoning science and technology, they have opened new worlds of problems and, if anything, deepened the mysteries of the universe yet to be plumbed. Small wonder, then, that men, since 1914, have increasingly seen the need to take a hand in the management of human affairs.

Thanks to two world wars and the Great Depression in between, Europe not only ceased to be the pivot of global politics, she ceased to be the pivot of the world economy. Beginning in 1914, European capital available for export began to decline, and by 1945 much capital invested abroad had been liquidated to pay for wartime imports. World War II, in particular, had been extremely destructive of capital equipment, and Europe experienced a sharp decline in her agricultural and industrial production, crippling her export trade. Consequently, she could not expect to import commodities essential to recovery, nor could she, by 1945, expect even to recover the standard of living of 1939 without outside help. That outside help could only come from the United States, which had gradually become the center of global economic power in the twentieth century, and especially so after World War II.

While the second war was more truly global than the first war, the first was far more destructive of the European population. If one is to understand the catastrophic effect of the casualties upon the morale and vitality of Europeans ever since, one must include in the calculation of the losses not simply battle casualties, but the rise in the civilian death rate and the reduction in the birthrate for which World War I was responsible. In other words, several generations have to pass before population losses can be reasonably reckoned, and we can as yet have no figures for the second war that are comparable to those of the first. World War I cost Europe, excluding Russia, between 20 and 22 million people, approximately 7 percent of the population. Russian losses, to which must be added those lost in the revolution and the civil war, are estimated to have been 28 million, or about 18 percent of the population. In the 1930s it was already noticeable that the western European populations were aging, a factor in both economic vitality and social welfare. By 1945, a continent that in the nineteenth century had experienced a population explosion and peopled all parts of the world with emigrants, had reached a point of near stabilization of population growth with little emigration.

As we have seen, liberals had traditionally opposed government regulation as champions of individual liberty. But the very magnitude of the disaster between 1914 and 1918 shocked liberals into a reversal of position. Led by Lord Keynes in Britain and Gunnar Myrdal of Sweden, they came to see that economic life in the highly complex modern society is not self-regulating. If economic recovery and social welfare were to be attained, governments would have to engage in economic planning and management. Keynes recommended such devices as the regulation of interest rates, of production ceilings, of subsidies, the raising or lowering of taxes to encourage or restrict investment, and programs of public works to provide employment. Beginning in 1932, the Social Democratic Party in Sweden used such devices to eliminate unemployment at a moment when it was widespread elsewhere. Keynes meant to revolutionize "the way the world thinks about economic problems," and since the alternative to the Keynesian revolution in the twentieth century became total economic planning by the State, as in Nazi Germany or in the Communist states of eastern Europe, it is fair to support Keynes' own contention that he meant to preserve liberal capitalism by the use of limited controls to prevent the ruinous "boom and bust" cycles of laissez-faire capitalism. The international economic planning in the years after 1945 simply confirmed and extended the Keynesian principles.

European recovery after 1945 also depended upon new technologies and new efficiency, as well as upon American financial aid. Industrialization and urbanization, long a fact of European economic life, continued to intensify, dependent in part on new forms of power and on the techniques of mass production—really a new degree of the specialization of production processes and labor—as well as upon new technologies born in the laboratory. The older industrial pioneers (Britain, France, and Belgium, in particular) had a more difficult time adjusting to the new techniques than those countries who came later to industrialization: Germany, Russia, Japan, and the United States. As diesel and internal combustion engines began replacing those powered by steam, the new demand for petroleum matched the decline in the demand for coal. Though it is true that by 1950 European productivity surpassed the capacity of 1929, one gets a better perspective by also noting that the productivity of 1928 had barely exceeded that of 1913. Two wars and a depression had clearly left their mark. Yet, by 1970, European productivity amazed all who knew the earlier devastation.

While the political division of Europe between East and West after 1945 was particularly the offspring of antagonisms born during World War I, we should not overlook the historical administrative and doctrinal differences that have divided the continent along the iron curtain since Roman times. From the Middle Ages onward, there were really two Europes, albeit similar in their common Roman and Christian foundations. Moreover, only eastern Europe endured lengthy occupation by Asian conquerors, Mongols and Turks, whose exactions of tribute left the occupied regions impoverished. And the East never enjoyed the river and ocean communications of the West. The economic underdevelopment of eastern Europe, in other words, when compared to that of the West, is both a contemporary and an historical phenomenon. In our own time, eastern Europe has been relatively unproductive: The rates of disease have been higher, and there has been more infant mortality, more malnutrition, and more bad housing than in the West. In Europe, at any rate, such conditions have not fostered political democracy. East European democratic governments have proved to be vulnerable to extremist movements that fed on popular desperation. When one charts the interwar political record, one notes that democracy survived in only the few countries with the highest per capita income. By that standard, eastern Europe had little chance, either before or after 1945, to make a success of western-style democracy.

Economic productivity, if an important key to the standard of living, is not the only key. In the twentieth century we have come to add as important measures of standard of living a sense of economic stability and security, the social services that are available, the shortening of work hours, physical health, and life expectancy. Creation of a mass market for nonessential consumer goods has perhaps been the most recent measure of the affluent society. In all such categories western Europe has the superior standard of living, but eastern Europe has been the scene of notable economic development since 1945; though some insist that eastern development could have been greater than it has been if the region had not been so rigidly tied to Russian economic and political requirements.

This recent progress, on the other hand, should not obscure the enormous damage to the European economy and psyche that the twentieth century brought. Europe has lived almost continually with either war, revolution, or economic crisis since 1914; a period of relative insecurity of life and property, a period of many and great purges and confiscations, of refugees and displaced peoples, an era of concentration camps and genocide unexampled in Western Civilization. Such insecurities and imperfections, in view of the democratization of society and the general awareness that European civilization held the promise of a better life for all, produced increasing demands for social justice.

Universal manhood suffrage was a commonplace in Europe after 1918. What was new after that date was a growing tendency to give the vote to women, a movement more precisely egalitarian than democratic. Norway was the first European nation to extend the vote to women (1907); and except for Switzerland, the practice was general by 1950. Democracy and industrialization had always implied the need to provide increased public instruction for an expanding electorate and the technical requirements of a complex economy. Especially after World War II, European opportunities for secondary, technical, and higher education were multiplied; but with an uneasy awareness, thanks to interwar memories, that a rising literacy rate in itself did not necessarily guarantee a more enlightened electorate.

Mass literacy opened the door to greater learning but at the same time it made the population more reachable by propaganda and advertising. The dilemma harkened back to the cultural despair of many intellectuals in the later nineteenth century, who had equated democratization with vulgarization. A resolution of that dilemma has since become clearer: a more sophisticated public education dedicated to making each citizen aware of the complexity of causality and aware of the "two cultures" whose rift remains to be bridged. The historical alternative to a democratic society is just as clear: an authoritarian society governed by an elite of some kind. This was the preference of some European university students in the 1960s who declared their abandonment of liberal democracy.

Meanwhile, the most systematic response to the clamor for social justice, especially intense after the economic collapse of the

1930s, came from an economist named William Beveridge in his *Report on Social Insurance and Allied Services* (1942). His formula to provide social security "from the cradle to the grave" and to eliminate extremes of wealth and poverty became a creed for postwar social reformers. It meant state responsibility for full employment as well as for education, insurance, and health. It often meant public ownership of resources or industries to force social progress.

Some nationalization of property had already begun, it is true, in the 1930s as a response to economic disaster. For example, the coalition of Leftist parties in France known as the Popular Front in 1936–1937, established the French National Railways Company, a mixed corporation with the state holding 51 percent of the stock. The most striking example of the welfare state in action, however, came after the British Labour Party took office in 1945: a National Insurance Act, a National Health Act, the Coal Industry Nationalization Act, the nationalization of the Bank of England, and the Transport Act to supervise all public transport, all enacted in 1946 and 1947. Similar developments took place under the new Fourth Republic in France. It would be wrong, consequently, to think of postwar Europe as divided into two communities: one of total free enterprise, one of total collectivization. Everywhere in Europe national economies functioned under greater regulation than ever before—and for the general good. In the East, the economies were controlled by single-party dictatorships; in the West, certain enterprises were nationalized only after popular vote had sanctioned such policies.

It is clear, in sum, that the society and economy of Europe, especially that of western Europe, had become far more democratic by the 1970s than it was at the turn of the century. Moreover, prosperity has touched ranks of society that had no expectation of welfare 70 years ago. It is no small matter, therefore, that the new generation of Europeans, more particularly the intellectuals, exhibits restlessness and discontent. Perhaps in part this malaise is a manifestation of what has been called a revolution of rising expectations, namely, that rapid progress always kindles greater expectations than reality allows, so that enthusiasm melts into disenchantment. But it is equally likely that the malcontents are the children of the literary culture, the victims of that divorce in our civilization that began long before the twentieth century. And the literary culture is to be understood to include all the arts and the humanities.

The Literary Culture

The vitality of the sciences in twentieth-century Europe has been in sharp contrast to the spiritual despair revealed in arts and letters. Although this sense of despair is largely a reflection of the political and social crisis in which Europe has lived since 1914, European intellectuals had already felt threatened by violence and vulgarity in the later nineteenth century, and were often further benumbed by their inability to perceive any purpose in the universe. Having for the most part rejected metaphysical truths and put their faith in science to provide the ultimate answers, they lived to learn that modern science, almost by definition, could not provide the answers they sought. Their growing alienation from science, therefore, went beyond their earlier objection to the birth of a materialist society founded on technology. The road to new metaphysical truths lay open to those who came to understand the limits of science, but it has been a road not overburdened with traffic. Instead, the tendency has been to close the shutters and to seek a private truth within the recesses of the self.

The sudden increase in the size of the reading public, by contributing to a mass of writing that reflected popular taste rather than literary merit, aggravated the literary agony. The cheap press did attract some eminent writers, men like G. K. Chesteron and G. B. Shaw, who may well have influenced people to acquire an interest in better literature, ideas, and politics. On the other hand, radio and television came to share with literature and journalism the task of informing the public; and the educational possibilities inherent in such media have too often been offset by their exceptional effectiveness in spreading partisan propaganda. We are only beginning to suspect, however, that the most critical aspect of the new media is to blunt the mind by encouraging the notion that learning is an easy and passive thing. The necessary present-mindedness of much journalism, radio, and television may also have contributed to popular indifference to traditional values, to anything that may be of permanent value, to history itself.

This abandonment of time-honored traditions and truths could already be seen after the turn of the century in the tendency to reject conventional art forms. The discord and lack of melody in music, the disappearance of subject matter in the plastic arts, and the absence of rhyme in verse, all reflected the increasing discord between man and an environment that was expanding in complexity. The new emphasis in the arts was upon abstraction, suggesting that the natural world was to be avoided in life itself, not merely in artistic representation. It is undeniable that abstract art has revealed new aesthetic truths; but we must recognize also the cultural crisis which these experimental forms reveal.

Thus, if the literary culture has to a certain extent lost its market to the new media, the fault is not entirely due to the attractive slickness of the new media. Twentieth-century poets, for instance, have been passionately concerned about violence and social issues, yet much less effective than their nineteenth-century counterparts in influencing national thought. New poetic techniques, while innovative and subtle, have amounted to a failure to speak to people, thus limiting the poet's audience to an élite of critics and other poets. The same tendency has occurred in the fields of serious music, art, and fiction. Novelists like James Joyce, Virginia Woolf, and Franz Kafka have been much akin to the new poets, developing a highly symbolic, often obscure narrative to be interpreted by each reader—really an appeal to a very limited audience.

Some of the early twentieth-century novelists revealed the optimism of scientific humanism which had occurred earlier in Flaubert; but the farther this group got into the century the more they saw science as nothing more than nonmoral, manipulative technology, as in H. G. Wells, *The Shape of Things to Come*, or in Aldous Huxley's *Brave New World*. The ultimate horror—the use of technology to enslave mankind entirely—was predicted in George Orwell's *1984*.

In the French literary world, André Gide was one of the giants, exerting tremendous influence upon the writers in the decades between the two world wars. While the novel was his usual medium, it is better to think of him as a moralist investigating the deep conflict between social values and individual sensuality, a conflict of which he was a tragic victim and for which his *Journal* covering the years 1889 to 1949 is the best source.

Beyond the tendency to portray social conflict or social decay, writers increasingly built their novels by drawing on inward experience. Novelists like D. H. Lawrence, James Joyce, and Marcel Proust were representative of what one might call the Freudian tradition, emphasizing not our rational selves but the unconscious or the irrational, and imbued with a pessimistic view of man's nature and his fate. The most astounding practitioner of inward analysis was Proust, whose literary achievement may well be the most impressive in the first half of our century. Although his lengthy work is generally published in a number of volumes, Proust's *Remembrance of Things Past* was intended to be one long novel. Appearing in sections between 1913 and 1927, the novel has been variously described as the revelation of a decaying society and as a pessimistic analysis of love. While this is true, the real subject of Proust's novel is the unreality of the external world where life goes by and time is lost. He discovered through sensation-memory, not merely the materials for his novel, but a device for recapturing time—of making time stand still, as if in eternity. The past then becomes the present, but only within the mind of the individual.

The dominant schools in the plastic arts during the 1920s and 1930s were cubism and surrealism. The surrealist movement, led by Salvador Dali, was influenced by Freudian psychology. The principal idea was to explore the subconscious through the use of free association. Cubism had the greater impact upon contemporary art. Here deliberate distortions were obtained by using either abstract or geometric linear arrangements, methods most brilliantly employed by Pablo Picasso and Henri Matisse.

The rejection of ancient and refined traditions was also evident in music. Arnold Schönberg, for instance, insisted that there is no real difference between concord and discord, and that man must learn to perceive all tonalities. Thus it followed that all possible tonal combinations ought to be accepted as chords. Schönberg's music has sometimes been called *Augenmusik* (eye music) because its intricacies can be more easily seen on the page than heard by the ear. An art form more likely to appeal to the few could hardly have been devised. It must be added that Igor Stravinsky and Béla Bartók moved in a different direction from Schönberg. Dissonance was evident in their music, too, but they made much use of primitive sounds and rhythms and, in the case of Bartók, of folk music, devices calculated to reach a larger audience.

The sense of alienation within the literary culture also emerged in the most sensational histories published in the twentieth century. In 1918, Oswald Spengler published his massive work *The Decline of the West,* a curious mishmash of learning and fantasy. He drew a parallel between European civilization in the twentieth century and that of the ancient world in its last stages. Using analogies drawn from the human life cycle, he portrayed the rise and fall of civilizations as a matter of inevitability and beyond our rational control: just as a human being must die so, too, must a civilization. This prophet of doom was widely quoted by European intellectuals in the interwar period, congenial as his message was to the literati, although in retrospect it seems unlikely that many of the quoters were qualified to judge the validity of his analogies. Part of Spengler's popularity derived from a willingness to pronounce on the state of civilization's health. This organic approach to history was also used by Arnold J. Toynbee in his 12-volume *Study of History,* which became well known through the publication of an abridgment after World War II. His results were less pessimistic than Spengler's. Despite the controversial nature of Toynbee's views in historical circles, it is notable that he became the outstanding historian of our time in the public mind; because, like Spengler, he reflected on the state of our civilization's health.

During World War I, Karl Barth, a Swiss theologian, began to preach what has been called a "theology of crisis," clearly a response to deep shock. He became a modern prophet defining sin for modern man, condemning the sinfulness of modern civilization, and called for repentance, for men to live in awe, fear, and trembling. Barth represented a revival of Kierkegaard's view (and perhaps Calvin's) that God cannot be intellectually investigated. In this view, only God's love makes possible the otherwise unbridgeable distance between man and God; and His revelation in the Bible is the unique source of His truth for us. Thus, Biblical revelation was a miracle. Barth's fundamentalism has been in sharp contrast to the social gospel of many contemporary churchmen, who have devoted themselves to practical, secular social programs. Whereas Barth would argue that they mistake temporal goals as the Kingdom of God, they would argue that there can be no salvation for men reduced to a brutish state by social or economic oppression.

The private agony of many in the literary culture was especially revealed in the philosophy of existentialism. With its roots deep in the nineteenth century, notably in the ideas of Kierkegaarde and Nietzsche, existentialism did not really flourish in Europe until after the holocaust of two world wars. Existentialism is difficult to define, because by 1945 it encompassed a variety of creeds, some of them Christian like Paul Tillich's, some of them atheist like Jean-Paul Sartre's. The most popular writer in the movement was Albert Camus, whose principal existentialist work, *The Myth of Sisyphus* (1942), argued for the absurdity of human existence.

Whatever their other differences, all existentialists opposed a systematic philosophy, seeing truth or reality only in subjective, personal terms. Thus thought has to do with a particular person in a particular situation, but always against a background of deep anxiety. For the existentialist, man cannot know reality through the use of detached or objective reason, almost suggesting an anti-intellectualism. Existence alone becomes reality, a fearful and agonizing plight. Men are seen as cast into an alien and hostile world with death as the final absurdity, each man inevitably alone both in his knowledge and his values. This view goes beyond the idea that we are all unique and that some things can be known to us alone (a Romantic view). It means to assert that there are no eternal or universal truths, and that human life has no meaning or purpose beyond what we ourselves invent in our search for security. It means that man has no place in the rationale of nature.

When the novelist-physicist C. P.

Sir Charles P. Snow (Wide World Photos)

Snow commented in 1961 on the rift between the scientific and the literary cultures, he did so as a man who had bridged them and who knew that the incomprehension and mistrust separating the two cultures is as unnecessary as it is dangerous. The literati, who had had no part in the technical advances of the two previous centuries, hated the Industrial Revolution for its presumed brutalization of the working classes and its emphasis on material gain. Remaining relatively indifferent to man's social condition, these "humanists" were preoccupied with man's tragic destiny as an individual. They saw scientists as blindly optimistic, since the scientists were confident in the possibility of improving the social condition of man. Snow argued that the two views of man can and must coexist: that they are not incompatible perceptions of man's lot. In essence the message was not new, however timely. Man requires bread to live, but cannot live by bread alone.

Others who bridged the two cultures also

avoided the agony of despair so common after 1914. In his *Science and the Modern World* (1925), the philosopher-mathematician Alfred North Whitehead noted that "successful organisms modify their environment," and that the various species, if often regarded as hostile, are actually mutually dependent. "A forest," he put it, "is the triumph of the organization of mutually dependent species." Similarly in society, different races and nations are necessary if a higher civilization is to be produced. Racial or national uniformity would produce stagnation, not to speak of boredom. Whitehead believed modern science to be the enterprise that challenges us to change, to grow, to modify our environment for the better. Science, Whitehead argued, forces us to see the future as necessary change and forbids us the "placidity of existence" that may be comfortable for individuals but is suicidal for civilization.

Change no doubt involves us in dangers and uncertainties, but it avoids the certain disaster of clinging to the present. Indeed, as the philosopher-mathematician Bertrand Russell claimed, hope for the future is at least as rational as fear. As for those who seek to make their peace with the two cultures and to reconcile themselves to the mysterious, the uncertain, and the unknown, there has been no better guide than history.

SUGGESTED READINGS

The asterisk indicates a paperback edition.

I. *1914–1945*

P. Birdsall, *Versailles Twenty Years After* (*New York: Reynal, 1941).

John C. Cairns, *France* (*Englewood Cliffs, N.J.: Prentice-Hall, 1965).

Gordon A. Craig, *From Bismarck to Adenauer: Aspects of German Statecraft* (Johns Hopkins Press, 1958).

John S. Curtiss, *The Russian Revolutions of 1917* (Princeton, N.J.: Princeton University Press, 1957).

Keith Eubank, *The Origins of World War II* (*New York: Thomas Y. Crowell, 1969).

Herbert Feis, *The Road to Pearl Harbor: The Coming of the War between the United States and Japan* (Princeton, N.J.: Princeton University Press, 1950).

Herbert Feis, *Churchill, Roosevelt, Stalin: The War They Waged and the Peace They Sought* (Princeton, N.J.: Princeton University Press, 1957).

Herman Finer, *Mussolini's Italy* (*New York: Grosset & Dunlap, 1965).

Fritz Fischer, *Germany's Aims in the First World War* (*New York: Norton, 1967).

Wallace Fowlie, *A Guide to Contemporary French Literature from Valéry to Sartre* (*New York: Meridian Books, 1957).

Felix Gilbert, *The End of the European Era, 1890 to the Present* (*New York: Norton, 1970).

Nathanael Greene, *From Versailles to Vichy, The Third French Republic 1919–1940* (*New York: Thomas Y. Crowell, 1970).

Hajo Holborn, *The Political Collapse of Europe* (New York: Knopf, 1957).

H. Stuart Hughes, *Consciousness and Society: The Reorientation of European Social Thought, 1890–1930* (New York: Knopf, 1958).

W. M. Jordan, *Great Britain, France, and the German Problem, 1918–1939* (Oxford: Oxford University Press, 1943).

George F. Kennan, *Soviet-American Relations, 1917–1920*, 2 vols. (Princeton, N.J.: Princeton University Press, 1956–1958).

Milton Mayer, *They Thought They Were Free* (*Chicago: University of Chicago Press, 1955).

George L. Mosse, *The Culture of Western Europe: The Nineteenth and Twentieth Centuries* (Chicago: Rand McNally, 1961).

Ernst Nolte, *Three Faces of Fascism: Action Francaise, Italian Fascism, National Socialism* (New York: Holt, Rinehart & Winston, 1966).

Richard Pipes, *The Formation of the Soviet Union: Communism and Nationalism, 1917–*

1923 (Cambridge, Mass.: Harvard University Press, 1954).

Joachim Remak, *The Nazi Years, A Documentary History* (*Englewood Cliffs, N.J.: Prentice Hall, 1969).

John L. Snell and others, *The Meaning of Yalta, Big Three Diplomacy and the New Balance of Power* (Baton Rouge: Louisiana State University Press, 1956).

Hugh Thomas, *The Spanish Civil War* (*New York: Harper, 1960).

David Thompson, *Democracy in France since 1870* (*Oxford: Oxford University Press, 1969).

Christopher Thorne, *The Approach of War 1938–39* (*New York: St. Martin's, 1967).

S. P. Tillman, *Anglo-American Relations at the Paris Peace Conference of 1919* (Princeton, N.J.: Princeton University Press, 1961).

Donald W. Treadgold, *Twentieth Century Russia* (Chicago: University of Chicago Press, 1959).

Robert C. Tucker and Stephen F. Cohen, eds. *The Great Purge Trial* (*New York: Grosset & Dunlap, 1965).

F. P. Walters, *A History of the League of Nations* (Oxford: Oxford University Press, 1960).

Eugen J. Weber, *The Action Française* (Stanford, Ca.: Stanford University Press, 1962).

Gerhard L. Weinberg, *Germany and the Soviet Union, 1939–1941* (Leyden: E. J. Brill, 1954).

II. *Since World War II*

Karl W. Deutsch, *et al., France, Germany and the Western Alliance—A Study of Elite Attitudes on European Integration and World Politics* (New York: Scribner's, 1967).

Theodosius Dobzhansky, *Mankind Evolving* (New Haven, Conn.: Yale University Press, 1962).

André Fontaine, *History of the Cold War* (3 vols. New York: Pantheon, 1968–1969).

Herbert Feis, *Between War and Peace: The Potsdam Conference* (Princeton, N.J.: Princeton University Press, 1960).

Herbert Feis, *Japan Subdued: The Atomic Bomb and the End of the War in the Pacific* (Princeton, N.J.: Princeton University Press, 1961).

Carl J. Friedrich, *Europe: An Emergent Nation?* (New York: Harper, 1970).

Will Herberg, ed., *Four Existentialist Theologians* (*New York: Doubleday Anchor, 1958).

H. Stuart Hughes, *The Obstructed Path* (*New York: Harper, 1968).

John Lukacs, *A New History of the Cold War* (*New York: Doubleday Anchor, 1968).

Charles S. Maier and Dan S. White, *The Thirteenth of May: The Advent of de Gaulle's Republic* (*Oxford: Oxford University Press, 1968).

Ortega y Gasset, *The Dehumanization of Art and Other Writings on Art and Culture* (*New York: Doubleday Anchor, 1956).

Roy Pierce, *Contemporary French Political Thought* (*Oxford: Oxford University Press, 1966).

David Rees, *The Age of Containment: The Cold War 1945–1965* (*New York: St. Martin's, 1967).

Morris H. Shamos, *Great Experiment in Physics* (New York, London: Holt, Dryden, 1957).

C. P. Snow, *The Two Cultures and a Second Look* (*New York: Mentor, 1964).

Alfred North Whitehead, *Science and the Modern World* (*New York: Mentor, 1948).

F. Roy Willis, *France, Germany and the New Europe 1945–1967* (*Oxford: Oxford University Press, 1968).

Index

Abelard, Peter, 155
  rationist philosophy of, 171-172
Abraham, 4-5
Academies of science, and scientific
  revolution, 298
Accademia del Cimento, 298, 299
Acropolis, function of, 17-18
  reconstruction of, 42
*Address to the Cristian Nobility of
  the German Nation* (Luther), 231
Administrative reform, of enlightened
  despots, 357
Adoration of the Magi (da Vinci),
  210, 211
Aeneid (Virgil), 67
Aeschylus, 40
Aestheticism, 469
Agamemnon (King), 15
Agora, 18
Agrarian life, during High Middle
  Ages, 135
Agrarian Revolution, in England,
  374-375
Agrarian slavery, of ancient Near-
  East, 2-3
Agrarian technology, in Carolingian
  Europe, 116-117
Agriculture, and European economy
  (16th Century), 286
  of High Middle Ages, 129
  in Roman Empire, 91
Alaric, 94
Albert of Wallenstein, 266
Albigensian Crusade, 157
Albigensianism, 157, 158
Alcuin, and Carolingian Renais-
  sance, 117
Alexander I (Czar), 411
Alexander II (Czar), 451-452
Alexander III (Czar), 486
Alexander the Great, accession of, 29
  campaigns of, 45
  characterized, 44
  style of, 45-46
  successor to, 46-47
Alexander of Parma, and religious
  wars, 263
Alfred the Great, cultural impact of,
  123
  military leadership of, 121-122
Algeria, 542-546
Alliance of 1879, 435
Allies, African campaign of, 524
  offensives of, 524-525, 528
  reconstruction policy of

(post-WWII), 534-535
All-Russian Extraordinary Commission (Cheka), 489
Alphonso XIII of Spain, 512
Alsace-Lorraine, 430
  and Treaty of Versailles, 490
Altaic peoples, during middle ages,
  104
Ambrose, impact of, 87
America, and aid to British (1940),
  521, 523
  and French colonialism, 276
  influence in Europe of, 548-549
  and League of Nations, 495-496
  and post-WWI attitudes, 493-494
  Soviet relations of (1945-73), 531-
  533
  and Vietnam War, 546-547
  in WWI, 483
  and WWI debts, 499
  in WWII, 524, 528
American Indians, and colonialism,
  279
American Revolution, 359
  conservatism of, 360-361
Amsterdam, 294
  vs. *Stadhouder*, 321
Anabaptism, and Peasants'
  revolt, 231-232
Anabaptists, characterized, 249
Anarchism, 450
Anatomy, progress in, 308
Anaximander, and theory of
  evolution, 32, 33
Ancient Greece, and Homeric epics,
  15-16
Ancient Jews, history of, 4-8
  impact of, 8
Anglo-French rivalry, and Hundred
  Years' War, 185
Animism, 16-17
Anschluss, 517
Anselm, Saint, scholastic philosophy
  of, 171
Anticlericalism, 356
  in late-medieval Christianity, 181-
  182
  in Renaissance literature, 204-205
Antigone (Sophocles), 40-41
Antigonids, 46
Antoninus, 69
Antony, Mark, 66
Antwerp, commerce in (during
  Reformation), 222, 223
Appeasement, of Fascist

regimes, 515-516
Aquinas, St. Thomas, 158
  philosophical system of, 173
  views on, 196, 197-198
Aragon, royal power in, 328
Archetype, in Platonic philosophy,
  36-37
Archilochus, 32
Archimedes, 51
Architecture, during High Middle
  Ages, 165-167
  during Renaissance, 206-208
Arianism, 86, 87
Ariosto, Ludovico, 251
Aristarchus of Samos, theories of,
  301
Aristocracy, in classical Greece, 18
Aristophanes, 41
Aristotelian physics, 304
Aristotle, life of, 37
  scholarship of, 37-38
  translations of (during High
  Middle Ages), 172-173
Arkwright, Richard, 378, 379
Arms Limitation Treaty, 549
Arnold, Matthew, 468
Art, death in (pre-Reformation), 227
  of Golden Age, 38
  of Hellenistic Age, 47-48
  late medieval, 198
  of Reformation, 250
  and Renaissance, 212, 213-214
  of 20th Century, 555, 556, 557
Aspasia, 39
Asper, collapse of, 289
Assembly of Notables, 369
Assignats, 389
Association Movement, 365
Assumption of the Virgin, 247
Astronomy, ancient-medieval, 299-
  300
  and scientific revolution, 300-303
  in 20th Century, 550
Atheism, and Enlightenment, 352-353
Athenian empire, evolution of, 26-27
  and Peloponnesian War, 27-28
Athens, 22-24
  citizenship in, 23
  Golden Age of, 26-27
  and Persian Wars, 24-26
  politics of, 20, 22, 23-24
Atomic bomb, and American
  decision (WWII), 528
  cultural impact of, 530
Atomism, 33

of Epicureans, 50
Attila, 95
Attlee, Clement, policy of, 542
Audiencia, 273
Augustan Age, 66-68
Augustine, Saint (Benedictine), 88-89, 111
August the Strong, 326
Augustus, deification of, 75
leadership after, 68-69
Roman Empire under, 66-68
Aurelius, Marcus, 69
Austria, administrative centralization in, 320
and Bosnia-Herzegovina, 439-440
and Bulgarian unification, 436
and Crimean War, 426
German absorption of, 517
political climate of (1919-1934), 501
vs. Prussia (18th Century), 339
and Thirty Years War, 266-267
and Treaty of Vienna, 413
vs. Turks (17th Century), 336-337
see also Austrian Empire; Austria-Hungary
Austria-Hungary, and politics, 450, 456
in World War I, 481, 484
and Treaty of Versailles, 491
see also Austria; Austrian Empire
Austrian Empire, uprisings in, 363-365, 423-424; See also Austria; Austria-Hungary
Austrian National Socialists, 517
Autarky, 510
Autobiography (Franklin), 346
Averroes, 172
Avogadro, 461

Babeuf, Gracchus, 396
"Bacchanale" (Titian), 213
Bacon, Sir Francis, ideas of, 281, 310
Bacon, Roger, 159, 173-174
Badoglio, Marshal, 525
Bakunin, Michael, 470
Balance of power diplomacy, 331
Balboa, 221
Balbo, Count Cesare, proposals of, 422
Balfour Declaration, 544
Balzac, Honore, 467
Bangladesh, 544
Bank of Amsterdam, 294
Banking, 193-194, 287-288
Bankruptcy, in Europe (16th Century), 287-288, 292
Barbarossa, Frederick, 144
Barere, Bertrand, 392
Barometer, 304
Barth, Karl, 557-558
Bartok, Bela, 557
Bastille, storming of, 387
Battle of Lechfeld, 119-120, 128
Baudelaire, Charles, 469
Bauhin, Kasper, 308
Bayle, Pierre, 344, 348, 349
Beccaria, Cesare de, political theories of, 351

Bede the Venerable, Saint, 112
Belgium, and revolution, 363-364, 417-418
in World War I, 480-481
Benedict of Nursia, Saint, impact on monasticism of, 109-110
Benedictines, impact of, 109-110, 111-112
Benedictinism, crisis in (during High Middle Ages), 153-154
and urbanization, 154
Benefice, 124
Benoist, Elie, 348
Bentham, Jeremy, 446
Bergson, Henri, on mankind, 472
Berkeley, Lord, 277
Berlin Decree, 400
Berlin Wall, 537
Berlioz, Hector, 466
Bernard of Clairvaux, Saint, career of, 155
Bernouilli family, 347
Berthollet, Claude, 347
Beveridge, William, 555
Bible, as historical source, 4
Big Deal, 285
Bill of Rights (English), 278
Birth rate, in France (1930's), 514
Bismarck, Otto von, and Congress of Berlin, 435-436
factors confronted by, 432-433
and German unification, 429-430
resignation of, 436-437
and socialism, 455-456
Black Death, 180, 194, 195
Blacks, and slavery, 279
Blanc, Louis, 421, 448
Blitzkrieg, 520
Block, Marc, on feudalism, 125
Blum, Leon, 513, 514
Boards of Trade, 277, 278, 282
Boccaccio, 202, 203, 204, 205
Bohemia, and Thirty Years War, 266-267
Boleyn, Anne, and Henry VIII, 235, 236
Book of the Courtier, The (Castiglione), 203
Bolsheviks, 486
Bonaparte, Josephine, 397
influence of, 398
Bonapartist Constitution, 415
Bonaventure, Saint, 159, 173
Boniface, Saint, 112
Boroughs, 325
Bosnia, 435
Bosnia-Herzegovina, annexation of, 439, 440
Botany, advances in, 308-309
Botero, Giovanni, on states, 314
Boulanger, General Georges, 458
Bourbon family, and religious wars, 258
in Spain (18th Century), 329
Boyle, Robert, 311
contributions of, 304
Bracciolini, Poggio, 205
Braddock, General, 340
Brahe, Tycho, contributions

of, 301-302
Brave New World (Huxley), 556
Brethren of the Common Life, 181
Bretton Woods (New Hampshire), 532
Breviary, 248
Brindley, James, 376
Britain, agrarian revolution, 374-375
and Cambrai breakthrough, 484
and centralization of power, 444
Christianization of, 111-112
colonial empire of, 277-279, 544-545
and Common Market, 540
conditions in (post-WWII), 535
vs. Cutch, 293-294
democratization in, 458
depression in, 515
foreign agreements of (1899-1907), 438-439
vs. Germany (1917), 482-483
German blockade of, 482
vs. Holland (1780), 361-362
and Hundred Years' War, 185-186
industrialization in, 372
vs. Italians, 523
vs. Napoleon, 400, 402
Navigation Acts of, 282
vs. Nazis, 521
Parliament vs. monarchy in (17th-18th Centuries), 322
Parliament in, 147-148, 184-185
population growth in, 374
prosperity in (17th Century), 292-293
Protestant Reformation in, 234-238
radicalism in (19th Century), 446-447
recovery of (post-WWII), 542-543
and religious war, 267-268
socialism in, 448
vs. Spain, 264
and Triple Alliance, 437
unification of, 121-123, 146-147
and Wars of the Roses, 186
as welfare state, 555
British East India Company, 177
Brittany, and privilege, 368
Brutus, 66
"Buchlau bargain," 439
Bulgaria, 502
vs. Serbs, 436
and Treaty of Versailles, 491
Bundesrat, 455
Burckhardt, Jacob, 179
Bureaucracy, French management of, 317-318
Burial of the Count of Orgaz, The (El Greco), 250
Byron, Lord, 465
Byzantium, cultural significance of, 106
cultural sources of, 104
transformation of, 105-106
during Middle Ages, 101

Cabot, 221
Caesar, 63

Caesaropapism, in Byzantium, 105, 106
doctrine of, 87
Cahiers, 386, 388
Caligula, 69
Calonne, Marquis de, and fiscal reform, 369
Calvert, Lord, 277
Calvin, John, career of, 238-239
theology of, 239-240
Calvinism, 238-241
and conscience, 250
republicanism of, 249
see also Calvinists
Calvinists, characterized, 249
revolt of (1566), 262-263
and state churches, 258
see also Calvinism
Camisards, 292
Canaanite civilization, influence on Jews, 5
Canada, British capture of, 341
French colonization of, 176
Canal du Languedoc, 283
Candide (Voltaire), 345
Canisius, Saint Peter, and Poland, 245
Canizzaro, Stanislo, 461
Canon law, during High Middle Ages, 169
Canterbury Tales (Chaucer), 198
Capetians, accomplishments of, 148-151
French kings of, 123
Capital investment, and industrialization, 373
Capitalism, and Calvinism, 241
Marx on, 449
Caporetto, 483
"Captive Slaves" (Michelangelo), 212
Capuchins, 244
Carmelites, 245
Carnot, Lazare, 392, 394
Carolingian Europe, agrarian technology in breakdown of, 118
chronology of, 118
intellectual revival in, 117-118
invasions of (800's and 900's), 118-120
overview of, 115-116
"Carolingian Renaissance," 117-118
Carolingians, and feudalism, 124
rise of, 113-115
Carteret, Sir George, 277
Carthage, development of, 55
and Rome, 60
Carthusian order, during High Middle Ages, 154-155
Casablanca, 524
Casa de la Contratacion, 273, 274, 281
Cassiodoris, 95-96
Cassius, 66
Castiglione, 203
Castile, royal power in, 328
Castlereagh, Viscount Robert Stuart, 411, 414
Cathari, 157
Catherine de Medici, and religious wars, 258, 259

Catholic Inquisition, in Spain (during late Middle Ages), 189-190
Catholic League, and Thirty Years War, 266
Cavour, Count Camillo Benso di, and Italian unification, 426-427
Cellini, Benvenuto, 202
Centralization of power, overview of, 443-445, 450-452
Centuriate, in early Rome, 57-58
Ceremony, under Louis XIV, 318
Cervantes, 203, 250-251
Ceylon, 544
Chamberlain, Neville, 521
and Hitler, 517
Chamber of Deputies, 456
"Chambers of Reunion," 335
Champlain, Samuel de, 276
Chansons de Geste, 162-163, 164
Charlemagne, 101, 104
becomes emperor, 115
and feudalism, 124
military campaigns of, 115
Western Christendom under, 115-118
Charles Albert of Sardinia-Piedmont, 422
Charles I of England, vs. Parliament, 322-323
and Puritans, 267-268
Charles II of England, colonial policy of, 277
and Parliament, 323
on trade, 282
Charles II of Spain, 329
Charles III of Spain, and administrative reform, 357
Charles V of Spain, 246
Charles XII of Sweden, and military, 337
Charles X of France, 417
Charles the Simple, 120
Charterhouse of Parma, The (Stendhal), 467
Chateaubriand, Rene, 464
Chaucer, Geoffrey, 198, 202
Cheka, 510
Chemistry, advances in, 347, 461-462
Chesteron, G. K., 556
Child, Josiah, 293
China, Japanese invasion of, 516
and Korean War, 537
Chivalry, development of, 126
Chrestien Le Clercq, 279
Christian church, hierarchy in, 78
Christian Democrats (Italy), 540, 541
Christian IV, 266
Christianity, appeal of, 80
conversion to (under Constantine), 85-87
and dualism, 104-105
emergence of, 76-78
Enlightenment attacks on, 349
and Hellenism, 78-79
during High Middle Ages, 152-160
impact of, 80-81, 161
Irish (during Early Middle

Ages), 109
and Judaism, 76-77
in late-medieval Europe, 181
and Roman Empire, 78, 80-81
sacraments in, 78
syncretic quality of, 76
see also Christians
Christians, persecution of (under Roman emperors), 80-81
and Roman religion, 76
see also Christianity
Christianization, of England, 111-112
and Germanization (during High Middle Ages), 139, 141
of Iberian Peninsula (during High Middle Ages, 136-137
of Scandinavia, 120
Churchill, Winston, 521
Churchill, 542
Church-state controversy, in Western Europe (during High Middle Ages), 142-145
Cicero, 63
murder of, 66
Cistercianism, during High Middle Ages, 155-156
City of God (Augustine), 88
Citizenship, in Athens, 23, 39
City-states, and Alexander the Great, 44-45
decline of, 29-30
of Greece, 17-18, 19-20
of Hellenistic Age, 47
and Peloponnesian War, 29
see also Greek city-states
Civil Constitution of the Clergy, 388, 389
Civil History of the Kingdom of Naples (Giannone), 349
Civil law, during High Middle Ages, 169
Civil liberties, under enlightened despots, 359
Civilization, definition of, 2
Civil War in France, The (Marx), 452
Clarendon Code, 323
Class conflict, during late Middle Ages, 194, 195
and industrialization, 379
Classical Greece, colonization by (750-550 B.C.), 18-19
decline of, 29-30
social structure in, 18, 19-20
philosophical outlook in, 31
Cleisthenes, leadership of Athens by, 23
Clemenceau, Georges, 489
Cleopatra, 66
Clive, Robert, 341
Clouds, The (Aristophanes), 41
Clovis, 96
Cluniac movement, 154
Clusius, 308
Cobbett, William, 446
Cobden, Richard, 448
Cockayne project, 293
Coined money, and social structure (in classical Greece), 19, 20
Colbert, Jean Baptiste, 287

and French depression, 292
mercantilism of, 283
Cold War, thawing of, 547-548
Colet, John, 205
Collectivization, 511
Coloni, 72
Colonial empire, overview of, 279-280
of western European nations, 271-279
see also Colonialism
Colonialism, decline of, 284, 544-546
turning point in, 270
see also Colonial empire
Columbus, Christopher, career of, 220-221
Comedy, of Golden Age, 41
Comitatus, 93
Commentaries on the Gallic Wars (Caesar), 64
Commerce, of Carthage, 55
in Greece, 18, 19, 22
during Reformation, 222-223
and European economy (16th Century), 286
trends in (during High Middle Ages), 134-135
Commercialism, attack on, 468
Committee of Public Safety, 393
Commune of Paris (1871), 452-453
Communism, in Enlightenment, 353
Communist Manifesto (Marx), 449
Communist parties, Western attitudes toward, 538
Commynes, Phillip de, 203-204
Comte, August, positivism of, 448-449
Comte de Segur, on French Revolution, 366
Concert of Europe, 414, 415
Conciliarism, in late medieval church, 183
Concordat, The, 398
Condorcet, Marquis de, 345-346
Confederation of the Rhine, 400
Confederation of Targowica, 363
Confessions (Augustine), 88
Congress of Berlin, 435, 436
Congress of Paris, 426
Congress of Verona, 415
Congress of Vienna, 410
Consolation of Philosophy (Boethius), 95
Conspiracy of Equals, 396
Conspiracy of Tavoras, 356
Constantine, Roman Empire under, 84-87
Constantinople, founding of (A.D. 330), 85
Constitution, in France, 389, 397
of Sparta, 21
Convergence, and scientific revolution, 298
Copernicus, 391
career of, 300-301
Cordeliers, 391
Corpus Juris Civilis, 105
Corpus Juris Civilis (Justinian), 169

Cort, Henry, 382
Cortes, 222
Cosmopolitanism, of Hellenistic age, 47
vs. nationalism, 409-410
Cotton gin, 380
Council of Basel (1431-1449), 183
Council of Constance (1415-1418), 183
Council of Five Hundred, 23-24
Council of People's Commissars, 510
Council of Pisa, 183
Council of Trent, 245-246
doctrine of, 247-248
impact of, 248
Counterreformation, development of, 244-245
and scientific progress, 298-299
Covenant, of Jews, 4-5, 7
Cranmer, Thomas (Archbishop of Canterbury), and English Reformation, 235, 237
Creation of Adam, The (Michelangelo), 212
Creative Evolution (Bergson), 472
Crete, and Ottoman Empire, 336
Crime and Punishment (Dostoevsky), 469
Crimean War, 425-426
Croats, 423, 424
Crompton, Samuel, 379
Cromwell, Oliver, career of, 323
Cromwell, Thomas, and English Reformation, 235-236
Crusades, Christian (during High Middle Ages), 138-139
Crusading orders, during High Middle Ages, 156
Cults, revival of (during Hellenistic Age), 48-49
in Roman religion, 75-76
Culture, of Athenian Golden Age, 27, 39-43
during early Middle Ages, 109-110
Greek-European comparison, 161
overview of (20th Century), 550-558
of late-medieval Europe, 196-198
Spartan, 20
Curie, Marie, 462
Currency, manipulation of (17th Century), 289
Cynics, 49
Czechoslovakia, creation of, 491
invasions of, 517, 548
politics in (post-WWI), 503, 504

da Feltre, Vittorini, 203
Daladier, Edouard, and Hitler, 517-518
Dali, Salvador, 557
Dalton, John, atomic theory of, 461
Dance of Death theme, in late-medieval art, 196
Dante, 164-165, 202
Danton, Georges, 391
Darby, Abraham, 381
Darius the Great, and Persian Wars, 24, 25

Darwin, Charles, 459-461
Dauphin Charles, 186, 187
David, 5
Dawes, Charles, 500
Dawes Committee, 500
Dead Souls (Gogol), 467
Death, in art (pre-Reformation), 227
Death-consciousness, pre-Reformation, 226-228
Decameron (Boccaccio), 204
Decembrist Revolt, 485
"Declaration of Independence," 361
Declaration of Rights, importance of, 324
"Declaration of the Rights of Man and the Citizen, The," 387
Decline and Fall of the Roman Empire, The (Gibbon), 351-352
Decline of the West, The (Spengler), 557
Defensor Pacis (Marsilius of Padua), 184
Degas, 468
De Gaulle, Charles, 546
and Common Market, 540
and NATO, 548-549
Deification, of Roman emperors, 75
Deism, 349
de La Court, Peter, on war, 294
Delacroix, Eugene, 465, 466
Delian League, 26
Democracy, Athenian, 22, 23-24
failure of (post-WWI), 513-514
Roman, 57-58
Democratization, of Europe, 455-458
Democritus, and atomism, 33
Denmark, 540
Nazi occupation of, 521
and Treaty of Vienna, 414
de Poitiers, Diana, 285
Depression, causes of (16th-17th Centuries), 285-289
in Europe, 289-292
overview of (16th-17th Centuries), 295-296
Descartes, Rene, 298
and analytic geometry, 306
world view of, 310-311
Detente, 532, 549
Deurbanization, of late Roman Empire, 91
De Witt, Jan, vs. *Stadhouder*, 321
Dia, Beatriz de, 164
Dialectical materialism, 449
Dialogues on Natural Religion (Hume), 353
Dialogue on Two New Sciences (Galileo), 304
Dialogue on the Two Principal Systems of the Universe (Galileo), 303
Dickens, Charles, 467
Dien Bien Phu, 545
Diet of Poland, 326, 327
Diet of Worms (1521), 230
Dilthey, Wilhelm, 472
Diocletian, Roman Empire under, 81, 83-84

Diogenes, 49
Directory, Government of, 396-397
Disputa (Raphael), 250
Dispute, The (Raphael), 211-212
Divers Thoughts on the Comet
   (Bayle), 344
Divine Comedy (Dante), 164-165,
   202
Divine right absolutism, 350
   rise of, 314, 316
Dr. Faustus (Marlow), 251
Doctors of Latin Chruch, 87-89
Dollfus, Engelbert, 501
Domesday Book, 146
Dominican order, during High
   Middle Ages, 158-159
Dominic, Saint, achievement of, 158-
   159
"Donation of Pepin," 115
Don Quixote (Cervantes), 203, 250-
   251
Doran Greeks, and Mycenean Greeks,
   15
Dostoevsky, Fyodor, 469
Drake, Sir Francis, and Spanish war,
   264
Drama, of Golden Age, 39-41
Dreyfus Affair, 458
Dualism, impact on Christianity,
   104-105
Dual Monarchy, 432, 433
Duke of Alva, and religious up-
   risings, 263
Duke of Guise, and Holy League, 260
Duke of Sully, 316
Duma, 485
Dumas, Alexandre, 466
Dunkirk, 521
Durer, 250
Dutch, and colonial empire, 274-276,
   279
   vs. England, 293-294
   see also Holland; Netherlands
Dutch East India Company, success
   of, 275
Dutch West India Company, failure
   of, 275

Early Middle Ages, Germanic peoples
   during, 92-96
   monasticism in, 109-110
Eastern Europe, and communism,
   535, 547-548
   diplomatic sphere in, 331
   economics of (20th Century), 55
   Germanic expansion (during
      High Middle Ages), 139, 141
   power shifts in (18th Century),
      338
"Eastern Question, The," 331
East Frankland, *see* Germany
East Germany, creation of, 536
Ecclesiastical History of England
   (Bede), 112
Ecclesiastical organization, 109, 128
Eckhardt, Meister, 181
Economics, changes in (20th Century),
   552-553
   and enlightened despots, 357-358

Economy, Hellenistic, 47, 51
   medieval, 134, 193-196
   of Roman Empire, 84, 91
   of Western Christendom, 108, 109
   see also European economy
Edict of Nantes, 260
Edict of Restitution, 266-267
Education, Enlightenment view of,
   346
   during Reformation, 223-224
   during Renaissance, 203, 206
Egypt, 523
   development of civilization in, 2
   Ptolemaic, 46
Einstein, Albert, and theory of
   relativity, 463
Elections, and Parliament (18th
   Century), 325-326
Electoral reform, in Parliament
   (1780's), 366-367
Elementary Treatise of Chemistry
   (Lavoisier), 347
Eleusinian Mysteries, 16
El Greco, art characterized, 250
Elitism, 468-470
Elizabeth (Czarina), 340
Elizabeth I of England, 277
   compared to Philip II, 265-266
   and Spain, 264
Emile (Rousseau), 346
Enclosures, 375
Encyclopedia, 348
England, *see* Britain
Enlightened despotism, 356-358
Enlightenment, intellectual climate
   of, 343-345
   legacy of, 353-354
   and legal reform, 356-357
   overview of, 343
   political theory in, 350
   reason in, 345-358
   and religion, 352-353
   and science, 346-347
   world view in, 345-346
Epicureanism, 50
Epicurus, teachings of, 50
Equestrian class, rise of (in Rome),
   61-62
Erasmus, 204, 205, 233
Eratosthenes, 51
*Essays Concerning Human Under-
   standing* (Locke), 311
*Essay Concerning Human Under-
   standing* (Locke), 344
Essay on the Inequality of the Races
   (Gobineau), 471
Estates General, 186, 187, 385-386
Ethiopia, Italian invasion of, 516
Etruscans, impact of Greek civiliza-
   tion on, 56
Euclid, 51
Eugene of Savoy, 331, 337
Euripides, 40
Europe, in A.D. 500, 96
   Christianity in (during High
      Middle Ages), 152-154
   commerce in (during Reformation),
      222-223
   population growth in (during

Reformation), 223-224
   post war periods, 491, 493-494,
      505, 533-534, 539
   see also Eastern Europe; Western
      Europe
European civilization, polarities in,
   454-455
European economy, and crisis of
   1557, 285
   instability of (16th Century), 286-
      287
   see also Depression
Eusebius, 87
Evolution, and Anaximander, 32, 33
   Darwinian theory of, 459-461
Exchange Bank, 294
Exchequer, development of, 146
Existentialism, 558
Exploration, during Reformation,
   220-222
Expressionists, 468

Fable of the Bees (Mandeville), 353
Fairie Queen (Spencer), 252
Falange, 512
Family patterns, during Reforma-
   tion, 223-224
Famine, in France, 292, 335
Faraday, Michael, contributions of,
   459
Farmers, in early Rome, 58-59
Fascism, in Europe, 504-506, 507-
   510, 512-514
   see also Nazis
Faust (Goethe), 464
Ferdinand of Styria, and Thirty Years
   War, 266-267
Ferdinand I of Naples, 415
Ferdinand II of Italy, 422
Ferdinand VII of Spain, revolt
   against, 415, 416
Fermat, Pierre, 306
Feudalism, decentralization of, 316
   in France, 123-125, 126
Fifth Republic, 542
Finland, Soviet attack of, 520-521
   and Treaty of Vienna, 414
First Balkan War, 440-441
First Estate, 386
First Hague Conference, 439
Fiume, 496-497
Five Year Plan, 511
Flaubert, Gustave, 467, 469
Flemish school, 207, 209
Florence, during late Middle Ages,
   193
   Renaissance in, 200, 201
Flowers of Evil (Baudelaire), 469
Fluit, 294
Flying shuttle, 378
Foch, General Ferdinand, 484, 494
Food crisis, 549
Fourier, Charles, socialism of, 447-
   448
Fourteen Points, 484
Fourth Republic, instability of, 541-
   542
France, administrative weaknesses in
   (17th-18th Centuries), 318-319

and Algerian independence, 542
bureaucracy in, 317-318
centralized government in, 450-451, 452
and colonial empire, 276-277, 545-546
decline of (1860's), 428
democratization, 456, 458
depression in, 291, 292
feudalism in (during Viking Age), 123-126
foreign ties of (early 20th century), 439
and German war debts, 500
and Hundred Years' War, 186, 187, 188
and Italian agreement, 438
mercantilism in, 283-284
military in (17th-18th Centuries), 316-317
Nazi defeat of, 521
in 1930's, 514, 516
poetry of (during High Middle Ages), 162-163, 164
political organization in (during late middle ages), 186-188
radicalism in (19th Century), 445-446
recovery of (post-WWII), 541-542
religious wars in, 258-260
revolutions in (1800's), 417
socialism in, 447-448
under Capetian kings (during High Middle Ages), 148-151
in WWI, 481, 483
see also French Revolution
Francis I (King), 224
Franciscans, 181, 182, 245
in High Middle Ages, 159-160
and urban evangelism, 134
Francis, Saint, career of, 159
Franco, General Francisco, emergence of, 513
Franco-Prussian War, 430
Frankland, rise of Carolingians in, 113-115
Franklin, Benjamin, 346
Franks, 96
Franz Ferdinand, Archduke, 441-442
Franz-Stefan, 373
Frederick-Henry, and royal absolutism, 321
Frederick of Bohemia, 266
Frederick the Great, economics of, 358
and law reform, 356
Frederick William, 320
and Prussian army, 317
Frederick William III, and antiliberal censorship, 414-415
Frederick William IV of Prussia, and liberal-national movement, 424
Frederick II, 144
Free Corps, 362
French Academy of Sciences, 306
French Revolution, beginning of, 370
chronology of, 404
and Constitution, 389
and Estates General, 385-386

heritage of, 443-444
and Paris, 387, 391-392
and pre-revolutionary atmosphere, 366-369
in provinces, 387
and Reign of Terror, 392-396
and Roman Catholic Church, 388-389
Freud, Sigmund, 3
theories of, 473
Fronde revolution, 317
Fuggers, 287

Galen, 73, 308
Galileo, 298-299
career of, 303, 304
Garibaldi, Giuseppe, 427
Gauguin, 468
Gaul, conquests of, 64-65, 96
Geer, Luis de, 295
Geocentrism, 299-300
Geography, and Rome, 56
Geology, advances in, 551
Geometry (Descartes), 306
George, Stefan, 470
George I of England, 324
George III, 325
Gerbert of Aurillac, 128-129
Gericault, J. A., 466
Germania (Tacitus), 92
Germanic Confederation, 414
Germans, culture of (during Early Middle Ages), 92-94
invasions by, 82, 94-96
German-Soviet Pact, 518
Germany, aggression of (1930's), 519
and Austria, 517
and Bosnia-Herzegovina, 439-440
and church-state struggle, 145
democratization of, 455-456
depression in, 291
economic recovery of, 539
expansion of (during High Middle Ages), 139, 141
foreign policy of (1890-1914), 480
invasions of (during Viking Age), 127
in late Middle Ages, 190
monarchy in, 127-129
Ottonian renaissance in, 128-129
post WWI, 499-500, 507
revolution in (1830), 418
surrender by, 528
Turkish policy of, 441
unification of, 428-430
in WWI, 480-481, 482-483, 484
WWII offenses of, 520-521, 523
see also Hitler, Adolf; Nazis
Gerusalemme Liberata (Tasso), 251
Ghiberti, Lorenzo, 209
Giannone, Pietro, 349
Gibbon, Edward, 351-352
Gide, Andre, 556
Gioberti, Vincenzo, compromise of, 422
Girondins, 391, 392
execution of, 394
Glorious Revolution, The, 324
Gnostics, interpretation of

Christ by, 79
Gobineau, Arthur, 471
Gods, in Homeric epics, 16
in Roman religion, 75
Goethe, J. W. von, 464
Gogol, N. V., 467
Golden Age, 26-27
cultural creativity of, 38
life in, 39-43
and drama, 39-41
Spanish, 190
Golden Bull, 190
Gomulka, Wladyslaw, 547
Gordon riots, 365
Gothic style, 166-167, 206-207, 208
Government Inspector, The (Gogol), 467
Government of National Defense, 430
Gracchus, Tiberius and Gaius, 62
Grand Trunk Canal, 376
Great Assembly of Divines, 268
Great Civil War, 497, 499
Great Ordinance of 1357, 186, 187
Great Remonstrance, 344
Great War for Empire, 284, 339, 340-341
Greece, 502
American aid to (post-WWII), 535
Antigonid, 46
city-states of, 17-18, 19-20
revolution in (1820's), 416
Roman conquest of, 60-61
study of (during Renaissance), 205-206
vs. Turkey (1920's), 496
see also Classical Greece
Greek Dark Age (1120-800 B.C.), 15
Greek literature, Minoan-Mycenaean era in, 13
Gregory the Great (Pope), impact of, 110
Gregory VII (Pope), and church-state controversy (during High Middle Ages), 144
and monastic reform, 154
Groot, Gerard, 181
Grosseteste, Robert, 173
Guadeloupe, 341
Guilds, development of (in high-medieval towns), 135
influence of (during Renaissance), 201
Guise family, and religious wars, 258, 259
Guizot, Francois, 421
Gunpowder, 196
Gustavus Adolphus, and Thirty Years War, 267
Gutenberg, John, 219
Gwynne, Nell, 323

Hadrian, 69
Halley's Comet, 344
Hamlet (Shakespeare), 252
Hannibal, 60
Hanseatic League, 134-135, 139, 141
Hardenberg, Prince Karl August von, 411
Hargreaves, James, 378

Harvey, William, on circulatory system, 308
Hawkins, Sir William, and Spanish war, 264-265
Hawley-Smoot Act of 1930, 508
Hegel, G. W. F., philosophy of, 463-464
Heliocentrism, advent of, 301
Hellenism, and Christianity, 78-79
Hellenistic Age, beginning of, 45
  characterized, 47-48
  legacy of, 51-52
  religion and ethics during, 48-50
  science in, 50-51
Hellenization, of Near East, 45-46
Helmholtz, H. L. F., 462
Henry Esmond (Thackeray), 467
Henry the Navigator, 272
Henry II of France, and bankruptcy, 287
  and Big Deal, 285
Henry III of France, and Holy League, 260
Henry IV of France, 276
  career of, 259-260
  and church-state controversy (during High Middle Ages), 144
  and French army, 316
Henry VIII, 235-236
Herodotus, 34
Hernani (Hugo), 465
Herzl, Theodor, 471
Herzegovina, 435
Hesiod, on social structure (in classical Greece), 18
High Middle Ages, architecture in, 165-167
  beginning of (in Western Europe), 129-130
  and culture, 134, 161-162
  Crusades during, 138-139
  definition of, 133
  literature of, 162-165
  monarchies during, 151
  monasticism during, 153-156, 158-160
  philosophy during, 169-173
  and religion, 142-145, 152-160
  science during, 173-174
  territorial expansion during, 135-136
  and towns, 134-135
Hipparchus, 51
Hippocrates, 34
Hiroshima, 529
Hispanic culture, spread of, 274
Historians, on Renaissance, 179
Historical and Critical Dictionary (Bayle), 349
History, Christian theory of, 88-89
  Greek contribution to, 34
  Renaissance approach to, 203-204
  20th Century approaches to, 557
  views of, 1
History of England (Hume), 351
History of My Calamities (Abelard), 171-172
Hitler, Adolf, appeasement of, 515-516
  compared to Stalin, 512
  death of, 528
  rise of, 508-509
Ho Chi Minh, 546
Holbach, Baron d', 352
Holland, vs. British (1780), 361-362
  parliament vs. *Stadhouder* in, 320-322
  prosperity in (17th Century), 292, 294-295
  revolution in (1780's), 361-362
  see also Dutch; Netherlands
Holy League, 260
Holy Roman Empire, disintegration of, 326
Homeric epics, 12, 15-16, 67-68
Hooker, Richard, 350
Hoplites, 19
Horthy, Admiral Nicholas, 502
House of Commons, 148
Hudson Bay Company, 277
Hugo, Victor, 465
Huguenots, and religious wars, 259-260
Huizinga, John, 179
Human Comedy, The (Balzac), 467
Humanism, and Luther, 233
  in Renaissance, 202-206
Human society, historical perspective on, 1
Hume, David, 351, 353
Humiliati, 157
Hundred Years' War (1337-1453), 184, 185-186, 187
Hungarians (Magyars), invasions by (800's and 900's), 119-120
Hungary, independence movements of, 424
  politics in (post-WWI), 501-502
  revolt in, 364, 548
Huns, and invasion of Western Roman Empire, 95
Hus, John, 182, 183
Hussites, 182
Huxley, Aldous, 556
Huxley, Julian, 552
Huygens, Christian, 298, 304-305
Hypothesis, in Hellenistic science, 50, 51

Iberian Peninsula, Christianization of, 135-136
Ibsen, Hendrik, 468-469
Iliad (Homer), 13, 15-16
Il Pastor Fido (Guarini), 251
Imitation of Christ, 181
Impetus, and scientific revolution, 298
"Impressionism," 468
Index, 246
India, and independence, 544
Indiana (Sand), 467
Individualism, during Hellenistic Age, 47, 48
Indochina, French withdrawal from, 545
  Japanese control of (WWII), 523-524
Indulgences, dispute over (during Reformation), 230
Industrial Revolution. *See* Industrialization
Industrialization, and agrarian revolution, 374-375
  causes of, 372-377
  and class conflict, 379
  defined, 371
  impact of, 372, 383-384, 444
  and population, 374
  and technological innovations, 377
Industry, and European economy (16th Century), 286
Inflation, 396
  in Europe (16th Century), 286-287
Ingres, J. A. D., 465
Innocent III, 144
Inquisition, during High Middle Ages, 157-158; *see also* Roman Inquisition; Spanish Inquisition
Instrumentation, and scientific revolution, 304
Investiture controversy, in high medieval Europe, 143-144
Ionia, culture of, 24
  and Lyric poetry, 32
  philosophers of, 32-33
  settlement of, 15
Irgens, 295
Iron industry, 380-383
Iron Law of Wages, The (Ricardo), 445
Islam, cultural sources of, 104
  development of, 105-106
  impact of, 107-108
  rise of (during Middle Ages), 101
Israel, formation of, 544-545
Italy, and church-state struggle, 145
  Fascism in, 504-506
  and French agreement, 438
  and national unity, 422-423
  Norman conquest of, 137
  political structure in (during Renaissance), 200-201
  post-war recovery of, 540, 541
  revolution in (1830's), 418
  and Tripoli, 440
  unification of, 426-427
  and WW I, 482, 483, 496
  and WW II, 516, 523
Iwo Jima, 528

Jacobins, 391, 392-393
Jacquerie Rebellion, 187
James I of England, on governing, 320
  reign of, 267-268, 322
Jan III Sobieski, 336
Japan, foreign policy of (20th Century), 438, 523
  and WW II, 516, 523-524, 528-529
Jellicoe, Admiral John, 483
Jerome, impact on Latin church of, 87-88
Jerusalem, Crusades in, 138-139
Jesuits, and anticlericalism, 356
  impact of, 245
Jesus, life and teachings of, 77
Jews, and Nazi racism, 509

and Roman religion, 75-76
see also Ancient Jews
Joan of Arc, 182, 186
  impact of, 187-188
John XXII (1316-1334), 182
John of the Cross, Saint, 244
Joseph II of Austria, and anti-
  clericalism, 356
  economics of, 358
  vs. revolt, 363-365
Joshua, 5
Joule, James, 462
Joyce, James, 556
Judaism, impact on Christianity
  of, 76-77
Judicial system, Athenian, 22
Julian "the Apostate," 86
Julius Caesar, assassination of, 66
  dictatorship of, 65
  military campaigns of, 64-65
July Monarchy, 445
  fall of, 420-422
Justinian (Emperor), impact of, 105-
  106

Kafka, Franz, 556
Kapp Putsch, 507
Karlowitz, treaties at, 337
Karolyi, Count Michael, 501-502
Kasmir, Jan, 338
Kay, John, 378
Kelvin, William, 462
Kepler, Johann, 302-303, 305
Kerensky, Alexander, 488
Keynes, John Maynard, 553
Kierkegaard, Soren, 464
Knox, John, 240
Koran, 107
Korean War, 537
Kornilov, General Laurent, 488
Kosciuszko, Thaddeus, 363
Kun, Béla, 502

Labor Party (British), 515, 542
Lamarck, Jean Baptiste de, 460
Lamartine, Alphonse de, 421
La Mettrie, Julian Offray de, 352
Land, and social status (in classical
  Greece), 18
Land and Liberty Society, 485
Land policy, in Roman republic, 61,
  62
Language, of Renaissance humanism,
  202-203, 205
La Salle, 276
Last Judgement, The (Van Eyck), 227
Last Supper, The (Tintoretto), 212-
  213
Late-medieval Europe, trends in, 180
Late Middle Ages, art and literature
  during, 198
  church and state (in Europe), 180-
    181
  culture during, 196-198
  economy during, 193-194
  France during, 186-188
  Germany during, 190
  philosophical trends during, 196-
    198

Spain during, 188-190
Latifundia, 61
Latin, rediscovery of (during
  Renaissance), 202, 203
"Latin Averroists," 172-173
Laud, Archbishop, 322
  and Purtitans, 268
Lavoisier, Antoine, 347
Law, reform of (Enlightenment),
  356-357
  and Rome, 57, 73-74
  see also Canon law; Civil law
League of Nations, 490
  and Italian-Greek dispute, 506
League of Schmalkald, 234
Leeuwenhoek, Anton van, 308-309
Legislative Assembly, 389
Legitimacy, 410-412
Legitimists, 421
Lelia (Sand), 467
Lend-Lease Act, 523
Lenin, Vladimir Ulianov, vs. Russian
  war effort (1917), 487
Leo I (Pope), 95, 96
Leo XIII (Pope), encyclicals of, 472-
  473
Leopold of Saxe-Coburg, 418
Leopold of Tuscany, tax policy of,
  358
*Letter of Christopher Columbus
  Concerning the Newly Discover-
  ed Islands, A* (Columbus), 220
*Letters Concerning the English
  Nation* (Voltaire), 311
Letters Concerning Toleration
  (Locke), 348-349
Leyden, 294
Liberal Empire (1870), 451
Liberalism, 415-416
  in Austrian Empire, 423-424
  and centralization of power, 444-
    445
  in Germany, 424
  in Italy, 422-423
  and radicalism, 445
Liberty of a Christian Man (Luther),
  231
Liebnitz, Gottfried, 298
  contributions of, 306
Linneaus, Karl, 309, 347
Linschoten, Jan, 294
Literature, of High Middle Ages,
  162-165
  late medieval, 198
  of Reformation, 250-253
  of Silver Age, 73
  of 20th Century, 555-557
*Lives of the Painters, Sculptors and
  Architects* (Vasari), 203
Lobelius, 308
Locke, John, 344, ideas of, 311,
  348-351
Logarithms, introduction of, 302,
  305
Lollards, 182
Lombard League, 135
Lomenie de Brienne, 369-370
London Exhibition of 1851, 462
Lords of Trade, 277, 282

Louis IX, Saint, reign of, 150
Louis XI, 188
Louis XIII, bankruptcy of, 292
Louis XIV, 292
  bureaucracy under, 318
  and military, 317, 333-335
Louis XV, characterized, 366
Louis XVI, 368, 370, 391
Lousi XVIII, 403
  reactionary measures of, 417
Louis-Napoleon Bonaparte. *See*
  Napoleon III
Louis-Philippe I of France, 417
Louvois, and French army, 317
Lovett, William, 448
Loyola, Ignatius, 247
  career of, 244-245
Luther, Martin, on Anabaptist
  movement, 231, 232
  and humanism, 233
  political stands of, 232-233
  and Protestant Reformation, 228,
    230-231, 234-236
Lutherans, characterized, 249
Lvov, Prince George, 487
Lyell, Charles, 459

MacArthur, General Douglas, 528
Macbeth (Shakespeare), 252
MacDonald, Ramsey, 515
Machault, 368
Machiavelli, 204
Magdeburg, sacking of, 267
Magellan, 222
Maginot Line, 521
Magna Carta, 147, 148
Magna Graecia, 18-19
  political evolution of, 56
Magnus, Albertus, 173
Malaya, 544
Malplaquet, battle of, 335-336
Malthus, Thomas, theories of, 445
Man: A Machine (La Mettrie), 352
Mandeville, Bernard, 353
Manet, 468
Manuel the Fortunate, 271
Marathon, battle of, 25
Marcel, Etienne, 186
Maria Theresa, 357, 358, 363
Marius, 63
Marlborough, duke of, 335
Marlow, Christopher, 251
Marselis, 295
Marshall, George, 536
Marshall Plan, 536
Marsilius of Padua, on sovereign
  state, 184
Martel, Charles, 113
Martinique, 341
Martov, Julius, 486
Marx, Karl, doctrines of, 449-450
Marxism, 449-450
Mary, Queen of Scots, 240-241
Masaryk, Thomas, 503
Massachusetts Bay Company, 277
Mathematics, advances in, 305-306
  during Hellenistic age, 51
  Pythagorian, 33
Matisse, Henri, 557

Maximilian of Mexico, 428
Mazzini, Giuseppi, 418, 422
Maudslay, Henry, 383
Maupeou, and Parlement, 368
Maurice (*Stadhouder*), vs.
    Oldenbarneveldt, 321
Mauriec de Saxe, 331
Media (Communications) of 20th
    Century, 556
Medici, Marie de, and French army,
    316
Medicine, advances in, 306-308
    Greek contribution to, 34
    in Hellenistic Age, 50-51
    in High Middle Ages, 168-169
Medieval Western Europe, overview
    of, 101, 104-105
Meditations (Marchs Aurelius), 73
Mehemit Ali, 419
Mein Kampf (Hitler), 517
Mendel, Gregore, genetic theories of,
    460
Mendeleyev, Dmitri, 461-462
Mendicantism, 158
Mensheviks, 486
Mercantilism, doctrines of, 281
    domestic, 282-284
    rise of, 280
Merchant of Venice, The (Shake-
    speare), 251-252
Merovingians, decline of, 113, 115
Mesopotamia, and civilization, 2
Messenia, and Sparta, 20-21
Metternich, Klement von, 411, 418
    and Concert of Europe, 414
    fall of, 420
Mexico, 222, 428
Michelangelo, 250
Microscope, impact of, 308-309
Middle Ages, impact of, 91-92
    Western Europe during, 101, 104-
    105
Milan Decree, 400
Military, of England (under Alfred
    the Great), 121-122
    and feudalism (in France), 124,
    125, 126
    organization of, 316-317
    under Romans, 63, 81-82
Mill, James, 446
Minoan civilization, 13-15
Minoan-Mycenean era, in Greek
    literature, 13
Missal, 248
Missionaries, in colonies, 271, 276
Mohacs, 327
Mohammed, teachings of, 106-107
Moltke, General Helmuth von, 430,
    481
Mona Lisa (da Vinci), 211
Monarchy, and medieval Europe, 180-
    181, 187, 188, 189-190
Monasticism, in middle ages, 109-
    110, 153-156, 160
Monet, 468
Monk, General, 323
Monnet, Jean, 541
Monotheism, of Aristotle, 37, 38
Monroe Doctrine, 415

Montaigne, 251
Montecuccoli, 336
Monteith, John, 380
Montesquieu, Baron de, 347
    political theories of, 351
Montmorency family, and religious
    wars, 258
Morality, Enlightenment view of, 346
More, Thomas, 205
Morelly, 353
Moriscos, expulsion of, 291
Morocco, riots in, 440
Moses, 5
"Mule," 379
Museum of Alexandria, 50
Music, of 20th Century, 556, 557
Mussolini, Benito, 525
    appeasement of, 515-516
    reign of, 505-506
Mycenean Greece, 14-15
Mysticism, 464
    in medieval Europe, 181-182
    rise of (Spain), 244
    in Roman religion, 76

Nagasaki, 529
Nagy government (Hungary), 548
Naples, and revolt of 1820, 415
Napoleon Bonaparte, innovations
    of, 397-399
    return of, 412
    at war, 399-403
Napoleon III, 421, 424-425, 429,
    450
    and Italian unification, 427
    and Mexico, 427-428
Naseby, 323
National Assembly, 387-388, 456
    economic policies of, 389
National Convention, 391
Nationalism, in Europe, 422-424
    vs. cosmopolitanism, 409-410
NATO, 538
*Natural and Social History of a
    Family Under the Second
    Empire, The* (Zola), 468
Natural Selection, 460
Nature, and Enlightenment, 345
Nature's Code (Morelly), 353
Navigation Acts, 277, 287
Nazis, policies of, 509-510
    political setting for, 507-508
    takeover by, 508-509
    see also Germany; Hitler, Adolf;
        Third Reich; World War II
Near East, ancient, 2-4
    Crusades in (during High Middle
    Ages), 138-139
    Hellenization of, 45-46
Nelson, Lord, 400
Neoclassicism, 465
Neoplatonists, 80
Nero, 60
Nerva, 69
Netherlands, Nazi defeat of, 521
    and religious wars, 262-264
    and Treaty of Vienna, 413
New Plan (Nazi), 510
Newton, Sir Isaac,

    career of, 303, 305, 306
Nicholas II, abdication of, 487
Nicholas Nickelby (Dickens), 467
Nietzsche, Friedrich, philosophy
    of, 471
Nihilism, 470
95 theses, of Martin Luther, 230
1984 (Orwell), 556
Nomilists, 171
Non-Proliferation Treaty, 549
Normandy, Allied invasion of, 525
    conquest of (during High Middle
    Ages), 137
    development of, 120
North Africa, and Islam, 108
North Korea, formation of, 537
Northumbrian Renaissance, 111-112
Norway, Nazi occupation of, 521
    and Treaty of Vienna, 414
Nystadt treaties, 337

Obrenovic, Prince Michael, 433
Octavian. *See* Augustus
Odovacar, 95
Odyssey, 16
    symbolism of, 13
OGPU, 510
Okinawa, 528
Oldenbarneveldt, Jan de, 275, 321
Old Regime, chronology of, 342
    colonial enterprise in, 284
    decay of, 355-356
    diplomatic sphere in, 331
Old Sarum, 325
Old Testament, 8
Oligarchy, of Roman republican
    government, 58
Oliva, Antonio, 299
Olivares, Count-Duke, *328n*
Oliver Twist (Dickens), 467
Omar Khayyam, 107
Onions, Peter, 382
*On the Babylonian Captivity of the
    Church* (Luther), 231
On Crimes and Punishments
    (Beccaria), 351
"On the Freedom of the Will"
    (Erasmus), 233
*On the Movement of the Heart and
    the Blood* (Harvey), 308
On the Reason of State (Botero),
    impact of, 314
*On the Structure of the Human
    Body* (Vesalius), 308
Opticks (Newton), 305
Optics, advances in, 305
Oratory of Divine Love, 246
    report of, 244
Order of Theatines, 244
Oresme, Nicholas, 197
Organization of Labor, The
    (Blanc), 448
Origen, religious system of, 79
Origin of Species (Darwin), 459-461
Orlando Furioso (Ariosto), 251
Orpheo (Montiverdi), 251
Orphism, 33
Ortega y Gasset, Jose, 474
Orwell, George, 556

Ostracism, in Athenian politics, 23
Othello (Shakespeare), 252
Otto ("the Great"), achievements of, 128
Ottoman Empire, decline of, 327-328
  and Eastern power balance, 419
  and Greek revolution, 416
  at war, 336-337, 425-426, 433, 434
  see also Turkey
"Ottonian Renaissance," 128-129
Owen, Robert, 448
Owenite movement, 448

Pacification of Ghent, 263
Pacific theater (WWII), 528
Pacifism, in Britain (Post-WWI), 515
"Pact of Steel," 520
Paganism, 80, 86
Pakistan, 544
Palestine, 544
Papacy, and Carolingian rise (in Frankland), 114-115
  in late medieval Europe, 180-181, 182-184
Papal Infallibility, 45
  roots of, 246
Para, 289
Paraphrases (Erasmus), 205
Pare, Ambroise, contributions of, 307
Pareto, Vilfredo, 505
Paris, and French Revolution, 387
Paris Commune of 1792, 391; *see also* Commune of Paris
Paris Exposition Universelle, 462
Parliament, 268
  growth of, 147-148, 184-185
Parliaments, vs. monarchies (17th-18th Centuries), 320-326
Parthenon, architecture and sculpture of, 42-43
Pascal, Blaise, 311
  career of, 306
Pasteur, Louis, contributions of, 461
Pastoral Care (Pope Gregory), 110
Pater, Walter, 469
Patricians, in early Rome, 57-58
Patriotism, and deified emperors (in Roman Religion), 75
Patronate real, 273
Paul, Saint, 77-78
Paul et Virginie (Saint-Pierre), 346
Paul III, and Oratory of Divine Love, 244
Peace of Amiens, 399
Peace of Augsburg (1555), 225
Peace of Paris, 341
Peace of the Pyrenees, 33, 329
Pearl Harbor, 523
Peasants, 194-195, 388
Peasants' rebellion of 1358, 187
Peasants War (1525), 232
Peloponnesian War, 27-28
  criticism of, 41-42
  impact of, 29
Peninsular War, 402
Penn, William, 277
Pennsylvania, as colony, 278

"People's Charter," 448
Pepin the Short, 113-115
Pericles, and Athenian Golden Age, 27
  leadership of Athens by, 24, 38-39
  and Peloponnesian War, 27, 28
  and public works policy, 42-43
Persia, conquest of (by Alexander the Great), 45
  and Ionia, 24
  and Peloponnesian War, 28, 29
Persian Empire, during Middle Ages, 101
Persian Letters (Montesquieu), 347-348
Persian Wars, 24-26
Petain, Marshal Philippe, 521
Peter the Great, bureaucracy under, 319-320
Petrarch, 202, 203, 205
Petition of Right, 344
Phidias, work of, 42-43
Philhellenism, 416
Philip of Macedon, 29, 44
Philip II of Spain, and bankruptcy, 285, 287, 288
  compared to Elizabeth I, 265-266
  and England, 264, 265
  and religious uprisings, 263
  rule of, 261-262, 265
Philip III of Spain, 289
Philip IV of Spain, 150
Philip V of Spain, 335
Philistines, 5
Philosophical Dictionary (Voltaire), 347-348, 349
Philosophy, Aristotelian, 37-38
  of Hellenistic Age, 49-50
  high medieval, 169-173
  Ionian, 32-33
  in late Middle Ages, 196-198
  and science, 309-312
  sophist, 34-35
Physics, 300
  advances in, 303-305, 462-463, 550-551
Picasso, Pablo, 557
Pico, Giovanni, 206
Pietism, 464
Pilsudski, Marshal, 502, 503
Pisistratus, and Dionysian drama, 39
  leadership of Athens by, 22-23
Pitt, Sir William, and Great War for Empire, 341
Pius IV, and Council of Trent, 246
Pius V, impact of, 248
Pius IX, and centralization, 451
  and Italian unity, 422, 427
Place, Francis, 448
Planck, Max, and quantum theory, 463
Plataea, battle of, 26
Plato, philosophy of, 34-37
Plebeians, in early Rome, 57-58
Plekhanov, Georg, 486
Plotinus, teachings of, 80
Poetry, Augustan, 67-68
  Greek lyric, 32
  Latin (of High Middle Ages), 162

vernacular (of High Middle Ages), 162-165
  see also Literature
Poland, foreign policy of (1930's), 517
  Nazi invasion of, 518-519, 520
  partitioning of (1790's), 337-338
  politics in, 326-327, 502-503
  recreation of, 490
  and revolution, 363, 418-419, 428
  vs. Russia (1919-22), 497, 499
  and Treaty of Vienna, 413
  vs. Turks (17th Century), 336
Polis, 17-19; *see also* Greek city-states
Political organization, in England (during High Middle Ages), 146-148
  in France (during late middle ages), 186-188
  and Germans, 93-94, 190
  Greek, 17-18, 19-20, 22-24, 47
  in Renaissance, 200-202
  and Rome, 61-62, 90-91
  of Spain (late medieval), 188
  of Sparta, 20-21
  of Western Christendom, 109
Political theory, in Enlightenment, 350
Politiques, 259, 260
Pombal, and administrative reform, 357
Pompey, 63
Poniatowski, Stanislas, 326, 363
Pope, Alexander, 345
Popular Front, 514, 555
Popular Republicans (MRP), 541
Population growth, 549, 551-553
  in England, 374
  in Europe, 458-459
  during Reformation, 223-224
Portugal, colonialism of, 271-272, 279
  and revolt of 1820, 415
  royal power in, 328
Positivism, 448-449
Potocki clan, 327
Praise of Folly (Erasmus), 204
Priestley, Joseph, 347
Primitive society, transformation to civilization of, 2, 3
Prince, The (Machiavelli), 204
Prince of Conde, 317
Prince Henry the Navigator, 222
Princip, Gavrilo, 441-442
Principia Mathematica (Newton), 303, 344
Principles of Geology (Lyell), 459, 462
Printing, 196, 219-220
Privilege, in pre-revolutionary France, 366-368
Prophets, in Jewish religion, 7-8
Protestant Reformation, 226-244
  in England, 234-238
  and Martin Luther, 228, 230-231
  in Scandinavia, 233-234
  social origins of, 226-228
  see also Reformation

Proudhon, P. J., anarchism of, 450
Proust, Marcel, 556
Provincial Letters (Pascal), 309
Prussia, vs. Austria (18th Century),
   339
   and centralized government, 320,
   450
   military in, 317
   vs. Napoleon, 400
   and Treaty of Vienna, 413
Psychoanalysis, 473
Ptolemies, 46
Ptolemy, Claudius, 73
   and geocentrism, 299-300
Puddling and rolling process, 382
Pufendorf, Samuel, 326
Punic Wars, 60
Puritans, vs. Anglicans, 267-268
Pythagorean school, 33
   and Platonic thought, 37
Pythermus, 19

Quadruple Alliance, 414
Quanta Cura, 451

Rabelais, 203
Racism, in 19th Century, 471
   in Third Reich, 509
Radicalism, of 19th Century, 446-
   447
Raleigh, Sir Walter, and Spanish war,
   265
Raphael, 210, 211-212
Realism, 467-468
Realpolitik, 425
Reason, in Enlightenment, 346-348
Reconstruction (post-WWII), 534-
   535
Red and the Black, The (Stendhal),
   467
Reflections on Violence (Sorel), 474
Reformation, art-literature of, 250-
   253
   and Catholicism, 243-248
   chronology of, 241
   commerce during, 222-223
   cultural aftermath of, 248-250
   early trends in, 219
   exploration during, 220-222
   population growth during, 223-
   224
   and Renaissance, 226
   see also Protestant Reformation
Reform Bill of 1832, 446
Reichsrat, 456
Reichstag, 455
Reign of Terror, 392-396
Reinsurance Treaty, 436, 437
Relativity, Theory of, 463
Religion, in Ancient Near-East, 4
   Enlightenment view of, 348-350
   in Hellenistic Age, 48-50
   in late medieval Spain, 189-190
   and science, 309-312
   see also under individual religions;
   Gods; Roman religion
Religious toleration, and Enlighten-
   ment, 344, 348-349
Religious wars, in Europe, 257-269

Remembrance of Things Past
   (Proust), 556-557
Renaissance, art-literature of, 206,
   207, 208, 209, 210, 211, 212-
   213
   concepts of, 199-200
   and French invasion, 214
   and Italian-Northern Europe
   comparison, 179-180
   perspectives on, 179
   political setting of, 200-202
   and Reformation, 205-206, 226
   world view during, 299
Renaissance humanism, 202-206
Renoir, 468
*Report on Social Insurance and
   Allied Services* (Beveridge), 555
Republic (Plato), 35
Republic of Virtue, 395
Restoration Parliament, 323
Revolutionary Era, legacy of, 403-
   404
Revolution of Heavenly Bodies, The
   (Copernicus), 300
Rhineland, German occupation of,
   516
Ricardo, David, theories of, 445
Richelieu, Cardinal, and French
   army, 316-317
   program of, 342
   on power, 326
Robespierre, Maxmillian, 391
   executions by, 394
   execution of, 395
Roebuck, John, 383
Roentgen, Wilhelm, 462
Roger the Great, reign of (in Sicily
   and Southern Italy), 137
Roman Catholic Church, and
   centralization, 451
   and French Revolution, 388-389
   in Late Middle Ages, 180
   and Reformation, 243-248
Romance, in poetry (during High
   Middle Ages), 163-164
Roman Empire, agriculture in, 91
   after Augustus, 68-69
   under Augustus, 66-68
   and Christianity, 78, 80-81, 85-87
   chronology of, 96-97
   and development of law, 73-74
   division of, 83-85
   economic problems of (during
   third century), 82-83
   "fall" in west of, 90-92
   fusion of cultures in, 87-89, 91, 92
   invasions of (during third
   century), 82, 83
   political disintegration in (during
   third century), 81-82
   slavery in, 72-73
   succession in, 69
   territorial expansion of, 70-72
   urbanization of, 72
Romanesque style, in high medieval
   architecture, 165-166
Romania, 502
   and Congress of Berlin, 435
Roman Inquisition, scope of, 247

"Roman Peace," 66
Roman religion, 75, 76
Roman republic, beginnings of, 56-
   58
   and Caesar, 64-66
   chronology of, 63-64
   evolution of, 56-58
   Hellenization of, 61, 62
   last century of, 62-63
   social and political changes in
   (264-146 B.C.), 61-62
Roman Synod of 1059, impact of,
   143
Romanticism, artists-writers of, 465-
   467
Rome, citizen-farmers of, 58-59
   conquests of, 59-61
   influences on, 56
   sack of, 94
Romeo and Juliet (Shakespeare), 252
Roosevelt, President Franklin D., 521
Roosevelt, President Theodore, 438
Roscellinus, philosophy of, 170-171
Rossbach, 340
Rotherham plow, 374
Rousseau, Jean-Jacques, 346
   political theories of, 351
Royal College of Physicians, 307
Royal Navy, in Great War for
   Empire, 341
Royal Society, 298
Rudel, Jaufre, 163
Rudiger, von Strahrenburg, 336
Rudolph of Hapsburg, 144
Ruskin, John, 468
Russia, and Balkan alliance, 440
   and Bosnia-Herzegovina, 439-440
   bureaucracy in (17th-18th
   Centuries), 319-320
   and Byzantium, 106
   and central government (19th
   Century), 451-452
   and Great Civil War, 497, 499
   and Treaty of Vienna, 413
   at war, 337, 400, 402, 424, 425,
   434, 438, 481, 482, 483, 497,
   499
   see also Soviet Union
Russian Revolution, and Bolshevik
   takeover, 488-489
   historical background on, 485-487
   and provisional government, 487-
   488
Russo-Japanese War, 438
Rutherford, Lord William, atomic
   research of, 550-551

Sacramental system, 152-153, 231
Sacrifice of Isaac (Ghiberti), 209,
   210
Saint-Andre, Jean Bon, 392
St. Bartholomew's Day Massacre, 259
Saint-Pierre Bernardin de, 346
Saint-Simon, Count Henri de,
   socialism of, 447
Salamis, battle of, 25-26
Sanctorius Sanctorius, 307
Sand, George, 467
San Luis Potosi, 272

Sappho, 32
Saracens, invasions of (800's and 900's), 118-119
Sardinia-Piedmont, 415
  and Italian unification, 426-427
Sarel, George, 474
Sartre, Jean-Paul, 558
Sassanid dynasty, 101
Saul, 5
Savonarola, career of, 243-244
Scandinavia, 120, 234
Schism, in late medieval church, 182-183
Scholastics, 300
Schleiffen Plan, 481
Schonberg, Arnold, 557
Schopenhauer, Arthur, 464-465
Science, Enlightenment view of, 346-347
  in Hellenistic Age, 50-51
  in High Middle Ages, 173-174
  late-medieval, 197
  prestige of, 459, 462
  vs. religion and philosophy, 309-312
  of Silver Age, 73
  state of (pre-16th Century), 297
  in 20th Century, 550-551
Science and the Modern World (Whitehead), 558
Scientific revolution, 297-300
Scotland, and Calvinism, 240-241
Scott, Sir Walter, 466
Scotus, Duns, 197
Sculpture, of Golden Age, 38-39
  in Hellenistic Age, 47
Sea, in Greek experience, 13
Second Balkan War, 441
Second Estate, 386
Second Reform Bill, 458
Second Republic, 421-422
Second Treaty of Paris, 414
Seed drill, 374
Seleucids, 46
Senate, in early Rome, 57, 58
  in France, 456
Septimius Severus (emperor), rule of (during third century), 81-82
Serbia, 433, 436, 442
Servan-Schreiber, 540
Seven Years War, 339-340
Shakespeare, William, 403
  and tragedies, 252
Shape of Things to Come, The (Wells), 556
Shaw, G. B., 556
Shelley, Percy Bysshe, 465
Shipbuilding, in Holland, 294
Sic et Non (Abelard), 172
Sicily, Norman conquest of, 137
Silesia, Prussian invasion of, 339
Silver Age, 73-74
Six Acts, 418
Six Weeks War, 429
Skeptics, 49
Slavery, in Athens, 23
  and European colonialism, 279, 447
  in Hellenistic Age, 47, 51

in Roman Empire, 72-73
Slavic states, vs. Turks, 433
Slavs, 423
Slovenes, 423
Snow, C. P., 455, 558
Social Contract (Rousseau), 351
Social Democratic party (Russia), 486
Social institutions, in late medieval Europe, 180
Socialism, rise of, 447-448
Socialist Revolutionaries (SR's), 486
Social Sciences, changes in (20th Century), 552
Society of Jesus. See Jesuits
Sociology, advent of, 448
Social structure, 2
  of ancient Near-East, 2-3
  in classical Greece, 18, 19-20
  and feudalism (in France), 125
  Hesiod on, 18
  and High Middle Ages, 129
  medieval, 135, 194-195
  of Mycenaen Greeks, 14
  and Rome, 57, 67, 84
  of Western Christendom, 108-109
Socrates (469-399 B.C.), 35
Solon, laws of, 22
Song of Roland, 162-163, 164
Sophists, 34-35
Sophocles, 40
Southeast Asia Treaty Organization (SEATO), 538
South Korea, formation of, 537
Southwest Asia, impact of Islam on, 108
Soviet Union, and America (1945-1973), 531-533
  Eastern European policy of, 547-548
  post-Civil War, 510-512
  in WWII, 520-521, 523, 525, 529
  see also Russia
Spain, and colonial empire, 272-274, 279
  decline of, 328-329
  depression in, 289-290
  vs. England, 264
  Fascism in, 512-514
  Islam in, 107
  in late Middle Ages, 188-190
  reconquest of (during High Middle Ages), 136-137
  and religious wars, 260, 261-264
  and revolt of 1820, 415
Spanish Civil War, 512-513
Spanish Inquisition, 247
  in colonies, 273
Sparta, 20-22
Spartacists, 507
Spencer, Herbert, 470-471
Spengler, Oswald, 557
"Spider King," 188
Spinning jenny, 378
Spinning machines, 378-379
Spirit of the Laws, The (Montesquieu), 351
Spiritual Exercises (Loyola), outline of, 245

Spiritual Franciscans, 160
Stadhouder, vs. States General, 321-322
Stadium generale, description of, 167-168
Stalin, Josef, policies of, 511-512
  rise of, 510-511
Stamp Act, 360
Staple Enumeration, 282
State church, and religious wars, 258
States, administration of, 316-320
  growth of, 341-342
States General, vs. Stadhouder, 321-322
Statistics, emergence of, 281
Statute of Cities, 363
Steam engine, 382
Stendhal, 467
Stephan, Saint (king), 139
Stock market crash of 1929, causes of, 507
Stoicism, 49-50
Stravinsky, Igor, 557
Stuart kings, 322-324
Students, medieval, 162, 168
Study of History, A (Toynbee), 557
Submarine warfare, in World War I, 482, 483
Succession, in Roman Empire, 69, 81
Succession states, problems of, 501
Sudetens, 517
Sugar Act (1764), 282, 360
Sulan Mahmoud II, 419
Sulla, 63
Summa Theologia (St. Thomas Aquinas), 173, 196, 248
surplus value, 449
Surrealism, 557
Sweden, vs. Russia, 337
  and Thirty Years War, 267
  and Treaty of Vienna, 414
Sylvius, Aeneas (Pope Pius II), 196
Symphonie Fantastique (Berlioz), 466
Syncretism, 49
  and Christianity, 76
Systema Naturae (Linnaeus), 347

Taaffe, Count Edward, 456
Talleyrand, Maurice de, 404, 410, 411
Tanucci, Bernardo, 356-357
Tasso, Torquato, 251
Taxation, and enlightened despots, 358
Technology, impact of, 377
  in Middle Ages, 195-196
  prestige of, 459, 462
Temple, Sir William, 331
Tennis Court Oath, 387
Tenth Penny, 262
Territorial expansion, in High Middle Ages, 135-136
  of Roman Empire, 70-72
  of Sparta, 20-21
Test Ban Treaty, 549
Teutonic Knights, conquests of, 141
Textile manufacturing, 377-380
Thackery, W. M., 466
Thales of Miletus, 32

"Theater of Dionysus," 39-40
Themistocles, 25-26
Theodoric, 95
Theodosius I, 86, 87, 94
Theresa of Avila, Saint, 244, 247
Thermodynamics, 462
Thermopylae, battle of, 25
Third Estate, 386
Third Reich, establishment of, 508-509
Third Republic, political turbulance of, 456, 458
39 Articles of Faith, 248
Thirty-Years War, 266-267
Thomson, Joseph, 550
Three Emperors' League, 433, 435
Thucydides, 34
Tillich, Paul, 558
Tintoretto, 212-213
Titian, 213
Tito, Marshal, 538
Tolstoy, Leo, 469
Torricelli, Evangelista, 298, 304
Towns, growth of (High Middle Ages), 134-135, 136
of late-medieval Europe, 194
Toynbee, Arnold, 557
Trade, and industrialization, 377-378
Tragedy, of Golden Age, 40-41
revival of, 251
Trajan, 69
and Christians, 81
Transportation system, reconstruction of, 375-376
Transylvania, revolt in, 364
Treaties of Aix-la Chapelle, 339
Treaties of Tilsit, 400
Treaties of Utrecht, 336
Treaties of Westphalia, 267, 333
Treatise on General Sociology (Pareto), 505
Treaty of Berlin, 435
Treaty of Brest-Litovsk, 483, 484, 488
Treaty of Campio Formio, 397
Treaty of Câteau Cambrésis, 224
Treaty of Hubertusburg, 340
Treaty of Neuilly, 491
Treaty of Nijmwegen, 333
Treaty of Ryswick, 335
Treaty of Verdun, 118
Treaty of Versailles, stipulations of, 490-491
Treaty of Vienna, stipulations of, 412, 414
Tribal Assembly, in early Rome, 57-58
Tridentine Profession of Faith, 247
Trip, Elias, 295
Tripartite Pact, 523
Triple Alliance, 435
Tripoli, 440
Trollus and Cressida (Shakespeare), 252, 413
Trotsky, Leon, 486
vs. Stalin, 510-511
Troubadours, tradition of, 163
Troyes, Chrétien de, 164
Truce of Vasvar, 336

Truman Doctrine, 536
Tudor, Mary (Queen), and Reformation, 237
Tulip Mania, 295
Tulips, in Dutch economy, 295
Tull, Jethro, 374
Turgot, A. R. J., 368-369
Turkey, American aid to (post-WWII), 535
and Treaty of Versailles, 491
and WW I, 482, 496
see also Ottoman Empire
Turnpike Acts, 375
Twelve Tables, 57, 74
Twenty Four Articles, 418
Twofold-truth doctrine, in philosophy, 172-173
Two Treaties on Civil Government (Locke), 344

Ukraine, 497
Unemployment, in Europe, 508
Union of Liberation, 486-487
"Unitarianism," 446
United Nations, 526, 531, 543
Universities, rise of, 167-168
University of Toledo, 245
Upper classes, status of (Middle Ages), 194, 195
Urbanization, and Benedictinism, 154
of Europe, 458-459
of Roman Empire, 72
problems of, 445
see also Deurbanization
Utopia, Platonic, 35-37
Utopia (More), 205
Utopian movement, and Anabaptism, 231-232

Valens (emperor), 94
Valla, Lorenzo, 204
van der Capellan tot der Pol, Jan, 362
van Eyck, Jan, 207, 208
Van Gogh, Vincent, 468
Vanity Fair (Thackeray), 467
Vasa, Gustavus, 234
Vasari, Giorgio, 203
Vasco de Gama, 222-279
Vassal, duties of, 126
Vauban, Marshal, 317
Vega, Lope de, 250
Venality, and French bureaucracy, 318-319
Venetian school, 212-213
Versailles, 318
Vesalius, Andreas, 298
on anatomy, 308
Vespucci, Amerigo, 221
Vienna, siege of (1683), 336
Vietcong, 546
Vietnam War, 546-547
Vietnam, and French, 545
Vikings, invasions of, 120, 121-122, 123
Villars, Marshal, 336
Villon, Francois, 198, 199
Vinci, Leonardo da, 202, 203,

210, 211, 212
Violence, 470, 473-474
Virginia Company of London, 277
Virtue, and Enlightenment, 353
Visigoths, 94, 95
Viviani, 298
Voltaire, 304, 311, 345, 348-349, 353

Wages, in European economy (16th Century), 286-287
Wagner, Richard, 471
Waldensianism, 157, 158
Waldo, Peter, 157
Walpole, Robert, 325
Waning of the Middle Ages (Huizinga), 179
War, and economy, 291, 294
objectives of (18th Century), 331
see also individual wars; Religious wars
War of Devolution, 333
"War of Jenkin's Ear," 339
War of the League of Augsburg, 335
Wars of the Roses, 186
War of the Sicilian Vespers, 189
War of the Spanish Succession, 335-336
Wars of the Austrian Succession, 331, 338, 339
Water frame, 378
Waterloo, 403, 412
Watt, James, 382
Weaving, mechanization of, 379-380
Weimar Republic, 507
Weissman, August, on heredity, 460
Welfare, in England, 447
Welfare State, 555
Wellington, Duke of, vs. Napoleon, 402
Wells, H. G., 556
Welsers, 287
Wergeld, 93
Western Christendom, church-state relationship in, 112
cultural sources of, 104-105
in High Middle Ages, 129-130
rise of, 101, 108
roots of, 2-3
territorial expansion in (during High Middle Ages), 136-137
under Charlemagne, 115-118
Western Europe, American influence in, 548-549
church-state struggle in (during High Middle Ages), 142-145
cultural trends in (during late Middle Ages), 196-198
cultural overview of (20th Century), 552-555
economic trends in (during late Middle Ages), 193-196
Western European civilization, development of, 92
West Germany, creation of, 536
Whigs, and radicals, 446, 447
Whitehead, Alfred North, 558
Whitney, Eli, 380
Wilkinson, John, 383

William the Conqueror, reign of, 146
William of Ockham, 197-198
William of Orange, 263, 364
William I (Dutch), and Belgian revolution, 417
William I of Prussia, 428-429
William II of Germany, abdication of, 484
  foreign policy of, 436, 438
William III of Holland, 321-322
William IV of Holland, 322
William V (Stadhouder), 361-362
Will of the People Society, 485
Wilson, President Woodrow, and World War I, 484, 490
Women, 23, 39, 58n, 493, 554
Woolf, Virginia, 556

Works and Days (Hesiod), 18
World War I, blame for, 478, 480
  campaigns of, 480-484
  conclusion of, 484, 485
  debts and reparations for, 499-501
  longrange impact of, 552-553
  postwar settlements of, 489-491
  precipitating events, 439-442
World War II, and American entry, 523-524
  destructive impact of, 533-534
  end of, 528-530
  offensives of, 520-521, 523, 524-525
  outbreak of, 519
Worsley Canal, 376
Wycliffe, John, 202

doctrines of, 181-182

Xavier, Saint Francis, 245
Xerxes, 25
X rays, 462

Yalta Conference, 526
Yorktown, 360
Ypsilanti, Alexander, 416
Yugoslavia, 491, 502, 538

Zeno, philosophy of, 49-50
Zhukov, Marshal, 528
Zionism, 471
Zola, Emile, 467
Zoology, advances in, 308-309
Zoroastrianism, 104
Zwingli, 234